Are They Thinking?

Are They Thinking?

A Thinking-Skills Program for the Elementary Grades

By Greta and Ted Rasmussen

ISBN 0-936110-18-X
Library of Congress Catalog Card Number: 95-062182
Copyright © 1996 by Greta Rasmussen
All rights reserved. Printed in the U.S.A.

TIN MAN PRESS
BOX 219
STANWOOD, WA 98292

Contents

Introduction

One afternoon some years ago, while working with a group of third-grade students, I asked a question that went something like this:

> "You need to buy five loaves of bread for a picnic. The loaves are big, and only two will fit into one bag. How many bags will you need in order to carry the bread?"

I was more than a little surprised when several of the youngsters answered, "2 1/2 bags." Good math but bad thinking! It turned out just a couple of them grasped the idea that three bags would be needed.

In school, we teach handwriting, spelling, reading, math, science, etc., but thinking—the process of making use of knowledge—is often neglected. As educators, it is our duty to help students learn how to analyze information, draw inferences, generate ideas, make connections, and solve problems.

This book addresses these needs by providing a structured, 30-week program of short thinking exercises that are interesting to children and very easy for you to implement. Those of you who already use Tin Man Press materials may notice some familiar themes. However, all of the activities are brand-new.

Here is how the program works: Each day of the week a particular thinking skill is featured. The five skill groups and their definitions are as follows:

Analytical Thinking—To separate something into parts in order to identify key elements. To examine a particular concept to discern its essential qualities.

Flexible Thinking—To try various approaches and take alternate points of view. To present different ideas, shifting perspectives with ease.

Problem Solving—To define a problem, determine the desired outcome, select possible solutions, choose strategies and apply the best solution.

Elaborative Thinking—To expand on an idea, providing additional information or insights, thus widening its possibilities.

Originality—To see something in a fresh way. To generate creative responses that often result in unexpected solutions.

Each activity consists of a one-page reproducible sheet which children should be able to complete in just a few minutes. We have attempted to give these reproducible pages an open and inviting look. For example, each exercise is accompanied by a cartoon which is usually both humorous and thought-provoking.

It is also worth noting that many of the exercises will work on an overhead if you do not want to offer them as reproducibles. Some, such as the paper-folding activities, can be done orally.

To save you time, we have provided short scripts for introducing the activities. We have tried to make them lively and motivational, but they are guidelines only. Introduce the activities in your own style.

It is probably best to begin this program after the mechanics of the first two or three weeks of the school year are out of the way. Also, you may want to suspend the program for the week before Christmas vacation.

How you schedule the activities is up to you. Here are some thoughts:

- Block out ten or fifteen minutes at a certain time each day and have the whole class work on the activity then. Discuss the previous day's activity during this period, also.

- Set aside several minutes at the beginning or end of each school day to assign the activity, which children complete when they have time. The previous day's activity could also be discussed during this period.

- For those of you in pull-out programs, the day-to-day organization of these activities may not be possible. So tailor them to your needs. You might want to try doing all the analytical-thinking activities first, followed by flexible, etc. Every activity in the program has been designed to stand alone, so you can "mine" the ideas at random rather than using them sequentially.

Notice that I have mentioned the need for discussion and follow-up. Students need to know that you take these assignments seriously. Your enthusiastic response, including evaluation, is essential.

Let me also express the hope that every child in your class will be fully involved in these exercises. Children of all abilities can learn to be better thinkers. Once you have developed a plan for using the program, stick with it.

Finally—remember my bread and bag story? Who knows? Perhaps after doing these activities, one of your students might give you an answer like this: "Well, I could carry four loaves of bread in two bags and tuck the fifth one under my arm." Let's see . . . that would be good math plus flexible thinking, problem solving, originality . . . you get the picture.

I hope you and your students enjoy the ideas in this book.

Greta Rasmussen
Camano Island, Washington

WHICH FACE?
Week 1/Analytical Thinking

The Premise:
Students will match drawings of facial expressions with statements.

Comment:
The subject of faces is a natural, since we all happen to have them and "use" them every day! This activity takes its cue from the common expressions we make when we're mad, sad, etc. By analyzing the visual information presented, students should be able to surmise that a somewhat disgruntled expression will NOT go with the sentence, "Mmm. I'm going to eat all that pizza."

Script:
(Draw this very surprised face on the board:)

Look at the face I have just put up on the board. How would you describe its expression? *(Response)* Think of a sentence this person might be saying. *(Response)* Today, you'll be matching nine faces and their expressions with nine sentences. Look at all the pictures and read all the sentences before you decide which picture goes with which sentence. Good luck.

Answers:
(1) 8 (2) 3 (3) 7 (4) 2 (5) 6 (6) 9 (7) 5 (8) 4 (9) 1.

_____

Which Face?

Name_____

What expression are you wearing on your face
right now as you read this? Let's hope it is more
like the Number 9 face than the Number 4 face.
Match the pictures with the words.

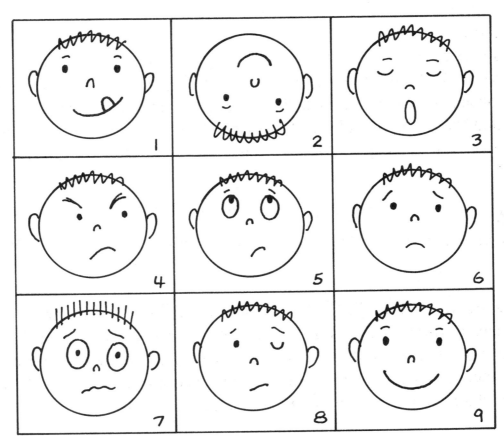

1. I have something in my eye. _____
2. I'm very tired. _____
3. This is a scary movie. _____
4. I like to stand on my head. _____
5. I don't feel so good. _____
6. I'm glad it is Saturday. _____
7. I hope that ball doesn't land on me. _____
8. You stop that! _____
9. Mmm. I'm going to eat all that pizza. _____

WHO ASKED?
Week 1/Flexible Thinking

The Premise:
Students will analyze questions in order to determine who is asking them.

Comment:
Youngsters may not have had all of these experiences, but their common sense should help them come up with acceptable responses. Don't be overly generous when accepting answers. To our knowledge, Question 6 could only be asked by a child or teenager.

Script:
I'm going to ask a question and you tell me who might be saying it. *(In a whiny tone of voice, ask:)* "How long before we get there?" *(Response)* Yes, it probably would be a child taking a long car trip.

Today, I am going to give you an activity containing ten questions. Your job is to figure out who is doing the asking. Good luck.

Answers:
(1) dentist (2) teacher (3) grocery checker (4) shoe salesperson (5) waiter
(6) child (7) doctor (8) mother or father (9) ice-cream clerk
(10) photographer.

Who Asked?

Name_____

Question: Who might be doing the talking in the sentences below? Answer: That's for you to figure out! Read the sentences and think of someone who might be asking each of these questions. Good luck!

1. Can you open your mouth a little wider? _____

2. What is the capital of Colorado? _____

3. Paper or plastic? _____

4. How do you feel when you walk in them? _____

5. Soup or salad? _____

6. Can I stay overnight at Susan's? _____

7. How long have you had your sore throat? _____

8. Could you watch Joey while I go to the store? _____

9. Do you want nuts on that? _____

10. Can you stand a little more to the left, please? _____

STRAIGHT-LINE RABBIT
Week 1/Problem Solving

The Premise:
Students will proceed from start to finish by using straight lines and making just three turns.

Comment:
The "three-turns" requirement makes this activity quite rigorous. Had the activity's goal been to reach the finish by using "just straight lines," the objective would have been less well-defined and, therefore, not as challenging.

Script:
(Put this diagram on the board—minus the dotted lines, which show a solution.)

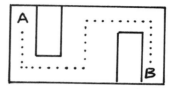

Today, you are going to be working on an activity where you will have to get from one place to another by drawing straight lines and making just three turns. For practice, I have put a similar problem on the board. How could you get from A to B by making just four turns—without touching the rectangles or the border? Who wants to do it? *(Response)*

Now, you're ready to try "Straight-Line Rabbit." Use your ruler and draw very light lines at first until you figure out how to do it.

Possible solution:

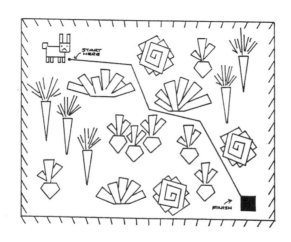

Straight-Line Rabbit

Name_____

This square rabbit lives in a square rabbit hole in a square garden, and it can only run in straight lines! Your job is to find a way for the rabbit to get to its hole by making JUST THREE TURNS. (There is a way to do it!)

Use a pencil and ruler to show the path the square rabbit takes. One more thing: The square rabbit cannot touch the fence or any of the vegetables on the way!

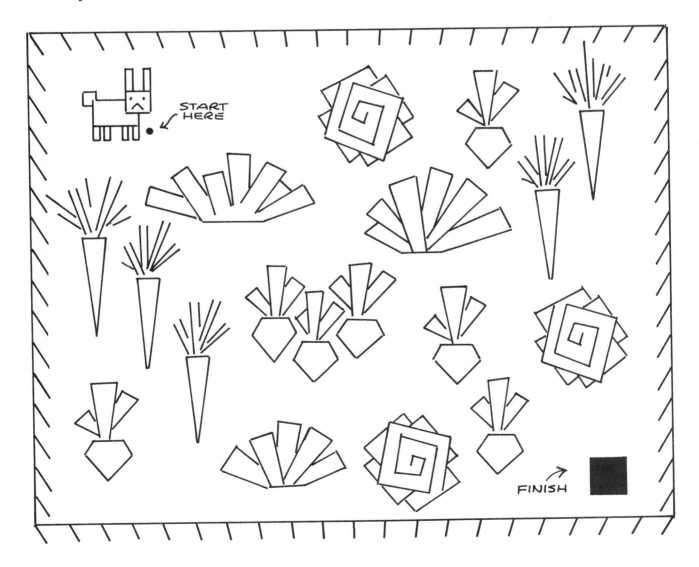

17

EYES
Week 1/Elaborative Thinking

The Premise:
Students will expand their thinking on the subject of eyes.

Comment:
This is the first of a number of subject-oriented activities designed to encourage children to think in depth about a particular topic.

How students handle Number 3 should be interesting. The obvious answer is that you wink with one eye and blink with both eyes. However, a youngster might say, "You can't help it when you blink but you wink on purpose," and that's fine, also.

If you and your students enjoy this activity, you might also like our book, "Nifty Fifty," which asks interesting questions about 50 common objects, such as a stick, fly, hanger, etc.

Script:
They're in your head, you have two of them, and they come in various colors. What am I talking about? *(Response)* Yes, eyes. Today's activity centers around the subject of eyes, so open yours and see how well you can do.

Answers:
(2) to protect their eyes, and to darken them when they're sleeping. (3) you blink with both eyes (usually to protect them), and you wink with one eye. (4) nose - yes; ear - no; elbow - yes; neck - no.

Eyes

Name_____

This activity focuses on those two things on your face called EYES. Everyone should be an expert on this subject, so do a good job and have fun!

HOO HAS GREAT EYESIGHT? I DO!

1. What color are your eyes? _____

2. Why do people have eyelids? _____

3. How is blinking different from winking? _____

_____

4. Without using a mirror . . .

   • can you see your nose? _____
   • can you see your ear? _____
   • can you see your elbow? _____
   • can you see your neck? _____

5. Eyes seen from the front look different than eyes seen from the side. Draw a close-up picture of an eye from the front and from the side.

Front   Side

ART POEM
Week 1/Originality

The Premise:
Students will make drawings based on visual and written prompts.

Comment:
Drawing is a natural form of communication for elementary-age children, who are usually more concerned about the ideas they are expressing than the aesthetics.

Although the assignment seems simple, there is structure. For example, drawing a person in the act of sneezing requires some thought.

Script:
(Do you have the nerve to stand up and recite this poem? Try it!)

> Your assignment today
> Isn't work, it is play—
> Not with scissors or rulers
> Or crayons or clay,
> But just with a pencil.
> How simple, hooray!

Art Poem

Name_____

Are you feeling art smart? It's time to show off by making the most interesting drawings you can. They must have something to do with the poem and with the words beneath each frame.

Who's making these sounds?
Well, that's up to you.
Finish these drawings
And we will know, too.

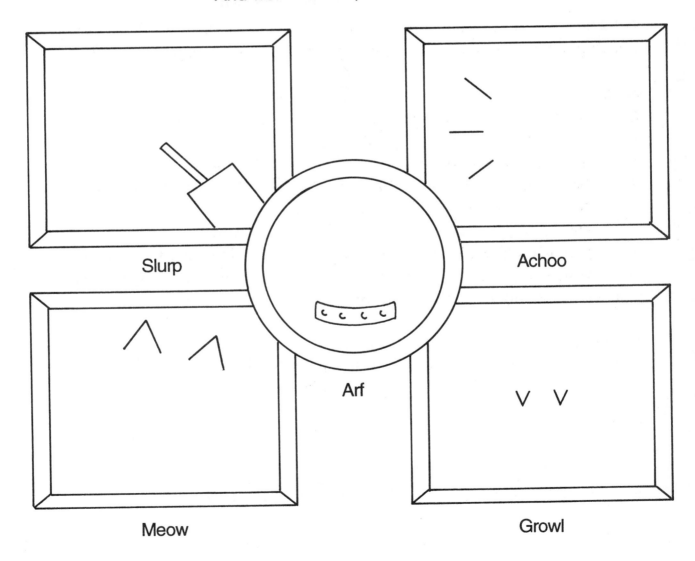

Slurp

Achoo

Arf

Meow

Growl

PICK THE WORDS
Week 2/Analytical Thinking

The Premise:
Students will match word descriptions with drawings.

Comment:
Part of the process of becoming an astute thinker is the ability to observe things precisely. This exercise in observational thinking is provided now so that more complicated analytical tasks can take place later.

Many children need this practice. For the ones who don't, a little reinforcement won't hurt.

Script:
(Put these figures on the board:)

Look at what I have drawn on the board. If I wished to describe one of the drawings by saying "circle, line," which one would I be talking about? *(Response)* Yes, the one on the right. To describe the other drawing, I'd have to say "circle, line, line."

In today's activity, you will be looking at nine drawings and then finding the exact words that describe them. Why is this important? Because it gives you practice in looking at things carefully.

Answers:
(1) 6 (2) 3 (3) 7 (4) 8 (5) 1 (6) 9 (7) 4 (8) 2 (9) 5.

Pick the Words

Name_____

Which words EXACTLY describe the drawings you see below? Match the pictures and the words. Hint: Start with the first words—dot, dot, dot—and look through all the pictures. You'll get the idea.

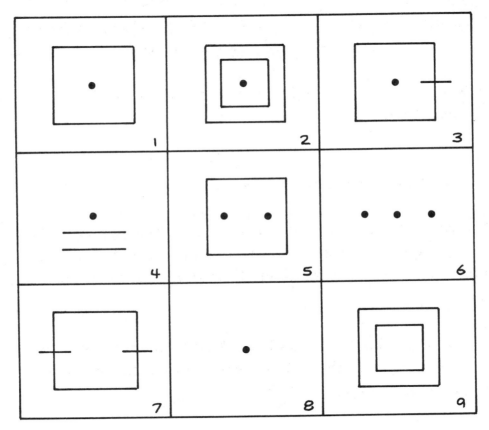

1. Dot, dot, dot _____
2. Square, dot, line _____
3. Line, line, square _____
4. Dot _____
5. Dot, square _____
6. Square, square _____
7. Line, line, dot _____
8. Square, square, dot _____
9. Square, dot, dot _____

BETWEEN
Week 2/Flexible Thinking

The Premise:
Students will examine various sequential relationships.

Comment:
This activity is offered as a sprightly, lighthearted way to encourage children to think flexibly. The concept of between-ness has all sorts of possibilities. Let children generate their own lists of "What is between . . ." when they finish this assignment.

Script:
(Hold up a book and then say:)

What is between the covers of this book? *(Response)* Yes, pages. What is between your foot and your shoe? *(Response)* Yes, your sock.

The activity today deals with things that are between other things. Sometimes, more than one answer is possible, but I want you to choose just the one answer you think is most important.

Answers:
(1) nose (2) neck (3) lunch (4) eggshell (5) net (6) wall (7) roof (8) night (9) day.

Between

Name_____

What is between you and your teacher right now? Desks? Other students? In this activity, you are asked to think of ONE thing which comes between two other things.

You'll need to use the space BETWEEN your ears to do a good job!

What is between . . .

1. your eyes and your mouth? _____

2. your shoulder and your head? _____

3. breakfast and dinner? _____

4. an egg yolk and an egg carton? _____

5. two tennis players? _____

6. the outdoors and the indoors? _____

7. the sky and a ceiling? _____

8. sunset and sunrise? _____

9. sunrise and sunset? _____

TAKE AWAY
Week 2/Problem Solving

The Premise:
Based on classification clues, students will cut away shapes until they are left with one final shape, which contains the answer-word.

Comment:
Categorization comes first, cutting comes next, and the suspense mounts as children work their way to the conclusion of this activity—discovering the word on the final shape.

The hands-on nature of this project is a good change of pace. Most children shouldn't have any trouble cutting out the simple shapes.

Script:
(Put these words on the board: stir, sweep, mix, boil, whip, dust, bake.)

If I asked you to pick out only those words that have something to do with cooking, which ones would you choose? *(Response)* Yes, stir, mix, boil, whip, and bake.

In this activity, you will be reading some clues and then looking for certain words that appear on various shapes. You will cut away the shapes until you get to one last shape. That shape will contain the word which is the answer.

Read the instructions carefully. They are very clear and will tell you what to do. One piece of advice—think carefully before you cut. Good luck.

Answers:
(1) bib, diaper (2) policeman, soldier, nurse, pilot (3) avenue, street (4) watch, calendar, clock (5) sand, shell, starfish (6) cough, sniffle. The word on the remaining shape: bridge.

Take Away

Name_____

Today, you will be cutting away shapes until you get to one final shape. Which shapes do you cut? You will learn that by following the directions. Three rules:

- Cut only the number of shapes listed after each direction.
- Do not work ahead. Complete each direction in the order given.
- As you work, put all the shapes in a pile. You won't need them.

Look for and then cut out:

1. Things babies wear. (2)
2. People in uniforms. (4)
3. Names for roads. (2)
4. Things that measure time. (3)
5. Things on a beach. (3)
6. Sounds of a cold. (2)

The word on the remaining shape is: _____

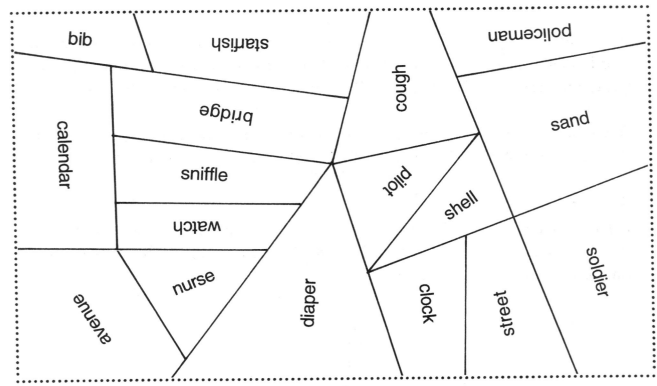

First, cut along the dotted lines.

BOTTLES AND JARS
Week 2/Elaborative Thinking

The Premise:
Students will examine the general characteristics of bottles and jars.

Comment:
What youngster hasn't poured ketchup from a bottle or dipped into a jar of pickles? Though admittedly unspectacular, these containers are a part of every child's experience.

Regarding Number 3, it is probably safe to say that the biggest difference between a bottle and a jar involves the size of the mouth. Other answers might be: a bottle has a neck and a jar does not; a bottle holds liquids (or semi-liquids) while a jar usually holds things that are more solid.

Script:
What's wrong with this sentence? "One day, Jose went to the refrigerator for a bottle of pickles and a jar of ketchup." *(Response)* Yes, pickles come in jars and ketchup comes in bottles.

You will be thinking about jars and bottles in this activity. You'll even get to do some drawing. Have fun.

Answers:
(1) Soda pop, vinegar, lemon juice, soy sauce, ketchup, syrup. (2) Olives, mayonnaise, mustard, pickles, jam, peanut butter. (3) a bottle has a narrow mouth while a jar has a wide mouth.

Bottles and Jars

Name_____

This activity should be a JARRING experience for you, but please, don't BOTTLE up any private feelings you have about this subject. Ready?

1. List three things that come in bottles.

_____

_____

_____

Draw a bottle.

2. List three things that come in jars.

_____

_____

_____

Draw a jar.

3. What is one important difference between a bottle and a jar?

_____

_____

_____

® Tin Man Press

FUNNY QUESTIONS
Week 2/Originality

The Premise:
Students will answer questions containing words which have been shortened and/or manipulated.

Comment:
Original thinking involves the ability to see things in new ways. This activity certainly encourages that process by asking students to decipher some new "words." To be sure they have understood—and to make them accountable—students must then respond by answering the questions.

Script:
(Write on the board: U can X-pect some fun B-4 today is over.)

This is a funny way to write a sentence, isn't it? What does it say? *(Response)* In this activity, you will have to answer 10 questions, but first you'll have to figure out what the words are.

Translations:
(1) What grade are you in? (2) Do you like to play ball? (3) Who's sitting next to you? (4) What color are your eyes? (5) Do you like cookies? (6) Have you ever been to the seashore? (7) Are you always wise? (8) What is today? (9) What comes after Tuesday? (10) Were these questions too easy for you?

Funny Questions

Name_____

Do U like 2 have fun with words and letters? If you do, U should enjoy this activity. Reading the questions is the hard part. The answers should be E-Z 4 someone as smart as U!

1. What grade R-U in? _____

2. Do U like 2 play ? _____

3. Who's sitting next 2-U? _____

4. What color R your I's? _____

5. Do you like cook E's? _____

6. Have U ever been 2 the C shore? _____

7. R-U always Y's? _____

8. What is 2 day? _____

9. What comes after 2's day? _____

10. Were these questions 2-E-Z-4-U? _____

ZOO CLUES
Week 3/Analytical Thinking

The Premise:
Students will identify various abstractions of zoo creatures.

Comment:
This is the first of many abstractions in this program. The focus here is on dominant features of zoo animals—an elephant's trunk, a zebra's stripes, a turtle's shell. Students must think about these characteristics and then match the drawings with the words.

Abstractions are useful tools in the analytical process because they encourage children to break their thinking into parts. This search for key elements is at the center of analytical thinking.

Besides their obvious educational value, abstractions are also fun. There is real satisfaction to be gained when you hook up a sparely-drawn image to a familiar concept.

Script:
(Put these drawings on the board:)

If I told you these were common animals, what do you think they could be? *(Response)* Yes, the one on the left could be a porcupine. The one on the right is probably a cat, or a tiger perhaps. How did you know one was a porcupine? *(Response)* Yes, the slanted lines look like the quills of a porcupine.

Today, you are going to be doing some similar thinking about zoo animals. You will have to think about primary characteristics. For example, what makes a camel look like a camel? If you do that, you'll have a lot of fun doing this activity.

Answers:
(1) 7 (2) 4 (3) 2 (4) 9 (5) 8 (6) 5 (7) 1 (8) 6 (9) 3.

Zoo Clues

Name_____

These pictures have something to do with creatures you might see at the zoo. Think about what makes animals—and birds and reptiles—different from each other. Then, match the pictures with the words.

1. Ostrich _____
2. Camel _____
3. Zebra _____
4. Leopard _____
5. Lion _____
6. Turtle _____
7. Elephant _____
8. Snake _____
9. Monkey _____

CRAZY RHYMES
Week 3/Flexible Thinking

The Premise:
Students will complete rhymes based on visual clues.

Comment:
As the saying goes, "All work and no play makes Jack a dull boy." This activity shouldn't be very difficult for children to do. However, it is a good chance for students to think like poets and have some fun.

If one of your children says, "A <u>rabbit</u> with lots of money," you have a job on your hands. More of this sort of thing can be found under the title, "Silly Rhymes," in our book, "Ideas To Go."

Script:
(As you hand out the papers, say:)

To do this assignment and finish on time,
You'll have to be able to think of a rhyme.
Just look at the pictures and when you are through,
I'm sure I'll be very happy with you.

Answers:
A bunny with lots of money. A soggy doggy. Where's your tooth, Ruth? This pig wears a wig. A witch with an itch. A bow on a toe. A parrot with a carrot.

Crazy Rhymes

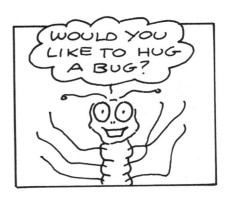

Name_____

How good are you at rhyming? Here's your chance to find out. Finish the sentence or phrase with a word that rhymes with the underlined word.

A _____ with lots of <u>money</u>.

A <u>soggy</u> _____ .

Where's your

_____, <u>Ruth</u>?

This <u>pig</u> wears a _____ .

A <u>witch</u>

with an _____ .

A _____ on a <u>toe</u>.

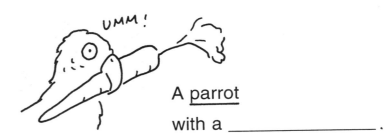

A <u>parrot</u>

with a _____ .

CIRCLE FUN
Week 3/Problem Solving

The Premise:
Students will draw lines to solve problems presented by dot-and-circle arrangements.

Comment:
This assignment sets a trap for students who tend to rush through their work, for without careful direction-following, there is trouble ahead.

The instructions are clearly worded, so don't rush to interpret them for students. They need to learn how to work independently.

Script:
(Put this diagram on the board:)

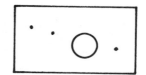

If I asked you to connect all three dots with one straight line, but I also told you that the line could not touch the circle, could you do it? *(Response)* No, you couldn't, could you?

This is the kind of thinking you'll be doing today. Take your time and read all of the directions very, very carefully before you begin.

Solutions:

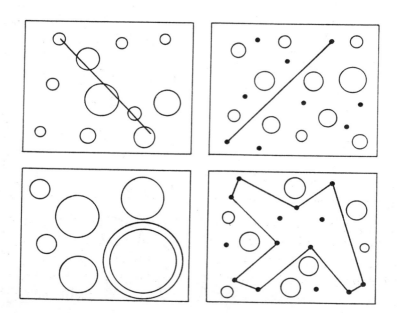

Circle Fun

Name_____

A ruler is necessary for three of the four challenges below. And remember to think before your pencil strikes the paper! Good luck.

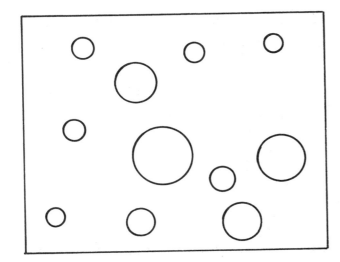

Draw one straight line that goes through as many circles as possible.

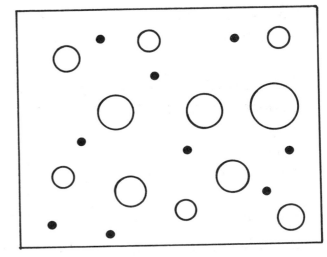

Draw the longest straight line you can that connects any two dots, but the line must not touch any of the circles.

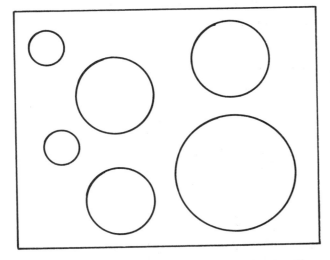

Without touching any circle or the border, draw another circle that is bigger than any of the circles you see here. Hmmmm, where can you put it?

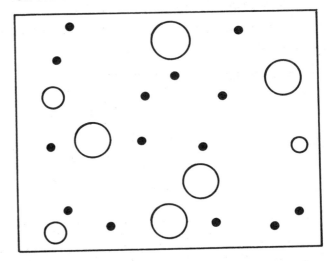

Make the largest shape you can by connecting any dots you wish with straight lines. Your lines cannot touch any circles, and there can't be any circles inside your shape.

CARTOONS
Week 3/Elaborative Thinking

The Premise:
Students will expand their thinking on the subject of cartoons.

Comment:
Isn't Number 3 interesting? The answers should give you some insight into how your students perceive reality! As for Number 4, youngsters will need to be able to think like marketing experts—as they digest their morning cereal.

You might extend this activity by encouraging children to draw their own cartoon characters. How about: Colossal Man, The Masked Donut, Clock Woman, or the Box Heads?

Script:
Today, you are going to be thinking about TV cartoons. What is a cartoon, anyway? *(Response)* Yes, it is a story with characters that are drawn in a very funny or strange way.

Here's your assignment. Do a good job.

Cartoons

Name_____

No, it is not Saturday morning, but it's cartoon time anyway. Today, you are being asked to think about the subject of TV cartoons, so have some fun with this one!

1. What is your favorite cartoon? _____

2. Why do you like it? _____

_____

3. Write a sentence about something you've seen in a cartoon that couldn't happen in real life. _____

_____

4. When you're watching cartoons on TV, you see more commercials for cereal than for coffee. Why? _____

_____

5. Finish these cartoon starts any way you like.

 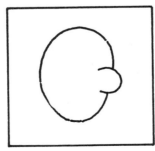  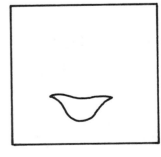

INVENTING FLOWERS
Week 3/Originality

The Premise:
Using defined design elements, students will originate nine kinds of flowers.

Comment:
The point of this assignment is not the flowers, it is the components of the flowers. A little flower made of scribbles, a little flower made of circles—we guarantee they've never drawn flowers like these!

If given the instruction, "Make a picture of a flower," children will probably draw flowers as they always have in the past. Nothing new there. Shake them out of their flower schema and watch creativity bloom.

Script:
Close your eyes. Imagine that it is spring. The days are getting longer and the sun feels nice and warm.

Using some seeds that a friend gave you, you plant a flower garden. Then you wait for the seeds to sprout.

It takes them just a day or so to sprout and you are surprised! You thought it would take at least a week! The next day, something else happens. The sprouts have turned into beautiful flowers no one has ever seen before!

Your job today: Follow directions, of course—but make the flowers in this activity just as strange and beautiful as you can.

Some possible versions:

Inventing Flowers

Name_____

How are you at inventing flowers? In this activity, you will design nine different kinds. Follow the directions beneath each box and make your flowers just as interesting as you can. Remember, these are new types of flowers no one has ever seen before!

HURRY UP! I NEED SOME FLOWERS!

A flower made of little triangles. △

A flower made of little circles. ○

A flower made of little dashes. / | \

A flower made of little scribbles.

A flower made of many U's.   U

A flower made of little spirals. ☺

A flower made of rectangles. ▭

A flower made of little dots. ●

A flower made of anything you wish!

VERB PUZZLERS (C)
Week 4/Analytical Thinking

The Premise:
Students will match C words with visual clues.

Comment:
To complete this challenge correctly—(sorry, C's are habit-forming)—children will have to determine what has been done to the letters.

You will find two other versions of this idea later in the book. Not only do they provide practice in analytical thinking, but they are fast-paced and entertaining.

Script:
(Put this drawing on the board:)

I am looking for a word that is a verb, that begins with the letter you see on the board, and has something to do with what I've done to the letter. What could the word be? *(Response) (If another hint is needed, point out the teeth and ask what you do with teeth.)* Yes, the word is "chew."

Today, you will be thinking about some other C verbs. Look at the pictures, read the words below the pictures, and you'll know what to do.

Answers:
(1) 5 (2) 8 (3) 6 (4) 1 (5) 4 (6) 7 (7) 9 (8) 3 (9) 2.

Verb Puzzlers (C)

Name_____

CAN you CHOOSE which C verbs match up with these C pictures? CHECK out what has been done to the C pictures and you should be fine!

1. Count _____
2. Carry _____
3. Cough _____
4. Cook _____
5. Climb _____
6. Crumble _____
7. Cry _____
8. Curl _____
9. Cut _____

CHANGE A LETTER
Week 4/Flexible Thinking

The Premise:
Students will change one letter in an existing word to make a new word that fits a clue.

Comment:
By having to keep two things in mind—the one-letter change and the clue—children will need to think flexibly about their answers.

Script:
(Write the word "pear" on the board.)

I want you to change this word into another word, but you can change only one letter, and it must fit this clue. *(Write the words, "an animal," on the board.)* Based on the clue, what would the new word be? *(Response)* Yes, the new word is "bear."

In this activity, you'll be turning 10 words into 10 different words.

Answers:
(1) bang (2) chair (3) ant (4) fire (5) nose (6) peach (7) jar (8) March (9) wind (10) plant.

Change a Letter

Name_____

Change one letter in the words on the left to make new words which fit the clues on the right. For example, if you were working with the word, "sheep," you could change one letter and make a new word, "sleep."

HI. I'M A TROG.

1. Hang _____ A loud noise.

2. Chain _____ It has four legs.

3. Act _____ An insect.

4. Fare _____ This is very hot.

5. Lose _____ It's on your face.

6. Beach _____ A fruit.

7. Jam _____ A container.

8. Match _____ A month.

9. Wild _____ A big breeze.

10. Plane _____ Often seen in a pot.

A BIRD
Week 4/Problem Solving

The Premise:
Using only scissors and paper, students will cut and fold a bird shape.

Comment:
Some students will plunge into this project with enthusiasm, inventing as they go, while others will try to get you to tell them how to proceed. These are the ones who need this activity the most. If they remain stumped, you might suggest that they think of a bird in flight, with its wings spread.

Have plenty of extra rectangles available. There will be some youngsters who will want to make several versions.

Script:
Today, you are going to be making something out of nothing. Well, almost nothing. Your job will be to make a bird shape out of a piece of paper. Sounds easy, doesn't it? But there is one important rule. You can't make just a flat shape of a bird; it has to have folds in it somewhere to make it more interesting.

Questions? *(Response)* Let's get started. I expect to see some fantastic birds!

Possible versions:

A Bird

Name_____

Cut out the rectangle below. Then, using only your scissors, make a shape that looks like a bird. One rule: Your shape must have some folds in it so that it isn't flat.

If you're really puzzled about how to begin, think of all the paper airplanes you have folded. That should get you started!

SHIRTS
Week 4/Elaborative Thinking

The Premise:
Students will expand their thinking on the subject of shirts.

Comment:
Here's an ancillary activity you might try:

Ask students to write about a favorite shirt. Encourage them to list at least six details about it. (Possible details: where they got it, color, fabric, style, kind of collar, what they wore with it, what happened to it, etc.)

Be firm about the six-detail requirement. It won't hurt them to strain their brains a bit. A little elaborative angst is good for them.

Script:
Put your heads down on your desks and close your eyes. Now, without looking, guess how many people in the room are wearing shirts with collars right now. How many do you think there are, (name)? *(Response)* How many do you say, (name)? *(Response)* Now, everyone look up. If you are wearing a shirt or blouse with a collar, stand up. Did anyone guess the actual number? *(Response)*

Now that you're thinking about shirts, you know what the subject of today's assignment will be, don't you?

Answers:
(1) 4 (2) the size (3) I outgrew it, it has a hole in it, the style isn't "in" any longer, I tore it, I moved to a different climate, etc. (4) A-3, B-5, C-1, D-6, E-4, F-2.

Shirts

Name_____

Think of something that has a collar and a tail. The answer, at least for this activity, is not a dog but a shirt! We all wear shirts sometimes, so you should know a lot about this topic.

1. Think of a shirt that is buttoned up. How many openings does it have—not counting the spaces between the buttons? _____

2. You have gone to a store and found a shirt you like. The price is right. The color is right. The style is right. What other thing do you need to know?

_____

3. List three reasons you might never wear a certain shirt again.

_____

_____

_____

4. Match these shirt clues with the words below.

A. Football player _____
B. Person on vacation _____
C. Referee _____

D. Soldier _____
E. Baby _____
F. Business person _____

DRAW A RHYME
Week 4/Originality

The Premise:

Students will make drawings based on short rhymes.

Comment:

Hold them responsible! If the rhyme says, "long tooth," then the drawing better have a long tooth in it somewhere.

If students have fun with this, let them create drawings of other strange animals and display them on the bulletin board or in the hallway.

Script:

(As you hand out the assignment, read this poem:)

Your assignment today
Has to do with some creatures
Who have funny names
And need funny features.

How you will do it—
Well, that's up to you.
Just pretend that you're in
The world's weirdest zoo!

Possible versions:

  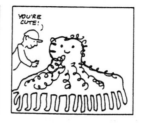 

A Zooth   A Skyle   A Nurr   A Zeek

Draw a Rhyme

Name_____

Read the poems and then draw the creature the little person has seen. Make your drawings as interesting as you can!

I saw a big Zooth
With a fat tail
And a long tooth.

I saw a Skyle
With funny eyes
And a twisted smile.

I saw a Nurr
With sixteen legs
And curly fur.

I saw a Zeek
With spotted wings
And a pointed beak.

HUMAN BEINGS
Week 5/Analytical Thinking

The Premise:
Students will match symbolic versions of facial characteristics with words.

Comment:
In this exercise, children will be working with symbolic representations of things they know very well—eyebrows, freckles, teeth, etc.

Suggest to them that they solve the most obvious matches first. The rest of the challenges will then become easier. For example, "nose" and "eyebrows" are quite obvious while "mouth" and "ear" are less so.

Script:
Today, you have an interesting assignment. You will be doing an activity which has something to do with your eyes, your nose, your teeth and other features. That sounds pretty easy, doesn't it?

Surprise! This activity isn't as easy as it sounds! But if you go slowly and examine everything first before you decide on the answers, you'll be fine.

Answers:
(1) 7 (2) 6 (3) 9 (4) 2 (5) 8 (6) 5 (7) 4 (8) 1 (9) 3.

Human Beings

Name_____

You should know a lot about this subject because it's all about human beings! These things don't look exactly like what they are, but you should be able to get some good ideas from the clues. Match the pictures with the words.

1	2	3
4	5	6
7	8	9

1. Eyebrows _____
2. Freckles _____
3. Mole _____
4. Mouth _____
5. Nose _____
6. Eyes _____
7. Hair _____
8. Ear _____
9. Teeth _____

ALPHABET CLUES
Week 5/Flexible Thinking

The Premise:
Students will think of words beginning with the letter shown in the drawings.

Comment:
The chance to play with words—and think flexibly about them—is at the heart of this activity.

First, students must find the alphabet letter in each drawing and determine what has been done to it. Then, they must read the word or words under the drawing. Finally, they must fill in the blanks with an answer that carries out the theme of the drawing and fits into the rhythm of the phrase.

For those who find this activity fun—and there are some adults who have been known to fall into that category—our book, "T is for Think," contains more than 300 of these challenges.

Script:
(Put this drawing on the board:)   ⊢ ⊣

Beneath the drawing, write: This H has been cut in _____ .

What has happened to this H? Has it been cut in two? Has it been cut apart? Yes it has, but if I asked you to fill in the blank using an H word that fits the drawing, what would you say? *(Response)* Yes, the best answer would be "half."

This is the kind of work you will be doing today. Have fun!

Answers:
We like to play tennis. Open wide. An H showing its hands and feet. I have a stomachache. There are nine N's in this pile. An umpire. A big bunny and a small bunny.

Alphabet Clues

Name_____

You'll find a letter of the alphabet in every one of these little pictures. Your assignment is to fill in the blanks with words which begin with that letter.

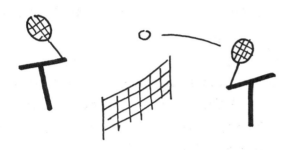

We like to play _____ .

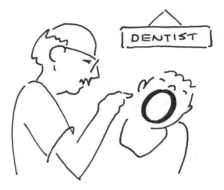

_____ wide!

An H showing its

_____ and feet.

I have a

stomach

_____ .

There are _____

N's in this pile.

An _____ .

A _____ _____

and a small

_____ .

FROM ALSTOV TO BEZOT
Week 5/Problem Solving

The Premise:
Students will go from start to finish, touching every planet on the way, without retracing their path or crossing any lines they have already made.

Comment:
This challenge may seem impossible at first, until the proverbial light bulb comes on. Then, the solution becomes apparent. The trick is to snake a line back and forth until the destination is reached.

Script:
Who would like to be an astronaut some day? *(Response)* Today, you are going to be visiting 20 little planets on your journey to a very important planet called Bezot.

Oh, I forgot to mention one thing. This all happens on paper. In this trip, you cannot retrace your path or cross any lines you have already made. It may not seem easy, but it can be done.

Be sure to make your lines light at first until you decide which way to go. Then, make them darker so I'll know what you did.

Possible solution:

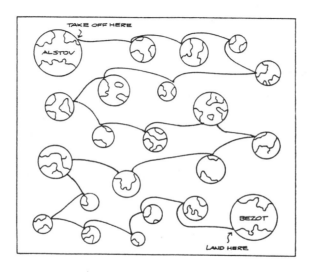

From Alstov to Bezot

Name_____

You are an astronaut. You must fly your spaceship from Planet Alstov to Planet Bezot. But first, you must land on each of the other planets you see. Draw a line to show how you will do this. (Hint: Your line will be wavy, not straight.)

But here's the hard part: Your line must never cross a line you have already made and you may not retrace any lines. (Whew!) Have a good flight.

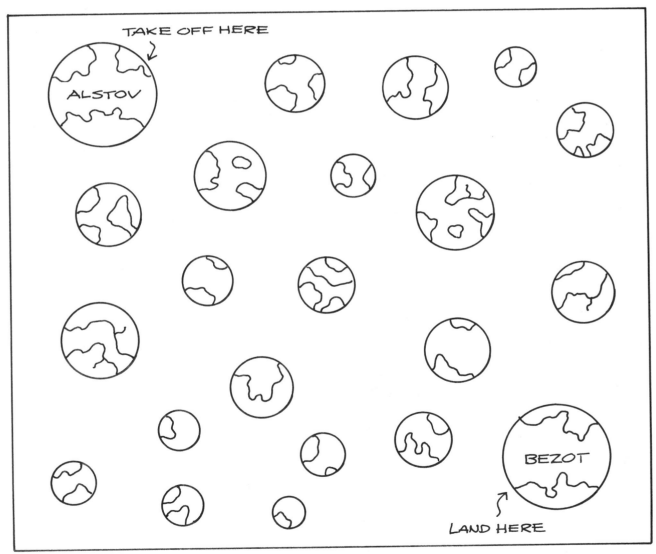

BRUSHING MY TEETH
Week 5/Elaborative Thinking

The Premise:
Students will describe every step they take when they brush their teeth.

Comment:
Get ready for varying degrees of success. It's hard to think of everything you do in a process that is almost automatic. (Some students will turn the water faucet on but forget to turn it off.) For the record, here is one version:

> I picked up my toothbrush.
> I opened the medicine cabinet to get the tube of toothpaste.
> I picked up the tube of toothpaste.
> I unscrewed the cap of the toothpaste tube.
> I squeezed the toothpaste onto the toothbrush.
> I turned on the cold water.
> I put water on my toothbrush.
> I put the cap back on the tube of toothpaste.
> I brushed my teeth.
> I rinsed out my mouth.
> I rinsed off my toothbrush.
> I turned off the water.
> I put away the tube of toothpaste.
> I put away my toothbrush.

Script:
Just for fun, let's think of all the things you do when you prepare a bowl of cold cereal for yourself in the morning. What is the first step in the process? *(Response)* Yes, opening the cabinet door to get the cereal. What is the second step? *(Response)* Yes, getting a bowl. What is the third step? *(Response, and continue.)*

Today, you are going to be writing down every step in a process I hope you do at least twice a day. I won't tell you what you'll be describing. That's for you to find out!

Brushing My Teeth

Name_____

Your job today is to make a list of every single thing you do when you brush your teeth. Start with the first step you take and then go on from there. Don't forget to take off the toothpaste cap and turn on the water!

WRITE YOUR NAME
Week 5/Originality

The Premise:
Students will write their names five different ways.

Comment:
Occasionally, it's good to toss youngsters a softball. This activity isn't too rigorous, but it is entertaining and inventive. Since it focuses on children themselves, they will respond readily to the subject matter.

The name-writing idea also appears in our book, "WakerUppers," in which students begin each of 50 assignments by writing their names in a different way.

Script:
(Student's name), come up to the board and write your name with the hand you usually don't use when you write. *(Response)* (Student's name) come up to the board and write your name with very tall, skinny letters. *(Response)*

Now, everyone gets a chance to do some name-writing! Follow these directions carefully and do your best.

Possible versions:

Lynette Smith

Ernesto Diaz

Doug Wilson

Write Your Name

This is an activity about you. At least, it's about a very important part of you—your name. Here's your chance to be creative and even a little crazy if you like. Follow the directions, of course, but have some fun.

1. Write your full name as if all the letters were made out of sticks.

2. Close your eyes and try to write your name inside this little box.

3. Write your name so it is very hard to see.

4. Write your name so the letters look as if they are about to tip over.

5. Write your name using fat letters. Then give the letters eyes, noses, and mouths.

WRONG!
Week 6/Analytical Thinking

The Premise:
Students will match check marks with statements.

Comment:
Consider this project the cousin of handwriting analysis.

Since most students already know more than they probably want to know about check marks, they should welcome a somewhat frivolous look at them here. Little do they know that this exercise provides excellent practice in analytical thinking.

Script:
Today, you are going to be detectives, working on an activity involving check marks. These check marks were made by several make-believe students as they checked their papers. Your assignment is to figure out who made each mark.

Answers:
(1) 6 (2) 8 (3) 4 (4) 3 (5) 1 (6) 5 (7) 2 (8) 9 (9) 7.

Wrong!

Name_____

Nine students have just finished checking their own papers. By looking at the way they made their marks, can you figure out who did what?

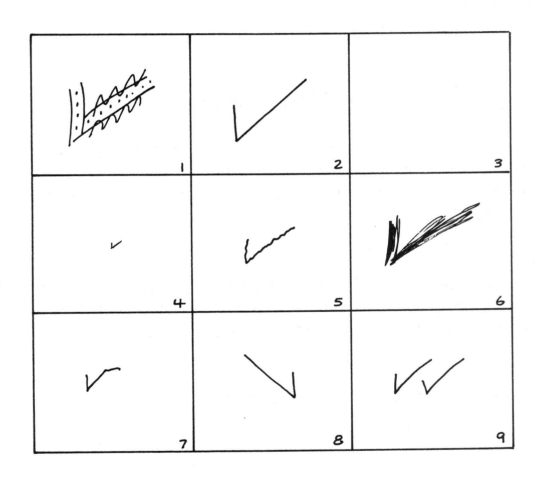

1. Very angry about missing a question. _____
2. Writes left-handed. _____
3. Hoping the teacher won't see it. _____
4. Got them all right. _____
5. A doodler. _____
6. Nervous and uptight. _____
7. Very neat and proper. _____
8. Missed two parts of one question. _____
9. Just broke her pencil. _____

MYSTERY THINGS
Week 6/Flexible Thinking

The Premise:
Students will determine the identity of common objects by analyzing complicated descriptions.

Comment:
You may have to help them with the word "device" in Number 1—or at least point them in the direction of the dictionary. Whenever possible, we have tried to describe the common objects in words they already know.

Some students may argue for "French fries" as the answer for Number 4. We think the words "thin" and "slices" more accurately describe potato chips.

Script:
I am thinking of a common object, but I am going to describe it in a very different way. This means you will have to think very hard to figure out what it is. Are you ready? Okay.

"A row of evenly-spaced pieces of thin plastic which are joined together and used to part and smooth hair." What am I describing? *(Response)* Yes, a comb.

Now, it's your turn to figure out four other mystery objects. Good luck.

Answers:
(1) toaster (2) fingernail polish (3) teddy bear (4) potato chips.

Mystery Things

Name_____

These aren't really mystery objects at all. They are things you know about already. Read the definitions and see if you can figure out what is being described.

1. An electrical device for making bread crisp.

_____

2. A colored liquid applied to the hard surface at the ends of fingers.

_____

3. A small, stuffed cloth object, often found in bedrooms, which is made to look like a large, brown mammal.

_____

4. Thin, crisply fried slices of a white vegetable, usually sold in plastic bags.

_____

HOW MANY CUTS?
Week 6/Problem Solving

The Premise:
Students will cut along as many straight lines as possible without cutting the square in two pieces.

Comment:
Tell your students to get out their scissors and their patience. This activity is not easy. Many youngsters won't be able to make the maximum number of cuts. (The magic number is 10.) There will be some false starts, so have extra copies available.

Some children may even want to draw out a plan before they do any cutting.

Script:
Today, you are going to be solving a problem by cutting along some straight lines. But the real problem is this: As you make your straight-line cuts, you must keep the paper you are working with in one piece.

One other point: *(Draw this diagram on the board:)*

You are not allowed to cut just part of a line and count it as one cut. For example, A-C is one line, and B-D is another. But you cannot cut from A to B and count it as one cut, or from A to B to D and count it as two cuts. You must cut the whole line or not cut it at all.

Plan out what you're going to do before you start cutting. Then, give it a try.

Solution:

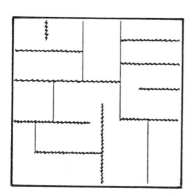

How Many Cuts?

How many straight cuts can you make without cutting the square below into two pieces?

Begin by cutting out the square along the dotted lines. Then, make any cuts you wish along the lines that are shown. Write the number of cuts you made and your name somewhere on the square so your teacher can see how well you did.

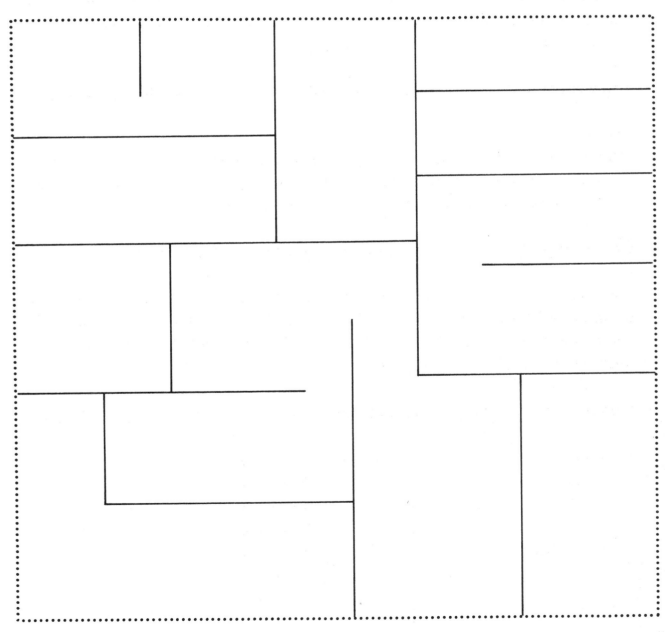

THROWAWAYS
Week 6/Elaborative Thinking

The Premise:
Students will expand their thinking on things that are commonly discarded.

Comment:
We must admit that one of our earlier versions of Number 2 asked for a "reason you might throw away a newspaper." Fortunately, we substituted "calendar," since everyone (including us) knows that newspapers should be recycled.

Which brings us to another point: Why not follow up on the subject of "things you throw away" with a list-making activity on "things you recycle?"

The drawings in Number 3 will be fun. It should be a challenge for children to figure out how to draw items that have been broken or used up.

Script:
Here's a question for you. What is something you would never, never throw away? *(Response)* Now, I am going to give you an activity in which you will be thinking the opposite way—about things you do throw away.

At the end of this activity, you will be drawing three objects. Go slowly and do your drawings as carefully as you can.

Answers:
(1) candy bar - wrapper; Popsicle - stick; banana - peel; peach - pit
(2) pencil - it's too short; light bulb - it burned out; calendar - it's out of date.

Throwaways

Name_____

Don't throw away this paper—it's important! But think about how many things are thrown away every day. That's the focus of this activity.

HEY! PICK ME UP AND PUT ME WHERE I BELONG.

1. What do you throw away after you have eaten . . .

    •   a candy bar? _____

    •   a Popsicle? _____

    •   a banana? _____

    •   a peach? _____

2. Give one reason why you might throw away . . .

    •   a pencil? _____

    •   a light bulb? _____

    •   a calendar? _____

3. Draw these things people have thrown away. Remember, they must have something wrong with them—otherwise, they wouldn't be thrown away!

Comb	Tube of Toothpaste	Sunglasses

E DRAWINGS
Week 6/Originality

The Premise:
Students will turn the letter E into six drawings based on specific descriptions.

Comment:
This is a very nice little exercise in original thinking. Who would expect the quite ordinary letter E to end up as the face of a robot? Or a chest of drawers?

Script:
(Draw a big capital E on the board.)

What is on the board? *(Response)* Yes, a capital E. What if I said, "Turn this E into a picture of a sock and shoe?" How could you do it? *(Response, letting a couple of students try it.)*

This is how I would do it. *(Add curved lines and other details as shown:)* And I would probably give the sock some ribs, and I would give the shoe a lace, a sole, and a heel.

Today's activity is similar to what we have just done. It involves drawing and thinking—and using your imagination. Have fun!

Possible solutions:

E Drawings

Name_____

Turn these E's into the six things listed below. You may use the E's in any way you wish, but they must be part of your drawing.

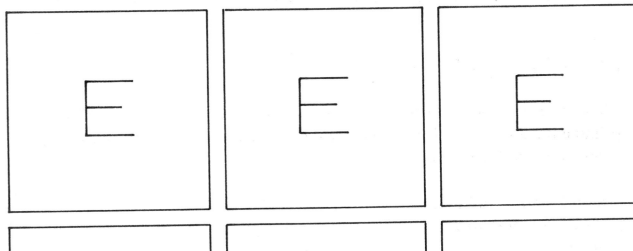

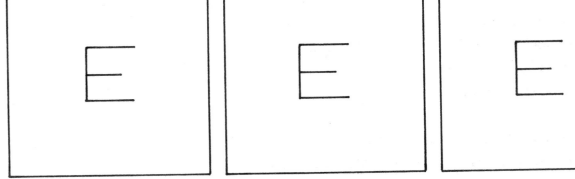

- A window with fancy curtains.
- A stack of four books.
- A chest of drawers.
- A jungle gym with two kids playing on it.
- A fish tank with fish.
- The face of a robot.

BIRD TALK
Week 7/Analytical Thinking

The Premise:
Students will match drawings about birds with statements.

Comment:
Consider the cognitive processes students must go through to solve this activity. For example, to match Number 9 with Picture 3, students must:

- examine the five drawings in which a bird's head is portrayed.

- notice that there are motion lines above the head of the bird in Picture 3.

- surmise that the straight line in Picture 3 represents the edge of a tree trunk.

- realize the bird is probably a woodpecker and that by pounding his beak into the tree, he is getting a headache! (Actually, woodpeckers don't really get headaches from pecking, as some aspiring junior ornithologists will probably inform you.)

Script:
How many of you have bird feeders or birdhouses in your yard? *(Response)* No doubt, all of you know a great deal about bird behavior because you see birds every day, don't you?

This activity is about birds, so anything you know about them will be helpful to you.

Answers:
(1) 4 (2) 5 (3) 1 (4) 7 (5) 9 (6) 8 (7) 2 (8) 6 (9) 3.

Bird Talk

Name_____

If birds could talk, here are some things they might say. Your job is to match the statements with the pictures. Use each picture and statement just once.

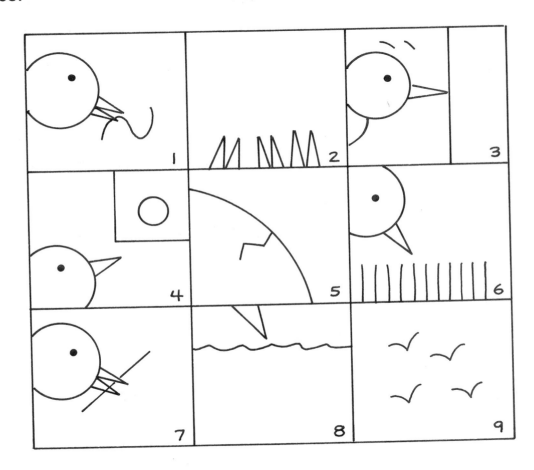

1. Anybody home? _____
2. I want out! _____
3. Mmmm. Dinner. _____
4. I'm building a home. _____
5. Sometimes, I like to be with my friends. _____
6. I'm getting a drink. _____
7. We're hungry. _____
8. You can't hide from me. _____
9. I think I'm getting a headache! _____

NOUNS, PLEASE
Week 7/Flexible Thinking

The Premise:
Students will supply nouns that are appropriate for certain verbs.

Comment:
The first noun/verb combinations are easy—a ball rolls, a baby cries, etc. Later, students will encounter verbs such as "begins" and "falls," which are harder to associate with an appropriate noun.

Some students will do very well with this activity. Others, who have trouble "moving around" in the language, may have some difficulty. For example, a good answer for Number 9 would be " day" or "game." An answer such as "person" or "breakfast" does not really fulfill the spirit of the activity. As an extender, ask students to brainstorm as many nouns as possible for one of the verbs on the sheet.

Script:
(Write on the board: A _____ smiles.)

What is a noun? *(Response)* Yes, a noun is a person, place, or thing. In this activity, the noun serves as the subject of a very short sentence. Look at what I have put on the board. Can you think of a noun that would turn this into a sentence? *(Response)* Yes, "a baby smiles," "a child smiles." You couldn't say, "a fish smiles" because it wouldn't make sense, would it? Fish don't smile!

Your job today will be to come up with nouns that make sense with certain verbs.

Possible answers:
(1) ball (2) baby (3) clock (4) cookie (5) snake (6) string (7) star (8) car (9) day (10) sprain (11) bite (12) tree (13) rock (14) snowman (15) merry-go-round (16) leaf (17) jet (18) spider (19) balloon (20) door.

Nouns, Please

Name_____

Here are some verbs which describe what certain nouns do. Supply a noun that MAKES SENSE. (Some of these are not easy!) You'll need to be a flexible thinker to do this well.

1. A _____ rolls.

2. A _____ cries.

3. A _____ ticks.

4. A _____ crumbles.

5. A _____ slithers.

6. A _____ breaks.

7. A _____ shines.

8. A _____ runs.

9. A _____ begins.

10. A _____ hurts.

11. A _____ itches.

12. A _____ grows.

13. A _____ sinks.

14. A _____ melts.

15. A _____ turns.

16. A _____ falls.

17. A _____ flies.

18. A _____ climbs.

19. A _____ pops.

20. A _____ closes.

GLORFS
Week 7/Problem Solving

The Premise:
Students will analyze characteristics of faces to determine whether or not they belong in a specific group.

Comment:
There is one property that makes a Glorf a Glorf: All Glorfs have closed shapes for heads. Of course, it will take students some time to figure this out, but not everything in this life should be easy.

Script:
(Put these drawings on the board:)

Which one of these heads is different? Why? *(Response)* Yes, the middle head is not like the other two. It has no ears.

Today, you are going to be doing the same kind of thinking in an activity called "Glorfs." Glorfs are very strange people. Your job will be to figure out what makes a Glorf a Glorf.

Be good detectives and find those Glorfs!

Answers:

Glorfs

Name_____

What in the world is a Glorf? There's a way to tell—if you think hard and look closely. Figure out what is the same about all of the Glorfs and you'll be on the right track.

These are Glorfs.

These are not Glorfs.

Which of these are Glorfs? Circle them.

PIZZA
Week 7/Elaborative Thinking

The Premise:
Students will expand their thinking on the subject of pizza.

Comment:
Do they perhaps know more about this subject than you do?

Don't let them off the hook for Number 3. All students should be able to list at least three similarities.

Despite what the introduction on the activity page says, this would be an excellent opportunity to surprise them with a taste of the real thing. That's easy for us to suggest, we realize.

Script:
Not counting school lunches, how many of you have eaten pizza in the past week? *(Response)* Today's topic focuses on this popular food, so I know you'll have fun.

Answers:
(2) crust, topping (3) both are flat, they are usually round, they have flour in them, they taste good, they are baked, etc. (4) how hot it is.

Solution for Number 5:

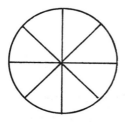

Pizza

Name_____

Juicy mushrooms, Italian sausage, green olives, tasty cheese . . .Too bad you'll just be THINKING about pizza in this activity!

1. What's your favorite kind of pizza? _____

2. Name the two main parts of a pizza. _____

   _____

3. How is a pizza like a cookie? List as many similarities as you can.

   _____

   _____

   _____

4. What is the most important thing you need to know before you take your first bite of pizza? _____

5. Four people have ordered a large pizza. Each person wants two pieces. Show how you could cut the pizza to give everyone two pieces of the same size.

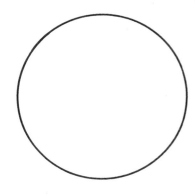

ART POEM
Week 7/Originality

The Premise:
Students will make drawings based on a poem.

Comment:
The drawings should contain the three elements mentioned in the poem—hairiness, lumpiness, and chin-ness!

Script:
In today's activity, you'll be reading a poem and then drawing the things that are mentioned in the poem.

I don't need to say anything more about this activity—just that I will be interested in seeing the results. Have fun, and use your imagination!

Possible versions:

Art Poem

Name_____

Are you feeling art smart? It's time to show off by making the most interesting drawing you can. It must have something to do with the poem. Take your time and put in lots of details.

Here is a creature
That has just a grin.
Give it some hair
And some lumps and a chin!

DRAW IT!

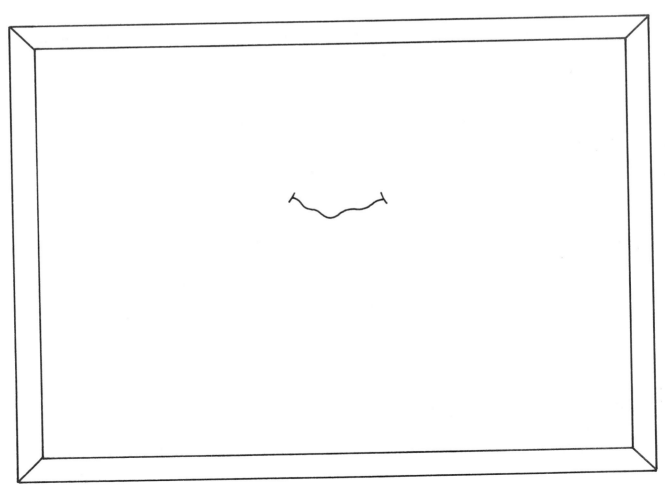

SLOPPY SHAPES
Week 8/Analytical Thinking

The Premise:
Students will match drawings with statements.

Comment:
No clean straight lines here! No perfectly-drawn objects! Which brings us to our soapbox . . .

Effective critical thinking depends on the ability to see things from a number of perspectives. Fixed ideas about how things "ought" to be (or look) tend to produce predictable, unimaginative thinking. Since all of us—students included—are surrounded these days by slick graphics, a little imperfection is a good thing.

That's why we feel handmade bulletin boards are better than those which are commercially prepared, and that's why we dislike all those bashful little lambs and smiling teddy bears you see in so many activities for students. Children need to be able to see things in a variety of ways. Hence, Sloppy Shapes.

You'll find another version of this activity in our book, "Ideas To Go."

Script:
The person who drew the activity you're going to be doing today was in a really big hurry. He didn't have time to make all his drawings as carefully as he should have. See if you can figure out what the things are that he drew in such a sloppy way.

Answers:
(1) 2 (2) 7 (3) 6 (4) 1 (5) 8 (6) 3 (7) 4 (8) 9 (9) 5.

Sloppy Shapes

Name_____

These are certainly sloppy drawings, aren't they?
But they almost look like real things. Figure out
which drawing goes with which sentence.

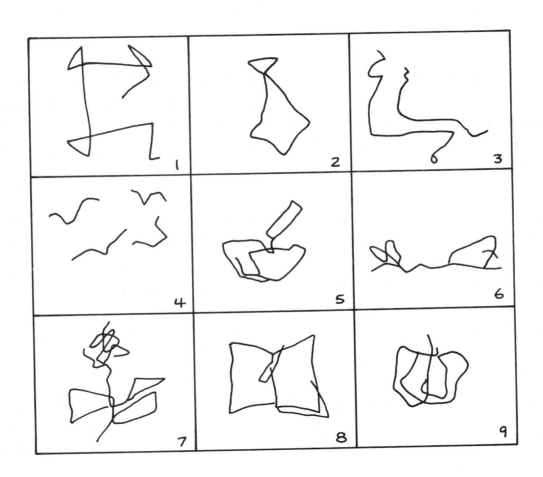

1. It's a nice necktie. _____
2. The flower is growing well. _____
3. Sharks scare me. _____
4. I am kneeling to shoot with my bow and arrow. _____
5. It's a good book. _____
6. The boy sat on his father's lap. _____
7. Several birds flew over at once. _____
8. I love apples. _____
9. I like ice cream in a dish. _____

NAME GAME
Week 8/Flexible Thinking

The Premise:
Students will finish sentences with words that rhyme.

Comment:
Youngsters often get frustrated when they have to write formal poetry. Ask them to participate in a two-word rhyming scheme, however, and that's a different story. Any child can think of a way to rhyme "flea" or "ball."

Since there are 10 sentences here, children will have to shift gears often to come up with 10 rhyming schemes.

Script:
I'm going to get you in the mood for this activity. Please think of a rhyming word that finishes these nonsense sentences. I like <u>mice</u>, but not on *(Response)*. Yes, the word is "rice," or it could be "ice." I think that <u>bat</u> is wearing a *(Response)*. Yes, the word is "hat." Tiny <u>roads</u> are only for *(Response)*. Yes, the word is "toads."

In this activity, you will do some more thinking about words that rhyme. However, the words you use must also make sense in the sentences.

Answers:
(1) bike (2) silly (3) head (4) zoo (5) tree (6) pony (7) ham (8) sad
(9) hill (10) candy.

Name Game

Name_____

MY NAME IS JOE, AND THIS IS MY TOE.

If your name were Sally and I saw you at a place where people play a game with a ball and pins, I could say, "I saw Sally at the bowling alley."

"Sally" and "alley" rhyme, don't they? You'll need to do more rhyming to finish the sentences below. Try to think of a word that rhymes with the name and also makes sense in the sentence.

1. I saw Mike on his _____ .

2. I saw Billy acting _____ .

3. I saw Ted scratch his _____ .

4. I saw Sue at the _____ .

5. I saw Lee climb a _____ .

6. I saw Tony on a _____ .

7. I saw Sam eating _____ .

8. I saw Chad looking _____ .

9. I saw Jill climb a _____ .

10. I saw Mandy eating _____ .

TAKE AWAY
Week 8/Problem Solving

The Premise:
Based on classification clues, students will cut away shapes until they are left with one final shape, which contains the answer-word.

Comment:
This is the second in a series of three Take Away activities. Naturally, the categories—and the word on the final shape—are different.

Again, the main point to stress is that they think before they cut.

Script:
(*Put these words on the board: sum, many, add, divided, plus.*)

If I asked you to pick out only those words that have to do with addition, which ones would you choose? *(Response)* Yes, sum, add, and plus.

In this activity, you will be reading some clues and then looking for certain words that appear on various shapes. You will cut away the shapes until you get to one last shape. That shape will contain the word which is the answer.

Read the instructions carefully. They will tell you what to do. If you think about what you want to cut <u>before</u> you cut, you will do very well.

Answers:
(1) pencil, paper, eraser, scissors (2) washcloth, soap, tub (3) shoe, sock, boot (4) knee, elbow (5) bleachers, bench, chair, sofa (6) crackers, cereal. The word on the remaining shape: dog.

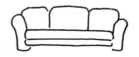

Take Away

Name_____

Today, you will be cutting away shapes until you get to one final shape. Which shapes do you cut? You will learn that by following the directions. Three rules:

- Cut only the number of shapes listed after each direction.
- Do not work ahead. Complete each direction in the order given.
- As you work, put all the shapes in a pile. You won't need them.

Look for and then cut out:

1. Things in a desk. (4)
2. Bath things. (3)
3. Things worn on the feet. (3)

4. Things on your body that bend. (2)
5. Things to sit on. (4)
6. Things that come in a box. (2)

The word on the remaining shape is _____

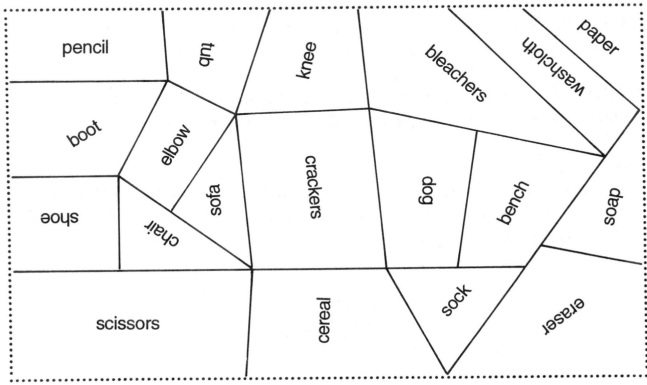

First, cut along the dotted lines.

CL WORDS
Week 8/Elaborative Thinking

The Premise:
Students will think of "CL" words that fit various descriptions.

Comment:
They must tap into their repository of "CL" words for this activity. If they can do that, with words that fit the clues, they should have no trouble.

It might be fun to see if students can invent their own elaborative exercise. Give them something easy, such as "SL" or "DR," and see how well they do. (The best way for them to begin would be to make a list of words which start with a particular letter-combination, and then do the clues.)

Script:
Some of the activities you've done in the past have centered around a single subject, such as eyes or pizza. The subject of this activity is not a thing, like pizza, but a combination of two letters that are used to start many words. The letters are "CL." So, if your brains are CLuttered with "CL" words, you'll be in good shape to do this assignment.

Answers:
(1) clean (2) claws (3) clock (4) closet (5) cloud (6) clap (7) clown
(8) climb (9) clerk (10) closed.

CL Words

Name_____

First, CLear the cobwebs from your head, and get your mind CLicking. In case you still don't have a CLue, all of the answers start with CL.

1. The opposite of dirty. _____

2. Cats have them. We don't. _____

3. It keeps track of time. _____

4. A place for clothes. _____

5. It's in the sky. _____

6. A sound made with your hands. _____

7. Circus guy. _____

8. A ladder helps you do this. _____

9. This person works in a store. _____

10. Not open. _____

SIDE BY SIDE
Week 8/Originality

The Premise:
Students will put together complete drawings of specific objects by positioning the sides of two rectangles.

Comment:
Another hands-on activity! Not only will students be cutting out the rectangles, they also will be turning them around until they find the object they are looking for.

In other words, every answer is a surprise.

You will find three other versions of this activity in our book, "Smart Snips."

Script:
Today, you are going on a picture hunt. You will be hunting for a bird, a candle, a glass of juice and some other things, but there's a problem—they're all in two pieces, and you'll have to put them together.

First, you'll need to do some careful cutting, so be sure to have your scissors handy.

Answers:
(1) Sides 3 and 8 (2) Sides 2 and 6 (3) Sides 2 and 6 (4) Sides 1 and 7
(5) Sides 4 and 8 (6) Sides 2 and 7.

Side by Side

Name_____

Today, you'll be looking for complete drawings. Right now, part of each drawing is on one rectangle, and part is on the other. Your job will be to put the two parts together. The six sentences will tell you what drawings to look for.

First, cut out the rectangles. Then, look for the thing mentioned in the sentence. In the blanks at the end of the sentence, write the numbers of the two sides you put together to make each thing. (You may need to use some drawing parts more than once.)

1. Find a bird. (I used Sides _____ and _____ .)
2. Find a glass of juice and a straw. (I used Sides _____ and _____ .)
3. Find a big letter "L." (I used Sides _____ and _____ .)
4. Find a diamond shape. (I used Sides _____ and _____ .)
5. Find a person walking. (I used Sides _____ and _____ .)
6. Find a candle. (I used Sides _____ and _____ .)

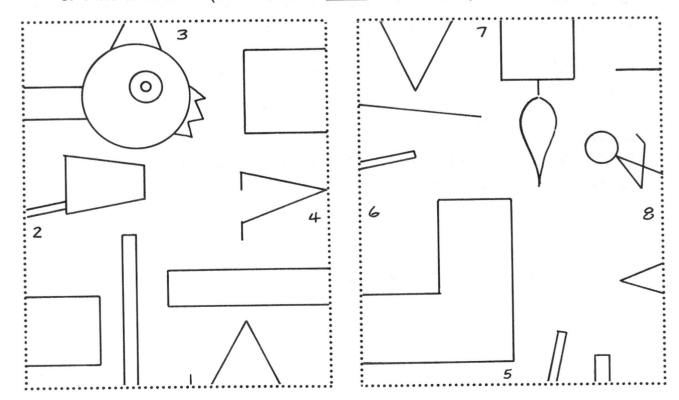

91

NOT TIC-TAC-TOE
Week 9/Analytical Thinking

The Premise:
Students will match drawings with word descriptions.

Comment:
Familiar tic-tac-toe frames, along with dots, are called into service here to challenge students with an analytical exercise that is mostly about feelings.

We particularly like the answer to Number 3 (Drawing 6). The center space is the only place where the dots can't exit.

Script:
(Put this drawing on the board:)

I am going to say three words, and you tell me which word best expresses the drawing. The words are: uneven, straight, scattered. *(Response)* Yes, the best answer would be "straight."

Today, you'll be doing similar work, so think and look carefully.

Answers:
(1) 4   (2) 1   (3) 6   (4) 5   (5) 2   (6) 3.

Possible versions for the second part:

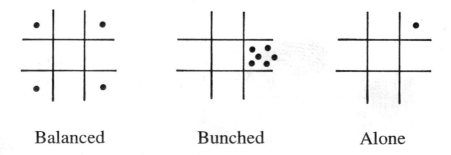

Balanced   Bunched   Alone

Not Tic-Tac-Toe

Name_____

This activity may look like tic-tac-toe, but the "game" is completely different. Study the drawings and read the words below. Which drawing best expresses each word?

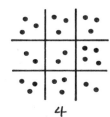
1

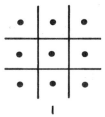
2

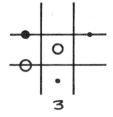
3

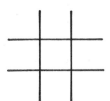
4

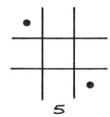
5

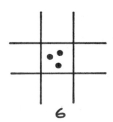
6

1. Crowded _____
2. Even _____
3. Trapped _____
4. Opposite _____
5. Empty _____
6. Different _____

Now, put your own dots in the drawings below to express these ideas:

Balanced   Bunched   Alone

THE ZALDA WORD
Week 9/Flexible Thinking

The Premise:
Students will determine the real word which "zalda" represents.

Comment:
As you know, many good readers actually hear each word as they read to themselves. Those students will probably have no trouble with this activity.

The key to solving this puzzle, of course, is studying (and hearing) the other words around the zalda word.

Script:
Before I give you this exercise today, I want you to pretend for a minute. Pretend that you know every single word in the English language.

This morning, though, someone has come along and invented a new word, which you do not know. The new word is "zalda," and it will replace a very ordinary word you already know.

Your assignment is to figure out the ordinary word which is being replaced by the zalda word. Good luck.

Answer:
The zalda word is: very.

The Zalda Word

Name_____

In the paragraph below, a strange little made-up word—zalda—has taken the place of a real word. Your job: Figure out what the real word is.

How do you decide what "zalda" stands for? Well, read the whole paragraph first. The words around the zalda word should give you a clue. Good luck.

Spiders always scare me, especially the zalda big ones. Some spiders have zalda short legs. Some spiders have zalda long ones. Of course, big spiders with long legs are the zalda scariest!

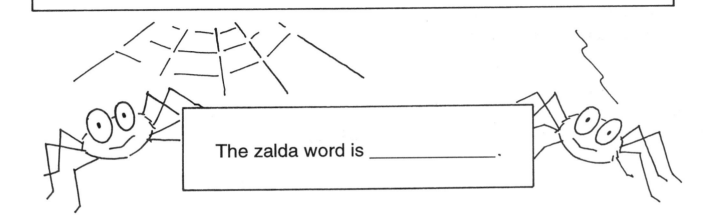

The zalda word is _____.

HARD PROBLEMS
Week 9/Problem Solving

The Premise:
Students will solve problems by analyzing visual information.

Comment:
These are fun, and if youngsters take their time, the answers should be well within their grasp.

It might be interesting for children to try inventing their own string drawings (in the manner of Problem 1). They could then pass their drawings around to other students for solutions.

Problem 4 is a good object lesson, isn't it? We must constantly remind students not to jump to conclusions. For those who see three blocks in the drawing FOR SURE, there is work to be done.

Script:
The activity you are about to do is called "Hard Problems." Don't be scared off by the title, though. If you take your time, it could be called "A Piece of Cake."

Answers:
(1) 4 strings (2) 2 more lines (3) uphill (4) no.

Hard Problems

Name_____

Look carefully at these four drawings and then answer the questions.

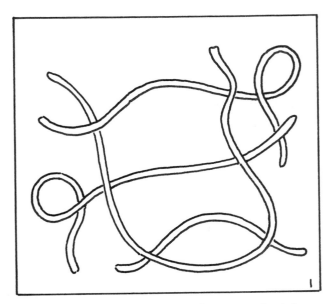

How many separate pieces of string do you see? _____

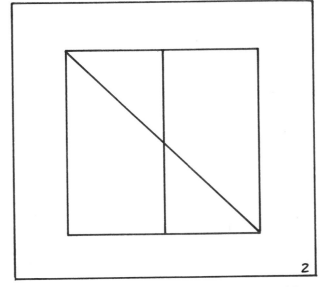

How many more lines are needed to make eight triangles of the same size? _____ lines.

This man is out for a walk. Do you think he is probably walking uphill or downhill? _____

Can you say for sure how many blocks there are here?
Yes _____ No _____

WHAT I SEE
Week 9/Elaborative Thinking

The Premise:
Students will list things they see on their way to school.

Comment:
This is the first of four activities in the program devoted exclusively to list-making. We have not included many, since children do quite a bit of list-making during the normal course of school.

Lists are an effective way to encourage elaborative thinking. When children brainstorm about a particular subject, they expand their awareness—and that builds confidence.

Script:
What is one thing you see when you open your eyes every morning? *(Response)* Today, you are going to be making a list of things you see every day <u>after</u> you leave your home and <u>before</u> you walk through the door of the school building.

Write down as many things as you possibly can. Let's see who can make the longest list.

What I See

Name_____

There are some things you see every day on your way to school. What are they? Make the longest list you can, and don't forget the obvious things. You see the sky, don't you? Start with the very first thing you see when you walk out your front door.

_____   _____

_____   _____

_____   _____

_____   _____

_____   _____

_____   _____

_____   _____

_____   _____

_____   _____

_____   _____

DECIDE AND DRAW
Week 9/Originality

The Premise:

Students will decide which of three sentences has the best visual possibilities and then illustrate it.

Comment:

If they try to draw a picture of Sentence 2, they have their work cut out for them. Sentence 3 is the obvious choice, while Sentence 1 could be drawn by those few free spirits (in every class) on a different wavelength.

Script:

Are you feeling art smart? Today, you are going to be drawing a picture. You can't draw just any picture, however.

First, you must read three sentences. Then, you must decide which sentence would be the easiest to show in a drawing. After that, you get to be an illustrator and draw what is described in the sentence.

Have fun with this assignment. I can hardly wait to see what you do!

Decide and Draw

Name_____

Read the three sentences. Which one would be easiest to show in a drawing? You decide . . . and then make your drawing in the rectangle below.

1. It was raining so hard I could barely see the road.

2. The sound of music filled the room.

3. My dog has a lot of spots.

This drawing is about Sentence _____.

PICK THE WORDS
Week 10/Analytical Thinking

The Premise:
Students will match word descriptions with drawings.

Comment:
Students have already done one of these exercises, so this is added practice.

The objective, of course, is to sharpen observational skills. This time around, you could extend the activity by presenting them with the words below, and letting them make their own precise drawings.

Line, line, square.
Square, square, line.
Triangle, square.
Triangle, triangle, line.
Square, line, triangle.

Script:
(Put these figures on the board:)

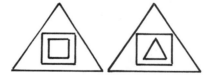

Look at what I have drawn on the board. If I wished to describe one of the drawings by saying "triangle, square, square," which one would I be talking about? *(Response)* Yes, the one on the left.

In today's activity, you will be studying nine drawings and then finding the exact words that describe them. Good luck.

Answers:
(1) 8 (2) 4 (3) 2 (4) 9 (5) 7 (6) 3 (7) 1 (8) 5 (9) 6.

Pick the Words

Name_____

Which words EXACTLY describe the drawings you see below? Match the pictures and the words. Hint: Start with the first words—line, line—and look through all the pictures. You'll get the idea.

1. Line, line _____
2. Circle, circle, circle _____
3. Circle, square _____
4. Square, line, line, line, line _____
5. Circle _____
6. Line, line, line _____
7. Circle, line, line, line _____
8. Square, circle, line _____
9. Square-line, circle-line _____

CHANGE A LETTER
Week 10/Flexible Thinking

The Premise:
Students will change one letter in an existing word to make a new word that fits a clue.

Comment:
This is the second in a series of three similar activities.

In this brain-flexing assignment, students will make one-letter changes to existing words while meeting certain clue requirements.

Script:
(Write the word "road" on the board.)

I want you to change this word into another word, but you can change only one letter, and it must fit this clue. *(Write the words, "Something you do in school," on the board.)* Based on the clue, what would the new word be? *(Response)* Yes, the new word is "read."

What new words will you be making today? That's for you to figure out. Let's see what you can do.

Answers:
(1) kite (2) mouth (3) warm (4) drool (5) and (6) tent (7) bitter (8) what (9) red (10) pickle.

Change a Letter

Name_____

Change one letter in the words on the left to make new words which fit the clues on the right. For example, if you were working with the word "sheep," you could change one letter and make a new word, "sleep."

1. Bite _____ Something you fly.

2. Month _____ Body part.

3. Worm _____ Not hot.

4. Droop _____ Babies do this.

5. End _____ A connecting word.

6. Test _____ A camping item.

7. Batter _____ Not sweet.

8. That _____ A word that starts a question.

9. Rod _____ A color.

10. Tickle _____ Something you eat.

A SPIDER
Week 10/Problem Solving

The Premise:
Using only scissors and paper, students will cut and fold a spider shape.

Comment:
They already made a bird (Week 4). Now comes a bigger challenge, involving four times as many legs!

Let them struggle with the assignment before you offer any assistance. It's good for their character!

Script:
Today, you will be turning a simple piece of paper into a spider! And I don't mean you will be drawing a spider on the paper. No, it's not quite that easy.

Using only scissors and paper, you must make a spider that stands up! This means your spider can't be flat.

I expect to see some pretty scary results. Good luck.

Possible versions:

A Spider

Name_____

Cut out the dark rectangle below. Then, using only your scissors, make a shape that looks like a spider, and don't forget the legs! One important rule: Your shape MUST be folded in some way so that the spider is not flat.

Remember, just the outline of a spider isn't good enough. It must stand somehow on its eight legs. Good luck.

RADIOS
Week 10/Elaborative Thinking

The Premise:
Students will expand their thinking on the subject of radios.

Comment:
All children begin this exercise knowing quite a lot about radios. The thinking problems build on this knowledge base.

Number 1 is a case in point. Students must organize information they already possess in order to formulate correct answers.

Number 4 once again draws on children's experience, challenging them to think analytically and elaboratively.

Script:
How many of you listened to the radio this morning before you came to school? *(Response)* How many of you have your own radios? *(Response)* Today, you are going to be doing an activity about radios. Good luck.

Answers:
(1) volume, station (2) because people can listen when they drive a car, but they shouldn't take their eyes off the road. (4) A-6, B-4, C-1, D-5, E-2, F-3.

Radios

Name_____

WXIO. KXOB. 710 on the dial. 92 FM. You probably already know that this is not a strange new language. It's just radio talk!

1. What controls do you need to check when you turn on the radio?

_____

2. Why do most cars have radios but not TV's? _____

_____

3. Write a short paragraph about something you have heard on the radio recently that has interested you.

_____

_____

_____

4. Help! The radio signal is fading and you can hear just part of these programs. Match the words on the left with the programs on the right.

A. . . . buy two and save. _____
B. Today will be clou . . . _____
C. The mayor said today that . . . _____
D. . . . John on the line. _____
E. Number 1 on the charts . . . _____
F. . . . big win over . . . _____

1. News program
2. Music program
3. Sports program
4. Forecast
5. Call-in talk show
6. Commercial

DRAWING STARTS
Week 10/Originality

The Premise:
Students will determine which drawing start would be most appropriate to use in illustrating each sentence.

Comment:
Fun but not easy! If students don't develop an overall strategy before they begin, they're in for a real challenge by the time they reach Sentence 4.

Script:
(Make these drawings on the board:)

Today, you will be completing drawings that have already been started. Sounds pretty simple, doesn't it? However, there is a catch. There are also four sentences on the activity sheet, and each drawing start must illustrate one of the sentences. So your job is to figure out which drawing start would be best for each sentence.

To give you a better idea, look at these drawing starts. Now, listen to these two sentences: "The bird has a sharp beak." "I saw a person walking."

(Finish the two drawing starts in this way:)

Well, the drawing start on the right is better for making a bird than the one on the left. And there's a nifty way to make a "person walking" out of the left drawing start, isn't there? Now, here are your drawing starts. If you plan ahead, you should have fun!

Possible solutions:

 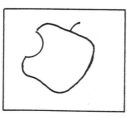  

| Sentence 1 | Sentence 2 | Sentence 3 | Sentence 4 |

Drawing Starts

Name_____

Today, you will be making drawings that tell what is happening in each of the sentences. But there is one catch: The drawings have already been started! It will be up to you to decide which drawing start would be best to use for each sentence.

Be sure to read all of the sentences first, so that you can figure out how you are going to do this activity.

1. I am eating an ice-cream cone.
2. Someone took a bite out of my apple.
3. The girl is skipping rope.
4. The clown rode a bicycle.

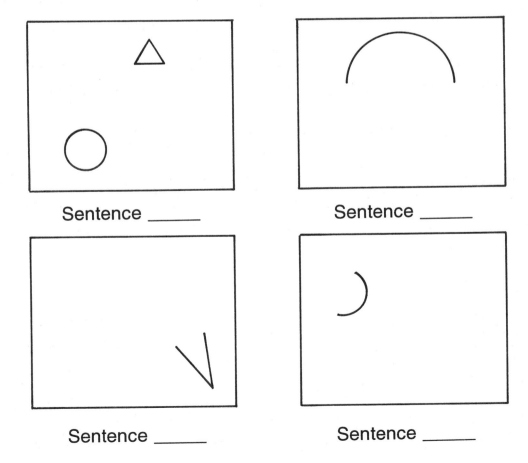

Sentence _____

Sentence _____

Sentence _____

Sentence _____

PHONE TALK
Week 11/Analytical Thinking

The Premise:
Students will match drawings with word descriptions.

Comment:
We have some sympathy for that person in Drawing 6 who can't get a word in edgewise.

Activities using visual symbols and abstractions are very entertaining—especially when the subject is familiar. Children probably have experienced most of these situations, so they should be able to relate to what is happening.

Script:
(Pretend you're holding a telephone up to your ear.)

Hello, (student)? This is (your name). I'm calling to tell you about a very special assignment. Are you interested? *(Response)* What have you been doing this morning? *(Response)* Well, I've got to run. Talk to you again soon. Goodbye. *(Response)*

The subject today, if you have not guessed already, is the telephone. I'm going to give you an activity which should be a lot of fun to do. Be sure to look at all the pictures and read the words before deciding on your answers.

Answers:
(1) 4 (2) 1 (3) 7 (4) 6 (5) 3 (6) 5 (7) 2.

Phone Talk

Name_____

Do you like to talk on the phone? Here are some people using the telephone. See if you can match the pictures with the words.

1. Long conversation. _____
2. Busy signal. _____
3. Talking to someone who doesn't hear well. _____
4. Other person is doing all the talking. _____
5. Wrong number. _____
6. Conversation with a special person. _____
7. Short conversation. _____

SENTENCE SENSE
Week 11/Flexible Thinking

The Premise:
Students will complete sentences based on picture clues.

Comment:
Children develop a feel for the flow of language at a very young age. This syntactic ability will stand them in good stead in this activity.

There are many more of these activities in our book, "WakerUppers."

Script:

(Put this on the board:)   The cloud is in _____
of the _____ .

Look at the picture and the words I have written. How would you finish the sentence in a way that makes sense? *(Response)* Yes, "The cloud is in front of the sun." Today, you're going to be solving some similar problems. Have fun and do a good job.

Answers:
In space, there is no up or down. This bottle is too big for this baby. This water isn't very deep. Mom, have you seen my other sock? This basketball needs more (or some) air. Is this the head or the tail?

Sentence Sense

Name_____

The sentences below are missing some words. First, look at the pictures and read the words that are there. Then, complete each sentence in a way that makes sense. (Put one word in each blank.)

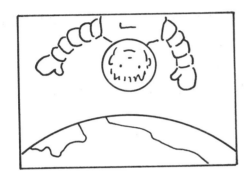

In space, there is

no up _____ _____ .

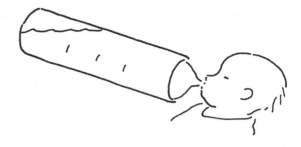

This bottle is _____ _____

for this baby.

This water isn't _____ _____ .

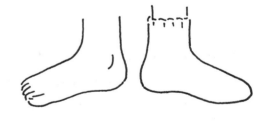

Mom, have

you seen my

_____ _____ ?

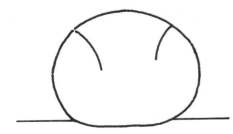

This basketball

needs _____ _____ .

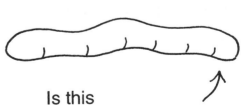

Is this

the _____

_____ the tail?

115

WHAT WORD NEXT?
Week 11/Problem Solving

The Premise:
Students will write the next word in the pattern.

Comment:
This activity is a warm-up for two additional pattern activities which will come later. Even though this project is the easiest of the three, it does shift gears nicely—with patterns that go backwards, forwards, etc.

Script:
(Call two girls to the front of the room and have them stand side by side. Then, call one boy to stand in between them. Next, call two more boys to stand on either end of the line, so that the pattern is boy-girl-boy-girl-boy.)

Today, you are going to be doing an activity in which you must think about patterns. I've made a "people pattern" for you just now. What is it? *(Response)* Yes, the pattern is boy-girl-boy-girl-boy.

Now, it's time to look for some patterns on paper. Once you know what the pattern is, you must think of a word that would come next in the pattern. Good luck!

Answers:
(1) evening or night (2) October (3) Friday (4) year (5) adult (6) house (7) summer (8) red (9) elbow (10) empty.

What Word Next?

Name_____

Can you you do do do this this this this? Patterns are fun, aren't they? Try to figure out what the pattern is in each of these groups of words. Then, write the word which you think should come next.

1. morning, afternoon, _____

2. December, November, _____

3. Monday, Wednesday, _____

4. day, week, month, _____

5. baby, child, teenager, _____

6. cow, barn, chicken, coop, person, _____

7. December, winter, July, _____

8. tan, brown, grey, black, pink, _____

9. leg, knee, arm, _____

10. on, off, up, down, full, _____

A GLASS
Week 11/Elaborative Thinking

The Premise:
Students will expand their thinking on the subject of glasses.

Comment:
The way children respond to Number 4 should be interesting. A circle (representing the rim) would suffice. However, some of your more sophisticated thinkers may realize that in looking down on the glass shown in the drawing, both the rim and the bottom of the glass would be visible.

Script:
Just for a minute, let's brainstorm some things that are made out of glass or have glass in them. *(Response)* Yes, windows, eyeglasses, drinking glasses, binoculars, cameras, cars, buses, etc. Today, you are going to be thinking about just one kind of glass—the kind you drink from.

Answers:
(1) soda pop, milk, chocolate milk, orange juice, tomato juice, water, etc.
(2) Glass A, because it has the broadest base and would be less likely to tip over, it would also be the easiest to wash (3) I dropped it on the bed, it was made out of plastic, I was close to the floor when I dropped it.

A Glass

Name_____

A glass you drink from, which is made out of glass, is called a glass, isn't it? Does that mean a plastic cup should be called a plastic? Today, you will be thinking about that ordinary item—a glass.

1. Make a list of some things you have drunk from a glass.

_____

_____

_____

2. Which of these glasses would probably be best to use every day? _____

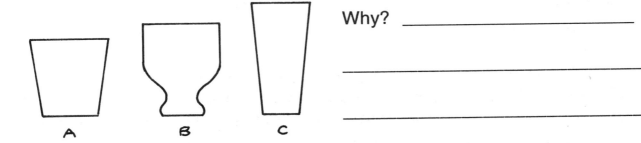

Why? _____

_____

_____

3. Name two reasons a glass might not break if you dropped it. _____

_____

4. If you were looking directly down on the glass at the right, what would it look like? Draw it in the box.

BE A DESIGNER
Week 11/Originality

The Premise:
Students will create four different designs.

Comment:
Directing students to design the graphics for a sweatshirt is a good assignment. Directing them to design graphics for a sweatshirt that promotes a specific thing—such as peace—is a better assignment. As the poet Robert Frost said, "Freedom is pulling easy in the harness." In other words, creativity is usually enhanced by imposing some structure.

Since the formats we have presented are small, be sure children do their designing with pencils, not crayons, so they can include enough detail.

Script:
Are you feeling like artists today? In this assignment, you will be making some designs for four important projects. Keep in mind what the items are to be used for when you make your designs.

Possible versions:

Be a Designer

Name_____

You are famous. You are known all over the world for your artwork. Here are a few projects you're working on right now. Show us your designs.

This sweatshirt design promotes peace and millions will buy it.

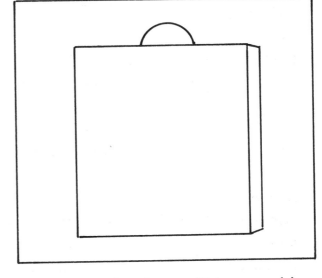

This shopping bag will be used by a huge music store.

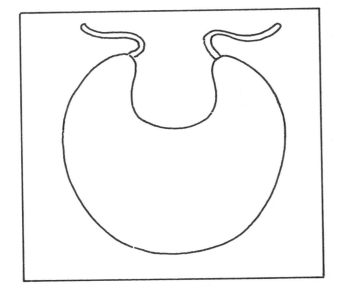

This design will appear on thousands of baby bibs.

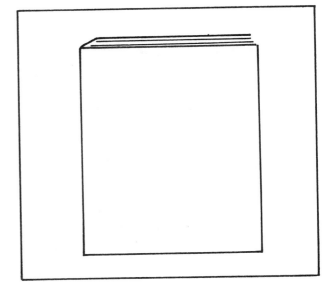

This book is entitled "Trees," and you must design its cover.

GOOD EATS
Week 12/Analytical Thinking

The Premise:
Students will match word descriptions with abstract drawings of food.

Comment:
Not only will students have to think about the way food looks from the side, they must also deal with the abstract nature of the drawings.

Drawings 4 or 6 might have been the answer for "pancake," if the description had been in the singular. But since we asked for "pancakes," the best answer is Drawing 8. (The only other possible candidate for "pancakes" would have been Drawing 9, but upon closer inspection, this drawing shows something thin in the middle, which probably means sandwich meat. So the answer for that one is "sandwich!")

This is the kind of thinking students must do if they are to be successful with this activity.

Script:
Today, you will be doing an activity which features drawings of food. These drawings have been done as if you were seeing the food from the side.

If at first the drawings look kind of strange, don't worry. You'll be able to figure out what they are if you look at them carefully.

Answers:
(1) 8 (2) 3 (3) 9 (4) 6 (5) 2 (6) 5 (7) 1 (8) 10 (9) 4 (10) 7.

Good Eats

Name_____

Gulp! The pictures below are drawn to look as if you are seeing different kinds of food from the side. Figure out what the food items are and match them with the words.

SIDE VIEW OF A PERSON ABOUT TO EAT AN APPLE.

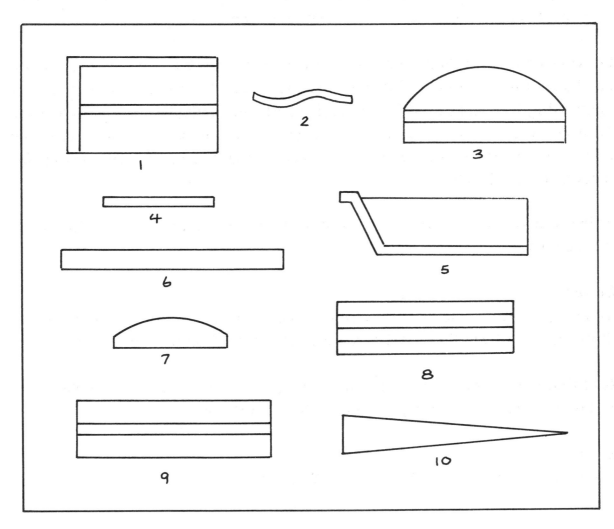

1. Pancakes _____
2. Hamburger _____
3. Sandwich _____
4. Celery _____
5. Potato chip _____

6. Slice of pie _____
7. Slice of cake _____
8. Carrot _____
9. Cracker _____
10. Cookie _____

PLAYFUL PLATES
Week 12/Flexible Thinking

The Premise:
Students will determine occupations based on vanity-plate clues.

Comment:
Now and then, a little humor stirs things up a bit. If that is the case, students should be well-churned after they've done this activity!

The unifying concept here is that all of the license plates have something to do with jobs. Granted, the auto repairman down the street may not think of himself as a "dent gent" or the mattress salesman as a "pad lad," but in the world of vanity plates, anything goes.

Script:
Who knows what a vanity plate on a car is? *(Response)* Yes, it is a license plate that uses numbers or letters in a very imaginative way to express a thought—or to say something about the person who owns the car.

Today, you'll be looking at some very unusual license plates. On them, you'll find funny descriptions of jobs. YOUR job will be to figure out which plate goes with which job.

Answers:
(1) 7 (2) 4 (3) 8 (4) 5 (5) 2 (6) 3 (7) 6 (8) 1.

Playful Plates

Name_____

You're riding down the highway and you keep noticing funny license plates! A lot of them seem to describe what people do in their jobs. Here are a few. Match the pictures with the words.

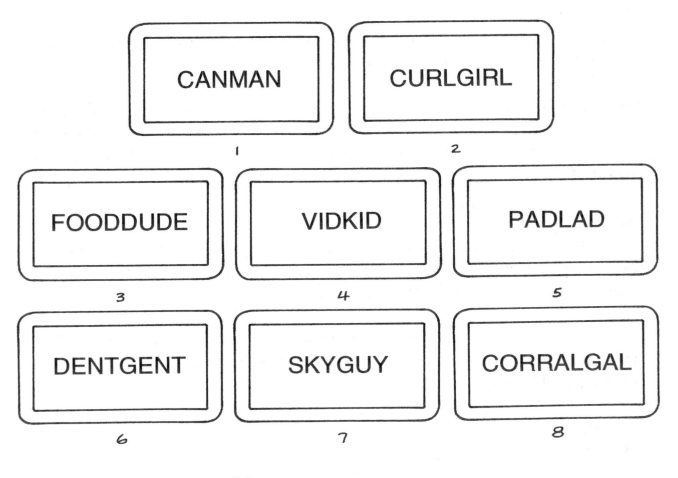

CANMAN
1

CURLGIRL
2

FOODDUDE
3

VIDKID
4

PADLAD
5

DENTGENT
6

SKYGUY
7

CORRALGAL
8

1. Pilot _____
2. Works in TV shop _____
3. Horse trainer _____
4. Mattress salesman _____
5. Beautician _____
6. Chef _____
7. Auto repairman _____
8. Grocery store stocker _____

CATCH SOME BUGS
Week 12/Problem Solving

The Premise:
Students will draw straight lines between dots, making shapes that capture various bugs.

Comment:
Children must be very careful when they read the directions. Do not accept any solutions that do not carry out the instructions.

The problems presented here are quite ambitious. For those students who do a good job, this is an excellent opportunity to give them some recognition.

Script:
Today, you are going to be hunting some bugs. These bugs are only on paper, but catching them still won't be easy. Pay close attention to the directions.

You will need a ruler because all the lines you make must be straight.

Solutions:

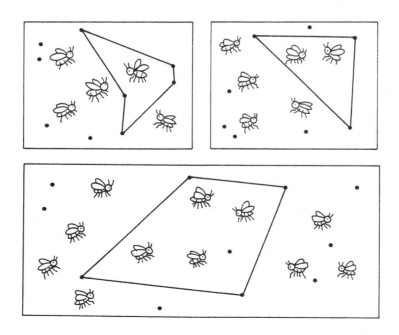

Catch Some Bugs

Name_____

Bugs, bugs, and more bugs! Before you begin each activity, come up with a plan for the best way to catch the critters below. Use a ruler for the lines you make between the dots.

IF YOU DON', THINK FIRST, THIS ACTIVITY WILL BUG YOU!

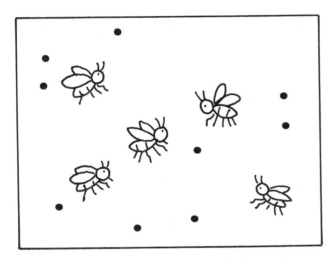

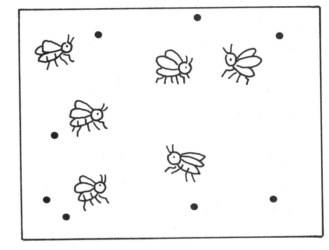

Connect FIVE dots to make a shape that goes all the way around ONE of these bugs. Your lines cannot touch any of the bugs.

Connect THREE dots to make a triangle that goes all the way around TWO bugs. Your lines cannot touch any of the bugs.

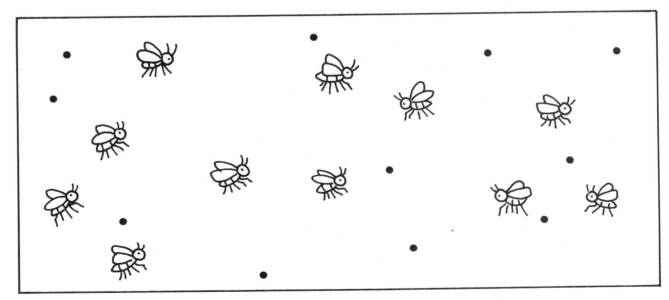

Connect any FOUR dots with straight lines to make a shape that goes all the way around as many bugs as possible. Your lines cannot touch any bugs.

BR WORDS
Week 12/Elaborative Thinking

The Premise:
Students will think of "BR" words that fit various descriptions.

Comment:
By searching through their BRains for "BR" words that fit the clues, students will be getting good practice in the process of elaborative thinking.

If they answer that the way to cross a river (Number 8) is "briskly," so much the better!

Script:
When you do this activity, everyone will be starting each answer the same way—with the letters "BR." The hard part will be figuring out what to put after the "BR's." Take a deep BReath and begin—and if you do a good job, BRavo!

Answers:
(1) brain (2) bread (or bratwurst!) (3) branch (4) bricks (5) brush
(6) breeze (7) bride (or bridesmaid) (8) bridge (9) brown (10) brook.

BR Words

Name_____

Here's a BRand new activity waiting for you to do!
Take a deep BReath. Every answer will begin
with (you guessed it) the letters BR.

1.   It's in your head. _____

2.   Used in sandwiches. _____

3.   Part of a tree. _____

4.   Some buildings are made of these. _____

5.   What you do to your teeth. _____

6.   A gentle wind. _____

7.   She's in a wedding. _____

8.   One way to cross a river. _____

9.   A color. _____

10. A little stream. _____

V DRAWINGS
Week 12/Originality

The Premise:
Students will turn the letter V into six drawings based on specific descriptions.

Comment:
If students expect all the drawing challenges to be as easy as the first one—the ice-cream cone—they're in for a surprise. By the time they get to the cheerleader, they'll be considerably less cocky.

You might want to display the results on the bulletin board, since there should be some interesting approaches.

Script:
(Draw a big V on the board.)

What is on the board? *(Response)* Yes, a V. What if I said, "Turn this V into a picture of a kite?" Could you do it? How? *(Response, letting a student try drawing it.)*

(Here's one version you could use:)

Today's activity is similar to what we have just done. Be creative and have a lot of fun!

Possible solutions:

V Drawings

Name_____

Turn these V's into the six things listed below. You may use the V's in any way you wish, but they must be part of your drawing.

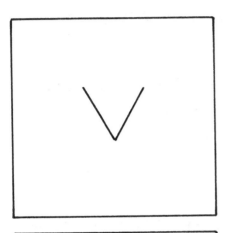 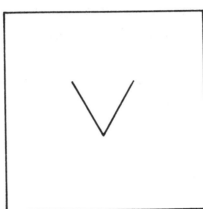 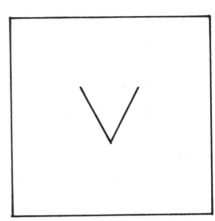

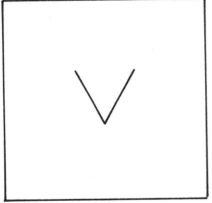 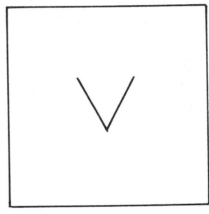 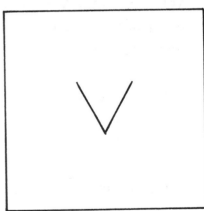

- An ice-cream cone.
- A bird's head from the top.
- A tree in the winter.
- A star.
- A cheerleader.
- A pair of scissors.

DOG TALK
Week 13/Analytical Thinking

The Premise:
Students will match drawings about dogs with statements.

Comment:
Youngsters should be able to solve most of these challenges, whether or not they have dogs in their own homes. After all, a wagging tail (Drawing 7) is universally understood to mean that a dog is happy. Therefore, the best answer would be Number 9, "Wow! Here comes my family."

Script:
How many of you have dogs at home? *(Response)* Let's make a list of some of the words dogs know. *(Write responses on board.)*

Based on the list we have made, what do you think will be the subject of our activity today? Yes, a very interesting assignment about dogs!

Answers:
(1) 8 (2) 6 (3) 4 (4) 9 (5) 5 (6) 3 (7) 2 (8) 1 (9) 7.

Dog Talk

Name_____

If dogs could talk, here are some things they might say. Your job is to match the statements with the pictures. Use each picture and statement just once.

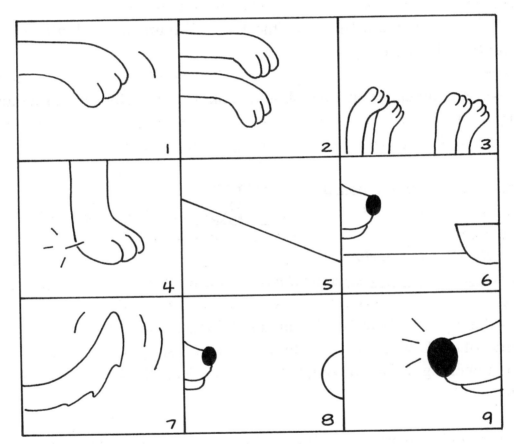

1. I like to chase balls. _____
2. I think I'll go get a drink. _____
3. Ouch! _____
4. I like to smell things. _____
5. I'm on a leash. _____
6. I can roll over. _____
7. I can sit up and beg. _____
8. I can shake. _____
9. Wow! Here comes my family. _____

ALPHABET CLUES
Week 13/Flexible Thinking

The Premise:
Students will think of words beginning with the letter shown in the drawings.

Comment:
The corn-on-the-cob drawing uses the letter C quite well, don't you think? Mr. O isn't bad, either.

Emphasize to students that they should look for the alphabet letter in each drawing first.

Script:
(*Put this drawing on the board:*)

Beneath the drawing, write:
This L is _____ against the tree.

What is the alphabet letter in this picture? *(Response)* Yes, an L. Now, can you think of an L word that would work in the sentence—and also describe what is happening in the drawing? *(Response)* Yes, the best answer would be "leaning."

This is the kind of work you will be doing today. Your answer must start with the alphabet letter which is featured in the drawing, and it must make sense in the phrase or sentence.

Answers:
I wish these bugs would go away. This dog is under the table. I smell the toast burning. "O" is the only (or one) letter in this face. This D is made of dots. I love to eat corn on the cob. A pilot in a plane.

Alphabet Clues

Name_____

You'll find a letter of the alphabet in every one of these little pictures. Your assignment is to fill in the blanks with words which begin with that letter.

I wish these bugs

would _____ away.

This dog is

_____ the table.

I _____ the

toast burning.

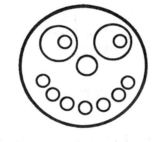

"O" is the

_____ letter

in this face.

This D is

made of _____ .

I love to eat

_____ on the _____ .

A _____

in a _____

LOOK CAREFULLY
Week 13/Problem Solving

The Premise:
Students will make observations in response to written instructions.

Comment:
These circle problems give students additional practice in looking closely and critically at visual information.

The way they handle Problem 3 should indicate how seriously they have approached this activity. If they really try, they can devise a way to come very close to replicating the size of Circle D.

Script:
Today, you will be doing an activity involving circles. To get you in the mood, let's take a minute and see how many circular things we can see in the room right now. *(Response)*

(As you hand out the activity, say:)
While we've been talking, there have been some other circles present in the room—right here on this paper!

Answers:
(1) 3 (2) Circle B appears to be in front of Circle C. (Or Circle B appears to be the same size as Circle C.)

(3) Size of completed circle:

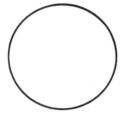

Look Carefully

Name_____

You'll need to do some careful looking and thinking in this activity. Be sure to take your time. When you draw a circle for Number 3, don't worry if it's not completely round. It doesn't have to be perfect.

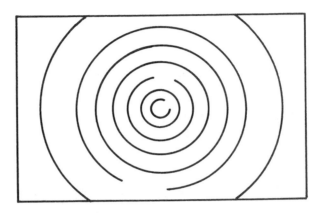

1. How many complete circles can you count in the drawing above? _____

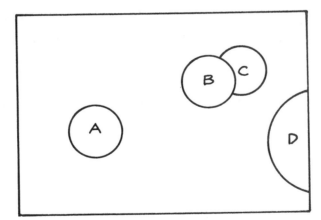

2. Finish this sentence: Circle B appears to be _____

_____

3. Draw a circle around Circle A that is about as big as Circle D would be IF YOU COULD SEE ALL OF IT.

WIND
Week 13/Elaborative Thinking

The Premise:
Students will expand their thinking on the subject of wind.

Comment:
Sometimes, it is important to pause and think about the obvious. Number 1 is an example of this. Every child knows that wind is air in motion, but the actual answer when "formalized" on paper, is surprising.

Script:
Every day, the weather can be different. What are some words which describe the weather? *(Response)* Yes—hot, sunny, cold, windy, rainy, cloudy, clear, warm, etc.

Today's topic is about one of those words—windy. You'll even be doing a little experiment at the conclusion of this activity, so have fun!

Answers:
(1) moving (or in motion) (2) west (4) fan (5) from the side.

Wind

Name_____

How's the weather today? Was it windy when you came to school? If you think carefully, this assignment should be a "breeze."

THERE WAS A CARTOON HERE, BUT THE WIND BLEW IT AWAY!

1. Finish this sentence: Wind is air that is _____ .

2. If someone outside looked like this, would the wind be coming from the west or the east? _____

WEST    EAST

3. Write a short paragraph describing something you have seen happen on a very windy day.

_____

_____

_____

_____

4. A machine for making a breeze inside a house is called a _____ .

5. Cut out the square on the right. Put it on your desk. Blow on it from above. Then, blow on it from the side. Did the paper move more easily when you blew from above or from the side?

_____

DECIDE AND DRAW
Week 13/Originality

The Premise:
Students will decide which of three sentences has the best visual possibilities and then illustrate it.

Comment:
To take a cue from the first sentence in the activity, it would probably not be a good idea to try to draw Sentence 1.

If you receive a lot of creative "tired" drawings, it might be fun to display them. You might even assign some "wide-awake" self-portraits and feature them at the same time.

Script:
Are you feeling art smart? Today, you are going to be drawing a picture. You can't draw just any picture, however.

First, you must read three sentences. Then, you must decide which sentence would be the easiest to show in a drawing. After that, you must illustrate the sentence you have chosen.

Make your drawings just as good as you can. I'm looking forward to seeing some masterpieces!

Decide and Draw

Name_____

Read the three sentences. Which one would be easiest to show in a drawing? You decide. . . and then make your drawing in the rectangle below.

1. It was not a good idea.

2. I am looking very tired today.

3. Spelling some words is difficult.

This drawing is about Sentence _____ .

VERB PUZZLERS (D)
Week 14/Analytical Thinking

The Premise:
Students will match D words with visual clues.

Comment:
We decided to stay away from "disparage" or "delineate."

When students are assigned analytical exercises such as this one, encourage them to skip around and solve the simple problems first. The process of elimination will make the tough problems a little less formidable.

Script:
(Put this drawing on the board:)

I am looking for a word that is a verb, that begins with the letter D. Take a look at this drawing and see if you can think of the word I have in mind. *(Response)* Yes, the word is "drive."

Today, you will be looking for other D verbs. Look at the pictures, read the words below the pictures, and do your best.

Answers:
(1) 4 (2) 3 (3) 1 (4) 9 (5) 6 (6) 8 (7) 5 (8) 2 (9) 7.

Verb Puzzlers (D)

Name_____

Can you DECIDE which D verbs match up with these D pictures? Look at what has been DONE to the D pictures and you should be able to DO it.

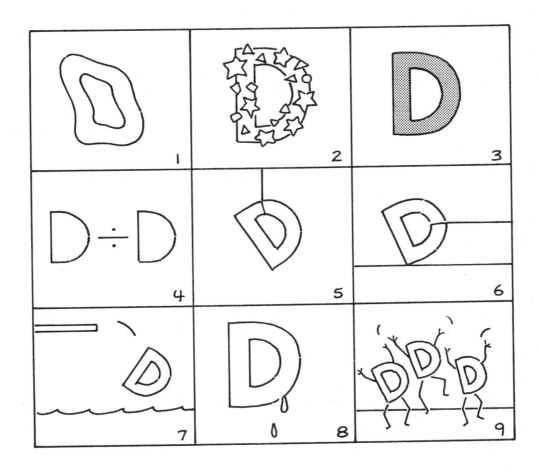

1. Divide _____

2. Darken _____

3. Droop _____

4. Dance _____

5. Drag _____

6. Drool _____

7. Dangle _____

8. Decorate _____

9. Dive _____

IF YOU THINK OF . . .
Week 14/Flexible Thinking

The Premise:
Students will determine what drawings represent when they are paired with other drawings.

Comment:
The same drawing can mean different things. It all depends on the context. For example, while the dots in Drawing 1 represent salt in the first sentence, the same dots become something else (leaves) in the context of the fourth sentence.

This is an excellent assignment for encouraging flexible thinking.

Script:
(Draw a rectangle on the board.)

Here's a riddle for you: How can one thing be more than one thing? Well, here's one way. If I say the words, "new shoes," what could this rectangle be? *(Response)* Yes, a shoe box. If I say the word, "basketball," what could the rectangle stand for now? *(Response)* Yes, a basketball court, but if you said "towel" or "score sheet," you would have been right, too.

That's the kind of thinking you'll be doing in this exercise.

Answers:
(1) pepper (2) baking sheet, table, or pizza box (3) lake (4) leaves (5) water
(6) comb (7) thread (8) bologna or sandwich meat (9) eye or mouth.

If You Think Of ...

Name_____

If you think of this assignment with some imagination, it should be a lot of fun. Just keep a wide-open mind.

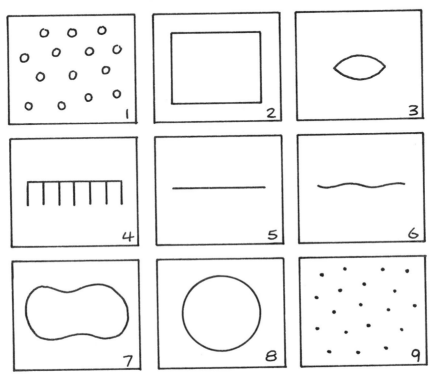

If you think of . . .

1. Number 1 as salt, what could Number 9 be? _____

2. Number 8 as a pizza, what could Number 2 be? _____

3. Number 3 as a canoe, what could Number 7 be? _____

4. Number 4 as a rake, what could Number 1 be? _____

5. Number 5 as a diving board, what could Number 6 be? _____

6. Number 6 as hair, what could Number 4 be? _____

7. Number 5 as a needle, what could Number 6 be? _____

8. Number 2 as bread, what could Number 8 be? _____

9. Number 8 as a face, what could Number 3 be? _____

HOW MANY CUTS?
Week 14/Problem Solving

The Premise:
Students will cut along as many straight lines as possible while keeping the square intact.

Comment:
Students were presented with a similar activity in Week 6, so that experience should help them this time.

This is the kind of activity which should not be judged too rigidly. The maximum number of cuts is 13, and some of your best students will come up with that number. However, other youngsters may not see all the possibilities. Still, if they try—and follow directions—they have done a good job.

Script:
Today, you are going to be solving a problem by cutting along some straight lines. But the real problem is this: As you make your straight-line cuts, you must keep the paper you are working with in one piece.

One other point: *(Draw this diagram on the board.)*

You are not allowed to cut just part of a line and count it as one cut. For example, A-C is one line, and B-D is another. But you cannot cut from A to B and count it as one cut, or from A to B to D and count it as two cuts. You must cut the whole line or not cut it at all.

Make some plans before you cut. Then, cut!

Solution:

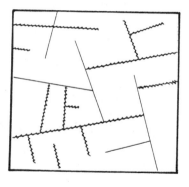

How Many Cuts?

How many straight cuts can you make without cutting the square below into two pieces?

Begin by cutting out the square along the dotted lines. Then, make any cuts you wish along the lines that are shown. Write the number of cuts you made and your name somewhere on the square so your teacher can see how well you did.

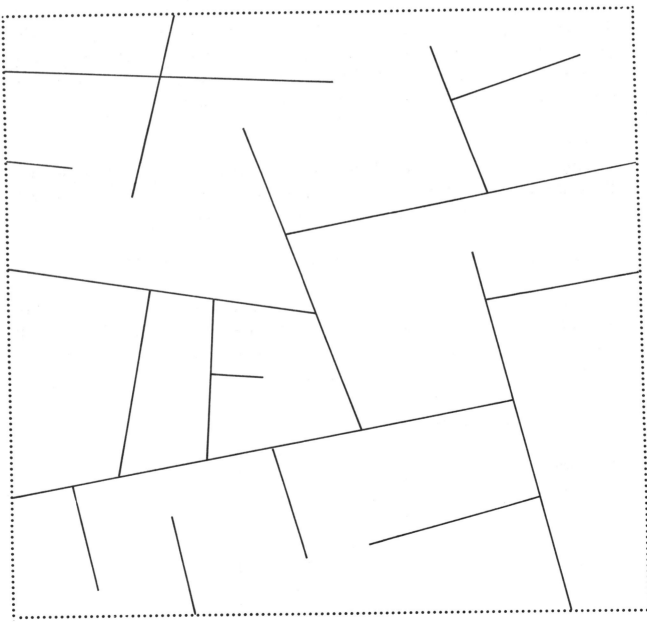

PEOPLE-MADE
Week 14/Elaborative Thinking

The Premise:
Students will make a list of manufactured things they have touched this day.

Comment:
Certainly, their desk and the pencil they write with should be included on the list. Otherwise, how could they do the assignment? Other things that probably should be listed: sheet, bed, blanket, clothes, toothpaste, toothbrush, soap, faucet . . . you get the idea.

Script:
Today, you are going to make a list. I hope it will be a long, long list. I hope your list is so long that you have to use the back of your paper.

What will your list be about? It will be a list of everything you have touched today that has been made by people—not things in nature. Notice that I have said things you have touched, not things you have seen.

The best way to begin is to think back to this morning when you first woke up, and start your list from there. Good luck!

People-Made

Name_____

Make a list of everything you have touched today that has been made by people. Oops, here's one: this paper. Use the back of this sheet if you run out of room. There should be many possibilities.

ART POEM
Week 14/Originality

The Premise:
Students will make drawings based on word prompts.

Comment:
So what if the "Hoo" under the box on the lower left is missing its "t?" We are taking poetic license.

Again, hold them to the basic rules of the activity—their drawings should be about the words. In other words, if they haven't drawn a cow, ghost or goblin, zoo animal, owl and baby, they've missed the point.

Also, insist that students use pencils. Many children automatically reach for their crayons, but crayons can be inhibiting if the format is small, as is the case here.

Script:
Today, you'll be making five different drawings. First, read the poem. Then, read the words under each drawing frame. That will help you decide what you wish to draw.

Even though the spaces for your drawings are small, put in as many details as you can. I'm looking forward to seeing the results!

Art Poem

Name_____

Are you feeling art smart? It's time to show off by
making the most interesting drawings you can.
They must have something to do with the poem
and with the words beneath each frame.

Finish these drawings
And don't be too slow.
Show something about
The word that's below.

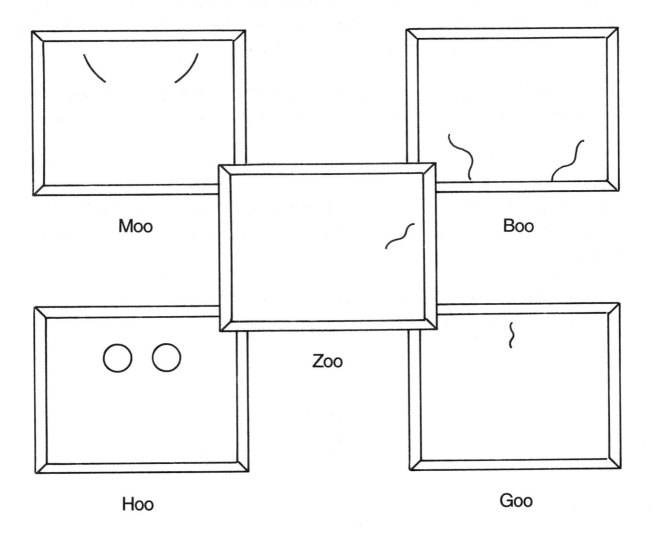

Moo

Boo

Zoo

Hoo

Goo

ARM TALK
Week 15/Analytical Thinking

The Premise:
Students will match gesture drawings with statements.

Comment:
This little character has quite a lot to say! If students take their time, they should have no trouble. For example, it is quite obvious that she (or he) is covering her eyes in Drawing 4 and covering her ears in Drawing 9.

Another part of the anatomy will be featured later in the activity, "Leg Lines."

Script:
(Hold your arms straight out from your body, with your palms toward your students.)

Which one of these statements expresses what I'm doing right now? "Get in line for lunch." "Stay in your seats." "Fix me a peanut butter and jelly sandwich." *(Response)* Yes, what I'm doing with my arms best expresses the statement, "Stay in your seats."

Today, you'll be working on an activity about things people do with their arms. Have fun with this one!

Answers:
(1) 5 (2) 1 (3) 6 (4) 2 (5) 8 (6) 3 (7) 9 (8) 4 (9) 7.

Arm Talk

Name_____

People talk with their mouths, but they also talk with their arms. And this little person certainly has busy arms! Match the pictures with the words.

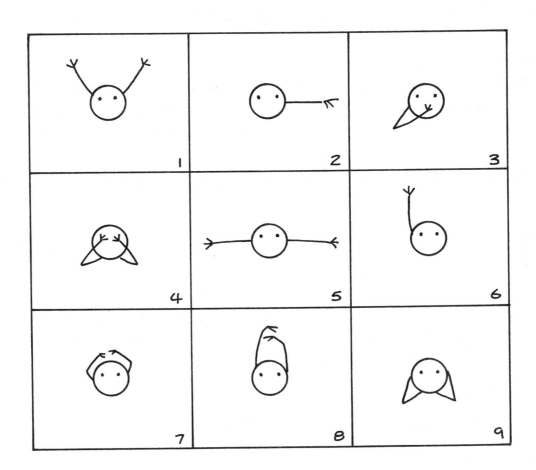

1. I won't let you get by me. _____
2. Yippee! I got an A! _____
3. I know the answer. _____
4. Your dog ran that way. _____
5. I'm taking ballet lessons. _____
6. Excuse me, I burped. _____
7. I won't listen to you! _____
8. I'm not watching! _____
9. Don't drop that on me. _____

CHANGE A LETTER
Week 15/Flexible Thinking

The Premise:
Students will change one letter in an existing word to make a new word that fits a clue.

Comment:
You may want to encourage your students to develop their own versions of this activity. All they have to do is:

- Compile a list of fairly simple words.

- Select the words that can be turned into new words by changing one letter.

- Think of descriptive clues for the new words.

Script:
(Write the word "hand" on the board.)

I want you to change this word into another word, but you can only change one letter, and it must fit a clue. *(Write the words, "music group" on the board.)* Based on the clue, what would the new word be? *(Response)* Yes, the new word is "band."

You get the idea. Now, let's see what you can do.

Answers:
(1) pie (2) glue (3) mood (4) nine (5) shore (6) giggle (7) ear (8) sock (9) gold (10) book.

Change a Letter

Name_____

Change one letter in the words on the left to make new words which fit the clues on the right. For example, if you were working with the word, "sheep," you could change one letter and make a new word, "sleep."

1. Pit   _____   A dessert.

2. Blue   _____   It's sticky.

3. Food   _____   State of mind.

4. None   _____   A number.

5. Short   _____   Where ocean meets land.

6. Wiggle   _____   A happy sound.

7. Eat   _____   Body part.

8. Sack   _____   Something you wear.

9. Good   _____   A certain metal.

10. Boot   _____   This has many words.

GALOOPS
Week 15/Problem Solving

The Premise:
Students will analyze characteristics of faces to determine whether or not they belong in a specific group.

Comment:
There is one property that makes a Galoop a Galoop: All Galoops have heads whose outlines are made with curved lines.

If some students are having trouble with this activity, tell them to concentrate on the three heads which are NOT Galoops. What makes them different from Galoops? (Straight lines)

Script:
(Put these drawings on the board:)

Which one of these heads is different? Why? *(Response)* Yes, the head on the right is not like the other two. The nose is pointing in the opposite direction.

Today, you are going to be doing an assignment called "Galoops." You must figure out who the Galoops are. Look, look, and look—you'll find them!

Answers:

Galoops

Name_____

What in the world is a Galoop? There's a way to tell—if you think hard and look closely. Figure out what is the same about all the Galoops, and you'll be on the right track.

These are Galoops.

These are not Galoops.

Which of these are Galoops? Circle them.

REFRIGERATORS
Week 15/Elaborative Thinking

The Premise:
Students will expand their thinking on the subject of refrigerators.

Comment:
As a follow-up activity, ask students to turn their papers over and draw what a refrigerator looks like from the front, with the door open. Tell them to draw shelves, bottles, jars, milk cartons, leftovers, whatever.

Script:
Question: What is the biggest object in a kitchen? *(Response)* Yes, a refrigerator. What are some popular colors for refrigerators? *(Response)* What are some popular brands of refrigerators? *(Response)*

Today, you will be doing an activity about refrigerators. You'll even get to do a bit of drawing.

Answers:
(1) It keeps food cold. (2) they are found in the kitchen, they control temperature, they have doors, they are made of metal, they are heavy, etc.
(3) magnets will stick on refrigerators because they are made of metal and walls aren't.

Refrigerators

Name_____

Chances are, you or someone at your house opened a refrigerator this morning. That big boxy object in your kitchen is the subject of this activity.

1. Write the shortest complete sentence you can explaining what a refrigerator does. _____

2. Even though a stove and a refrigerator do different things, they still have many things in common. Name as many as you can.

_____

_____

_____

3. Many people put little magnets on refrigerators to hold notes or pictures. Why do they put magnets there rather than on kitchen walls?

_____

4. Finish this drawing of a refrigerator. Show where the doors and the handles should be.

SIDE BY SIDE
Week 15/Originality

The Premise:
Students will put together complete drawings of specific objects by positioning the sides of two rectangles.

Comment:
In some ways, this activity reminds us of those old "hidden pictures," in which birds and rabbits were so cleverly disguised in clouds and grass. In this case, however, the objects to be found require some hands-on effort, as students manipulate the two rectangles to find the object they are after.

Script:
How are you at locating some missing objects? It might not be easy because right now, they're in two pieces. You've done an activity like this before, so you should know what to do. It's called "Side by Side." Have fun!

Answers:
(1) Sides 3 and 5 (2) Sides 1 and 8 (3) Sides 4 and 8 (4) Sides 4 and 5 (5) Sides 4 and 7 (6) Sides 2 and 6.

Side by Side

Name_____

Today, you'll be looking for complete drawings. Right now, part of each drawing is on one rectangle, and part is on the other. Your job will be to put the two parts together. The six sentences will tell you what drawings to look for.

First, cut out the rectangles. Then, look for the thing mentioned in the sentence. In the blanks at the end of the sentence, write the numbers of the two sides you put together to make each thing. (You may need to use some drawing parts more than once.)

1. Find a boy with a balloon. (I used Sides ____ and ____ .)
2. Find a dog. (I used Sides ____ and ____ .)
3. Find a jellybean. (I used Sides ____ and ____ .)
4. Find a pair of eyeglasses. (I used Sides ____ and ____ .)
5. Find a cowboy twirling a rope. (I used Sides ____ and ____ .)
6. Find an eye. (I used Sides ____ and ____ .)

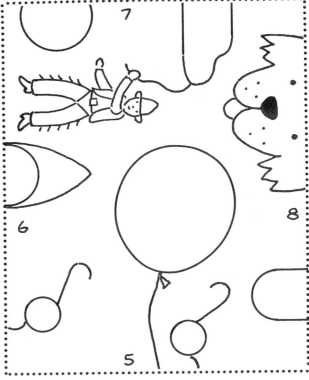

FOOD X-RAYS
Week 16/Analytical Thinking

The Premise:
Students will match symbolic drawings of food with word descriptions.

Comment:
Though the food items in Pictures 1 and 2 are somewhat similar in shape, everyone knows that raisins are darker than corn flakes. (Yes, yes, we know there are golden raisins, but our raisins are the kind children eat!)

What is interesting about this exercise is how much sophisticated information is transmitted with just a few lines and shapes.

Script:
Today, we're going to pretend that you are in a grocery store and all the labels have fallen off the food. But that doesn't matter, because you have X-ray vision.

(Draw this on the board:)

What could be in this can I have drawn? *(Response)* Yes, cashews. *(Or lima beans, etc.)* Here's another can.

(Erase the can of cashews and draw this on the board:)

What could be in this can? *(Response)* Yes, peas. Now, I'm going to give you an activity in which you'll be using your X-ray vision to look through boxes rather than cans. But the idea is the same.

Answers:
(1) 6 (2) 4 (3) 8 (4) 1 (5) 7 (6) 5 (7) 2 (8) 3.

Food X-Rays

Name_____

What has happened? You're in the grocery store and suddenly, you have X-ray vision! You can see right through boxes!

What kinds of foods are in these boxes? Look at the pictures and match them with the words.

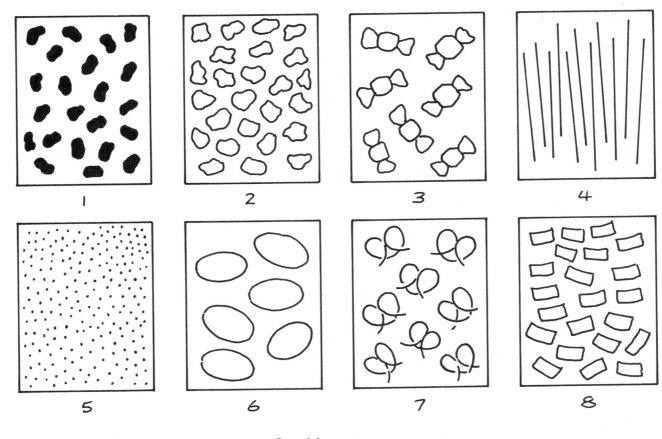

1. Cookies _____
2. Spaghetti _____
3. Noodles _____
4. Raisins _____
5. Pretzels _____
6. Brown sugar _____
7. Corn flakes _____
8. Candy _____

163

CRAZY RHYMES
Week 16/Flexible Thinking

The Premise:
Students will complete rhymes based on visual clues.

Comment:
Basically, when you have an activity in which a goat uses a remote and a head is on a bed, you are being a little silly. What else can you say?

Script:
You are going to be doing some rhyming today, so let's get in the mood. *(Write on the board the word, "sand.")* What rhymes with this word? *(Response)* Yes, band, hand, land, brand, strand, grand, stand, etc.

You're pretty good at this, so now you get to do some more rhyming on your own. Your assignment is called "Crazy Rhymes." One thing's for sure—some of these rhymes are really crazy!

Answers:
There's a rock in this sock. A flower in a shower. A head on a bed. These are twins with fins. A clown in a gown. This jet is getting wet. A goat using a remote.

Crazy Rhymes

Name_____

How good are you at rhyming? Here's your chance to find out. Finish the sentence or phrase with a word that rhymes with the underlined word.

There's a _____ in this <u>sock</u>.

A <u>flower</u> in a _____

A _____ in a <u>gown</u>.

A _____ on a <u>bed</u>.

These are _____ with <u>fins</u>.

This <u>jet</u> is getting _____ .

A <u>goat</u> using a _____ .

WHAT'S THE PATTERN?
Week 16/Problem Solving

The Premise:
Students will determine sentence patterns based on simple clues.

Comment:
Patterns are often very difficult to recognize, unless you are the pattern-maker. That is why we have included a corresponding list of clues. The clues themselves have been written in a kind of shorthand to give students a little bit of help—but not too much!

Script:
(Write on the board: Tacos taste terrific.)

Then write: T x 3

Today, you are going to be doing an activity in which you must think about patterns. I've just written a sentence. I've also written a clue which should help you figure out what the pattern is in the sentence.

What is the pattern—based on the clue? *(Response)* Yes, each of the three words in the sentence begins with a "T." Did the clue help? *(Response)*

Now, it's time to look for patterns in other sentences. Good luck.

Answers:
(1) C—words begin with consecutive alphabet letters (2) A—all words start with an "R" (3) E—all 5-letter words (4) B—all words end in an "N"
(5) D—three-letter words between other words.

What's the Pattern?

Name_____

There is something unusual about the sentences below. Each one has its own special pattern. The problem is—you must find it.

Read all of the sentences and all of the clues before you begin. Then, match the clues with the sentences by putting the clue letter in the right blank. Hint: Skip around and find the easiest patterns first!

SENTENCES

1. Allen breaks chairs daily. _____

2. Robert really reads rapidly. _____

3. Sally likes lemon candy. _____

4. Even Marilyn can learn German. _____

5. Cake and muffins are my top choices. _____

CLUES

(A) R x 4

(B) Last letter

(C) A-B-C-D

(D) ___3___3___3___

(E) 5/5/5/5

SP WORDS
Week 16/Elaborative Thinking

The Premise:
Students will think of "SP" words that fit various descriptions.

Comment:
This is the last in a series of three activities which focus on words that start with consonants. After yesterday's pattern challenge, this should come as a giant relief.

As an extra challenge, ask your students to use five of their answers in a very long, crazy sentence. It can be done. Here's one version: "Chills went up my spine this spring when I saw that the spinach in my garden contained spider spit."

Script:

(Write this on the board:)
    etty

    ogram

    etzel

    om

Point to the list and say: These aren't words, but they want to be words. The problem is that they are missing the same two beginning letters. Can anyone figure out what those two letters are? *(Response)* Yes, the letters are "PR."

Today, you are going to be doing an activity in which you will be thinking of answers which start with "SP." Do your best, won't you?

Answers:
(1) spill (2) spinach (3) spine (4) sports (5) spider (6) spring (7) spit
(8) sprinkle (9) split (10) spin.

SP Words

Name_____

Just to put a SParkle in your day, think of some SP answers for this activity. No groaning, please. After all, you could be practicing SPelling!

1. An accident with milk, juice, etc. _____

2. A vegetable Popeye likes. _____

3. It's part of your back. _____

4. Football, basketball, baseball, etc. _____

5. It has eight legs. _____

6. A season. _____

7. It's liquid and in your mouth. _____

8. When it rains just a little bit. _____

9. Made of ice cream, it's called a banana _____.

10. If you do this, you'll get dizzy! _____

DRAWING STARTS
Week 16/Originality

The Premise:
Students will determine which drawing start would be most appropriate to use in illustrating each sentence.

Comment:
Students have already done one of these activities and there are four more to come! Obviously, we like the concept. Why? Consider some of the skills children are using when they do these exercises. They are:

- assessing the overall problem. (What kind of drawings are required?)
- deciding upon a strategy. (I'll use the first square for Sentence 2.)
- thinking creatively. (How can I make interesting drawings?)

Script:
(Make these drawings on the board:)

Today, you will again be completing drawings that have already been started. You did a similar activity a few weeks ago, but let me refresh your memory. Look at the drawing starts I have put on the board. Now, listen to these two sentences. "That is a nice umbrella." "The man is laughing."

(Finish the two drawing starts in this way:)

Well, the drawing start on the right is better for making an umbrella, isn't it? The drawing start on the left looks sort of like a mouth already, so it is easy to use it to draw a laughing man. Now, here are your drawing starts.

Possible solutions:

Sentence 1   Sentence 2   Sentence 3   Sentence 4

Drawing Starts

Name_____

Today, you will be making drawings that tell what is happening in each of the sentences. But there is one catch: The drawings have already been started! It will be up to you to decide which drawing start would be best to use for each sentence.

Be sure to read all of the sentences first, so that you can figure out how you are going to do this activity.

1. What a pretty flower!
2. I have a bug in this jar.
3. That man has a large beard.
4. The lady looked angry.

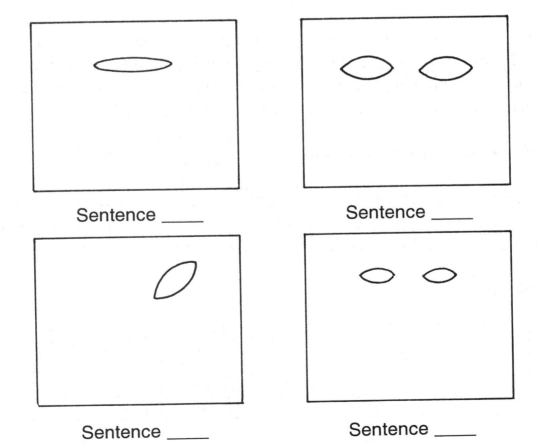

Sentence _____

Sentence _____

Sentence _____

Sentence _____

THE LINE PEOPLE
Week 17/Analytical Thinking

The Premise:
Students will match line drawings with statements.

Comment:
We developed a "Line People" activity for our book, "Ideas To Go," and had so much fun doing it that we decided to try it again with some new "people."

Children seem to understand body language about as well as adults do, so this is a fair challenge. Tell them to put a little "X" beside a drawing after they've used it, so they won't use it twice.

Script:
(Put this drawing on the board:)

Today, you have a most interesting assignment. You will be working with some "Line People," and figuring out what they are doing.

Look at the drawing I have made on the board. Now, I am going to read three sentences. Ready? "I like to do sit-ups." "I know the answer." "I can stand on my hands." Which sentence most closely describes the drawing on the board? *(Response)* Yes, the sentence, "I can stand on my hands."

Now, it's time to see what you can do. Look over everything carefully before you start writing your answers. Good luck!

Answers:
(1) 5 (2) 3 (3) 8 (4) 6 (5) 1 (6) 9 (7) 7 (8) 4 (9) 2.

The Line People

Name_____

What are all of these little people doing? They are waiting for you to match them up with the sentences. One rule: You can use each picture only once. Good luck!

1. I'm a fast runner. _____
2. My shoes are muddy. _____
3. I'm practicing karate. _____
4. I'm brushing my teeth. _____
5. I can't reach it. _____
6. I'm about to start the race. _____
7. I'm taking a cake out of the oven. _____
8. Hmm. That's a neat cloud. _____
9. I'm feeling very lazy today. _____

NAME GAME
Week 17/Flexible Thinking

The Premise:
Students will finish questions with words that rhyme.

Comment:
If you have a Miguel in your class, ask, "Miguel, are you feeling well?" If you have a Jennie, ask, "Jennie, do you have a penny?" If you have a Shawn, ask, "Shawn, did I see you yawn?" You get the picture. Personalize this assignment if you can.

Script:
Your activity today is called "Name Game." As the title suggests, you will be working with names, and you'll also get to do some rhyming. Have fun.

Answers:
(1) sick (2) back (3) table (4) go (5) sale (6) story (7) park (8) cake
(9) ready (10) phone.

Name Game

Name_____

If your name were Bob and you had just started to work as a grocery-store clerk, I could say, "Bob, how's your new job?"

"Bob" and "job" rhyme, don't they? You'll need to do more rhyming to finish the sentences below. Try to think of a word that rhymes with the name and also makes sense in the sentence.

1. Rick, are you feeling _____ ?

2. Jack, is that a fly on your _____ ?

3. Mabel, would you please dust the _____ ?

4. Jo, where shall we _____ ?

5. Gail, did you get that shirt on _____ ?

6. Laurie, did you read the _____ ?

7. Mark, shall I meet you at the _____ ?

8. Jake, do you want a piece of _____ ?

9. Eddie, are you _____ ?

10. Joan, will you answer the _____ ?

HARD PROBLEMS
Week 17/Problem Solving

The Premise:
Students will solve problems by analyzing visual information.

Comment:
Piaget's influence shows up in Problems 2 and 4, doesn't it? This means that very young children may have some conceptual difficulty. On the other hand, it will help you assess how far along your students are in the developmental process.

Script:
Today, you are in for a real challenge. You are going to be thinking about four "Hard Problems." Relax, take a deep breath, and see what you can do!

Answers:
(1) no (2) Box A (3) eight cookies (4) left side of the house.

Hard Problems

Name_____

Look carefully at these four drawings and then answer the questions.

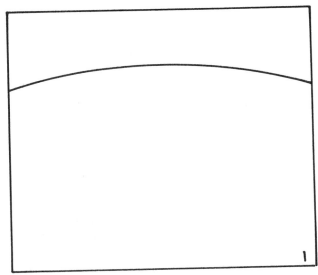

You are looking through a tiny window at the edge of a ball. Can you tell whether it is a basketball or a football?_____

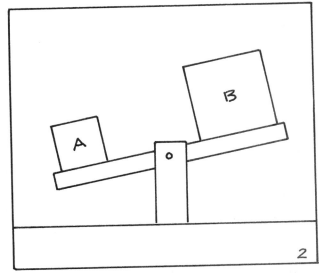

Which of these two boxes is heavier, A or B? _____

This cookie sheet was full of evenly spaced cookies, but someone ate all but four. How many did they eat? _____ cookies.

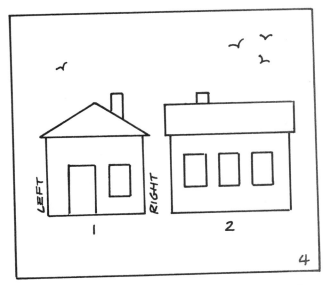

In Drawing 2, are you looking at the left or right side of this house? _____ side.

ROOMS
Week 17/Elaborative Thinking

The Premise:
Students will expand their thinking on the subject of rooms.

Comment:
Here is an example of a thinking-skills activity in which our central philosophy is apparent. We believe that productive thinking comes most readily out of a child's own experience.

When you start with something a child already knows a great deal about, two things happen: (1) that child is almost always interested in the subject matter (2) that child is inclined to use this knowledge as a launching pad for further intellectual exploration. So whether it is an analytical exercise about body language or a problem-solving activity on making a spider, no child using our materials starts from scratch.

Which brings us back to this assignment: What child doesn't know a lot about a room?

By the way, the "design your ideal bedroom" project (Number 5) allows for some daydreaming on paper, regardless of whether or not children have their own bedrooms. Everyone should have dreams.

Script:
What is this thing that we're in right now? *(Response) (If another hint is required, look at the ceiling, the floor, the walls, and they should get it.)* Yes, it is a room. Today, you are going to be doing an activity that asks you to think about rooms. So let's see what you can do.

Answers:
(1) four walls, a floor and a ceiling (2) book (3) living room (4) doorway.

Rooms

Name_____

Right now, you are sitting in a room. This morning, you woke up in a room. You were probably in other rooms today, too. So now it is time to make room in your head for . . . ROOMS!

1. A room usually has _____ walls, a _____ and a _____ .

2. A room is to a house as a page is to a _____ .

3. The largest room in a house is usually the _____ .

4. A room is still a room without windows but it has to have a _____ .

5. If you could design your ideal bedroom, what would it be like? Use the space below to make a little drawing of how it would look from above.

C DRAWINGS
Week 17/Originality

The Premise:
Students will turn the letter C into six drawings based on specific descriptions.

Comment:
Probably the hardest drawing to make, because of perspective, is the "roll of paper towels." A "bird sticking its head out of a birdhouse" isn't too easy to depict, either.

This assignment really forces children out of old drawing habits, encouraging them to find new ways of illustrating their ideas. (Hello, creativity!)

Script:
(Put a rather small letter C on the board.) C

What is on the board? *(Response)* Yes, the letter C. What if I said, "Turn this C into a picture of a paper clip?" How could you do it? *(Response, letting a couple of students try it.)*

This is how I would do it.
(Add lines
as shown.)

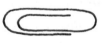

Today, you will be making some other C drawings. I think you'll enjoy working on this activity. I know I'll enjoy seeing the results!

Possible solutions:

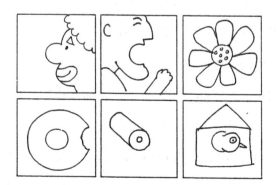

C Drawings

Name_____

Turn these C's into the six things listed below. You may use the C's in any way you wish, but they must be part of your drawing.

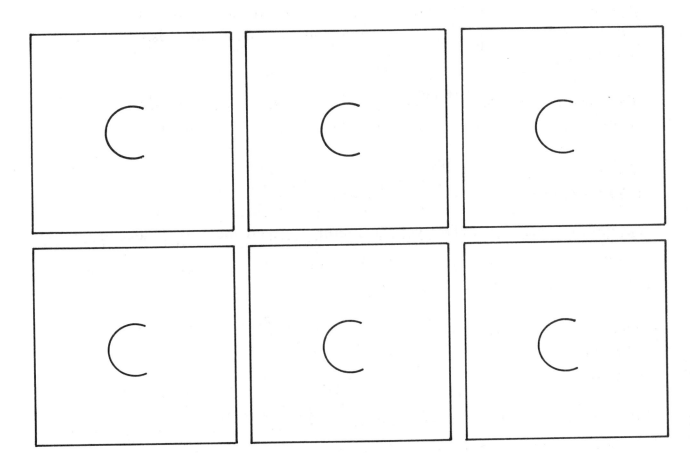

- A clown with a big nose.
- An angry man shouting.
- A big flower.
- A doughnut with a bite out of it.
- A roll of paper towels.
- A bird sticking its head out of a hole in a birdhouse.

CAT TALK - Week 18/Analytical Thinking

The Premise:
Students will match drawings about cats with statements.

Comment:
Even though some children may not have spent much time around cats, they still should be able to do this assignment. For example, Statement 6 ("I can see very well") obviously relates to Picture 7, and any student can make that connection.

A harder challenge, for those with or without cats, is Statement 5 ("I hope I land on my feet"). At first glance, the statement seems to go with either Picture 1 or Picture 5. But the word "hope" in the statement implies that the cat hasn't landed on its feet yet. So Picture 1, with the feet in the air, is the better choice.

Script:
How many of you have cats at home? *(Response)* What are their names? *(Response)* What colors are they? Describe them. *(Response)*

Today, you will be doing an activity called "Cat Talk." Look at all the pictures and read all the sentences before you decide on your answers. This is fun!

Answers:
(1) 9 (2) 6 (3) 8 (4) 5 (5) 1 (6) 7 (7) 3 (8) 2 (9) 4.

Cat Talk

Name_____

If cats could talk, here are some things they might say. Your job is to match the statements with the pictures. Use each picture and statement just once.

1. That flea is driving me crazy. _____
2. That dog is scaring me. _____
3. I like to climb trees. _____
4. I'm a very quiet walker. _____
5. I hope I land on my feet! _____
6. I can see very well. _____
7. Hi, Tom. Hi, Tabby. _____
8. He has to come out some time. _____
9. I hope that bird lands in my yard. _____

SENTENCE SENSE
Week 18/Flexible Thinking

The Premise:
Students will complete sentences based on picture clues.

Comment:
Common sense is what is needed here. For example, students must look at the drawing of a doorknob, consider its placement on the door, and then finish the sentence in a logical way.

Script:

(Put this on the board:)   This cat has _____ _____ ear.

Look at the picture and the words I have written. How would you complete the sentence in a way that makes sense? *(Response)* Yes, "This cat has only one ear," or "This cat has just one ear."

Today, you are going to be working on some similar problems. Good luck.

Answers:
One person is outside looking in, and one person is inside looking out. To make a dark mark, you have to press hard. On Saturdays, I get to sleep late. The knob on this door is in the wrong place. This dog has a long leash. This clock has too many hands (or one extra hand.)

Sentence Sense

Name_____

The sentences below are missing some words. First, look at the pictures and read the words that are there. Then, complete each sentence in a way that makes sense. (Put one word in each blank.)

One person is outside

looking _____ , and one

person is inside

looking _____ .

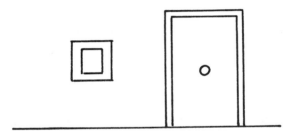

To make a dark mark,

you have to _____ _____ .

The knob on

this door is

in the _____ _____ .

On Saturdays,

I get to _____ _____ .

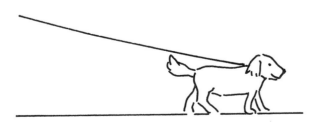

This dog has

a _____ leash.

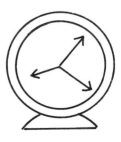

This clock has

_____ _____ _____ .

185

CUT IT OUT
Week 18/Problem Solving

The Premise:
Students will cut their way to the dark shape—and remove it—while keeping the square of paper intact.

Comment:
This is really just a kinetic maze. Unlike conventional mazes, however, where there is no penalty for backtracking and false starts, this version must be done right the first time. Best to have extra copies available!

Script:
(Take out a piece of notebook paper and a pair of scissors. Stand in front of the class, and begin to cut the paper in the manner shown at right.)

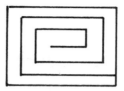

(In other words, make a rectangular "spiral.")

The kind of snipping I have been doing is easy. I really didn't have to think about it much. You are going to be doing some snipping today also, but there's a catch. You are going to have to think before you snip. Be sure to read the instructions carefully. You'll notice that you are to cut ON the lines, not BETWEEN them.

Solution:

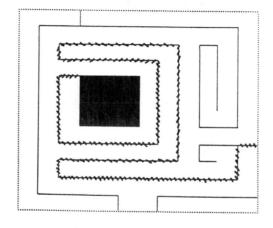

Cut It Out

In this activity, your goal is to cut out the dark shape you see below. But your job won't be easy because there are two rules:

1. You must not cut the big square in two as you try to get to the dark shape.

2. You must cut only along the lines.

Begin by cutting out the big square along the dotted lines. When you are finished, write your name somewhere on it, so your teacher can see how well you did.

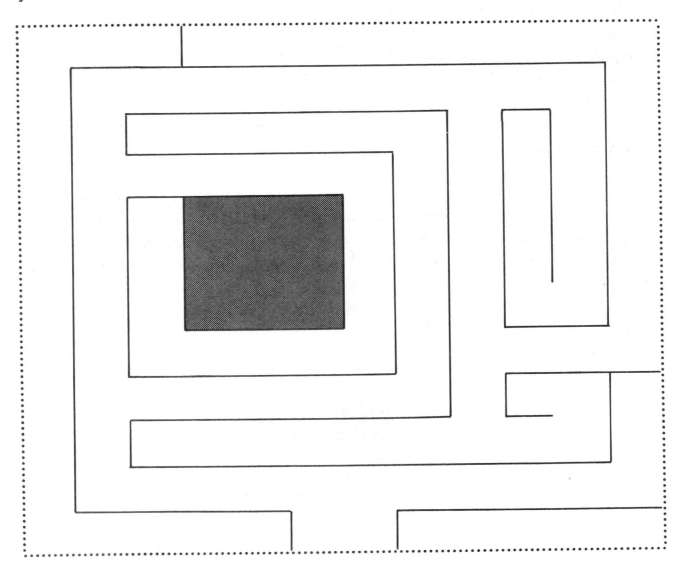

TEMPERATURE
Week 18/Elaborative Thinking

The Premise:
Students will expand their thinking on the subject of temperature.

Comment:
After students perform the "experiments" in Numbers 4 and 5, they still won't know the scientific reasons for their answers—and that's okay for this assignment. As a matter of fact, the best way to promote interest in science (and thinking generally) is to take advantage of the "gee whiz" factor first. Theory can come later.

Script:
What's the coldest weather you've ever experienced? *(Response)* What's the hottest weather you've ever experienced? *(Response)* Today's activity is about temperature, and you'll be making a couple of lists. If you run out of room, use the back of the paper.

Answers:
(1) open their windows, put on cool clothes, go swimming, turn on air conditioning, go to a movie, turn on a fan, drink a cold beverage, etc. (2) stay indoors, turn on the heat, eat hot soup, put extra blankets on their beds, build a fire, put on a coat, get a hot-water bottle, etc. (3) because the sun is not out (4) warmer (5) cooler.

Temperature

Name_____

Have you ever burned your finger? Have your teeth ever chattered? If you answered yes to these questions, then you already know a lot about temperature!

1. Make a list of things people do to keep cool when the weather is hot.

   _____

   _____

   _____

2. Make a list of things people do to keep warm when the weather is cold.

   _____

   _____

   _____

3. Why is it usually cooler at night than during the day? _____

4. Hold the back of your hand about an inch from your mouth. In a whisper, say "haaaa" (stretching out the "a" sound for a few seconds). Did it make your hand feel warmer or cooler? _____

5. Now, blow really hard on your hand for a few seconds. Did it make your hand feel warmer or cooler? _____

DOT
Week 18/Originality

The Premise:
Students will draw four pictures showing "Dot" in action.

Comment:
Dot has been with us a long time.

He (or she) first turned up as a bulletin board in our book, "The Great Unbored Bulletin Board Book II." The little character was so well-received that we decided Dot deserved even bigger and better things. So next came a series of activities called "Adventures of a Dot," in which all sorts of thinking experiences take place (Dot goes to the mall, school, beach, eats out, etc.)

Not long ago, we received a batch of Dot drawings from a third-grade teacher. Her students had fun putting Dot in all sorts of new situations—on a bulldozer, on water skis, etc. That was the inspiration for this activity. So turn your students loose and see what they can do!

Script:
(Go up to the board and make one big dot. ● *Point to the dot and say:)*
Today, I want you to meet Dot, the star of this assignment. Who is Dot? Dot is a little person who likes to do exciting things.

Wave to the class, Dot! *(Go to the board and add an arm, like this:)*

Now, it's your turn to make some Dot drawings. Good luck!

Dot

Name_____

This is Dot. ●~HI Dot is a little person who goes places and does things. Dot has a lot of fun! How old is Dot? Is Dot a boy or girl? We don't know. Do you?

This is Dot sky diving.   This is Dot bungee jumping. ●WHEE!

Use the boxes below to show Dot doing four other things. Also, complete the sentences under your drawings.

Dot is _____

Dot is _____

Dot is _____

Dot is_____

BUSY BOB
Week 19/Analytical Thinking

The Premise:
Students will match visual clues with the various places "Bob" has visited.

Comment:
Bob always seems to be carrying something!

Some of these clues are easy, others are hard. The hard ones become easier after the most obvious clues have been used. For example, as soon as students ascertain that Picture 9 is "toy store," and Picture 2 is "library," and Picture 3 is "football game," the more difficult challenges become less daunting.

Script:
Today, you are going to meet Bob. Bob has been very busy. Bob is always going places and buying things, and now Bob is carrying everything home.

In this activity, you'll have to figure out what Bob is carrying in order to know where he has been. So do some good detective work!

Answers:
(1) 3 (2) 5 (3) 2 (4) 8 (5) 7 (6) 6 (7) 4 (8) 9 (9) 1.

Busy Bob

Name_____

Bob has really been busy lately. He has had a lot of things to do! Where has he been? Match the pictures with the words.

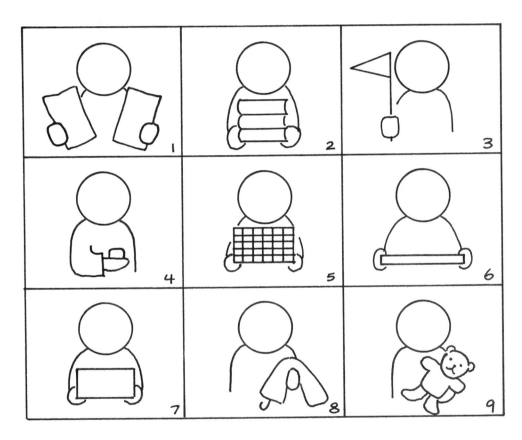

Bob has been . . .

1. to the football game. _____
2. to the pet store. _____
3. to the library. _____
4. to the cleaners. _____
5. to the bakery. _____
6. to the pizza parlor. _____
7. to the jewelry store. _____
8. to the toy store. _____
9. to the grocery store. _____

MYSTERY THINGS
Week 19/Flexible Thinking

The Premise:

Students will determine the identity of common objects by analyzing complicated descriptions.

Comment:

Developing definitions such as these without using obscure language or making the identity of the object too obvious is not easy. If children wish to try some versions of their own, let them do so and they'll get a quick lesson in the difficult job of writing precisely.

One interesting variation would be to ask them to write the most complete description they can of a commonplace thing such as a door—without giving away the fact that they are thinking about a door. (What is its function? Its shape? What is it made of?)

Script:

I am thinking of a common object, but I am going to describe it in a very different way. This means you will have to think very hard to determine what it is. Are you ready? Okay.

"A simple tool designed to remove marks made on a large surface in a classroom." What am I describing? *(Response)* Yes, an eraser.

Now, it's your turn to figure out four other mystery objects. Good luck.

Answers:

(1) table (2) window (3) weed (4) ice cubes.

Mystery Things

Name_____

These aren't really mystery objects at all. They are things you know about already. Read the definitions and see if you can figure out what is being described.

1. A flat surface held above the floor by legs.

_____

2. An opening in a wall that lets in light.

_____

3. A plant not considered useful which often grows in a place where it is not wanted.

_____

4. Water frozen into chunks that will fit easily into a glass.

_____

ABC
Week 19/Problem Solving

The Premise:
Students will determine how to connect three alphabet letters by using the fewest number of straight lines.

Comment:
This is good training in learning how to focus on the forest and not the trees. In other words, students will need to consider the overall arrangement of letters in order to choose the best pathway.

There may be some false starts, so have extra copies of this activity available. Better yet, encourage them to make light marks at first and use those funny rubber things on the ends of their pencils.

Script:
In today's activity, "ABC," you are going to connect the letter A to the letter B, the letter B to the letter C, and the letter C back to the letter A, using the fewest straight lines possible. Sounds pretty easy, doesn't it? But there's a problem. Some other pesky letters—H's, K's, T's, Q's and others—just happen to be in the way! Try your best!

Solution:

ABC

Name_____

Danger! Read all of these directions before you do anything, because this assignment takes some planning in advance. (You'll need a ruler as well as a pencil.)

Connect the A to the B, the B to the C, and the C back to the A, using the FEWEST number of straight lines possible. Your lines cannot touch the border or any other letters.

To do this, you will have to make your lines turn like this:

I made _____ straight lines.

THINGS I CAN DO
Week 19/Elaborative Thinking

The Premise:
Students will compile a list of things they can do that very young children can't do.

Comment:
After your students are finished with this list-making activity, they should be able to say, "I know how to do a lot of things!"

Obvious answers such as "read, write, add," are acceptable, but encourage them also to list specific skills, such as, "I can sew on a button."

Script:
Today, you are going to be making a list, and I will be very interested in what you have to say. You are going to be writing down things you can do that a three-year-old child can't do, and I hope you will be very detailed when you write about your skills and abilities.

For example, if I were doing this activity, here are several things I could write:

(*Write on the board several specific abilities, such as "I can look up a phone number in the directory. I can drive a car. I can make a chocolate cake."*)

I couldn't put "I can run," or "I can sleep" on my list because a three-year-old child could also do those things.

Have fun, and make your list as long as you can!

Things I Can Do

Name_____

What things can you do that a three-year-old child cannot do? Think about it! Make a list of all the skills you have that a very young child doesn't have. Your list should be a long one!

_____   _____

_____   _____

_____   _____

_____   _____

_____   _____

_____   _____

_____   _____

_____   _____

_____   _____

_____   _____

DRAWING STARTS
Week 19/Originality

The Premise:
Students will determine which drawing start would be most appropriate to use in illustrating each sentence.

Comment:
Even though the lower-left box would be best to use for a "baby crawling," it would be possible to turn the curved line in the upper-right box into the back of a crawling baby. One could then turn the marks in the lower-left box into some strange-looking underwater plants in a tank containing one fish. That's the kind of creativity this activity engenders!

Script:
(Make these lines on the board:)

Today, you will again be completing some drawings that have already been started. As an example of what you'll be doing, look at the drawing starts I have put on the board, and listen to these two sentences: "The building is very big." "The pyramid is a tourist site."

(Finish the two drawing starts in this way:)

Well, it would be very hard to use the drawing start on the left as a pyramid, wouldn't it? But it would make a fine building!

Here are your drawing starts. Have a good time.

Possible solutions:

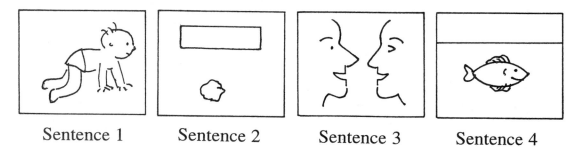

| Sentence 1 | Sentence 2 | Sentence 3 | Sentence 4 |

Drawing Starts

Name_____

Today, you will be making drawings that tell what is happening in each of the sentences. But there is one catch: The drawings have already been started! It will be up to you to decide which drawing start would be best to use for each sentence.

Be sure to read all of the sentences first, so that you can figure out how you are going to do this activity.

1. Babies love to crawl.
2. This is gum before and after chewing.
3. Two people are having a nice talk.
4. There is just one fish in the tank.

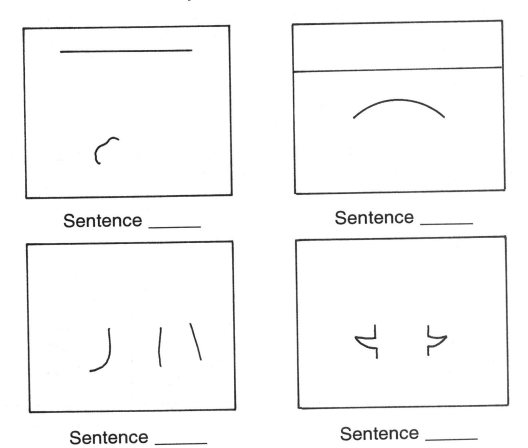

Sentence _____

Sentence _____

Sentence _____

Sentence _____

WHAT'S GOING ON?
Week 20/Analytical Thinking

The Premise:
Students will match abstractions of simple concepts with statements.

Comment:
In a way, this is very difficult. In a way, this is very simple.

The difficulty lies in the fact that the symbols crowd into the frames so aggressively that at first glance, it is hard to "read" them. Like many of our other abstract activities, however, this becomes easier once you focus on one abstraction and then read through the list of possibilities. At that point, you realize that "uncle's bald head" could only be Picture 2—unless he has a pointy head!

Script:
(Put this drawing on the board:)

Take a look at the drawing. Now, I'm going to read three sentences, and I want you to decide which sentence best fits the drawing. Ready? "The clouds are pretty today." "The hill is not very steep." "The lake is very calm." Which sentence best describes what you're looking at? *(Response)* Yes, the sentence, "The hill is not very steep," because the drawing looks more like a hill than a cloud or a lake.

Now, you have some of your own problems to solve. Look at the pictures, think about the meaning of the sentences, and hook up the right pictures and sentences!

Answers:
(1) 5 (2) 1 (3) 4 (4) 6 (5) 2 (6) 3.

What's Going On?

Name_____

These are simple sentences and simple drawings, but will you be able to put them together? To do it, you'll need to be a careful thinker. Read all of the sentences first. Then, match them with the pictures.

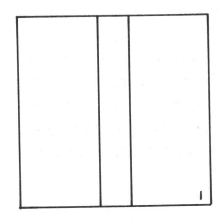
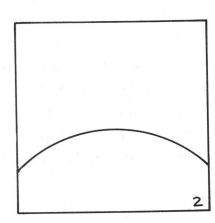
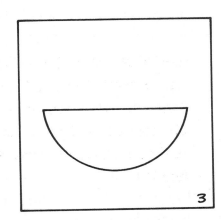

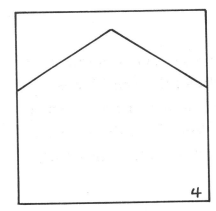
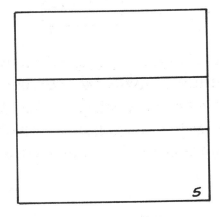
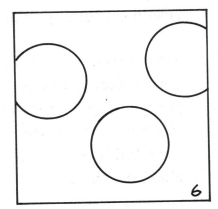

1. The tree blew down. _____
2. There is a space between each fence board. _____
3. I live in a tall house. _____
4. Eat your peas! _____
5. There is no hair on top of my uncle's head. ___
6. Is that bowl clean? _____

NAME ONE THING
Week 20/Flexible Thinking

The Premise:
Students will think of a property unique to one item in a pair.

Comment:
This activity encourages children to think about the essential properties of the things that have been listed.

In some cases there really is only one obvious answer. For example, a doughnut can be frosted or sprinkled with coconut, but so can a cookie. The only real difference is that doughnuts have holes and cookies do not (at least most of them).

A few of the pairs present more difficulty. There are several things a bicycle sometimes has that a tricycle doesn't—a light, reflectors, gears—but the biggest difference, apart from the number of wheels, is brakes. Similarly, a Popsicle usually comes wrapped and an ice-cream cone doesn't, but the biggest difference is the stick.

Script:
In today's activity, you will be thinking about how things are different from one another. Here's an example of what I mean. If I said, "Name one thing a television set has that a radio doesn't have," what could be the answer? *(Response)* Yes, a television set has a screen and the radio doesn't, so "screen" would be the best answer.

Now, get ready to do some tough thinking about some other things.

Answers:
(1) sleeves (2) hole (3) lid (4) legs (5) handle (6) laces (7) brake (8) stick.

Name One Thing

Name_____

Think of one thing you have that a bed doesn't have. Well, let's see. A bed has a head and you have a head. A bed has a foot and you have a foot. But how about a nose?

That's the kind of thinking you'll need to do in this activity. Read the sentences carefully and put your best answers in the blanks.

1. Name one thing a shirt has
   that a vest doesn't have. _____

2. Name one thing a doughnut has
   that a cookie doesn't have. _____

3. Name one thing a garbage can has
   that a wastebasket doesn't have. _____

4. Name one thing a lizard has
   that a snake doesn't have. _____

5. Name one thing a cup has
   that a glass doesn't have. _____

6. Name one thing tennis shoes have
   that slippers don't have. _____

7. Name one thing a bicycle has
   that a tricycle doesn't have. _____

8. Name one thing a Popsicle has that
   an ice-cream cone doesn't have. _____

CONNECT THE DOTS
Week 20/Problem Solving

The Premise:
Students will solve various challenges by connecting dots.

Comment:
Remember all those connect-the-dot activities you used to do? Well, this is the cerebral version! Students will have to make good choices to succeed in this activity.

Script:
(Put this dot pattern on the board:)

Here's a problem for you. What is the biggest triangle you can make by connecting any four of these dots? You have to draw straight lines and your lines can only touch four dots. *(Response, letting a student try it.)*

(If necessary, show class this solution:)

Today, you will have other dot decisions to make. Have fun selecting which dots to use!

Possible solutions:

Connect Some Dots

Name _____

If you think this is just another connect-the-dots game, you're wrong! Yes, you will be connecting dots, but you will also have to use your brain to figure out which dots you want to connect!

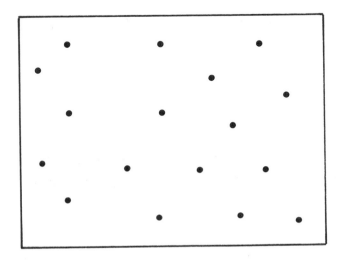

Make the biggest number 5 you can by connecting as many dots as you wish.

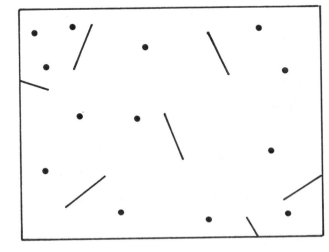

Make the largest rectangle you can by connecting any four dots. The lines of your rectangle cannot touch any lines that are already there.

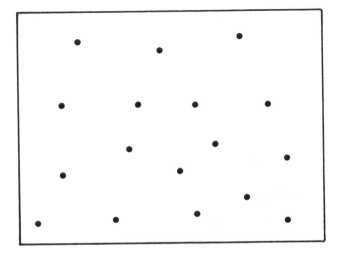

Make the biggest star you can by connecting as many dots as you wish.

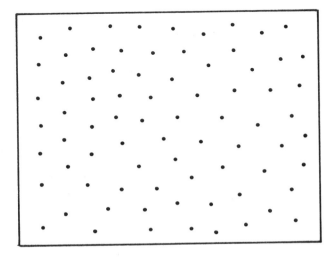

Connect the dots in any way you like to make a scary face. If you want to add eyes, ears, etc., that's okay, too.

WORDS
Week 20/Elaborative Thinking

The Premise:
Students will expand their thinking on the subject of words.

Comment:
Isn't Number 3 interesting? Of course, there are no right answers, but it is fun to speculate! At the top of the list: "I." Or would it be: "You?" And probably everyone uses "and" and "the." At the very least, this should provoke some spirited discussions.

If students think about it, they could write their own first names as the answer for Number 4.

Script:
(Write this on the board:)
Tod ayyo uwill bed oing af unactiv ityab out wo rds.

I'm really making a lot of mistakes today. I decided to write your assignment on the board and somehow, the spaces between the words got all mixed up. What did I mean to say? Well, if you can figure it out, you'll know what the subject of today's activity is. Good luck.

Possible solutions for Number 6:

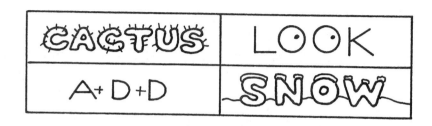

Words

Name_____

What are you doing right now? You're reading, aren't you? And what are you reading? Words! You already know a lot about this subject, so choose your words carefully.

1. Write the shortest word you know. _____

2. Write the longest word you know. _____

3. Write five words everyone
   probably uses every day. _____

   _____

4. Write a word that is always capitalized. _____

5. Write three words you would find near the middle of a dictionary.

   _____

6. Look at the words below. What can you do to them to tell something important about them? Here's one example: THE

CACTUS	LOOK
ADD	SNOW

SIDE BY SIDE
Week 20/Originality

The Premise:
Students will put together complete drawings of specific objects by positioning the sides of two rectangles.

Comment:
These days, children spend too many passive hours watching videos and television. This makes it even more important that they have some hands-on, manipulative experience. "Side by Side" gives them that opportunity. They begin the assignment by cutting out the rectangles. Then they must turn the pieces around until they find the objects they are looking for.

Script:
Today, you are going to be doing another "Side by Side." You'll be looking for some neat things, such as a turtle and an astronaut, but right now (poor things), they're in two pieces! So put on your detective's cap and see what you can do.

Answers:
(1) Sides 4 and 6 (2) Sides 2 and 8 (3) Sides 3 and 6 (4) Sides 4 and 6
(5) Sides 2 and 5 (6) Sides 3 and 7.

Side by Side

Name_____

Today, you'll be looking for complete drawings. Right now, part of each drawing is on one rectangle, and part is on the other. Your job will be to put the parts together. The six sentences will tell you what drawings to look for.

First, cut out the rectangles. Then, look for the thing mentioned in the sentence. In the blanks at the end of the sentence, write the numbers of the two sides you put together to make each thing. (You may need to use some drawing parts more than once.)

1. Find a kite and string. (I used Sides _____ and _____ .)
2. Find an astronaut. (I used Sides _____ and _____ .)
3. Find a face from the side. (I used Sides _____ and _____ .)
4. Find a turtle. (I used Sides _____ and _____ .)
5. Find a needle and thread. (I used Sides _____ and _____ .)
6. Find a tired person. (I used Sides _____ and _____ .)

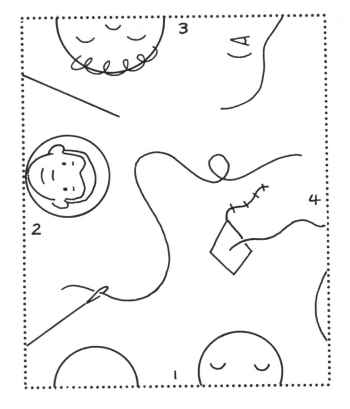

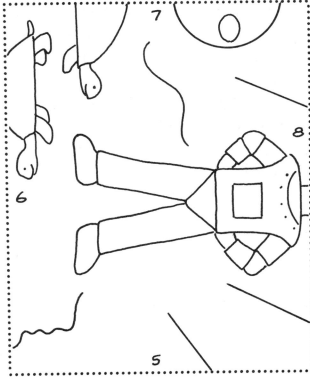

VERB PUZZLERS (S)
Week 21/Analytical Thinking

The Premise:
Students will match S words with visual clues.

Comment:
We have tampered playfully with alphabet letters in a couple of earlier products, "OPQ, Offbeat Adventures with the Alphabet," and "An Alphabet You've Never Met." These situations are brand-new, however.

Script:
(Put this drawing on the board:)

I am looking for a word that is a verb, that begins with the letter S. Take a look at this drawing and see if you can think of the word I have in mind. *(Response)* Yes, the word is "sip."

Today, you will be looking for other S verbs. Match the pictures with the words, and have fun.

Answers:
(1) 6 (2) 1 (3) 5 (4) 7 (5) 3 (6) 4 (7) 9 (8) 2 (9) 8.

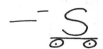

Verb Puzzlers (S)

Name_____

Can you SEE if you can figure out which S verbs
match up with these S pictures? Look at what has
been done to the S's and SOLVE the puzzle!

1. Sit _____
2. Swim _____
3. Smell _____
4. Scream _____
5. See _____
6. Sparkle _____
7. Stand _____
8. Slide _____
9. Scatter _____

PLAYFUL PLATES
Week 21/Flexible Thinking

The Premise:

Students will determine occupations based on vanity-plate clues.

Comment:

There are actually three vanity plates which could apply to "English teacher." Want to guess what they are? (We're not entirely serious, of course, but a case could be made for Pictures 1 and 2 as well as the real answer, Picture 8.)

Script:

Pretend for a moment that you are on a long car trip. You're getting a little bored. To help you pass the time, you start looking at license plates. You see that a lot of them are fun to read, because they're vanity plates.

Now, come back to reality. You've done an assignment on vanity plates before, haven't you? Who remembers what vanity plates are? *(Response)* Yes, they are license plates that use numbers or letters in a very imaginative way to say something about the person who owns the car.

All of the vanity plates in this exercise today have something to do with what a person does in his or her job. You will really need to think hard, but you should also have a lot of fun. Good luck.

Answers:

(1) 3 (2) 5 (3) 4 (4) 6 (5) 7 (6) 1 (7) 8 (8) 2.

Playful Plates

Name_____

You're riding down the highway and you keep
noticing funny license plates! A lot of them seem
to describe what people do in their jobs. Here are
a few. Match the pictures with the words.

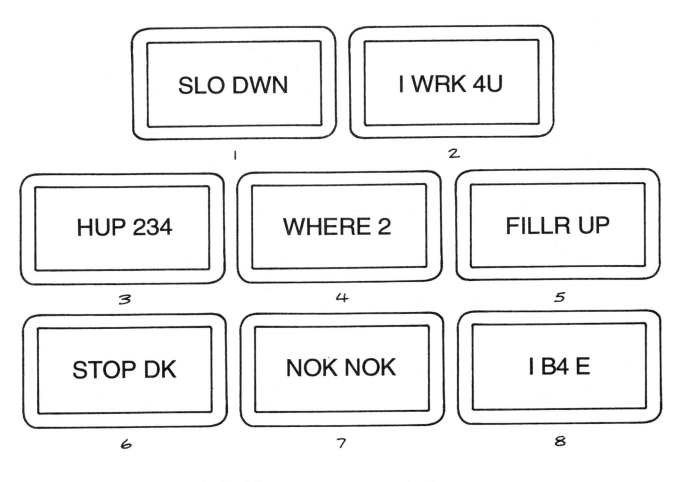

SLO DWN
1

I WRK 4U
2

HUP 234
3

WHERE 2
4

FILLR UP
5

STOP DK
6

NOK NOK
7

I B4 E
8

1. Soldier _____
2. Gas station attendant _____
3. Taxi driver _____
4. Dentist _____
5. Door-to-door salesperson _____
6. Police officer _____
7. English teacher _____
8. Senator _____

TAKE AWAY
Week 21/Problem Solving

The Premise:
Based on classification clues, students will cut away shapes until they are left with one final shape, which contains the answer-word.

Comment:
Take Aways are good for building categorization skills. You can find more of this activity in our book, "Smart Snips."

Since children will be cutting away shapes until they reach the final shape—which is in fact the answer—they are also gaining experience in using scissors. Some students, as you know, need to develop better hand-eye coordination, and this will help.

Script:
(Put these words on the board: climb, sit, bend, ride, walk:)

If I asked you to pick out only those words that have to do with getting from one place to another, which words would you choose? *(Response)* Yes, climb, ride, and walk.

In today's assignment, you are going to do more thinking about groups. The activity is called "Take Away," and you've done a couple of them before. Remember when you had to cut your way to an answer? Here's your chance to do it again.

Answers:
(1) joke, clown (2) lawn, rug, sidewalk (3) brown, blue, green (4) peas, spinach, beans, carrots, lettuce (5) postcard, birthday card (6) frown, scowl. The word on the remaining shape: robin.

Take Away

Name_____

Today, you will be cutting away shapes until you get to one final shape. Which shapes do you cut? You will learn that by following the directions. Three rules:

- Cut only the number of shapes listed after each direction.
- Do not work ahead. Complete each direction in the order given.
- As you work, put all the shapes in a pile. You won't need them.

Look for and then cut out:

1. Things that make you laugh. (2)
2. Things you walk on. (3)
3. Colors for eyes. (3)
4. Vegetables. (5)
5. Things you mail. (2)
6. Expressions that show how you feel. (2)

The word on the remaining shape is _____

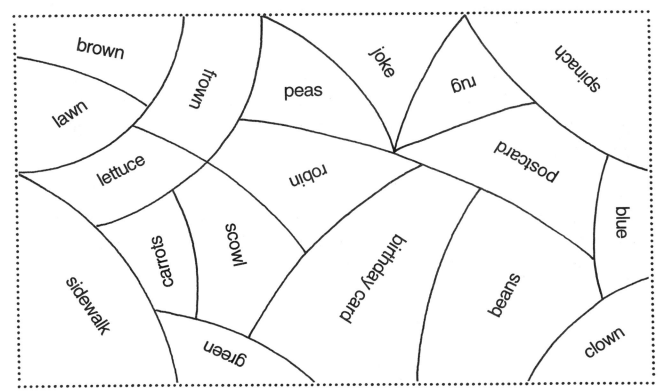

First, cut along the dotted lines.

ROCKS
Week 21/Elaborative Thinking

The Premise:
Students will expand their thinking on the subject of rocks.

Comment:
The abstractions in Number 5 were fun to develop. Of course, students must zero in on the verbs in order to be successful. In each situation there is just one clue provided. For example, the inclined plane in Picture 4 provides the only hint that the rock is rolling.

Script:
Let's play a guessing game. I'm thinking of an object that is found outside. There are millions and millions of them, and no two are exactly alike. They come in various sizes and shapes and colors. They feel quite hard to the touch. What am I thinking of? *(Response. If more hints are needed, say:)* They can be found on the ground or under the ground. *(Response)* Yes, I'm thinking of a rock!

Now, you get to dig into the subject of rocks even more deeply! Good luck.

Answers:
(1) sand (2) pebble (3) rocks (4) Sometimes, I rock the baby to sleep. This pizza crust is as hard as a rock. He must have rocks in his head to pass up a chance like that. I love rock and roll. (5) A-3, B-6, C-4, D-5, E-2, F-1.

Rocks

Name_____

Do you think everyone in the world has seen a rock? Held a rock? Skipped a rock? Rocks are quite interesting, aren't they?

1. What would you call a rock this size? _____

2. What would you call a rock this size? _____

3. Do you think there are more rocks or trees in the world? _____

4. Here are several sentences which use a form of the word, "rock." You should be able to figure out the missing words by reading the other words in the sentence. Write the missing words in the blanks.

    •   Sometimes, I rock the baby to _____ .
    •   This pizza crust is as _____ as a rock.
    •   He must have rocks in his _____ to pass up a chance like that.
    •   I love rock and _____ .

5. Match these pictures with the words below.

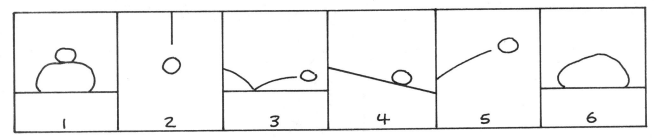

A. I skipped a rock. _____   D. I threw a rock. _____
B. I hid behind a rock. _____   E. I dropped a rock. _____
C. I rolled a rock. _____   F. I balanced a rock. _____

DECIDE AND DRAW
Week 21/Originality

The Premise:
Students will decide which of three sentences has the best visual possibilities and then illustrate it.

Comment:
You should get some hilarious ladder-and-cat drawings. Display them. Less adventuresome students who don't think they can draw themselves going up a ladder to get a cat, will probably show lightning streaks in the sky, hoping that suffices for "I heard thunder in the distance."

No one in the world will draw "It was a boring movie." Or will they?

Script:
How is the art part of you feeling today? Are you up to making a good drawing? This activity is called "Decide and Draw." Read the three sentences first, decide what you are going to illustrate, and then do it!

Decide and Draw

Name_____

Read the three sentences. Which one would be easiest to show in a drawing? You decide . . . and then make your drawing in the rectangle below.

1. It was a boring movie.

2. I heard thunder in the distance.

3. I climbed up the ladder to get my cat.

This drawing is about Sentence _____ .

TV TALK
Week 22/Analytical Thinking

The Premise:
Students will match drawings of television sets with statements.

Comment:
Whether they watch TV from the perspective of a favorite chair, a sofa, or sprawled out on the floor, most youngsters are sure to relate to these situations.

As an ancillary activity, ask them to draw a close-up view of a TV set in their own house, with a picture of their favorite program on the screen.

Script:
How many of you watch TV each day? Raise your hands if you do. *(Response)* Where do you usually sit when you watch TV? *(Response)* Today's activity has a lot to do with how the TV screen looks when you watch it from different places in a room.

I think you know a lot about this subject already, so I expect to see some good results.

Answers:
(1) 5 (2) 3 (3) 6 (4) 1 (5) 7 (6) 8 (7) 4 (8) 9 (9) 2.

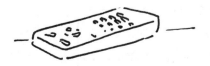

TV Talk

Name_____

Here are nine different views of television sets. Look at the pictures and read the sentences. Then decide which sentence goes best with each picture. Good luck!

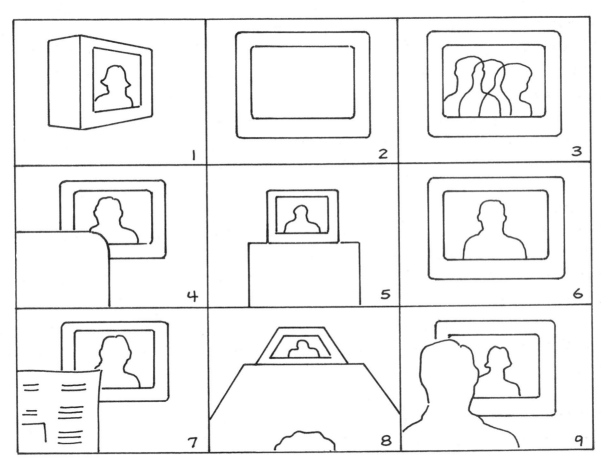

1. I'm sitting too far away. _____
2. There's something wrong with the picture. _____
3. I can see perfectly. _____
4. I can't see too well from over here. _____
5. I like to watch TV and read the newspaper at the same time. _____
6. I like to lie on the floor and watch television. _____
7. The chair's in the way. _____
8. Move over. You're in the way. _____
9. The TV went off! _____

MYSTERY THINGS
Week 22/Flexible Thinking

The Premise:
Students will determine the identity of common objects by analyzing complicated descriptions.

Comment:
After students identify the four objects, it might be fun to have them answer these questions:

- Which of the objects is the heaviest? (The doughnut)
- Which of the objects can be folded? (The bill)
- Which of the objects would you least likely take camping? (The light bulb)
- Which two objects would a person use only once? (The doughnut and the bill)
- Which three objects are probably in this room right now? (Pencil, bill, and the light bulb)

Script:
I am thinking of an object, but I am going to describe it in a very unusual way. This means you will have to think very hard to figure out what it is. Are you ready? Okay.

"A small circular object, usually having two or more holes, which is designed to help hold two parts of something you wear together." What am I describing? *(Response)* Yes, a button.

Now, see if you can guess these four mystery objects.

Answers:
(1) doughnut (2) pencil (3) money (a bill) (4) light bulb.

Mystery Things

Name_____

These aren't really mystery objects at all. They are things you know about already. Read the definitions and see if you can figure out what is being described.

1. A circular piece of baked sweet dough with an opening in the middle.

_____

2. A long, narrow piece of wood containing black material which will make a mark.

_____

3. A piece of paper shaped like a rectangle that can be traded for something you want.

_____

4. A glass object containing wires that glow brightly when electricity is passed through them.

_____

GUMBOS
Week 22/Problem Solving

The Premise:
Students will analyze characteristics of faces to determine whether or not they belong in a specific group.

Comment:
There is one property that makes a Gumbo a Gumbo. All Gumbos have open mouths.

Script:
(Put these drawings on the board:)

Which one of these heads is different? Why? *(Response)* Yes, the head on the left is not like the other two. It has straight hair.

Today, you are going to do an assignment called "Gumbos." You must figure out just who the Gumbos are. Or, let me put it another way—what makes a Gumbo a Gumbo?

Answers:

Gumbos

Name_____

What in the world is a Gumbo? There's a way to tell—if you think hard and look closely. Figure out what is the same about all of the Gumbos, and you'll be on the right track.

These are Gumbos.

These are not Gumbos.

Which of these are Gumbos? Circle them.

           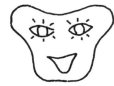 

SINKS
Week 22/Elaborative Thinking

The Premise:
Students will expand their thinking on the subject of sinks.

Comment:
About Number 3: All children know how to regulate a faucet in order to get warm water. Nevertheless, the desired answer will stump some, surprise others. It's another one of those "gee whiz" revelations that comes from having to formulate an answer on paper.

Go easy in judging how students handle Number 4. Most likely, they have never been asked to do anything like this before. A couple of students will probably surprise you by having a pretty good idea where water pipes go, while others will be clueless. It should be interesting.

Script:
(Pantomime washing your hands at a sink by turning on the water, reaching for the soap, and scrubbing both hands together. Then say:) What am I doing? *(Response)* Yes, I am washing my hands. Where am I? *(Response)* Yes, probably in the bathroom. What am I standing in front of? *(Response)* Yes, I'm in front of a sink.

Today, you are going to be thinking about sinks. Since you all use them, you should approach this activity with a lot of confidence. Have fun!

Answers:
(1) bathroom, kitchen (2) a sink is smaller, it is higher, it is for washing hands and face and not one's whole body (3) warm.

Possible version of sink:

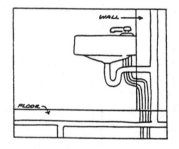

Sinks

Name_____

Today, you'll need to sink about a think. Oops! Make that think about a sink. You'll either "sink or swim" in this activity!

1. Two rooms in a house usually have sinks. What are they? _____

   _____

2. Think of two ways in which a bathroom sink is different from a bathtub.

   _____

   _____

3. Complete this sentence: In a sink, hot and cold water come out of the same place because sometimes people want _____ water.

4. Draw a sink from the side. The sink should be attached to the wall. Pretend you have X-ray vision and show where all the pipes would be.

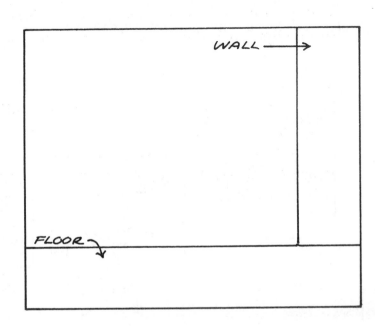

DRAWING STARTS
Week 22/Originality

The Premise:
Students will determine which drawing start would be most appropriate to use in illustrating each sentence.

Comment:
Although most of the drawing starts in this program have some flexibility built into them, this version is different. Two of these drawing starts are appropriate only for specific sentences. The top-right box is the only place where a student could illustrate the sentence, "I stacked six blocks of the same size into a triangle." The lower-right box is the only start that would work for the sentence, "I stacked three blocks of the same size into a triangle."

Script:
(Make these lines on the board:)

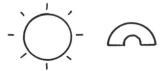

By now you are familiar with drawing starts, but let's refresh your memory anyway. If I had to illustrate these two sentences using these two drawing starts, how could it be done? The sentences are: "The sun was shining brightly." "We made an igloo."

Here is how I would do it.
(Finish the drawing starts this way.)

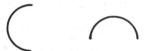

Now, you have some drawing starts of your own to do.

Possible versions:

  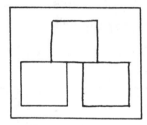 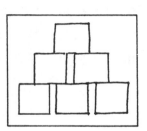

Sentence 1   Sentence 2   Sentence 3   Sentence 4

Drawing Starts

Name_____

Today, you will be making drawings that tell what is happening in each of the sentences. But there is one catch: The drawings have already been started! It will be up to you to decide which drawing start would be best to use for each sentence.

Be sure to read all of the sentences first, so that you can figure out how you are going to do this activity.

1. The robot's mouth was open.
2. I had a surprised look on my face.
3. I stacked three blocks of the same size into a triangle.
4. I stacked six blocks of the same size into a triangle.

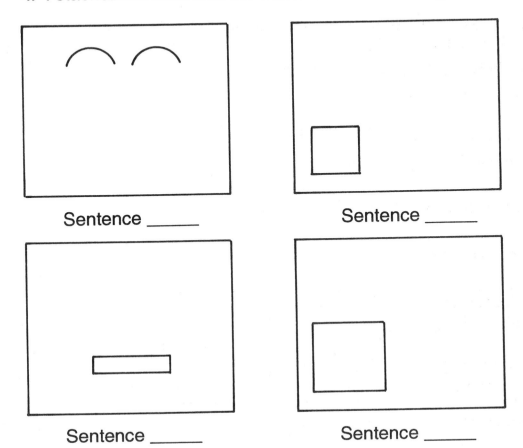

Sentence _____

Sentence _____

Sentence _____

Sentence _____

PET PLACES
Week 23/Analytical Thinking

The Premise:
Students will match types of pets with places where they might be found.

Comment:
One interesting aspect of this activity is that scale is not a clue. The solution to each problem depends solely upon the setting.

As for the cat on the couch (Picture 6), many ideas in this book come from personal experience!

Script:
Today's activity has a lot to do with where pets spend most of their time. To get you in the mood for this, let's think about where other things are usually found. For example, where do you usually find a spoon? *(Response)* Yes, in a drawer. Where do you usually find a car? *(Response)* Yes, in a garage or a carport or parked on the street. Where do you usually find a coat? *(Response)* Yes, in a closet.

Now, you are ready to do "Pet Places."

Answers:
(1) 4 (2) 3 (3) 1 (4) 6 (5) 5 (6) 2.

Pet Places

Name_____

Those aren't circles in these drawings, they're pets! Your job today is to figure out which pet is shown in each drawing. To do that, you'll have to think about where pets spend a lot of their time. Match the pictures with the words.

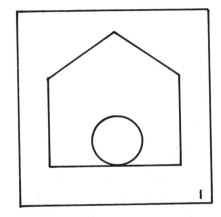

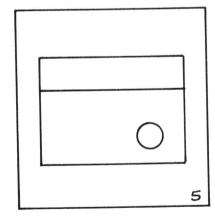

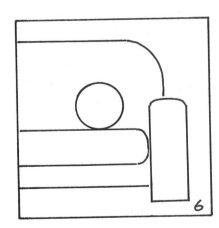

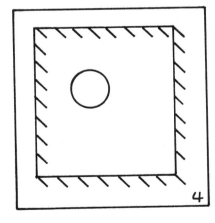

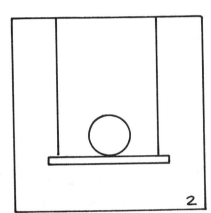

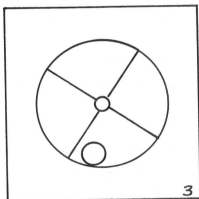

1. Horse _____

2. Hamster _____

3. Dog _____

4. Cat _____

5. Goldfish _____

6. Canary _____

THREE REASONS WHY
Week 23/Flexible Thinking

The Premise:

Students will think of plausible motives for everyday activities.

Comment:

This should make children a bit more thoughtful about why they do what they do. Hold them responsible for giving serious answers. Nothing far-fetched allowed!

Script:

Today, you are going to be doing an activity called "Three Reasons Why." Your task is to give reasons why you may or may not do something.

Just so you understand what I want from you in this assignment, let me give you an example. If I asked you to list reasons why you might not go to a store, what could you say? *(Response)* Yes, you might not go to a store because:

- It was evening and the store was closed.
- You didn't have any money to spend.
- You were busy doing something else.
- You didn't need anything that the store had to sell.
- You don't like the way the clerks treat you.
- You don't like the brands the store sells.

Notice that all of these reasons are believable. That is the way I hope you will handle this exercise today. Think carefully about your answers.

Possible answers:

(1) It is too hard to read. I am not interested in the subject. I have read it already. (2) I am going to visit a friend. I am going to the store with my dad. I am playing ball. (3) I am in school and everyone is working. I have lost my voice. I am telling someone a secret.

Three Reasons Why

Name_____

In this activity, you are asked to think about the reasons certain things happen as they do. Try to make your reasons believable. In other words, you can't say, "I might not read a book because I'm vacationing on Mars and there aren't any books there." (You haven't been to Mars lately, have you?)

Three reasons why . . .

1. you might not read a book.

    _____

    _____

    _____

2. you might leave your home on a Saturday.

    _____

    _____

    _____

3. you might talk in a whisper.

    _____

    _____

    _____

HARD PROBLEMS
Week 23/Problem Solving

The Premise:
Students will solve problems by analyzing visual information.

Comment:
Here's an extending activity for Problem 4. Put a shoelace at a center—or let them use their own—and have them arrange the lace so that it makes a loose knot. Then let them try drawing it. Will they be able to do it? A nice art challenge.

Script:
(Cut three pieces of notebook paper into several large pieces, tape them to the wall in a random arrangement, and then say:) Today's activity is called "Hard Problems," but they're actually quite easy, if you really examine what's happening. To get you into the spirit of things, I have taped some pieces of notebook paper to the wall. My "Hard Problem" to you is—how many full sheets of paper did I use? *(Response)*

Now, it's time to tackle some other problems.

Answers:
(1) 3 plates (2) 8 or 9 bites (3) no (4) no.

Hard Problems

Name_____

Look carefully at these four drawings and then answer the questions.

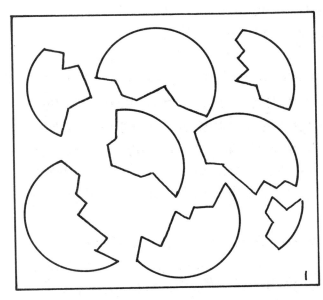

Oops! Somebody dropped some dinner plates. How many plates do you think they dropped? _____

About how many more bites do you think it will take for the bug to eat the whole leaf? _____ bites

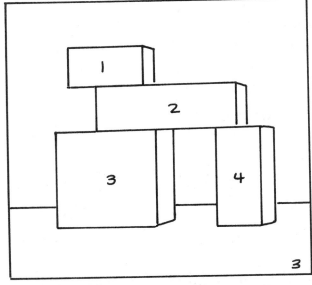

If you take away Block 4, will Blocks 1 and 2 fall for sure?
Yes _____ No _____

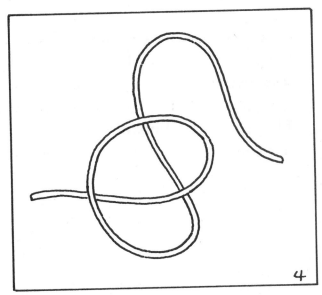

If you pull on the ends of this string, will you make a knot?
Yes _____ No _____

NUMBERS
Week 23/Elaborative Thinking

The Premise:
Students will make a list of things that have numbers on them.

Comment:
Encourage students to be as creative as possible. Tell them to think of ways numbers are used in various places—on a street, at a store, in a football stadium, etc. Some of the answers you might be looking for: street addresses, speed–limit signs, maps, scoreboards, sports jerseys, price tags, money, stamps, newspapers, page numbers in books, dog tags, license plates, telephone directories, backs of cereal boxes, calculators, keyboards, size numbers in shoes, calendars, clocks, etc.

Script:
Look around you. Can you see numbers anywhere? *(Response)* Yes, on the calendar, on the clock, etc. Today, you are going to be making a list of all the things you can think of that have numbers on them. I hope you can make a very long list.

One rule before you begin. You cannot write, "geography book, English book, math book," because that would be too simple! Instead, if you are thinking about books, a good answer would be "page numbers in a book."

I hope you can think of at least 26 things. I'll write that number on the board, but sorry, you can't use it on your list!

Numbers

Name_____

Make a list of things that have numbers on them. There are a zillion possibilities! Well, maybe not a zillion, but your list should be long. Just to get you started, here are a couple of ideas: telephone, microwave. And don't forget about that little label on the inside of your shirt.

_____   _____

_____   _____

_____   _____

_____   _____

_____   _____

_____   _____

_____   _____

_____   _____

_____   _____

_____   _____

SIX-LINE DESIGN
Week 23/Originality

The Premise:
Students will make nine designs, each of which is made up of six lines.

Comment:
If you told children to make a design using lines, they probably would have some trouble getting started. But by limiting the scope of the challenge—using only six lines—the activity becomes instantly approachable.

Script:
(Draw several different kinds of lines on the board—such as the ones shown here.)

I've just made some lines which I think are interesting. Can anyone come up and make a different kind of line? *(Response, letting several students do it.)*

Today, you are going to be artists, but you won't be making pictures of anything real. Instead, you are going to be making nine designs. There is one rule, however—you have to use exactly six lines in each of your designs. Your lines can be wiggly, short, straight, thick, thin—it's up to you. Be creative!

Possible versions:

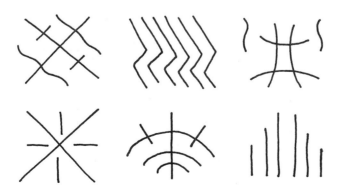

Six-Line Design

Name_____

How many ways can you put six lines together? Actually, there are many, many possibilities—if you just use your imagination!

Here's an example:

Now, make nine interesting designs using exactly six lines for each. Your lines can be short, long, wiggly, straight, curved—anything you like. Just be inventive.

AT THE MOVIES
Week 24/Analytical Thinking

The Premise:
Students will match drawings with word descriptions.

Comment:
A couple of easy beginning clues ("soft drink," "popcorn") should get students comfortable with the concept, and lead them quite easily to Pictures 9 and 4.

The hardest challenge is probably Number 6. To be successful, students will have to determine that the parents and children are identifiable only by their "shirts," which all share the same pattern.

Script:
When was the last time you went to the movies? *(Response)* What did you see? *(Response)* Today, you are going to do an activity called "At the Movies." You won't really be going to the movies, you will just be thinking about some of the people who might be there. Have fun!

Answers:
(1) 9 (2) 4 (3) 10, 11 (4) 8 (5) 16 (6) 13, 14 (7) 7 (8) 2.

At the Movies

Name_____

It's Saturday, and there's quite a crowd at the movies. Here are the people who came. Study them closely. Then, match the seat number or numbers with the words.

1. Having a soft drink. _____
2. Likes to eat A LOT of popcorn. _____
3. Talking to each other. _____ and _____
4. Wishes the person in front of her would move. _____
5. A healthy eater. _____
6. Kids sitting apart from their parents. _____ and _____
7. In the lobby getting a snack. _____
8. Thinks the movie is VERY scary. _____

FUN WITH UN
Week 24/Flexible Thinking

The Premise:
Students will complete sentences using words that begin with "un."

Comment:
As an extender, ask youngsters to brainstorm other words starting with "un" which don't carry the meaning of "not." Possible answers would include: understand, under, union, unit, unicorn, unite, uncle, uniform, and unique.

Script:
Please give me your UNdivided attention, because today you are going to be doing a little activity that centers around the word-part "un."

What does "un" usually mean? If I say, "The book I wanted at the library was unavailable," what would that mean? *(Response)* Yes, it is another way of expressing the idea of "not."

Please do not leave any of this activity sheet UNdone. I am UNaware of any reason why you can't do all of it.

Answers:
(1) unlock (2) unzip (3) untie (4) unwrap (5) unfold (6) unplug
(7) unscrew (8) unhappy (9) unfinished or undone.

Fun with UN

I'M NOT AS UN- FRIENDLY AS I LOOK.

Name_____

You're not UN-smart, are you? Of course you're not. That means you'll be able to do this activity without any difficulty. UNless you aren't trying . . .

This is really a little story with many "un" words. Only, the "un" words haven't been completed. Write the missing parts of the "un" words in the blanks. The words you use should make sense in the sentences.

Joe had a lot of things to do:

1. He had to un_____ the door.

2. He had to un_____ his jacket.

3. He had to un_____ his shoes.

4. He had to un_____ a candy bar.

5. He had to un_____ a map.

6. He had to un_____ the lamp.

7. He had to un_____ the lid on a jar of pickles.

8. All of these things he did with a smile on his face, because he was not un_____ .

9. He said to himself, "I never like to leave things un_____ ."

A TABLE
Week 24/Problem Solving

The Premise:
Using only scissors and paper, students will make a table that stands up.

Comment:
This is a difficult assignment. To accomplish the task, students will need to make the legs fairly wide (and fairly short) so they won't bend.

Script:
An interesting assignment is in store for you today—you will be making a table. The table won't be made out of wood, however. It will be made out of paper.

The challenge is that you will be using just a simple rectangle of paper to make your table. No other materials are allowed. Also, your table must stand up, so you're going to have to do some folding.

To get started, think about what makes a table a table. Think of legs. That's all I'm going to say. Now, it's your turn to figure out how to make it!

Possible version:

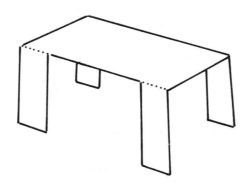

A Table

Name_____

Are you able to make a table? Cut out the rectangle below and figure out a way to make a table that will stand up on its own.

Of course, you will have to do some folding as well as some cutting.

If you wish to draw some plates, cups, food, etc. when you finish, go ahead and "set the table."

INSECTS
Week 24/Elaborative Thinking

The Premise:
Students will expand their thinking on the subject of insects.

Comment:
You might want to go over some of the characteristics of insects, so students won't waste their time on spiders. At least, remind them that all insects have six legs and most have two wings.

Script:
Today, you are going to be doing an activity about a certain subject. The subject rhymes with "hugs." What do you suppose it is? *(Response)* Yes, bugs. What's another name for a bug? *(Response)* Yes, insect. I think that you'll find some of the questions to be very interesting, so do a good job.

Answers:
(1) ladybug, honeybee, bumblebee, fly, mosquito, cricket, grasshopper, cockroach, beetle, aphid, praying mantis, dragonfly, wasp, firefly, ant, etc. (2) so they are hard to see when they are in grass or leaves (3) because insects don't blink, smile, frown, or show any emotions (4) A-3, B-4, C-2, D-1.

Insects

Name_____

How many insects do you think are within a mile of you right now? Ten? A thousand? A million? In this activity, you are going to be thinking about those cuddly six-legged creatures.

1. Name all the different kinds of insects you have seen in the past year.

_____

_____

_____

(Use the back of the paper if you need more room.)

2. Why are many insects green? _____

_____

3. Why can't you tell if an insect is happy? _____

_____

4. Which insects would be most interested in the things below? Match the words with the pictures.

A. Bee _____
B. Moth _____
C. Mosquito _____
D. Fly _____

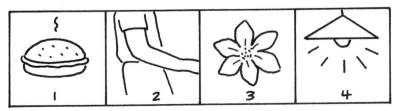

DOTS AND A CIRCLE
Week 24/Originality

The Premise:
Students will use one circle and as many dots as they wish to make simple drawings that express the idea of short sentences.

Comment:
This activity will provide a real challenge for your students. It takes an imaginative leap to think of a mother duck as a circle and the baby ducks as dots, or to represent a necklace as a large circle with dots for beads. However, once children get the general idea, the solutions will begin to occur to them.

Script:
First, I'm going to read you a sentence and then I'm going to show you a little drawing. Ready? Here's the sentence. "I like chocolate chip cookies." Now, if I had to express the idea of this sentence using just one circle and some dots, what could I do? *(Response)* Sure, I could make a drawing like this.

(Put this drawing on the board:)

Now, you are going to get a chance to do your own dot-and-circle drawings.

Possible solutions:

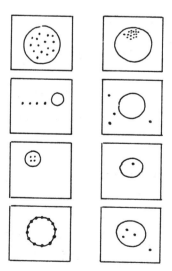

Dots and a Circle

Name_____

Show what is happening in the descriptions below by using just one circle and as many dots as you wish. The example will give you the idea.

MMM! I LOVE FRIED DOTS.

Example: The bugs are bothering me.

Mmm. There's a nice bowl of peas.

I always leave my rice on the plate until last.

The baby ducks followed their mother.

The planet has four moons.

I just found my missing button.

Ick. That apple has a worm in it.

I love my new beads.

Three shots hit the target and one missed.

OUTDOORS
Week 25/Analytical Thinking

The Premise:
Students will determine which set of symbols matches word descriptions.

Comment:
This is an activity which looks formidable until you break it into bite-sized chunks. Then, it becomes very satisfying because it is so logical! It certainly reinforces the value of careful reading and looking.

Script:
(Put these drawings and words on the board:)

person
table
floor
chair

 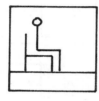 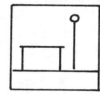 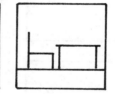

Look at these pictures and read the words. If I asked you to pick a picture that describes the words "table, floor, chair," which would you choose? *(Response)* Yes, the picture on the right. If I asked you to pick a picture that describes the words "person, table, floor," which would you choose? *(Response)* Yes, the middle picture. What are the three words which would describe the picture on the left? *(Response)* Yes, "chair, person, floor."

In today's challenge, you will be doing something similar. Just read one description at a time and look for the matching picture. It should be fun.

Answers:
(1) 4 (2) 1 (3) 5 (4) 2 (5) 6 (6) 3.

Outdoors

Name_____

There are five things that appear over and over in the drawings below. They are: tree, mountain, lake, moon, and tent. Match the drawings with the words below.

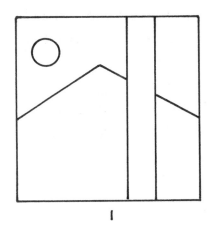
1

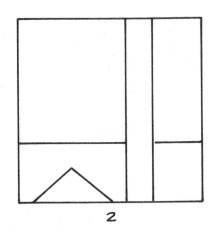
2

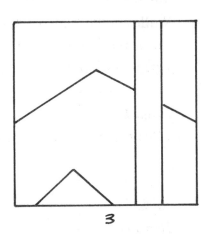
3

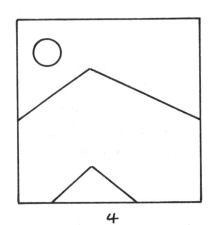
4

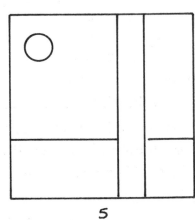
5

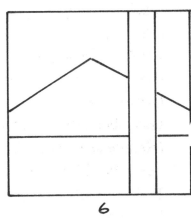
6

1. Mountain, tent, moon _____

2. Tree, mountain, moon _____

3. Lake, moon, tree _____

4. Lake, tree, tent _____

5. Tree, mountain, lake _____

6. Tent, mountain, tree _____

SENTENCE SENSE
Week 25/Flexible Thinking

The Premise:
Students will complete sentences based on picture clues.

Comment:
This is the third and final version of this activity. As an extender, try giving students this super sentence and see if they can fill in the blanks with words that make sense. The sentence is:

I like to sleep _____ on Saturday because I don't _____
to get _____ and go to _____ . (*I like to sleep late on Saturday because I don't have to get up and go to school.*)

Script:

(Put this on the board:)

$$\begin{array}{r} 4 \\ +3 \\ \hline 8 \end{array}$$

Sometimes, I make _____ when I do _____ .

Look at what I have written on the board. How would you complete the sentence in a way that makes sense? *(Response)* Yes, "Sometimes, I make mistakes when I do math (or arithmetic or addition)."

Today, you are going to be completing some other sentences. Have fun.

Answers:
I always chew my food carefully. There is something wrong with this hanger. This spider was drawn with a ruler. Most rabbits like to nibble (or eat) carrots. Someone probably dropped this egg. There is a pig behind (or in) this bush.

Sentence Sense

Name_____

The sentences below are missing some words. First, look at the pictures and read the words that are there. Then, complete each sentence in a way that makes sense. (Put one word in each blank.)

I always _____ my _____ carefully.

There is something _____ with this hanger.

This spider was drawn with _____ _____ .

Most rabbits like to _____ carrots.

Someone probably _____ this egg.

There is a _____ _____ this bush.

MAKE SOME LETTERS
Week 25/Problem Solving

The Premise:
Students will follow directions in order to turn seemingly random lines into alphabet letters.

Comment:
Every student begins at the same point in this exercise, since all children know their alphabet letters. The tricky part is applying that knowledge to solve these particular problems. Children with the most patience will probably fare the best.

Script:
(Put this on the board:) ⊢A\⊏ ⌐U∨ ∖IT⊣ T⊢I⊂ ∠C⌐I ∕IT∨

I guess I was in too big of a hurry when I wrote this on the board because I forgot some parts of the letters. Can anyone figure out what I meant to write? *(Response)* Yes, I meant to write, "Have fun with this activity."

Today, you will be doing something similar. The assignment is called "Make Some Letters." If you work carefully, you will be successful. Good luck.

Possible solutions:

Make Some Letters

Name_____

The squares below are filled with curves and lines that would like to become letters of the alphabet, BUT . . . they need your help! Follow directions, and make some alphabet letters happy.

Add three straight lines to the lines you see to make three different capital letters.

Add five straight lines to the lines you see to make five different capital letters.

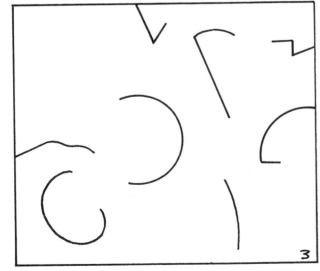

Add two curved lines and one straight line to make three different capital letters.

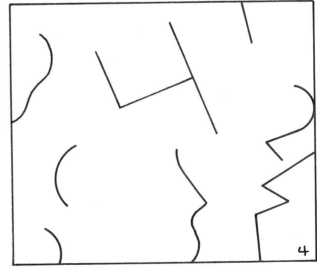

Add one curved line and one straight line to make two different capital letters.

POCKETS
Week 25/Elaborative Thinking

The Premise:
Students will expand their thinking on the subject of pockets.

Comment:
Obviously, "postcard" is the best answer for Number 3 because it is the only item on the list which cannot hold something.

Number 5 is an interesting assignment. Thoughtful students may not draw anything in the last pocket, since a stick of gum would be completely out of sight.

Script:
(Put this drawing on the board:)

What could this be? *(Response. If they don't guess that you have drawn a pocket, draw a simple shirt outline around the pocket.)* Yes, this is a pocket, and today's activity is about pockets. So here we go!

Answers:
(2) a pocket is a little pouch attached to clothes (3) postcard (4) shirt pocket.

Number 5 possible versions:

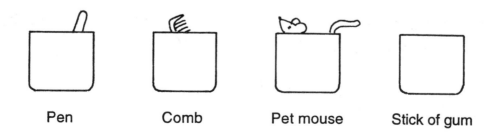

| Pen | Comb | Pet mouse | Stick of gum |

Pockets

Name_____

Kangaroos have them and you have them—
pockets. In this activity, you will do some digging
into the subject of pockets. Are you ready?

I NEED
A POCKET!

1. How many pockets are on the clothes you are wearing now? _____

2. What is a pocket anyway? Write a short description. _____

_____

3. Which of the things below is LEAST like a pocket? _____

Envelope   Backpack
Paper Bag   Postcard
Purse   Wallet

4. Would it be better to carry a candy bar in your shirt or pants pocket? Why?

_____

5. Pretend these are shirt pockets. Draw how you think the things below
would look if they were in a shirt pocket.

Pen   Comb   Pet mouse   Stick of gum

DRAWING STARTS
Week 25/Originality

The Premise:
Students will determine which drawing start would be most appropriate to use in illustrating each sentence.

Comment:
After students have completed this activity, it might be interesting to call for more ambitious "tree house" drawings (Sentence 1). Provide large sheets of white paper and tell them to draw any kind of tree house they wish.

Script:
(Draw these lines on the board:)

Today, you will be doing another "Drawing-Starts" activity. To reacquaint you with the idea, look at the marks I have made on the board. Now, listen to these two sentences. "That is a nice stack of pancakes." "There are two candles on the cake." Which set of marks would give you the best start in illustrating the sentences? *(Response)* Here is how I would do it.

(Finish the drawing starts in this way:)

Now, you have some drawing starts of your own to do. Think before you begin to draw!

Possible solutions:

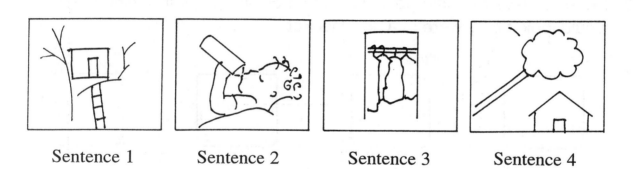

Sentence 1   Sentence 2   Sentence 3   Sentence 4

Drawing Starts

Name_____

Today, you will be making drawings that tell what is happening in each of the sentences. But there is one catch: The drawings have already been started! It will be up to you to decide which drawing start would be best to use for each sentence.

Be sure to read all of the sentences first, so that you can figure out how you are going to do this activity.

1. We made a great tree house.
2. The baby loves her bottle.
3. The closet door is open and I can see the clothes.
4. A tree is falling on the house.

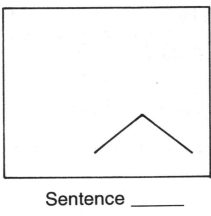

Sentence _____

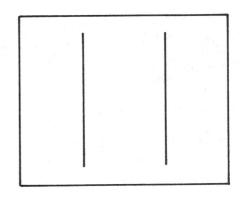

Sentence _____

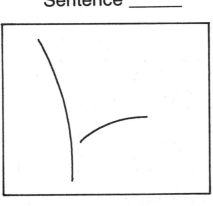

Sentence _____

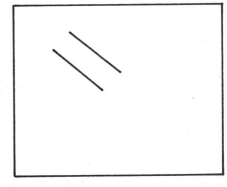

Sentence _____

LEG LINES
Week 26/Analytical Thinking

The Premise:
Students will match symbolic drawings of legs with verb descriptions.

Comment:
The differences in the various leg positions shown in the drawings are sometimes subtle, but there is well-defined logic at work here, whether students know it or not.

Suggest to youngsters that they put a little X beside each drawing after they use it to avoid duplication. Also tell them to write their answers lightly. They may change their minds several times as they work through the list.

Script:
Here's a riddle for you. What has a calf but is not a cow? *(Response)* Yes, I'm thinking of a leg. In today's activity, you will have to do a lot of thinking about legs! Good luck.

Answers:
(1) 5 (2) 4 (3) 1 (4) 8 (5) 9 (6) 3 (7) 2 (8) 6 (9) 7.

Leg Lines

Name_____

What are these? They're leg lines! You may have
to use your imagination a bit, but try to figure out
what these leg lines are doing. Then, match the
pictures with the words.

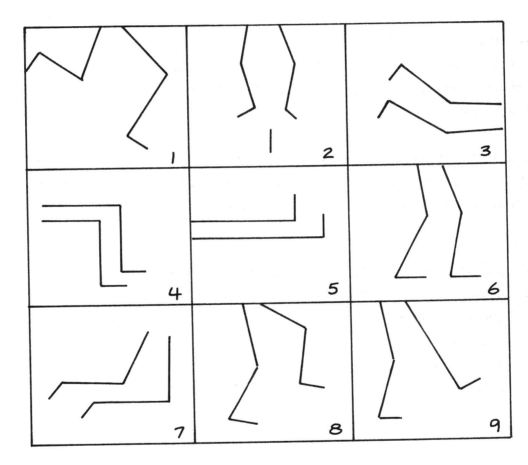

1. Lie _____
2. Sit _____
3. Run _____
4. Climb _____
5. Kick _____
6. Fall _____
7. Jump _____
8. Walk _____
9. Crawl _____

THE GLETCH WORD
Week 26/Flexible Thinking

The Premise:
Students will determine the real word which "gletch" represents.

Comment:
What is intriguing about this exercise is that an everyday word such as "my" can make its presence known so readily, even though it is disguised—which emphasizes the important part context plays in the understanding of language.

Script:
Gletch. What is a "Gletch?" By the time you finish today's assignment, you are going to encounter the gletch word several times. You'll also find out that it takes the place of a very ordinary word.

Your job? Figure out what that ordinary little word is.

Answer:
The gletch word is: my.

The Gletch Word

Name_____

In the paragraph below, a strange little made-up word—gletch—has taken the place of a real word. Your job: Figure out what that real word is.

How do you decide what "gletch" stands for? Well, read the whole paragraph first. The words around the gletch word should give you a clue. Good luck.

I think gletch tooth is about to fall out. Yesterday, I was eating an apple when I heard a sound. It was coming from gletch mouth. It sounded as if gletch tooth were tearing away from gletch gum. I told gletch Dad about it, and he said, "Get ready for a visit from the tooth fairy."

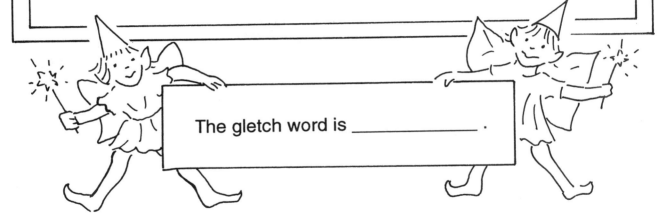

The gletch word is _____ .

CUT IT OUT
Week 26/Problem Solving

The Premise:
Students will cut their way to the dark shape—and remove it—while keeping the square of paper intact.

Comment:
We really like the hands-on nature of this activity. Since some students don't use scissors very often, this is good practice for them.

Script:
Today, you are going to be doing another "Cut It Out" activity. This means you'll need your scissors. You'll also need to make a plan to figure out where to cut. Good luck.

Solution:

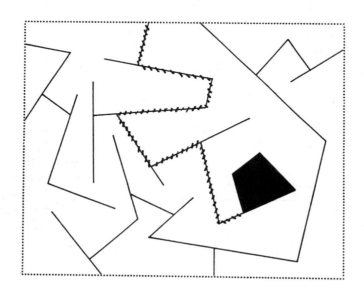

Cut It Out

In this activity, your goal is to cut out the dark shape you see below. But your job won't be easy because there are two rules:

1. You must not cut the big square in two as you try to get to the dark shape.

2. You must cut only along the lines.

Begin by cutting out the big square along the dotted lines. When you are finished, write your name somewhere on it, so your teacher can see how well you did.

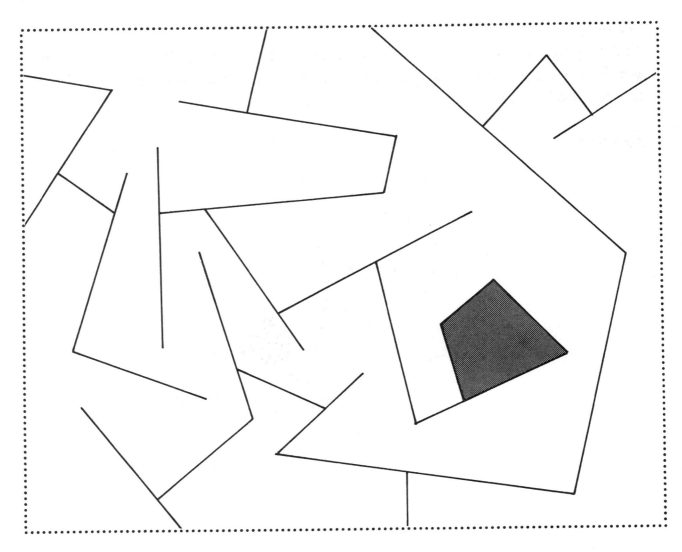

SOUND
Week 26/Elaborative Thinking

The Premise:
Students will expand their thinking on the subject of sound.

Comment:
The outcome of the simple experiment in Number 3 is satisfying. The paper wad dropped on the raised paper is much louder than the paper wad dropped on the desk.

Script:
What are some sounds a cat makes? *(Response)* Yes, a meow, a purr, a hiss. What are some sounds a dog makes? *(Response)* Yes, a bark, a growl, a whine. In today's assignment, you will be thinking about sound. You'll even get to do a little experiment. Good luck.

Answers:
(2) possible answers: coughing, breathing, yawning, street noises, swallowing, talking, laughing, door opening, footsteps, etc. (3) wad hitting the paper (4) radio.

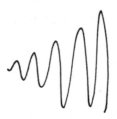

Sound

Name_____

Listen! What can you hear right now? Sound is around us all of the time, isn't it? Today, you will be doing some thinking about sound.

1. What is the loudest sound you've ever heard? _____

2. Listen carefully for about a minute and write down every sound you hear.

   _____

   _____

   _____

3. Tear off a little corner of this paper and wad it into a ball.

   A.   Hold the paper wad a few inches above your desk and drop it.

   B.   Hold this sheet of paper a couple of inches above your desk. Hold the wad a few inches above the paper and drop it onto the paper.

   C.   Which made a louder sound, the wad hitting the desk or the wad hitting the paper? _____

4. Circle the one thing below that depends THE MOST on sound.

   Book   Movie   TV   Radio

CIRCLES AND A SQUARE
Week 26/Originality

The Premise:
Students will make nine designs, each of which is made up of four circles and the square which is provided.

Comment:
Most youngsters will have no trouble coming up with nine different designs. But if some students choose to satisfy the requirements of the activity without "digging in" in a creative way, the results will be ho-hum. For those children who truly try to make varied and interesting designs, the assignment will be a lot of fun. You might wish to display some of the best efforts.

Script:
Today, you are going to be artists. You will be making designs, but not just any designs. You must follow the directions.

In this activity, you will be making lots of circles, but the circles you make don't have to be perfect. Who can make a perfect circle anyway? I can't.

I want you to think carefully about how to make each one of the designs different from all the others. If you want to use the back of your paper to make some little "idea" drawings before you do the real thing, that might be a good idea.

Possible versions:

 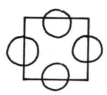 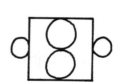

Circles and a Square

Name_____

How many different ways can you put four circles and a square together? If you're a good designer, there are lots and lots of combinations!

Here's an example:

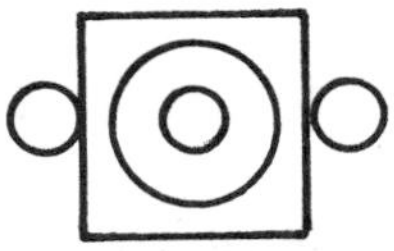

Now, your job is to make nine interesting designs. Each design should include one of the squares below, along with four circles which you draw. The circles can be large, small, inside the square, outside the square, touching the lines of the square, etc. Just be inventive.

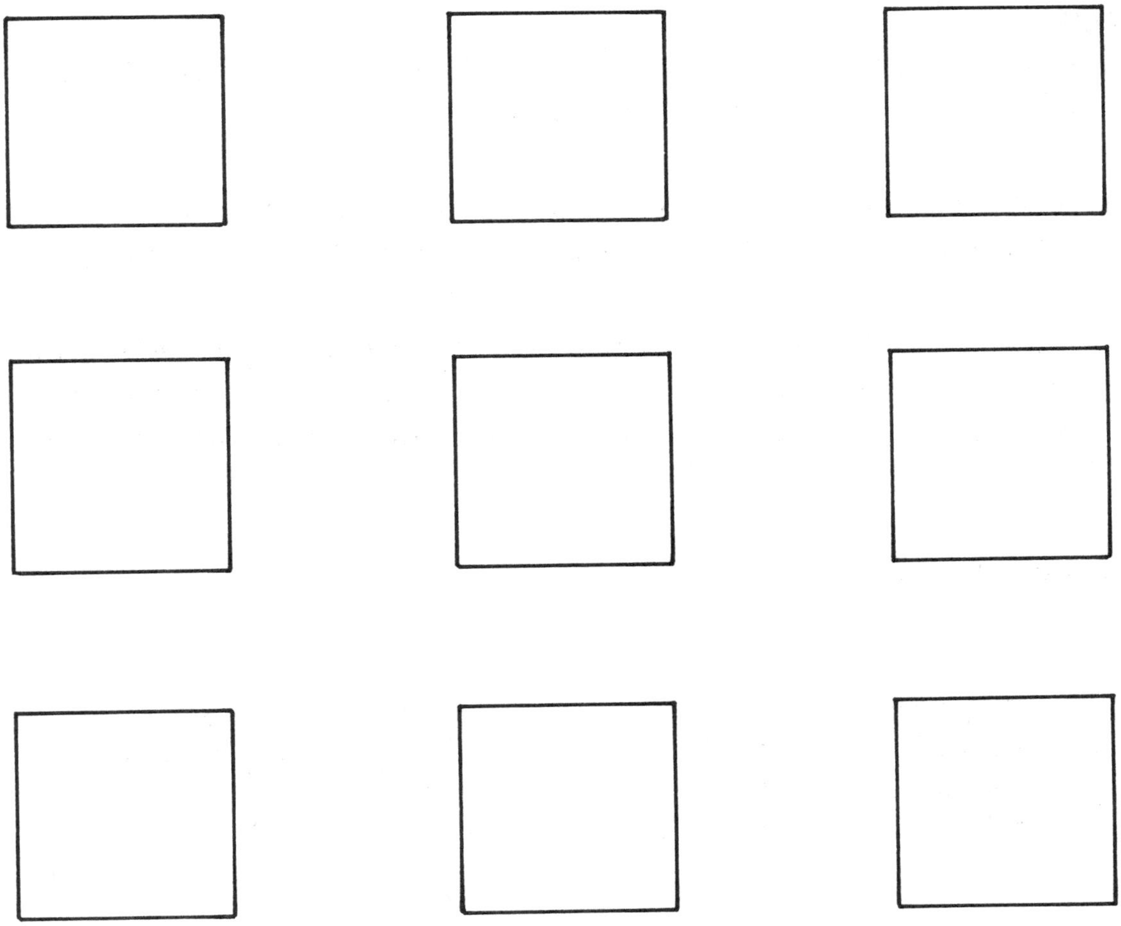

WHAT'S GOING ON?
Week 27/Analytical Thinking

The Premise:
Students will match abstractions of simple concepts with statements.

Comment:
Students were exposed to a similar activity in Week 20.

Again, encourage them to focus on one drawing (or sentence) at a time. If they have trouble, tell them to go on to another one and come back to the tough one later.

Script:
(Put this drawing on the board:)

Take a look at this drawing. Now, I'm going to read three sentences, and I want you to decide which sentence best fits the drawing. Ready? "The television set is unplugged." "I love to eat bread." "I received a birthday card." Which sentence best describes what you're looking at? *(Response)* Yes, the sentence, "I love to eat bread," because the drawing looks more like a slice of bread with a bite out of it than a television set or a birthday card.

Now, you have some similar problems to do. Probably the best way to begin is to read all of the sentences first and then look at all of the pictures. Then, take one sentence at a time and try to find the picture that describes it.

Answers:
(1) 5 (2) 3 (3) 1 (4) 6 (5) 2 (6) 4.

What's Going On?

Name_____

These are simple sentences and simple drawings, but will you be able to put them together? To do it, you'll need to be a careful thinker. Read all of the sentences first. Then, match them with the pictures.

BREAKFAST AT SUNRISE!

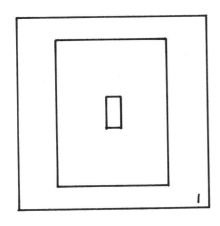

1

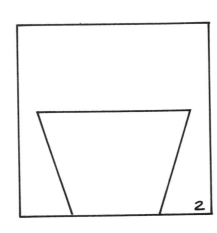

2

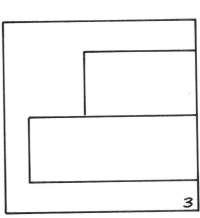

3

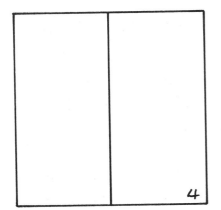

4

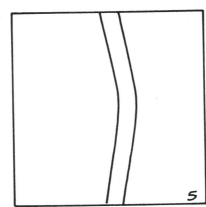

5

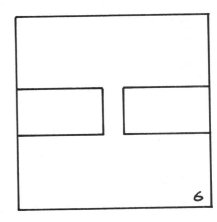

6

1. The nail is bent. _____

2. I cut one of the boards too short. _____

3. I don't know whether it's on or off. _____

4. This belt doesn't reach all the way around. _____

5. My seeds haven't sprouted yet. _____

6. Who closed the curtains? _____

NAME ONE THING
Week 27/Flexible Thinking

The Premise:
Students will think of a property unique to one item in a pair.

Comment:
This really is a great flexibility challenge because students have to go back and forth from one thing to another, comparing the properties of both. In other words, you can't come up with the answer of "fingers" for Number 1 without having given thought to the properties of mittens.

Script:
In today's challenge, you will be thinking about how things differ from each other. For example, if I said, "Name one thing a sheet of notebook paper has that a sheet of drawing paper doesn't have," what could be the answer? *(Response)* Yes, notebook paper has lines. It also has holes.

Now, I'm going to give you a list of some other interesting pairs for you to think about.

Answers:
(1) fingers (2) wheels (3) dot (4) legs (5) strap (or band) (6) drawers
(7) eraser (or lead) (8) bark (or trunk).

Name One Thing

Name_____

Think of one thing you have that a chair doesn't have. Well, let's see. A chair has legs and you have legs. Some chairs have arms and you have arms. But how about a brain?

That's the kind of thinking you'll need to do in this activity. Read the sentences carefully and put your best answers in the blanks.

1. Name one thing gloves have
   that mittens don't have.   _____

2. Name one thing a skateboard
   has that a sled doesn't have.   _____

3. Name one thing an "i" has
   that a "b" doesn't have.   _____

4. Name one thing a turtle has
   that a clam doesn't have.   _____

5. Name one thing a watch has
   that a clock doesn't have.   _____

6. Name one thing a chest has
   that shelves don't have.   _____

7. Name one thing a pencil has
   that a crayon doesn't have.   _____

8. Name one thing a tree has
   that a flower doesn't have.   _____

HARD PROBLEMS
Week 27/Problem Solving

The Premise:
Students will solve problems by analyzing visual information.

Comment:
The fun of this activity lies in its variety. The problems move around from something akin to geometry (Problem 1) to counting (Problem 2) to common sense (Problem 3) to rudimentary physics (Problem 4).

Script:
Today, you are going to be doing another version of "Hard Problems." Let's see how many of you can turn "Hard Problems" into "Easy Solutions."

If you have time, you may want to turn your paper over and invent a "Hard Problem" of your own for someone else to solve.

Answers:
Number 1:

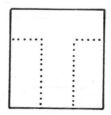

(2) 7   (3) untie the string   (4) direction A.

Hard Problems

Name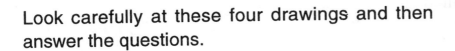

Look carefully at these four drawings and then answer the questions.

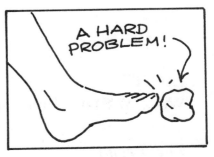

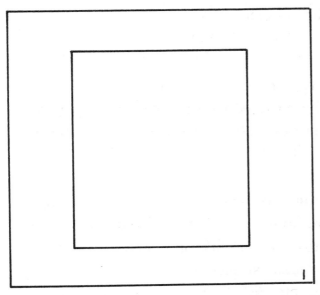

How could you cut the letter T out of this rectangle with just four cuts? Draw lines where you would cut.

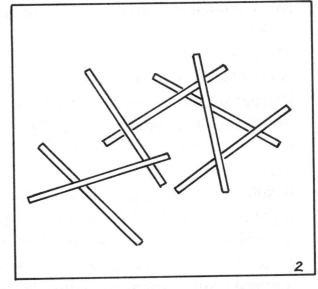

How many sticks are there in this pile? _____ sticks

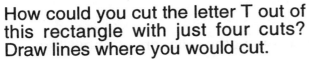

How could you make this balloon smaller without popping it?

_____

This car is rolling down the hill. Are the wheels turning in direction A or direction B? _____

LIGHT
Week 27/Elaborative Thinking

The Premise:
Students will expand their thinking on the subject of light.

Comment:
About Number 5: If children have a hard time discerning that it seems a bit darker when they put their hand over their closed eyes, have them repeat the process while looking toward a light or out the window.

Script:
In today's assignment, you will be thinking about the subject of light. But first, let's do a bit of brainstorming. What are some things that have lights? I will start by saying "cars." What other things have lights on them or in them? *(Response)* Yes, refrigerators, stoves, trucks, streets, stores, houses, closets, airplanes, ships, trains, stadiums, bicycles, etc.

Now, it's time to see what you can do with some other challenges about light.

Answers:
(1) sun, light fixtures (2) X should be placed to the lower right of figure (3) probably a flash from a camera, a spotlight, a strobe, etc. (4) bulb from flashlight or penlight (5) It was darker when I put my hand over my eyes because my hand blocked out the light.

Light

Name_____

Light can mean "not heavy." Light can mean "not dark." Light, in this case, means the light which lets you see this paper and read these words. So switch on your brain and see what you can do.

1. The room where you are right now has light in it. What's making the light?

_____

2. Without light there would be no shadows. Put an X where the shadow should be in this picture.

_____

3. What is the brightest light, other than the sun, that you have ever seen? Where did you see it?

_____

4. What is the smallest light bulb you have ever seen?

_____

5. Close your eyes and count to ten. Then, without opening your eyes, put your hand over your eyes. Describe what happened when you put your hand over your eyes.

_____

LINE TIME
Week 27/Originality

The Premise:
Students will match symbolic line drawings with sentences.

Comment:
This kind of symbolic thinking is probably new to most children, since they don't often encounter such material in regular curricular work. However, it is an excellent way to encourage original thinking.

Each of the sentences expresses certain elements of everyday life that even young children can understand. The challenge, of course, is to equate a particular line with a particular thought or experience.

If students take their time, they should be able to make these creative leaps!

Script:
(Draw this line on the board:)

Look at the line I have made on the board. Now, I am going to read two sentences, and I want you to tell me which sentence is best expressed by the line. Ready? "I have the hiccups." "I sneezed." *(Response)* Yes, the line looks more like hiccups, which happen over and over, than a sneeze, which usually happens all of a sudden once or maybe twice.

This is the kind of thinking you will be doing in the activity today. Have fun!

Answers:
(1) 4 (2) 5 (3) 1 (4) 3 (5) 2 (6) 6.

Line Time

Name_____

Look at the lines in the boxes and then read the sentences. Which line fits best with each sentence? Put your answers in the blanks.

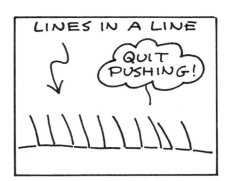

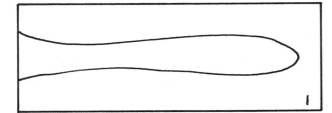

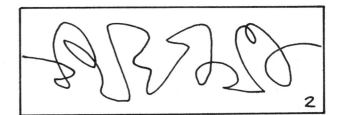

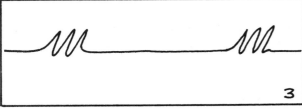

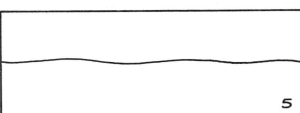

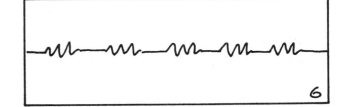

1. I was sound asleep, and then I had a bad dream and woke up, but later I went back to sleep. _____

2. It was a very boring day. _____

3. I forgot my lunch money and had to go back home for it. _____

4. I like mornings and evenings the best. _____

5. I can't make up my mind. _____

6. Lately, every day has seemed the very same to me. _____

A CROWD OF PEOPLE
Week 28/ Analytical Thinking

The Premise:
Students will match abstractions with sentence descriptions.

Comment:
If students take these problems one by one, they will be successful—and have some fun in the process. We especially like that person with very broad shoulders.

Script:
When you see an ant on the ground, what does it look like? Who wants to draw it on the board? *(Response)* Good. Now, pretend you are an ant on the ground looking at another ant on the ground. What would your drawing of an ant look like now? Anyone care to draw it? *(Response)*

In today's assignment, you must think as imaginatively as we did just now. In this activity, you will be thinking about how people would look from the window of a tall building. Make good choices.

Answers:
(1) 5 (2) 9 (3) 1 (4) 2 (5) 3 (6) 7 (7) 4 (8) 6 (9) 8.

A Crowd of People

Name_____

You're looking out the window of a tall building. Down below, there is a park filled with a lot of people. Since you're seeing the people from above, they look a little strange! Can you figure out what is going on? Match the pictures with the sentences.

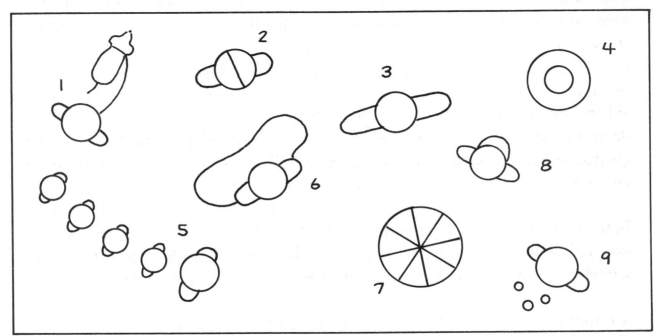

1. This teacher is taking a class on a field trip. _____

2. This person just dropped some money. _____

3. This person is walking a dog. _____

4. This person parts her hair in the middle. _____

5. This person has very broad shoulders. _____

6. This person is using an umbrella. _____

7. This person is wearing a hat with a very large brim. _____

8. This person is jumping rope. _____

9. This person is wearing a baseball cap. _____

IF YOU THINK OF . . .
Week 28/Flexible Thinking

The Premise:
Students will determine what drawings represent when they are paired with other drawings.

Comment:
The process of "if this is a this, then that must be a that" is important. It has everything to do with the understanding of contextual relationships. For example, a white line on a parking lot means one thing, while a white line of exactly the same width on a baseball field means something entirely different.

Script:
(Draw a circle on the board.)

Question: What is this? *(Response)* Yes, a circle. If I say the words "dinner table," what could this circle represent? *(Response)* Yes, a plate, a saucer, a bowl, or even the table itself. If I say the word "car," what could the same circle represent? *(Response)* Yes, a wheel, steering wheel, or headlight.

This is the kind of flexible thinking you get to do in today's exercise.

Answers:
(1) bun (2) road (3) buckle (4) paper clip (5) teeter totter (6) batteries
(7) glass of water (8) hill (9) remote.

If You Think Of...

Name_____

If you think of this assignment with some imagination, it should be a lot of fun. Just keep a wide-open mind.

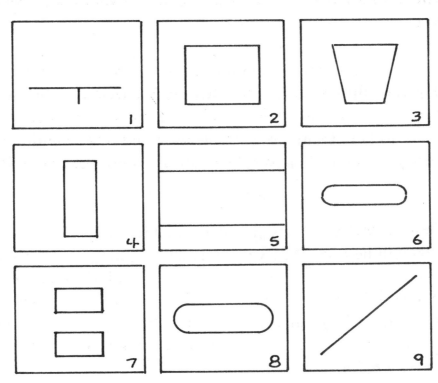

If you think of . . .

1. Number 6 as a hot dog, what could Number 8 be? _____

2. Number 4 as a school bus, what could Number 5 be? _____

3. Number 5 as a belt, what could Number 2 be? _____

4. Number 7 as sheets of paper, what could Number 6 be? _____

5. Number 9 as a slide, what could Number 1 be? _____

6. Number 4 as a flashlight, what could Number 7 be? _____

7. Number 8 as a pill, what could Number 3 be? _____

8. Number 7 as two sleds, what could Number 9 be? _____

9. Number 2 as a TV, what could Number 4 be? _____

LOOK CAREFULLY
Week 28/Problem Solving

The Premise:
Students will make observations in response to written instructions.

Comment:
If students approach this assignment nonchalantly, they will probably come up short. Looking carefully and closely is what this activity is all about.

Resist the urge to help them solve Problems 3 and 4. All children should be able to come up with satisfactory solutions if they work at it.

Script:
Your assignment today mostly involves looking at squares. If you look carefully, you will be fine. Take your time and see how well you can do.

Answers:
(1) three (2) corners (3) squares

Solution for Number 4:

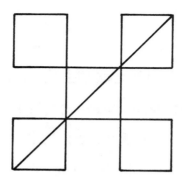

Look Carefully

Name_____

You'll need to do some careful looking and thinking in this activity. Be sure to take your time. When you get to Numbers 3 and 4, you may want to draw directly on this sheet.

1. How many complete squares can you count in this drawing? _____

LOOK AT THE DRAWING BELOW AND THEN COMPLETE

SENTENCES 2, 3, 4.

2. All the squares touch other squares only at their _____ .

3. By drawing four lines you can make four more _____ .

4. You can make _____ triangles by drawing just one straight line somewhere on this drawing.

RULERS
Week 28/Elaborative Thinking

The Premise:
Students will expand their thinking on the subject of rulers.

Comment:
As an ancillary activity, have students measure their math books. Then, look to see if they have provided measurements for length, width, and thickness. Check also to see if they have included the unit of measurement, either inches or centimeters.

Script:
Let's play a guessing game. I'm thinking of something that is in this room right now. Actually, there are many of these things in the room right now. Want to ask me some "yes or no" questions? *(Response, letting them ask questions which can be answered with "yes or no.")* Yes, I'm thinking of a ruler.

You'll be thinking about rulers today and you'll also be using them. Try to do a first-rate job.

Answers:
(2) It can measure things. It can help me make straight lines. (3) a carpenter (4) I could spread out my hand and say how many hands wide it is.

A straight-line example:

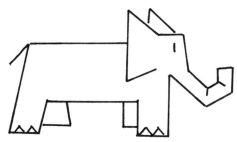

Rulers

Name_____

Will you be able to "measure up" to this activity? Today, you will be thinking about rulers. Let's get one thing "straight"—you've got to do your best.

I'M MEASURING A RULER.

1. Try to remember the last time you used a ruler. What did you use it for?

_____

2. List two important things a ruler can help you do.

_____

_____

3. Who would use a ruler more often, a carpenter or a cook? _____

4. If you didn't have a ruler handy, and you needed to tell someone how wide your desk was, how could you explain it to them?

_____

5. Use the space at the right to make a drawing of any animal you wish. BUT— every line you make must be made with a ruler. Hint: you may need to make some very short lines.

LINE WORK
Week 28/Originality

The Premise:
Students will draw lines that cross themselves a specified number of times.

Comment:
One thing's for sure: No two papers will look alike. That's the beauty of this assignment.

Be sure students follow the line-crossing directions, because the structure is important. The "unstructured" part comes later, when youngsters must turn what they've done into various little creatures. It should be fun to see how they handle it.

Script:
(Draw these lines on the board:)

Here's a question for you. Which of these three lines crosses itself in two places? *(Response)* Yes, the one in the middle. Which line doesn't cross itself at all? *(Response)* Yes, the one on the right.

Today, you will be making some other lines which cross themselves a certain number of times. Follow the directions and make your lines as interesting as you can. I'll be anxious to see the results!

Line Work

Name_____

Lines can be fat or thin. Lines can be straight or curved. Lines can also cross themselves, like the ones in this activity.

Follow the instructions beneath each box to make your own lines that cross themselves. For example, here is a line that crosses itself in 2 places.

Make a line that crosses itself in 3 places.

Make a line that crosses itself in 4 places.

Make a line that crosses itself in 5 places.

Make a line that crosses itself in 6 places.

Now, turn each of the line drawings you have made into a crazy creature—a bug, fish, animal, monster, etc. Do something surprising!

AT SCHOOL
Week 29/Analytical Thinking

The Premise:
Students will determine which set of symbols matches word descriptions.

Comment:
Children did one of these activities in Week 25. In that exercise, they analyzed "outdoor" things, such as a mountain, tree, lake, etc. Now they get to come inside, where they will work with five school elements—a book, blackboard, desk, teacher, and student.

Script:
(Put these words and drawings on the board:)

window
floor
light
door

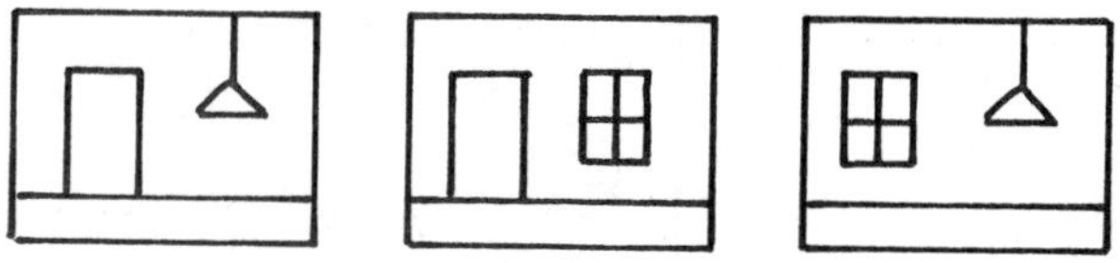

Look at these pictures and read the words. If I asked you to pick a picture that describes the words "window, light, floor," which would you choose? *(Response)* Yes, the picture on the right. If I asked you to pick a picture that describes the words "window, floor, door," which would you choose? *(Response)* Yes, the middle picture. What are the three words which would describe the picture on the left? *(Response)* Yes, "floor, door, light."

Today, you will be doing something similar. Just read one description at a time and look for the matching picture. Good luck.

Answers:
(1) 3 (2) 1 (3) 4 (4) 2 (5) 6 (6) 5.

At School

Name_____

There are five things that appear over and over in the drawings below. They are: teacher, student, blackboard, desk, and book. Match the drawings with the words below.

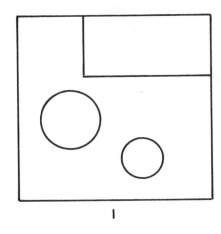

1

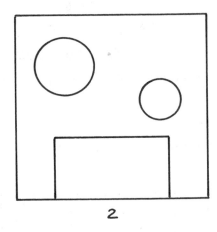

2

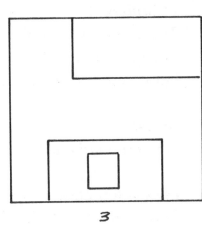

3

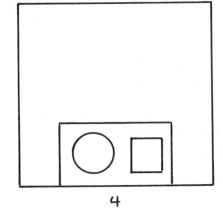

4

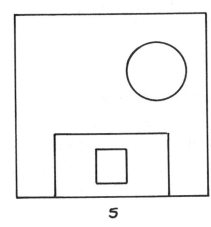

5

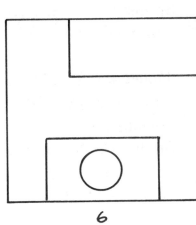

6

1. Book, desk, blackboard _____

2. Teacher, student, blackboard _____

3. Student, book, desk _____

4. Student, teacher, desk _____

5. Blackboard, student, desk _____

6. Desk, teacher, book _____

CRAZY RHYMES
Week 29/Flexible Thinking

The Premise:
Students will complete rhymes based on visual clues.

Comment:
There could be collective cringing if you tell students it is now time for Poetry with a capital P. This exercise hardly qualifies as a poetry assignment, but it is a first step. With its visual clues, it can be quite entertaining.

Script:
(As you hand out the papers, say:)

I hope you know
Where these sentences will go,
So just finish each rhyme
And you'll have a good time.

Answers:
These hills are so steep that the lake must be deep. At night you need a light. Something furry in a hurry. This fish made a wish. This kite had a bad flight. This thing is tied with string. I had a dream about ice cream.

Crazy Rhymes

Name_____

How good are you at rhyming? Here's your chance to find out. Finish the sentence or phrase with a word that rhymes with the underlined word.

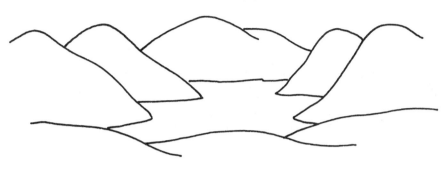

These hills are so <u>steep</u>

that the lake must be _____ .

At <u>night</u>

you need a

_____ .

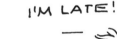

Something <u>furry</u>

in a _____ .

This <u>fish</u>

made a _____ .

This <u>kite</u>

had a bad _____ .

This <u>thing</u>

is tied with _____ .

I had a _____

about ice <u>cream</u>.

A HOUSE
Week 29/Problem Solving

The Premise:
Using only two rectangles, students will make a three-dimensional house shape.

Comment:
Don't let children use glue or tape for this assignment. The challenge is to make a house by doing some clever folding. Later, they can use their pencils to draw doors, windows, etc.

Some of your students will probably be able to visualize a three-dimensional house shape immediately and will surprise you with how quickly they launch into the construction process. Others may need more time to do some trial-and-error folding.

Script:
Today, you are going to build a house, but you are not going to need hammers or nails. Your house is going to be made with just two little pieces of paper. How will you do it? That's for you to figure out.

You are not allowed to use tape or glue to put your house together. Obviously, you must do some folding to make your house stand up.

After you have made your house, you can use a pencil to give it a door, some windows, and whatever other details you think are important.

Good luck. If everybody does a good job, we will have a neighborhood full of houses right here in our room!

Possible version:

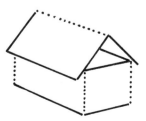

A House

Name_____

A very small person needs your help building a very small house. But there is a problem: The plans have been lost.

All we know is this:

- The walls are made out of the long skinny rectangle.

- The roof is made out of the other rectangle.

First, cut out the two rectangles. Then, see if you can figure out a way to do some clever folding to make the house. Use a pencil to give the house a door and windows if you wish.

FEET
Week 29/Elaborative Thinking

The Premise:
Students will expand their thinking on the subject of feet.

Comment:
Number 1 is hard, isn't it? If students are really stumped, tell them to think about their own feet. Where are their big toes? Of course, there may be those pragmatic types who decide to take off their socks and shoes and find the answer that way.

Script:
Today, you are going to be thinking about the subject of feet. To get you in the mood, let me ask you a couple of questions. What's another name for a cat's foot? *(Response)* Yes, a paw. What's another name for a horse's foot? *(Response)* Yes, a hoof. Now, it's your turn to think about feet—and in this activity, you'll be thinking only about people's feet. Have fun.

Answers:
(1) right foot (2) fingers (3) four (4) big toe (5) A-8; B-6; C-1; D-5; E-7; F-4; G-3; H-2.

Feet

Name_____

Get off on the right foot with this activity by figuring out which foot is pictured in Number 1. From there, you'll be off and running!

1. Here is a drawing of the BOTTOM of a foot. Is it the person's left foot or right foot?

_____

2. Toes are to a foot as _____ are to a hand.

3. How many spaces are there between the toes on one of your feet? _____

4. Try to wiggle your big toe. Then, try to wiggle your little toe. Which is easier to wiggle? _____

5. Match these things you wear on your feet with the pictures:

A. Basketball shoe _____
B. Boot _____
C. Sock _____
D. Roller skate _____
E. High heel _____
F. Sandal _____
G. Bootie _____
H. Shoe _____

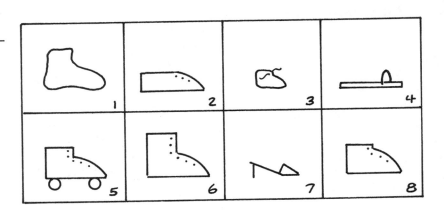

DRAWING STARTS
Week 29/Originality

The Premise:
Students will determine which drawing start would be most appropriate to use in illustrating each sentence.

Comment:
By this time, students should have learned to approach this activity with some caution. After all, they've already tackled five similar challenges.

Script:
(Draw these lines on the board:)

Today, you will again be completing some drawings that have already been started. As an example of what you will be doing, look at the drawings starts I have put on the board, and listen to these two sentences: "I stacked up three boxes." "This is my new comb."

(Finish the two drawing starts in this way:)

Well, if you are stacking up three boxes, you probably need to use the drawing start on the right, since things that are stacked go up, don't they? This is the kind of thinking you will have to do today. Have fun!

Possible solutions:

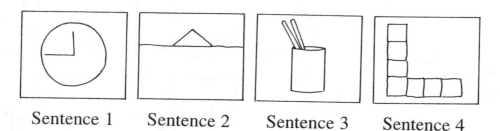

Sentence 1   Sentence 2   Sentence 3   Sentence 4

Drawing Starts

Name_____

Today, you will be making drawings that tell what is happening in each of the sentences. But there is one catch: The drawings have already been started! It will be up to you to decide which drawing start would be best to use for each sentence.

Be sure to read all of the sentences first, so that you can figure out how you are going to do this activity.

1. It's a quarter to twelve.
2. I saw a pyramid in the distance.
3. There were two straws in the glass.
4. I used seven blocks to make the letter L.

Sentence _____

Sentence _____

Sentence _____

Sentence _____

PARKING LOT
Week 30/Analytical Thinking

The Premise:
Students will analyze an abstract version of a grocery store parking lot.

Comment:
This is one of those "situational" abstractions we like very much. The analytical thinking that goes on here is varied, engaging, and educationally valuable.

The first question should lead children to the conclusion that dots stand for people. From there, they must evaluate other factors until the final revelation is reached—that the "X" in Car 12 is a dog!

Script:
When was the last time you were in a parking lot? *(Response)* Where was it? *(Response)* Can someone describe what a parking lot looks like? *(Response)* Yes, it has painted lines to show where people should park their cars. It usually has lights. There is an entrance and an exit.

Today, you will examine what is happening in a grocery store parking lot. If you take your time and really think, you are going to have a lot of fun.

Answers:
(1) 17 (2) Space 8 because it is nearer to the store and the only other available space is partially blocked by a car (3) shopping carts (4) a carry-out person is helping the driver put groceries into the car (5) going the wrong way (6) a motorcycle (7) Space 14 (8) Space 12.

Parking Lot

Name_____

The grocery store parking lot is especially crowded today. Look at what's happening in the drawing below and then answer the questions.

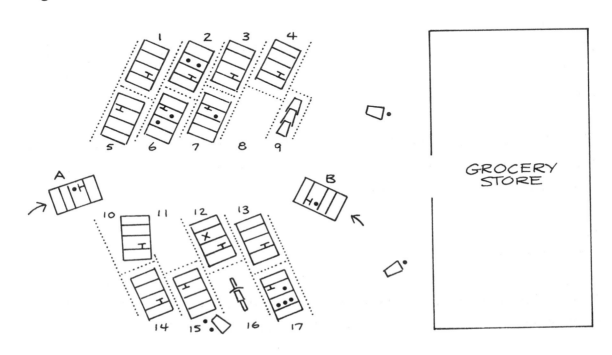

1. One car has several people in it. Which space is it in? _____

2. Which space will Car "A" probably take, and why? _____

3. What is "parked" in Space 9? _____

4. What is happening in Space 15? _____

5. The driver of Car "B" is about to make a mistake. What is it? _____

6. What is parked in Space 16? _____

7. One driver backed in rather than coming in forwards. Which space is the driver's car in? _____

8. One car has a dog in the back seat. Which space is it in? _____

THE SPLOOGE WORD
Week 30/Flexible Thinking

The Premise:
Students will determine the real word which "splooge" represents.

Comment:
When we developed this activity, we realized that many words wouldn't work very well as the mystery word. For example, to have used the word "cat" would have been too obvious. It is only those unassuming, inconspicuous, ordinary words that are candidates for sploogery.

Script:
(Write on the board: splooge.)

Who can pronounce this word for me? *(Response)* I think that everyone in the room will know what "splooge" stands for after this assignment. Be good detectives and find out!

Answer:
The splooge word is: and.

The Splooge Word

Name_____

In the paragraph below, a strange little made-up word—splooge—has taken the place of a real word. Your job: Figure out what that real word is.

How do you decide what "splooge" stands for? Well, read the whole paragraph first. The words around the splooge word should give you a clue. Good luck.

I love my new cat. Her name is Lucy. She is the first cat I've ever had. She likes to eat tuna splooge liver splooge (would you believe it?) spaghetti! If you give her a ball of string, she jumps up splooge goes crazy. She is always doing strange splooge wonderful things!

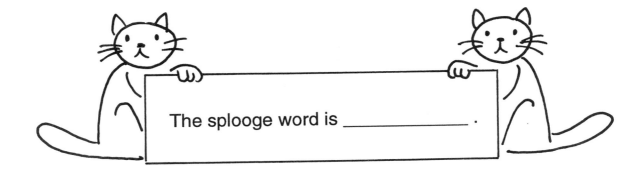

The splooge word is _____ .

WHAT'S THE PATTERN?
Week 30/Problem Solving

The Premise:
Students will determine sentence patterns based on simple clues.

Comment:
Even though the clues are scanty, they should help students recognize the various patterns in the five sentences.

Script:
(Write on the board: Can the dog fly?)

Then write: 3-3-3-3.

Today, you are going to be doing an activity in which you must think about patterns. I've just written a sentence. I've also written a clue which should help you figure out what the pattern for the sentence is.

What is the pattern—based on the clue? *(Response)* Yes, each of the four words in the sentence has three letters. Did the clue help you? *(Response)*

Now, it's your turn to look for patterns in other sentences. Good luck.

Answers:
(1) B—all words begin with an M (2) C—the first word is one letter, the second word is two letters, the third word is three letters, etc. (3) D—each word has double letters (4) E—the last letter of the first word is the same as the beginning letter of the next word, etc. (5) A—all words start with vowels.

What's the Pattern?

Name_____

There is something unusual about the sentences below. Each one has its own special pattern. The problem is—you must find it.

Read all of the sentences and all of the clues before you begin. Then, match the clues with the sentences by putting the clue letter in the right blank. Hint: Skip around and find the easiest patterns first!

SENTENCES

1. Mother made more muffins. _____

2. I am the best eater. _____

3. Cookies really seem sweet. _____

4. All ladies sing grandly. _____

5. Even I owned an umbrella. _____

CLUES

(A)   Vowel starts

(B)   M x 4

(C)   1-2-3-4-5

(D)   Twin letters

(E)   Last-first, last-first, last-first

307

ONE THUMB TALL
Week 30/Elaborative Thinking

The Premise:
Students will consider what their world would be like if they were just one thumb tall.

Comment:
This activity presents students with an unusual situation and encourages them to speculate on the consequences.

Upon completion of this exercise, ask students to draw some one-thumb-tall people. Then, respond to the drawings by writing a thank-you note to the class on a tiny piece of paper in your tiniest script. Tape it to the wall, approximately three inches from the floor, where one-thumb-tall people can read it.

Script:
What if you were just one thumb tall? Hold up one thumb to get an idea of how tall you would be.

In today's activity, you must pretend that you are just that size. I wonder what your voice would sound like. Here's what I think. *(Speak in a very small voice.)* I will be interested in how you handle this assignment now that you are suddenly one thumb tall.

Answers:
(4) cookie crumb, raisin, sugar grain, chocolate chip, blade of grass, etc. (5) bottle cap, peanut, marble, short pencil, stick of gum, etc. (6) in my desk, on a shelf, in my lunchbox, in a drawer, etc. (7) being stepped on by normal-sized people, going down stairs, getting into a car, cats, dogs, etc.

One Thumb Tall

Name_____

Suddenly you have turned into a tiny person as big as your thumb. Everything you're wearing has shrunk, too. Pretend you are that person as you do this activity. The world looks pretty strange, doesn't it? Good luck.

1. You are wearing glasses. Draw them the size they would be.

2. How big is that hat you're wearing? Draw it.

3. How big is one of your fingernails? Draw it.

4. Think of three things that you could carry easily.

   _____

5. Think of three things you could carry but which would seem heavy.

   _____

6. List three places in this room where a normal person could not hide, but where you could.

   _____

7. Think of one thing that wouldn't scare a normal person, but would scare someone one thumb tall. _____

MOST LIKE
Week 30/Originality

The Premise:
Students will match generalized shapes with word descriptions.

Comment:
This activity is bound to frustrate some children because it is impressionistic, and some of the problems have no clear answers. It is our opinion, however, that such ambiguities are very good for students.

There are, however, some choices which are more logical than others. The answer for Number 8, "a nose from the side," though not obvious, pretty much settles on Drawing 5 because. . . what other drawing could it be? The circle in Drawing 1 looks something like a clown's nose from the front, but not from the side.

Script:
(Put this drawing on the board:) ⬛▭▭▭▭▭⬛

In today's assignment, you are going to be looking at little drawings that ALMOST look like something real, but not quite. So you must figure out what they look MOST like.

For example, look at the shape on the board. Is it MOST like a table, a book or a belt? *(Response)* Yes, it looks MOST like a belt. It doesn't look like a real belt because it doesn't have a buckle or holes. But we know that it looks more like a belt than a table or a book.

Now, I want you to shake your shoulders and loosen up. *(Response)* The next thing is to get your thinking loose, and then you're ready to begin!

Answers:
(1) 1 (2) 2 (3) 4 (4) 3 (5) 5 (6) 1 (7) 2 (8) 5 (9) 4 (10) 2 (11) 3 (12) 1.

Most Like

Name_____

This is hard, because the little drawings you see here don't really look like anything—exactly. But, if you use your imagination, they should remind you of something real.

In this activity, you will be using the pictures more than once. Do your best to match them with the words below.

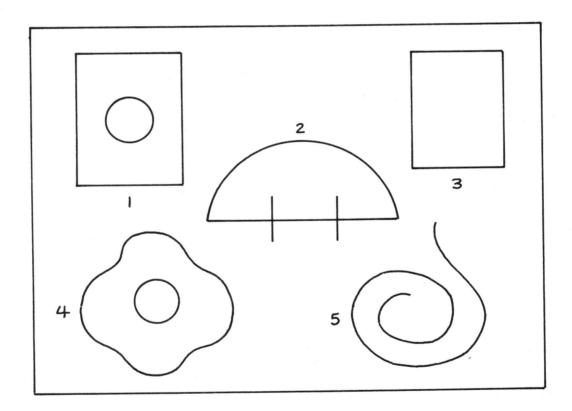

Which looks most like . . .

1. a stoplight. _____
2. an umbrella. _____
3. an egg. _____
4. a blanket. _____
5. a snail. _____
6. a doorknob. _____
7. an anthill. _____
8. a nose from the side. _____
9. an island in a lake. _____
10. a mushroom. _____
11. a price tag. _____
12. a birdhouse. _____

Publications by Tin Man Press

Is It Friday Already? Learning Centers That Work – 30 weeks of centers in nine subject areas.

Are They Thinking? – A comprehensive, year-long thinking skills program.

Loosen Up! – Art activities designed to build confidence.

T is for Think – More than 300 drawings spur thinking excitement.

OPQ – Offbeat Adventures with the Alphabet – A center approach based on the alphabet.

Waiting for Lunch – Sponge activities for those little moments in the day.

Great Unbored Bulletin Board Books I and II – 20 great board ideas in each book.

Great Unbored Blackboard Book – Quick analytical activities you do on the board.

WakerUppers – 50 friendly hand-drawn reproducible sheets to motivate thinking.

Nifty Fifty – 500 provocative questions about 50 everyday things.

Smart Snips – Each of the 50 reproducible activities starts with something to cut.

Ideas To Go – 50 different assignments cover a broad range of thinking skills.

Brain Stations – 50 easy-to-make centers promote creative and flexible thinking.

Play by the Rules – 50 scripted challenges turn students into better listeners.

The Discover! Series – 24 card sets provide hands-on experiences with everyday objects.

Adventures of a Dot Series – 10 card sets use a Dot character to encourage thinking.

Linework – Jumbo card set centers around the concept of line.

An Alphabet You've Never Met – Jumbo card set plays creatively with letters.

Going Places – Students participate in five interesting imaginary adventures.

Letter Getters – Letter clues encourage language development and deductive thinking.

1-800-676-0459

Index

Originality

WORLD
RESOURCES
2005

WORLD
RESOURCES
2005

The Wealth
of the Poor

Managing Ecosystems to Fight Poverty

United Nations Development Programme

United Nations Environment Programme

World Bank

World Resources Institute

WORLD RESOURCES INSTITUTE   WASHINGTON, DC

The World Resources Institute wishes to acknowledge three organizations whose support has been indispensable in bringing *World Resources 2005* to publication:

Netherlands Ministry of Foreign Affairs

Swedish International Development Cooperation Agency

United States Agency for International Development

World Resources 2005: The Wealth of the Poor—Managing Ecosystems to Fight Poverty

Cite as: World Resources Institute (WRI) in collaboration with United Nations Development Programme, United Nations Environment Programme, and World Bank. 2005. *World Resources 2005: The Wealth of the Poor—Managing Ecosystems to Fight Poverty.* Washington, DC: WRI.

Published by
World Resources Institute
10 G Street, NE
Suite 800
Washington, DC 20002

The **World Resources Series** is produced collaboratively by four organizations: the United Nations Development Programme, the United Nations Environment Programme, the World Bank, and the World Resources Institute. The views expressed in this volume are those of the contributors and do not necessarily reflect the judgments of the organizations' boards of directors or member governments.

ISBN 1-56973-582-4

WORLD RESOURCES 2005

CONTENTS

PART II DATA TABLES

MAKING THE WEALTH OF NATURE WORK FOR THE POOR

PROFOUND POVERTY IS A FUNDAMENTAL OBSTACLE TO THE dreams and aspirations of people in every nation. Even after five decades of effort to support development and growth, the dimensions of poverty still stagger us. Almost half the world's population lives on less than $2 per day; more than a billion live on $1 or less. Poverty at this scale ripples beyond the boundaries of any particular country or region and affects the well-being of us all.

The publication of *World Resources 2005* comes at a particularly critical time. Economies in many developing countries have been growing at a rapid pace for several years. That growth has made us aware of two stark realities: in the largest of those countries it has lifted millions out of extreme poverty; but the price these nations are paying in accelerated degradation of their natural resources is alarming.

At the same time, there have been a number of key events this year, 2005, that provide a clearer focus on the future. At the G-8 Summit in Scotland, attention to the problems of global poverty, especially in Africa, was unusual for its single-mindedness and for the acknowledgment of poverty's far-reaching consequences.

In the spring of this year, the Millennium Ecosystem Assessment (MA), an international appraisal of the health of the world's ecosystems, published the first of its series of reports after five years of intensive study. The MA findings sound an alarm bell for the future, but they also contain within them a framework to address the challenges we have created for ourselves.

The MA has shown beyond any question the degradation we have caused to the ecosystems of the earth. At the same time, the MA has demonstrated unequivocally that we can better manage these assets, and, by so doing, secure their benefits for the future.

World Resources 2005 is about simple propositions:

■ Economic growth is the only realistic means to lift the poor out of extreme poverty in the developing world; but the capacity of the poor to participate in economic growth must be enhanced if they are to share in its benefits.

■ The building blocks of a pro-poor growth strategy begin with natural resources. These provide the base upon which the vast majority of the poor now depend for their fragile existence, but over which they exercise little control, and therefore can't exercise full stewardship.

■ The role of governance—transparent and accountable governance—is critical to fostering pro-poor growth and essential to ensuring that the engine of that growth, natural resource wealth, is managed wisely.

There are some things we know for sure. We know that the great majority of the world's poor are concentrated in rural areas. They depend on fields, forests, and waters—the bounty of ecosystems—for their livelihood. These ecosystems provide a natural asset base that the rural poor can use to begin a process of wealth creation that will boost them beyond subsistence and into the mainstream of national economies—but only under the right circumstances.

If the natural resource base is not managed for the long term, if it is exploited and polluted for short-term gain, it will never provide the fuel for economic development on the scale demanded to relieve poverty.

And that is what is happening today, as the Millennium Ecosystem Assessment has dramatically shown. If the ecosystems of the world represent the natural capital stock of the planet, we have drawn down that account at an alarming pace in the past decades. Over the last 50 years, we have changed ecosystems more rapidly than at any time in human history, largely to meet growing demands for food, freshwater, timber, and fiber.

The changes have not been without benefit. The resulting increase in food, fiber, and other services has contributed to improved human well-being. However, the gains are unevenly distributed, and the poor have more often borne the associated costs.

As populations and economies grow, the pressures on ecosystems will inexorably increase. Yet thanks to the MA, we finally understand, in terms even the most hard-bitten economist or banker can appreciate, the economic value of our natural capital account. And like the banker or economist, we now understand that we must manage that capital account—a trust fund, if you will—so that it not only provides for our needs today but also for the needs of future generations.

This volume documents that such stewardship of nature is also an effective means to fight poverty. When poor households improve their management of local ecosystems—whether pastures, forests, or fishing grounds—the productivity of these systems rises. When this is combined with greater control over these natural assets, through stronger ownership rights, and greater inclusion in local institutions, the poor can capture the rise in productivity as increased income. With greater income from the environment—what we refer to as *environmental income*—poor families experience better nutrition and health and begin to accumulate assets. In other words, they begin the journey out of poverty.

For some time now we have known that economic growth, growth that expands the availability of opportunities, is necessary to any permanent effort to alleviate poverty. But the quality of that growth is crucial if its economic benefits are truly to extend to the poor. Pro-poor growth based on the sustainable use of natural resource capital requires a fundamental change in governance. *World Resources 2002-2004* demonstrated that the wisest and most equitable decisions about the use of natural resources are made openly and transparently. Those most affected by such decisions must have full access to information and the ability to participate.

Change in governance must necessarily include reforms that give the poorest a real stake in their future. The issues of land tenure, of responsibility for resources held in common, of control, and of accountability must be addressed in a way that acknowledges and catalyzes the role of individual and community self-interest in managing natural resources as a long-term asset.

Included in these reforms must be a clear mandate to end corruption, which particularly oppresses the poor. The graft of government officials, the inside deals of vested interests, and the exploitation of natural resources for the immediate gain of a few creates an environment where the resource rights of the poor are violated and pro-poor growth cannot flourish.

The growth of free and uncorrupt institutions in developing countries provides the catalyst that will help us solve these two inextricably linked challenges: the eradication of extreme poverty and the management of our natural capital to provide for future needs.

Access to the natural capital to create wealth, control and responsibility for that capital, information and basic technology to make that control useful and productive, and the ability to reach markets that bring the poor into the global economy are the tools at hand. The pay-off for countries that take up these tools is the prospect of a far better future than what they face today, and a social stability based on choice, access, and economic opportunity.

Achieving these goals will not come without a price for the developed world, but it is one developed countries should be eager to pay, given the return. Aid programs will have to become more targeted and accountable. Free trade will have to mean just that. Tariffs, import quotas, and crop subsidies will have to be modified, minimized, or eliminated so that the promise of a better life that starts on a farm in central Africa is not dashed on the docks of Europe, Japan, or the United States.

Consider the consequences of inaction or misguided action: continued poverty. The unchecked ravages of preventable diseases. Lost generations whose talent and promise are denied to us. Depletion of resources vital to our future. And the social corrosion born of inequality and political instability that national boundaries can no longer contain.

Much of what we call for in this latest Report is captured in the Millennium Development Goals, adopted by the United Nations in 2000, and committed to by the wealthiest nations of the world. *World Resources 2005* shows us how important pro-poor management of ecosystems is to attaining these goals

What *World Resources 2005* argues eloquently and unequivocally is that the path forward is clearer now than at any time. The Report presents a wealth of examples to adopt and replicate, demonstrating how nations can support a bottom-up approach to rural growth that begins naturally with the assets that the poor already possess. We know so much more than we did at Rio in 1992. We know the folly of extending aid without the tools to make use of it, of granting debt relief without improved governance, of stimulating production without access to markets. And we know the promise of ecosystems for poverty reduction. Delivering on that promise can allow the bounty of nature to become the wealth of the poor. At no time has so much been at stake, and at no time are we better able to respond.

Kemal Derviş
Administrator
United Nations Development Programme

Klaus Töpfer
Executive Director
United Nations Environment Programme

Ian Johnson
Vice President for Environmentally and
Socially Sustainable Development
World Bank

Jonathan Lash
President
World Resources Institute

The Wealth
of the

Poor

For many of the 1.2 billion people living in severe poverty,

nature has always been a daily lifeline—an asset

for those with few other material assets.

NATURE, POWER, AND POVERTY

ECOSYSTEMS ARE—OR CAN BE—THE WEALTH OF THE POOR.
For many of the 1.1 billion people living in severe poverty, nature is a daily lifeline—an asset for those with few other material means. This is especially true for the rural poor, who comprise three-quarters of all poor households worldwide. Harvests from forests, fisheries, and farm fields are a primary source of rural income, and a fall-back when other sources of employment falter. But programs to reduce poverty often fail to account for the important link between environment and the livelihoods of the rural poor. As a consequence, the full potential of ecosystems as a wealth-creating asset for the poor—not just a survival mechanism—has yet to be effectively tapped.

The thesis of *World Resources 2005* is that income from ecosystems—what we call *environmental income*—can act as a fundamental stepping stone in the economic empowerment of the rural poor. This requires that the poor manage ecosystems so that they support stable productivity over time. Productive ecosystems are the basis of a sustainable income stream from nature.

But for the poor to tap that income, they must be able to reap the benefits of their good stewardship. Unfortunately, the poor are rarely in such a position of power over natural resources. An array of governance failures typically intervene: lack of legal ownership and access to ecosystems, political marginalization, and exclusion from the decisions that affect how these ecosystems are managed. Without addressing these failures, there is little chance of using the economic potential of ecosystems to reduce rural poverty.

Making governance more friendly to the poor means tackling issues of property rights, access to information and decision-making, adequate representation, institutional transparency, and fairness in sharing the costs and benefits of resource management. These are all aspects of *democratic governance*—decision-making that respects the rights and needs of those who depend on resources. For the poor, democratic governance is the door to equity and one of the building blocks of sustainability.

This fusion of ecosystem management and good governance is also necessary to achieve the Millennium Development Goals, the set of eight goals adopted by the international community in 2000 to address world poverty. As the foundation of rural livelihoods, ecosystems are central to real progress toward the health, nutrition, sanitation, and environmental targets embedded in the Millennium Development Goals. Indeed, without empowering the poor to responsibly manage their environment for economic gain, we cannot effectively attend to rural poverty in its many dimensions. *(See Box 1.1.)*

The goal of this report is to highlight the vital role of ecosystems and their governance—of nature and power—in poverty reduction. The report's central question is: Who controls ecosystems, and how can this control be reconfigured to allow the poor to use their natural assets as sustainable sources of wealth creation, vehicles of political empowerment, and avenues of integration into the national and global economies?

Linking Ecosystems, Governance, and Poverty

Ecosystem management, democratic governance, and poverty reduction are each essential elements of sustainable economic growth. Moreover, these elements are inextricably linked. More than 1.3 billion people depend on fisheries, forests, and agriculture for employment—close to half of all jobs worldwide (FAO 2004:169-174). This dependence of livelihoods on natural systems is nowhere more important than among the rural poor (MA 2005:7, 48). *(See Table 1.1.)* In Africa, more than seven in ten poor people live in rural regions, with most engaged in resource-dependent activities, such as small-scale farming, livestock production, fishing, hunting, artisanal mining, and logging (IFAD 2001:15). This small-scale production accounts for a significant percentage of the GDP of many African nations (Kura et al. 2004:36-39; IFPRI 2004:2).

Making wise choices about the use of natural resources and the distribution of environmental benefits and costs is central to maximizing the contribution that a nation's resource endowment makes to social and economic development. Many of the poorest regions of the world are, however, also the least democratic. That means much of their resource wealth is typically diverted from the public good through corruption, mismanagement, and political patronage. It is no coincidence that fundamental democratic principles such as transparency,

---

DEFINING ECOSYSTEMS AND GOVERNANCE

An ecosystem is a community of interacting organisms and the physical environment they live in. We know ecosystems as the forests, grasslands, wetlands, deserts, coral reefs, rivers, estuaries, and other living environments that surround us. They also include the farms, pastures, and rangelands—collectively known as agroecosystems—that feed us. They are the earth's living engines of production, providing the goods and services—air, food, fiber, water, aesthetics, and spiritual values—that make life possible for rich and poor alike.

In *World Resources 2000-2001: People and Ecosystems—The Fraying Web of Life,* we explored the threats to global ecosystems and stressed the need to adopt an "ecosystem approach" to environmental management. *View the report online at http://www.wri.org*

Governance is the exercise of authority—the decisions, regulations, and enforcement that determine how we will act and who will benefit. It encompasses the laws, institutions (such as government agencies or village councils), and decision-making processes that embody this authority. **Democratic governance** implies the participation of those who are governed in the decision-making process—either directly, through representatives, or both.

In *World Resources 2002-2004: Decisions for the Earth—Balance, Voice, and Power,* we showed how the conditions and quality of governance influence our environmental decisions, and stressed that good governance that ensures adequate representation, access to information, and public participation is crucial to the sustainable and equitable management of ecosystems. *View the report online at http://www.wri.org*

In *World Resources 2005,* we argue that prudent ecosystem management, enabled by pro-poor governance, can reduce poverty. Without attention to poverty, the goal of sustainable development recedes beyond reach.

---

public participation, accountability, and the separation of legislative, judicial, and executive powers are often absent in developing countries where poverty is greatest.

Many people in developing countries are thus not only poor, they are voiceless. Dependent directly on natural resources, they have little say in how those resources are used, but suffer the consequences when the decisions are corrupt and the use is destructive. For example, rural peoples' livelihoods are often in direct conflict with extractive industries such as large-scale fishing, logging, or mining, but they have little say in resolving that conflict. Access to decision-makers—government bureaucrats, lawmakers, or the courts—is typically for the powerful, not the poor.

Rectifying this imbalance means supporting democratic practices. History shows, however, that efforts to promote democratic principles in a vacuum rarely succeed. To take root, they must engage citizens, and they must deliver on matters that are immediate and important to citizens. As the source of livelihoods, the environment is arguably the most

important issue that democracy must deliver on in the developing world. Put differently, the environment is not only a powerful tool for promoting democratic reform, but good environmental governance is fundamental to strengthening and consolidating democracy. Democratic institutions, in turn, are an important factor supporting strong economic growth (Kaufmann et al. 1999:18).

This emphasis on good governance and environment is particularly relevant when addressing poverty. The case studies in this report and the experiences of an increasing number of villages and communities in many nations suggest that efforts to promote sustainable livelihoods among the poor are more successful when they simultaneously promote ecosystem stewardship and democratic governance. For that reason, a number of development agencies and nongovernmental organizations (NGOs) are beginning to focus on this integration of environment and governance.

In spite of increasing interest in this integration, its application to the alleviation of poverty is still new. Success will demand a new openness to go beyond traditional economic development strategies, or at least to add a more deliberate recognition of the linkages among nature, power, and poverty.

The Persistence of Poverty

The persistence of global poverty is both disturbing and humbling. Policymakers have long recognized the moral and practical need to address the substantial number of people who lack basic amenities such as adequate nutrition, housing, education, or opportunity. But decades of piecemeal efforts have brought only limited success. *(See Box 1.1.)*

More than a half century of persistent efforts by the World Bank and others have not altered the stubborn reality of rural poverty, and the gap between rich and poor is widening.

—World Bank Strategy for Rural Development, 2003

Ending world poverty first become a stated goal of politicians from industrialized countries in the 1940s, when U.S. President Franklin Roosevelt stated his desire to extend "freedom from want" not only to the people of the United States, but to people in every nation (Roosevelt 1941). The United Nations Charter, crafted in the same era, explicitly acknowledged the need to promote "social progress and better standards of life" across the globe (UN 1945). Almost 60 years later, at the United Nations Millennium Summit in 2000, more than 100 heads of state committed to reach the eight Millennium Development Goals (UN General Assembly 2001:55).

These commitments confirm the simple fact that poverty remains an obstacle to the development aspirations of most

Continues on page 10

BOX 1.1 THE DIMENSIONS OF POVERTY

What is Poverty?

DEFINING AND MEASURING POVERTY ARE essential to any discussion of poverty reduction. Definitions of poverty have traditionally focused only on material—and specifically monetary—measures of well-being. But key concepts behind poverty have evolved considerably in recent years. Today, a more holistic, multi-dimensional perception of poverty has emerged, drawn from interviews with the poor themselves. Definitions of poverty have expanded to include the social and psychological burdens of daily survival on the bottom rungs of society. This broader conception is described by Amartya Sen as a lack of capabilities that enable a person to live a life he or she values, encompassing such domains as income, health, education, empowerment, and human rights (Sen 1999:87-98).

As researchers and policymakers struggle to understand these complexities, they have begun to use "participatory assessments" to let the poor speak in their own voice and identify their own priorities. The authors of the *Voices of the Poor* series interviewed 60,000 poor people in 60 countries in one of the better-known assessments (Narayan et al. 2000a, 2000b, 2002). Complex descriptions of the "ill-being" associated with poverty emerged, with dimensions other than material deprivation given strong significance.

Such studies make it clear that, in addition to being without financial resources, being poor often means suffering sickness, chronic pain, or exhaustion. It means enduring difficult social relations, sometimes facing exclusion from the community or family. Poverty also translates into insecurity and powerlessness, a lack of access to information and institutions, and often a lack of self-confidence and voice. Psychological suffering is also associated, in the form of humiliation, anguish, grief, and worry (Narayan et al. 2000b:37-38).

These varying aspects of poverty tend to be self-reinforcing, making it all the more difficult to move out of poverty and construct a stable life. It is hard to plan ahead or to seize new opportunities when you are exhausted, stressed, or hungry. In addition, the poor often live in dangerous and degraded environments, since that is all they can afford. They are thus the most vulnerable to violence, crime, and natural and economic catastrophes (Narayan et al. 2000a:72, 84-88).

Finally, living in poverty often means facing a truncated view of the future. The poor are often averse to risk, having suffered from mistakes or false expectations in the past and lacking assets to fall back on. Whereas those with means can save for emergencies and plan for the future, the poor do not have that luxury. A poor person's planning horizon—how far ahead they can plan or foresee—is often determined by when food will run out. It may be as soon as the end of the day. This element of poverty—the lack of ability to reasonably plan for the long term—has real significance for anything related to ecosystem management, which works over extended periods of time, often yielding benefits in the future.

Quantifying Poverty

Poverty estimates are usually constructed from household survey data. The head of a household is typically asked about income and consumption levels, and these are used as the measure of well-being (World Bank 2001:17). Most governments have established national "poverty lines" by compiling and pricing a basket of goods meant to reflect the basic human necessities, such as food, clothing, and housing. Many countries have a "food" or "absolute" poverty line calculated from a food basket representing minimum nutritional requirements, and a "basic needs" line that is slightly higher (Deaton 2004:3-4; Coudouel et al. 2002:34).

In 1990, the World Bank began using the measure of $1 per day as an official "international poverty line," meant to roughly approx-

PROFILING HOUSEHOLDS IN BOLIVIA, 1999-2003	
Population of Bolivia	8.8 million
Number of Bolivians Living on Less than $1 a Day	1.3 million
Number of Bolivians Living Below the Basic Needs Poverty Line	5.1 million
Percent of Urban Population Living Below the Poverty Line	39
Percent of Rural Population Living Below the Poverty Line	91
Percent of Poor Bolivians Living in Rural Areas	59
Percent of Total Spending Accounted for by the Poorest 20%	4
Percent of Total Spending Accounted for by the Richest 20%	49
Percent of Rural Households in Lowest Income Decile with Electricity	5
Percent of Rural Households in Highest Income Decile with Electricity	46
Percent of Rural Households Using Dung for Cooking	6
Percent of Adults Who Are Literate	87
Percent of Poor Rural Children Attending School	83
Percent of Poor Rural Children Working	51

Sources: Demographic and Health Surveys, 2005; UNESCO 2004; World Bank 2002, 2004a

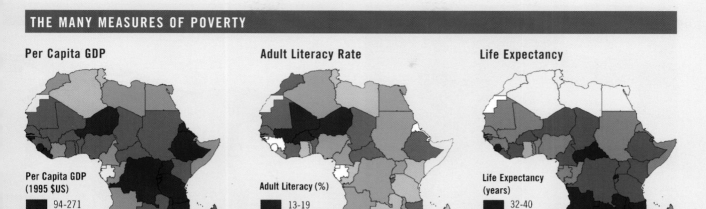

Per Capita GDP

Adult Literacy Rate

Life Expectancy

Per Capita GDP
(1995 $US)
- 94-271
- 272-644
- 645-1,456
- 1,457-2,472
- 2,473-5,850
- No data

Adult Literacy (%)
- 13-19
- 20-51
- 52-69
- 70-90
- 91-100
- No data

Life Expectancy
(years)
- 32-40
- 41-46
- 47-57
- 58-68
- 69-64
- No data

Well-being can be measured using indicators other than income poverty. Three maps of Africa show country-by-country variations in the three indicators used by the United Nations Development Programme to annually measure human development: adult literacy, life expectancy at birth, and gross domestic product per capita.

Sources: World Bank 2004a; United Nations Population Division 2003; UNESCO 2004

imate the poverty lines of low-income countries (Ravallion et al. 1991; World Bank 1990:27). This measure remains controversial, but has provided a starting point for international comparison and for important poverty initiatives, including the United Nations' Millennium Development Goals.

The World Bank's most recent estimate is that some 1.1 billion people lived below the $1 per day line in 2001. About 46 percent of the population of Sub-Saharan Africa and 31 percent

of South Asians live on less than a dollar a day (Chen and Ravallion 2004:1, 30). These numbers have not been static; the distribution of world poverty has changed significantly over the last quarter-century, due in large part to a dramatic drop in the number of poor people in East Asia. Chen and Ravallion broadly estimate that between 1981 and 2001, the number of people living below $1 per day in China declined by over 400 million, while in the rest of the world, the number rose from 850 to 880 million. The number of poor in Sub-Saharan Africa almost doubled over this period (Chen and Ravallion 2004:17, 20). In addition, many more people around the world live only slightly above the $1 per day line, suffering many of the symptoms of $1 per day poverty. Some 2.7 billion—almost half the world population—live on less than $2 per day (Chen and Ravallion 2004:16).

As useful as these aggregate numbers are, they tend to mask some important elements of the poverty landscape. For example, not all the poor fall into a single category—some are poorer than others. The depth and distribution of material poverty in different countries can be extremely varied. Weighing how far below the poverty line households fall—their "poverty gap," or gap between household income and the national poverty line—offers a useful measure of the depth of a nation's poverty (World Bank 2001:320).

PERCENT OF POPULATION LIVING ON $1 PER DAY, 1981-2001

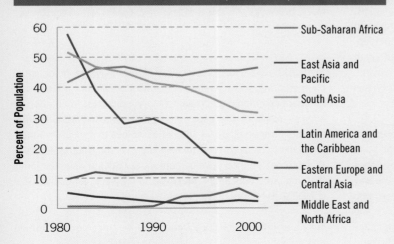

- Sub-Saharan Africa
- East Asia and Pacific
- South Asia
- Latin America and the Caribbean
- Eastern Europe and Central Asia
- Middle East and North Africa

Sources: Chen and Ravallion 2004:30; World Bank 2004b

7

BOX 1.1 THE DIMENSIONS OF POVERTY

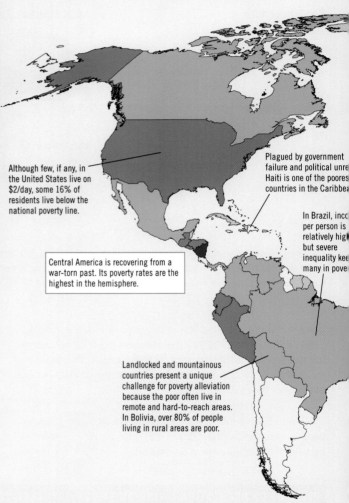

Although few, if any, in the United States live on $2/day, some 16% of residents live below the national poverty line.

Plagued by government failure and political unre[st] Haiti is one of the poores[t] countries in the Caribbea[n]

In Brazil, inco[me] per person is relatively hig[h] but severe inequality kee[ps] many in pove[rty]

Central America is recovering from a war-torn past. Its poverty rates are the highest in the hemisphere.

Landlocked and mountainous countries present a unique challenge for poverty alleviation because the poor often live in remote and hard-to-reach areas. In Bolivia, over 80% of people living in rural areas are poor.

Another variation on the standard poverty line looks at "relative poverty" by assessing the proportion of a country's population that lives at less than one-third the national consumption average. When this measure is applied, the poverty numbers for Sub-Saharan Africa and South Asia stay relatively similar to those calculated using national poverty lines. But the numbers in other regions soar, rising to 51 percent in Latin America and the Caribbean, and 26 percent in Europe and Central Asia (Hulme et al. 2001:18).

Still another way to measure poverty is to assess whether a household's total assets—cash, property, livestock, transport, and other possessions—fall below a critical level (Barrett and Swallow 2003:9). This approach is consistent with the perceptions of the poor themselves. When poor people are asked about their material concerns, they tend to focus not just on income, but on their lack of assets in general and the insecurity this brings (Narayan et al. 2000b:49).

Because poverty has so many dimensions, monetary measures are not the only, nor necessarily the best, way to count the poor. For example, the conventional household survey approach does not reveal disparities within households, and hence has no way of measuring income or consumption poverty among women, who often hold lower status. Education and health statistics, on the other hand, can be used to get a better perspective on many aspects of poverty, including those that are gender-related (World

Sources: Chen and Ravallion 2004:29-30; Kryger 2005; Ritakallio 2002; UNAIDS 2004:191; UNESCO 2004; UNICEF 2004; UNICEF 2005:25; World Bank 2004a

Bank 2001:27). Life expectancy, child mortality, the incidence of child stunting, literacy rates, and school enrollment are some of the more commonly used nonmonetary indicators. In an effort to address some of the gaps left by money-based assessments, analysts have developed a number of indices that measure multiple dimensions of poverty. The best known is the UN Development Programme's Human Development Index (HDI), a weighted index that includes education, life expectancy, and per-capita GDP (UNDP 2004:139).

For more information, see Data Table 4, "Income Distribution and Poverty."

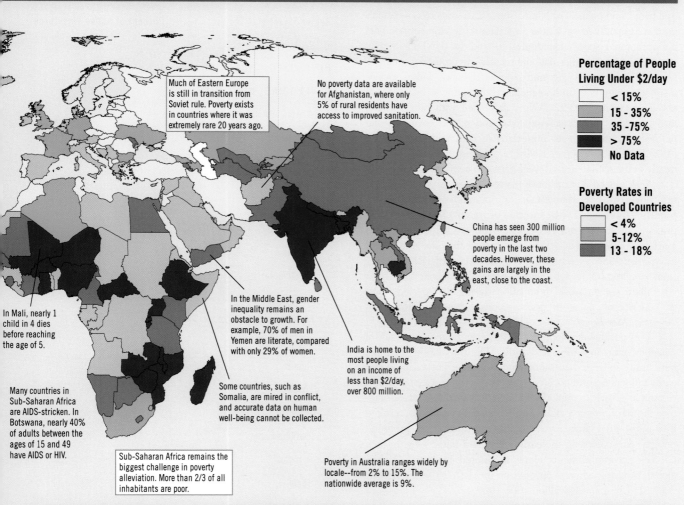

Percentage of People Living Under $2/day

- < 15%
- 15 - 35%
- 35 - 75%
- > 75%
- No Data

Poverty Rates in Developed Countries

- < 4%
- 5-12%
- 13 - 18%

Much of Eastern Europe is still in transition from Soviet rule. Poverty exists in countries where it was extremely rare 20 years ago.

No poverty data are available for Afghanistan, where only 5% of rural residents have access to improved sanitation.

China has seen 300 million people emerge from poverty in the last two decades. However, these gains are largely in the east, close to the coast.

In Mali, nearly 1 child in 4 dies before reaching the age of 5.

In the Middle East, gender inequality remains an obstacle to growth. For example, 70% of men in Yemen are literate, compared with only 29% of women.

India is home to the most people living on an income of less than $2/day, over 800 million.

Many countries in Sub-Saharan Africa are AIDS-stricken. In Botswana, nearly 40% of adults between the ages of 15 and 49 have AIDS or HIV.

Some countries, such as Somalia, are mired in conflict, and accurate data on human well-being cannot be collected.

Sub-Saharan Africa remains the biggest challenge in poverty alleviation. More than 2/3 of all inhabitants are poor.

Poverty in Australia ranges widely by locale--from 2% to 15%. The nationwide average is 9%.

$1 AND $2 PER DAY POVERTY TRENDS, 1981-2001

	NUMBER OF PEOPLE (MILLIONS)						REGIONAL POPULATION 2001 (MILLIONS)
	LIVING ON $1 PER DAY			LIVING ON $2 PER DAY			
	1981	2001	Change since 1981	1981	2001	Change since 1981	
East Asia and Pacific	796	271	-66%	1,170	864	-26%	1,823
Eastern Europe and Central Asia	3	18	468%	20	94	363%	474
Latin America and the Caribbean	36	50	40%	99	128	30%	518
Middle East and North Africa	9	7	-22%	52	70	35%	300
South Asia	475	431	-9%	821	1,064	30%	1,378
Sub-Saharan Africa	164	316	93%	288	516	79%	673
Global Total	**1,482**	**1,093**	**-26%**	**2,450**	**2,736**	**12%**	**6,127**

Sources: Chen and Ravallion 2004.

nations. It goes without saying that poverty levies heavy personal costs on the poor themselves. It robs families of security, opportunity, and health. In so doing, it also robs nations of the potential contributions these families could make to economic growth, social well-being, and political stability. Poverty thus squanders a nation's human capital. It acts as a drag on economic development, requiring substantial state expenditures to address (UNDP 1996:5). Poverty also undermines national security by promoting disaffection and magnifying class and political divisions within society, increasing migration, and potentially contributing to international terrorism (Sachs 2003:27). When combined with other driving forces, it also can exacerbate local and global environmental problems, contributing to unsustainable land and resource use (ASB 2003:2; Duraiappah 1998:2177). Given this list of ills, it is clearly in the self-interest of every nation to confront poverty.

And, indeed, nations have made some progress in combating poverty. The percentage of people suffering severe poverty—those who live on incomes of roughly $1 per day (1993 prices)—has fallen from 40 percent of the world's population in 1981 to 21 percent in 2001. This means that the number of impoverished people has dropped by an estimated 400 million—from roughly 1.5 to 1.1 billion—over 20 years, in spite of a 1.6 billion rise in world population during that period, most of which took place in poor nations (Chen and Ravallion 2004:31). *(See Box 1.1.)*

This positive development is, however, largely the result of rising incomes in China and India. The populations in these nations are so large that improvements in their poverty rates can easily influence world poverty totals. For example, China's robust economic growth, coupled with de-collectivization of agriculture, stronger property rights, and other policy changes, resulted in a substantial drop in the number of people in profound poverty, particularly in the early 1980s and mid-1990s. In fact, China's accomplishments alone accounted for much of the global progress against poverty in the last 20 years (Dollar 2004:31; Chen and Ravallion 2004:18).

There are other success stories as well. The poverty rate in Vietnam dropped sharply over five years—from 58 percent in 1992 to 37 percent in 1998—on the strength of its economic growth and pro-poor policies (Glewwe et al. 2000:39; Kakwani 2004:6). In just eleven years—from 1987 to 1998—Chile succeeded in cutting its poverty rate in half (World Bank 2001a:5). The rate of primary-school completion in the developing world rose from 73 percent to 81 percent during the 1990s (Bruns et al. 2003:3). Over the past 40 years, life expectancy in developing countries has increased by 20 years—about as much as was achieved in all of human history prior to the middle of the twentieth century, although this is being sharply eroded by the AIDS epidemic today (Goldin et al 2002:iii; WHO 2004:5).

These successes notwithstanding, poverty is very much present in the world today. In fact, in many countries poverty continues to worsen. Between 1981 and 2001, the number of people living on less than $1 per day in Sub-Saharan Africa

TABLE 1.1 ECOSYSTEMS BRING JOBS	
Percent of Global Workforce Employed in Agriculture, Fisheries, and Forestry, 2001	
Region/Country	**Percent of Active Workforce**
WORLD	44
DEVELOPED COUNTRIES	7
DEVELOPING COUNTRIES	54
ASIA AND PACIFIC	60
Cambodia	70
China	67
India	59
Nepal	93
LATIN AMERICA AND THE CARIBBEAN	19
Bolivia	44
Guatemala	45
Haiti	62
NEAR EAST AND NORTH AFRICA	33
Afghanistan	67
Turkey	45
Yemen	50
SUB-SAHARAN AFRICA	62
Burkina Faso	92
Ethiopia	82
Niger	88
Tanzania	80
COUNTRIES IN TRANSITION	15
Albania	48
Azerbaijan	26
Tajikistan	33

Source: FAO 2004:169-174, Table A4

doubled from 164 million to 313 million people. In Latin America and the Caribbean it climbed from 36 million to 50 million (Chen and Ravallion 2004:31). The percentage of people living on less than $2 per day in Eastern Europe and Central Asia rose from 2 percent in 1981 to 20 percent in 2001, largely as a result of the collapse of communism in those regions (Chen and Ravallion 2004:19). The scourge of AIDS adds to the problem, particularly in Africa, where the disease is wiping out many of the gains against poverty made over the last few decades (Wines and LaFraniere 2004:1; WHO 2004). Even in China, the incidence of poverty increased during the late 1990s as the nation's torrid pace of economic growth slowed for a few years (Kakwani 2004:6).

To be sure, progress against poverty has been held back in many poor nations by a lack of economic growth. Experience shows that such growth is an important component of large-scale poverty alleviation. Over the last two decades, however, economic growth has often not kept pace with population growth in the poorest countries. From 1981 to 2001, per capita GDP dropped in 43 percent of developing nations (Hufbauer 2003:31, 33, 35). This lack of economic growth is particularly acute in rural areas, compounded by the political weakness of these areas and consequent underinvestment in rural development. For example, from 1999-2002, the World Bank directed just 25 percent of its total lending toward rural areas, in spite of the predominance of poverty there (World Bank 2003:10-11).

Growth Alone is Not Enough

Even where there is economic growth, many poor people are left behind. Economic growth alone does not necessarily translate to poverty reduction. In Latin America, for instance, the number of people in poverty has increased in the last decade even as the GDP per capita has increased, indicating that economic inequality has intensified (Chen and Ravallion 2004:31; World Bank 2005:24).

We all know the basic facts. Half the people in the world live on less than $2 a day. A fifth live on less than $1 a day. Over the next three decades, two billion more people will be added to the global population—97 percent of them in developing countries, most of them born into poverty.

—James D. Wolfensohn, President, World Bank, Oct. 3, 2004

In China, too, the nation's growing wealth has by-passed many families, with the benefits often captured by rapidly industrializing regions and cities, and missing many rural residents. One result has been a widening of the income gap between urban and rural areas over the last two decades, as well as greater growth and poverty reduction in China's coastal provinces where the engine of economic growth runs hottest (Ravallion and Chen 2004:15-16, 25). Moreover, the rural poor often suffer the environmental costs of China's industrialization and rapid growth disproportionately. Highly polluting industries have routinely relocated from cities to China's rural areas to avoid clean-up costs, leaving a legacy of water and air pollution that

REDUCING INEQUALITIES REDUCES POVERTY

Working toward economic equity—toward a more equal distribution of economic benefits within a nation—is a powerful means to fight poverty. It is a necessary complement to strategies that expand the national economy, so that some of the benefits of growth make their way to those in the lowest income bracket. Even when economic growth is slow, policies that more equally distribute economic gains can help reduce poverty, as shown by the success of Jordan in lowering its poverty rate from 1992-1997.

In 1989, following a currency devaluation, Jordan suffered an economic crisis that increased the poverty rate sixfold. At the same time, the nation's level of economic inequality—the difference between the incomes of the rich and the poor—increased dramatically as well, prompting a significant rethinking of economic strategy among government policymakers (Shaban et al. 2001:iv).

Beginning in 1991, Jordan changed its spending policies to increase the proportion of economic benefits flowing to the lowest income sector. One of the most effective changes was the gradual replacement of general food subsides, from which richer families benefited most, with direct cash payments to poor families only (Shaban et al. 2001:iv, 15-20). This reprogramming reduced the nation's economic inequality, with the gap between the wealthiest segment of Jordanian society and the poorest narrowing over the next six years (Shaban et al. 2001:viii, 10-13).

Subsequent analysis showed that it was this reduction of inequality that helped Jordan reduce its poverty rate from 14.4 percent in 1992 to 11.7 percent in 1997, even though the nation experienced little or no economic growth during this period (Shaban et al. 2001:viii, 7). In addition, those who remained poor were not as far below the poverty line, and extreme poverty had declined (Shaban et al. 2001:8). The reduction in inequality was driven by a greater percentage of government expenditures being captured by the poor. Had this trend toward reduced inequality been accompanied by genuine economic growth, Jordan's poverty rate would likely have dropped even more.

JORDAN: LESS INEQUALITY, LESS POVERTY

	1992	1997
Percent of Population in Poverty[1]:	14.4	11.7
Level of Inequality (Gini Index[2])	0.40	0.36

[1] Annual per capita consumption is below 314 JD or US $443 at 1997 prices.

[2] The Gini index is scaled between 0.0 and 1.0; 0.0 indicates perfect equality and 1.0 indicates perfect inequality.

Source: Shaban et al. 2001:10,12

many rural residents are too poor to escape (Yardley 2004:1). All too often, such inequalities in income and vulnerability among groups are exacerbated by rapid economic growth, with the poor falling further behind (Kakwani 2004:6).

Perhaps the most striking examples of the difficulty of spreading the benefits of growth equitably occur in the indus-

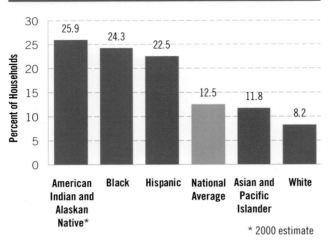

FIGURE 1.1 UNITED STATES HOUSEHOLDS FALLING BELOW THE NATIONAL POVERTY LINE, 2003

Percent of Households

American Indian and Alaskan Native*	Black	Hispanic	National Average	Asian and Pacific Islander	White
25.9	24.3	22.5	12.5	11.8	8.2

* 2000 estimate

Source: DeNavas-Walt et al. 2004:10; United States Census Bureau 2001:7

Historically marginalized groups such as Native Americans, African Americans, and Hispanics continue to suffer significantly higher rates of poverty. For example, 24.4 percent of African Americans fell below the poverty line in 2003, compared to the national rate of 12.5 percent. Among Native Americans and Hispanics, poverty rates were 23 percent and 22.5 percent, respectively (DeNavas-Walt et al. 2004:10). *(See Figure 1.1.)*

In general, research shows that to benefit the poor most, economic growth must be coupled with policies that reduce inequalities and improve how income is distributed in a society (Kakwani 2004:6). Where dependence of the poor on natural resources is high, as it is in most developing nations, these policies must necessarily involve the environment. And they must translate to governance practices that increase the poor's access to vital natural resources and their ability to govern those resources so that they share in the income from them.

Environment Matters to the Poor

The link between environment and poverty reduction is strong. Since the Rio Earth Summit in 1992, the importance of a sound environment to sustainable livelihoods has been widely acknowledged, particularly for the rural poor in Africa, Asia, and Latin America (UN 1992; UN 2002:2). Income derived

trialized world, where poverty persists in spite of the general affluence of the population. In the United States, the number of poor has risen steadily since 2000, reaching almost 36 million people in 2003—some 1.3 million more than in 2002.

WHY FOCUS ON RURAL RATHER THAN URBAN POVERTY?

Although poverty in urban areas is substantial and increasing, global poverty is still predominantly a rural phenomenon. Some 75 percent of the poor live in rural areas despite the global trend toward urbanization. Even in 20 years, 60 percent of the poor are expected to live outside of cities (IFAD 2001:15). Providing a route out of poverty for these rural residents will remain a priority for national governments and the international community for decades to come (Reed 2001:13; World Bank 2003:1).

In addition, while urban ecosystems such as parks, waterways, and green spaces provide important services, it is rural ecosystems that provide the bulk of the goods and services on which humans depend for survival. The forest areas, fisheries, grasslands, agricultural fields, and rivers that provision both urban and rural residents, be they poor or rich, exist primarily in rural areas, and this is where most ecosystem governance and management occurs.

However, even as we focus on rural ecosystems and the rural poor, we recognize the intimate connection between the urban and rural spheres. Much urban poverty, for example, begins as rural poverty, exported from the countryside through rural-to-urban migration. Working for a healthier rural economy thus helps address urban poverty too, by lessening this migration. At the same time, the rural and urban economies are deeply intertwined, particularly through the flow of remittances from the city back to family members in the country. In fact, being able to tap into such remittances is often one of the dividing lines between poverty and sufficiency, and modern rural economies could hardly function without this net flow of income out of urban areas. In the end, then, we realize that addressing rural poverty has an important urban dimension as well. Urban and rural poverty can never be completely disentwined.

URBAN-RURAL COMPARISONS

	VIETNAM Urban	VIETNAM Rural	INDIA Urban	INDIA Rural	ZIMBABWE Urban	ZIMBABWE Rural
Percent Below Poverty Line	7	36	25	30	8	48
Under-Five Mortality (per 1,000 live births)	16	36	63	104	69	100
Access to Improved Sanitation (percent of households)	84	26	58	18	69	51
Median Years of Schooling (men)	8.5	6	8.3	4.6	8.8	4.9

Sources: Macro International 2000; ORC Macro 2000; ORC Macro 2003; UNICEF 2005; World Bank 2004

FIGURE 1.2 CLIMATE CHANGE AND FOOD SECURITY

Changes in Projected Growing Season, 2000-2050

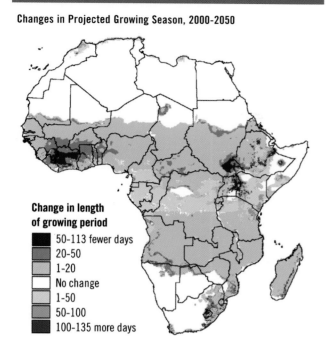

Change in length of growing period

- 50-113 fewer days
- 20-50
- 1-20
- No change
- 1-50
- 50-100
- 100-135 more days

Source: Thornton et al. 2002:89

(See Chapter 2 for a thorough discussion of how ecosystems contribute to the livelihoods of the poor.)

Common Pool Natural Resources Are a Key Source of Subsistence

The poor make extensive use of goods collected from lands or waters over which no one individual has exclusive rights—resources known generally as common pool resources (CPRs) or simply the "commons" (Jodha 1986:1169; Ostrom 1990:30). Common pool resources exist in many different ecosystems and under a variety of public or community ownership regimes. Typical examples include village pastures, state or community forests, waste lands, coastal waters, rivers, lakes, village ponds, and the like (Jodha 1986:1169).

Materials gleaned from CPRs consist of a wide range of items for personal use and sale including food, fodder, fuel, fiber, small timber, manure, bamboos, medicinal plants, oils, and building materials for houses and furniture. Fish, shellfish, seaweed, and other items harvested from coastal waters, rivers, and other aquatic environments are also of major importance to the poor. Nearly all rural families—both rich and poor—benefit from CPR income, but it is particularly important to landless households, for whom it provides a major fraction of total income. Researchers estimate that common pool resources provide about 12 percent of household income to poor households in India—worth about $5 billion a year, or double the amount of development aid that India receives (Beck and Nesmith 2001:119).

When access to common pool resources is unrestricted, as it is often is, it is difficult to keep them from being overexploited. Degradation of open access resources in the form of overfishing, deforestation, and overgrazing is an increasing burden on the poor—a trend that leads away from wealth.

Natural Resources Are Vital Social Safety Nets During Lean Times

Natural resources play a key role as a subsistence source of last resort in times of economic decline and when other food supplies are constrained. In southeastern Ghana, for example, recession and drought in 1982 and 1983 coincided with the normal lean season—the time before harvest when food supplies are naturally low. During this lean season, the poorest households depended on the "bush" for 20 percent of their food intake, compared to the highest income bracket, for which the bush provided only 2 percent of the household food intake. Women and children in particular relied on wild products such as roots, fibers, leaves, bark, fruit, seeds, nuts, insects, and sap. Men also hunted and trapped small mammals, reptiles, and birds (Dei 1992:67).

Environmental Factors Add to the Health Burden of the Poor

Environmental risks such as unclean water, exposure to indoor air pollution, insect-borne diseases, and pesticides account for almost a quarter of the global burden of disease, and an even

from the environment is a major constituent of the livelihoods of the rural poor, and this direct dependence on nature does not appear to be decreasing.

The environment is also a source of vulnerability. Environmental factors contribute substantially to the burden of ill-health the poor suffer. In addition, low-income families are especially vulnerable to natural disasters and environment-related risks such as the growing impacts of global climate change. As these environment-poverty links have become clear, major development institutions and donors have begun to make the environment a more central feature of their efforts to tackle poverty (USAID et al. 2002; Duraiappah 2004; UK DFID et al. 2002; UK DFID 1999; UNDP and EC 1999; World Bank 2001b).

Natural Resources Play a Vital Role in the Livelihoods of the Poor

Poor rural families make use of a variety of sources of income and subsistence activities to make their livings. Many of these are directly based on nature—like small-scale farming and livestock-rearing, fishing, hunting, and collecting of firewood, herbs, or other natural products. These may be sold for cash or used directly for food, heat, building materials, or innumerable other household needs. This "environmental income" is added to other income sources such as wage labor and remittances sent from family members who have emigrated. The decline of natural systems through soil depletion, deforestation, overexploitation, and pollution represents a direct threat to nature-based income and is a contributor to increasing poverty.

Continues on page 16

BOX 1.2 LIFE ON A DOLLAR A DAY

TO BE OFFICIALLY POOR IN INTERNATIONAL TERMS is to live below the World Bank's poverty line of US$1 per day. In actuality, the incomes of poor people vary by nation and by region, but by definition always add up to less than what is needed to make ends meet. To be poor is to have to choose among a range of necessities, not all of which you can afford. Food, shelter, health care, clothes, fuel, transportation, and tools or equipment needed for work are all basic expenditures vying for the limited family budget. Social obligations such as weddings, funerals, and gifts add to these basic needs. With little means and many needs, what do you spend your income on?

The Necessities

Food is the primary and immediate concern, and by far the major expense, for poor households. Studies show that the poorer the household, the greater the percentage of income spent on food. This is in spite of the fact that the poor often grow some of their own food. In Tanzania, the average rural household survived on just 32 cents a day in 2001, with 21 cents—65 percent—going for food (National Bureau of Statistics of Tanzania 2002:68-70). Food spending among the poor shows similar patterns in other regions: food purchases account for 60 percent of household spending in rural Morocco ($0.37/day) (World Bank 2001:4, Table 5) and 75 percent ($0.50/day) in Georgia (Yemtsov 1999:15, Table 5, 42). By comparison, a family in the United States spends an average of 14 percent of the household budget on food (U.S. Dept. of Labor 2004:4).

With food accounting for so large a share of daily finances, other critical necessities must receive proportionately less—often only pennies a day. Housing and the fuel or electricity to heat and cook with, for example, account for only 12 percent of spending among Argentina's poor (Lee 2000:8, Table 2). Health care, another priority for low-income families, receives only three cents of every dollar spent by Morocco's rural poor, the same amount spent in rural Georgia (World Bank 2001:9, Table 17; Yemtsov 1999:15, Table 5). Clothing and transportation costs account for a similarly small share of the daily dollar.

WHAT CAN YOU BUY FOR A DOLLAR?

Country	$1 buys
Bangladesh (Chittagong)	1 Dozen Eggs
Kenya	8 Cups of Milk
Ghana	2 1/3 Bottles of Palm Oil
Ghana	4 1/3 Bottles of Coke
Philippines	4/5 of a Big Mac
USA	1/3 of a Starbucks Tall Latte
Uganda	1/46 of a Bicycle
Bangladesh	1/3 of a Sari
Ghana	1 1/2 Pairs Rubber Sandals
Bangladesh	7 Bars of Soap
Ghana	87 Tablets of Penicillin
India (Andhra Pradesh)	1/2 Unit of Blood for a Transfusion
USA	1/150 of the Average Daily Cost of Nursing Home Care
Tanzania (Nzanza)	1/3 of a Liter of Pesticide
Ghana	4 1/3 Rolls of Toilet Paper
Ecuador (Quito)	1/500 of a Washing Machine
India (Andhra Pradesh)	2-3 Pieces Bamboo for Building
Uganda (Mbale)	1/1500 of the Cost of Building a New Home
India (Mumbai)	1/3 of a Regular Price Evening Movie Ticket

A family of four interviewed in rural Bangladesh calculated that they spent roughly 80 cents a day on food and fuel, allowing them to buy and cook two meals of rice and beans, as well as an occasional piece of meat. Medical costs came to 3.3 cents a day ($12 per year), mainly on medicines for the husband's coughs and colds. Other family expenses included 4.1 cents per day on clothes ($15 per year), 1.6 cents on school books ($6 per year), and 2.2 cents ($8 per year) visiting and giving presents to relatives. Family health and food costs thus accounted for more than 90 percent of the household's basic expenses (Rutherford 2002:10).

What You Can't Afford

When income does not fully cover even daily necessities, everything else becomes a luxury. Thus there are a great many things that the poor cannot afford to buy. Tools, materials, and upkeep for income-generating assets like transportation or farm equipment are all expenses that are routinely left out of the family budget. To cover gifts, dowries, and funerals—expenses at the heart of many social structures and customs—the poor must often sell what little land or livestock assets they have (Narayan et al. 2000a:149-150). Furniture, stylish clothing, or appliances—all items taken more or less for granted in the developed world—are largely an extravagance. Investments in hard assets or insurance to cushion against future hardships are even more difficult to afford. With no insurance or provision for emergencies, an already marginal income becomes an even more precarious foundation for the future.

Poverty often means not being able to take advantage of opportunities and investments that are open to others with more secure incomes. Education is a good example. Although the benefit of an education can dramatically increase a child's chance of leaving poverty, a poor family's budget does not always permit this. School costs can include tuition, supplies, and the loss of labor that the child could have contributed had he or she stayed home (Narayan et al. 2000b:242-244). Other investments that require savings or start-up capital are also out of reach, such as launching a small business, buying fertilizer or a fishing boat, or advertising to reach a wider market. Lacking such investment ability, the poor are often confined to subsistence activities and low-value wage labor that make it hard to get ahead.

WHAT THE RURAL POOR SPEND IN MOROCCO

Daily Per Capita Expenditures of Rural, Low-Income Individuals in Morocco 1998/99 (US$)

	Amount Spent	% of Total
Food	$0.35	61.4
Housing	$0.13	22.8
Clothing	$0.02	3.2
Health	$0.02	3.2
Transport and Communications	$0.01	2.5
Leisure	$0.01	1.8
Other	$0.03	5.1
TOTAL	**$0.57**	**100**

Adapted from World Bank 2001:9, Table 17

greater proportion of the health burden of the poor (Cairncross et al. 2003:2; Lvovsky 2001:1). The poor are far more likely to be exposed to environmental health risks than the rich by virtue of where they live. They also have much less access to good health care, making their exposure more damaging. In turn, poor health is an important obstacle to greater income and a contributor to diminished well-being in every dimension of life. *(See Box 1.3.)*

Climate Change Adds to the Vulnerability of the Poor

The adverse impacts of climate change will be most striking in developing nations—and particularly among the poor—both because of their high dependence on natural resources and their limited capacity to adapt to a changing climate. Water scarcity is already a major problem for the world's poor, and changes in rainfall and temperature associated with climate change will likely make this worse. Even without climate change, the number of people impacted by water scarcity is projected to increase from 1.7 billion today to 5 billion by 2025 (IPCC 2001:9).

In addition, crop yields are expected to decline in most tropical and sub-tropical regions as rainfall and temperature patterns change with a changing climate (IPCC 2001:84). *(See Figure 1.2.)* A recent report by the Food and Agriculture Organization estimates that developing nations may experience an 11 percent decrease in lands suitable for rainfed agriculture by 2080 due to climate change (FAO 2005:2). There is also some evidence that disease vectors such as malaria-bearing mosquitoes will spread more widely (IPCC 2001:455). At the same time, global warming may bring an increase in severe weather events like cyclones and torrential rains. The inadequate construction and exposed locations of poor people's dwellings often makes them the most likely victims of such natural disasters.

Nature as an Economic Stepping Stone

Nature has always been a route to wealth, at least for a few. Profit from harvesting timber and fish stocks, from converting grasslands to farm fields, and from exploiting oil, gas, and mineral reserves has created personal fortunes, inspired stock markets, and powered the growth trajectories of nations for centuries. But this scale of natural resource wealth has been amassed mostly through unsustainable means, and the benefits have largely accrued to the powerful. It is the powerful who generally control resource access through land ownership or concessions for logging, fishing, or mining on state lands; who command the capital to make investments; and who can negotiate the government regulatory regimes that direct the use of natural resources. The poor, by contrast, have reaped precious little of the total wealth extracted from nature. But that can change.

Natural Resources Are a Key Determinant of Rural Wealth

Even though they do not currently capture most of the wealth created by natural systems, the livelihoods of the poor are built around these systems. Indeed, natural resources are the fundamental building block of most rural livelihoods in developing nations, and not just during lean times. Chapter 2 offers many examples of the environmental income that both the poor and rich derive from nature.

The ability to efficiently tap the productivity of ecosystems is often one of the most significant determinates of household income. For example, studies show that the key variable explaining income levels for rural households in Uganda is access to land and livestock. In Ugandan villages near Lake Victoria, the key variable explaining wealth is access to fishing boats and gear. Income-wise, these are found to be even more important than other wealth-associated factors such as access to education (Ellis and Bahiigwa 2003:1003).

Beyond Subsistence: Natural Endowments as Capital for the Poor

Ecosystem goods and services—the natural products and processes that ecosystems generate—are often the only significant assets the poor have access to. These natural endowments, if managed efficiently, can provide a capital base—a foundation for greater economic viability, and a stepping stone beyond mere subsistence. Yet the potential of these assets is often overlooked.

Typical commercial evaluation of natural resources tends to undervalue the total array of ecosystem goods and services, which includes not just the crops, lumber, fish, and forage that are the usual focus of exploitation, but also a wide variety of other collectibles, agroforestry products, small-scale aquaculture products, as well as services such as maintenance of soil fertility, flood control, and recreation (Lampietti and Dixon 1995:1-3; Pagiola et al. 2004:15-19). One of the consequences of the difficulty of assigning a monetary value to ecosystem benefits is that it has led to the systematic undervaluation of the assets of the poor and the underestimation of the potential benefits of improved environmental management.

But the potential for strategic management of ecosystems to raise the incomes of the poor is real. In fact, good ecosystem management can become one of the engines of rural economic growth more generally. Experience shows that the poor use several strategies to make their ecosystem assets a stepping stone out of poverty.

Restoring Productivity

Where ecosystems are degraded, it limits their potential as a source of environmental income. Many communities have found that restoring the productivity of local forests, pastures, or fisheries has the opposite effect, raising local incomes substantially. Often this entails a community effort to more carefully control the use of common property areas and even private lands. For example, the village of Sukhomajri in Haryana, India, has gained widespread recognition for its success in raising village incomes through community efforts to restore and maintain the productivity of local forests and farmland. Careful land management and rainwater harvesting produced large gains in agricultural production, tree density, and available water, increasing annual household incomes by 50 percent in five years (Agarwal and Narain 1999:16).

Many other watershed management projects in India have also reported benefits to village residents, including poor families who do not own land. In the Adgaon watershed in Maharashtra, annual days of employment (wage labor) per worker increased from 75 days at the project's inception to over 200 days after restoration was complete. In Mendhwan Village, laborers found eight months of agricultural work per year after four years of watershed management, compared with only three months before the community began its restoration and management project (Kerr et al. 2002:56).

Marketing Niche Products and Services

One common way to translate ecosystem assets into economic gain is to create or take advantage of niche markets for nontimber forest products, such as bamboo, mushrooms, herbs, and other collectibles. In Nam Pheng village in northwestern Laos, villagers began a cooperative effort in 1996 to expand the market for bitter bamboo and cardamom. They created a coordinated management plan for sustainable harvest of these traditional products, improved the harvest technology, and

TABLE 1.2 BITTER BAMBOO AND CARDAMOM VS. OTHER INCOME SOURCES

NAM PHENG VILLAGE, LAO PDR

Income Activity	Income Per Day of Labor (in Lao Kip)
Collection and Sale of Bitter Bamboo	13,500-19,600
Collection and Sale of Cardamom	11,200
Heavy Labor: Road Construction	20,000
Heavy Labor: Agriculture	20,000
Collection and Sale of Fuelwood	17,000
Light Labor: Agriculture	10,000
Slash and Burn Cultivation	1,500

Note: 1000 Lao Kip = US$0.13

Source: Morris 2002:14

established a marketing group to both increase sales and obtain higher prices for their wares. By 2001 a day's harvest of bitter bamboo brought ten times the wages of slash-and-burn cultivation, which had been the villagers' main livelihood activity (Morris 2002:10-24). *(See Table 1.2.)*

By 2002, harvesting bitter bamboo and cardamom provided the main source of income for most villagers and the community had made considerable progress toward higher incomes and more secure livelihoods. *(See Figure 1.3.)* The village poverty rate had fallen by more than half, food security had increased, and the mortality rate for children under five had fallen to zero. In addition, enough community funds from the joint marketing group had been raised to build a school, prompting school enrollment to double, with more than half of the students being girls. While the income potential from bamboo and cardamom is not unlimited, it has clearly provided a stepping stone to larger capital investments, such as livestock, and allowed villagers to diversify their income sources. It has also brought villagers an appreciation of the forest as an economic asset, providing an incentive for long-term care of the forest ecosystem (Morris 2002:10-24).

In addition to marketing forest products like bamboo, poor households can find substantial income marketing ecosystem services, such as recreation. In Namibia, communities have successfully tapped the ecotourism trade built around viewing and hunting the area's springbok, wildebeest, elephants, giraffes, and other animal populations. To accomplish this, the communities have formed legally constituted "conservancies" to regulate the hunting, sightseeing, camping, and other activities that affect local wildlife. The conservancies have generated direct benefits ranging from jobs and training to cash and meat payouts to community members. In 2004, total community

FIGURE 1.3 A TREND TOWARD WEALTH, Nam Pheng Village, Lao PDR

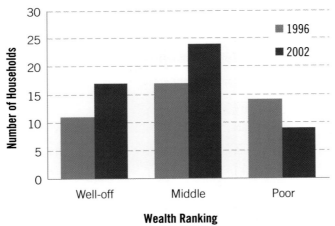

Well-off: Permanent house, equipment, and accessories (e.g., truck, TV/VCR); enough money and rice for one year; some livestock; and enough labor.

Middle: Semi-permanent house (i.e., thatched grass roof, stripped bamboo walls), insufficient money or rice for half the year, few livestock, and enough labor.

Poor: Temporary house (bamboo or small trees for beams and pillars), insufficient rice for entire year, no livestock, and insufficient labor.

Source: Morris 2002:17

benefits reached N$14.1 million (US$2.5 million) in value. Studies have documented that, over the course of 10 years, the conservancies have enhanced the livelihood security of local people while spurring major recoveries in wildlife populations (WWF and Rossing Foundation 2004:v-vi; Vaughan et al. 2003:18-19).

Capturing a Greater Share of the Natural Resource Value

Maximizing environmental income involves not only improved resource management or creation of new markets for nontraditional or underexploited products. It also requires greater attention to marketing traditional products such as fish, so that more of the revenue generated is captured by the fishers themselves in the form of higher prices for their harvests. In Kayar, a community along the coast of Senegal, local fishers worked together to regulate their fish catch, with the idea of stabilizing the catch and insuring a good price at market (Lenselink 2002:43). By limiting the quantity of fish each boat owner could deliver to market each day, they successfully raised fish prices to the point that fishers had surplus income to save. At the same time, fish stocks were better managed by limiting the number of fishers allowed in a given area, the number of fishing trips allowed per day, and the kinds of permissible fishing gear (Lenselink 2002:43; Siegel and Diouf 2004:4, 6). The Kayar fishers made economics and ecosystem management work hand in hand. (*See the case studies in Chapter 5 for other examples of how communities have used better ecosystem management to improve their economic prosperity and reduce poverty.*)

The examples described above involved a different understanding of nature's wealth from the conventional view of large-scale extraction—a different view of what natural wealth is, how it can best be tapped, and who is to benefit from it.

Ecosystem Management as a Basis for Agriculture Growth, Rural Diversification, and General Economic Growth

Making ecosystems work as an economic asset for the poor should be seen not as an isolated goal but part of a larger strategy for rural development. Utilizing the natural assets of the poor is not a "silver bullet" for poverty reduction that can single-handedly bring wealth to poor families. It is rather part of a general transition of rural economies from subsistence to wealth accumulation, working first to support a more profitable small-scale agriculture and natural resource economy—the current mainstays of rural livelihoods—and eventually to build a complementary rural industrial and service economy (World Bank 2003:xix-xxvi).

Agriculture is a particularly important piece of the rural poverty equation. There is a well-established connection between improvements in small-scale agriculture and poverty reduction. One study in Africa found that a 10 percent increase in crop yields led to a 9 percent decrease in the number of people living on $1 per day (Irz et al. 2001 in World Bank 2003:xix). Indeed, rapid agricultural growth is considered a primary avenue for poverty alleviation (Smith and Urey 2002:71). From the 1960s to the1980s, the Green Revolution's use of modern seeds and fertilizers, irrigation, better credit, roads, and technical assistance helped bring this kind of rapid agricultural growth to many rural areas, with a corresponding reduction in poverty. For example, from 1965 to 1991—the period of greatest Green Revolution gains—rural poverty rates in India declined from 54 percent of the population to 37 percent (Smith and Urey 2002:17).

But spreading the Green Revolution's success to the poor families and the marginal lands it has by-passed will require something more than the technocratic approach of those earlier decades. It will also require good ecosystem management by the poor that helps build and retain soil fertility and allows small farmers to harvest and efficiently use water resources. Failure to take this approach has resulted in fertility loss, salinization, and overdrafting of groundwater on many of the Green Revolution farms—environmental problems that have begun to erode productivity gains in many areas (Smith and Urey 2002:10).

Sustained agricultural growth, augmented by other forms of environmental income, from forest products to forage to aquaculture, can help many poor rural families to create an asset base that allows them to begin the transition away from sole dependence on farming and nature-based activities. Research shows that as growth proceeds, agriculture eventually begins to play a less crucial role in the overall development process and subsequently declines as a share of economic output (Timmer 1988:276, 279). Rural residents begin to depend more on rural industry and so-called "off-farm" income, which provide an additional and quicker route out of poverty to complement agriculture.

But even as rural economies slowly diversify, nature will still play an important role. Many rural industries—such as local processing of agriculture or fishing products, crafts production, and ecotourism—will themselves be indirectly dependent on natural resources. They will thus benefit from a sound approach to ecosystem management. For example, when the shrimp-processing company Aqualma was established in 2000 in a remote corner of Madagascar, it brought permanent jobs to 1,200 rural workers, most of whom had never held a wage-paying job. But Aqualma's future relies entirely on sound fishing practices that insure a continuing shrimp supply. In other words, a good relationship to ecosystems and environmental income supports many dimensions of rural growth and is beneficial at several points in the economic evolution of the rural poor from subsistence to wealth (World Bank 2003:xxii).

Better Governance Is Vital for Higher Incomes

Maximizing environmental income for the poor requires changes in the governance of natural resources. The need for such changes is pressing because the poor are at a great disadvantage when it comes to controlling natural resources or the decisions surrounding them. They often lack legal ownership or tenure over land and resources, which restricts their access and makes their homes and livelihoods insecure. They also suffer from a lack of voice in decision-making processes, cutting them out of the decision-making loop. Natural-resource corruption falls harder on the poor as well, who may be the victims of bribe-demanding bureaucrats or illegal logging and fishing facilitated by corrupt officials who look the other way. The poor are also subject to a variety of policies—such as taxes and various regulations—that are effectively anti-poor.

These governance burdens make it hard for poor families to plan effectively, to make investments that might allow them to profit

from their assets or skills, or to work together effectively to manage common areas or create markets for their products. In other words, governance burdens quickly translate to economic obstacles.

Tenure Security is a Primary Obstacle

Ownership and access are the most fundamental keys to the wealth of nature. Unfortunately, many poor people do not own the land or fishing grounds they rely on for environmental income. This lack of secure tenure makes them vulnerable to being dispossessed of their homes and livelihoods, or, if they rent homes or land, subject to sometimes exorbitant rent payments.

The importance of tenure—or the lack of it—to the ability to tap nature's wealth can't be stressed too much. The rights to exploit, sell, or bar others from using a resource—the bundle of rights associated with tenure or ownership—are essential to legal commerce. Ownership also provides an incentive to manage ecosystems sustainably by assuring that an owner will be able to capture the benefits of long-term investments like soil improvements, tree planting, or restricting fishing seasons to keep fish stocks viable.

Tenure issues affecting the poor involve not only private ownership of land, but also the use of common lands. Many areas

Continues on page 23

Box 1.3 HEALTH, ENVIRONMENT, AND POVERTY

GOOD HEALTH IS A BASIC COMPONENT OF HUMAN well-being and a necessity for earning a livelihood. Unfortunately, the poor are much more vulnerable to ill health, and ill health is itself an important factor in reinforcing the poverty cycle. The health vulnerability of the poor has many facets, with environmental exposure being one of these faces.

Health as an Asset

Good health is among the most valuable assets the poor possess. Not only is good health essential to almost any income-generating activity, but most of the other assets of the poor—such as livestock and farmland—yield few returns without the physical capacity to maintain or use them (Barrett and McPeak 2003:8; Lawson 2004:20). Individuals who are sick or disabled are less likely to be hired for wage work, may have difficulty working effectively, and will often be paid less for their services (Narayan et al. 2000:96).

Ill health is not just the lack of an asset, but a negative asset. Having a household member fall ill can destroy a poor family's standard of living. Household and village-level studies show that the illness of a key income-earner—a so-called "health shock"—is one of the leading causes of a household's decline into abiding poverty (Krishna 2004:11; Lawson 2004:3). The immediate loss of income is only the start: health bills can mount quickly and create an urgent need for cash, and since the poor possess few liquid assets that can be used for such emergencies, they may have to sell land or items central to sustaining their livelihoods. Families facing a health shock very often fall into substantial debt, from which they can only emerge with difficulty. One common coping strategy is to pull children out of school and send them to work, depriving them of training they will need in the future to keep themselves out of poverty (Narayan et al. 2000:98).

THE HIGH PRICE OF ILL HEALTH

Serious back problems required a hospital stay for Susan, a poor Kenyan farmer. Even before purchasing medicines, Susan's hospital bill cost her US$27 (2,100 Kenyan shillings). She sold her only 2 goats, her bean crop from the previous year, kitchen utensils, and her few pieces of furniture to raise the money. Even if her back recovers, Susan has been reduced to destitution, and will be hard-pressed to earn a livelihood. Her friends remain as her only source of help in the future (Hamilton 2003:21).

DALYs ATTRIBUTED TO ENVIRONMENTAL HEALTH RISKS

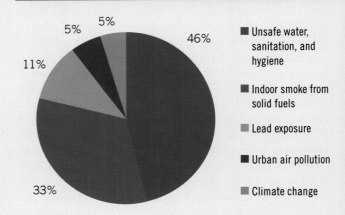

- Unsafe water, sanitation, and hygiene
- Indoor smoke from solid fuels
- Lead exposure
- Urban air pollution
- Climate change

The Disability-Adjusted Life Year (DALY) is a statistical measure of the human costs of sickness in terms of the number of healthy years lost to illness and disability (Ezzati et al. 2004: 2142-3). Time spent in poor health will translate into a loss of income, making the DALY a helpful measure of the impact of health hazards upon the livelihoods of the poor.

Source: Ezzati et al. 2004:2144-45

Elevated Risk of the Poor

The poor are more likely to suffer serious illness during their lifetime. They tend to live in higher-risk areas, with greater exposures to pollution, disease agents, and natural hazards such as floods. They also tend to work more dangerous jobs and have less access to services than the wealthy. Once ill, they face greater challenges in receiving adequate care. A shortage of trained health personnel and gaps in clinics and hospitals may mean that the poor must travel substantial distances and wait in long lines to receive treatment, particularly in rural areas (Narayan et al. 2000:72, 95; World Bank 2004:135).

Corruption in the public health care sector is also widely reported among the poor in the developing world. Patients may be forced to pay for services and medicines that should be free, and are turned away or given inferior care if they cannot afford to pay (Narayan et al. 2000:102;World Bank 2001:83). In Pakistan, a survey found that 96 percent of patients reported some type of corruption associated with visiting the local hospital, such as having to pay extra for beds, X-rays, tests, or medicines (Transparency International 2002:22). As a result, the public health care system is often the last resort of the poor, and many avoid using it at all (Narayan et al. 2000:100; Narayan and Petesch 2002:33-34).

Hunger

Malnutrition is the leading health risk among the poor, accounting for 1 in 15 deaths globally (WHO 2002:54). Of the 1.1 billion people living below the "dollar-a-day" threshold, 780 million suffer from chronic hunger (FAO et al. 2002:8). Because they are often marginalized in society, women and female children in particular may eat last and eat less than the principal breadwinner in the family. Undernourishment of women and children alone accounts for almost 10 percent of the global burden of disease (WHO 2002:54; Economist 2004:68).

Hunger is not only an outcome of poverty but a prime cause for remaining in poverty. Chronically hungry people are less productive at whatever labor they are able to obtain, and thus find it harder to accumulate the financial capital they need to take them out of poverty (FAO et al. 2002:10). The effects of poverty reach across generations as well. Children suffering from malnutrition may suffer physical stunting and impeded cognitive development, and are more susceptible to other forms of disease, both during youth and later in life. An estimated 40-60 percent of children in developing countries suffer from iron deficiencies severe enough to impede cognitive development (Economist 2004:68; WHO 2001:7-8). These disabilities are likely to limit their capacity to generate income in the future, extending the cycle of poverty for yet another generation (FAO 2002:10; WHO 2002:53).

Environmental Health

Environmental hazards comprise a significant portion of the health risks facing the poor. By one estimate, environmental causes account for 21 percent of the overall burden of disease worldwide (the combination of days spent sick and deaths due to sickness) (WHO 2002 in Cairncross et al. 2003:2). Acute respiratory infections and diarrhea rank among the highest contributors to the disease burden in the developing world, and these are mostly diseases of the poor (WHO 2002:83).

A disproportionate share of environmental health risk is borne by the very young. Although children under five constitute just 10 percent of the world's population, they suffer 40 percent of the environment-related burden of disease. Diarrhea, caused by unclean water and inadequate sanitation, is responsible for the deaths of an estimated 1.8 million people worldwide each year, 1.6 million of which are children under five (Gordon et al. 2004:14).

Respiratory ailments are caused in large part from exposure to high levels of indoor smoke from cooking with dung, wood, or other biomass fuels. More than half the world's population— 3.5 billion people—currently depend on such fuels as their main energy source (Desai 2004:vii). Analysis by the International Energy Agency shows that this dependence will likely increase in the years ahead, with an additional 200 million people—most of them poor—relying on these fuels by 2030 (IEA 2002:30).

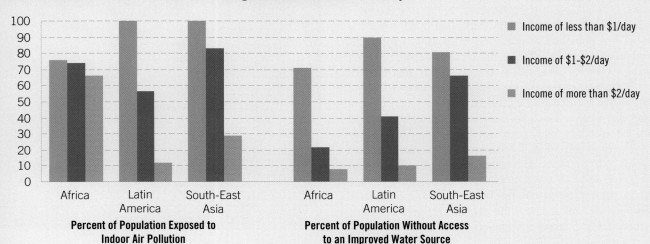

THE POOR ARE MORE VULNERABLE TO HEALTH RISKS

Environmental risk factors in countries with high adult and childhood mortality

Source: Blakely 2004:1990, 1992, 2003

Box 1.3 HEALTH, ENVIRONMENT, AND POVERTY

Indoor air pollution is linked to over 1.6 million deaths a year, 500,000 of them in India alone. More than half of those who die of respiratory infections related to indoor air pollution are children under the age of five (Warwick and Doig 2003:2). In urban areas, ambient air pollution from auto exhaust, industrial smoke stacks, dust, and other particulates is also a significant health risk. Ambient air pollution causes some 800,000 deaths a year, most of them in the developing world (WHO 2002:69).

Looking to the future, climate change comprises a considerable environmental health risk, since it can intensify existing environmental health threats. Vector-borne diseases such as malaria, dengue fever, schistosomiasis, and Chagas disease could expand their ranges as temperature and rainfall patterns change. Mosquitoes are among the first organisms to expand their range when climate conditions become favorable, so cases of malaria and dengue fever may increase their already heavy toll among the poor (WRI et al.1998:70). Diarrheal organisms are also sensitive to changes in temperature and humidity, with the health risk they pose increasing as average temperatures rise. A study in Peru found that hospital admissions for diarrhea increased as much as 12 percent for every 1 degree C increase in temperature (McMichael et al. 2003:215). On a broader scale, the World Health Organization estimates that in 2000, climate change was responsible for 2.4 percent of all cases of diarrhea and 2 percent of all cases of malaria worldwide (WHO 2002:72).

The Scourge of AIDS

AIDS poses one of the most potent health threats to poor households. High rates of infection are common in many of the poorest nations in Africa and Asia, and the disease has begun to ravage rural household economies in many areas. When AIDS strikes a family member—particularly a key wage-earner—it administers the kind of health shock that often drives the family into profound poverty. In the Tanzanian village of Kagabiro, households with an AIDS patient spent between 29 and 43 percent of household labor on AIDS-related duties—time that previously was available for earning money (Tibaijuka 1997 in Stover and Bollinger 1999:5). A study in Côte d'IVoire found that when a family member with AIDS died or moved away for treatment, average consumption in the family fell by as much as 44 percent the following year due to loss of income (Bechu 1998 in Stover and Bollinger 1999:4). Research on AIDS-afflicted families in rural Ethiopia found that the average cost of medical treatment, funeral, and mourning expenses amounted to several times the average household income (Demeke 1993 in Stover and Bollinger 1999:4).

AIDS also has profound effects on food security. In eastern Africa, AIDS-related labor shortages have led to lower crop yields, smaller amounts of land being cultivated, and a move from cash crops to subsistence crops, as the rural agricultural economy retrenches.

under state ownership provide the resource base for poor communities, but these communities often have no legal basis for their use of common pool resources. In many instances, these resources—whether they are forests, grazing areas, or fishing grounds—have been governed locally for centuries under traditional forms of "communal tenure," in which resources are owned in common by a group of individuals, such as a village or tribe.

Unfortunately, such customary arrangements are often not legally recognized, and conflicts between communal tenure and modern state-recognized ownership frequently threaten rural livelihoods. State recognition of such traditional ownership arrangements or new power-sharing agreements between local communities and the state that grant specific rights to use and profit from the state commons are often important ingredients in successful efforts to tap the wealth of natural systems (Meinzen-Dick and Di Gregorio 2004:1-2).

Lack of Voice, Participation, and Representation

When important decisions about local resources are made, the poor are rarely heard or their interests represented. Often these decisions, such as the awarding of a timber concession on state forest land that may be occupied by poor households, are made in the state capitol or in venues far removed from rural life. Even if they could make it to these decision-making venues, the poor—and other rural residents as well—would still be unlikely to find a seat at the table. The right for local resource users to participate in resource decisions is still a relatively new concept in most areas and often not embodied in law. Language barriers, ignorance of their legal rights, and a lack of full information about how resource decisions are likely to affect them are also potent obstacles to the participation of the poor. Lack of money, of political connections, and of lawyers or other advocates that can articulate their needs are all sources of political isolation and marginalization (WRI et al. 2003:44-64).

The Wealthy Dominate the Economic Machinery

Wealthier landowners and traders tend to dominate the resources and economic tools necessary to turn natural resources to wealth. In addition to owning more and better land, livestock, farm machinery, boats, or other assets directly relevant to profiting from ecosystems, the rich also tend to have greater access to resources like irrigation water, seed, fertilizers, pest control, and labor (Narayan and Petesch 2002:58-59, 188; Narayan et al. 2000:49-50; Kerr et al. 2002:61). The wealthy also have easier access to credit, which is a key constraint for the poor wishing to improve their ecosystem assets by planting trees, undertaking soil or water conservation projects, or developing new products or markets.

These advantages are often magnified by the dense and inter-linked social networks in rural areas, which tend to reinforce the near-monopoly position enjoyed by some wealthier families, leaving poorer families with fewer options and sometimes all-or-nothing choices (Bardhan 1991:240). For instance, surveys from West Bengal, India, found that laborers tied to their landlords through credit were less likely to take part in group bargaining and agitation for raising rural wages. These indentured workers felt it was a choice between a low wage or no job at all—a cycle of dependence that can be self-perpetuating (Bardhan 1991:240).

Capture of State-Owned Natural Resources by the Elite—Facilitated by Corruption

In many cases, state-owned resources like forests and fisheries are opened to exploitation by granting individuals or companies concessional leases or harvest licenses. The wealthy are much more likely to be able to take advantage of these. In Bangladesh, the government leases rights to fish in state-owned water bodies for a period of one to three years through a public auctioning system that generates considerable revenue for the state. Unfortunately, poor fishermen can rarely afford to bid, so the licenses are purchased by rich investors known as "waterlords." These entrepreneurs hire fisher-men as daily laborers at low wages, keeping most of the profits for themselves. This has led, in effect, to the institutionalized exploitation of the fishermen by a small rural elite (Béné 2003:964). In other instances, lease holders will exclude the poor altogether from their concession, even though they may have tradition-ally lived on and collected from these lands.

This problem of the capture of state resources by the elite is worsened by corruption, political patronage, and sweetheart deals for insiders. Such corruption and favoritism often focuses on natural resource concessions in remote areas far from official concern and public scrutiny—precisely those areas inhabited by the poor. In 2001, Bob Hasan, Indonesia's former Minister of Industry and Trade, was sentenced to prison for forest-related graft worth $75 million. For years, the timber magnate and close associate of former President Suharto dominated Indonesia's lucrative plywood trade, at one point controlling nearly 60 percent of world tropical plywood exports (Borsuk 2003:1; Barr 1998:2, 30).

Apart from its role in enabling the elite capture of state resources, corruption also stands as a fundamental obstacle to the sustainable management of resources and thus another way in which the natural assets of the poor are diminished. Illegal logging and fishing are prime causes of the depletion of common pool resources that the poor depend on, short-circuit-ing effective state management of ecosystems and undermining customary management arrangements at the village or tribal level as well (WRI et al. 2003:36-38). *(See Figure 1.4.)* Demands by local officials for bribes or other considerations for access to resources place a special burden on the poor and encourage low-income families to themselves engage in illegal logging, fishing, and other unsustainable resource uses. At a national level, corruption acts as a drag on the economy, behaving essentially as a tax on legitimate businesses. Research shows that corruption suppresses national economic growth—one of the main require-ments for effective and widespread poverty reduction (Thomas et al. 2000:144-150).

Anti-Poor Taxes and Regulations Work Against Economic Empowerment

In many countries, natural resource-related activities such as timber extraction, fishing, grazing, small-scale agriculture, and water use are subject to controls and taxes that are regressive with respect to the poor. In China, grain farmers—many of whom are poor—until recently were obliged to sell

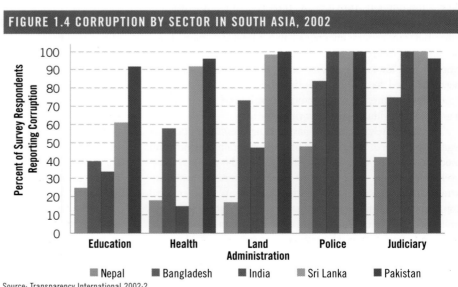

FIGURE 1.4 CORRUPTION BY SECTOR IN SOUTH ASIA, 2002

Percent of Survey Respondents Reporting Corruption

Education · Health · Land Administration · Police · Judiciary

■ Nepal   ■ Bangladesh   ■ India   ■ Sri Lanka   ■ Pakistan

Source: Transparency International 2002:2

the government a fixed quota of their production at below-market prices, essentially lowering their potential income (Ravallion and Chen 2004:21-22). In Uganda, households face a confusing array of resource-related taxes, which often appear arbitrary to rural families. These include taxes on activities as diverse as smoking fish, growing maize, and slaughtering cows or goats (Ellis and Bahiigwa 2003:1008-1009). Around Lake Chad in central Africa, fishery fees are levied by three distinct groups: by traditional authorities, by the central government, and by soldiers (Béné 2003:970). Such overlapping fees discourage low-income families from engaging in market transactions that would help them generate returns from their access to natural resources.

In addition, well-intentioned environmental regulations are sometimes introduced in a draconian way that hurts the poor. For example, there is evidence that China's 1998 ban on tree felling in the upper watersheds of the Yangtze and Yellow River Basins has had very negative impacts on some poor households. The ban was meant to restore the health of the watersheds and avoid repeating the disastrous floods on the Yangtze that had occurred earlier that year. However, expansion of the logging ban beyond state-owned forests into private and collectively owned land has cost numerous jobs and restricted local communities' access to forest products in these areas (Xu et al. 2002:6, 8). In Mali, a 1986 forest law banned bush fires, made felling of certain species illegal without Forest Department permission, and made wood-saving stoves compulsory. In response, the wood trade was forced underground, and poor people unable to pay fines levied against them had their livestock confiscated (Benjaminsen 2000:97, 99-100).

The Environment as a Route to Democratic Governance

The environment provides a powerful tool to promote democratic reform. Particularly among the poor, it offers a unique opening for localizing and building demand for democratic practices because of its connection with livelihoods. In turn, good environmental governance is essential to developing, strengthening, and consolidating democracy in the world's poorest nations because it is a prerequisite for the poor to realize greater income from the environment.

Counteracting the bias against the poor that is embedded in government policies, institutions, and laws will require significant political change. That in turn demands greater access by the poor to true participation, accurate information, and fair representation. The environment itself provides one effective route for this needed transition to democratic decision-making. In countless communities in Africa, Asia, and Latin America, control over and use of natural resources are matters of everyday survival. These are governance issues with immediate bearing. The prospect of more equitable decisions about land and resources gives the ideals of democracy personal relevance to the

poor. And it provides a motive for the kind of public activism that brings political change.

There are many examples of poor people organizing around environmental issues to prompt government action, gain rights, or call attention to gross inequities. The 1980s saw poor fishermen in the Indian state of Kerala organize to demand a seasonal ban on industrial trawlers that directly competed with local fishers and reduced their catch. Using tactics such as public fasts, road blocks, and marches against the government, the fishers became a political force that eventually coaxed fisheries managers to adopt a three-month seasonal ban on trawlers (Kurien 1992:238, 242-243). In Brazil's Amazon region, rubber tappers joined forces with the Indigenous People's Union to form the Alliance of Forest Peoples in the mid-1980s, demanding greater recognition of their resource rights. By 1995, their efforts had gained widespread support and the government designated some 900,000 ha of rainforest as Extractive Reserves (Brown and Rosendo 2000: 216).

Although initially the Green Belt Movement's tree planting activities did not address issues of democracy and peace, it soon became clear that responsible governance of the environment was impossible without democratic space. Therefore, the tree became a symbol for the democratic struggle in Kenya. Citizens were mobilized to challenge widespread abuses of power, corruption, and environmental mismanagement....

—Wangari Muta Maathai, Kenyan Environmental Activist and 2004 Nobel Peace Prize Winner, from her Nobel Laureate Lecture

Civil society in general has used the environment to great effect to push the process of democratization in regimes where civil liberties had been restricted. During the turn towards democracy in Chile and East Asia in the 1980s, and Eastern Europe in the 1990s, protests led by environment-focused civil society groups played an important role (McNeill 2000:347-348, WRI et al. 2003:67). For example, WAHLI, a prominent Indonesian environmental group, was one of the few NGOs tolerated by the Suharto government in the 1980s (Steele 2005).

The power of the environment as a stage for social action arose for two reasons. First, environmental problems were serious and were widely known, and second, environmental protests were seen—at least initially—as less overtly "political" and hence were more tolerated by government authorities. This ability for the environmental movement to maneuver where other civil society groups have not been given as much latitude is now manifesting in China, where activity by environmental NGOs is increasing (Economy 2005:1).

Linking Environment and Governance in the Global Poverty Fight

More than ever, national governments, international institutions, and donors are focused on poverty reduction. But their efforts have often given limited attention to the role of healthy ecosystems in providing sustainable livelihoods, and equally limited attention to the importance of environmental governance in empowering the poor. The models of economic growth that nations continue to rely on for poverty reduction—job creation through increased industrialization, intensified large-scale agriculture, industrial fishing fleets, and so on—do not fully appreciate the realities of rural livelihoods.

For example, these strategies miss the fundamental fact that if ecosystems decline through poor governance, the assets of the poor decline with them. Findings from the recently concluded Millennium Ecosystem Assessment—a five-year effort to survey the condition of global ecosystems—confirm that the burden of environmental decline already falls heaviest on the poor (MA 2005:2). This often results in an immediate drop in living standards—a descent into greater poverty. This in turn precipitates migration from rural areas to urban slums or a resort to unsustainable environmental practices—overfishing, deforestation, or depletion of soil nutrients—for bare survival's sake. For this reason alone—simply to prevent an *increase* in poverty—greater attention to ecosystem management and governance practices that serve the poor is vital. The promise that environment can be one of the engines of rural growth is all the more reason to keep environment as a focal point in poverty reduction efforts.

Refocusing the Millennium Development Goals

One way to increase the profile of environment and governance in poverty reduction is to make them more dynamic players in the global effort to achieve the Millennium Development Goals (MDGs). The MDGs represent a new commitment by the world community to concentrate on poverty alleviation. Nations have endorsed a limited set of universally accepted goals and time-bound targets, and have promised to measure progress toward these goals and hold the community of nations accountable. Goal 7 of the MDGs recognizes the connection between environmental sustainability and poverty reduction, with a specific commitment to "[i]ntegrate the principles of sustainable development into country policies and programs and reverse the loss of environmental resources" (UN General Assembly 2001).

Unfortunately, this sustainable development target is the least specific and the least understood by nations of all the MDG

targets, making it easy to pass over in favor of targets that are simpler to understand and measure, such as the provision of safe drinking water, or the reduction of infant mortality. In addition, no specific measures of governance (with the exception of measuring the tenure security of urban slum dwellers) are included in the sustainable development target, so the essential tie between a healthier environment and the governance of natural resources is missing.

Furthermore, the idea that the sustainable development goal is basic to the achievement of all the other goals and central to lasting progress against poverty is acknowledged in the MDG structure, but it is not elaborated in a way that guides nations to act or gives them adequate measures of how well they are integrating sustainable development principles in their work to meet the other MDGs (UNDP 2005:3-5). Addressing these important lacks requires clearer guidance on the links between ecosystems, governance, and each MDG, as well as an expanded slate of indicators that better encompasses the governance dimension of these goals.

Refocusing Poverty Reduction Strategies

Much the same kind of criticism can be made of the process that developing countries are using to design their national efforts to reduce poverty. Guided by the World Bank, poor nations are drawing up formal plans—called *poverty reduction strategy papers*, or PRSPs—that describe how they envision creating the conditions for growth and social development that will raise incomes and lower national poverty rates (Bojö and Reddy 2003:3).

PRSPs themselves represent a significant step toward pro-poor development. They arose out of the realization that the structural economic reforms recommended in earlier decades by the International Monetary Fund and the World Bank—polices such as market liberalization and an emphasis on export-oriented trade—have not yet produced enough growth in many poor nations to result in sufficient progress against poverty (Reed 2004:7-9). Therefore the Bank and the IMF have encouraged poor nations to draw up their own blueprints for poverty reduction through a process of national consultation. Being self-generated, it is hoped these strategies will better engage poor nations' poverty efforts and provide a guide for development aid from the World Bank and wealthy nations (IMF 2004:3).

Just as with the Millennium Development Goals, however, the initial attempts at poverty reduction strategies have taken little note of the centrality of ecosystems in the lives of the poor and the need to enhance the ability of the poor to govern them as sustainable sources of income. For example, a survey of initial PRSPs in 11 West African nations showed that they paid little attention to the small-scale fishing sector, even though this sector provides one of the major sources of livelihoods for the poor in the region and is faced with a declining resource base (FAO 2002:iv). More generally, analysis has shown that environmental concerns are often poorly mainstreamed in PRSPs.

This is beginning to change as PRSPs mature from draft to final versions (Bojö et al. 2004:xii). For example, Cambodia's poverty plan emphasizes the importance of increasing environmental income through community forestry and small-scale fisheries management, as well as better market access for small farmers (Cambodia PRSP 2002:53, 60-61). Still, few PRSPs contain quantified, time-bound targets for improved environmental conditions or better resource management (Bojö et al. 2004:xii).

Since PRSPs provide a national roadmap to poverty reduction, it is particularly important that they do a better job of highlighting the role of natural resources in rural development and prioritizing the need to strengthen local capacity to manage ecosystems. This means they must grapple with the issue of how best to devolve control over natural resources to local communities in a way that empowers the poor rather than simply transferring power to local elites. PRSPs must also adopt a long-term perspective that identifies lasting poverty reduction with sustainability, rather than focusing totally on short-term economic growth. Typically, PRSPs do not reflect long-term strategic thinking about the environment (Bojö and Reddy 2003:1, 9) or the consequences of possible environmental change from climate instability, land use change, pollution, population, or other forces.

From Vulnerability to Wealth

Progress on incorporating ecosystems and governance into the Millennium Development Goals and the PRSP process is only a first step in the effort to make the environment a way out of poverty, rather than another source of vulnerability for the poor. Completing this transition will require much more. It will demand local institutions that are accessible to the poor and empowered to manage local ecosystems; secure tenure that gives the poor a legal stake in good resource management; and viable models to commercialize nature-based products and services, including access to credit, transportation, and marketing savvy. And it will demand scientific guidance and technical help to optimize ecosystem management at low cost, and to ensure that local uses of nature do not threaten ecosystems at larger geographical scales and are consistent with national environmental goals. Facilitating this must be pro-poor political change that increases the accountability of government officials and service providers to the poor, and recognizes the potential role of the poor in national economic growth.

The chapters that follow expand on these themes, providing examples of the vital role that nature can play in poverty alleviation if governance, economic, and management factors are aligned. In doing so, it shows how both social and environmental goals depend on each other for their achievement and must be pursued simultaneously. *World Resources 2005: The Wealth of the Poor* is not only an exploration of the power of nature to provide sustainable livelihoods and support rural growth that increases the incomes and options of the poor. It is equally an exploration of the power of nature as a means toward democratic change and greater social equity.

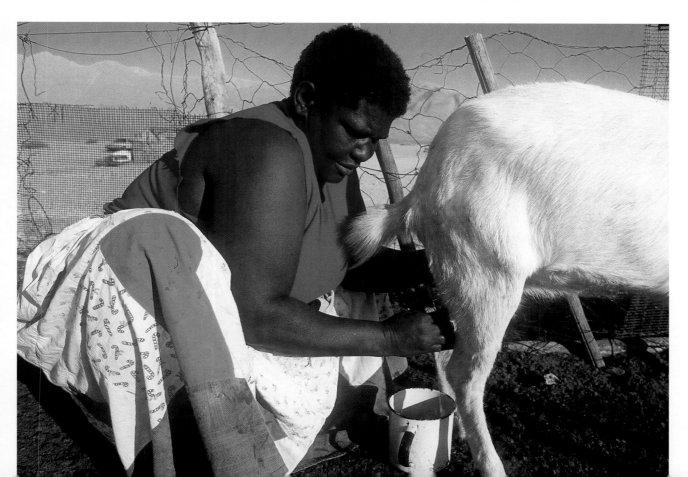

BOX 1.4 POVERTY AND GOVERNANCE IN A GLOBAL FRAME

MANY OF THE OBSTACLES THE POOR FACE IN turning their natural assets into wealth manifest themselves at the local and national levels. But these governance and economic obstacles often have their roots in policies and practices at the global level. The arenas of international trade, development aid, and international finance and investment influence global poverty trends, in as much as they influence the broad economic and political setting that poor people find themselves in.

Over the past five years, the controversy over the benefits and dangers of globalization has highlighted the power of international policies to affect poverty. This influence can be positive: inflows of capital, goods, and services to developing countries exceeded US$2.5 trillion in 2003 (World Bank 2005). Several East Asian countries like China, Korea, and Taiwan have used export-oriented trade to spur the economic growth that helped many of their citizens escape poverty. China has also attracted large quantities of foreign direct investment, another growth accelerant. Remittances that immigrants to industrialized countries send back home provide a vital source of funds for many developing nations. In addition, industrialized countries provide significant amounts of technical assistance and foreign aid to developing countries—more than US$76 billion in 2003 (World Bank 2005).

But the fact remains that just as national power is generally controlled by a limited group of powerful individuals and companies, international economics and politics are also dominated by a limited group of wealthier countries. Even when benefits to poor countries do occur, they tend to be restricted

RICH COUNTRIES DOMINATE GLOBAL EXPORTS

Global Exports of Goods and Services, 1990-2002

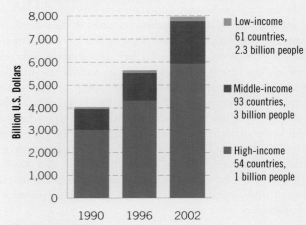

Source: World Bank 2005

to a few countries with the ability to compete in the global marketplace. In 2003 only ten percent of all exports from developing countries originated in the 61 nations classified as "Low Income" by the World Bank (World Bank 2005).

The resulting inequality in global power can exacerbate the causes of rural poverty, dampen growth in developing nation economies, or encourage models of development that may be less effective at reducing poverty. This is why decisions made in industrialized countries are the focus of so much attention in the worldwide debate over poverty reduction.

FINANCIAL FLOWS TO DEVELOPING COUNTRIES, 1980-2002

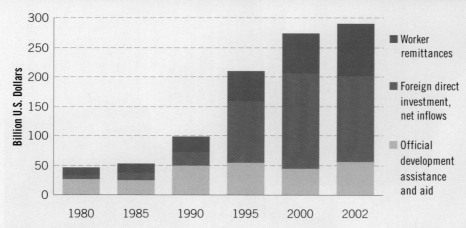

Source: World Bank 2005

Capital inflows can act as a growth accelerant to developing economies. They typically take one of three forms: (1) Official aid includes grant and loans by governments and international institutions to developing countries to promote economic development and welfare; (2) foreign direct investment (FDI) is private investment in a foreign economy to obtain an ownership interest in an enterprise; (3) Worker's remittances include the transfer of earned wages by migrant workers to their home country.

Total Investment in Billion US Dollars

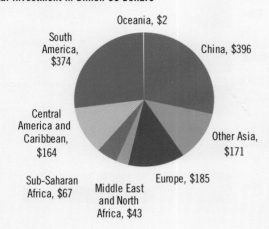

Source: World Bank 2005

The Effects of Private Investment Are Mixed

Foreign direct investment (FDI)—the acquisition of an ownership interest in a private enterprise—became the dominant route for money flowing from rich to poor countries after the liberalization of global financial markets in the 1970s (Oxfam 2002:11, 15). In 2002 the overseas investments of 64,000 corporations supported 53 million jobs worldwide (UNCTAD 2003:4).

Private investment does not necessarily benefit the poor, however. In the past decade, 80 percent of the private investment in developing countries has gone to just 15 countries—and they are not the world's poorest countries (World Bank 2005). In 2003, for example, the 50 least-developed countries received only 4 percent of private investment to developing countries (UNCTAD 2004:48; World Bank 2005). The investment environment in poor countries is often unattractive, for they lack the economic stability, coherent legal system, and physical infrastructure that investors seek.

In addition, FDI is typically channeled into infrastructure and larger-scale investments, rather than small or medium-scale enterprises that might benefit the poor. Thus FDI investments may help the poor in the long term, but have not been proven to reduce poverty in the near term. In Latin America, foreign private investment has increased sixfold since 1981 due to expansion in the oil, gas, timber, water, and mining sectors. However, the percentage of the population living below the poverty line has not changed significantly, and the absolute number of poor people in Latin America actually increased from 200 million in 1990 to 225 million in 2003 (World Bank 2004; FAO 2004).

Private investment can help developing nations acquire capital to fund domestic projects, receive new technology and skills, and improve productivity. Without proper regulations, however, it can also increase economic volatility if investors lose interest and pull out. Economic volatility has historically hurt the poor. Since the 1970s, wages have declined in developing countries during economic contractions without expanding to previous levels during periods of growth. An analysis of 32 developing countries experiencing currency crises shows a total wage loss of $545 billion between 1980 and 1998; subsequent recoveries only offset about one-third of this loss (Oxfam 2002:33-36).

International Aid Can Miss Its Target

The international community plays an important role in providing technical and financial support to developing countries. From 1998 to 2003, official development assistance increased by more than one-third, to US$76 billion (World Bank 2005). There has been a concerted effort by donors in the last decade to focus more on poverty reduction in the broadest sense, and most aid agencies are now actively working to support the Millennium Development Goals (MDGs).

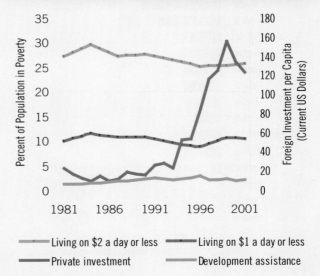

Source: World Bank 2004, 2005

BOX 1.4 POVERTY AND GOVERNANCE IN A GLOBAL FRAME

Accompanying this move towards a greater poverty focus has been a shift by donors away from funding individual projects and toward more programmatic support. While this is a welcome development, many countries still formally "tie" their aid, requiring it to be used to purchase goods or professional services from the donor country. This has been estimated to reduce aid effectiveness by roughly 25 percent compared to untied aid (World Bank 2005).

Technical assistance (TA) is earmarked in many aid packages to provide countries with the knowledge to utilize aid effectively; in 2003 it accounted for more than 25 percent of all aid transfers. While TA can build capacity in developed countries, it can also divert much-needed funds away from their intended recipients. For example, records from the United Kingdom Department for International Development reveal that the 34 largest recipients of its TA contracts are private firms in developed countries (Greenhill and Watt 2005:22).

There has been an ongoing international campaign to reduce the debt that many low-income countries have accumulated over the years. Some debt relief has been forthcoming, but many argue

CONDITIONALITY OF DEVELOPMENT AID, 2002

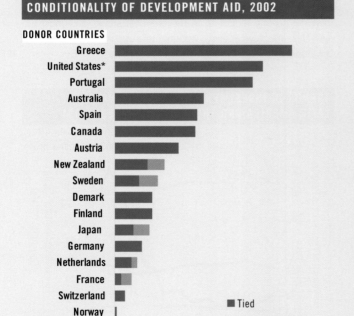

DONOR COUNTRIES

Greece
United States*
Portugal
Australia
Spain
Canada
Austria
New Zealand
Sweden
Demark
Finland
Japan
Germany
Netherlands
France
Switzerland
Norway
United Kingdom
Ireland

■ Tied
■ Partially tied

Percent of Net Disbursements

* Data are from 1996.

Source: United Nations Millennium Project 2004

U.S. AGRICULTURAL PRICE SUPPORTS, 2002

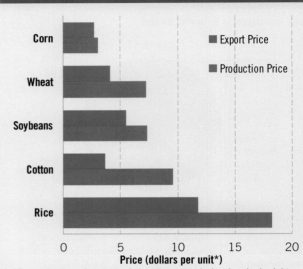

Corn
Wheat
Soybeans
Cotton
Rice

■ Export Price
■ Production Price

Price (dollars per unit*)

*Corn, wheat, soybeans: bushel; cotton: pound; rice: hundredweight

Source: Environmental Working Group 2005; World Bank 2005

that more is needed (UNDP 2003:14-15, 49). Advocates of development assistance worry, however, that aid agencies measure debt relief in a way that exaggerates its importance relative to other types of aid, since it does not represent actual monetary transfers to a country or contribute directly to poverty reduction (Greenhill and Watt 2005:20).

Agricultural Trade Policy Favors Industrialized Countries

The world's existing trading system puts most developing countries at a disadvantage. Agricultural products, which make up the main exports of many developing countries, still face heavy tariffs in rich countries. It has been estimated that developing countries would gain well over US$100 billion a year from trade liberalization resulting in reduced tariffs—much more than they receive in current aid flows (Anderson 2004:14-15, 49).

At the same time, rich countries often subsidize their own farmers and the agricultural products they sell abroad. These subsidies enable the products to be sold on world markets at prices below the cost of production. Such "dumping" practices deprive developing countries of vital export markets and suppress world agricultural commodity prices (Murphy et al. 2004:2-5).

Agricultural subsidies are currently high on the agenda of the World Trade Organization (WTO), which provides a forum for

AFRICAN COUNTRIES' DEPENDENCE ON SINGLE-COMMODITY EXPORTS

Country	Commodity	PERCENT SHARE OF		
		Gross National Income	Total Merchandise Exports	Total Agricultural Exports
Malawi	Tobacco leaves	23.8	59	74
Sao Tome and Principe	Cocoa beans	16.9	69	97
Burundi	Coffee	7.2	75	83
Kenya	Tea	6.5	26	42
Guinea-Bissau	Cashew nuts	6.3	48	91
Chad	Cotton	5.7	37	71
Ethiopia	Coffee	5.4	62	69
Burkina Faso	Cotton	4.9	39	77

Source: FAO 2002

Many developing nations depend heavily on agricultural exports. These nations are susceptible to fluctuations in prices for the commodities they export, and are hurt by subsidies and dumping in these markets by developed nations.

FAIR TRADE?
U.S. COTTON SUBSIDIES AND THE GROSS DOMESTIC PRODUCT OF SELECTED COTTON-EXPORTING COUNTRIES, 2003

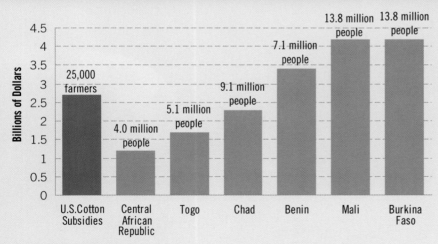

Source: Environmental Working Group 2005

Annual subsidies for 142,000 cotton growers in the United States have averaged $3 billion in recent years. Eighty-five percent of these subsidies go to 25,000 farmers. This is roughly comparable in size to the entire economy of some African countries dependent on cotton exports. Country populations in 2003 are shown above each bar.

negotiating global trade agreements. The WTO offers some advantages for developing countries in that each country has an equal vote, so developing countries comprise the largest group. Still, the world's largest trading nations have historically dominated the WTO's trade negotiations. That may be starting to shift, as shown by the coordinated action taken by developing nations at the WTO's meeting in Cancun in 2003, where they refused to back down from their demands (CAFOD 2003).

Nonetheless, wealthy nations continue to hold enormous trade advantages. Using export credit agencies, they invest millions of dollars each year to build markets for their own exports (Maurer 2003:13). They also pursue bilateral trade agreements with individual or small groups of developing nations. In bilateral negotiations with strong trading powers such as the United States or the European Union, developing countries have a much weaker negotiating position than at the WTO.

Harvests from forests, fisheries, and farm fields are the primary source of income for the rural poor worldwide. Yet the full potential of ecosystems as a wealth-creating asset for the poor has yet to be effectively tapped.

ECOSYSTEMS AND THE LIVELIHOODS OF THE POOR

ECOSYSTEMS PROVIDE THE FOUNDATION FOR ALL HUMAN survival, since they produce the food, air, soil, and other material supports for life. Everyone, rich and poor, urban and rural, depends on the goods and services that ecosystems provide.

But the rural poor have a unique and special relationship with ecosystems that revolves around the importance of these natural systems to rural livelihoods. By *livelihoods*, we mean the whole complex of factors that allow families to sustain themselves materially, emotionally, spiritually, and socially. Central to this is *income*, whether in the form of cash, or in the form of natural products directly consumed for subsistence, such as fish, fuel, or building materials.

As this chapter will show, the rural poor derive a significant fraction of their total income from ecosystem goods and services. We refer to such nature-based income as *environmental income*. Because of their dependence on environmental income, the poor are especially vulnerable to ecosystem degradation.

Of course, environmental income is not the only important component in rural livelihoods. A poor family's total income is generally derived from at least four different sources:

- environmental income (including small-scale agriculture),
- income from wage labor (such as agricultural labor) and home businesses,
- remittances (money or goods sent from relatives outside the community), and
- other transfer payments, such as assistance from state agencies.

All these sources are important, and none can be ignored without losing sight of the reality of the rural economy. However, this chapter's primary concern is exploring how environmental income fits into rural livelihoods. This includes asking how important it is compared to other types of income, where it comes from, how it is obtained, and what role it plays in the total livelihoods of the poor. Even though this chapter dwells primarily on income, it does so with the cognizance that maximizing income is only one component of a total *livelihoods approach* to development.

How Important is Environmental Income?

Environmental income—the income generated from ecosystem goods and services—is a major constituent of the household incomes of the rural poor. It includes income from natural systems such as forests, grasslands, lakes, and marine waters. It also includes agricultural income—the output of agroecosystems.

Researchers often make a distinction between agricultural income and what in this report we term "wild income"—that is, income from less manipulated natural systems like forests and fisheries. This distinction means that these two income streams are often counted and analyzed separately. Wild income deserves special attention, since it is often the element that is not accurately accounted for in most considerations of rural livelihoods. But both agricultural and wild income are important to an accurate assessment of the dependence of the poor on ecosystems for income. In addition, there is overlap between the two, as in the use of forest grasses for livestock forage, or forest leaf litter as a soil amendment or crop mulch.

Environmental income can be derived in several distinct ways. Income might accrue to households through direct use of ecosystem services, for instance, by consuming bushmeat and other wild foods, cutting fodder for livestock, using wood products in home construction, or eating produce grown in a home garden. Where markets exist, goods harvested from ecosystems, such as fish, herbs, or fuelwood, can be sold for cash or exchanged for services like school tuition. In addition, communities may charge stumpage fees for providing loggers

---

WHAT ARE ECOSYSTEM GOODS AND SERVICES?

Just as the physical forms of ecosystems vary widely—from delicate coral reefs to arid deserts—so do the array of goods and services available to local communities. The benefits that humans obtain from ecosystems fall into four main categories (MA 2003:53-60):

Provisioning services comprise the production of basic goods such as crops and livestock, drinking and irrigation water, fodder, timber, biomass fuels, and fiber such as cotton and wool.

Regulating services are the benefits obtained as ecosystem processes affect the physical and biological world around them. These services include flood protection and coastal protection by mangroves and reefs; pollination; regulation of water and air quality; the modulation of disease vectors; the absorption of wastes; and the regulation of climate.

Cultural services are the nonmaterial benefits people obtain from ecosystems through spiritual enrichment, cognitive development, reflection, recreation, and aesthetic experiences. These provide the basis for cultural diversity, spiritual and religious values, as well as the more prosaic experience of tourism.

Supporting services are those that are necessary for the production of all other ecosystem services. Their impacts are indirect or extend over long time-scales. They include primary production of biomass through photosynthesis, soil formation, production of atmospheric oxygen, and nutrient cycling.

TABLE 2.1 NUMBER OF PEOPLE DEPENDENT ON ECOSYSTEMS

Dependent on forests in some way	**1.6 billion**
■ Smallholder farmers who grow farm trees or manage remnant forests for subsistence and income	500 million to 1 billion
■ Indigenous people wholly dependent on forests	$60 million
Poor dependent on agriculture in Sub-Saharan Africa	**>500 million**
Rural poor who keep livestock	**600 million**
■ Landless rural poor who keep livestock	150 million
Fishers and fish-farmers in the Lower Mekong River basin	**40 million**

Source: Angelsen and Wunder 2003; IFAD et al. 2004; Kura et al. 2004; Haggblade et al. 2004

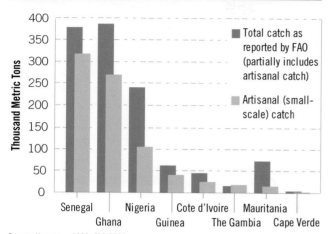

FIGURE 2.1 ARTISANAL AND TOTAL CATCH FOR SELECTED WEST AFRICAN COUNTRIES, 1996

Legend:
- Total catch as reported by FAO (partially includes artisanal catch)
- Artisanal (small-scale) catch

Y-axis: Thousand Metric Tons

Countries: Senegal, Ghana, Nigeria, Guinea, Cote d'Ivoire, The Gambia, Mauritania, Cape Verde

Source: Horemans 1998; FAO 2004

At the national level, environmental income is also important, not only to the poor, but to national economies. Small-scale fisheries, for example, are not only common sources of income for the impoverished but are major contributors to the economies of many nations. In Asia small-scale fisheries contributed 25 percent of the total fisheries production of Malaysia, the Philippines, Thailand, and Taiwan for the decade ending in 1997 (Kura et al. 2004:38). In West Africa the importance of small-scale fishing is greater still, constituting three-fourths of the region's total fish catch (Kura et al. 2004:39). In Indonesia, small-scale fishers are responsible for almost 95 percent of the total marine catch (FAO 2000a:2). *(See Figure 2.1.)*

At the same time, export revenues from small-scale agriculture are vital to many poor nations. In Mali, cotton grown by small-holder farmers generates 8 percent of the nation's GDP and 15 percent of all government revenues. Some 30 percent of all Malian households grow cotton on small plots, and it is second only to gold as the nation's most important export (Tefft 2004:1).

access to timber, or they may collect taxes or levees from hunters or tourists, or royalties for access to minerals or the use of local species for pharmaceutical research. The income benefits of these public revenues may then be passed on to households in the form of public infrastructure like roads, schools, and clinics, or public services like agricultural extension programs.

Ecosystems have several characteristics that make them attractive as a source of income. Environmental resources are renewable, widespread, and they are often found in common property areas where the poor can access them without owning the land (Cavendish 2000:1980). In addition, exploiting natural systems often can be done with little need for investment or expensive equipment, making the cost of entry low—an important consideration for poor families with limited assets.

Important at Every Scale

The importance of environmental income to the poor can be judged at different scales. At the global scale, estimates of nature's contribution to livelihoods are impressive. For example, the World Bank estimates that 90 percent of the world's 1.1 billion poor—those living on $1 per day or less—depend on forests for at least some of their income (World Bank 2002:1). Agriculture is likewise essential to poor families. Small-scale agriculture—the kind the poor practice—accounts for more than 90 percent of Africa's agricultural production (Spencer 2001:1). In addition, over 600 million of the world's poor keep livestock, a critical cash asset for many (IFAD et al. 2004:1).

The Food and Agriculture Organization estimates that over 90 percent of the 15 million people working the world's coastal waters are small-scale fishers, most of them poor. That does not count the tens of millions of the poor who fish inland rivers, lakes, ponds, and even rice paddies (FAO 2002 in Kura et al. 2004:35). *(See Table 2.1.)*

THE COMPONENTS OF ENVIRONMENTAL INCOME

Environmental Income *is the value derived—in cash or direct use—from ecosystem goods and services.* As we use the term in this report, environmental income is the sum of two important income streams.

- **Wild Income:** Income from wild or uncultivated natural systems, such as forests, marine and inland fisheries, reefs, wetlands, and grasslands. This includes commodities such as fish, timber, and nontimber forest products such as fuelwood, game, medicinals, fruits and other foods, and materials for handicrafts or art. It also includes income from nature-based tourism, as well as payments that rural landowners might receive for environmental services such as carbon storage or preservation of watershed functions.

- **Agricultural Income:** Income from agroecosystems—all agricultural lands, such as croplands, pastures, or orchards. In the context of the poor, agricultural income is mostly generated through small-scale agriculture, including commodity crops, home gardens, and large and small livestock. Income from aquaculture would also fit in this category.

Environmental income could also reasonably include a third component:

- **Mineral and Energy Income:** Income from mining or extraction of oil, gas, hydrothermal energy, or hydroelectric energy. Large-scale mineral and energy exploitation is not usually a direct source of income for poor rural households, so in this report we do not consider this income stream as part of rural livelihoods.

We should note that other definitions of environmental income exist that are not as broad-reaching as ours (see Vedeld et al. 2004:5-6). Our aim is to account for all sources of income based on nature that figure into the household budgets of the poor or can be tapped by them for sustainable wealth creation.

ADOPTING A *LIVELIHOODS APPROACH* TO DEVELOPMENT

Livelihoods are our means of everyday support and subsistence. As commonly conceived, a livelihood generates financial resources that come from employment or subsistence activities. But livelihoods also draw on other resources: human and social resources that give structure and context to our daily lives, as well as the natural and physical resources that underpin our work. In the 1990s, development agencies began to adopt this more holistic view of livelihoods, with the goal of focusing development activities more effectively. The UN Development Programme's *Human Development Reports* in particular drew attention to human well-being—defined by health, education, opportunity, a healthy environment, and a decent standard of living—as the core of development practice (Solesbury 2003:vii).

The United Kingdom's Department for International Development (DFID) made the "sustainable livelihoods approach" a core principle of its development strategy in 1997 (Solesbury 2003:vi). Building in part from the *Human Development Reports* and the 1987 Brundtland Commission Report, *Our Common Future,* DFID's approach assesses the strengths and vulnerabilities of poor people in terms of five types of capital: human, social, natural, physical, and financial (UK DFID 1999:2.3). As opposed to the more traditional focus on macroeconomic policies, this approach puts people at the center of development and is inherently nonsectoral. It also explicitly concerns itself with the condition of the natural resource base.

The "sustainability" element of the livelihoods approach is achieved by helping people to build resistance to external shocks and stresses, maintain the long-term productivity of natural resources, move away from dependence on unsustainable outside support, and avoid undermining the livelihood options of others. Addressing these challenges requires that development agencies view the poor as a mixed, rather than a homogenous, group, and tailor policies to the various sub-groups. Listening to the poor and involving them in the policy process is a key part of this approach (UK DFID 1999:5, 7; Chambers and Conway 1991:6).

The sustainable livelihoods approach has been recognized and adopted to varying degrees by a number of development agencies. One of the challenges of its application is finding ways to match such a dynamic framework to existing policies and institutions (Hussein 2002:55). That is why an emphasis on governance—dealing with who wields power and how decisions are made—has become a key element in modern development practice.

HOW IS ENVIRONMENTAL INCOME CALCULATED?

Environmental Income of a Small-Scale Fisher

Gross Value of Natural Resource
- Value of fish consumed by producer (subsistence income)
- Sales at market* (cash income)

Labor and Materials Costs
- Labor Costs: fishing, repairing equipment, etc
- Capital Costs: purchase or rental of nets, fishing rods, boats, etc.

TOTAL ENVIRONMENTAL INCOME =
Gross Value of Resource − Labor and Materials Costs

* Includes value added by producer through preparation such as smoking, preserving, etc.

Environmental income—the value of goods and services from ecosystems—can be difficult to measure. Typically, it is calculated as the gross value of natural resource goods minus the cost of labor and materials needed to collect and sell these goods (Vedeld et al. 2004:6). The environmental income for a family dependent on fisheries is illustrated above. The gross value of the natural resource (fish) would include both the value of the fish consumed by the household and the price of any fish sold at market. The total environmental income is calculated by subtracting from the gross value any labor and materials costs, such as rental fees for boats or the purchase price of fishing rods and nets.

Assessing environmental income at the household level is the most difficult, but also the most valuable in judging how much of a factor nature-based income is in the lives of the poor and whether it can be increased or at least made more secure. Household surveys have been used for decades to measure income and consumption patterns, but they have not traditionally assessed what portion of this income was from natural resources (Cavendish 2000:1980). As a result, the kind of comprehensive data needed to quantify the dependence of the poor on environmental income has been scarce, increasing the tendency of policymakers to minimize the environment in their poverty prescriptions.

In recent years, researchers have begun to fill this breach with quantitative studies of environmental income at the village and household level. While the amount and dependence on environmental income differs depending on the ecosystem, the community, and other social and economic factors, these studies have confirmed that environmental income is near-universally important to poor households.

Estimating the Importance of Wild Income

William Cavendish's study of 30 villages in the Shindi ward of Zimbabwe in the late 1990s provides a careful look at how the poor make use of nature-based income. Cavendish's survey of nearly 200 households excluded farm income, concentrating on wild income from forests and other natural sources, particularly common areas in the public domain. He found that this kind of environmental income constituted over 35 percent of total household income. It was not usually obtained from one source, but many small sources combined. Households derived direct subsistence value from collecting firewood, consuming fruits and berries, and browsing their livestock. They received cash income from the sale of materials, fruits, medicines, or meat they had collected or hunted. They even derived some income from small-scale gold panning. Cavendish also found that the dependence of households on environmental income decreased as their average incomes rose. Although the poor tended to get more of their total income from the environment, the rich still made heavy use of natural products for income (Cavendish 2000:1979, 1990, 1991).

TABLE 2.2 DIVERSE USES OF ENVIRONMENTAL INCOME

Location	Ecosystem	Goods or Services Used	Benefit to Households
Shindi Ward, Southern Zimbabwe	Forests and grasslands	Wild fruits, timber, thatching grass, livestock fodder	Ecosystems contribute an average of 35% of total income. Cavendish 2000
Southern Malawi	Forest	Firewood, fruit, mushrooms, bushmeat, insects, honey	Forest income contributes up to 30% of total income. Fisher 2004
Gulf of Mannar, India	Reefs	Seaweed, shellfish, sea cucumber, medicines, lobster	Reefs are often the only source of cash income for poor families, providing up to $199 of income annually. Whittingham et al. 2003
Coquimbo Region, Chile	Semi-Arid	Pasture, fodder	80–90% of poor households use common pool resources. Bahamondes 2003
Iquitos, Peru	Tropical forest	Non-timber forest products, including fruits, latexes, medicines, tourism and carbon sequestration	Forests provide $422 of potential sustainable income per hectare annually. Lampietti and Dixon 1995
Budongo Forest, Uganda	Semi-deciduous tropical forest	Fuel wood, building materials, wood for furniture, food, medicinal plants	Biomass provides 90% of the energy needs for the country and between 6% and 25% of household income in Bundongo village. Aryal 2002
Bushbuckridge District, South Africa	Agriculture	All crops including maize, cassava, morogo, various fruits	Total value of wild and crop plants was US$269 per household per year. High and Shackleton 2000
Chimaliro Forest Reserve, Malawi	Agriculture	Maize, cassava, ground nuts, pulses, soy beans, potatoes	Food crops contributed between 45% and 55% of household income. Botha et al. 2004
Jhabua, Madhya Pradesh, India	Agriculture	Agriculture, fuelwood, timber, fodder for livestock	Environmental income (including agriculture and resource collection) was the largest household income source for the poorest 25%. Narain et al. 2005

MISUNDERSTANDING THE WEALTH OF THE POOR

It is often difficult to assign a monetary value to the ecosystem goods and services on which the poor rely. Some have a market value when sold, but many are consumed locally or at home, and do not enter into the formal economy. In effect, the poor exist in an informal, and often unrecognized, economy. This has led to the systematic undervaluation of the assets of the poor and the underestimation of the potential benefits of sound ecosystem management.

Several studies have tried to delineate this "other economy" of the rural poor. A recent World Bank analysis, for example, found that the poor derive, on average, one-fifth of their household income from forests, mostly from nontimber products like wild foods, fuel, fodder, and thatch grass (Vedeld et al. 2004:27-29). Regretfully, much of the economic value of forests to the poor is missed in official state accountings of the forest economy.

Kenya is a typical example. By official estimate, the formal forest sector only generates about $2 million in earnings per year for sawn timber, pulp, and other industrial wood products. This is dwarfed by the value of the informal forestry sector, which contributes some $94 million in value to rural households in the form of charcoal, fuelwood, and the panoply of other forest products. And this does not include the recreational value of forests for leisure and tourism, which could come to $30 million or so. Since so much of this forest value accrues to the informal sector, most of its value is missed (Mogaka et al. 2001:17).

This undervaluation causes decision-makers to assign a lower priority to intact forest ecosystems as an economic asset than they should. For example, in spite of their place in rural livelihoods, woodfuels are generally not seriously considered in rural development plans and poverty reduction strategies, even though they provide the majority of the energy requirements of poor families on every continent (Arnold et al. 2003:25; IEA 2002:27).

A similar situation exists with small-scale fisheries. Despite the unquestioned importance of coastal and inland fisheries to the poor, small-scale fisheries are also an overlooked resource in most poverty alleviation strategies (Béné 2003:949). Again, this reflects the fact that fisheries income for the poor frequently escapes official notice, since fish are often locally consumed, and often at home. A survey in four rural Cambodian provinces found that, even though three-fourths of households engage in fishing as a primary or secondary occupation, fully half of them never sell any fish in the open market (Degen et al. 2000:1, 20).

If programs to alleviate poverty continue to undervalue the assets of the poor and misunderstand the dynamics of the informal economy, they will remain only partially effective. Better valuation and accounting of wild income, as well as income from home-based agriculture, is part of any sensible strategy to incorporate environmental income into poverty reduction programs.

Other studies confirm Cavendish's general findings. Research in South Africa found communities regularly using between 18 and 27 wild products, the most valuable again being fuelwood, construction wood, wild fruits and herbs, and fodder (Shackleton et al. 2000a:2). Quantities consumed per household can be substantial. Average annual usage figures of 5.3 metric tons of fuelwood, 104 kg of edible fruits, 58 kg of wild vegetables, and 185 large poles for house construction and fencing are typical in rural South Africa (Shackleton and Shackleton 2004:658; Shackleton et al. 2000a:2).

Subsistence use represents the greater part of the value of these natural products to households. Home use of wild products brings a direct reduction in cash expenditures of households—a form of income that is essential to the survival of the very poor. Estimated cash equivalents for subsistence use of wild products ranged from US$194 to US$1,114 per year over a series of seven studies in South Africa—a significant income fraction (Shackleton et al. 2000a:2).

But wild products can be a considerable source of cash income. In the Indian state of Kerala, residents in the Wayanand district sell wild foods such as honey and mushrooms, along with coveted gooseberries and other medicinal plants, earning an annual average of Rs. 3,500 (US$75) per household (Shylajan and Mythili 2003:109, 112-113). Likewise, medicinal-plant vendors in rural South Africa bring in significant cash, with a mean annual income of 16,700 rand (US$2,680) (Botha et al. 2004). At the other end of the scale, rural charcoal makers in Kenya sell a 30-35 kilogram bag of charcoal for a mere 280 Ksh (US$3.50) to middle men who transport it to Nairobi for cooking fuel (Kantai 2002:16). *(See Table 2.2.)*

Gauging the importance of wild income to a poor family's total income is difficult, of course, because the amount of such income is highly variable across families and across the seasons. In general, however, wild income tends to be more an auxiliary source rather than the main income source for most poor families. But there are many exceptions to this rule. For example, in some alpine villages in the Western Himalayas, wild income provides around 70 percent of household income, mostly from grazing of sheep and goats and the collection of medicines and herbs (Asher et al. 2002: 20). If markets—such as tourists—are handy, wild income can be impressive. A skilled wood carver using native materials in Namibia, for example, can earn as much as US$1,800 per year by plying the tourist trade. In general, however, wild income contributes more modestly to total income, providing perhaps 15-40 percent of family income, if current studies are any guide (Shylajan and Mythili 2003:100-102; Cavendish 2000; Beck and Nesmith 2001).

Although the value of many wild products seems small when considered in isolation, their aggregate value can be substantial, and their contribution to rural economies crucial. In South Africa, Shackleton has estimated the value of wild products extracted by households in the savanna biome alone at 8 billion rand (US$1.3 billion) per year—a figure that works out to about R750-1,000 (US$120-160) per hectare of accessible land. That compares favorably with the economic productivity of cattle ranching and plantation forestry in these areas. In fact, when collection and sale of wild products is compared head to head with other rural employment options, it often proves to be more lucrative. In Nigeria, research shows that returns on labor are 3-4 times higher for harvesting and selling woodland products than for agricultural wage labor (Shackleton et al. 2001:583; Shackleton and Shackleton 2004).

Unfortunately, the size and importance of these economic contributions often goes unnoticed. Such transactions belong to the informal economy, and are generally unaccounted for in official economic statistics.

Adding in Agricultural Income

Income from wild products is only a part of the environmental income equation. Agricultural income is just as crucial. Only when income from agriculture is combined with the income from wild products do we begin to get a clear idea of how important ecosystem goods and services are as a source of rural livelihoods.

A study of households (rich and poor) in the Masvingo Province in southeastern Zimbabwe provides a good example of how agricultural income complements wild income and how it compares with other income sources such as wages and remittances. As Figure 2.2 shows, agricultural income—from crops and home gardens—contributed 30 percent of total household income (cash and subsistence income combined). Livestock rearing—a modified form of agriculture that relies on wild forage—contributed another 21 percent. Wild products from woodlands contributed 15 percent. Together, these elements of environmental income sum to 66 percent of total income. In other words, *goods and services from ecosystems contribute two-thirds of family incomes in rural Zimbabwe.* The remaining 34 percent came from wage labor, income from home industries, and remittances. For the poorest of these rural households, dependence on these different kinds of environmental income is even higher, providing a full 70 percent of total income when combined (Campbell et al. 2002:89-95).

The balance between agricultural income and wild income varies by location, with agriculture supplying more income in some areas, and wild income more in others. For example, a recent survey in the Jhabua district of Madhya Pradesh, India, found that agriculture provided 58 percent of total income of the poorest families, with livestock and wild income providing another 12 percent. In this district, farming is the main occupation, with over 90 percent of the workforce employed in agriculture. But families in Jhabua also supplement their incomes with livestock-rearing and collection of various forest products, such as wood fuel, fodder, tendu leaves, and mahua flowers (Narain et al. 2005:6, 14). *(See Figure 2.3.)*

Common Pool Resources as a Source of Environmental Income

Much of the environmental income earned in the developing world comes from common pool resources (CPRs). Common pool resources are forests, fisheries, reefs, waterways, pastures, agricultural lands, and mineral resources that no individual has exclusive rights to. They are typically owned and administered by the state, a village, a tribe, or other social grouping, with the idea that the benefits will accrue to many people rather than one person or family. Local and distant residents go there to collect fire wood, graze their cattle, gather nontimber forest products like medicinal herbs or mushrooms, hunt, fish, collect water, or make use of a variety of other services such as visiting sacred groves. Because these "commons" or "public domain" lands are such a rich source of environmental income, they are a crucial element in the livelihood strategies of the poor, particularly those who do not own land themselves (Jodha 1986:1169).

Just how important are they? Research over the past two decades has amassed a fair amount of evidence on this topic, particularly in India. N.S Jodha, in his pioneering study of 80 villages across seven semi-arid states in India, found that the poor make extensive use of common areas, with CPRs contributing 15-25 percent of household income (Jodha 1986:1177). Other studies from different states in India have found that CPRs contribute up to 29 percent of the income of poorer households (Adhikari 2003:5). Altogether, CPRs contribute some US$5 billion a year to the incomes of India's rural poor, according to one estimate (Beck and Nesmith 2001:119).

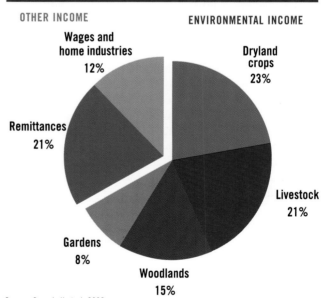

FIGURE 2.2 HOUSEHOLD INCOME BY SOURCE, MASVINGO PROVINCE, ZIMBABWE

OTHER INCOME

ENVIRONMENTAL INCOME

Wages and home industries 12%

Dryland crops 23%

Remittances 21%

Livestock 21%

Gardens 8%

Woodlands 15%

Source: Campbell et al. 2002

FIGURE 2.3 SOURCES OF INCOME FOR POOR HOUSEHOLDS IN JHABUA, INDIA

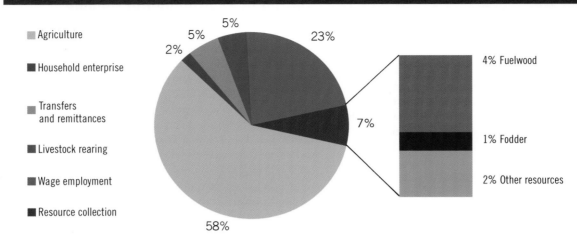

- Agriculture
- Household enterprise
- Transfers and remittances
- Livestock rearing
- Wage employment
- Resource collection

5%
5%
2%
23%
58%
7%

4% Fuelwood
1% Fodder
2% Other resources

Source: Narain 2005

Fewer studies have been done in other parts of the world, but there are indications that many of the rural poor derive a similar or higher percentage of their income from the commons (Beck and Nesmith 2001:119). In Botswana, researchers found that the poorest 20 percent of the population earn 51 percent of their household income from CPRs (Kerapeletswe and Lovett 2001:1). In southeastern Zimbabwe, households (both rich and poor) get 35 to 40 percent of their income from the commons (Cavendish 1998:7). Over 90 percent of Cambodians reported they make use of common property fish resources from lakes, rivers, flooded ricefields, and even flooded forests (Ahmed et al. 1998 in UK DFID 2000:31).

Without access to these resources, poor families would be virtually unable to support themselves. For example, poor households in Jodha's study met 66-80 percent of their fuel requirements from CPRs. Common areas also contribute a great deal of fodder, allowing poorer families to raise more livestock than they would otherwise be able to support (Jodha 1986:1173).

The Commons as a Safety Net and Employment Source

Even where dependence is not as high, CPRs function as an irreplaceable safety net for the poor. When farm and financial assets are scarce, the commons can provide secondary income and sources of food and fuel for basic survival. Researchers in western Africa have found that common pool resources are of particular importance to the poor during seasonal food shortages and times of crisis. According to one study, the poorest households rely on "bush" sources to supply 20 percent of their food requirements during the lean time before harvest, when food supplies are low. Wealthier families relied on the bush for only two percent of their food during this period (Dei 1992:67).

The dependence of poor households on the commons is typically highest after crop production has finished and when other alternatives for wage labor are unavailable (Jodha

1986:1177). Indeed, CPRs can generate significant self-employment opportunities, and often serve as an important and flexible source of secondary income for poor households. Jodha found that collection activities alone provided 36-64 days of work annually per worker in poor households in his study area (Jodha 1986:1175). In Haryana, India, collection of foods and other products, stone quarrying, and livestock grazing in common areas generate an annual average of 88 days of employment per household. Importantly, the numbers break down very differently by socio-economic class, with wage laborers working an average of 213 days per year in the commons, and higher-class households only 25 (Quereshi and Kumar 1998:350).

Gender also strongly influences reliance on the commons. Women head a disproportionate number of poor households, and their reliance on wild income is higher than men, who often have more schooling and greater wage-earning capacity. Studies show that women are often the primary gatherers and sellers of non-timber products such as fruits, medicinals, and handicraft materials (Shackleton et al. 2001:583; Shackleton et al. 2002:135; Shackleton 2005).

The Commons in Decline

A combination of factors, including privatization, agricultural intensification, population growth, and ecosystem degradation have caused common property areas to dwindle in size, quality, and availability to the poor in much of the world (Beck and Nesmith 2001:123). In some areas, common lands are converted to private parcels as a form of land reform or decentralization, or to spur development. Or common property resources may be leased out to private enterprises in the form of fishing or timber concessions. In either case, the poor may lose access to resources they once relied on.

Jodha estimates that in the areas covered by his study the extent of common lands has declined by 31 to 55 percent since the 1950s, mainly because of privatization through land reform (Jodha 1995:23). He estimates that in 1951 the average number of persons per 10 hectares of CPRs ranged from 13 to 101; by 1982, that number had risen to over 47,000 per 10 hectares in some villages. The increased pressure this has put on the remaining commons has led to overexploitation and a decline in the quality and quantity of services they yield (Jodha 1995:23). Degraded common lands undoubtedly make up a large part of the 75-130 million hectares of India's land that has been classed as "wasteland"—land that is both unproductive and ecologically depleted (Chopra 2001:25, 29).

Such declines in the ecosystem quality of public-domain lands are increasingly hard on rural livelihoods. A recent study in Ethiopia found most of the commons there in a state of either exhaustion or stress. Depleted grazing lands there have led to ethnic clashes and a decline in total livestock numbers, while the growing scarcity of woodfuel from common areas has forced more households to depend on purchased fuel (Kebede 2002:133-134). *(See Box 2.1.)*

Degradation from overuse is not inevitable, however, and examples of collective action to manage the commons are growing in number. In Caprivi, Namibia, good management and sustainable harvesting techniques of palm fronds from common areas have enabled local women to supplement household incomes by selling woven palm baskets to tourists. As one of the few sources of cash income for women, the market has grown from 70 producers in the 1980s to more than 650 by the end of 2001, a jump that the resource has been able to sustain thus far (Murphy and Suich 2004:8-9). In another example, rural harvesters of marula fruits in Bushbuckridge district of South Africa have planted marula trees in their home gardens and fields and selected for those with greater yields in the face of the dwindling number of marula trees in the communal lands (Shackleton et al. 2003:12, 13). *(For more examples of sustainable use of the commons by poor households, see Chapters 4 and 5.)*

Who Gets More Environmental Income: Rich or Poor?

Environmental income is not only important to the poor. Richer families also make extensive use of income from ecosystem goods and services. ("Rich" here does not necessarily imply high income by developed-world standards, but a greater relative level of wealth and opportunity compared to lower-income households within the same community.) In fact, several recent studies have shown that the rich commonly derive more environmental income, in absolute terms, than the poor do (Cavendish 2000:1990-1991; Fisher 2004; Narain et al. 2005:10,14; Twine et al. 2003:472). This generally reflects the fact that they have greater ability to exploit what ecosystems can provide. For example, higher-income families may have more livestock and can therefore make better use of forage resources in common areas, whereas a poor family's forage demand may be more limited due to their smaller herd size.

A study in the Jhabua district in the Indian state of Madhya Pradesh showed wealthier families using more fodder resources to feed their larger herds (Narain et al. 2005:5). In addition, the rich frequently have greater access to hired labor, transportation, credit, arable land, or other factors needed to maximize harvest of natural products or agriculture and bring

Continues on page 44

BOX 2.1 FINDINGS OF THE MILLENNIUM ECOSYSTEM ASSESSMENT: HOW DO THE POOR FARE?

THE MILLENNIUM ECOSYSTEM ASSESSMENT (MA) was a four-year, international effort to document the contribution of ecosystems to human well-being, assay the current state of ecosystem health, and offer a prognosis for how the capacity of ecosystems to support human needs may change under different management scenarios. The intent was to provide decision-makers scientifically credible information to help them manage ecosystems more sustainably while meeting human development goals.

The MA was a remarkably broad-based effort. Completed in 2005, it involved over 1300 scientists from 95 countries. It found that humans have altered the structure and functioning of the world's ecosystems more substantially in the second half of the twentieth century than at any time in human history. As a result, 15 of the 24 ecosystem services the MA assessed are now being degraded or used unsustainably (MA 2005a:viii, 1, 6).

This unsustainable use stems from the fact that humans often favor some kinds of ecosystem production—such as the provisioning services of food and fiber production—at the expense of other services that ecosystems can render, such as biodiversity, water purification, or natural pest control. The MA showed that such trade-offs among different ecosystem services are the norm. Particularly over the past hundred years, human management of provisioning services (food, timber, water, and other commodities) has degraded the ability of ecosystems to provide regulating services, such as flood control or pollination. Cultural services such as recreation and the aesthetic and spiritual appreciation of nature have also suffered.

At the same time, the findings of the MA have shed new light on the importance of ecosystems to the poor and how ecosystem degradation impairs the livelihoods of the poor. Poor people, particularly those in rural areas in developing countries, are more directly dependent on ecosystem services and more vulnerable when those services are degraded or lost (MA 2005a:2-14).

The MA findings document many examples of the human toll on ecosystems. Approximately 35 percent of mangroves have disappeared in the last two decades. Twenty percent of the world's coral reefs have been lost and an additional 20 percent are degraded. Water withdrawals from rivers and lakes have doubled since 1960. Nitrogen flows to the environment have also doubled, while phosphorous flows have tripled between 1960 and 1990. Landings from inland and marine fisheries have declined due to overexploitation. Fuelwood used for energy is scarce in many parts of the world. Some 10-20 percent of drylands are degraded (MA 2005a:2, 26, 31, 34).

Ecosystem Degradation and the Poor

The MA highlights the relationship between the poor and ecosystem goods and services. While everyone is affected by ecosystem degradation, the poor suffer the harmful effects disproportionately. In fact, the disparities between the poor and rich have grown in recent decades. For instance, despite global increases in the amount of food available per capita, over 800 million people remain undernourished, and food production per capita has actually decreased in Sub-Saharan Africa. While water availability has increased in many regions of the world, half of the urban population in Africa, Asia, Latin America, and the Caribbean suffer from contaminated water and its burden of disease. Ecosystem degradation has very real human and financial costs. The burning of 10 million hectares of Indonesia's forests in 1997-8 resulted in additional health care costs of US$9.3 billion and affected some 20 million people (MA 2005a:2, 13, 51, 57, 62).

The poor have also suffered from loss of access to ecosystems through privatization of what were formerly common pool resources. Examples include inland and coastal fisheries, which the MA findings reveal to be in steep decline. Small-scale fisheries are of great value to the poor, providing an inexpensive source of protein and supplemental income. Increasingly, coastal areas that were once open fishing grounds are being converted for use in shrimp farming and other forms of aquaculture. The harvest from aquaculture ponds or cages is typically exported, and both the income and the protein bypass the local poor. Countries where extensive conversion of coastal habitats for aquaculture is taking place include Ecuador, Thailand, Vietnam, Honduras, Chile, Indonesia, the Philippines, Bangladesh, and India (MA 2005b:25.13).

The MA findings also confirm that the substantial degradation of ecosystems that is now occurring is a barrier to achieving the Millennium Development Goals. For example, the MA warns that meeting the goals of eradicating hunger and reducing child mortality by 2015 will be unattainable if ecosystems continue to be used unsustainably. Soil degradation and water scarcity are two important sources of risk to the production of agroecosystems, and thus to the food supply, particularly as it affects the poor. The MA makes it clear that failure to tackle the current decline of ecosystem health will seriously erode efforts to reduce rural poverty (MA 2005a:61).

For more information on the Millennium Ecosystem Assessment and its findings, see: http://www.maweb.org.

GLOBAL STATUS OF PROVISIONING, REGULATING, AND CULTURAL ECOSYSTEM SERVICES EVALUATED IN THE MILLENNIUM ASSESSMENT

The table below summarizes the MA's finding on ecosystem services. The "Status" column indicates whether in the recent past the condition of the service globally has been enhanced (▲) or degraded (▼) or whether there has been no consistent global pattern (▲+▼)

Service	Subcategory	Status	Notes
PROVISIONING SERVICES			
Food	crops	▲	Substantial production increase
	livestock	▲	Substantial production increase
	capture fisheries	▼	Declining production due to overharvest
	aquaculture	▲	Substantial production increase
	wild foods	▼	Declining production
Fiber	timber	▲+▼	Forest loss in some regions, growth in others
	cotton, hemp, silk	▲+▼	Declining production of some fibers, growth in others
	wood fuel	▼	Declining production
Genetic resources		▼	Lost through extinction and crop genetic resource loss
Biochemicals, natural medicines, pharmaceuticals		▼	Loss through extinction, overharvest
Fresh Water		▼	Unsustainable use for drinking, industry, and irrigation; amount of hydro energy unchanged, but damns increase ability to use that energy
REGULATING SERVICES			
Air quality regulation		▼	Declining ability of atmosphere to cleanse itself
Climate regulation	global	▲	Net source of carbon sequestration since mid-century
	regional and local	▼	Preponderance of negative impacts
Water regulation		▲+▼	Varies depending on ecosystem change and location
Erosion regulation		▼	Increased soil degradation
Water purification and waste treatment		▼	Declining water quality
Disease regulation		▲+▼	Varies depending on ecosystem change
Pest regulation		▼	Natural control degraded through pesticide use
Pollination		▼	Apparent global decline in abundance of pollinators
Natural hazard regulation		▼	Loss of natural buffers (wetlands, mangroves)
CULTURAL SERVICES			
Spiritual and religious values		▼	Rapid decline in sacred groves and species
Aesthetic values		▼	Decline in quantity and quality of natural lands
Recreation and ecotourism		▲+▼	More areas accessible but many degraded

Source: Millennium Ecosystem Assessment 2005a

FIGURE 2.4 DEPENDENCE ON NATURE FOR INCOME IN BOTSWANA

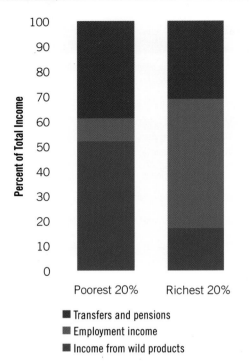

Percent of Total Income

Poorest 20%   Richest 20%

■ Transfers and pensions
■ Employment income
■ Income from wild products

Source: Kerapeletswe and Lovett 2001

them to market. In the Jhabua study, these factors allowed rich families to earn nearly five times as much environmental income—from a combination of farming, livestock rearing, and collection of wild products—as the poorest families.

On the other hand, even if the rich capture greater environmental income, they tend not to be as dependent on such income as are the poor. Environmental dependency and poverty seem to go hand in hand. A 1999 study of 12 Himalayan villages found that the poor relied on natural resources for 23 percent of their income, compared to only 4 percent for the rich (Reddy and Chakravarty 1999:1145). In Botswana's Chobe region, the difference was even greater, with the poor depending on wild products from nearby common property lands for half their total income, while the rich depended far more on employment income and remittances,

deriving less than 20 percent of their income from the nearby commons. *(See Figure 2.4.)* This was in spite of the fact that rich families in Chobe earned four times as much actual income as poor families from natural resources (Kerapeletswe and Lovett 2001:6-7).

The poor and the rich also tend to use natural resources differently to derive income. The poor tend to pursue a variety of different sources of environmental income, while the rich often concentrate on one or two that allow them to make use of their greater assets for agriculture or livestock rearing. In the Chobe example, three-fourths of the income that the rich derive from the commons comes from livestock rearing, while the poor diversify their efforts, spending time in at least five different activities, from collecting wild foods to making baskets and carvings from natural materials. *(See Figure 2.5.)*

The continued dependence of the poor on ecosystems for their livelihoods stems from several factors, but these generally reduce to the fact that nature is their best—and often only—option. The poor often lack the education and social access to find consistent wage labor. Without wage income, households lack the cash to purchase fuel, food, and services like health care. To substitute, they use small-scale agriculture and other forms of nature-based income, often collected from common areas. When given options for other forms of employment, the poor often reduce their dependence on environmental income.

In any case, the clear implication of most detailed studies of environmental income is that increasing the productivity of ecosystems, and therefore the potential to derive more income, would benefit all income classes in rural areas, not just the poor. Both the poor and the rich stand to gain more income, and rural economies more stability, if ecosystems are managed for greater productivity.

FIGURE 2.5 POOR VS. RICH: DIFFERENT STRATEGIES FOR ENVIRONMENTAL INCOME IN BOTSWANA

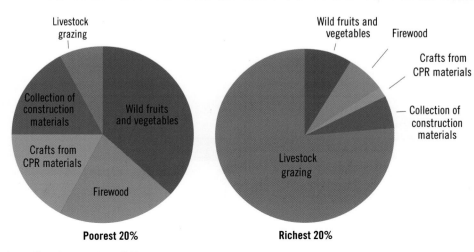

Poorest 20%   Richest 20%

Source: Kerapeletswe and Lovett 2001

Environmental Income by Ecosystem

By looking directly at individual ecosystems and the value that they provide to the poor, their importance to livelihoods becomes more obvious.

Agroecosystems

The most important source of environmental income in the world is agriculture—the goods derived from agroecosystems. Agroecosystems differ from other types of ecosystems because of the high degree to which they have been modified by people. Large-scale agriculture, driven by expensive inputs and technology—fertilizer, pesticides, irrigation, tractors, and harvesters—is responsible for much of world food production and agricultural exports. But small-scale agriculture—the farming that the poor pursue—is the silent giant that supports the great majority of the rural residents in poor nations.

This kind of farming looks much different than large-scale farming. While most farms in developed countries are owned by corporations and dominated by physical rather than human capital, in the developing world farms are still largely family-owned and operated. Small-scale farming remains labor-intensive and often lacks access to irrigation, fertilizer, or other inputs that raise productivity. The producer and consumer is frequently the same household. Despite the successes of the Green Revolution, this characterization still describes the majority of the agriculture practiced in the world today (FAO 2000b).

Smallholder farmers—those who own less than 5 hectares of land—cultivate lands in several ways: home gardens and small orchards that largely produce subsistence goods for home consumption; cultivation of commodity crops such as cotton or maize; and grazing of family-owned livestock. This can occur on very small parcels—sometimes on quite marginal land—and is often intermixed with other land uses like forestry. The goods which these small-scale "farms" produce can also be sold in local markets, sold to collectives that combine goods for resale, or even exported to other countries. Each of these modes of production plays a role in the household economy of the poor. Perhaps the most common and important benefit of these farms is that, combined with livestock, they meet a large portion of the nutritional requirements of many poor households.

Malawi, where small-scale farmers account for 70 percent of all farm production, provides a window onto the importance of such farming. Nearly eight of ten Malawians farm their own land—most cultivating less than a hectare (Fisher 2004:136). Maize is the staple crop, with cassava, sorghum, groundnuts, and beans also important. Nearly half of all households own chickens, and one-fifth own goats. Together these agricultural assets provide more than half of household income. Income from forests contributes another 30 percent. Only 10 percent of Malawi's population is engaged in wage employment, highlighting how critical environmental income—and particularly farm income—is to survival (Dorward 2002:9-24).

NATURE AS A DIVERSIFICATION STRATEGY

Why is it that environmental income is so important to the household economies of the poor? Environmental income comes from a variety of sources, each with a fairly low cost of investment. This allows poor households to pursue several different income-generating activities at once, diversifying their income sources and reducing their risk if any one activity fails. Specializing in a particular commodity or trade might be the most profitable, but poor households often lack the income buffer to take the chance. For example, if a household produces only maize, and the market for maize falls, or a pest or drought damages the crop, the family would lose its entire income. Or the household may simply lack the means to invest in the equipment, land, or training needed to specialize in a single trade or business.

Diversification is the answer. A poor family may raise rice for sale and home consumption, harvest fish cultured in the rice paddies for protein, collect wild materials for construction use and fuel, pursue home crafts such as basket making or wood carving for sale to tourists, and keep cattle for milk production and as a quickly saleable asset in time of need. All these are strategies for smoothing out the family-income stream over time and over a variety of sources of risk, such as weather, illness, or market downturns (Ellis 1998:17, 18).

An ecosystem, then, acts as a natural buffer to income shocks for a poor family (Campbell et al. 2002:102). Since it often provides some income even after wage income or remittances fall, it is where the poor often turn to in times of duress. But dependence on an array of low-income nature-based activities, while safest from a survival point of view, is often not a route to substantial wealth. For accumulating wealth, nature-based activities need to tap more lucrative markets, be supported with adequate financial, social, and physical infrastructure—credit, roads, training, marketing cooperatives, and the like—and be coupled with the development of a rural enterprise sector that gradually creates wage opportunities to supplement environmental income.

Understanding the role of small-scale agriculture in poor households requires an appreciation of the interplay between selling crops for cash and consuming them at home.

A study of home gardens in the Bushbuckridge district in South Africa exemplifies this interplay and the substantial contribution that home gardens often have in the livelihoods of the poor. In this district, households grow an average of four to five plant species on their residential plots. Households consume nearly three-quarters of the plants that they grow and sell the rest. The total cash value of all plants sold and consumed at home per year was US$266 per household—a sizable contribution to income in an area with few employment opportunities (High and Shackleton 2000: 148, 154). *(See Table 2.3.)*

Forests

After agriculture, forests are probably the greatest generators of environmental income for the poor. Rural communities are

Continues on page 47

IT IS NOT SURPRISING THAT POOR FAMILIES IN rural forested areas would draw upon the nearby trees for income from the use or sale of nontimber forest products (NTFPs) like wild fruits, construction materials, or medicinals. But the economic value of these forest products can be captured by the urban poor as well, particularly those who have recently migrated to the city.

A study conducted between 1996 and 1999 in the outskirts of Riberalta, a rapidly growing city in northern Bolivia, showed that households gain a significant proportion of their income from the collection and processing of Brazil nuts and palm hearts. These peri-urban neighborhoods are peopled largely by poor families, many of them recent immigrants from rural areas. The study found that households benefited from NTFPs in two ways: some family members (men, mainly) go out to the forest for a few months each year to collect Brazil nuts and palm hearts to sell to processors; other family members (mostly women) work in the processing plants in and around Riberalta where Brazil nuts are graded, shelled, washed, and packaged.

Nearly 60 percent of the surveyed households participated in one form or another in the Brazil nut or palm heart industries (Stoian 2003:4, 11). The poorest income group was the most dependent on NTFP income, getting 47 percent of their income from it. Even the better-off families derived more than a quarter of their income from NTFPs (Stoian 2003:12).

Many recent immigrants were driven to the city in search of employment after the decline of the Bolivian rubber industry in the late 1980s. New arrivals found that their lack of education and formal training, as well as social stigmas, acted as barriers to entry into most sections of the urban labor force. For these migrants, as well as other marginalized sectors of the population, the Brazil nut industry serves as the largest employer because of its high demand for unskilled labor. For example, migrants with only primary school education or less relied on NTFPs for 60 percent of their income (Stoian 2003:10, 14, 16).

The dependence of the urban poor on forest-related income highlights the rural-urban continuum that exists in many nations, where environmental income continues to play an important role in the income profile of poor households even when these families leave the countryside (Stoian 2003:10, 14, 16).

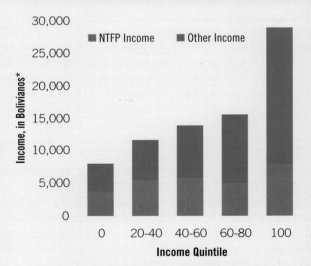

HOUSEHOLD INCOME FROM NON-TIMBER FOREST PRODUCTS IN RIBERALTA, BOLIVIA, 1998

■ NTFP Income ■ Other Income

Income, in Bolivianos*

Income Quintile

*At the time of the survey (1998), 1 Boliviano was equivalent to US$0.19.

Source: Stoian 2003

TABLE 2.3 THE VALUE OF HOME GARDENS TO HOUSEHOLDS IN BUSHBUCKRIDGE, SOUTH AFRICA, 1996

Crop	Cash Equivalent for Crops Consumed at Home (Rand)*	Cash Value of Crops Sold (Rand)*
Bean	57	4
Cabbage	445	46
Cassava	296	10
Cauliflower	100	0
Chili	48	13
Dintlo	124	109
Ground nut	184	41
Madanda	60	0
Maize	267	42
Onion	30	10
Pumpkin	52	0
Spinach	92	24
Sugar cane	277	217
Sweet potato	175	7
Tomato	126	0
Water melon	35	0

*Average income of households cultivating each crop

Source: High and Shackleton 2000

frequently found in or near forest areas, which vary widely in density and composition, from closed canopy rainforests to alpine coniferous forests to woody savannas. The productivity and variety of forest ecosystems, as well as their habitat value for game species, make them important contributors to the local subsistence and commercial economies.

Substantial research corroborates the importance of forests to the world's poor. In 2004 the World Bank completed a review of studies on the income that forests provide to those who live in or near them. The review examined cases from 17 countries on three continents, focusing especially on Africa. The results were striking: environmental income from forests was found to be important at every income level and on every continent, providing an average of 22 percent of total income—the equivalent of $678 per year (adjusted for purchasing power parity (PPP) worldwide)—in the households examined (Vedeld et al. 2004:28-29). (*See Table 2.4.*)

As many other studies have concluded, the Bank found that the most significant income from forests came from wild foods, fuel, fodder, and thatch grass. Timber and medicines were also

found to be important to total income. Unfortunately, much of the economic value of forests to the poor is missed in the official state accounting of the forest economy (Mogaka et al. 2001:4).

Woodfuels

The poor rely overwhelmingly on woodfuels as their household energy source. In developing nations alone, some 2.4 billion people—more than a third of the world population—rely on wood or other biomass fuels for cooking and heating (IEA 2002:26). For example, nearly all rural households in Kenya, Tanzania, Mozambique, and Zambia use wood for cooking, and over 90 percent of urban households in these countries use charcoal imported from the countryside (IEA 2002:26). In India, 62 percent of rural households depend on woodfuels (Vadivelu 2004:5).

Wood used as fuel is fundamentally important in the household economies of the rural poor. It is not only a source of energy in the home, but a supplemental source of cash income through the collection, processing, and sale of firewood and charcoal. Charcoal in particular, due to its high energy content and easy portability, is an important income-producer and a sole source of employment for many. In Kenya alone, the charcoal economy is estimated at about 23 billion Kenyan shillings per year—on a par with tourism as an income generator (Kantai 2002:16).

Non-Timber Forest Products

The poor have traditionally not been able to capture much of the income generated from the harvest and sale of timber.

TABLE 2.4 ANNUAL HOUSEHOLD INCOME FROM FORESTS

Source	Average Forest Income* (US$)	Share of Forest Income (% of total)
Wild Foods	287	38.3
Fuelwood	216	31.7
Fodder	124	5.8
Timber	28	2.3
Grass/Thatch	83	5
Wild Medicine	47	3.7
Gold Panning	6	0.2
Others	129	13
Total	**678****	**100**

* Average amount of environmental income based on 54 empirical studies, reported in Purchasing Power Parity (PPP) dollars.

**Average total forest income is less than the sum of all sources because many studies do not measure income from every source.

Source: Vedeld et al. 2004

Because of its high value, more powerful interests—in private commerce and in the state bureaucracy—have generally dominated this resource. For the poor to reap greater benefits from timber production, forest ownership and governance regimes would have to change substantially.

TABLE 2.5 USES OF SELECTED NON-TIMBER FOREST PRODUCTS (NTFPS)

Product	Primary Use	Location
Ant Larvae	Bird food	Banten, Indonesia
Bamboo (Moso)	Bamboo mats and handicrafts	Zhejiang, China
Bark (Cape Onionwood)	Medicine	Eastern Cape, South Africa
Resin (Benzoin)	Incense	North Sumatra, Indonesia
Brazil Nuts	Food	Vaca Díez and Iturralde, Bolivia
Cardamom	Food, medicine	Bac Kan, Vietnam
Woody Vine (Cat's Claw)	Medicine	Puerto Inca, Peru
Fruit (Allspice)	Spice	Puebla, Mexico
Garcinia Fruit	Medicine	Karnataka, India
Hearts of Palm	Food	São Paulo, Brazil
Marula Trees	Fruit, beer, livestock feed, medicine, woodcarvings	Bushbuckridge district, South Africa
Mulberry Bark	Paper	Sayaboury and Luang Prabang, Laos
Pine Resin	Turpentine	Pinar del Río, Cuba
Rattan (African Rattan Palm)	Rattan furniture	Central Cameroon
Rattan (Calamus)	Rattan handicrafts and mats	East Kalimantan, Indonesia
Roots (Fáfia)	Medicine	Paraná, Brazil
Rubber	Rubber handicrafts	Acre, Brazil
Sandalwood	Essential oils for perfume	East Nusa Tenggara, Indonesia
Tendu Leaves	Cigarette wrappers	Madya Pradesh, India
Wood (Silver Oak)	Woodcarvings	Coastal Kenya
Wood (Parasol Tree)	Woodcarvings	Mpigi, Uganda

Source: Ruiz-Pérez et al. 2004; Shackleton et al. 2000b

But forests produce many other goods and services—collectively known as "nontimber forest products (NTFPs)"—that are critical income sources for the poor. Typical NTFPs include various foods, fodder, fuel, medicines, and many other collectibles—literally every product derived from a forest besides timber (Wickens 1991:4). *(See Table 2.5.)* The variety can be staggering. Forest dwellers in the Brazilian Amazon, for example, regularly sell some 220 NTFPs at Belem's daily open market—140 of which are wild products, and the rest cultivated in the forest (Shanley et al. 2002, in Molnar et al. 2004:35). If harvested correctly, NTFPs can make not only a substantial, but a sustainable, contribution towards livelihoods. In addition to their market value, many NTFPs have social, cultural, or religious significance as well.

The use of NTFPs is quite varied, and it is well documented that they provide a wide range of subsistence and cash income to a large number of households in many nations (Neumann and Hirsch 2000:53-55). On Mexico's Yucatan peninsula, for example, the market value of palm thatch used or sold as roofing material is estimated at US$137 million per year (Bye 1993, in Molnar et al. 2004:35). In India, NTFP production contributes about 40 percent of total official forest revenues and 55 percent of forest-based employment. (Tewari and Campbell 1996:26). In Botswana, the government recently admitted the value of NTFPs exceeds that of timber (Taylor 1996:76-77).

As impressive as these national-scale estimates are, they tend to understate the importance of NTFPs to households. Since the values of NTFPs are generally difficult to calculate, they are often underestimated (Lampietti and Dixon:1995:1-2). This undervaluation causes decision-makers to assign a lower priority to intact forest ecosystems as an economic asset than they should.

Fisheries and Reefs

For those living near the coast, or near inland water bodies, fisheries are nearly always an important aspect of household income. Like forests, fisheries are generally accessible, in some form, by people of all income levels, making them a last refuge for many poor households. An estimated 250 million people in developing countries are directly dependent on small-scale fisheries for food and income. In Thailand, for example, 90 percent of the nation's fishers are still small-scale operators (World Bank 2004:17).

SMALL-SCALE FISHERIES IN RURAL THAILAND

The average small-scale fisher in rural coastal Thailand earns probably half of the income of the average Thai citizen. He is from one of the almost 50,000 households in Thailand fishing with a vessel that weighs less than 10 tons. He lives in one of the 2,500 rural fishing villages around the country, 80 percent of which are located beyond municipalities, without basic infrastructure such as roads and electricity (World Bank 2004:17).

The small-scale fishing that the poor do differs markedly from the industrial fishing of factory trawlers and long-line fishers. Small-scale fishing is usually a low-capital operation with owner-operated vessels, such as those using cast nets and small traps. Many times it is carried out from small non-mechanized canoes or rafts, or from small motorized boats and dinghies crewed by one or a few people. But sometimes it is done from the shore without even the use of a boat. In Indonesia, for example, half of the nation's 2 million ocean fishers use unmotorized canoes; another 25 percent use small boats with outboard engines; 80 percent live below the national poverty line (FAO 2000a:2-3).

Marine fisheries often contribute enormously to the livelihoods of the coastal poor. In coastal communities studied in Mozambique, fishing contributes 34-38 percent of cash income, with additional environmental income coming from the sale of mollusks, seaweed, and sea cucumbers (Wilson et al. 2003:96). Likewise, families in coastal Tanzania supplement subsistence agriculture and forestry with fishing, seaweed and shrimp farming, and salt production (Bayer 2003:1). Households living in coastal villages along Korangi Creek in Pakistan rely on mangroves as their primary source of woodfuel and animal fodder, and rely on the mangrove fisheries for both wage labor and food (Khalil 1999:9-10). For families too poor to own boats in Indiranagar, India, labor on the fishing boats of others provides a crucial source of income (Rengasamy et al. 2003:128).

Inland fisheries—in lakes, rivers, streams, rice paddies, and fish ponds—are just as important a resource for the poor as marine fisheries. In the Lower Mekong River basin, for example, a recent study found that 40 million rural farmers—many of them poor—engage in seasonal fishing activities. In Laos, where

the incidence of rural poverty is quite high, 70 percent of all farm households augment their family food supplies and incomes with fish (Sverdrup-Jensen 2002:8).

These statistics make it clear that fisheries are a key—and often overlooked—aspect of food security for the poor. In East Asia and in Africa, fish provide more than 50 percent of the animal protein intake in the diet of 400 million people (World Bank 2004:18). In Liberia, Ghana, and Cambodia, fish and fish products constitute 65 to 70 percent of animal protein consumed (FAO and UK DFID 2002:20, 21; UK DFID 2000:18).

In areas of the world that support coral reefs, these systems also provide a crucial portion of people's livelihood. *(See Table 2.6.)* Reefs provide fish for daily consumption, shells and corals for use in house construction and for sale to tourists, and a variety of marine species for medicinal purposes (Rengasamy et al. 2003:130-133). Rural households in the Fiji Islands—a third of which are poor—routinely subsist on fish and shellfish such as *kaikoso* clams they catch themselves on

TABLE 2.6 NATURE-BASED LIVELIHOOD STRATEGIES BY INCOME LEVEL ON AGATTI ISLAND, INDIA

	Poor	Lower Middle Class	Upper Middle Class	Rich
Annual Income	Below Rs 15,000 (<US$319)	Rs 15,000–60,000 (US$319–1,276)	Rs 60,001–250,000 (US$1,277–5,319)	Above Rs 250,000 (>US$5,319)
% of Population	10%	50%	39%	1%
Reef Use	Subsistence and survival	Supplementary income or subsistence during monsoon	Collecting bait fish, octopus, etc.	Pay others to collect building materials and fish
Selected Assets	No land or coconut trees	Few trees	Land, coconut trees	Land, coconut trees
	No livestock	Goats, chickens	Goats, chickens	Goats, chickens, calves
	Cast net	Small wooden boat (thoni) with outboard engine. Fishing rod and various nets	Boat with outboard engine	Cargo vessel (manju)

Source: Hoon 2003

local beaches, reefs, and other inshore waters, and sell the remainder for cash. *(See Chapter 5 for a complete case study of Fiji's fisheries.)* In the Caribbean and parts of South East Asia, coral reefs play an important role in a growing ecotourism market, bringing money and jobs into these regions. The combined benefits of dive tourism, fisheries, and shoreline protection provided by reefs bring an estimated net value of US$3.1-3.6 billion to the Caribbean region every year (Burke and Maidens 2004:58).

Many fisheries—particularly marine fisheries—are dominated by large-scale fishing operations, and conflicts between local small-scale fishers and commercial operations are common. Often, poor communities operate at the margins, fishing what large-scale operators leave behind (Kura et al. 2004:87-88). In Chad's Chari delta and along the western shore of Lake Chad (Nigeria), a comparative analysis found that the poor have access only to marginalized fishing grounds, while the more well-to-do have access to all water bodies (Béné 2003:960). Even where the poor do have access, they often lose out to richer fishers when competing directly, due to inferior equipment.

The Role of Livestock

Livestock are an important and sometimes overlooked element of the livelihood strategies of the poor. As much as 70 percent of the rural poor depend on livestock to some degree. Livestock holdings are diverse and include cattle, goats, sheep, pigs, poultry, horses, camels, yaks, and llamas. An estimated 600 million poor people, including 150 million landless poor, own livestock (Delgado et al. 1999; IFAD et al. 2004:9,10; Thornton et al. 2002).

Livestock are a crucial source of financial capital for the rural poor. For many, livestock ownership is the only form of savings available. In fact, for pastoralists and often for poor women, livestock are the most important fungible asset they own. Livestock provide a critical reserve against emergencies and decrease vulnerability to financial shocks from ill health, crop failures, and other risks. They yield direct benefits in the form of food, wool, or hides, and can raise farm productivity by providing manure and draught power (PPLPI 2003:1). In a comparative study of poor livestock keepers in Bolivia, India, and Kenya, households in all three countries ranked livestock above business and housing as their best investment (Heffernan et al. 2002 in IFAD et al. 2004:14).

In 40 percent of Kenya's districts, livestock represent more than a quarter of total household income (Thornton et al. 2002:75). In rural Nepal, they contribute 9-14 percent of production for home consumption, and are even more important as a source of cash income. For Nepal's isolated mountain communities, livestock are among the few items exchanged for cash, constituting nearly half of total farm cash income (Maltsoglou and Taniguchi 2004:24-25). Studies have found that livestock generally contribute significantly more to the income stream of poor households—particularly the income controlled by women—than to the incomes of those living above the poverty line (Thornton et al. 2002:75; Heffernan 2001:60; Delgado et al. 1999).

The benefits from livestock can even extend to those who don't own livestock—often the poorest members of the community. Non-owners are sometimes able to obtain milk, dung for fuel, or help with ploughing of fields. These may be given free of charge from livestock owners, or at greatly reduced prices (Shackleton et al. 2000b:53; Shackleton 2005).

Perhaps not surprisingly, livestock figure prominently in the movement of households into and out of poverty. In a study of household poverty dynamics in 20 communities in Kenya, researchers found that more than 40 percent of families that escaped poverty did so by diversifying their farm income, primarily by acquiring livestock (Kristjanson et al. 2004:12).

When the poor have access to markets, livestock can serve as a source of collateral, giving households access to other forms of capital and opening pathways for further income diversification (IFAD et al. 2004:3).

The role of livestock in rural communities extends significantly beyond their economic value. Most notably, livestock play a prominent role in social and cultural relationships. Loans and gifts of livestock contribute to family and community ties and often play a central role in cultural traditions such as weddings and funerals. Owning livestock can also bring better nutrition to some of the most vulnerable groups, including women and children (IFAD et al. 2004:19-20).

Despite the benefits, livestock rearing is also risky for the poor. Production risks—from harsh weather to predators to lack of proper veterinary care—are greater among low-income producers (IFAD et al. 2004:14). Loss of livestock holdings can have a long-term impact on a family far beyond the value of the individual animals, because herds generally take such a long time

to build up. Catastrophic losses from natural disasters or having livestock stolen can therefore have a devastating effect on family finances. Even intentional loss, such as use of livestock for funeral feasts, can be hard on the poor. In western Kenya, slaughter of livestock for funerals has been identified as a major cause of falling into poverty (Kristjanson et al. 2004:iv).

The Social Benefits of Ecosystems

Deriving income from the environment is clearly a powerful tool for improving the lives and livelihoods of individual families, but it can also bring significant societal benefits by making the distribution of wealth in a community more equal. If environmental income is not counted, the income distribution in rural communities is often significantly skewed, with a large gap between rich and poor. However, if environmental income is included in the income profile, the gap between rich and poor shrinks somewhat (Vedeld et al. 2004:36-38; Jodha

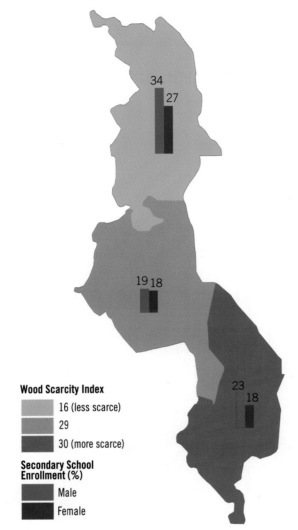

Wood Scarcity Index

- 16 (less scarce)
- 29
- 30 (more scarce)

Secondary School Enrollment (%)

- Male
- Female

Time spent collecting woodfuel is one factor that limits the social and educational development of children—particularly girls—in impoverished areas.

Source: Nankhuni and Findeis 2003

words, natural resources are often a binding element of communities. Community-based resource management can increase this bond, fostering community cohesion and strengthening the social safety net for poor community members.

Conversely, degradation of resources can harm communities and poor households by increasing the effort and time required to meet basic needs. Deforestation and scarce or polluted water supplies can increase the amount of time required to collect adequate fuelwood and water for daily use. Since women are usually charged with providing wood and water, longer collection times usually translate to less time to prepare food, care for young children, and help with agricultural activities. In low-income households, this can translate into poorer nutritional status and can harm the general household welfare (Kumar and Hotchkiss 1988:55-56).

Often, a portion of the collecting burden falls on the children in a household. Greater collection times can reduce the chances that children, especially girls, will remain in school. In Malawi, where more than 90 percent of households use firewood as their main source of energy, children in fuelwood-scarce districts are 10 to 15 percent less likely to attend secondary school (Nankhuni and Findeis 2003:9). *(See Figure 2.6.)* A study in Nepal found that educational attainment of girls in poor households dropped as fodder and water availability decreased, suggesting that the additional labor fell to school-age girls in the household (Cooke 1998:19). On the other hand, restoration of traditional forest enclosures in the Shinyanga region of Tanzania has dramatically increased forest cover in the district and reduced collection times for fuelwood by several hours per day, on average—a direct benefit to poor families. *(See Chapter 5 case study, Regenerating Woodlands in Tanzania: The HASHI Project.)*

These social and community benefits of nature point to how intact ecosystems can support many non-income aspects of rural livelihoods, adding weight to the argument that better ecosystem management is a crucial element of rural poverty reduction.

Building on the Strength of Ecosystems

As this chapter demonstrates, environmental income is critical to the survival of the poor within the typical rural economy in developing countries. On average, income from small-scale agriculture and the collection of wild products such as nontimber forest products together account for some two-thirds of the household incomes of families in poverty. Without income from ecosystem goods and services, rural poverty would unquestionably be deeper and more widespread—a lesson to remember as the pace of ecosystem degradation picks up worldwide.

But as important as environmental income is to the poor today, it is typically not used as a route out of poverty. Usually, the poor use environmental income more as a support for current levels of consumption or as a safety net to keep from

1986:1177). This supports the contention that ecosystem goods and services act as community assets, whose benefits reach beyond the individual household level. By providing an income source to those without other assets, ecosystems moderate and buffer the rural economy and increase economic equity. This provides another rationale for sound management of local ecosystems.

The use of natural resources and especially their degradation also has other implications for households and for communities. Rural communities are often bound together by shared professions based on nature—fisher, pastoralist, or farmer—or their use of a specific set of forest resources. In other

falling further into poverty. They generally do not have the means or empowerment to use environmental income as a tool for true wealth creation. As Chapter 3 will show, behind this failure to capitalize on the potential of ecosystems for income is an array of governance failures. The challenge is to alter this state of affairs, increasing the access of the poor to local ecosystem potential and their capacity for managing this potential sustainably and profitably, with viable models for turning nature's productivity into income.

Essential to meeting this challenge is realizing that environmental income is not separate from but part and parcel of today's rural economies. It is intimately tied to other forms of income, such as wage labor and self-employment income. It is tied also to the urban economy through remittances as well as the inevitable reliance of cities on the environmental output of ecosystems. Helping the poor to increase their environmental income, then, must be seen as supporting rural economic growth more generally. It both widens and secures the range of income options available, and can support a transition to higher-paying employment that carries the poor beyond the subsistence level.

The patterns and institutions of governance are the critical factors determining how effectively the poor can harness ecosystems for their livelihoods.

THE ROLE OF GOVERNANCE

CHAPTER 3

AN ABUNDANCE OF NATURAL RESOURCES DOES NOT necessarily translate into wealth for the poor. To make nature a source of prosperity for poor communities requires supportive governance conditions: policies and laws that protect the rights of the poor, coupled with responsive institutions that promote their interests. Without these, the presence of high-value resources like timber, gold, diamonds, or oil can actually be detrimental to poor communities, providing a target for exploitation by outside business interests and politicians. Too often, the result is that most of the revenues are appropriated by others, leaving the community—and local ecosystems—worse off than they were prior to "development."

Even where high-value resources are not present, the patterns and institutions of governance are usually the critical factor determining how effectively the poor can harness ecosystems for their livelihoods. Where laws are biased against the poor and government practices disenfranchise them, the potential for better management of ecosystems to alleviate poverty is greatly diminished.

This chapter examines key governance conditions that influence whether nature becomes a source of wealth and prosperity for many, or merely a select few. It focuses on the three governance factors with the most concrete impacts on the poor and their capacity to derive environmental income: *resource tenure and property rights; decentralization of resource management; and the rights to participation, information, and justice.*

These factors revolve around the rights of the poor to physically access and control natural resources, and their right to be heard in decisions about how to utilize these natural resources.

Resource Tenure and Property Rights: Access and Ownership

A person or community's rights to land and other natural resources defines their natural resource tenure. Legally, tenure is a bundle of both rights and obligations: the rights to own, hold, manage, transfer, or exploit resources and land, but also the obligation not to use these in a way that harms others (Bruce 1998a:1; FAO 2002:10). In other words, tenure defines *property* and what a person or group can do with it—their *property rights*.

However, tenure is not only a legal concept but a complex social institution, often involving traditional practices and customary authorities as much as formal laws. It governs ownership and access to natural resources, which is the gateway to use and benefit from these resources. As such, tenure is at the heart of the poor's ability to derive income and subsistence from ecosystems—to make them part of a sufficient and sustainable livelihood. *(See Box 3.1.)*

In many parts of the world today, resource tenure systems and property rights regimes are undergoing an important evolution. Fundamental shifts are occurring in the way that people and institutions think about the ownership of land, water, forests, fisheries, and other natural assets—about who controls these assets, who benefits from them, and where the power to make decisions about them is vested.

Two countervailing global trends in the evolution of resource tenure are evident. One trend stems from globalization. The growing economic integration of nations and societies has increased the sphere of private property and private responsibility, with government assuming a lesser role with respect to the private sector and civil society. This has important implications for how public lands and natural resources—often common pool resources—are managed, with more power over resources transferred to corporate interests through privatization or the granting of resource concessions (Johnson et al. 2001).

At the same time, there is a trend toward decentralization of natural resource management. Local and community-level institutions have become more assertive in the management of local resources, and this decentralized approach also has important implications for resource tenure. Indigenous groups have, for example, been more vigorous in pressing their ancestral claims to lands they inhabit but to which they lack formal title.

These two trends are shaping—and promise to profoundly transform—the capacity of the poor to earn environmental income from natural resources. For example, as illustrated in a study on the impact of globalization on the implementation of community-based natural resources management (CBNRM) in the Philippines, these global trends have the potential to both undermine and strengthen governance conditions that benefit

ENVIRONMENTAL INCOME AND THE POOR: CRITICAL GOVERNANCE QUESTIONS

Resource Tenure: How do property rights enhance or restrict the ability of poor people to derive environmental income? In particular, what is the role of resource tenure in enabling the poor to transform nature into an economic asset? How crucial is security of land tenure to the poor's ability to benefit from natural resources? How important to the poor are community-based forms of tenure?

Decentralization: What effect do institutions such as national forestry or fishery departments, district governments, or village councils have on the ability of the poor to access or sustain environmental income? What is the role of the state in natural resource management, and how does the transition to decentralized and community-level institutions (such as tribal structures, local levels of government, cooperatives, user groups, or watershed committees) affect the poor? When is decentralization the solution to poverty, and when does decentralization work against the poor?

Participation, Information, and Justice: How does political disenfranchisement prevent the poor from utilizing their natural endowments for more than mere subsistence livelihoods? Conversely, what is the role of democratic rights in ensuring that poor people benefit from natural resources? How can poor people use better access to information, public participation through their representatives, and access to the courts when their rights are violated to increase their capacity to earn environmental income? What are the challenges of providing appropriate information, participation opportunities, and real judicial or administrative access to poor communities?

the poor (La Viña 2002:24). Growing economic integration through increased trade and the emergence of multilateral environmental agreements, such those as on climate change and biodiversity, pose both threats and opportunities for poor communities worldwide.

The significance for the poor of changes in resource tenure systems and property rights systems is not limited to their economic impacts. For many rural communities, resource tenure is a central social institution that governs not only their relationship to the land and natural resources but also the relationships between families, between members of the community and those outside it, and between villages, communities, and peoples. Therefore, changes in tenure and property regimes have implications for the entire social fabric of rural communities. This is true for all tenure and property systems relevant to natural resources, but is particularly evident in the evolution of land tenure.

The Insecurity of the "Landed Poor"

Most of the rural poor in developing countries have some access to land on which they can collect forest products, graze animals, grow crops, gather medicinal plants, or in other ways benefit from nature. These "landed poor" typically remain poor not only because their land holdings are small, but because their rights to the land are weak, their tenure insecure (Bruce 2004:1).

Insecure tenure translates to a lack of assurance that one's land or resource rights will be respected over time (Meinzen-Dick et al. 2002:1). In many countries of Southeast Asia, for example, long-term forest dwellers such as indigenous peoples and local farmers often have *de facto* access to forests, but their tenurial control over trees, timber, and the right to manage forest uses is often limited in scope and unrecognized in law (Lynch and Talbott 1995:29). For instance, the traditional system of forest tenure (called *adat*) recognized by many forest dwellers in Indonesia has often been ignored by the government, which asserts legal ownership of all forest areas in spite of customary or historic uses (WRI et al. 2000:36-37).

In addition, the ability of the rural poor to participate in political decisions that affect their livelihoods often is limited by the power of other, more politically connected, parties with an interest in the same resources. Government agencies, corporations, large landowners, poor farmers, indigenous peoples, and different ethnic or cultural groups frequently make overlapping and conflicting claims on the same set of natural resources. Unfortunately, unless the tenure rights of the poor are secure, they usually lose out in these conflicts over competing claims (Alden Wily 2004:5).

While many forms of resource tenure are important, land tenure—rights over the land itself—is often the most fundamental building block of prosperity for the poor (Deininger et al. 2003:5). That is because land rights underpin most other resource rights, with the exception of offshore marine resources.

Without secure land tenure, it is difficult to conceive of the poor being able to generate wealth from nature.

Tenure Security and Environmental Investment

Security of tenure exerts tremendous influence on how land and resources are used. Secure tenure can be defined as the certainty that a person's rights to continuous use of land or resources will be recognized and protected against challenges from individuals or the state. This kind of certainty provides an incentive to make long-term investments in maintaining or enhancing the productivity of that property. For instance, a person with the right to use an agricultural field for decades or a lifetime may invest in an irrigation system whereas a farmer leasing a field for only a year will not (Bruce 1998a:2).

When insecurity of tenure acts as a disincentive to long-term investments in soil conservation, irrigation, and the like, land quality can deteriorate and agricultural productivity suffer. For this reason, tenure reform is frequently a component of development projects aimed at enhancing food security and sustainable livelihoods for the rural poor. Tenure reform is distinct from land reform in that it does not redistribute parcels of land per se, but rather makes adjustments in the rights to hold and use land. Examples of land tenure reforms include strengthening informal tenure rights by making them legally enforceable and transforming state-issued permits for specific land uses into leases that provide more protection for users of the land (FAO 2002:20).

Continues on page 59

BOX 3.1 UNDERSTANDING THE SCOPE OF RESOURCE TENURE

UNDERSTOOD BROADLY, "TENURIAL RIGHTS" over natural resources are synonymous with "property rights." Tenure covers all the means by which individuals and communities gain legitimate access to and use of natural resources. To know who has tenure over a natural resource is to identify who owns the resource, who can use or extract it, who can exclude others from having access to it, and who benefits from exploiting it. As such, the details of how tenure is determined and recognized—particularly through national laws and policies—greatly affects the rural poor, whose lives depend on access to ecosystems.

Typical tenure rights and obligations include:

- The right to use the resource (the "usufruct" right) or control how it will be used
- The right to exclude others from unauthorized use
- The right to derive income from the resource
- The right to sell all or some of these rights to others, either permanently, or for a limited time (such as through a lease)
- The right to pass these rights down to one's successors (the right of descendants to inherit land or resource rights)
- Protection from illegal expropriation of the resource
- An obligation not to use the land in a way that is harmful to others
- An obligation to surrender these rights through a lawful action, (e.g., in a case of insolvency, the rights are surrendered to creditors; in the case of default on tax payments, the rights are surrendered to the state) (FAO 2002:10)

Resource tenure includes rights over land, but it encompasses other natural resources as well. Land tenure is the usual focus of public interest, but distinct tenure arrangements apply as well to forest resources (Lynch and Talbot 1995), fisheries (Kinch 2003; Pereira 2000), mangroves (Hue 2002), wetlands (Rahman et al. 1998), watersheds (Kumar et al. 2004; Ayudhaya and Ross 1998), wildlife (Alinon 2002; Hasler 2002), and other natural resources. In a forest, tenure might translate not just to the right to harvest timber but to the ability to harvest fruit from certain trees, to collect fallen branches for fire wood, or bamboo for building materials. In fisheries it might mean the right to fish certain waters, harvest certain species but not others, or fish at certain times of the year.

Resource tenure covers not only formal property rights recognized by the legal system and enforced by the government, such as land titles or forestry licenses. It also refers to traditional practices—often unwritten and informal—through which rural people secure access to natural resources. Official

documents issued by the government are not the only ways that tenure is recognized in rural areas. Evidence of long-term occupation or of observance of customary law are other recognized ways of establishing tenure. Experience shows that where states emphasize the use of formal processes and official documents to acknowledge resource tenure rights, it is likely that poor communities, particularly indigenous peoples, will be disenfranchised (Lynch and Talbot 1995:7).

Tenurial rights include but are not equivalent to ownership. The absence of full ownership over a natural resource does not preclude the possibility of other tenure rights over a natural resource (Schlager and Ostrom 1992:256). For example:

- The state may own the forests in its territory but recognize the right of occupants to utilize timber or non-timber resources through some kind of permitting system.
- Protected areas may be part of the public domain, but the right of indigenous peoples and other long-term occupants to inhabit these areas may be legally recognized.
- Coastal waters may be claimed by the state, but local fishers may be granted rights over customary, near-shore fisheries.

This is true as well for tenure rights over forests, fisheries, and other natural resources where the benefits of good stewardship can only be gained over time. For example, given their limited resources, it is unlikely that the poor would see a value in investing in sustainable forest management practices, including reforestation, if their tenure over forests is restricted and they can't count on reaping the benefits of such practices. Tenure reform, in this context, would require addressing these tenure insecurities by providing longer time-frames for forest management agreements, or by recognizing the communal ownership rights of groups who have long occupied forest lands. Thus, one study of joint forest management agreements in India—agreements between local communities and the state allowing limited local management and use rights on state forest lands—notes an urgent need to first resolve the issue of tenure security to give these community-state agreements a foundation for success (Reddy and Bandhii 2004:29).

Security of tenure is important for poverty reduction because it allows poor people to grow more food, harvest

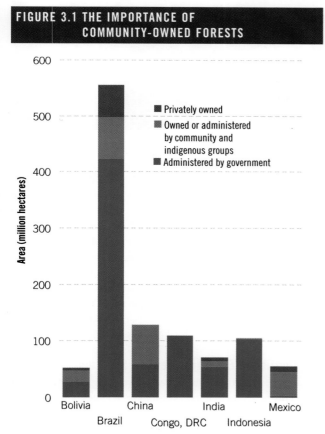

FIGURE 3.1 THE IMPORTANCE OF COMMUNITY-OWNED FORESTS

■ Privately owned
■ Owned or administered by community and indigenous groups
■ Administered by government

Area (million hectares)

Communities own or manage a significant percentage of the world's forests, some 22 percent in developing countries. However, the fraction of forest under community management varies widely by country. In Mexico, over 80 percent of commercially harvested forests are controlled by the people who live in and around them.

Source: White and Martin 2002; Antinori et al. 2004

products for consumption or trade, invest more in economically productive activities, or use property to obtain credit. Some studies report that investment doubles on land where tenure is strengthened (Feder 2002, cited in Deininger et al. 2003:8). Recent research also indicates that countries with equitable, efficient land tenure systems, ensuring property rights for both women and men, tend to achieve faster, more sustainable economic development with high levels of food security, health, and welfare (FAO 2002:5; Deininger 2003:17-20).

Case studies from Asia, Africa, and Latin America have also shown that tenure security affects people's long-term investments in modern management practices that can raise productivity, such as agroforestry techniques, livestock feeding practices, or integrated pest management (Meinzen-Dick et al. 2002:1). Failure to invest in agriculture, fisheries, and forest management due to tenure insecurity can greatly impede development goals. In Ethiopia, the nation's tenure regime changed radically in 1975 as the government nationalized all rural land with the intent to distribute land rights more equitably. Unfortunately, continued changes in tenure laws, a growing rural population, and insufficient land to meet demands, have led to markedly insecure land tenure for many. This has undermined investment in agriculture, worked against food security, and contributed to land degradation (Kebede 2002:138-140).

The Importance of Communal Tenure

Property rights can be held by private entities or by the state, and by an individual or a group. Property rights experts generally identify four basic kinds of tenure or ownership (FAO 2002:8):

- *Private,* or owned by an individual, corporation, or institution;
- *Communal,* or owned in common by a defined group of individuals, such as a village, tribe, or commune;
- *State,* or owned by the government;
- *Open access,* or owned by no one.

The term "communal" has been used to cover a plethora of ownership situations, ranging from resources that can be used by virtually anyone (more accurately described as open-access) to resources that are used simultaneously or serially by multiple users, such as land on which all community members have grazing rights or traditional fishing grounds where they can fish. It also applies to tenure arrangements in which ownership is vested in the community, which in turn allocates land or other resources among households for cultivation, resource extraction, and other uses. Communal tenure systems thus may encompass strong household and individual rights to use a particular resource or parcel of land, often passed down by inheritance through a family. In fact, holding exclusive use-rights in a traditional, community-based tenure system can be as secure as private, individually titled property rights in Western countries (Rukuni 1999:4). *(See Figure 3.1.)*

Property rights regimes involving significant communal control over land or resource use have been the prevailing land

tenure arrangements in Africa and Asia for centuries. More recently, however, European colonial powers introduced the western concept of private, individual property. In colonial Africa, both the British and the French created enclaves of individually owned property in urban areas as well as white settler farms, but only cautiously expanded the concept of individually titled property to selected Africans (Bruce 2000:17). Among West African countries, individualized tenure often appeared in tandem with the introduction of cash crops for export (Elbow et al. 1998:5).

Contrary to the belief of some Western observers, communally owned resources (which are a form of common pool resources) are not inevitably subject to overuse and destruction—the so-called "tragedy of the commons" popularized by Garrett Hardin in his scholarly article in 1968 (Hardin 1968). Hardin's thesis—that natural resources held in common will inevitably be overused—more accurately pertains to open-access resources rather than to communally owned and managed resources. With open-access resources, such as ocean fisheries in international waters or state forests where the government presence is weak or absent, all potential users have equal access to the resource and none can be excluded. In contrast, in well-functioning communal tenure situations, the community itself is able to exclude outsiders from using the resource and to enforce norms of behavior—such as fishing or grazing limits—for its own members' resource use (Ostrom et al. 1999:278).

Recent research has shown that community-based tenure systems can be quite compatible with sustainable resource use under the right conditions. For instance, a study of two Guatemalan communities, Las Cebollas and Moran, found that when community members perceive a resource as both necessary and scarce, they invest in efforts to protect it from overuse (Jensen 2000:641). In Jordan, herder cooperatives with management rights on their traditional pastures are achieving higher range productivity than state-managed reserves, without requiring expensive fencing and guarding (Ngaido and McCarthy 2004:1).

The Duality of Emerging Tenure Systems

In practice, property rights in many developing countries reflect a diversity of tenure regimes. Customary regimes based on local traditions, institutions, and power structures such as chiefdoms and family lineages may exist alongside the formal legal tenure system sanctioned by the state. Customary tenure systems have evolved and adapted over time to meet the needs of community members, and they continue to do so in response to modern-day pressures (Elbow et al. 1998:10). This includes the introduction of more individualized property rights arrangements in traditional communal arrangements.

A rural community's customary tenure system is often composed of several different kinds of tenure, each of which defines different rights and responsibilities for the use of diverse resources. Clear individual or household rights are generally allocated for more or less exclusive use of arable and residential land, while group rights may prevail for use of pastures, forests, mountain areas, waterways, and sacred areas (Rukuni 1999:2).

But customary tenure systems today do not exist independently. They inevitably live in relationship—often uneasily—with modern state-sanctioned tenure systems. The upshot is that in many parts of the developing world, land tenure systems exhibit a dual nature—that is, property rights that are partly individualized and formalized in legal statutes, and partly community-based and grounded in customary practices (Elbow et al. 1998:16).

For example, in many African countries—including the Republic of the Congo, Cote d'Ivoire, Ghana, Mali, and Togo—land markets based on individualized tenure have developed in response to a perceived commercial potential. For instance, in Cote d'Ivoire, immigrants to forest areas "buy" land from the local population in order to produce cash crops (Elbow et al. 1998:10).

Tenure systems are also evolving because of changing patterns in herding versus sedentary agriculture. In parts of Burkina Faso, Mali, Mauritania, and Niger, tenure systems traditionally have been based on overlapping rights to use land. For example, herders might leave their animals on croplands during the dry season, effectively exchanging the soil nutrients in animal manure for the right to graze their animals on crop stubble, while sedentary farmers might grow crops on pasture land during the rainy season. Increasingly, however, cultivators are expanding into herding, and herders into sedentary agriculture. This has led to a breakdown in traditional tenure arrangements, growing tensions between competing groups, and an apparent shift from overlapping rights to exclusive rights over particular land parcels (Elbow et al. 1998:10).

The state frequently adds to these conflicts through changes in national land policies that weaken customary or community-based tenure practices. In Niger, tenure reforms in the 1960s and 1970s abolished the system of "tithe" payments that tenant farmers paid to local chiefs under customary tenure practice and asserted state ownership over all lands. The intent was to give greater land rights to tenant farmers. However, later reforms in the 1980s reasserted the right of traditional chiefs to control land use by allocating pasture and agricultural land. The confusion brought on by these land policies has created conflicts between farmers, pastoralists, and customary chiefs and landowners, and has weakened tenure security for all parties (Bruce et al. 1995:19-21.)

The dual nature of land tenure arrangements persists whether national policies explicitly recognize customary tenure systems, ignore them, or actively work to dismantle them. Attempts to completely overturn customary tenure systems and replace them with formalized systems of purely individual property rights have rarely been effective, prompting a shift in approach from replacement to adaptation (Bruce 1998b:81). For instance, in the case of forest land claimed by the state, the state may grant individuals from a community the right to collect medicinal plants or fallen branches for firewood, and local groups might have the right to plant trees, but the state might reserve the right to approve any felling of trees and to collect revenue from timber users (Meinzen-Dick et al. 2004:7). Joint forest management agreements between communities and state governments in India often follow this pattern, recognizing in law certain community use-rights but retaining for the state many of the other prerogatives of property ownership, including ultimate title.

The balance between the two components of dual tenure systems is dynamic and ever-shifting. In general, however, customary systems operate as the de facto allocators of land and natural resources in rural areas, with the rules of such allocation increasingly subject to modification by national policies and institutions and in response to changing economic conditions (Elbow et al. 1998:16-17).

Grassroots Pressure for Effective, Equitable Tenure Reform

Today there is mounting pressure for government tenure reform, a mark of the centrality and dynamism of the rural tenure issue. In part, rural populations themselves are responsible for this pressure, as land sits idle and grossly unequal land holdings coexist uneasily with landlessness, poverty, and the hovering specter of hunger in many parts of the developing world.

Additional impetus comes from research showing that unequal access to land and other productive assets is a defining feature of persistent poverty (Riddell 2000). Peruvian economist Hernando de Soto argues that the lack of a well-defined system for recording, transferring, and enforcing the property rights of the poor is a major source of continued poverty, since it does not allow the poor to make use of their assets for collateral and credit, thus barring them from productive investments (de Soto 2000).

These and other findings have contributed to a growing consensus that establishing secure property rights and making rural land markets work for poor farmers and rural producers is one of the keys to effective poverty reduction. In fact, de Soto goes so far as to predict that the countries that achieve substantial economic progress over the next two decades will be those that have developed strong property rights institutions (Riddell 2000).

Against this backdrop, tenure reform has emerged as an essential component of a broader sociopolitical transition to greater democracy and decentralization in developing countries. Governments are starting to recognize that customary, community-based tenure systems are legal in their own right. They are beginning to put these systems on an equal legal footing with Western, individualized property rights (Alden Wily et al. 2000). Tenure reform movements are active in all regions of the developing world, including Sub-Saharan Africa, Asia, Latin America, and Central and Eastern Europe, with dozens of countries initiating major tenure-reform efforts in the

past decade. For example, Thailand has recently completed a major initiative to provide the country's rural population with access to modern land registration, deeds, and credit institutions (Riddell 2000). Mexico has undertaken reforms to strengthen land and credit markets and improve the access to land among poorer households (Carter 2003:52).

Whether tenure reforms positively or adversely affect the poor depends on who designs and ultimately implements them. The extent to which the interests of the poor are represented and promoted by national and local institutions—both critical players in enforcing tenure rights—is key to ensuring that tenure reforms do in fact assist the poor.

Decentralization: Can It Help the Poor?

Across diverse economic and policy sectors, from health care and education to parks and wildlife management, decentralization is one of the most frequently pursued institutional reforms in developing countries today.

Decentralization is a process by which a central government transfers some of its powers or functions to a lower level of government or to a local leader or institution. In the natural-resource sector, an example of decentralization might be transferring from central to local government the responsibility for managing a tract of forest land, including the right to collect some of the income from sales of timber harvests in that forest. Or the central government might give a farmers group responsibility for managing an irrigation system, or grant a village

TABLE 3.1 DECENTRALIZATION: WILL IT HELP THE POOR?

Pros	Cons
Promotes democracy because it provides better opportunities for local residents to participate in decision-making.	Undermines democracy by empowering local elites, beyond the reach or concern of central government.
Increases efficiency in delivery of public services; delegation of responsibility avoids bottlenecks and bureaucracy.	Worsens delivery of service in the absence of effective controls and oversight.
Provides a chance for poor households to participate in local institutions and have their concerns recognized.	Local institutions mirror the anti-poor biases present at the state level.
Leads to higher quality of public services because of local accountability and sensitivity to local needs.	Quality of services deteriorates due to lack of local capacity and insufficient resources.
Enhances social and economic development, which rely on local knowledge.	Gains arising from participation by local people offset by increased corruption and inequalities among regions.
Increases transparency, accountability, and the response-capacity of government institutions.	Promises too much and overloads capacity of local governments.
Allows greater political representation for diverse political, ethnic, religious, and economic groups in decision-making.	Creates new tensions or ignites dormant ethnic and religious rivalries.
Increases political stability and national unity by allowing citizens to better control public programs at the local level.	Weakens states because it can increase regional inequalities, lead to separatism, or undermine national financial governance.

Source: Adapted from ICHRP 2005

council the right to manage wildlife and run a commercial tourism operation in a national park (WRI et al. 2003:97).

Decentralization is being driven by powerful economic, political, and technological forces. International development agencies such as the World Bank have placed decentralization in a prominent position on their agendas, and nongovernmental organizations (NGOs) and governments alike have promoted the concept, although often for different reasons. Advocates of decentralization cite the potential for greater efficiency, equity, and accountability when decision-making is brought "closer to the people" (Ribot 2004:7; WRI et al. 2003:92-97). In theory, devolving power from central government means empowering local institutions that can better discern how to manage resources and deliver services to meet the needs of local people. Modern communication options like the Internet, television, and mobile phones help make local people and organizations more aware of their rights, more able to communicate and organize, and therefore more capable of asserting their rights.

But are central governments really so eager to give up some of the powers they have traditionally wielded? In the 1980s and early 1990s, decentralization emerged as a priority in an era of economic and budget crises. Shifting responsibility for health care, education, parks, and other planning and service functions to local governments offered opportunities to reduce central government budget deficits. Central governments are all too willing to pass on to local and community institutions the responsibility for managing resources and delivering services without providing them with necessary financial or technical support. They tend to be much more reluctant, however, to give up their powers to collect and allocate user fees, fines, or other revenues (WRI et al. 2003:98).

Areas with rich natural resource endowments tend to be geographically isolated and far from centers of political power where the most momentous development decisions are made. Furthermore, central governments are often run by and for elites, and people from poor rural communities or ethnic minority groups seldom occupy senior positions in the decision-making levels of bureaucracies (Sibanda 2000:3). (*See Table 3.1.*)

Not All Decentralization Is Created Equal

Some decentralization advocates—governments, donors, and NGOs—view the poor as particular beneficiaries of decentralization. They envision reforms that make policies more useful to the poor, and processes that encourage the involvement of the most socially disenfranchised people in natural resource decision-making—those people who have the greatest stake in the outcome of management decisions (Asante and Ayee 2004:3-6, 21-22). These advocates point out that effectively implementing poverty reduction strategies often requires specific local knowledge that is best found in local institutions, and that strengthening local delivery capacity for services requires genuine devolution of authority to these institutions (Asante and Ayee 2004:5).

Some countries have responded positively to these arguments. Bolivia, for example, made decentralization across

several sectors part of a package of anti-poverty reforms in the 1990s (Pacheco 2004:85, 90). Most West African countries have also declared local development a prime goal of their decentralization efforts (Ribot 2002:8).

Despite its theoretical potential, the record of decentralization has been decidedly mixed. This is true both in general and with respect to poverty reduction. In some instances, efforts to decentralize management of forests, land, water, and fisheries have shown positive outcomes: rural citizens conserving their natural resources; local councils that are increasing revenues from resource use; the poor more involved in local governance institutions and reaping more monetary benefits from local resources; and local governments providing better basic services. One of the longest-standing cases of decentralized environmental management with evident benefits to livelihoods is in Kumaon, India. Since the 1930s, elected forest councils, called van panchayats, have had the right to manage forest use, raising revenue from the sale of fodder and dead trees and enforcing regulations on forest use (Ribot 2004:22).

Similarly, some wildlife co-management schemes in Africa have yielded improved local infrastructure such as roads and schools, while community forest management in Mexico that has come about through decentralization has enabled communities to build water networks, schools, and clinics

(Shyamsundar et al. 2004:9). In Ghana, devolution of power to district assemblies has improved provision of basic services and infrastructure in rural areas through construction of more feeder roads, clinics, public toilets, classrooms, and the like (Asante and Ayee 2004:8).

Yet in most decentralization efforts to date, the intended benefits for local democracy and for the poor remain largely unrealized, due to flawed implementation of the reforms. The choice of which institutions to empower with new management or decision-making responsibilities, and the ways in which those institutions are held accountable to the people, have profound implications for the effectiveness of decentralization—and whether the benefits reach the poor (Ribot 2004:25).

How Decentralization Can Harm the Poor

Governance reforms that are truly empowering for the poor, responsive to their needs, and effective in reducing poverty are rare (Crook and Sverrisson 2001:iii). In a 2001 analysis of decentralization cases from about a dozen locations in Asia, Africa, and Latin America, only Brazil, Colombia, and the Indian states of West Bengal and Karnataka showed good results in terms of increasing policy responsiveness to the poor, or reducing poverty and inequality (Crook and Sverrisson 2001:14-15).

Most reforms in the name of decentralization come up short in two areas that are critical to bringing about benefits to

local populations and the poor: they don't create *accountable, representative local institutions,* nor do they *transfer meaningful powers* to them (Ribot 2004:15). Such incomplete or partial decentralization undermines the potential benefits of governance reforms, particularly for the poor.

Decentralization without Accountability

Often, powers over natural resources are handed over to a person or body not elected by the people, and thus not wholly accountable to them, such as a traditional chief, or to a civil-society organization such as a women's association, or to a "user group" such as a forestry cooperative, or a pastoralists' group. Such groups may help broaden grassroots participation in local decisions, but they speak for only a segment of the citizenry. For example, Cameroon's community forest law devolves power to local forest-management committees. While the law requires these groups to consult "representatives" of all segments of the community, it is unclear by whom these representatives are chosen, and the results of the consultation are not binding in forest management plans (Ribot 2004:35). Similarly, in Uganda, the wildlife authority created a committee of beekeepers, but its mandate was so narrow that only interested parties participated—and these beekeepers then excluded other forest users from the committee's deliberations (Namara and Nsabagsani 2003 in Ribot 2004:37).

Retention of Central Government Control

Another common implementation flaw is to empower a district office of the government or a local representative of the central government. Such an office or official is accountable only to central government authorities, not to the people in the town or municipality. Central governments frequently choose to transfer power to a local branch of the bureaucracy, rather than a locally elected body, as a means of maintaining central control over natural resources (Larson and Ribot 2004:6). In China, the central government devolved management of community forests in name, but in practice has shifted greater power to the provincial level, and has implemented national-level policies that override and often contradict local policies (He 2005).

Lack of Power to Generate Revenue

Even where local democratic institutions or bodies are charged with natural resource management, they are commonly entrusted with duties that are circumscribed in scope, and rarely with the power to generate revenue by setting fees or levying fines. The central government often retains the most lucrative powers—such as the right to assess wildlife hunting fees or allocate revenue from a logging or mining concessions—while granting rural communities or governments the less valuable rights to subsistence-scale harvesting, such as the collection of firewood or bamboo.

Elite Dominance of Elections, Participation, and Decisions

All too often, the fundamental differences in power between rich and poor warp the decentralization process, allowing members of elite, wealthier, more empowered groups to shape decentralization to their own ends and derive most of its benefits (Ribot 2004:41). Decentralization then becomes largely a transfer of power from national to local elites. In Indonesia, for example, many of the benefits of rural timber extraction during the Suharto era accrued to powerful business interests in Jakarta, the capital, and illegal logging was widespread. In the decentralization that followed the fall of the Suharto regime in 1998, a realignment of influence occurred, with district governments taking more control over managing timber extraction. Now the influence of local elites and business interests predominates. Rather than cracking down on illegal logging, this has tended to perpetuate the cycle, often with similar inequities and environmental damage (McCarthy 2002:879, 881-82; Djogo and Syaf 2003:9-13, 20-22).

Elites can also slant the electoral process, giving them the upper hand in local governance, and, accordingly, in the decisions made about natural resources by those institutions. Fair and competitive elections are a key means to make policies more responsive to the poor, and create a local government that is accountable to local people (Crook and Sverrisson 2001:50). But elites often have a disproportionate influence on which candidates will run for election—candidates that may then be beholden to their interests. Indeed, party politics are often dominated by local elites.

Parties, in turn, often run slates of party candidates, putting independent candidates at a disadvantage. When officials are elected from party slates rather than independently, research suggests that these officials have less accountability, in particular to the poorest citizens (Ribot 2004:27). In contrast, when independent candidates are given a fair shake, elections are more competitive, and the interests of the poor may be better served. Unfortunately, independent candidates are often barred from local elections. In a 2001 assessment of decentralization in 14 countries, only five (India, Mali, Mexico, Uganda, and Zimbabwe) permitted independent candidates in local elections (Ribot 2004:27).

Senegal shows the shortcomings, especially for poor populations, of electoral systems that do not admit independent candidates. In 1998 a new decentralized forestry law granted rural communities and their councils various rights over forests, including the right to authorize or deny commercial production of charcoal by the forest service and wealthy urban merchants—a forest use rural communities had long opposed. Yet years after the forestry law was enacted, the forest service continued charcoal production. Surprisingly, the forest service's charcoal extraction had the approval of rural council presidents, despite the fact that almost everyone in the communities in the region opposed it. Elected from a party slate, these council presidents were beholden to the party, rather than the local popular will (Ribot 2004:27-29).

Inadequate Participation by the Poor in Decentralized Bodies

Even when decisions and policy-making are devolved to a body made up of independently elected local people, there are inherent biases against equal participation by the poor. Because of their greater confidence, literacy, or other advantages, the better-off members of a community tend to assume positions of leadership in committees and councils. A study in West Bengal, India, showed that *panchayat* (village council) members from lower castes or tribes rarely spoke in meetings and, if they did, they tended to be ignored (Westergaard 1986 in Crook and Sverrisson 2001:16).

Moreover, the poorest members of the community are less able to shoulder the costs of participating in decentralized natural resource management, including membership fees, time spent in meetings or monitoring forests for poachers, and providing labor for maintenance of infrastructure such as irrigation systems (Shyamsundar et al. 2004:10). In addition, the earliest participants in projects often have more voice and opportunity to shape outcomes; the poor, joining in later stages, if at all, are less able to garner benefits (Ribot 2004:39).

Shortcomings of "User Committees"

Decentralized natural resource management often fosters the creation of user committees or user groups, which have proliferated in developing countries since the 1990s (Shyamsundar et al. 2004:5). Intended to give ordinary people a voice in local

Continues on page 68

BOX 3.2 HOW COMMUNITY-BASED RESOURCE MANAGEMENT CAN BENEFIT THE POOR

COMMUNITY-BASED NATURAL RESOURCE MANAGEMENT (CBNRM) is one of the most important manifestations of true decentralization as it relates to control of rural resources. CBNRM programs, if successful, can be models of local empowerment, imbuing communities with greater authority over the use of natural resources. Under the right circumstances, they can also bring important benefits to poor people and poor communities.

Improved Livelihoods

In many countries, community-based management of forests and other natural resources has improved livelihoods for the poor. The benefits of CBNRM can range from job creation to substantial management rights and long-term revenue-generation. For instance, in Nepal, community management of forests has created new jobs, including nursery staff and forest watchers, as well as wage labor for tree planting and weeding (Malla 2000:41). Community forestry concessions along the borders of the Mayan Biosphere reserve in Guatemala have generated more than 100,000 days of labor per year (Cortave 2004:26).

Where high-value resources such as timber are involved, CBNRM can generate significant revenues. A large forestry project in the Indian state of Madhya Pradesh earns an estimated $125 million per year for the communities involved, through sales of sustainably harvested timber and non-timber forest products (Shilling and Osha 2003:13).

Improved Resource Condition

A crucial element of community-based management is its potential to improve the condition of the resources being managed. The Krui people of southwestern Sumatra have practiced a complex form of agroforestry for generations, planting a succession of crops that culminate in a full forest canopy. Their agroforests support about ten times more biodiversity than conventional palm plantations in the area, and have economic uses ranging from resin tapping to timber sales (ASB 2001:1-2).

In northeastern India, the Khasi School of Medicine and others are working to re-establish traditional laws and practices of forest management to safeguard sacred groves of medicinal plants, which had been depleted under centralized management of the resource since the 1950s (Varshney 2003:46). In 1996 the Guatemalan government began awarding forest management concessions to settler communities living on the borders of the two million-hectare Mayan biosphere reserve in the lowland Petén region. Satellite imagery indicates that the 388,000 hectares under community management show better forest cover than adjacent areas (Molnar et al. 2004:19).

Development of Village Infrastructure

In some communities, a portion of the revenues from community-based enterprises has been directed to investments in key infrastructure needs, such as the construction of schools and libraries, development of drinking water and irrigation systems, and extension of electricity service (Malla 2000:42). Community management of land and water use in Gandhigram, Gujarat, has increased both the area and yield of lands under cultivation, despite three successive years of drought. The increase in income has gone toward village improvements, including fencing to keep out wild animals, construction and maintenance of irrigation structures, tractor and equipment purchases, and to pay down village debt (Down to Earth 2002). In another example, the mountain village of Lazoor, Iran, was one of a number of villages granted substantial control over their land and water resources by the Iranian government in 1999. With technical support from outside experts, the community built an extensive irrigation and erosion-control infrastructure, increasing productivity and opening new lands to cultivation (WRI et al. 2003:183-184).

Representation in Decision-Making Roles

CBNRM is most successful at benefiting the poorest members of the community when it empowers them to play a full decision-making role in resource management. One example of a community-based enterprise featuring equitable participation comes from the village of Deulgaon in Maharashtra State in India, where the community's forest-management committee includes representation by one male and one female member from each household, and all decisions regarding forest use are made by the general membership at its monthly meeting, rather than by an executive committee (Ghate 2003:9). CBNRM in Tanzania has sometimes spurred significant social change within the community itself, such that villagers gradually become less deferential to existing leaders and eventually may replace underperforming managers who serve their own self-interest rather than the interests of the community as a whole (Alden Wily et al. 2000:44).

In Lazoor, Iran—mentioned above—the land management program gave women a direct voice in priority-setting, with a positive impact on their confidence and role in broader village decision-making (WRI et al. 2003:184-185). In the Mapelane Reserve on the northeast coast of South Africa, a partnership between the local Sokhulu people and the government Parks Board resulted in the regeneration of mussel beds that had been a source of bitter conflict. The co-management scheme that emerged altered the community's role from illegal harvesters to resource managers. The Joint Mussel Management Committee, consisting of elected community members, park representatives, and university researchers, established management rules only after an extended process of experimentation and consultation with Sokhulu harvesters (WRI et al. 2003:176-179).

Reason for Caution

CBNRM can suffer from the same flaws that threaten all forms of decentralized management. Devolving decision-making power to the local level does not guarantee the poor a role in the process. An examination of Bolivia's effort to decentralize forest management found that the process did create new opportunities for marginalized groups to gain control of local resources and capture more of the economic benefits. However, only the better-organized groups have thus far been able to capitalize on the process; elsewhere, decentralization has simply strengthened the local elites (Kaimowitz et al. 1999:13-14).

Forest-user communities are often socially and politically diverse, with a range of different income levels represented (Malleson 2001:18). Unless these distinctions are taken into account, CBNRM will often end up favoring the more powerful. When the government of Laos introduced its land and forest allocation Policy in the early 1990s, it meant to foster local control over some of the country's agriculture and forest lands. However, the policy resulted in wealthier farmers reinforcing their rights to the best land, while small farmers and landless households found their access to both agricultural land and forest resources greatly reduced (Fujita and Phanvilay 2004:12).

Gaps in access to information about resource rights can also cause community forestry programs to work against the people they should support. In a blatant manipulation of the system in Cameroon, local elites in one region used community forestry laws to gain management rights over forests in another region, taking advantage of communities that were not yet aware of how to use the forestry law to protect their rights (Smith 2005:14). Studies from Nepal, one of the first countries to make a serious attempt to devolve forest management, show that lack of access to information and elite capture of forest-user groups have cut many of the poor out of benefits from community forestry (Neupane 2003:55-56, 58).

Finally, high transaction costs and complicated application and management requirements can deter communities from participating in CBNRM, or make it financially unsustainable for them to do so. In Cameroon, the application procedure to gain legal recognition of a community forest is lengthy and centralized. The costs for communities are significant—even more so because management rights are granted for only a ten-year period. Due in large part to these difficulties, only seven official community forests were established from 1995 to 2001 (Alden Wily 2002:18).

resource management, user committees do draw citizens into the policy process and give them significant influence over some programs. However, these committees aren't usually democratically elected, and they don't always benefit the poorest members of society. They also tend to have a short lifespan, which disadvantages poorer members of the community who need more time to develop the skills, confidence, and organizational capacities to participate on an equal footing. The only situations in which poor people are consistently able to wield influence in user committees is when the groups consist largely or entirely of poor people—for example, gatherers of non-timber forest products for subsistence use (Manor 2004:188 in Ribot and Larson 2004).

Project Bias Toward Wealthier Villages and Participants

Government agencies, donors, and nonprofit groups engaged in decentralization of natural resources management often have incentives to avoid poorer constituents and invest in wealthier groups or villages with better skills or higher-quality lands needed to make projects succeed. For example, managers of a state-funded watershed development program in the Indian state of Madhya Pradesh tended to work with more prosperous farmers in the valleys, where projects were more likely to gener-

ate dramatic results, rather than engaging with poorer hill farmers (Baviskar 2004:30-31 in Ribot and Larson 2004). Similarly, selection for anti-poverty employment programs in the Indian state of Karnataka was based on information provided by village leaders—who tended to be wealthier than other participants—resulting in the inclusion of many better-off families (Sivanna 1990:200 in Crook and Sverrisson 2001:20).

Gender Inequalities in Decision-Making

Women are typically among the poorest and most disadvantaged groups in developing countries. It is no surprise that they tend to be under-represented in positions of authority in local governments, village committees, and other decentralized decision-making bodies to which powers over natural resources are increasingly being devolved. Husbands often do not like their wives to attend group activities, and traditional working patterns and government structures tend to favor men's dominance in public decision-making. For example, in state-approved village forest management groups in India and Nepal, women are likely to be relegated to a peripheral role (Shyamsundar et al. 2004:92-93).

In Bangladesh, an analysis of local elected governance bodies, known as Union Parishads, found that women tend to head committees related to community welfare with little

FIGURE 3.2 LOCAL GOVERNMENT OFFICES OCCUPIED BY WOMEN

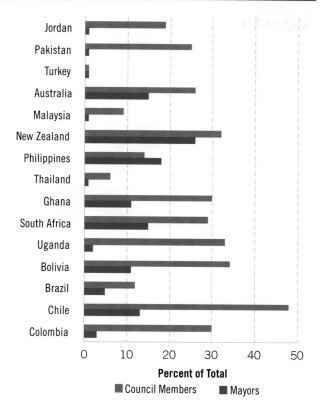

Percent of Total

■ Council Members ■ Mayors

Source: United Cities and Local Governments 2005

influence over disbursement of resources, while men typically ran and served on committees clearly related to resource allocation, like finance, agriculture, fisheries, livestock, and infrastructure (Mukhopadhyay 2003:59). Women also have a much smaller chance of becoming elected officials in local government. A study of over 15,000 municipalities in 42 countries found that only 8 percent of all local mayors are women (UCLG 2003). *(See Figure 3.2.)*

When women are absent from decision- making, issues that affect them are more likely to be overlooked. The inequity of this situation is all the more glaring in light of the fact that women are often charged with responsibility for collecting and using natural resources such as water, fuelwood, and other resources for the family's benefit.

New Demands on the Poor

Decentralization that transfers responsibility for managing services and projects to local institutions and communities without providing the financial resources needed to do so can end up creating extra burdens for the poor. For example, in Mongolia, local governments were given new responsibilities for winter preparedness and the cold-weather provisioning of livestock herds, but no new financial resources to meet this

responsibility. The result was massive livestock mortality during the brutal winters of 1999-2002, and loss of one-fifth of the nation's herd (Mearns 2004:137). In other cases, newly empowered local governments may enact new revenue-raising measures that hurt the poor. In Malawi, local governments with new decentralized responsibilities have established village-level enterprise taxes that could stifle fledgling efforts of the rural poor to build their assets and diversity their incomes by starting small businesses (Ellis et al. 2003:1507-1508).

Loss of Access to Natural Resources

Privatization—the transfer of public resources such as forests to private individuals and corporations—is often done in the name of decentralization. This transfer of management authority excludes the public from participation in decisions about the resource and often means the direct physical exclusion of people from the land or water as well, with the poor generally suffering most from such loss of access (Ribot 2004:52).

Devolving power over local resources to communities or groups within those communities can also bring problems of exclusion. For example, a community granted the power to manage a tract of public forest might decide to contract with a logging company in one area of the forest to raise revenue. In the process, it may limit local people's collection of non-timber forest products in that section of the forest. This can impose immediate costs on poor households who depend on fuelwood and other subsistence products gleaned from the forest (Shyamsundar et al. 2004:10, 95).

Making Decentralization Work for the Poor

Decentralization can be structured in ways that make it more effective and beneficial for the poor.

Ensuring Democratic Accountability

The best way to ensure that decision-makers are accountable to local people and decision-making reflects the interests of local people is to vest powers in elected authorities who are chosen through competitive local elections (Crook and Sverrisson 2001:50). While it is often difficult to rein in the political forces that stifle open elections, the benefits can be substantial. For example, competitive local elections in West Bengal, India helped make policy more responsive to the poor, and in Colombia, competitively elected mayors— challengers to the dominant party politics—brought about better education, roads, and water supply (Crook and Sverrisson 2001:15-16, 42).

Special Measures Promoting the Interests of the Poor

A central government can increase the chances of pro-poor decentralization by making an explicit commitment to promote the interests of the poor at the local level and to ensure that marginal groups get a voice in public decisions (Ribot 2004:41). Elected local governments tend to have a poor record of serving the interests of women, the poor, and other marginal-

FIGURE 3.3: VOICE AND ACCOUNTABILITY, 2004

0 -30 (Less Voice)

30 -50

50 - 70

70 -100 (More Voice)

No Data

The voice and accountability scores assigned here are based on indicators of political and civil liberties extended to a country's citizens, as well as the independence of the media, which plays an important role in monitoring governance performance. These scores reflect the extent to which citizens are able to participate in the political and decision-making processes, give voice to their concerns, and hold their government representatives accountable.

Source: Kaufmann et al. 2005

ized populations unless required to do so by the central government (Crook and Sverrisson 2001 in Ribot and Larson 2004: 6). Special measures are needed to ensure that decentralization benefits the poorest people and most vulnerable groups—women, indigenous people, the landless, migrants, and minority castes. In 1978, for example, the government of West Bengal specifically sought to increase the power of poor and landless peasants by devolving implementation of government programs to the village councils, and mobilizing poor peasants to participate. As a result, 44 percent of those on village councils in Birbhum District are now small farm owners, sharecroppers, or agricultural laborers, and the benefits of government development programs are increasingly going to the poorer members of the community (Crook and Sverrisson 2001:15-16). Kerala State's approach in 1996 was to give 35-40 percent of the state budget to local governance bodies for development planning, with detailed guidelines to make planning processes both participatory and equitable (Mukhopadhyay 2003:56).

Compensating the Poor for Short-Term Costs

Local institutions can find ways to compensate the poor for any rights they lose when a new management scheme restricts their access to a forest or other resource. For example, the community of San Antonio, Mexico, asked residents to forego cutting pine trees for use as roofing shingles so that they could be harvested as lumber. In return, the local logging business supplied free tin roofing materials and lumber to residents (Shyamsundar et al. 2004:96).

Community-Based Natural Resource Management

One specific approach to pro-poor decentralization of environmental resources is community-based natural resource management (CBNRM). Central governments in many parts of the developing world have begun to shift toward CBNRM in recognition of the limitations of centralized management and in response to the legitimate claims of indigenous groups and local communities to a share in the benefits of local resources. Worldwide, some 380 million hectares of forest land are now owned by or reserved for local communities—over half having been legally transferred to local control within the last 15 years (White and Martin 2002:11). This transformation in forest ownership and management began in Latin America in the late 1970s, moved through Africa in the late 1990s, and spread more recently to Asia. *(See Box 3.2.)*

The Rights to Information, Participation, and Justice: The Importance of a Voice

The democratic rights of the poor and their capacity to participate in environmental decisions affecting their livelihoods are central to their ability to escape poverty. Yet despite their greater reliance on natural resources to earn their livelihoods, the poor have less say than their richer counterparts in how environmental decisions are made.

In much of the developing world the policies, practices, and institutions of political life serve to exclude a majority of citizens from full participation in public decision-making—especially the poor and socially marginalized. This is true even in many nations that are nominally democratic. Democratic governance is more than merely casting a ballot in periodic elections. It means having opportunities beyond the ballot box to make one's voice heard, including participation in public hearings, review of official documents, and involvement in official processes, such as the preparation of environmental impact assessments. Full democratic engagement also means having opportunities not just to consult on projects already slated for implementation but also to play a role in shaping the design of public policies, in agenda-setting and establishing priorities for public policy, and in monitoring ongoing projects to ensure that they produce the benefits originally anticipated. *(See Figure 3.3.)*

These principles of democratic empowerment in the arena of environmental decisions were articulated over a decade ago at the 1992 Earth Summit in Rio de Janeiro. Principle 10 of the Rio Declaration, adopted by 178 nations at the close of the Earth Summit, put forth a ground-breaking proposition: that every person should have access to information about the environment, opportunities to participate in decision-making processes affecting the environment, and access to redress and remedy—that is, access to justice—to protect their rights to information and participation and to challenge decisions that do not take their interests into account. These three rights—the rights to information, participation, and redress—are often referred to as the *Access Principles. (See Box 3.3.)*

PRINCIPLE 10 OF THE RIO DECLARATION

"Environmental issues are best handled with the participation of all concerned citizens, at the relevant level. At the national level, each individual shall have appropriate access to information concerning the environment that is held by public authorities, including information on hazardous materials and activities in their communities, and the opportunity to participate in decision-making processes. States shall facilitate and encourage public awareness and participation by making information widely available. Effective access to judicial and administrative proceedings, including redress and remedy, shall be provided."

Adopted by 178 nations at the United Nations Conference on Environment and Development, Rio de Janeiro, June 1992

In 2002, during the World Summit on Sustainable Development, governments reaffirmed their commitment to Principle 10 and the Access Principles. At the same time, a coalition of governments, civil society organizations, and international institutions formed the Partnership for Principle 10 to help implement these principles at the national and local levels. Unfortunately, the record of most nations in conferring these basic rights is still far from perfect. A 2001 assessment of nine nations—both rich and poor—found a variety of systemic

MEASURING ACCESS TO INFORMATION, PARTICIPATION, AND JUSTICE

How well are governments upholding the commitments they made at the 1992 Rio Earth Summit to strengthen public participation in environmental decision-making? Are they making sufficient effort to include the poor? Answering these questions requires assessing a nation's governance performance so that it can be tracked over time and compared with good practices in other nations. Since 2000, *The Access Initiative (TAI)*, a global coalition of civil-society groups, has worked to insure this basic level of government accountability. Using a shared methodology, TAI coalition members conduct national-level assessments of laws and practices regarding public access to information, participation, and justice. For complete assessment results, visit http://www.accessinitiative.org.

weaknesses. For example, many nations have improved their laws granting public access to government data and analysis, but implementation of these laws is weak. Information on water or air quality that average citizens can understand and use is often hard to find, and documents about the environmental effects of development projects are frequently not made available in a timely manner (Petkova et al. 2002:1-8).

Even if information is made available, the public's ability to participate in resource-related decisions such as timber harvesting or the siting of mines is still limited. Although the process of preparing and publicly airing environmental impact assessments has greatly increased in the last two decades, the public's involvement still tends to be in the later stages, after many major decisions have already been made. And even when public comment is invited, many people do not have the capacity or time to take advantage of the opportunity. Performance on the Access Principles is weakest when it comes to access of ordinary citizens to redress. The ability of local people to appeal decisions they don't agree with is often constrained by obstacles of cost, lack of clarity about procedures for appeal, and also the lack of "standing" as a legally recognized party with a legitimate interest in the case (WRI et al. 2003:48-61).

These access deficits are not restricted to the poor, but the poor tend to suffer them more acutely. Indeed, most of the world's poor are excluded from interacting fully within the political processes of their country—and environmental decisions are decidedly political in many cases. They are held back by lack of education and literacy, by deficits of information and awareness, and by a lack of understanding of their rights and how to exercise them. Even where the poor are aware of their rights, other barriers may prevent them from becoming involved. People who are barely managing to eke out a subsistence livelihood often cannot afford the luxury of devoting time and resources to participation or even information-gathering. And they may be even less able to pursue a legal challenge to decisions with which they disagree, given the expense and time burden. *(See Figure 3.4.)*

Continues on page 73

BOX 3.3 EMPOWERING COMMUNITIES THROUGH FREE, PRIOR, AND INFORMED CONSENT

COMMUNITY-BASED NATURAL RESOURCE MANAGEMENT offers local people the chance to participate directly in decisions about local ecosystems and to benefit economically from their efforts. But in the real world, poor communities often do not initiate the large-scale resource development projects—such as mines, oil and gas development, or major forest concessions—that account for most natural resource wealth. More often, they are bystanders or second-class participants in these negotiations, inheriting the ecosystem costs of these projects with little gain.

The practice of "free, prior, and informed consent"—or FPIC—is designed as an antidote to this state of affairs. FPIC consists of giving local people a formal role—and some form of veto power—in the consultations and ultimate decisions about local development projects. It is intended to secure the rights of indigenous peoples and local communities: their rights to self-determination, to control access to their land and natural resources, and to share in the benefits when these are utilized by others. Many experts believe that without such informed consent on large projects, a community's land and resource rights are compromised.

In fact, without the kind of substantive participation that FPIC mandates, the tenure security of rural communities is always at the mercy of decisions made by others. It is well documented that such insecurity perpetuates poverty. In contrast, with the bargaining power that FPIC provisions bring them, communities can demand direct compensation for damages or a continuing share of the profits of resource extraction. They can even require the backers of development to invest part of the profits from these ventures to meet community needs. In this respect, FPIC is a tool for greater equity and a natural pathway to a co-management role for local communities in large development projects (Permanent Forum on Indigenous Issues 2005).

FPIC is relevant when governments make regulatory decisions—for example, allowing logging in forests traditionally occupied by indigenous peoples, or displacing riverside communities in order to construct a large hydropower dam. It can also be incorporated into infrastructure planning—from the building of roads that traverse through ancestral domains, to tourism development decisions such as providing access to sites considered sacred by tribal peoples. It is equally important in making decisions about bioprospecting for genetic resources as it is for making choices about locating major energy projects, from power plants to pipelines. To date, however, FPIC has been most relevant and critical in cases involving mining projects in countries as diverse as Australia, Canada, Peru, and the Philippines (Bass et. al. 2003:vii; Tebtebba 2002:7).

The potential poverty impact of FPIC in decisions on extractive industries such as oil, gas, and mining is particularly relevant and contentious. In order for communities to reap greater benefits from such development, their rights to sustainable livelihoods must be protected. Rules enforcing these rights will not only promote "cleaner" extraction, but also empower local communities to take the risks and share the benefits of future development. Without FPIC, these projects may further the economic marginalization of peoples and communities that are already poor and vulnerable.

These projects often require involuntary resettlement and all the negative economic consequences such dislocation brings. An FPIC requirement would enable affected people to negotiate more favorable relocation terms, including legally binding provisions on compensation, support for new housing, and the necessary infrastructure not only for shelter, but for livelihoods and education as well. Requiring FPIC could even allow these people and communities to negotiate fair, equitable, and enforceable terms of revenue- and other benefit- sharing. The inclusion of FPIC as a legal condition for financing, investment, or regulatory decisions could become a critical means to make poverty alleviation programs more sustainable (Goodland 2004; Kamijyo 2004).

To date, countries like the Philippines (Congress of the Philippines 1997) and Australia (Commonwealth of Australia 1976: Sections 66-78) have enacted laws requiring that FPIC be obtained by the government for projects within the ancestral domains of indigenous peoples. Internationally, the World Commission on Dams (WCD 2000:xxxiv-xxxv,98-112) and the Extractive Industries Review (World Bank Group 2003 Executive Summary: 2-3, Volume 2:29-33, 47-50; MacKay 2004) of the World Bank have recommended the adoption of FPIC in making decisions about dams and oil, gas, and mining projects. In addition, FPIC as a principle has been acknowledged in the Convention on Biological Diversity, with regard to access to and benefit-sharing of genetic resources (Perrault 2004: 22; Casas 2004:2728).

Putting the principles of free, prior, informed consent into practice remains a challenge. Important questions remain:

- How can we define "free" in practice? How far ahead does "prior" mean? What are the formal terms of "informed consent"?
- What is the role of customary law in FPIC? And what is the role of official processes, such as public hearings or referenda?
- In a diverse community, how is consent given and who gives the consent? Is a majority enough or is full consensus required? Is a written, legally binding agreement necessary?
- How is FPIC verified? Does the government verify it or is oversight by an independent party necessary?
- In implementing FPIC, how do we ensure a balance between the state, the general public interest, and affected community interests, particularly in the distribution of benefits?

FIGURE 3.4 THE POOR'S PERCEPTION OF RURAL INSTITUTIONS

Poll: Name the Most Effective and Least Effective Institutions in your Community

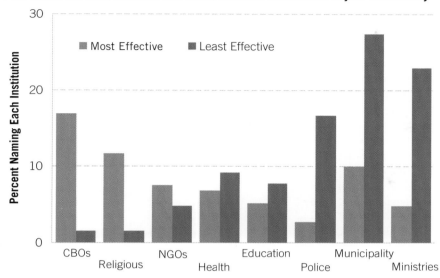

In discussion groups held worldwide, poor people were asked to name the five institutions they considered most and least effective. The bars to the left show the most frequently named institutions. Religious and community-based organizations (CBOs) were considered the most effective. Local governments and state ministries were considered the least effective.

Source: Narayan 2002

The sections below detail some of the ways in which the poor are particularly affected by deficits in their rights to information, participation, and justice. Also discussed are some of the successful steps that have been taken to address these shortcomings.

Access to Information

Information for Livelihood Choices

The rural poor face a keen need for information directly relevant to their livelihoods—information such as market prices for their crops, alternative cropping or pest control options, the availability of government assistance or training programs, or opportunities for developing new products or markets for environmental goods, from local crafts to ecotourism. Agriculture-related information is often one of the most immediate needs, since small-scale agriculture is so important to household incomes in rural areas. Information on current crop prices, fertilizer and pesticide costs, and the availability of improved seeds and low-cost improvements in farm technology can help guide the purchases of farm inputs and equipment, or help farmers successfully obtain credit.

Without information of this type, poor families find it harder to take advantage of new opportunities for generating income and increasing their assets. Numerous organizations, from multilateral agencies to local NGOs, are trying to improve access to livelihood-related information. One such effort is the farmer field schools developed by the UN Food and Agriculture Organization (FAO) as part of an Integrated Pest Management project in Indonesia. Using a participatory learning approach aimed at incorporating local knowledge and experience, these farmer field schools are yielding lessons that are being applied to information activities on sustainable livelihoods in other sectors, such as community forestry (Chapman et al. 2003:5).

Information for Public Accountability

Access to information on laws, mandated government services, and government expenses is fundamental for poor people to hold governments accountable for their performance. Unless citizens can find out what governments are doing and how they spend their funds, governments have little incentive to improve performance, deliver on their promises, or even provide basic services at adequate levels.

In Bangalore, India, citizen groups conducted surveys of municipal government performance and used the information to create "report cards" on the quality and efficiency of services such as water, transport, electricity, and police, and to press for reforms. In Rajasthan, India, citizen efforts to gain access to information on government spending and employment rolls led to exposure of local corruption, initiation of corrective action, and prompted consideration of a national right-to-information law. In Argentina, citizens can access a website—audited by a coalition of 15 NGOs—to find easily understandable information on public expenditures across a variety of government programs (Narayan 2002:32).

In Francophone Africa, cooperatively produced radio programming provides listeners of 48 rural radio stations in 10 countries with access to information on laws, legal systems, and justice. Developed during a workshop on law in Senegal, an initial radio program featured lawyers from six West African countries and provided information on land rights, women's rights in marriage, and other legal matters. Following enthusiastic listener response, the producers developed a series of subsequent broadcasts on related legal issues, such as divorce, inheritance, access to justice, and conflict resolution (Chapman et al. 2003:22).

Language Barriers to Information Access

In many developing countries, language is the most important vehicle for excluding the poor and socially marginalized groups from access to information (Sibanda 2000:9-10). For the mature democracies of Europe, Asia, North America, and Oceania, the language of government is an indigenous language or a language in which the vast majority of ordinary citizens are fluent. However, across the developing world, a significant proportion of the population typically does not use or understand the language of government, which often is a European language—French, English, or Spanish—imposed during the colonial era. It is expensive to produce multiple versions of official documents in indigenous as well as colonial languages, and the process of designating which indigenous languages are to be used in official documents can aggravate existing ethnic rivalries. But the alternative is continued high costs in social exclusion and political instability. *(See Figure 3.5.)*

Choice of Information Technologies

Whether the rural poor have adequate access to information for environmental decision-making is not only a function of the quality and quantity of information supplied. It also depends on whether the delivery technologies are appropriate for the target audience. Different groups may have different information needs and preferences for information delivery, and efforts to increase the poor's information access are most effective when they involve these groups in decisions about the information technologies to be used. For instance, in most developing countries radio and television remain much more widely accessible than the Internet. Technologies such as the wind-up radio make information dissemination possible in communities without electricity or access to batteries (Chapman et al. 2003:19-20).

Nonetheless, experience with pilot efforts indicates that it is possible to reach large numbers of people in developing countries with electronic sources of information. In the Philippines, a pilot project in the *barangays* (townships) on the island of Mindanao is using modern communications technologies to improve local access to information on topics such as agriculture, rural enterprise development, education, and health. The project features multipurpose community telecenters with telephone and Internet access (Chapman et al. 2003:17-18). The challenge remains to apply these pilot approaches more widely in Africa, Asia, and Latin America as well.

Equitable Access to Information

Despite new technological capacity for broad-based information dissemination, evidence suggests that if access to information is not universal, growing supplies of information may simply serve

FIGURE 3.5 ENGLISH DOMINATES THE INTERNET

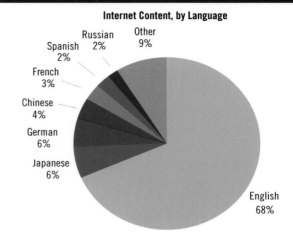

Internet Content, by Language

Russian 2%
Other 9%
Spanish 2%
French 3%
Chinese 4%
German 6%
Japanese 6%
English 68%

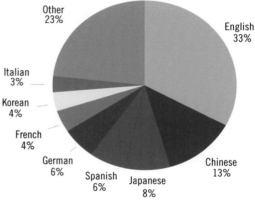

Internet Users, by Language Spoken

Other 23%
English 33%
Italian 3%
Korean 4%
French 4%
German 6%
Spanish 6%
Japanese 8%
Chinese 13%

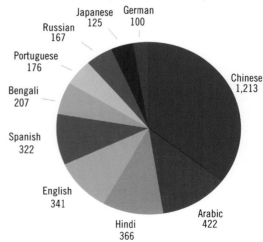

Top 10 Languages, by Millions of Speakers

Japanese 125
German 100
Russian 167
Portuguese 176
Bengali 207
Spanish 322
English 341
Hindi 366
Arabic 422
Chinese 1,213

Despite the growing diversity of internet users, the majority of content on the Internet remains in English.

Source: Global Reach 2005; Internet World Stats 2005; Encarta 2005

to exacerbate existing social, economic, and political inequalities. Historically, information on agriculture-based livelihoods in developing countries was viewed as a global public good that should be made available at no charge to all interested parties. More recently, donor agencies have emphasized private-sector provision of agricultural extension information, which can involve cost recovery and user fees that the poorest farmers cannot afford to pay (Chapman et al. 2003:vii). Involving the poor in decisions about who should pay for information services and how the sustainability of information services can be ensured is vital to ensuring the poor have access to such information.

Demand-Driven, Location-Specific Information

Rural producers in developing countries value locally generated, locally specific information much more than general information. Because farmers and fishers are unlikely to adopt new practices without substantial discussion of local examples, improved access to information is most effective when the information is focused on local conditions and local processing and marketing systems. Modern communications technologies such as the Internet and teleconferencing can enable rural farmers and fishers to discuss specific local problems with technical specialists based outside their area.

In India, the M.S. Swaminathan Research Foundation is using innovative information technologies in community-managed "e-villages" to respond to the information needs of local groups. For example, weather forecasts and information on wave height are being routed to fishers in the village of Veerampattinam. Such initiatives can also stimulate two-way information flow between villages and researchers, so that farmers and fishers can contribute their specialized knowledge to enrich national and international information systems (Chapman et al. 2003:19).

Inclusion of Women and Socially Marginalized Groups

In Swaminathan's e-villages, information centers are run mainly by semi-literate women and by students, with the aim of empowering them through their roles as information managers. By specifically targeting women and marginalized groups in knowledge management, initiatives to enhance the poor's access to information can also promote social equity (Chapman et al. 2003:19).

Access to Participation

Decision-Making About Livelihood Choices

Direct involvement in institutional processes that affect their livelihoods, such as determining the course of agricultural research, is crucial for poor farmers. Often, there is no route for their input, but that does not have to be so. The West African Rice Development Agency uses participatory methods to involve farmers in selecting which new rice varieties should be developed, thus giving poor farmers an opportunity to share

information on their preferences and needs with rice breeders (Chapman et al. 2003:20).

Participation in Broader Policy Processes

In many poor countries, poor people have participated in broader development initiatives dealing with poverty and poverty reduction. Citizen participation has been part of the process of crafting national poverty-reduction strategies in several countries, such as Bolivia, Kenya, and Uganda. The poor have also participated in creating citywide strategies for poverty reduction in approximately 80 cities around the world, including Cali, Colombia; Johannesburg, South Africa; Kampala, Uganda; and Haiphong, Vietnam (Narayan 2002:46, 70).

Citizen involvement is a central element in so-called "participatory poverty assessments"—an important tool to inform national policies and budgets. In several countries, participatory approaches to poverty assessments provided insights that had not been obvious from official survey data. In Uganda, for example, citizen participation led to increased investment in water supply and more flexible budget allocations allowing districts to respond to local needs. In Vietnam, people's participation led to the targeting of urban as well as rural poverty, steps to address the ethnic and gender dimensions of poverty, and the piloting of "citizen report cards" on the delivery of basic services (Narayan 2002:38).

Participation in Planning and Budgeting

Pioneered by the city of Porto Alegre, Brazil, participatory budgeting processes enable the poor to have more say in how government resources are distributed. In participatory budgeting, citizen meetings generate information about people's priorities for government budget allocations, which are then aggregated into neighborhood-level priorities. In Brazil, more than $260 million was allocated between 1996 and 1998 to projects selected by participants in citizen meetings, the vast majority of which addressed needs in poorer, underserved districts. As of 2003, some 180 municipalities in Brazil were engaged in some form of participatory budgeting processes (Serageldin et al. 2003:8-9).

Inclusion of Women and Marginalized Groups

In many countries, remedying deep, long-standing social inequality necessarily entails enacting laws requiring the inclusion of previously excluded groups. One example of such an initiative comes from Bolivia, where the Law on Popular Participation provides for the participation of indigenous people's organizations in municipal decision-making. Under this law, which is meant to improve local governance and aid poverty-reduction efforts, "community vigilance committees" are empowered to investigate municipal decisions. These citizen committees even have the power to halt the distribution of central government funds to local governments if they determine that planning and expenditures are not in line with community demands (Narayan 2002:42-43). In India, it took a constitutional amendment mandating that women must make up at least a third of the councilors in *panchayats* (village-level councils) to create real opportunities for women's voices to be heard in municipal leadership.

Access to Justice

Research shows that the poor are less likely to access the legal system to secure or enforce their rights to use natural resources. A study of seven countries in Africa and Asia found that poor communities are often reluctant to pursue legal claims based on their environmental grievances. In general, economically disadvantaged groups lacked familiarity with legal institutions as well as the necessary financial resources to use legal remedies effectively (Boyle and Anderson 1996, cited in ESRC/GECP 2001:18). Intimidation by local elites and government officials can also make the poor and others of low social status hesitant to assert their right to live in an environment adequate for their health and well-being. For the poor who lack formal, legally recognized tenure to their land and natural resources, the threat of retribution is especially chilling.

Securing and Enforcing Property Rights

Clearly defined property rights, and confidence that these rights can be efficiently defended against interlopers, are fundamental to governance systems built on the rule of law. As mentioned earlier, appropriate property rights regimes are also central to encouraging the poor to invest in their land or in resource management in ways that bring economic development and poverty reduction. However, in many developing economies, corruption, excessive regulation, and complicated property registration procedures significantly burden citizens, especially the poor.

In Guayaquil, Ecuador, for example, it has been three decades since the passage of land reform laws, and most households are aware of their property rights and the importance of securing title to land. But the majority of these poor households are incapable of navigating the legal labyrinth—including long delays and high costs—surrounding the land titling process. In theory, the process costs about $350, or as much as three months of a typical worker's salary. In practice, the actual cost is closer to $750—a prohibitive sum for most poor families (Moser 2004:42-44). A similar situation exists in Peru, where land registration processes to secure property rights requires land holders to engage with 14 different agencies involved in conferring a single title (Narayan 2002:54).

In several countries, poor people's associations and cooperatives are working with local authorities and financial institutions to address the need for secure land tenure rights and housing. In Mumbai, India, a slum-dwellers' organization has been able to acquire land, housing, and basic infrastructure services for its members. In the Philippines, a scavengers' association whose members live on a 15-hectare municipal dump in Quezon City has helped mobilize member savings to acquire legal rights to land through land purchase. And in

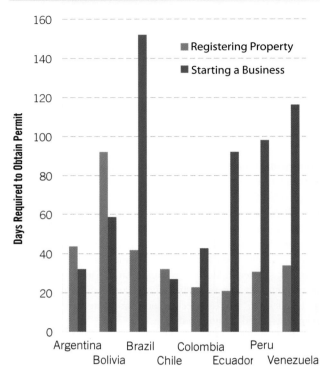

FIGURE 3.6 BARRIERS TO DOING BUSINESS

Days Required to Obtain Permit

- Registering Property
- Starting a Business

Argentina · Bolivia · Brazil · Chile · Colombia · Ecuador · Peru · Venezuela

Source: World Bank 2005

Guatemala, 50,000 squatters have formed cooperatives, acquired land through legal means, and are now repaying long-term loans (Narayan 2002:66). Meanwhile, Ghana's land-registration law specifically provides for registration of customary land rights, and pilot projects are now underway to build capacity among traditional-land administrators to improve record-keeping and land registries (Bruce 2005).

Procedural Injustice

The poor typically are most affected by procedural injustices in the legal and court systems. For instance, the poor are least able to afford the costs imposed by long delays in court proceedings. Also, the poor are more likely to be disadvantaged by language barriers in the legal system, such as court documents or hearings in languages not widely spoken by the rural poor (Girishankar et al. 2002:289).

Mechanisms for Alternative Dispute Resolution

For poor people living in remote rural areas, the existence of decentralized local processes for resolving disputes may make the difference in their ability to secure or enforce their rights. However, if such decentralized alternatives are poorly executed, they can end up disadvantaging the poor by reinforcing the dominance of local elites and incorporating local norms that discriminate against women, children, and other socially marginalized groups (Girishankar et al. 2002:289).

Fair Permitting and Licensing

A key element of access to economic justice for the poor is the ability to obtain permits and licenses for small business enterprises via processes that are transparent, fair, and efficient. The state of affairs in many developing countries departs considerably from this norm. In Zimbabwe, for instance, red tape and expensive licensing fees constrain the ability of poor communities to launch small businesses based on wildlife tourism or other products and services. Registration of a tourist company in Zimbabwe takes more than a year and costs about US$14,000 to obtain needed certificates and guarantees (Narayan 2002:55).

In Lima, Peru, registering a small garment workshop employing a single owner-operator takes on average 289 days and costs in excess of US$1,200, or more than 30 times the monthly minimum wage. In Indonesia, the official license fees for registering a small business are about US$400, but the actual costs often are typically triple that amount (Narayan 2002:54-55). *(See Figure 3.6.)*

Fortunately, some state and local governments are starting to make it easier for small entrepreneurs to secure their rights to operate. In Bali, one municipality introduced "one-stop shops" for business licenses and permits. This has not only helped businesses obtain licenses more efficiently but has also augmented government tax revenues by 75 percent. In India the government of the state of Gujarat removed the requirement that gum collectors—virtually all of them poor women—must sell gum at artificially low prices to a handful of government-selected buyers (Narayan 2002:56).

As the numerous examples cited above show, progress in empowering the poor in their rights to information, participation, and justice can be made. Such progress is central to giving the poor the political and business tools to take advantage of their nature-based assets and to participate in rural commerce that leads to sustainable economic progress—the route out of poverty.

Empowering the poor with resource rights can enable them to manage ecosystems better and significantly increase their environmental income.

FOUR STEPS TO GREATER ENVIRONMENTAL INCOME

THE WEALTH OF NATURE, IN THE FORM OF ENVIRONMENTAL income, is already a key component of rural livelihoods for both the rich and poor. But there is great potential for this component to grow, given the right conditions, and contribute to higher household incomes that lessen poverty. The first condition is an acceptance that better management of ecosystems can increase their productivity—immediately and over the long term. And, since the wealth of nature flows directly from the productivity of ecosystems, better management brings the potential for greater environmental income.

The second condition is that the access to and control of nature shifts so that the rural poor can both see the advantages of good ecosystem management and claim the benefits from it, overcoming the obstacles of disenfranchisement that have kept them economically and politically marginalized.

In this chapter we explore both these conditions—prudent management of ecosystems and governance that empowers the poor to profit from it. We consider the questions: What do we mean by better ecosystem management? What is its potential for poverty reduction? And what governance changes are required to route environmental income to the poor?

In addition, we examine the factors besides governance and eco-friendly practices that support the evolution of environmental income for poverty reduction. These revolve around the need to find successful models to commercialize ecosystem goods and services, coping with such constraints as marketing, transportation, and the need to capture greater value from nature-based enterprises than the poor often do. In addition, we consider the potential for "payment for environmental services" (payments for preserving the functions of ecosystems, such as water supply or carbon storage) to contribute to the portfolio of income-generating enterprises based on nature that the poor can tap.

In examining these factors, we put forth four steps to generate greater environmental income for the rural poor.

1 MORE INCOME THROUGH BETTER ECOSYSTEM MANAGEMENT

Healthy ecosystems work at peak productivity; degraded ecosystems produce less, particularly of the forest products, forage, clean water, crops, and bushmeat on which the poor tend to rely. In fact, degradation of ecosystem functions—in the form of nutrient-depleted soils, overgrazed pastureland, logged-over and fragmented forests, and overfished lakes and coastal waters—has become a serious impediment to the livelihoods of the poor.

As the findings of the recently concluded Millennium Ecosystem Assessment show, ecosystem decline is widespread. The global drop in ecosystem health not only undermines the natural resource base that anchors a substantial fraction of the global economy but erodes the planet's life-support systems more generally (MA 2005a:1-24). The most immediate victims of this decline are the poor, whose household economies, as shown in Chapter 2, depend heavily on ecosystem goods and services. The pressures on ecosystems are particularly intense on many common property lands and fisheries—the most important source of environmental income for the rural poor. Examples are many and distributed on every continent and sea: denuded hills in western India; exhausted forests in Madagascar and Haiti; and depleted catches off Indonesia, Jamaica, or Fiji are just a few of the many instances where overuse and abuse of ecosystems directly impacts the poor.

Better Management Requires an Ecosystem Approach

But ecosystem decline is not inevitable. Ecosystems are resilient and can be sustained through practices that accommodate their

inherent biological limits, recognizing that ecosystems are not simple production factories but living systems built on complex relationships among species and physical factors such as water, temperature, and nutrient availability. Practices that respect and preserve how ecosystems function are the building blocks of what in the past five years has come to be known as an *ecosystem approach* to natural resource management—that is, management that centers itself around the sustainable and equitable use of ecosystems. In this chapter, when we refer to "better ecosystem management," we mean adopting an ecosystem approach. *(See Figure 4.1.)*

In practice, "better ecosystem management" often translates to fairly simple principles, particularly in the context of the ecosystems that the poor use most frequently. For example, it may mean more moderate harvest levels of forest products, forage, or other vegetation, so that the ecosystem can retain its macrostructure, and so that watersheds maintain their ability to absorb rainwater and retain it as soil moisture. It may involve adopting different treatment of livestock, cultivation methods that reduce erosion, or cropping patterns that minimize depletion of soil nutrients. Where ecosystems have already degraded substantially, it may require a period of non-use and restoration, such as a closed fishing season or a logging or grazing ban. Or it may demand direct revegetation through tree-planting. In all cases, the effectiveness of such measures will be greater when they are actively supported by community members who see themselves as benefiting on a fair and equal basis in the short and medium terms. In this sense, an ecosystem approach is as much people-centered as it is ecosystem-focused.

Income Benefits of Better Management

When rural farmers, forest users, and fishers adopt more sustainable practices, considerable income benefits can follow. A recent study of four low-income farming villages in arid western India illustrates the potential for higher agricultural income. All four villages had participated in government-supported projects from 1995 to 2001 to better manage their degraded watersheds—part of a nationwide program known as Watershed Development. They used a variety of water and soil conservation techniques, such as check dams and contour tilling, as well as tree planting to revegetate denuded slopes. The idea was to capture the occasional but intense monsoon rains, preserving them as soil moisture, rather than letting them run off and erode the soil (Reddy et al. 2004:303-306).

The success of these measures from an ecosystem standpoint showed clearly in the recovery of groundwater levels, with the water table in local wells rising an average of 25 percent in spite of several years of scant rainfall. From this increase in soil moisture flowed other benefits. The amount of land under irrigation increased. Grass forage increased as well in most villages, including forage on common property areas, which, prior to the watershed treatments, had been too degraded to produce useable fodder. Crop yields rose significantly, both on

FOUR STEPS TO GREATER ENVIRONMENTAL INCOME FOR THE RURAL POOR

1. Manage Ecosystems Better for Higher Productivity
Improve the stewardship of ecosystems by adopting an ecosystem approach to management—recognizing the complexity of ecosystems and living within their limits. Good stewardship brings higher productivity, which is the foundation of a sustainable income stream.

2. Get the Governance Right to Insure Access to Environmental Income
Confer legally recognized resource rights (such as individual or communal title, or binding co-management agreements). Where possible, decentralize ecosystem management to the local level (community-based natural resource management), while providing for regional or national coordination of local management plans. Empower the poor through access to information, participation, and justice. Create local institutions that represent their interests and accommodate their special needs.

3. Commercialize Ecosystem Goods and Services to Turn Resource Rights and Good Stewardship Into Income
Improve the marketing and transport of nature-based goods produced by the poor. Make credit available for ecosystem-based enterprises. Capture greater value from the commodity chain. Partner with the private sector. Take care to keep successful commercial activities sustainable.

4. Tap New Sources of Environmental Income Such as "Payments for Environmental Services"
Make the newly developing market of payments for environmental services more pro-poor by expanding the array of eligible activities and payment schemes. Look upon ecosystem income as a portfolio of many different income sources. Diversify this portfolio to reduce risk and enhance the bottom line.

FIGURE 4.1 MAINTAINING THE VALUE OF NATURE

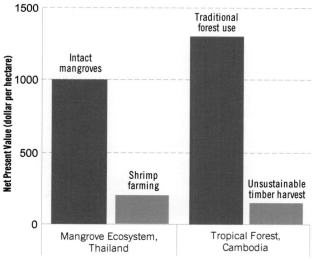

Value of Intact vs. Converted Ecosystems

Source: Millennium Ecosystem Assessment 2005b

irrigated and nonirrigated land: rice yields up 15-44 percent; peanut yields up 16-81 percent. Village land became more valuable too, because it was in better condition and had more agricultural potential (Reddy et al. 2004:308-312, 318).

With higher productivity, household incomes grew. Income from all sources—agriculture, livestock, and wage employment—increased from 50 to over 100 percent from their levels before the watershed rehabilitation. These increases, in turn, are reflected in higher spending on education and medical care. The benefits from adopting more sustainable watershed practices also extended beyond income. The availability of drinking water went up in all the surveyed villages and the time spent fetching water decreased—as much

as 80 percent in one village—a major benefit for women (Reddy et al. 2004:310, 313, 321). *(See Figure 4.2.)*

Likewise, indigenous communities in the Philippines' mountainous Kalinga province have revived traditional irrigation and forest-management techniques that protect local watersheds. Using a combination of reforestation, agroforestry plantings, environment-friendly irrigation, and fish production within active rice paddies, Kalinga families were able to greatly increase agricultural production and raise incomes. They have repaired over 90 traditional irrigation systems to sustainably supply their rice terraces, while on the watershed slopes individual families maintain and protect their own agroforest plantings. Between 1990 and 1996, the combination of watershed protection and good irrigation management raised annual incomes for over 1,000 poor families in seven indigenous communities by an average of 27 percent, all while maintaining over 80 percent of the original high-biodiversity forest cover (Southey 2004:1-2; UN Housing Rights Programme 2005:154).

Similar stories of income gains can be told for communities that have improved their management of local forest ecosystems, fisheries, or grasslands. In the Himalayan village of Waiga, villagers banned grazing and burning on the grasslands above the community in 1995, and planted 1500 alders. Over the next few years grassland recovery raised fodder production sevenfold—enough for all local livestock plus a surplus for sale—while the returning tree cover provided leaf litter for agriculture and stopped gully erosion in the steeply sloped terrain (Munsiari 2003:5, 15-19).

In Fiji, over 100 coastal villages have designated local *tabu* zones in nearshore waters where fishing and shellfish collection is banned to promote recovery of the marine life that forms a central element in local livelihoods and culture. Robust recovery in these local protected zones has spilled over into adjacent fishing areas, increasing the village marine harvest. In three villages where economic evaluations have been conducted, income from marine resources—typically half of all household income—increased 35-43 percent from 1997, when the *tabu* zones were established, to 2003. *(For details, see Chapter 5 case study, "Village by Village: Recovering Fiji's Coastal Fisheries.")*

In each of these instances, villagers have pursued more ecosystem-friendly practices because they visibly supported their resource-based livelihoods, boosting both their direct use of ecosystem goods and their cash incomes. These examples and many others clearly make the case that better ecosystem management pays off at both a household and a village level.

This is good news for rural economies in general. But how effective is this increase in environmental income at reducing village-level poverty? Unfortunately, evidence shows that the benefits of ecosystem improvements are often skewed toward higher income brackets. With more land, trees, cattle, or capital to invest in the increased farming potential of their recovered lands, the rich tend to capture more of the income bonus that healthier ecosystems provide (Reddy et al. 2004:318).

But poor families certainly do benefit also, for example by greater availability of wage employment, and greater ability to

PRINCIPLES OF AN ECOSYSTEM APPROACH

The goal of an ecosystem approach to natural resource management is to foster the sustainable use of ecosystems and the equitable distribution of their benefits. An ecosystem approach is successful if it preserves or increases the capacity of an ecosystem to produce the desired benefits in the future, and increases the capacity of society to fairly apportion benefits and costs.

Manage Within Natural Limits
Recognize the complex functioning of ecosystems and respect their biological thresholds. Conserve ecosystem structure in order to maintain ecosystem productivity.

Manage for the Long Term
Optimize ecosystem productivity—and benefits—over generations, not years. With care, managing for long-term productivity can be compatible with significant short-term gains.

Manage at Both the Micro and Macro Scales
Respect ecosystem processes at the micro level, but see them in the larger frame of landscapes. Decentralize management to the local level when possible. But recognize that ecosystems are interconnected and interactive, and exist on many scales. Local management efforts must be linked and harmonized at the larger scale so they do not work at cross-purposes.

Account for the True Value of Ecosystems
Include the full array of ecosystem goods and services when assigning economic value, not just the commodity value of extracted goods.

Make Trade-Offs Clear
Recognize that ecosystem management will involve trade-offs, since not every good or service can be maximized at the same time. Make trade-offs transparent so that costs can be shared equitably.

Involve All Stakeholders in Decisions
Be inclusive when making major management decisions, involving all stakeholders to foster equity and inspire active participation in the stewardship of ecosystems. Integrate social information with economic and environmental information in the decision-making process. Acknowledge that human modification of ecosystems is not incompatible with good stewardship.

meet their subsistence needs for firewood, fish, and the like. This provides a maintenance level of ecosystem support and greater income resilience for hard times. But it may not provide enough support to take a firm step out of poverty. For that, governance changes that free up access to ecosystems and promote information and market support to the poor are needed.

2 GETTING THE GOVERNANCE RIGHT: EMPOWERING THE POOR TO PROFIT FROM NATURE

As described in Chapter 3, lack of access—physical, political, and financial—is a critical roadblock to the ability of the poor to use ecosystems for poverty reduction. Bringing pro-poor governance to the management of ecosystems begins by removing this roadblock through improvements in tenure security, devolution of authority over nature to more local levels where the poor reside, and empowerment of the poor through information, participation, and the power of redress. The net effect of these actions is to secure the resource rights of the poor and give them the tools to exercise these rights responsibly and equitably.

Securing Property and Resource Rights Through Tenure Reform

Addressing the need for greater tenure security so that the poor can tap ecosystems and invest in their good stewardship is a top priority. It requires reform of the formal tenure regimes that currently make it hard for the poor to exercise property rights over land and resources. Interest in tenure reform has grown significantly in recent years as acceptance of the central role of tenure security in poverty reduction has spread. When well thought-out and appropriately implemented, tenure reform can produce considerable benefits for the poor. The most important is an acknowledgement by the state that traditional tenure

arrangements, including communal tenure, are legitimate and legally enforceable.

Recognition of Traditional Rights

Untitled, customary tenure remains the predominant form of tenure in many rural areas of the developing world. The persistence of untitled occupancy—the situation of many poor families who live on land they do not hold formal title to—is a common challenge for tenure-reform efforts. Experience shows that recog-

FIGURE 4.2 EFFECTS OF WATERSHED RESTORATION ON WATER AVAILABILITY AND TIME SPENT FETCHING DRINKING WATER						
	Drinking Water Used (liters/household/day)			Time Spent Fetching Drinking Water (hours/household/day)		
Village	Before Restoration	After Restoration	% Change	Before Restoration	After Restoration	% Change
Mallapuram	10.5	11.9	13%	10.5	11.9	13%
S. Rangapuram	10.7	12.8	20%	10.7	12.8	20%
Tipraspalle	11.8	14.3	21%	11.8	14.3	21%
Mamidimada	12.2	14.3	17%	12.2	14.3	17%

Source: Reddy et al. 2004

Continues on page 85

BOX 4.1 NEGOTIATING INDIGENOUS TENURE RIGHTS IN BOLIVIA

IN THE LOWLANDS OF EASTERN BOLIVIA, LAND RIGHTS lie at the heart of a pioneering agreement to preserve both an indigenous people's way of life and a unique tract of dry tropical forest. The deal shows the importance and difficulty of negotiating land tenure amidst differing land uses and user groups.

The setting is the Gran Chaco, an isolated, biodiverse region where the pre-Hispanic Guaraní-Izoceño people have sustainably farmed and hunted the parched, inhospitable land for centuries. In recent decades large-scale cattle ranching and commercial soybean, sunflower, and cotton farming have encroached upon traditional indigenous territory, damaging the land through deforestation and soil degradation. Lacking tenure rights over the public lands they lived on and utilized, the Guaraní-Izoceño were unable to prevent these incursions.

Negotiations in the 1990s between Bolivia's government and the Capitania del Alto y Bajo Izozog (CABI), a grassroots indigenous organization representing the Guaraní-Izoceño, resulted in two landmark agreements. The first preserved 3.4 million hectares of uninhabited Gran Chaco forest and scrub as a national park, designated in 1995. The second will grant the Guaraní-Izoceño title to 1.5 million hectares of land adjacent to the park as a communally owned indigenous territory.

For the Guaraní-Izoceño, the outcome was a pragmatic compromise. On the one hand, they relinquished any ownership claim to the land encompassed by the Kaa-Iya del Gran Chaco National Park (KINP), now the world's largest protected area of dry tropical forest (Winer 2003:181). On the other, the 10,000-strong community, which lives in 23 villages scattered along the Parapet River, will own the sole right to exploit the land and forests of their titled territory—a major step towards safeguarding their livelihoods and future survival (CABI 2004:1-2).

The Guaraní-Izoceño also negotiated a major influence over the park. The KINP is now the only national park in the Americas co-administered by an indigenous organization and a national government. Moreover, the group won the right to pursue sustainable activities, such as ecotourism and fishing, in some park areas, while closing the entire area to new settlers (CABI 2004:1).

CABI's successful land rights campaign was pursued in partnership with the New York-based Wildlife Conservation Society (WCS), which was anxious to protect the Gran Chaco's abundant and often rare wildlife, including jaguars, Chacoan peccaries and guanacos, giant armadillos, pumas, and tapirs (Roach 2004:1). Backed by WCS expertise, CABI submitted a successful proposal for a co-managed national park in 1995. To ensure community buy-in, the park proposal was reviewed in community meetings. To allay livelihood concerns, the border was determined in such a way as to minimize conflict—excluding from the park areas utilized by communities or occupied by third parties (Noss 2005).

In 1997, CABI presented a demand for a Tierra Comunitaria de Orígen (TCO)—designated indigenous territory—under Bolivia's new agrarian reform law. The government approved the request, while retaining ownership rights to underground minerals and awarding water rights to the local municipal government. By April 2005, 300,000 hectares of land had been titled. When the process is complete, 1.5 million hectares of formerly public land will be owned by CABI, as the indigenous people's legal representative, with the remainder of the 1.9 million hectares in private, nonindigenous ownership (Noss 2005).

While the new land rights afforded the Guaraní-Izoceño are clearly conditional, they offer significant potential to boost food and livelihood security. A revitalization of traditional production systems is already underway, with women villagers experimenting with the production of mesquite flour and fish meal for sale in the Isoso communities. Plant-based shampoo and honey are also being commercially developed for sale in Santa Cruz, the regional capital. These activities are managed by CABI's women's organization, CIMCI, whose goals are to empower women, promote traditional culture, improve food availability and nutrition and, ultimately, boost indigenous incomes (Winer 2001:13). CABI has also sought government permission for sustainable commercial trade in collared peccary and tegu lizard skins (Noss 2005).

According to a recent report on the land deals by an the independent consultant, the TCO, by increasing livelihood security, will enable the Guaraní-Izoceño to "retain their identity as an indigenous tribe of lowland Bolivia while building stronger, and more equitable, economic links with the expanding market-driven economy of Santa Cruz" (Winer 2001:12).

The conditional nature of the tribe's land rights, however, is underlined by the presence of the 1,900-mile Bolivia-Brazil pipeline, which bisects both the Kaa-Iya National Park and the TCO. The pipeline was approved before either the park or indigenous territory were created, and the government retains rights to energy resources in the area (Roach 2004:12). As a consequence, Bolivia's government has granted further gas and oil exploration concessions in both the KINP and the indigenous territory, although energy companies would be required to work with CABI to mitigate their social and environmental impacts. A trust fund contributed by the existing pipeline companies, following an agreement with indigenous organizations, including CABI, made up 43 percent of the park's budget between 1998 and 2003 (Noss 2005).

TABLE 4.1 RECENT LEGAL REFORMS STRENGTHENING COMMUNITY FOREST TENURE IN DEVELOPING COUNTRIES

Country	Year Enacted	Key Features of Reform
Bolivia	1996	Ancestral rights of community groups have precedence over forest concessions. Subsequent laws have strengthened community rights.
Brazil	1988	Constitution recognizes ancestral rights over land areas that indigenous groups and former slave communities traditionally occupied. Federal government is responsible for demarcating indigenous reserves on public lands and protecting land rights of indigenous groups.
Colombia	1991	Constitution of 1991 recognizes and outlines a framework for collective territorial rights for indigenous groups and Afro-Colombian traditional communities.
Indonesia	2000	New regulatory process has been recently established by which customary ownership can be recognized.
Mozambique	1997	Titles for customary rights are available.
Philippines	1997	Constitution of 1987 protects ancestral domain rights. Indigenous Peoples Rights Act of 1997 provides legal recognition of ancestral domain rights pursuant to indigenous concepts of ownership.
Tanzania	1999	Customary tenure is given statutory protection whether registered or not. Titles for customary rights are available.
Uganda	2000	2000 draft law currently under revisions. Government is embarking on an ambitious program of devolution to district and local councils.

Source: White and Martin 2002; used with permission, copyright Forest-Trends 2002

nizing and integrating such customary tenure into formal state tenure regimes is a key feature of successful reform. This may require greater flexibility about what is considered legitimate proof of "ownership" so that oral as well as written records of occupation or access to communal lands are accepted. *(See Table 4.1.)*

In Mozambique, Tanzania, and Uganda, new tenure laws simply recognize land held under customary tenure as fully legally tenured "as is." This includes using certification processes based on verbal endorsements (Mozambique), as well as using community-administered land recording and titling processes (Tanzania). In Eritrea, customary tenure has been recognized in the form of lifetime-use agreements, although they cannot be passed down to family members (Alden Wily and Mbaya 2001:15-18).

Other countries are slowly bridging between communal tenure and more individualized land rights. *(See Box 4.1.)* The key is that new individualized rights must be compatible with customary practices, so that they do not create or perpetuate a parallel tenure system that can give rise to conflicting claims later on. Simple and unambiguous procedures for recording land sales and transfers can also help avoid tenure disputes as customary systems interface with modern land markets and land uses (Deininger 2003:52-54).

Traditional rights to resources also extend beyond land rights per se into water rights, the use of fisheries, and pastoral rights. These too can be made more secure through formal recognition and delineation by the state. For example, the government of Fiji formally recognizes "customary fishing rights areas" where villagers have traditionally fished and collected shellfish. These nearshore zones, known locally as *qoliqolis*, have been surveyed and accurately mapped, with the records maintained by the nation's Native Fisheries Commission. Based on these designations, the state Fisheries Department has begun granting local communities the right to draw up their own management plans for *qoliqolis* with the aim of restoring these fisheries as a community asset.

It is important to recognize that increasing security of tenure for the poor does not always require gaining full title or private ownership of land or resources (Deininger 2003:39). In the case of common-property resources like state forests or fisheries, increased tenure security often takes the form of the legally sanctioned use of these resources, including the right to exclude others and manage the resource for optimum benefit. As in the Fiji example above, the key to increased security is that the physical extent of the land or resource, the exact limits of the use, the permissible forms of management, and the limits on the state's ability to modify or terminate the arrangement are specified and agreed to in a legally binding agreement. This kind of unambiguous and enforceable use-right is often a central feature of successful community-based natural resource management projects meant to extend ecosystem access to the poor.

Reduced Transaction Costs and Other Benefits

High transaction costs—the costs of doing business, both in money and time—have traditionally been an important obstacle to the poor in acquiring or disposing of land. Effective legal and land information systems typically form the core of successful tenure reform, thereby lowering property transaction costs, whether these be sales or leases of resources and use rights. This can help the poor access and manage land and resources as more flexible assets.

Other benefits can come from successful tenure reform as well. One is a decentralization of the bureaucracy that administers tenure and resolves resource and land disputes. When the government machinery for administering tenure rights moves closer to the small rural landowner, it increases the landowner's access to land registration and taxing authorities, as well as legal proceedings involving land disputes. Decentralization of tenure administration has been particularly dramatic in Tanzania and Uganda, with community-based mechanisms for resolving property rights-related disputes appearing in these countries, as well as Mozambique (Alden Wily and Mbaya 2001:14-18, 46).

Improved security of tenure has also, in many instances, fueled the development of more dynamic land markets in poorer communities. In such cases, poorer households can benefit through greater access to productive land if they have sufficient access to capital. Evidence from Mexico, for example, indicates that policy reforms of the early 1990s that opened up both land and credit markets enhanced access to land among poorer households with adequate access to capital, but not poorer families in general (Carter 2003:52).

Higher Rural Incomes

Greater security of tenure, especially when coupled with access to credit, can help poor farmers in developing countries invest more in their land, thereby improving agricultural productivity and raising farm income. In Thailand, evaluation of a 20-year initiative begun in 1987 to provide the country's rural populations with access to modern land registration and credit institutions revealed that midway through the effort, rural incomes, major investments, and use of formal credit is much higher among farmers with titled land than for those yet to be included in the program (Riddell 2000:10). In China, experimental land policy reforms granting clear ownership rights to village-based cooperatives for communal management of mountainous forest lands enabled villagers in Jiangsu and other provinces to create large, successful orchards (Bruce et al. 1995). In general, successful tenure reform creates both the perception of greater security and the reality of more enforceable rights—both important elements in the willingness and ability of the poor to invest their time and resources in expanding their environmental income. *(See Figure 4.3.)*

The Dangers of Ineffective Tenure Reform

Reforming something as central to wealth creation as a nation's tenure system is by no means easy. Even though modern tenure-reform efforts rarely attempt major land redistribution, they are still politically perilous, with vested interests often reluctant to change the status quo. Unfortunately, when changes to tenure systems are incomplete or poorly executed, the poor can end up worse off rather than better. Therefore, in designing tenure reforms, policymakers must be careful to avoid the following:

- **Failure to recognize important land uses and users.** Poorly designed attempts to increase security of tenure for some can end up reducing the security of others. For example, land titling and registration projects may overlook rights to important land uses, such as the right to gather non-timber forest products or to obtain water. These uses are most often exercised by women and the poor. If these rights are not legally recognized as part of the land registration process, they may be effectively destroyed (FAO 2002a:20).

- **Land grabs by urban elites.** In some instances, city-based government and business elites have made dramatic attempts at land grabbing through the process of shifting land out of customary tenure systems and into statutory tenure systems. This can take the form of government-granted concessions on indigenously held land over which the state claims ownership. Or it may simply be land purchases by the elite from those who hold land under customary tenure arrangements. Some countries, such as Cameroon, have initiated policies that appear to encourage land speculation, favoring privileged individuals with access to knowledge, influence, and money (Elbow et al. 1998:5).

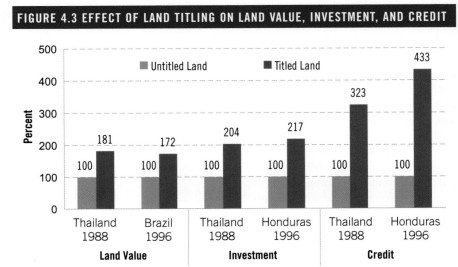

FIGURE 4.3 EFFECT OF LAND TITLING ON LAND VALUE, INVESTMENT, AND CREDIT

■ Untitled Land ■ Titled Land

Percent

	Land Value		Investment		Credit	
	Thailand 1988	Brazil 1996	Thailand 1988	Honduras 1996	Thailand 1988	Honduras 1996
Untitled	100	100	100	100	100	100
Titled	181	172	204	217	323	433

Source: Deininger 2003

- **Exclusion of women.** Women make up the majority of the world's agricultural producers, but they are usually the last to be included in land and tenure reform efforts. Traditionally, women in Africa and other parts of the developing world have only had access to land tenure through their husbands, fathers, or other male relatives. Registration of land in the name of male relatives precludes women from obtaining property rights at a time when women's access to land for cultivation is becoming increasingly important for AIDS widows and other female heads of households (Carter 2003:49).

- **Inadequate procedures for documenting communal rights.** The lack of appropriate procedures for expeditious, cost-effective documentation of untitled communal property rights can compromise the effectiveness of tenure reform. For instance, the government of Bolivia enacted legislation recognizing indigenous land rights in 1996; because of complicated and costly documentation procedures, however, by 1999 only 10 percent of eligible territories had received titles (White and Martin 2002:16).

- **Conditionality and other constraints to land markets.** Many new tenure laws do nothing to remove constraints and limitations that have long hampered land markets in developing countries. For example, none of the recent spate of African tenure legislation removes long-standing requirements to occupy and use agricultural land in order to maintain tenure (Alden Wily and Mbaya 2001:14). Agricultural use may not always be the best use of ecosystems, either economically or ecologically. For example, conversion to wildlife habitat may be a better use of some lands with high tourist potential, or conversion to other commercial purposes. Flexibility in land use may increase the value of the land assets of the poor, while conditions on use reduce the economic potential of the land.

Poor-Friendly Decentralization: Community-Based Natural Resource Management

Improving the tenure security of the poor and their ability to exercise property rights is only one step in the legal, economic, and political empowerment of poor families. A second important step is devolving management authority over ecosystems to local institutions that are more accessible to the poor.

As detailed in Chapter 3, decentralization that actually works for the poor is more the exception than the rule. It requires, at a minimum, that local institutions—whether they be official government institutions like village councils or informal institutions such as user groups, cooperatives, or watershed committees—are formed on democratic principles of representation, meaning that they are accountable to their low-income constituents. But this alone is not usually enough to overcome the structural bias against the poor in local institutions. Special efforts to include the poor are generally required. These can range from reserving gender-based or income-based slots in local institutions to insure participation; arranging for special outreach and training for members of these institutions; creating rules to insure equitable distribution of local benefits to low-income households; and using participatory rural appraisals and other survey techniques to help local institutions catalogue and quantify community needs and the potential trade-offs for any set of management actions. Of course, this is all predicated on the assumption that the state has granted these local institutions some actual authority over local resources—something that is still far from common.

Pro-Poor Decentralization: An Example

When these minimum requirements come together—true devolution of authority, local accountability, and an effort to acknowledge the special needs of the poor—the outlines of local empowerment can begin to take shape. Uganda provides an instructive example of democratic decentralization that is both ecosystem-friendly and serves the interests of the nation's low-income fishers. Until the late 1990s, management of fishing in Lake Victoria, Lake Albert, and other inland lakes was the province entirely of the central government. A government push for decentralization and the creation of new fishery rules led to the formation in 2003 of Beach Management Units (BMUs)—local institutions charged with regulating fishing along specific stretches of the lake and shore. Each BMU is headed by a

committee with 9 to 15 democratically elected members from each of four different stakeholder groups: 30 percent boat owners, 30 percent fishing crew members, 10 percent fish mongers, and 30 percent other stakeholders. In this way wage laborers, merchants, and other low-income families associated with local fishing can participate in the committee along with wealthier boat owners. To address gender disparities, BMUs are encouraged to have women make up 30 percent of the committee "whenever possible" (Waldman et al. 2005:65-68).

The duties of the BMUs cover the daily management of the local fishery: issuing fishing permits and limiting the size of the fishing fleet, registering fishing gear, and working with the government Fisheries Department to enforce regulations against illegal fishing practices. The BMUs also collect fishing data to help guide their management decisions. The local committees are allowed to keep 25 percent of money generated from licenses and landing fees to fund their operations (Waldman et al. 2005:65-68).

Results of the decentralization have been encouraging so far. The BMUs report better control over illegal fishing and improved working relations with central government authorities. The fishing statistics that BMUs have collected have brought greater local awareness to the need to reduce fishing pressure and fish more sustainably. On Lake Albert, BMUs have declared

three non-fishing zones designed to protect known nursery areas and thus maintain the fish stock. The committees report voluntary reductions in the use of illegal fishing gears, indicating a change in attitudes of the fishing community. It is too early to tell if these improvements in management have translated into more income for local fishers, but anecdotal reports of better daily catches are starting to come in. Women are also beginning to change their role. Local culture discourages women from joining fishing crews, but some women have started fishing from the shore; a few women have even become boat owners, hiring men to crew their boats (Waldman et al. 2005:65-68).

The Benefits of CBNRM

Uganda's Beach Management Units are just one example of the broad potential for community-based natural resource management (CBNRM)—one of the most progressive and potentially poor-friendly manifestations of decentralization. This kind of devolution of management authority over state-owned resources has the potential to be both inclusive enough to involve the poor and effective enough to generate increases in environmental income. Well-functioning community management arrangements have shown benefits in all three of the key areas highlighted in this chapter: household income, local empowerment, and ecosystem condition (Shyamsundar et al. 2004:7-13).

Income Benefits

Income benefits come from a variety of sources, including greater access to wage employment as well as to local subsistence goods like bushmeat and forest products (Shyamsundar et al. 2004:9). For example, community forestry arrangements often give rise to forest-related enterprises that can provide substantial local employment; revenue-sharing with the government from timber sales and the like; and greater control over sources of woodfuel and other forest goods in daily use. The same is true of devolving wildlife management to local communities. When the Namibian government in the late 1990s transferred to rural communities the authority to manage wildlife in certain demarked zones called conservancies, it included the right to regulate the substantial tourist trade in these zones and the right to harvest a modicum of bushmeat as well. Conservancy-related activities have created some 3800 jobs that did not exist before the decentralization took place; entrance fees and trophy-hunting fees have generated public funds for schools and other public investments, and even for cash payouts to conservancy members. Local incomes have risen substantially as a result. *(See the Chapter 5 case study, "Nature in Local Hands: The Case for Namibia's Conservancies.")*

Local Empowerment

Some of the most significant benefits of community management are in the area of empowerment. Shifting substantial management control over ecosystems to communities gives them a voice where often they had none. It often restores traditional rights—such as water use rights, forest collection rights, or fishing rights—that may have been lost as modern states central-

ized their authority. While these political and legal benefits are enormous, the shift in resource control also exerts a substantial psychological effect on communities that may be even more important, particularly for the poor. This manifests as a new sense of pride and control over one's life, as well as greater confidence in dealing with others outside the community and with government authorities. This empowerment dividend is often augmented as local community members gradually develop the accounting, monitoring, planning, and dispute-resolution skills that good resource management demands (Shyamsundar et al. 2004:11). The benefits of such new personal and group skills spill over into domains well beyond resource management.

Ecosystem Benefits

There is also evidence that community-based resource management can create incentives that foster good ecosystem management and contribute to conservation goals as well as economic development. Experiences in Africa, India, and Nepal demonstrate that community forestry management can result in healthier forests and improved tree cover (Shyamsundar et al. 2004:13). A notable example is the HASHI program in the Shinyanga district of Tanzania. With help from the central government, over 800 villages have revived a traditional conservation practice of creating "enclosures" that foster regrowth of the once-abundant forest by controlling grazing and harvesting within the enclosed area.

Management decisions about the enclosures are entirely a local matter controlled by village councils. So far, creating traditional enclosures through the HASHI program has reforested some 350,000 hectares of overgrazed and barren land. Economic benefits distributed to villagers—in the form of fodder, fuel wood, medicinal plants, and greater water availability—have made the HASHI program a popular success. The combination of income and ecosystem benefits made the HASHI program a finalist for the UN's Equator Prize in 2002, recognizing it as prime example of the conjunction of poverty reduction and conservation. *(See the Chapter 5 case study, "Regenerating Woodlands: Tanzania's HASHI Project.")*

Similar ecosystem improvements have also been documented in cases where wildlife management has been devolved to the local level. Wildlife censuses associated with the Selous Conservation Program in Tanzania showed increased animal numbers, and wildlife populations have rebounded impressively in Namibia's conservancy areas as poaching has fallen and conflicts with livestock have been reduced (Shyamsundar et al. 2004:12).

Keeping Community-Based Management Pro-Poor

These successes show the potential for community-based management to empower and enrich local communities and still manage ecosystems well. But CBNRM is no panacea, and it is by no means always pro-poor. Both the power and benefits associated with community management tend to be directed toward higher income classes unless specific accommodations are made. In pursuing pro-poor CBNRM, communities, governments, and NGOs must keep in mind several points:

Accounting for the Costs of CBNRM

Community management of ecosystems sometimes entails substantial costs that must be accounted for and minimized. One of the major costs of many community-management schemes is the short-term loss of the use of a resource to allow it to recover or to keep its use within sustainable levels (Shyamsundar et al. 2004:10). This "opportunity cost" may manifest as a restriction in the use of common areas for grazing or firewood collection, or a limit on how many game animals or fish can be harvested—restrictions that inevitably fall hardest on the poor. The loss is usually temporary—a typical grazing ban to restore a denuded watershed slope might last for three years. In addition, if the ban is successful, the long-term benefit from the closure will soon exceed the short-term costs. Nonetheless, the short-term costs can impact poor families considerably in the interim and are a frequent source of dissatisfaction (Kerr 2002a:1397).

For example, in a study of villages participating in watershed restoration projects in western India (part of India's Watershed Development program), nearly a fifth of the landless residents reported that the restoration projects harmed their interests because they could not graze their sheep on the commons due to grazing bans (Kerr 2002a:1396). Women too complained of their loss of access to common lands, which they used to collect grasses for brooms, tamarind pods, and tendu leaves—some of the few income sources that they controlled independent of their husbands (Kerr 2002a:1395-97).

This and other studies show that without a mechanism to compensate the poor for their short-term losses, achieving good ecosystem management and maximum benefit to the poor may be antagonistic goals, at least in the initial stages of ecosystem recovery. Offering wage labor to try to offset the income loss is one common way to avoid this trade-off. For example, watershed restoration may require seasonal labor for several years to build check dams, plant trees, install fencing, create ponds, or recontour croplands to retain water. However, this will only provide adequate support if the poor are hired preferentially for such jobs and the labor persists for as long as their access to resources is restricted. In the study of watershed restoration in western India, for example, wage labor, while helpful, was not sufficient to make up for loss of access to grazing on common lands (Kerr 2002a:1388, 1395-1396; Shyamsundar et al. 2004:17-18).

Other approaches to reducing short-term costs or providing compensation may also be useful. Staging the restoration of common areas so that they are not all closed at once, but in rotation, is one strategy to reduce the burden on the poor. Another approach is to provide extra services specifically to poor families, such as training in skills that open other employment options, or establishing credit or savings groups to help them manage household resources better and make investments in land (Kerr 2002a:1391-92).

Assuring Equity in Benefits Sharing

As has been stressed above, richer families in a rural community usually hold a structural advantage in capturing the benefits from good ecosystem management. For example, watershed restoration in arid climates will clearly advantage those with more land, especially if these are low-lying lands where the groundwater captured by the restoration is likely to accumulate most. Likewise, owners of large boats with more efficient gear will be able to harvest more of a healthy fish stock than the poorest fishers paddling small *piroques*. Even when local resource management projects try to make poverty reduction a goal, this natural advantage often intervenes (Kerr 2002a:1388-9, 1398; Kumar 2002:763).

Given the structural advantages of the rich, developing mechanisms to share benefits and costs equitably among all community members must be a priority when communities begin local management of common resources. But finding acceptable recipes for benefit-sharing is notoriously difficult. Successful attempts often require analyzing the benefits carefully so that they can be apportioned not just on the basis of the quantity of water, fish, or forest products produced, but on the economic value of these benefits.

The village of Sukhomajri in the Indian state of Haryana offers one famous example of the successful sharing of benefits. Watershed restoration there in the 1970s produced the same benefits seen in other successful restoration projects: revegetated upper slopes produced more fodder and more surface water in low-lying areas that could be used for irrigation and other income-producing activities.

The innovation came in giving each family an equal share of the water that collected in the village's new catchment ponds, with the option to use it or sell it to others if they wished. Landless families could thus sell their water to farmers with greater need for irrigation, turning their share to cash, as well as benefiting from wage labor that might result from more irrigated crops. Each family also received equal shares of the watershed's valuable *bhabhar* grass, which they could similarly use or sell. This arrangement resulted in considerable increases in household income throughout the community. By 1998, 70 percent of village households were earning Rs 2000 per month (US$47) (Agarwal and Narain 1999:14-17; Kerr 2002a:1390; Kerr 2002b:56).

Unfortunately, there is no easy formula for benefit-sharing arrangements, which are highly specific to both the resources being managed and the social structure of the community. In some instances, the resource is highly divisible and marketable, such as the harvest of high-priced medicinals, and sharing may be straightforward. Or community benefits may come in the form of access fees from tourists, timber revenues, or other income that can be split among community members. In

Namibian conservancies, for example, revenues from tourist access, campgrounds, and the sale of game hunting licenses to foreigners generate income that in some instances has been turned into a cash payout to each conservancy household—an easy way to assure equal treatment (US AID 2004:13).

But in other instances, easy division may be impossible. For example, in many restored watersheds the increase in water will not result in accumulation of surface water in ponds where shares can be calculated. Instead, extra water may manifest as more groundwater, which is legally the property of the land owner from whose well it is pumped to the surface. This makes the community benefit difficult to calculate and hard to tap by poor families without land or wells. Addressing this would require an arrangement where groundwater is considered community property no matter where it is pumped, with users paying a fee to the community to tap it (Kerr 2002a:1391-1392, 1399).

Another approach to community equity is to grant special arrangements just to the lowest income families. For example, one Indian village in Maharashtra state granted to the village's landless residents exclusive fishing rights in a run-off pond that the community had built (Kerr 2002a:1391-1392, 1399). Likewise, low-income families could be allowed special areas to fish, extra harvest or grazing periods, or an extra share of the resource being managed. In all cases, this requires a progressive view of benefits and a careful definition of user rights that is formalized and accepted by the community.

Acknowledging the Limits of Participation

There is a growing consensus that communities can establish functioning institutions capable of managing local resources, and that these institutions—from village councils to user groups—can function through community participation, making real the promise of local devolution. But there is also the realization that community processes are rarely egalitarian. Except in rare instances, communities are not homogeneous, and naturally break into various interest groups, making equity a challenge. Often, these are based along class, ethnic, and gender lines, with women and the poor usually being the least powerful of these groups (Kellert et al. 2000:705; Shyamsundar et al. 2004:16-17, 19; Kerr 2002a:1388-1389; Kumar 2002:765-766).

A scene several years ago from a village meeting about a new watershed restoration project in the Indian state of Karnataka illustrates the problem. At the front of the room sat the wealthiest landholders, who owned fertile, irrigated land in the valley bottom. Behind them sat middle-income farmers with less-desirable but still good land. In the back stood poor families with the least fertile land at the top of the watershed. The landless hung around the periphery; no women were present (Fernandez 2003:6-7).

In situations such as these, assuring true participation for the poor requires considerable institution-building so that mechanisms of inclusion can gradually work against ingrained social patterns. For example, one NGO in Maharashtra state that helps villages undertake watershed restoration programs insists on a consensus-based approach to all decisions about the watershed and spends a good deal of time facilitating such decisions and building the social basis necessary to foster them (Kerr et al. 2002:16, 34). Although it is more unwieldy than a majority vote, this approach offers an organic way to make sure the interests of the landless minority are not simply swept aside.

Another method that has proven effective in some situations is to encourage the poor to form a separate affinity group or self-help group—such as a credit or savings association—where they can discuss common concerns, develop skills such as bookkeeping and management of common funds, and come to common negotiating positions. One or more members of such self-help groups can then act as an official representative on the watershed committee or other local authority charged with managing the natural resource in question, insuring that the poor have an official voice and at least a modicum of representation. In Karnataka, such arrangements have, for example, resulted in better recognition of the need to provide forage to the landless during the watershed regeneration process (Fernandez 2003:5-10).

Often, these self-help and affinity groups have a high proportion of women. This points up the fact that achieving real participation of the poor inevitably means making special efforts to bring women, who head up many of the poorest households, into a greater decision-making role. Overcoming gender bias is particularly important in natural resource management because of the role women play in generating environmental income and their place in managing the household economy. They are usually the front-line users of natural resources on a day-to-day basis.

Unfortunately, there is abundant evidence that even when women are given places on village committees, they often are treated as tokens rather than full members, with their voices being lost among the male majority or their votes simply a proxy for their husbands' opinions. Techniques to increase the influence of women include requiring parity—or close to it—of representation on such committees, as well as deliberate scheduling of meetings to accommodate women's domestic and child-care responsibilities. Including women in technical training about managing the resource in question is also important to insure parity in skill levels and reinforce the idea of women as co-managers rather than dependents (Kerr 2002a:1398).

Nongovernmental organizations are frequently essential partners in helping communities devise decision-making processes that include the poor. Local NGOs often provide both technical help with the task of resource management, but also capacity-building in group dynamics and conflict resolution, as well as administrative capabilities such as bookkeeping, budgeting, keeping records, filing reports, and interacting with government officials. In Karnataka, the NGO MYRADA provides a series of 14 training modules for the use of local self-help groups covering topics such as crafting a common vision, developing internal rules and regulations, resolving conflicts, and maintaining proper books (Fernandez 2003:6). As with MYRADA, the involvement of local NGOs can be the catalyst for innovations in local governance that help the community reach beyond its traditional social hierarchy to recognize the need for greater equity in benefits-sharing (Kerr 2002a:1390-1392). Such groups can also bring isolated rural communities into contact with networks of similar communities to share experiences, as well as with a wider global community of ideas and funding that may offer new resources and partnerships (WRI et al. 2003:71-88).

While communities can look to civil-society groups for new approaches to local governance, they often need to revisit traditional community institutions as well. Customary sources of authority such as chiefs or village elders are frequently key players in helping communities to organize around the goal of local management. In many cases, community action could not proceed without at least the tacit blessing of the traditional leaders.

In some instances, these traditional institutions have acted in parallel with democratic institutions such as village councils, creating a synergy between new and old that has been key to the success of the management effort. In Fiji, it was the encouragement of the local district chief that led to the first experimentation with community management of a local fishery and the establishment of the no-fishing zone that helped rejuvenate it. In Tanzania's HASHI project, protected forest enclosures are officially managed by the local village councils, but the councils are guided by the villages' customary Council of Elders and informed by traditional village assemblies called *Dagashida*.

While traditional institutions generally engender the community's respect and buy-in to local management regimes, they can also be obstacles to equity and equal participation if they simply reinforce entrenched power arrangements or provide a route for powerful families to monopolize the benefits stream (Shyamsundar et al. 2004:7).

A Continuing Role for the State

The goal of devolving control over natural resource management from the national level to the local level is to give local residents a stake in management, thus increasing its effectiveness and equity. But the state still plays an essential role in helping such local management to succeed. For example, it is the state that must put in place the policy and legal framework to allow local management to take place at all. In addition, the state has a special responsibility to look beyond the level of community management to make sure that broader environmental standards are upheld and management efforts are coordinated. The state can also help local management to become a source of substantial income through training and capacity building, as well as deploying its more traditional economic development tools of transport, marketing, and credit assistance. More specifically, the state has an important role in eight areas:

1. **Defining the legal space for local management.** Without official state recognition, local management regimes can never be secure. This usually requires altering the framework of national laws that define the state's role in resource

ownership and management. Many nations have made significant progress in crafting new forestry, wildlife, and fishery laws that specifically sanction local management regimes. In South Africa, for example, the 1998 Marine Living Resources Act included a provision recognizing the legitimacy of managing local fisheries for subsistence use (WRI et al. 2003:180). In Africa alone, more than 30 countries have passed new forest laws since 1990 that mandate varying levels of decentralization and new opportunities for local participation in management (Shyamsundar et al. 2004:20). However, interpreting these laws and establishing the limits of local management authority are ongoing challenges that demand continued state attention and experimentation. This includes not only the details about technical management itself, but also such institutional questions as the structure of local management committees. The state, for instance, may play a progressive role by encouraging gender balance on such committees.

2. **Granting resource tenure.** As stated earlier, tenure is a central requirement for real access and control of resources. As it defines the parameters of local control, perhaps the state's most important contribution is to clearly establish the resource rights of communities in a legally unambiguous manner. This allows communities to make firm management plans and financial commitments without fear of disenfranchisement. It gives them the legal basis to seek redress through the courts if they feel their resource rights have been violated. This access to redress is essential to the exercise of true authority, and lack of this right is a frequent bugaboo of local management efforts.

3. **Requiring community consent.** One way that the state can safeguard local community management rights is to insist on a requirement of free, prior, and informed consent (FPIC) by the community whenever large-scale economic projects like mining, energy extraction, or major timber harvests are proposed nearby. Planning for such projects often excludes effective community participation and conflicts with local priorities. FPIC is both a principle and a process that some governments and international institutions are beginning to incorporate into their policies. As a principle, FPIC is the right of local communities and indigenous peoples to participate meaningfully, through consent procedures, in decisions about how the land they occupy and the natural resources they depend on are to be utilized. As a process, FPIC enables rural communities—who are often politically weak—to present their concerns to those proposing large-scale projects, whether they are from the government or the private sector. Its intent is to promote equal bargaining power among all parties and shield communities from coercion, threat, or manipulation. Without this shield, experience shows that poor communities often lose control of local resources. *(See Box 3.3.)*

CO-MANAGEMENT EXPERIENCES IN SAMOA

In 1995 the Fisheries Division of Samoa developed a co-management policy for the nation's small-scale coastal fisheries. It began to work with fishing communities to develop Village Fisheries Management Plans, providing villages with any technical assistance they needed to develop the plans. Provided the rules proposed in the management plans were consistent with national law, the government would help the communities make them legally binding by issuing them as by-laws. Once approved, the by-laws were disseminated via radio.

Within the first two years of implementing the co-management policy, the Fisheries Division had helped 44 communities adopt Fisheries Management Plans. These plans all contained elements of sound ecosystem management. For example, all of the plans banned the use of dynamite (a destructive fishing practice), 86 percent established local marine protected areas, and 75 percent set mesh size limits on fishing nets to reduce the accidental capture of juvenile fish. The government implemented the program gradually, providing extension services to roughly 10 new villages per year. Extension officers would first meet with the community; if it was interested, the officers would convene a community assembly to negotiate the co-management arrangement, including the various duties and obligations of the state and the community. Satisfaction with the program was generally high. An internal review in 2000 found that 86 percent of the villages were implementing management plans at or above average competency (King and Fa'asili 1999:138-140; World Bank 2004:42)

COMMUNITY-BASED FISHERY MANAGEMENT IN SAMOA

Management Technique	% of Villages Adopting
Banning the use of chemicals and dynamite to kill fish	100
Banning the use of traditional plant-derived fish poisons	100
Establishing small protected areas in which fishing is banned	86
Enforcement of limits on the size of mesh nets	75
Banning the dumping of rubbish in lagoon waters	71
Placing controls or limits on the number of fish fences or traps	<10
Offering prayers for the safe-keeping of the marine environment	<10

Source: King and Fa'asili 1999: FAO 2002b

4. **Creating local-state co-management partnerships.** In many cases, local management is best pursued as a partnership between the community and the state. Co-management regimes, as these partnerships are called, allow the state to contribute its expertise in some areas while devolving substantial control over most day-to-day management. Co-management regimes have become common in fisheries, where communities may not have the capability to take on some essential tasks such as fisheries research and stock assessment, or to manage an entire fishery. But they are

Continues page 96

BOX 4.2 **FAIR TRADE CERTIFICATION: RURAL PRODUCERS MEET THE WORLD**

A COFFEE DRINKER IN SAN FRANCISCO has little chance of ever meeting the small-scale farmer in Nicaragua who may have raised the original coffee beans. But if the coffee drinker has bought "Fair Trade" beans, he or she has made a conscious effort to support the coffee producer with a fair wage. Goods that are certified as "Fair Trade" are priced a little higher than the market rate, with the premium routed to the small rural producer in the form of a slightly higher profit. The Fair Trade concept aims to bring small farmers a fair price for their products and to support sustainable and socially responsible production methods (FLO 2004:3-8). Fair Trade is thus one of the more benign faces of globalization, with the potential to connect poor rural producers with global markets.

Besides coffee, Fair Trade items include tea, cocoa, sugar, honey, bananas, fresh fruit and vegetables, dried fruit, fruit juices, rice, wine, nuts and oilseeds, cut flowers, ornamental plants, cotton, and a variety of handmade crafts—but coffee remains the core of the Fair Trade system (FLO 2005; Young 2003:6). Fair Trade certification—where producer cooperatives commit to a series of labor and environmental practices and social equity goals—began in 1988, when Mexican and Dutch trading partners launched the Max Havelaar Fair Trade certification, sponsored by the Max Havelaar Foundation in the Netherlands. In 1997, the growing family of Fair Trade organizations formed an umbrella organization, Fairtrade Labeling Organizations International (FLO), which standardized labeling and certification procedures. In 2004 there were some 400 organizations and more than 800,000 producers certified under the FLO umbrella (FLO 2005).

Fair Trade producers can earn more than double the conventional market price for their beans. The 2004 price for Fair Trade Robusta coffee was set by the FLO at a minimum of US$1.01 per pound, with an additional $0.15 premium for organic coffee. This compares to prices on the conventional market that averaged US$0.40 per pound (FLO 2004:11; Bacon 2005:505). This can translate into a significant income boost for farmers. In Chiapas, Mexico, farmers in one coffee cooperative have reported 100-200 percent growth in income in recent years due to Fair Trade sales (Taylor 2002:19-23).

Direct gains in income are critical for small farmers, but some of the less visible benefits of Fair Trade can be even more important for producers in the long term. Members of the La Selva cooperative in Chiapas, Mexico, cite the importance of the "apprenticeship in commercialization" they have gained from working directly with buyers and learning about potential markets (Murray et al. 2003:12). Other important benefits include greater access to credit, broader networks of contacts, and technical training and information exchanges that help farmers produce higher-quality coffee (Taylor et al. 2002:20).

Finally, Fair Trade and shade-grown coffee can significantly reduce the vulnerability of small farmers, impacting livelihood security in ways that are often overlooked. A typical shade coffee farm consists of a mixed plantation that can produce fruit, firewood, timber, and other products in addition to coffee. This allows families to be less dependent upon a single crop, and provides resources that can be used directly or sold for cash. Studies in Guatemala and Peru suggest that these non-coffee products can provide as much as 25 percent of the total value earned on a small farm (Rice 2001 in Valencia 2001:2). Fair Trade cooperatives also offer a set price for a crop—this gives farmers the ability to plan ahead, a rare luxury (Murray et al. 2003:7). A survey of Nicaraguan farmers found that farmers participating in Fair Trade and other alternative markets were four times less likely to feel at risk of losing their land due to low coffee prices (Bacon 2005:506).

Fair Trade coffee production also has important environmental benefits. While Fair Trade cooperatives do not require their members to raise shade-grown coffee, they encourage it along with organic production methods. Most training and financing are linked to sustainable production methods, and organic coffee can earn an additional price premium (Taylor 2002:3-4).

The Samyukta Vikas Cooperative: A Fair-Trade Success

While coffee is the focus of much Fair Trade commerce, villagers near Darjeeling, India, have concentrated on tea. Residents of three remote hill villages located on a former tea plantation are now successfully exporting organic Darjeeling tea to U.S. consumers. The new tea enterprise has helped the villages of Harsing, Yankhoo, and Dabaipani become economically self-sufficient. Tea income has allowed residents to construct a community drinking water supply, and the villagers are developing plans to add ginger, cardamom, and oranges to their organic exports.

Life for the villages' 483 families, all of Nepali descent, has improved significantly in just eight short years. Since the tea estate they inhabit was abandoned in 1952, the isolated communities had survived on subsistence farming, cultivating maize, millet, and vegetables, and keeping a few cattle, goats, and chickens—almost all for domestic consumption. Most

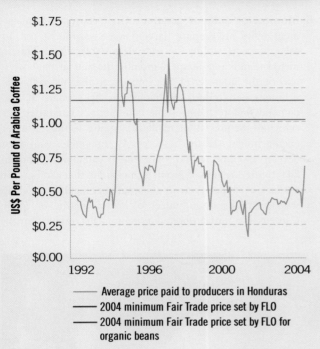

- Average price paid to producers in Honduras
- 2004 minimum Fair Trade price set by FLO
- 2004 minimum Fair Trade price set by FLO for organic beans

Source: FLO 2004, ICO 2005

families had small landholdings averaging 1.5 acres. Their soil's high acidity, the result of intensive tea cultivation, led to very low productivity. Local deforestation had also contributed to soil erosion, landslides, and the loss of forest products (RCDC 1996:5-7).

Most families lived a precarious existence, surviving on less than 12,000 rupees per year (US$275). A 1996 survey by a local development NGO, the Darjeeling Ladenla Road Prerna (RCDC), reported that the villagers "have very low self-esteem and display an attitude of despair." When asked their views on development priorities for their communities, 30 percent replied "no idea" (RCDC 1996:4).

All this changed in 1997 when RCDC persuaded the villagers to form the Samyukta Vikas Cooperative and use their own resources to improve their livelihoods. Three community members were chosen as "animators" and trained by RCDC in participatory decision-making and co-op management. These three explained what they had learned to households across the scattered hamlets. The villagers then voted to establish a cooperative of three levels, with farmer families as the bottom tier, elected

hamlet committees as the middle tier, and an elected board, with members from every village, as the highest decision-making authority (Down to Earth 2004:44). The board's first actions were to set up a milk cooperative and a small credit union through which villagers could sell milk and borrow small sums at far less interest than charged by middlemen (TPI 1999).

Once the cooperative was functioning, RCDC linked the villagers with Tea Promoters of India (TPI), a Calcutta-based, family-owned company that manages four organic tea gardens, all run according to Fair Trade standards. During a series of negotiations, the cooperative board voted that all members would convert to organic farming, while TPI undertook to buy the villagers' tea supply, distribute grasses used for soil rehabilitation to the farmers, and train them in organic techniques including composting, pruning, and use of natural pesticides. The company also supplied 4,800 tea saplings at a 50 percent discount (TPI 1999:1-2).

Tea-leaf production from the villages has grown steadily since the first collection for TPI in May 1998. Tea collectors are selected from the community by each hamlet committee, and paid a wage by TPI. Other co-op members transport the leaves to TPI's nearest tea garden, where they are processed and blended for export (Down to Earth 2004:44).

Samyukta Vikas Cooperative is the first non-plantation, cooperative tea supplier established in Darjeeling. Since 1999, organic English Breakfast, Earl Grey, and green tea sourced from its family-owned plots has been exported by Tea Promoters of India to the Fair Trade company Equal Exchange, based in Massachusetts. From there it is sold to food co-ops, health stores, churches, restaurants, and cafes around the United States. TPI, Equal Exchange, and Dritwelt Partners, a European certification organization, jointly bore the cost of the international organic certification process for the Samyukta Vikas Cooperative's tea supply. In 2004, Tea Promoters of India provided more than eight tons of tea to Equal Exchange (nearly 140,000 boxes), 10 percent of which came from the Samyukta Vikas Cooperative (Howard 2005).

While it remains a small-scale enterprise, the successful collaboration between community-owned farms in Darjeeling, local Fair Trade exporters, and overseas Fair Trade importers demonstrates one route by which global markets, when combined with fair prices and local governance over use of natural resources, can benefit poor producers in developing nations.

also common in forests, such as India's Joint Forestry Management agreements, where communities are granted limited management and use rights on state forest lands. The challenge for co-management regimes is to assure that the state cedes sufficient rights and authority to local communities but does not abandon them, leaving the communities without proper support.

5. **Accounting for the scale challenge.** Inherent in the management of ecosystems is the problem of scale. Ecosystems can exist simultaneously at different scales, from a forest block in a single watershed to interconnected forest tracts extending a thousand kilometers. Sustaining ecosystems requires keeping in mind the interconnections between these scales, from micro to macro. Forest management in one community's watershed may affect downstream communities and adjacent forests. Local communities cannot be expected to manage well at this macroscale, and thus the state retains an essential role here. This means helping to coordinate management plans in adjacent communities—and across the nation—so that they do

not conflict or overemphasize a single kind of use (Shyamsundar et al. 2004:20). The state also has an oversight responsibility to make sure that local management aligns with national environmental laws, and even with international treaties such as the Convention on International Trade in Endangered Species (CITES).

6. **Monitoring and enforcement.** Good ecosystem management relies on keeping harvest activities, tourist use, or other impacts within the ecosystem's tolerances. This in turn demands an attempt to monitor the state of the ecosystem or the intensity of the impacts so that management decisions can reflect conditions on the ground. It also demands enforcement of the community's harvest or use rules and the prevention of illegal logging, fishing, or other encroachment on the resource. Communities can often develop monitoring and enforcement capabilities, and, in fact, this is one area of group participation that can become a source of empowerment, as community members develop scientific skills or volunteer as forest guards or game wardens. But for transboundary monitoring or enforcement

actions where large-scale poaching or illegal activity is involved, the state can usefully intervene with personnel or funds or both.

7. **Capacity-building and networking.** Developing the management acumen required to effectively manage a fishery, game population, ecotourism trade, or forest concession takes time and training. While NGOs can help with much of this capacity-building and training, the state—as a repository of skills and budget in these areas—clearly has a part to play. The state, as overseer and coordinator, also has a natural role in helping communities share lessons and skills. It can also help communities participate in larger international networking efforts and partnerships, such as UNDP's Equator Initiative, which brings together governments, NGOs, businesses, and local communities to identify and support examples of sustainable community resource management that increases rural incomes.

8. **Supporting communities with transportation, credit, and market regulation.** If one of the prime goals of local management is to increase income from the community resource, then the state can help by fulfilling its traditional role of supporting economic development by assisting local communities to develop their transportation and marketing infrastructure. Without an outlet to viable markets and the knowledge and funding to create demand, local communities will not be able to maximize their gain and reward good management practices. At the same time, the state must do its part to insure that competitive markets exist for the products of rural enterprise. That means regulating markets to avoid the price-fixing and monopoly control of resource markets that frequently occurs in poor nations.

When the state supports communities by playing these roles well, it can greatly increase the chances for successful local management. In turn, the state can look forward to significant returns on its investment in the form of better management results, higher tax revenues, reduced resource conflicts, and smaller outlays for monitoring and enforcement (Shyamsundar et al. 2004:13-14).

3 COMMERCIALIZING ECOSYSTEM GOODS AND SERVICES

Success at managing ecosystems can bring the poor higher agricultural yields, more fodder, and higher fish catches. Success at creating local institutions that serve the poor can bring a fairer distribution of this enhanced productivity. But these steps alone do not necessarily bring wealth. They may enrich the household diet and stabilize daily subsistence, but they do not assure the kind of cash income that aids the transition out of poverty. That usually requires successful commerce. Success at commercializ-

ing ecosystem goods and services often marks the difference between using nature as a low-income livelihood support and making it a substantial source of cash and a path to the accumulation of economic assets (Marshall et al. 2003:128, 135-136; Neumann and Hirsch 2000:43). There are several important elements to successful commercialization:

Provide Marketing Assistance

Product processing, marketing, transport, and sales are the main aspects of commercialization. While emphasis is often placed on the process of production itself—the farming, fishing, or collection of wild products—the importance of the commercialization process is sometimes under-appreciated. That's unfortunate, because commercialization factors are the most frequent obstacles to higher cash income from ecosystems. A recent study in Mexico and Bolivia found that marketing and sales—not production issues—were the main constraints to successfully turning nontimber forest products like resins, basket-weaving materials, honey, bamboo, and bark into successful commercial products (Marshall et al. 2003:130, 135).

These constraints manifest in a variety of ways. Rural farmers and fishers may lack a way to get their products efficiently to market. Forest collectors may not know how to effectively price their product, may lack information on how to improve their product's quality or consumer acceptability, and may not know how to build demand in specialty markets in urban areas or among tourists. Guides or others serving the ecotourist market may lack contacts, experience, or language skills to market their unique services. It is not surprising that research suggests an urgent need for better business planning, market analysis, and market development if rural ecosystem users are to find commercial success (Marshall et al. 2003:135).

To a certain extent, sheer lack of information on current market conditions and trends contributes to lack of marketing power. New information services can help with this. In Uganda a coalition of NGOs, government agencies, and private companies operates FOODNET, a regional network that collects weekly or daily price information on commodities. Rural farmers access the information through radio broadcasts, the Internet, and cell phones. The service, which reaches seven million people weekly, prevents middlemen from manipulating prices to undercut producers. Farmers estimate that the service has raised their return on products by 5-15 percent (WRI 2005).

But the problem goes deeper as well—to a lack of training in business planning. NGOs and state extension services can be important partners in providing the training and technical support to meet these planning and marketing needs. For example, Mexico's PROCYMAF program, cofinanced by the government and the World Bank, offers training to community enterprises in forest management as well as marketing information for wood and nonwood products. The program has financed over 60 marketing studies and 10-12 pilot projects to test the viability of nontimber forest product enterprises (Scherr et al. 2003:50, 57).

Understand the Limitations of Transportation

Rural areas are notoriously difficult to reach. Roads and rail links are usually scarce, often in disrepair, and frequently impassable. This puts transportation high on the list of critical factors determining the commercial viability of ecosystem goods and services that the rural poor may wish to market. In the remote Iquitos region of Peru, for example, transportation costs are often the deciding factor in what is marketed (Neumann and Hirsch 2000:51-52).

Fresh fruits, vegetables, fish, milk, and other perishable items are particularly subject to the limitations of transport infrastructure. In Nigeria's Niger River delta region, marketing of the African or Bush Pear (*Dacryodes edulis*)—a nutritious and valuable fruit much in demand—is held back by impassable roads during the rainy season, just when the pear is bearing most heavily (Adewusi 2004:144). Likewise, a market analysis of palm fruits harvested in the one of Brazil's Extractive Reserves found that it was only profitable to market those fruits picked within 114 km of a market—about 3.5 days travel time. Beyond that, it was too slow and too costly to be worth the effort (Neumann and Hirsch 2000:52).

Of course, the need to provide efficient rural transportation goes well beyond its importance to building markets for ecosystem goods. It is a basic requirement for rural development more broadly. Studies show that transportation deficits and bottlenecks are an obstacle to economic growth. The connection of roads to poverty reduction is also well-understood. A recent study shows that living close to a highway decreases a household's chance of being poor by 17 percent and increases its access to work by 32 percent (Manasseh and Chopra 2004). Nonetheless, providing adequate rural transportation has been a constant challenge for national and local governments due to the high costs of transport infrastructure, and it is likely that getting products to market will remain a lingering problem for poor producers.

Make Credit Available

One of the most frequently cited constraints to commercializing environmental goods is a lack of financial services such as loans or credit. Credit is simply unavailable in many rural settings, handicapping the ability of the poor to use their environmental assets. By one estimate, 500 million economically active poor families have no access to credit or other financial services. Without access to credit, the poor must rely on their own savings to capitalize their enterprises, but these are frequently inadequate to fully exploit their economic opportunities (Marshall et al. 2003:135; IFAD 2004:9).

FIGURE 4.4 COFFEE MARKET VALUE CHAIN

	Total Value ($ per pound)	Value Added in Each Step	
Producing Country — Farm	$.68	$0.68	Coffee trees take 3-4 years to bear fruit after planting. On most small farms, coffee is picked from the tree by hand.
Factory	$1.36	$0.68	At the factory, the coffee beans are separated from the rest of the fruit and prepared for export.
Exporter	$1.70	$0.34	The beans are sent to an intermediary for export.
	$1.80	$0.10	Freight and export costs
Consuming Country — Importer	$2.14	$0.34	Coffee is received by the importing agent
Factory	$3.43	$1.29	The coffee is processed and roasted.
Retail	$4.40	$0.97	Retailers purchase roasted coffee and sell to coffee bars, restaurants, and the home market. The price of specialty coffee and coffee sold in cafes can reach $10 to $20 per pound.

Source: Wheeler in Fitter and Kaplinsky 2001

Considerable strides have been made in recent years in providing new credit channels for the poor, from informal savings clubs to more formal Grameen-type microfinance banks. These have dispelled the myth that the poor are not creditworthy or are unable to save (Morduch and Haley 2002:2-3). But the dimensions of the credit problem require continued progress in extending microfinance to diverse rural communities. One promising strategy involves taking advantage of the fact that the poor have already formed thousands of self-help groups and saving clubs to address their own finance needs. Linking these groups with traditional banks would allow the banks to extend their services to a ready-made clientele with a history of enterprise and saving. In turn, these small groups of poor households would then become connected to the larger financial market and could draw on its business expertise (IFAD 2004:15).

Other more traditional strategies will be needed as well if credit availability is to rise substantially. These include strengthening rural banks, both private and community owned; reforming agricultural development banks so that they become major microfinance providers; and helping current microfinance providers to create networks and take advantage of supporting services such as credit rating and refinancing (IFAD 2004:12-14).

Capture Greater Value

Increasing the economic return that the poor realize from nature-based products is an important element in any strategy to use nature for poverty reduction. Many of the goods that the poor produce or obtain from nature yield low prices relative to the labor involved. Changing this involves action at three different levels.

Improve Production and Processing

The first level of creating value is improving production or processing efficiency so that the same labor yields more or a higher-quality product. An important aspect of this is improving the storage and handling of products to reduce losses and improve quality. A high rate of post-harvest losses is typical for small producers. In Ethiopia, post-harvest grain losses from spoilage, insects, and rodents rob grain producers of 5-26 percent of their harvest (Gabriel and Hundie 2004:4). Losses of milk in Tanzania total some 60 million liters per year, worth over US$14 million (FAO 2005). Reducing losses involves a concerted effort to educate small-scale producers about good production hygiene and the use of low-cost technologies for storage and shipment. For example, FAO is currently helping to implement milk-hygiene programs for small producers in East Africa, and to explore the adoption of an inexpensive milk preservation system called the lacto-peroxidase system to extend shelf-life of small-producer milk (ILRI 2003:6).

Paying more attention to factors like appearance, packaging, or labeling, particularly for export or tourist markets, can also raise the value of products. State extension agents or NGO technical assistance can frequently help. In one example, small farmer cooperatives in Nicaragua have worked with the U.S.

Agency for International Development and the Thanksgiving Coffee Company to build "cupping labs" to taste their coffee after processing. Thanks to the labs, the Nicaraguan farmers have begun garnering international awards for coffee quality and are successfully reaching specialty markets in Europe and the United States (Bacon 2002:i-iii; USAID 2004:1).

Cooperatives Raise Marketing Power

The poor frequently capture only a small percentage of the value of the ecosystem products they sell, while middlemen and retailers higher up the commodity chain often capture a much greater share. Middlemen perform valuable services by transporting products to wider markets and tapping into distribution chains to which the poor have no access. But they are also key actors in keeping producer profits low. For example, small-scale coffee farmers capture, on average, only 4.5 percent of the retail price of coffee sold in U.S. supermarkets (Gresser and Tickell 2002:21). In Senegal, an analysis of the charcoal commodity chain likewise found that the profit of a typical woodcutter at the base of the chain is less than 4 percent of the profit that an urban charcoal wholesaler earns (Ribot 1998:318). *(See Figure 4.4.)*

A common way for rural producers to increase their market power and avoid middlemen is to form cooperatives or marketing groups. These groups can help poor producers receive better market information, increase their prices, and expand their markets. They also provide a natural forum for training, networking, and sometimes for management of the resource being marketed. In Nam Pheng village in northern Laos, villagers formed a marketing group in 1998 to coordinate their harvest of bitter bamboo and cardamom and to try to increase the price received at market. The marketing group collects the villagers' individual harvests, sells them on a large scale to traders, and delivers 85-90 percent of the final sale price to villagers (Morris 2002:4-5).

The effectiveness of the group was immediately apparent when, shortly after forming, they were able to raise the local price of cardamom from 500 Lao Kip per kilogram to 35,000 Kip. Although the price has since dropped to 14,000 Kip, it is still well above what villagers got when they marketed on an individual basis. The 10-15 percent of the sale price that the marketing group keeps goes into a community investment fund that has supported a new school and an improved water supply, as well as providing loans for a number of households. The marketing group has ventured into management by setting regulations for when and how much to harvest, and also providing training in collection techniques. Decisions are made jointly by the marketing group members, which include virtually all households in the village (Morris 2002:4-5). *(See Figure 4.5.)*

In Mexico, the Union de Ejidos de la Selva, a peasant organization, has helped organize small coffee producers in Chiapas state into an effective marketing force. The union collaborates with 1,250 families in 42 communities to ensure the adoption of better soil-management and environmental

FIGURE 4.5 MARKETING GROUPS RAISE PROFITS

Influence of Village Marketing Group In Nam Pheng, Laos

Marketing Group Formed

2002 price: 14,000 kip/kg

Initial price: 500 kip/kg

Local Price of Cardamom (Kip/kg): 0, 5,000, 10,000, 15,000, 20,000, 25,000, 30,000, 35,000, 40,000

1996 1998 2000 2002

Source: Morris 2002

practices, including certified organic techniques that limit erosion and water pollution. The union has partnered with a civil society organization called the Vinculo y Dessarrollo to create a chain of five up-scale coffee shops in Mexico City—the Café de la Selva—that serves the organic coffee produced by the Union de la Selva farmers. By controlling the entire vertical chain of coffee production, the Union de Ejidos de la Selva has been able to capture the full urban consumer value of coffee and use it to improve farmer income and self-sufficiency (Samperio 2002).

Use New Commercial Models

A third tactic for increasing commercial payoff is to make use of new models of commercialization, such as organic certification or the Fair Trade movement. These specialized markets, in which consumers purchase an item (often at a premium) in order to further social, environmental, and health goals, have continued to grow year by year. Although they do not account for a large percentage of total sales of any commodity, these markets can offer several advantages. The Fair Trade movement, for example, is targeted to support small rural producers, with the explicit goal of providing a fair wage for growing or crafting export items such as coffee, tea,

bananas, or any of a number of handicrafts. It essentially amplifies the idea of a typical cooperative or marketing group to the global level, offering low-income producers a route to high-value international sales they would otherwise have little chance of obtaining. *(See Box 4.2.)*

The markets for certified organic food, sustainably harvested lumber, and sustainably caught seafood also offer potential for low-income rural producers. Certification offers consumers a guarantee—through inspections or other verification methods—that a given product has met certain standards in its growth, harvesting, or processing. The kinds of small-scale production that the poor engage in often lend themselves to organic or sustainable methods. Many small coffee producers, for example, follow organic practices by default.

But certification offers challenges to the poor. The most significant is meeting the cost and technical requirements of certification. For example, fishery certification by the Marine Stewardship Council requires a time-consuming and expensive evaluation of the harvest levels and equipment used by fishers; forest certification similarly requires a verified forest management plan. For the poor to be able to participate, their certification costs will need to be reduced or subsidized by donors, NGO

CAPITALIZING ON THE COMPETITIVE ADVANTAGES OF THE POOR

Although they suffer some obvious disadvantages, small rural producers also hold some competitive advantages that can help them successfully commercialize their ecosystem assets. Exploiting these advantages increases their economic leverage.

- **Control of commercially valuable forest resources, land, or fishing rights.** Poor households and communities with well-established resource tenure are sometimes in a position to parley this into commercial opportunities. This is especially true for those communities within reasonable proximity of expanding centers of domestic or industrial demand, such as inland cities far from commercial ports. Constraints on the private sector's ability to meet wood demand in India, for example, have motivated more than a dozen companies to partner with rural farmers to grow trees on the farmers' lands (Mayers and Vermeulen 2002:45; Scherr et al. 2002:4-5).

- **Lower cost structure for some products.** For communities or farmers with excess labor or land not currently under crops, there may be little opportunity cost for growing trees or establishing low-tech aquaculture ponds. These operations may have lower costs than large-scale plantations or high-tech fish-raising enterprises run by outside business interests. Agroforestry systems, for example, may offer lower costs for tree production because trees are produced jointly with crops and livestock. For products like wood fuel and charcoal, transportation costs even from rural communities may be lower than importing these commodities from international markets (Scherr et al. 2002:4-5).

- **Sole providers of some products.** Because of their access to ecosystems and their traditional knowledge, poor households may be in the

best position to supply some niche markets, such as for medicinal plants, exotic fruits, or traditionally made handicrafts or art objects. They may also be in the best position to sell to "socially responsible" markets, which may value the fact that their products come from small community enterprises rather than factory farms or plantations (Scherr et al. 2002:4-5).

- **Ability to compete in domestic markets for some products.** Low-income producers may not always be able to be competitive in international trade, but they can frequently compete effectively in domestic markets. This is particularly true for certain products that do not offer high margins, such as "commodity grade" wood used for fencing, storage structures, crop and tree supports, or packing crates. Larger international producers typically do not compete in these markets with cheaper domestic products, which small-scale farmers can in many cases supply by growing trees in agroforestry schemes or wood lots (Scherr et al. 2002:4-5).

- **Better monitoring and enforcement abilities.** Local people may have greater ability than outside companies to prevent illegal logging or fishing. This may mean they are in a better position to assure the quality of certified wood or fish products (Scherr et al. 2002:4-5).

In general, low-income communities will find it easier to compete in commercial markets where there is less competition with large-scale producers, where there are few substitutes for their goods, where their low labor and start-up costs give them a lower overall cost structure, and where their deficits in transport are minimized.

partners, or the state. Innovations in the certification process to make it more inclusive can also help. One forest certification organization has experimented with videotaping community members as they describe their management and implementation plans, rather than making them submit a written plan (Shanley et al. 2002:296).

Another difficulty for the poor is that forest or organic certifications generally focus on the land where the timber or crop is grown, guaranteeing certain practices—such as absence of pesticide use for a specified number of years—on these lands. For those with secure ownership of land and resources, this may be fine. But many nontimber forest products are collected on common lands or by the landless, so guarantees about a given parcel of land cannot be made. In this case, certification may have to be modified so that it focuses on the training and practices of the harvesters themselves, with certification residing with a harvester association rather than with a land parcel (Shanley et al. 2002:296-298).

Partner with the Private Sector

It is hard to imagine successfully commercializing ecosystem goods and services without substantial participation of the private sector. The capital, facilities, know-how, and markets that businesses command make them strong potential investors and partners for nature-based enterprises of the poor. In Southwestern Ghana, the Swiss Lumber Company has entered into contracts with rural farmers to grow hardwoods on degraded lands, where they will not compete with agriculture. The company provides a lump-sum down payment, a 20-50 percent share (depending on the size of the down payment) of the timber at harvest, and an annual land rent. In return, Swiss Lumber—which does not own timber lands or have access to government timber concessions in the area—gets first option to buy the timber at market prices when the trees are ready for harvest (Mayers and Vermeulen 2002:141).

As the Swiss Lumber example shows, the business relationships that can develop between rural residents and companies can be beneficial to both. For poor households, benefits can include a more consistent income stream and access to credit, training, business planning, and marketing. One of the biggest benefits is that poor households can share the risks of a business venture rather than assume all the risks on their own (Mayers and Vermeulen 2002:viii, 97-101).

The obvious benefits to companies are access to raw resources such as timber, fish, nontimber forest products, or scenic sights and experiences for tourism. The poor also comprise a low-cost labor force for management tasks like tree pruning, growing of specialized crops, or hand-collection of wild fruits. In addition, despite their limited means, poor households can provide a substantial consumer pool for the products and services that companies sell. Targeting sales to the sizable consumer group at the "bottom of the pyramid" is a strategy that many companies are beginning to explore, and building brand recognition and engagement with rural communities is a first step to this end. *(See Box 4.3.)*

Continues on page 104

101

THE 4 BILLION PEOPLE WHO LIVE IN RELATIVE POVERTY are a potentially huge market. In the aggregate, their purchasing power is substantial, even if their individual means are limited. Increasingly, innovative companies are finding ways to serve these customers—meeting their basic needs and empowering them through access to information, access to credit, expanded consumer choice, and other benefits. These are not philanthropic endeavors; they are market-driven and intended to be profitable. Indeed, to be sustainable and scalable, they must be profitable. The hallmark of these private-sector approaches to poverty is close attention to the real needs and social and environmental circumstances of the intended customers. In many cases, new products or services are co-created with the communities for which they are intended.

An example of these poor-focused business models is the e-Choupal system deployed in rural farming areas in several Indian states by ITC, one of India's leading private companies with interests in agribusiness, packaged foods, and a range of other products. The e-Choupal system was designed to address inefficiencies in grain purchasing in the government-mandated marketplaces known as *mandis*. In the *mandi* system, traders who act as purchasing agents for buyers control market information and are well-positioned to exploit both farmers and buyers through practices that sustain system-wide inefficiencies. Farmers have only an approximate idea of price trends and have to accept the price offered them at auctions on the day they bring their grain to market (Annamalai and Rao 2003:1, 8-9).

The approach of ITC has been to place computers with Internet access in farming villages, carefully selecting a respected local farmer as its host. Each e-Choupal (*choupal* means gathering

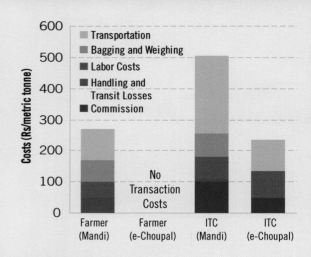

REDUCED TRANSACTION COSTS UNDER E-CHOUPAL

Costs (Rs/metric tonne)

Legend:
- Transportation
- Bagging and Weighing
- Labor Costs
- Handling and Transit Losses
- Commission

Farmer (e-Choupal): No Transaction Costs

Categories: Farmer (Mandi), Farmer (e-Choupal), ITC (Mandi), ITC (e-Choupal)

Source: Annamalai and Rao 2003

place in Hindi) is located so that it can serve 6-10 villages, or about 600 farmers. An e-Choupal costs between US$3,000 and $6,000 to set up, and about US$100 per year to maintain. Using the system costs farmers nothing, but the host farmer, called a *sanchalak,* incurs some operating costs and is obligated by a public oath to serve the entire community. The *sanchalak* benefits from increased prestige and a commission paid for all e-Choupal transactions (Annamalai and Rao 2003:1, 11).

Farmers can use the computer to access daily closing prices on local *mandis,* as well as to track global price trends or find information about new farming techniques. They also use the e-Choupal to order seeds, fertilizer, and consumer goods from ITC or its partners, at prices lower than those available from village traders. At harvest time, ITC offers to buy crops directly from any farmer at the previous day's market closing price; if the farmer accepts, he transports his crop to an ITC processing center, where the crop is weighed electronically and assessed for quality. The farmer is then paid for the crop and given a transport fee. In this way, the e-Choupal system bypasses the government-mandated trading *mandis* (Annamalai and Rao 2003:1, 13-14).

Compared to the *mandi* system, farmers benefit from more accurate weighing, faster processing time, prompt payment, and access to a wide range of price and market information. Farmers selling directly to ITC through an e-Choupal typically receive a price about US$6 per ton higher for their crops, as well as lower prices for inputs and other goods, and a sense

of empowerment. At the same time, ITC benefits from net procurement costs that are about 2.5 percent lower (it saves the commission fee and part of the transport costs it would otherwise pay to traders who serve as its buying agents at the *mandi*) and it has more direct control over the quality of what it buys.

The e-Choupal system also provides direct access to the farmer and to information about conditions on the ground, allowing the company to improve its planning and build relationships with farmers that increase its security of supply. The company reports that it recovers its equipment costs from an e-Choupal in the first year of operation and that the venture as a whole is profitable. As of late 2004, e-Choupal services reached more than 3.5 million farmers in over 30,000 villages, and the system is expanding rapidly (e-Choupal 2005).

What began as an effort to re-engineer the procurement process for cropping systems has also created a highly profitable distribution and product-design channel for the company—an e-commerce platform that is also a low-cost fulfillment system focused on the needs of rural India. Advocates for the e-Choupal system say that it has acted as a catalyst for rural transformation, helping to alleviate isolation, create more transparency for farmers, and improve their productivity and incomes. The increased system efficiencies and potential for improving crop quality also contribute to making Indian agriculture more competitive.

Although many farmers are happy with the e-Choupal system, not everyone has benefited from it. Since its success draws business away from the traditional *mandis,* many of the workers at the *mandi* exchanges have been severely affected. Laborers who used to weigh and bag the produce at the *mandis* have suffered from the drop in volume. Vendors at the informal bazaars that grew up around the *mandis* have also lost business as traffic has been diverted to the new ITC processing facilities. In the long run, these workers may be reemployed at the ITC exchanges, but in the short term many traditional *mandi* players have lost income (Annamalai and Rao 2003:25-26).

In spite of these transition costs, the e-Choupal experience and others like it are building confidence that private-sector actions can contribute substantially both to poverty alleviation and to sustainable commercialization of ecosystem services.

Engaging with rural communities can also help companies meet demand for specialized products such as certified lumber or organic foods. In 1990 the U.S. company Smith and Hawken faced growing consumer demand for sustainably harvested tropical hardwoods such as mahogany for furniture and other high-end home furnishings. In response, it helped *campesino* forestry groups in northern Honduras—community organizations of 5-50 members that manage state forests under use agreements with the government—attain certification for their mahogany and other hardwoods. The *campesino* groups are now using the publicity they have received to expand the market for less well-known woods (Mayers and Vermeulen 2002:147).

Arrangements like the ones undertaken by Swiss Lumber and Smith and Hawken to contract with rural farmers to supply trees are perhaps the most common arrangements between poor households and natural resource companies. These "outgrower" schemes are programs where timber companies pay small farmers to plant trees on their own (or sometimes communal) land in order to ensure a reliable supply of timber in the future. The schemes, which can be found in many countries on every continent, vary widely by company and by country. In some, the company provides seedlings, access to credit, technical help in planting and caring for the trees, and even the construction of roads for harvest. In other cases, the arrangements are more sparse, with no finance and little other than seedlings and an offer to buy the trees at market price (Mayers and Vermeulen 2002:140-154).

The poverty-reduction potential of outgrower schemes varies, but can be sizable. In the South African province of KwaZulu Natal, some 10,000 farmers—more than half of them women—participate in the outgrower programs of the Sappi and Mondi paper companies. With materials supplied by the companies, the farmers grow eucalyptus trees on their small plots of a few hectares. Sappi and Mondi agree to purchase the plantation wood after 6-7 years for their pulp mills. Studies have shown that participating in these outgrower programs contributes 12-45 percent of the income needed for a household to remain above the "abject poverty line," so outgrower programs can be important sources of stability in some rural economies (Scherr et al 2003: 51; Mayers and Vermeulen 2002:143).

For companies, outgrower programs can benefit the corporate image as well as securing the timber or pulp supply for the future. In Brazil, pulp-and-paper company Klabin works with timber outgrowers in a variety of joint ventures that have generated annual income for farmers ranging from US$76 to $217 per hectare. Klabin's stated reasons for running its outgrower program include the need to maintain a good company image. The company also tries to gets its outgrowers certified as sustainable timber producers in order to supply the demand from local furniture companies that want certified wood. Klabin has guaranteed 10 years of timber supply to these small furniture companies, which it hopes its outgrowers will provide (Mayers and Vermeulen 2002:143).

Despite the promise of such programs, nature-based investments in poor communities are not necessarily easy for companies or communities, and are by no means always successful. The history of such partnerships shows many missteps, reflecting the difficult circumstances of poor households that push them to seek quick returns at low risk, and demands investments of training and trust-building. For example, several outgrower programs in India were plagued with inconsistent participation by poor families. Free seedlings offered by the companies were often neglected; loan and credit deals were too complicated and cumbersome to be attractive; and participants often abandoned the programs when they learned they could find better prices on the open market than the prices offered by the companies (Mayers and Vermeulen 2002:v, 45-52).

For both companies and communities, partnerships sometimes have high transaction costs, and take negotiation and continued care to succeed. In addition, coping with government regulations can be confusing and time-consuming. Experience shows that it is important for both sides to enter an outgrower agreement with realistic expectations about the income potential and the responsibilities of each side. Outside legal advice, perhaps provided by an NGO, can help poor families clarify contracts, while a system of arbitration set up ahead of time can help resolve disputes. It takes energy and good faith to deal with these complexities, but where there is willingness on both sides, the local income gains and corporate benefits can be substantial (Mayers and Vermeulen 2002:xi-xv).

Keep Sustainability in Mind

Success in commercializing an ecosystem good or service creates its own problems. If a poor household or a rural community finds a winning formula for production, marketing, and delivery of a nature-based product, the temptation will be to push the formula to its limits to increase sales and income. This can easily lead to overexploitation of the type that typically degrades ecosystems. Reconciling the desire to maximize income with the need to sustain ecosystems so that they remain productive assets is one of the inherent challenges of using environmental income for poverty reduction (Neumann and Hirsch 2000:102).

Succeeding Too Well

An example of the dangers of succeeding too well with marketing a natural product can be found in Bolivia, where one indigenous community worked hard to commercialize the sale of string bags made of natural sisal fiber they collected and processed from the wild. They developed a low-cost marketing model to get their bags to customers in Europe, who paid a handsome price. As this enterprise began to succeed, local women involved in bag-making saw their purchasing power increase markedly. This, in turn, encouraged them to rely more on making sisal bags for income, abandoning other lower-profit activities such as subsistence agriculture. As economic reliance on sisal bags spiraled upward, pressure on native sisal plants grew, depleting local sisal sources around the community, and eventually forcing locals to lower their harvest to a more sustainable level (Shanley et al. 2002:279).

Many other examples of the potential for unsustainability can be found. African bushmeat hunting, for example, has reduced the population of primates like chimpanzees, whose low reproductive rates make them especially vulnerable to overharvest. The use of cyanide by poor fishers in Indonesia and the Philippines to catch prized fish for sale to high-end restaurants has decimated many coral reefs (Barber and Pratt 1997:10-21). In Southern Africa, the expanding market for handmade baskets has put pressure on some 30 indigenous plant species used for fiber and another 22 used for dyes. In western Zimbabwe, one weaving club that began with 20 members in 1986 had expanded to 500 by 1988. This is all the more remarkable given that handmade basket-making had only begun as a commercial enterprise in the 1970s as an economic development project in Botswana (Neumann and Hirsch 2000:102-103, 107).

In these examples, activities which, when pursued on a limited basis, might not harm the resource are pushed to unsustainability by sheer expansion of the scope of the activity. But there are other contributors to unsustainable commerce too. In some cases poor harvesting techniques or agricultural practices exacerbate the situation. Some harvesters of African *mbare* palm leaves—one source of basket-making fiber—engage in wholesale cutting of the palms, which kills them. A sustainable alternative is to simply cull individual leaves, which permits the palm to continue growing (Neumann and Hirsch 2000:103-104).

Governance Matters

Governance factors such as tenure—or lack or it—also play a role. Sometimes when a new market appears for a nontraditional product, there may not be a well-defined system of customary practices surrounding ownership and use of the product, and the resource essentially becomes an open-access resource subject to no practical controls on its use. Ecotourism can even fall into this category sometimes. In other instances, there may be well-defined customary or legal property rights over a valuable medicinal, fruit, or other resource, but it may break down as the market for the product—and its value—increases, leading to poaching. This emphasizes the important role of enforcement—through custom or law—in complementing well-defined resource tenure as foundations for viable commerce (Neumann and Hirsch 2000:105-106).

Diversity is Sustainable

Ultimately, the question of sustainability boils down to a question of ecosystem capacities and trade-offs. How much disturbance can an ecosystem tolerate and still remain healthy? What opportunities for environmental income are lost as other opportunities are emphasized? And perhaps most importantly, what is the best strategy to optimize environmental income without compromising ecosystem integrity?

The answer to this last question is not simple, but the idea of diversification of activities and income streams is one approach that many analysts have put forward. A mix of commercial uses of nature, including agriculture, agroforestry, collection of nontimber forest products, and commercial fishing may yield greater ecological resilience, at least at a landscape level. It may also offer greater economic stability for rural economies. From a household perspective, a portfolio of different products and activities will minimize risks for poor families. Neither a monoculture nor a monocommercial approach to environmental income is likely to give the best results (Chater 2003:3-4; May 1992:4; Scherr et al. 2003:22).

4 AUGMENTING NATURE'S INCOME STREAM: PAYMENT FOR ENVIRONMENTAL SERVICES

When the poor engage in good ecosystem stewardship, they create the conditions for higher productivity and greater direct environmental income for themselves. But they also safeguard ecosystem services whose benefits extend beyond their immediate surroundings. By maintaining a healthy forest cover, for example, they are helping to preserve watershed services like flood control, continuous water supply, and erosion control that landowners downstream will benefit from. In the past, these services have been considered "public goods" and available for free, but in recent years it has become clear that many of these

Continues on page 107

BOX 4.4 PAYING THE POOR
FOR ENVIRONMENTAL STEWARDSHIP

PROGRAMS THAT PAY LANDHOLDERS TO MAINTAIN ecosystem services like storing carbon, maintaining stable water flow, or preserving scenic landscapes for tourism have burgeoned in the last decade. Most of these "payment for environmental service" (PES) programs don't do a good job of reaching the poor, even though poor households are often active environmental stewards. A small but growing number of projects show that this does not always have to be the case. Two PES programs in particular—in the Cauca Valley of Colombia and in Chiapas, Mexico—demonstrate how PES can yield benefits for poor communities.

Cauca Valley, Colombia

In the late 1980s, private farmers initiated a voluntary system of payment for water use in the Cauca Valley, Colombia. The payment system was designed to improve the livelihoods of the upland poor as part of a strategy for sustainable watershed management. The uplands of the Desbaratado Watershed in the Cauca Valley were inhabited by poor farmers. Seventy-two percent lacked sanitary facilities and 83 percent had no electricity, but most held titles to their land (Echavarría 2002:6).

Overgrazing and deforestation on the slopes of the watershed had led to erratic stream flows and destructive seasonal flooding in the lower basin, the effects of which were being felt by landowners downstream. These landowners consisted mainly of wealthy sugarcane growers who had invested in costly farming technologies, including laser leveling and underground drainage and irrigation systems (Echavarría 2002:7). With the threat of continually escalating costs to protect their investment, the farmers became interested in regulating the stream flow by restoring and improving management of the lands in the upper watershed. They subsequently organized into twelve Water User Associations and instituted voluntary user fees to finance upland watershed management.

The Water User Associations came to the conclusion that the surest route to achieving long-term land-use change in the upper watershed was to improve the livelihoods of the land users. With the aid of the government, planners met with upland communities to identify community priorities for development. The result of these meetings was a series of programs with wide-ranging social benefits, including:

■ A "social program," providing education and skills training;

■ A "production program," which includes building home gardens to improve diets and increase earnings, as well as reforestation and crop-planting projects;

■ An "infrastructure program," which focuses on improving sanitary and drinking water facilities, building roads, and constructing erosion control structures (Echavarría 2002:7).

From 1995 to 2000, an estimated US$1.5 million was invested in the upper watershed—all from the water fees assessed by the Water User Associations (Echavarría 2002:5). So far, the environmental commitment of downstream users has remained strong, and upland projects have continued even in the face of armed guerilla activity in the region. Considering the length of the project, this suggests that benefits on both sides have been worthwhile.

Chiapas, Mexico: Scolel Té

The Scolel Té project in Chiapas, Mexico, represents one of the first efforts to make the international market for carbon storage benefit poor communities. Companies interested in offsetting their greenhouse gas emissions can purchase carbon credits from a local organization, Fondo BioClimático, with two-thirds of the revenue going to farmers (Scherr 2004:43; IUCN 2003:1). The largest buyer thus far has been the Fédération Internationale de l'Automobile, which purchased over 13,000 tons of credits to offset some of the emissions from professional auto racing (IUCN 2003:1).

Farmers who join the Scolel Té scheme must draw up a management plan for their land and agree, to the extent possible, to maintain the trees on their land over the long-term. Fondo BioClimático provides technical support and training to participants in managing their land (Phillips et al. 2002:8). Scolel Té is more than a strict reforestation program. It also allows participants to plant "live fences," shade-grown coffee plantations, and mixed agroforestry plantations. In addition to the PES payment they receive, farmers can make money on regulated sales of timber as well as non-timber products. They also commonly plant food crops under the trees until the canopy closes over (IUCN 2003:1). Because of this variety of income sources, the program is more attractive to farmers.

Since it began in 1996, Scolel Té has gained more than 700 participants in 40 communities. In 2002, sales of carbon credits at US$12 per ton amounted to $180,000, translating into $120,000 distributed among the participants (IUCN 2003:1). The project has also enabled farmers to penetrate markets in sustainable timber, organic coffee, and other agroforestry products. For many, access to these valuable markets has been the more important route to greater income (Rosa et al. 2003:27). The project has generated positive environmental benefits locally as well. Plantings on denuded hillsides are helping to reduce erosion and improve soil quality.

TABLE 4.2 PAYMENTS FOR ENVIROMENTAL SERVICES

Locale	Enviromental Service	Value to Community
Costa Rica	Forest conservation and reforestation for watershed maintenance and carbon storage	More than US$100 million disbursed under 10-15 year contracts with over 450,000 ha enrolled in program. Funded by a fuel tax and contributions from private companies. Rodriguez 2004
Pimampiro, Ecuador	Forest protection of headwaters to ensure clean water supply for the town	$1 per hectare payments constitute 30% of income for those households participating in forest protection. Grieg-Gran and Bishop
Cauca Valley, Columbia	Forest management to improve stream flows and reduce sedimentation of irrigation canals	US$1.5 million invested in poor communities in the upper watershed by downstream farmers. Scherr et al. 2004
Kerala, India	Discovery and maintenance of a continued supply of Jeevani, a commercially marketed medicine	500-1000 families will earn wage income from cultivation and harvesting of the fruit and leaves that are used to manufacture the drug. Ongoing royalty payments to the community from drug sales. Landell-Mills and Porras 2002
Botswana, Kenya, Namibia, South Africa, Tanzania, Zimbabwe	Support of ecotourism in southern and eastern Africa through the maintenance of landscapes, natural resources, and wildlife habitat	Direct employment of 3000 people; over US$100,000 reinvested in local economic development and conservation activities. Landell-Mills and Porras 2002
Scholel Té, Chiapas, Mexico	Forest management leading to carbon sequestration	Two-thirds of the value from the sale of carbon contracts goes to farmers. In 2002, US$120,000 was distributed to 700 participants. IUCN 2003

ecosystem services have a quantifiable economic value. If people downstream are being regularly flooded, the ability of the intact forest to moderate stream flows and lessen the flood risk will be worth something to them, and they may be willing to pay the upstream forest owners to preserve and protect this service—or even to restore it.

In the last decade or so, markets based on this kind of interchange—called *payment for environmental services* (PES)—have begun to develop worldwide. *(See Table 4.2.)* The most common environmental services marketed so far have been associated with forests and fall into four categories: watershed services like those described above, carbon storage, biodiversity conservation, and preservation of landscape beauty. Since the poor are the stewards of many rural ecosystems, it makes sense that they should be able to tap these payments for environmental services (PES) as an additional source of environmental income—another element of their "nature portfolio." In a few cases, they have been successful in doing so. But for the most part, the markets for environmental services, which are still in their infancy, do not yet serve the poor well.

Deals involving PES range in scale from local to international and are undertaken by a range of actors, including private companies, NGOs, communities, and state governments. Private businesses that depend on natural resources are sometimes willing to pay for protection of ecosystems, usually following

signs that a resource is threatened or already in decline. In one promising example in Colombia's Cauca Valley, downstream sugarcane growers hurt by flooding paid upland communities—predominantly poor—to change their land management practices to protect the watershed. This evened out the water supply on the valley sugarcane farms and reduced crop damages, while bringing public benefits—clean water supply, sanitation, and other economic development projects—to the upland communities. *(See Box 4.4.)*

Payments for preserving biodiversity and landscape beauty often come from conservation NGOs or local businesses involved in ecotourism. For example, Rainforest Expeditions, a private company in southeastern Peru, signed a 20-year agreement with the local Infierno community, splitting profits and management of the business in return for preservation and access to the forest and wildlife on the community's lands (Landell-Mills and Porras 2002:166).

Governments often act as originators or participants in PES schemes. In 1996 the Costa Rican government became a leader in PES when it established the first national program to dispense payments to farmers willing to maintain or restore forest ecosystems and their services. The program pays landowners to reforest their lands or conserve forest lands they already own, rather than convert them to pasture. By 2004, more than 450,000 hectares were included in the program, and the government had dispensed over US$100 million to farmers (Rodriguez 2004:13). The government has used a number of strategies to finance payments, including a national fuel tax, international sales of carbon credits, payments from private utilities and industry, and funding from the World Bank and GEF (Rosa et al. 2003:16).

In Brazil, the government took a different approach in the state of Acre, where it had set aside large extractive reserves for indigenous rubber tappers. To preserve the economic viability of the extractive reserves, it directly subsidized the rubber tapping industry, with the subsidy amounting to an indirect PES program to maintain the natural forest cover of the reserves. In Colombia, the government is experimenting with a regulatory approach, requiring hydroelectric utility companies to transfer a percentage of their earnings to support good land management in upstream communities, thus reducing reservoir siltation and preserving water flows (Tognetti 2001:17).

The Challenges of Pro-Poor PES

Despite the theoretical potential for PES programs to benefit the rural poor, many current programs present serious obstacles to the inclusion of poor households. This reflects the fact that PES programs were originally designed primarily to meet conservation goals rather than support the livelihoods of the poor. The Costa Rican program, for example, grew out of the Forestry Department, and its structure favored larger and wealthier landowners (Rosa et al. 2003:16-19). A survey in one Costa Rican watershed found that while all of the large landholders (owning more than 80 ha) were participating in the program, only one third of small landholders (owning less than 10 ha) had signed up (Miranda et al. 2003:21-22)

The obstacles to including the poor in PES programs mirror many of the problems holding them back from other forms of environmental income. The Costa Rican case, which has been one of the most thoroughly studied, has faced several of these:

- **Tenure and formal titles.** Secure property rights are one of the foundations of a PES program. Land ownership is almost always used to identify who should rightfully receive payments. That leaves those without secure tenure—particularly the landless—unable to benefit unless some special provision is made, or unless benefits are distributed to larger community associations that can then attempt an equitable distribution. In Costa Rica's original PES program, for example, only titled land holders could participate, which blocked many poor farmers. As PES programs mature and the market for environmental services builds, this may provide governments yet another incentive to improve tenure security for the rural poor. In the interim, however, a growing PES program could make things worse for the untenured poor if it makes rural lands more attractive to—and more liable to be snapped up by—large landowners.

- **Restrictions on land uses.** PES guidelines may bar grazing or other traditional forest uses that seem to conflict with the environmental services that the program is paying for. Without access to these or other replacement activities, poor families will not be able to afford to participate in PES programs. Costa Rica's program did not allow farmers to graze cattle or practice agroforestry on any lands enrolled in the program, yet the PES payments were not sufficient to serve as a primary income source. This left many small farmers no choice but to opt out. In 2002 the government amended its program to allow agroforestry activities (Rosa et al. 2003:20).

- **High transaction costs.** The costs of applying for a PES program, drawing up a contract, and monitoring performance can become a considerable burden on poor families. Applicants for the Costa Rican PES program have reported spending large amounts of time and money obtaining and certifying documents, paying for land management studies, and having quarterly visits from a forest manager. The government has committed to reducing these costs substantially and has also moved to allow groups of small farmers to join the PES program collectively, thereby spreading the costs over a larger group (Miranda et al. 2003:29-32; Pagiola 2002:43-44).

■ **Lack of credit and start-up funds.** Changing farming and other land-use practices or reforesting pastures to comply with PES requirements often requires a significant investment in new material, training, and lost income during the transition period. Covering these costs is difficult for poor families, who typically lack credit and cash savings. Costa Rica has tried to address this by front-loading payments to farmers, sending half of the total payments (normally dispersed over five or ten years) within the first year of joining the program (Pagiola 2003:11).

In spite of these obstacles, there is considerable hope that PES programs can be modified to make them work for the poor. The policy attention around PES programs in many nations has shifted to identifying reforms needed to increase their potential for poverty reduction. Costa Rica, for example, has striven in the past few years to modify its program so that it serves the poor better. It is no coincidence that many of the governance changes advocated in this chapter as pro-poor, such as establishing secure tenure and promoting community-based institutions that can collectively bargain for and represent the interests of the poor, are the same governance changes necessary to make PES programs better at poverty reduction.

Even in their current imperfect form, PES programs have managed to deliver some important benefits to low-income participants. Many times these are related more to social organization and skills training than the monetary payment. For example, small farmers in Costa Rica's PES program cite the technical training provided in the program as valuable enough to justify participation, even if the payments themselves are not large. The formation of local organizations to help small farmers take advantage of these schemes has also produced lasting gains in social capital, with the rural poor becoming more willing to demand compensation and ownership rights for natural resources (Rosa et al. 2003:23-26).

Participation in PES programs can also open doors to other sources of environmental income. The small farmers involved in the Scolel Té carbon sequestration scheme did not earn large sums from the environmental-service payments themselves. However, the project enabled farmers to penetrate markets in sustainable timber, organic coffee, and other agroforestry products (Rosa et al. 2003:27).

At their best, PES schemes offer a way to serve conservation goals while they add to the income profile of poor families and build social capital in poor communities. In contrast to the establishment of parks, which in many cases relies on excluding rural residents, the PES approach is more inclusive and based on a

positive role for rural communities in ecosystem management (Rosa et al. 2003:13). Like other forms of environmental income, PES by itself is not likely to allow poor families to escape poverty, but it can become an important contributor to livelihood security due to the regularity of the payments and the incentive they provide to manage sustainably.

BEYOND ENVIRONMENTAL INCOME

In this chapter, we have explored a bottom-up approach to generating environmental income by the poor. We have emphasized that better ecosystem management and a realignment of local resource governance to empower the poor can lead to significant increases in their household incomes. It is a strategy grounded in the belief that rural poverty reduction can begin with nature—the resource and employment base that already supports rural livelihoods.

At the same time, we realize that poverty reduction depends on many factors beyond our discussion in this chapter. For example, we have emphasized that good ecosystem management combined with effective commercialization of nature-based products helps reduce income risks for low-income families. But poor families face risks other than inadequate or uneven income, such as the risk of catastrophic loss from natural disasters or health shocks. Without mitigating these risks as well—through interventions such as crop insurance and access to better health care—the poor will not find a stable economic foundation in spite of good stewardship of their ecosystem assets.

Likewise, access to technology is another important factor we have only lightly touched on. Many examples show that innovations in technology and management practices have the potential to increase environmental income substantially, but there are considerable barriers to adoption of such innovations. For example, researchers in Brazil have found that a combination of planting legumes to enrich pasture soils and using solar-powered electric fences to better control where cattle graze on a given pasture could allow smallholders to sustainably double milk production and triple the carrying capacity of their land, bringing a marked increase in profits. But lack of credit and training, distance from markets, and lack of political commitment to extension programs means that few Brazilian farmers are likely to benefit from these innovations. Under the present economic incentives, poor farmers are likely to continue with their usual practices (Chater 2003:3).

This brings up the larger point that rural enterprises, although they may be physically remote, are connected to the national economy—and increasingly to the global economy— and therefore subject to macroeconomic and governance policies originating far from the village level. *(See Box 4.5.)* Without pro-poor policy changes at these higher levels, the ability of the poor to deploy their ecosystem resources for greater income will be greatly attenuated. For example, national fisheries ministries typically concentrate their attention and

budgets on industrial fisheries, ignoring the small-scale fisheries that the poor rely on. Without changing this dynamic, the poor will find their attempts at better ecosystem management frustrated by official inattention. Likewise, without high-level action to make credit and other financial services available for small rural enterprises, the poor will find it hard to capitalize on their governance and management successes.

On the other hand, this chapter shows that governments can create a foundation for greater environmental income by providing incentives for nature-based enterprises, empowering the poor by granting legally binding resource rights, and fostering responsive local institutions. In fact, as the case studies in Chapter 5 show, a high-level political commitment to expanding environmental income through local empowerment is crucial to scaling up village-level successes. When this happens, region-wide improvements in management practice and governance can occur that provide the poor a first step in economic advancement.

BOX 4.5 GLOBALIZATION, GOVERNANCE, AND POVERTY

THE CURRENT WAVE OF ECONOMIC GLOBALIZATION has lifted many people out of poverty and enhanced human welfare. But the benefits of globalization have not yet reached far enough: over three billion people still live impoverished lives, and the fields, fisheries, forests, and waterways they depend on are increasingly at risk.

As the Millennium Ecosystem Assessment points out, the transformation of ecosystems over the past five decades dwarfs the cumulative impact over the preceding centuries. This degradation is undercutting rural livelihoods (MA 2005:2). Half of all jobs worldwide depend on agriculture, forestry, and fishing. Yet agricultural subsidies and other import restrictions in developed countries make it difficult for developing country farmers to compete on the world market (WTO 2003:10, 22).

Improving this situation will require better and smarter globalization. Ultimately, a sophisticated market economy is the only mechanism capable of generating lasting prosperity. Market-based approaches, where informed by socially and environmentally responsible public policy, have also been effective in forging solutions to some environmental problems. Emissions trading has been successful in reducing sulfur dioxide and nitrogen oxides, and tradable fishing quotas have reduced over-fishing (Aulisi et al. 2005:11; Kura et al. 2004:92; Ellerman et al. 2000:315; NRC 1999:192). Innovative approaches are being used to assign value, and hence to protect, "ecosystem services"—from crops and fisheries to water filtration and flood prevention. All of these need to happen in ways that rural people can participate in and benefit from—which will only happen if they have a degree of control over the process and the ecosystem "assets."

The public equity markets steer billions of dollars every day to companies and projects around the world. While often inadvertent, this allocation of capital all too often hastens the loss of forests, fisheries, and watersheds, and underwrites the build-up of greenhouse gases in the atmosphere. To counter this trend, many private banks have committed to the "Equator Principles," which incorporate social and environmental criteria in investment decision-making. Major corporations are investing in environmentally cleaner technology because they are convinced it will increase their profits and make them more internationally competitive. In the energy sector, the International Energy Agency estimates that US$16 trillion will be required for global infrastructure investment over the next twenty-five years (IEA 2004:383). Redirecting this massive capital flow to clean energy and transport systems could reduce poverty, increase security, and stabilize greenhouse gas emissions.

To be pro-poor, investors and borrowers need to incorporate environmental sustainability in their activities. The developers of power, oil, gas, and mining projects will need to do a better job of managing risks to human health, as well as damage to rivers, fisheries, and other ecosystems. Borrowers from the Equator banks may have to drop or change their plans to meet environmental standards, as was done in many of ABN AMRO's projects last year. However, while steering private investment in pro-poor directions is critical, it cannot achieve the desired outcome where bad governance is pervasive.

Private investment in hydrocarbons and other extractive industries has sometimes been associated with corruption, environmental degradation, social dislocation, and impoverishment. Changing this will require more transparency, public participation, and accountability. The Extractive Industries Transparency Initiative (EITI), launched by the British government, is already proving successful. Royal Dutch Shell and BP have agreed to disclose detailed payment information on their oil operations in Nigeria and Azerbaijan, respectively. Investors representing over US$7 trillion have endorsed EITI, and civil-society organizations are using EITI as an instrument for government accountability. Endorsement of EITI by G-8 nations and oil-producing countries would make a decisive difference to the lives of the poor who live in the 60 countries that depend on oil, gas, and mining revenues (Soros 2005:43).

Economic globalization has led to a host of technologies that can aid efficient market functioning, promote sound governance of natural resources, and protect the interests of the poor. Low-cost environmental data collection using remote sensing and high-resolution satellite mapping is one example. Tracking and monitoring devices are helping to reduce over-exploitation of fisheries. In Malaysia conservationists use satellite transmitters to keep count of elephants (WWF 2005). Rural Indian farmers with high-speed Internet receive online updates about market prices and weather, making them more competitive (Annamalai and Rao 2003:1). Increasingly low-cost and accessible technologies are beginning to measure trends in deforestation, soil erosion, and climate change. India, China, and Brazil have launched their own satellites, and are sharing data with other developing countries. Hopefully, it will not be long before existing databases—including poverty maps and maps of ecosystem services—can be overlaid routinely on the sites of proposed mining operations, timber harvests, or industrial plants to identify how these developments might affect poor families in the region.

A smarter approach to economic globalization can work when the poor are empowered through access to information, participation, and justice, and when they have legally recognized resource rights that allow them to manage, sell, rent, and invest in ecosystem services. By partnering with the private sector to make credit available for ecosystem-based enterprises, and by improving the marketing and transport of goods produced, the poor can gain income and benefit from the wider marketplace that globalization affords. ◄

Each situation faced by the rural poor is unique, but the desire for better lives—materially, culturally, and spiritually— is universal.

CHAPTER 5

TURNING NATURAL ASSETS INTO WEALTH

In *World Resources 2005* we have argued that environmental income is the wealth of the poor, with the potential to provide not just subsistence but a path out of poverty if the right governance conditions prevail. In many communities, this argument is borne out every day, in on-the-ground, village-level experience.

he five case studies in this chapter come from far-flung parts of the world—communities in different physical environments and with different histories and cultural values. In each case, a poor rural community shows us how it has learned to restore and manage its local ecosystems for greater production, and how it has turned these natural assets into higher household income. But the heart of these stories is how communities have tried to meet the challenge of democratic governance. These cases are testaments to the difficulty and rewards of pursuing community-based natural resource management that is inclusive of the poor. Finally, these studies remind us that each situation faced by the rural poor is unique, but that the desire for better lives—materially, culturally, and spiritually—is universal.

Nature in Local Hands: The Case for Namibia's Conservancies
Devolving wildlife management and tourism to local conservancies for greater income opportunities. *Page 114.*

More Water, More Wealth in Darewadi Village
Village-led water management to conserve natural resources and improve livelihoods. *Page 124.*

Regenerating Woodlands: Tanzania's HASHI Project
Restoration of woodlands based on the traditional practice of restoring vegetation in protected enclosures. *Page 131.*

Bearing Witness: Empowering Indonesian Communities to Fight Illegal Logging
Training forest-dependent people to document illegal logging practices. *Page 139.*

Village by Village: Recovering Fiji's Coastal Fisheries
Restoring coastal resources by linking traditional conservation practices with modern techniques to create locally managed marine areas. *Page 144.*

NATURE IN LOCAL HANDS
The Case for Namibia's Conservancies

WHEN NAMIBIA GAINED INDEPENDENCE IN 1990, TEENAGER PASCOLENA FLORRY WAS herding goats in the country's dry, desolate northern savannah. Her job, unpaid and dangerous, was to protect her parents' livestock from preying jackals and leopards. She saw wildlife as the enemy, and many of the other indigenous inhabitants of Namibia's rural communal lands shared her view. Wildlife poaching was commonplace. Fifteen years later, 31-year-old Pascolena's life and outlook are very different. She has built a previously undreamed-of career in tourism and is the first black Namibian to be appointed manager of a guest lodge. Her village, and hundreds of others, have directly benefited from government efforts to devolve

wildlife management and tourism development on communal lands to conservancies run by indigenous peoples. "Now we see the wildlife as our way of creating jobs and opportunities as the tourism industry grows," she says. "The future is better with wildlife around, not only for jobs, but also for the environment" (Florry 2004).

Namibia's establishment of conservancies is among the most successful efforts by developing nations to decentralize natural resource management and simultaneously combat poverty. In fact, it is one of the largest-scale demonstrations of so-called "community-based natural resource management" (CBNRM) and the state-sanctioned empowerment of local communities. Most conservancies are run by elected committees of local people, to whom the government devolves user rights over wildlife within the conservancy boundaries. Technical assistance in managing the conservancy is provided by government officials and local and international nongovernmental organizations (NGOs). In late 2004, 31 conservancies were operating on 7.8 million hectares of desert, savannah, and woodlands occupied by 98,000 people. Fifty more were in development (WWF and Rossing Foundation 2004:iv).

Still in their infancy, Namibia's conservancies have their critics and remain to date imperfect vehicles of local democracy and poverty alleviation. Their active membership can be limited,

for example, and wildlife user rights are vested in committees, not directly in village households. Yet they have already delivered clear benefits for both wildlife and people. Zebra, oryx, kudu, and springbok populations are rebounding in many locations, and cash, jobs, and game meat are flowing to communities. Less tangible but equally important gains include the strengthening of local institutions and governance, women's empowerment, and greater community cohesion.

A New Idea for Wildlife Management

Namibia is a strikingly beautiful country of desert dunes, woodland savannah, open plains, and river valleys. Its small but growing population of 1.8 million people is highly dependent on natural resources for food and livelihoods. Large areas, primarily in the wildlife-rich plains of the north, are communally managed by more than a dozen different ethnic tribes.

In the apartheid era, when Namibia was governed by South Africa, game animals were declared protected, state-owned assets—a policy that discouraged those who inhabited communal areas from joining in conservation efforts (WWF and Rossing Foundation 2004:29). By the early 1980s ecosystems were rapidly deteriorating in the north, with rampant poaching

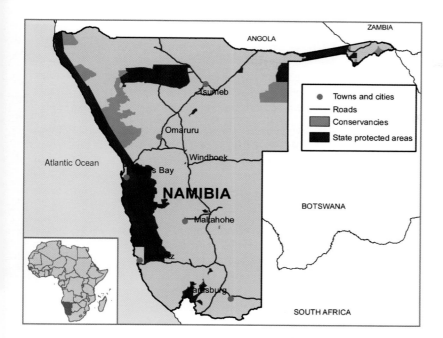

of elephant ivory and rhino horn and severe over-use of drought-prone land. Populations of Namibia's world-renowned wildlife, including the desert elephant, endangered black rhino, zebra, lion, impala, and oryx, plummeted.

In the mid-1980s an innovative anti-poaching program developed by Namibian conservationist Garth Owen-Smith provided an early template for community-based conservation. He won the trust of traditional leaders in the Kunene region, who agreed to appoint local people as community game guards and work with local NGOs to promote an increased sense of stewardship over wildlife (Long 2001:6). Meanwhile, Namibia's Nature Conservation Department (now the Ministry of Environment and Tourism, or MET) had devolved wildlife user rights to white-owned freehold farms. Private farm owners were allowed to sustainably utilize animals for game meat, trophy hunting, and tourism (Weaver 2004).

Following independence, these two models formed the basis of government action to extend the same kinds of use rights that farm owners had enjoyed to those who lived on communal lands. The Nature Conservation Act of 1996 enabled the establishment of conservancies—legally gazetted areas within the state's communal lands—through Namibia's Community Based Natural Resource Management Programme. Within the communal areas the state devolved limited wildlife rights to conservancy committees. These included rights to the hunting, capture, culling, and sale of "huntable game" (oryx, springbok, kudu, warthog, buffalo, and bushpig) and the right to apply to MET for permits to use quotas of protected game for trophy hunting (Long 2004:33).

To qualify, communities applying had to define the conservancy's boundary, elect a representative conservancy committee, negotiate a legal constitution, prove the committee's ability to manage funds, and produce an acceptable plan for equitable distribution of wildlife-related benefits (Long 2004:33).

Once approved, registered conservancies acquire the rights to a sustainable wildlife quota set by the ministry. The animals can either be sold to trophy hunting companies or hunted and consumed by the community. As legal entities, conservancies can also enter into contracts with private-sector tourism operators.

The first four conservancies were legally recognized in 1998. By October 2004, there were 31, with 31,000 registered members spread across six geographic regions. Conservancy committees had also set up 18 joint-venture agreements with private safari hunting and tour operators (WWF and Rossing Foundation 2004:iv)

This rapid expansion can be traced to a combination of factors. Government leadership and community enthusiasm were the prime ingredients. But an equally crucial factor was a strong commitment from support organizations. Collectively known as NACSO—the National Association of CBNRM Support Organisations—these included the University of Namibia and 12 national NGOs. The biggest support NGO, Integrated Rural Development and Nature Conservation (IRDNC), works with 40 conservancies in the wildlife-rich northern regions of Kunene and Caprivi, and is codirected by Garth Owen-Smith and Dr. Margaret Jacobsohn.

"Local people decide themselves if they want to form a conservancy. No pressure is put on anyone," says Dr. Jacobsohn. "Our experience is that a small group of people hear about the opportunities conservancies offer—on the radio, from MET, from neighboring conservancies and so on—and become a 'task force,' driving their community towards conservancy formation" (Jacobsohn 2004).

IN BRIEF: CONSERVANCY BENEFITS FOR PEOPLE

■ In 2004, total benefits flowing to conservancy communities, including employment income, cash from tourist fees and leases, and in-kind benefits like game meat, reached N$14.1 million (US$2.5 million).

■ Conservancy-related activities, including tourism, have provided 547 full-time and 3,250 part-time jobs since 1998.

■ Women's livelihoods and status have improved. Women fill almost 3,000 of the new part-time jobs, and more than half the full-time posts. They make up 50 percent of conservancy members, constitute 30 percent of conservancy committee members, and chair three conservancies.

■ Seven of the program's 12 support NGOs are now black-led (compared with none in 1995).

■ In 2003, conservancies and CBNRM support enterprises contributed an estimated N$79 million (US$9.6 million) to Namibia's Net National Income, and this contribution is expected to rise rapidly in the years ahead.

Source: WWF and Rossing Foundation 2004:v-vi

115

Some communities go it alone, while others seek help from ministry officials or a NACSO organization to hold public meetings, write a constitution, elect management committees, and consult households living within proposed conservancy borders. Not all resident adults need to sign up for a conservancy to be approved, but many community meetings are held in an effort to draw in all stakeholders. "At some point," says Dr Jacobsohn, "MET officials or the support NGO, if there is one, try to verify on the ground that there is majority support for the conservancy" (Jacobsohn 2004). The entire process takes two to three years (WWF and Rossing Foundation 2004:30).

While the success of Namibia's conservancies is dependent on local peoples' enthusiasm and commitment, the movement has also been significantly bankrolled by international donors. By late 2004, the development agencies of the United States, the United Kingdom, Sweden, and the Netherlands, as well as the World Bank and the European Union, had spent N$464 million on the effort to build a national community-based natural resource management program (WWF and Rossing Foundation 2004:17).

By 2004 this investment had begun to show strong economic results. Five of the longest-running conservancies—Torra, Uibasen, Nyae Nyae, Marienfluss, and Salambala—were financially self-sufficient, and four more are on track to become so in 2005 (WWF and Rossing Foundation 2004:v).

Conservancy Winners: Wildlife, Communities, Women

Wildlife Renaissance

Perhaps the most striking benefits of Namibia's experiment in people-led natural resource management are to wildlife. Populations of elephant, zebra, oryx, and springbok have risen several fold in many conservancies as poaching and illegal hunting has fallen. Northwest Namibia now boasts the world's largest free-roaming population of black rhino, while game in the large Nyae Nyae Conservancy have increased six-fold since 1995. In Caprivi's eastern floodplains, seasonal migrations of game between Botswana and Namibia have resumed for the first time since the early 1970s (WWF and Rossing Foundation 2004:v)

Income and jobs from tourism, lucrative sport hunting of trophy animals, and community hunting quotas have combined to make wildlife more attractive to communities as a managed resource than as a poaching prospect. To attract wildlife, and reduce conflict with humans, improved management techniques have also included new water holes for elephants, protection of domestic and livestock water sources from elephants, and land-use zoning to separate designated wildlife habitat from village and cropping areas (Long 2001:9) In some areas, including the Nyae Nyae, Uukwaluudhi, and

---

TORRA CONSERVANCY: EQUATOR INITIATIVE 2004 AWARD WINNER

■ Namibia's best-known conservancy is wildlife-rich Torra, which borders the celebrated Skeleton Coast Park. Registered in 1998, it covers 352,000 hectares of plains and rugged mountains in southern Kunene.

■ Benefits for the mixed community of Riemvasmakkers, Damaras, Herero, and Owambo, who live in the conservancy include cash payouts, jobs, game meat, and livestock protection measures such as new water points and electric fencing. Elderly residents have also received Christmas packages, including hats, scarves, socks, and blankets (Long 2001:16-17, Baker 2003:2).

■ The conservancy currently earns N$750,000 a year and has taken in enough revenue to cover its own running costs since 2000 (Long et al. 2004:19). In January 2003, Torra's conservancy committee distributed N$630 in cash (US$73) to every conservancy member over 18. This amounted to approximately half of the average annual income in conservancy households (USAID 2005:3).

■ Torra Conservancy has generated considerable income—about N$1.5 million as of October 2003—from ecotourism, trophy hunting, and sales of live game. Ecotourism activities include Damaraland Camp, a luxury lodge staffed entirely by local tribespeople. Damaraland Camp is a joint venture between Torra's conservancy committee and private tour operator Wilderness Safaris (Vaughan et al. 2004:2).

■ In 2004 Torra Conservancy won the Equator Initiative Prize awarded by the United Nations Development Programme for outstanding community projects that reduce poverty through sustainable use of biodiversity.

Salambala Conservancies, game animals have also been successfully reintroduced (Barnes 2004:4).

According to Chris Weaver, director of the Windhoek-based WWF-LIFE conservancy program, which funds several NACSO groups, these gains indicate "a massive shift in the attitudes of communal area residents towards wildlife. The strong embracement of the conservancy movement demonstrates a willingness and desire to incorporate wildlife into rural livelihoods, as they are now viewed as an asset to livelihoods" (Weaver 2004).

Namibia's conservancies have significantly altered the country's land-use landscape—to the benefit of biodiversity. Eighteen registered conservancies sit alongside or between national parks or protected game reserves. This facilitates the safe, seasonal movement of wildlife between parks and communal lands and adds an extra 55,192 km^2 of compatible land use to Namibia's protected area network of 114,080 km^2. Conservancies have also successfully adapted their traditional land-use pattern of subsistence activities—such as livestock grazing and dryland farming—to incorporate new tourism opportunities. Many, for example, have set aside large, dedicated wildlife areas for tourism and for sport or community hunting (WWF and Rossing Foundation 2004:iv).

Reducing Poverty, Empowering People

Benefits for human populations are also clear-cut, although they vary among conservancies. Over 95,000 Namibians have received benefits of some kind since 1998, according to the United States Agency for International Development (USAID), a funder and supporter of the conservancy effort (USAID 2005:1). These benefits include jobs, training, game meat, cash dividends, and social benefits such as school improvements or water supply maintenance funded by conservancy revenue (WWF and Rossing Foundation 2004:43).

In 2004 total income from the CBNRM program nation-wide reached N$14.1 million, up from N$1.1 million in 1998. Of this, N$7.25 million was distributed across communities in the form of cash dividends and social programs, with the rest earned by individual households through wages from conservancy-related jobs and enterprises. Tourist lodges, camps, guide services, and related businesses such as handicraft production employed 547 locals full-time and 3,250 part-time. In all, 18 conservancies received substantial cash income, averaging N$217,046 in 2004 (WWF and Rossing Foundation 2004:v,43).

Community hunting quotas provide another important direct benefit. Game meat distribution has proved highly popular with communities, providing both prized meat and a sense of community autonomy (Long 2001:9).

In each conservancy, once revenues are being generated (often within two years of registration), the membership and committee choose how to spend the conservancy's income and distribute benefits. Some opt for cash payouts to members or households. In January 2003, for example, Torra gave each adult conservancy member the equivalent of US$73. Others fund services such as school classrooms, new water pumps, or diesel fuel for operating pumps (USAID 2005:3).

A 2002 World Bank study of 1192 households in Caprivi and Kunene found benefits spread equitably across conservancy members. In Kunene the researchers recorded a healthy 29 percent increase in per capita income due to the combined direct and indirect effects of community-based natural resource management, and that did not include non-financial benefits such as bush meat (Bandyopadhyay et al. 2004:16,13). These findings suggest Namibia's conservancies are starting to play a significant role in fighting rural poverty.

Positive Gender Agenda

Conservancies are also having a major impact on women's empowerment and well-being. By 2004, women made up half of all conservancy members, and three in ten management committee members. They had also captured the majority of new jobs generated, boosting both their income and social status. At luxury Damaraland Camp in Torra Conservancy, for example, over 75 percent of employees are women (Florry 2004).

"These are local people who would never have found jobs anywhere else," says Pascolena Florry, whose own horizons expanded dramatically as she worked her way up from waitressing to camp manager. "The conservancy has given them training and skills and increased

FIGURE 1 WILDLIFE RECOVERY IN NYAE NYAE CONSERVANCY

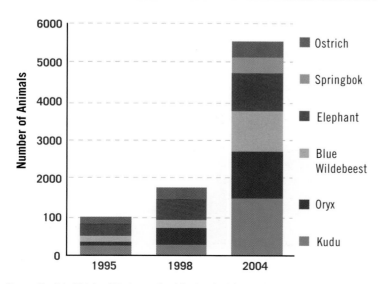

Source: Namibia Ministry of Environment and Tourism (aerial census)

117

their self esteem and sense of worth." Before tourism developed, she recalls, opportunities for paid work were almost nonexistent. "I grew up in a small village. The goats were our only income and there was no one to protect them from wild animals, so that is what I used to do. Life is better now. My family has more money, we are able to do more things" (Florry 2004).

Empowerment

The shift in power to local communities, after decades of centralized power, has also produced intangible benefits. Foremost among these are a greater decision-making role for citizens, a deepened sense of community, and growing pride in wildlife recovery and conservancy success.

The process of managing a new democratic institution has empowered those taking part, and given them new skills. Officials from the NGOs and MET train and mentor newly elected committee members on priority setting, decision-making, and conflict mediation (USAID 2005:5). In high-membership conservancies such as Torra, village households are also very involved in decision-making. "People understand that this is an opportunity that was not there previously. They feel conservancies give them power over how to take care of the animals…and a chance for a better future," says Paula Adams, Torra's community liaison officer. "They attend our meetings and tell us they want to build more tourist camps. If something is happening that's against the conservancy's interests, they report it. For example, if a farm's water pipes are damaged by elephants, they tell us, so we can go and fix it" (Adams 2004).

Citizens also come up with solutions and priorities that inform the Torra committee's actions. When problem animals became an issue, with lions killing livestock, local farmers requested a new, secure breeding station rather than cash compensation. The conservancy is now building one. A 2002 household survey

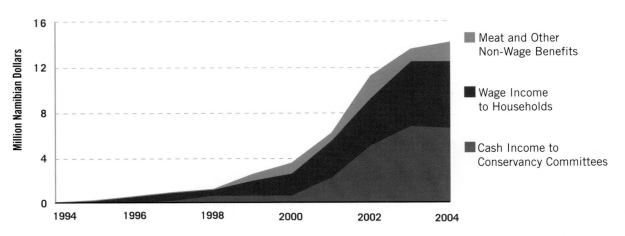

FIGURE 2 CONSERVANCY BENEFITS, 1994-2004

Legend:
- Meat and Other Non-Wage Benefits
- Wage Income to Households
- Cash Income to Conservancy Committees

Y-axis: Million Namibian Dollars (0, 4, 8, 12, 16)
X-axis: 1994, 1996, 1998, 2000, 2002, 2004

Source: World Wildlife Fund and Rossing Foundation, 2004.

TABLE 1 CONSERVANCY INCOME BREAKDOWN, 2003

Sources of Cash and In-Kind Income to Conservancies and Their Members, By Percentage

Community-based tourism enterprises and campsites	36%
Joint venture tourism	27%
Trophy hunting	17%
Thatching grass sales	7%
Crafts sales	4%
Game meat distribution	3%
Game donation	2%
Own-use game	1%
Live game sales	1%
Interest earned	1%
Miscellaneous	1%
	100 %

Source: Barnes 2004: 5

Limits to Poverty Alleviation

Every conservancy must produce a plan for equitably distributing benefits before it is registered by the government. In theory, the Ministry of Environment and Tourism could de-register a conservancy that violated this policy. But in practice, there is no blueprint for what constitutes "equitable" sharing of benefits, leaving conservancies to go their own way. Some specifically target poorer, more vulnerable households; others do not. Some spend revenue on social services such as school equipment or water supply maintenance, others on cash payouts. Some only distribute benefits to registered conservancy members, others to all households.

To promote self-governance, NACSO support organisations encourage communities to set their own priorities. Chris Weaver, WWF-LIFE program director, acknowledges this can create teething problems. "In some cases there has been a push-pull between wealthier households, who own livestock, and will have to give up grazing land for wildlife management, and poorer households who will benefit a lot more from conservancy-generated cash handouts than better-off households." He insists, however, that communities must run their own affairs if conservancies are to succeed long-term. "We don't prescribe. We believe the committees should make their own mistakes, learn from them, and adjust the next year" (Weaver 2004).

This laissez faire approach, however, was criticized by an international panel of social scientists that in March 2004 urged Namibia's government to ensure benefits were targeted to the

revealed that members "wanted to see a healthy community with healthy people," says Adams. The conservancy responded by starting HIV/AIDS workshops and distributing leaflets and condoms.

Active members across Namibia's conservancies also play a hands-on role in natural resource management. They collect and analyze wildlife population data, using a simple, standardized recording system, and conservancy committees apply the findings to management activities. This people-led monitoring has been so successful that it is now being introduced in national parks and protected areas in Zambia, Mozambique, and Botswana (WWF and Rossing Foundation 2004:vi).

Conservancy Failings

Despite their well-documented benefits, however, Namibia's conservancies remain a work in progress. Three issues, in particular, are raising concerns within the government, donor, and NGO communities. The first is that the ad hoc manner in which some conservancies distribute their benefits does not always favor the poorest households. The second is that limited participation in conservancies is hampering genuine local governance and empowerment. The third is that the recovery of wildlife populations has increased the number of natural predators of the livestock upon which many conservancy households depend. A deeper, more structural problem is the limited nature of local rights, with conservancy residents denied full property or tenure rights. Despite periodic discussion of land reform, ownership of all communal lands is retained by the government, in a holdover from colonial times.

poor. On the basis of an intensive three-year study covering eight conservancies, known as the WILD report, they recommended that the Ministry of Environment and Tourism:

- give conservancies strict guidelines on equitable distribution

- encourage them to target benefits to pre-identified groups of poor people

- help committees review whether their existing conservancy membership provided a fair basis for benefit distribution

- adopt a "pro-poor" national tourism policy, focusing on conservancy-based developments that "contribute directly to poverty reduction, enhanced livelihood security, and social empowerment" (Long 2004:xvii).

Limits to Local Governance

A second major challenge facing Namibia's conservancies is their democratic deficit. Many local people do not register themselves as conservancy members or vote for committee members. Although typically a majority of in-boundary adults join up, the WILD report identified several conservancies with a minority membership. A 2002 survey of a thousand households in seven conservancies found that only 34 percent identified themselves as "conservancy participants" (Bandyopadhyay et al. 2004:15).

In addition, the 1996 legislation originating conservancies vests legal ownership rights over wildlife in management committees, not directly in the conservancy membership. Conservancy committees are elected by the membership and hence are clearly meant to be directly accountable to conservancy members, but there is no legal obligation for this enshrined at the national level (Long 2004:35).

Limited participation in a conservancy's membership and activities can contribute to other problems, such as slow distri-

bution of cash and meat to resident families. Even flagship Torra Conservancy did not make any cash payouts to members until January 2003, three years after it became financially independent (Baker 2003:1).

In some conservancies there is also evidence that more highly educated community members disproportionately control management committees. Field researchers for the WILD project, working in eight conservancies in Caprivi and Kunene, also found that people employed in conservancy-based tourism tended to come from wealthier local families (Long 2004:17). On the other hand, the 2002 World Bank research team found no evidence that social elites were capturing a bigger slice of benefits than other community members. "In Caprivi there was some evidence that poor households benefited more than richer ones, whereas in Kunene we found that benefit distribution was poverty-neutral, with everybody benefiting equally," said Kirk Hamilton, lead economist at the World Bank Environment Department (Hamilton 2004).

According to Margaret Jacobsohn, high-handed behavior by wealthier residents has mainly been a problem during conservancy development. "In one area, an elite group blocked a conservancy for two years until a locally constituted Dispute Resolution Committee helped resolve the situation. A conservancy has since been registered, with a democratically elected committee that represents the whole community." While acknowledging that the conservancy movement is "a long way from perfect democracy," Jacobsohn remains optimistic. "The technical support providers—NGOs and government—are constantly adjusting to ensure that as much power as possible is devolved to the local, household level. It's an evolutionary process, improving year by year" (Jacobsohn 2004).

Some government officials have argued that every adult resident should automatically receive conservancy membership. But NACSO organizations have resisted, arguing that community-based management will only work if citizens accept responsibilities as well as rights (Jacobsohn 2004). Nevertheless, expert criticism of the limits to community participation is growing. The 2004 WILD report, submitted to the Ministry of Environment and Tourism, argued that higher membership levels were essential to increase pressure on committees to act competently, distribute benefits efficiently and equitably, and take actions approved by a majority of residents.

While praising the conservancies' achievements, the WILD report bluntly concluded that "the extent to which rural people will continue to support conservancies… depends on them gaining a stronger voice in local decision-making. The requirement now is to shift attention to supporting local capacity to address improved participation, and, in so doing, develop a more inclusive approach to planning that specifically addresses issues of livelihood security and diversification at household level, particularly for poorer groups" (Long 2004:9, 12).

Sensitive to such criticisms, NACSO and the Ministry of Environment and Tourism have drawn up plans to strengthen participatory democracy across conservancies. Performance indicators, to help residents and support organisations measure committee performance and hold management committees to account, are also in the works. "Getting more involvement from the community membership and more transparency in how a conservancy operates will be a key focus over the next five years," asserts Chris Weaver. Practical proposals include delegating decision-making down to the village level instead of conservancy committees, increasing information flow by posting regular financial and other bulletins in public locations, and making annual committee meetings more transparent (Weaver 2004).

Wildlife-People Conflict

While tourism based on the attraction of Namibia's majestic wild animals has brought undisputed benefits, the recovery of wildlife populations is not without trade-offs. Livestock in Kunene, and crops in Caprivi, are still the main breadwinners for many conservancy households. Tension is growing in some areas as cattle, goats, and crops succumb in increasing numbers to predators or marauding elephants. In Caprivi, for example, average crop losses equal 20 percent of local households' average annual income. Research suggests that poorer families suffer the most, which undermines the anti-poverty efforts of conservancies. It also encourages illegal, low-level wildlife poaching for food, a problem especially prevalent among poorer households (Long 2004:xxi).

Although the Ministry of Environment and Tourism acknowledges rising human-wildlife conflicts, it has no policy on how institutions should deal with the problem. In 2003 IRDNC (a support NGO) took action by successfully piloting a compensation scheme in four Kunene and Caprivi conservancies for households that had lost livestock to predators. In 2005 the compensation schemes will be extended to cover elephant-induced crop damage in some conservancies (Jacobsohn 2004).

A related problem, likely to get more urgent as wildlife numbers rise, is lack of land tenure. Unlike white-owned freehold farms, conservancies cannot bar outsiders from bringing their animals to graze on communal lands within their boundaries, even though this causes pressure on resources used by local wildlife and livestock. In Torra, for example, the conservancy committee zoned land for wildlife and tourism use and developed internal rules to regulate grazing access on this land. But livestock farmers from outside the conservancy simply ignored these rules, and continued to assert their open access grazing rights (Long 2004:148). The conservancy's lack of full property rights prevents it from legally excluding them.

Practice Makes Perfect: Sustaining and Reforming Namibia's Conservancies

The very success of Namibia's community-based natural resource management program is producing enormous, some say unrealistic, expectations for the future. With an estimated 100,000 people actively supporting the registration of 40-50 new conservancies, one in every nine Namibians may soon live in a communal area conservancy (WWF and Rossing Foundation 2004:iv). Namibia's government is anxious to use this expanding network of citizen-led local governance institutions as a broad vehicle for rural development in a poor nation.

In 2001 new legislation made provision for community-run forests, managed by community bodies (including conservancies) with ownership rights over forest products. In 2003 new freshwater fisheries laws allowed community institutions, including conservancies, to assume management of local fisheries (WWF and Rossing Foundation 2004:13). The government is also encouraging conservancies to diversify into social programs, including HIV/AIDS awareness and prevention.

But some NGOs caution that conservancies should not take on responsibility for implementing government programs or move too far from their original conservation objectives. As Chris Weaver sees it, "Conservancies were developed as a conservation initiative with spin-off benefits for development. They are contributing significantly to national income, but they are not going to solve all the poverty or rural development problems of Namibia" (Weaver 2004).

Conservancies also remain far from self-sufficient, with most still dependent on donor support. Of the more than 40 established and fledgling conservancies that IRDNC assists, only two are self-financing, although a majority are expected to be independent or earning significant income by 2010. While joint-venture tourism and sport hunting offer the best revenue-generating opportunities, they still provide a minority of jobs in most conservancies. Experts see a strong need to diversify livelihood options, especially among poor families, to avoid over-reliance on tourist income (WWF and Rossing Foundation 2004:44-45).

At the political level, pressure is also growing on government ministers to institute land reforms that will increase the security and long-term viability of conservancies by granting tenure to residents of communal lands. The WILD report recommended to Namibia's government that securing community tenure over conservancies was "a necessary step in strengthening conservancies' rights and authority with respect to resource use and allocation." Such rights were needed, the authors argued, to give conservancy committees legal grounds for excluding outside livestock herds which were depleting conservancy resources and revenues (Long 2004:157). New regional Communal Land Boards, to be established under the Communal Lands Act 2003, may provide

LEARNING FROM NAMIBIA'S CONSERVANCIES

Decentralization Can Bring Benefits. Devolving power over wildlife management to the local level can increase the local stake in good management, bringing benefits to both wildlife and local economies. The success of Namibia's decentralization effort was aided by grounding it firmly in law—the 1996 Nature Conservation Act—and through the active promotion by government, donors, and NGOs.

Conservation Benefits Follow Livelihood Benefits. Conservancies gain broad support and community compliance when they demonstrate a connection with greater income. Benefits to wildlife, in the form of reduced poaching, follow quickly. A combination of short-term community benefits such as bush meat and cash payouts may be necessary as longer term development gains such as better infrastructure and a more diverse local economy slowly manifest.

Targeting the Poor Takes Work. Conservancies have a fairly good record in terms of the equity of benefits distribution. But many need help in more directly targeting benefits to the poor. Performance indicators and distribution guidelines for conservancy committees may help.

Tenure Remains a Challenge. Devolution of user rights to wildlife may not be enough to sustainably manage conservancies over the long term or to maximize poverty reduction. Granting conservancies fuller tenure rights would give them the ability to better control access to conservancy lands, more effectively manage grazing pressures, and reduce conflicts.

Direct Accountability Needed. Conservancies can capitalize on their proven record and increase their broadbased support by making local conservancy committees more fully accountable and working to give conservancy members a stronger voice in decisions. Increasing the proportion of local community members that identify themselves as conservancy members is one important element of long-term viability.

Mature Institutions Take Time. Building the technical and governing capacity of local institutions such as conservancy committees takes time and requires steady financial and technical support. Local NGOs specially constituted to play this support role can play a vital part in institution-building, and in helping to construct and execute a workable business model for conservancy enterprises.

a vehicle for land reform, as both conservancies and traditional authorities will appoint representatives alongside those of various government departments. The boards will be responsible for granting land-use leases, but their full responsibilities and the influence that conservancies may wield on them are yet to become clear (Long 2004:157).

To address all these challenges and expectations, the Ministry of Environment and Tourism, USAID, and WWF launched a new five-year plan in October 2004 that aims to make most conservancies self-sustaining, with a broader rural development role, by 2009. Chris Weaver summarizes the approach as "an expanded conservation strategy with add-on benefits for development." Conservancies will be encouraged to expand beyond tourism and wildlife use into forestry, fisheries,

water management, and sustainable farming, and to use the income gained to invest in other enterprises such as small support businesses.

In six short years, Namibia's conservancies have developed from a hopeful experiment to the cornerstone of government plans to reform the management of the country's unique natural resource base. For local support NGOs, however, the central focus for the next five years will be on improving conservancy governance and participation.

On the front line in Kunene, Dr. Jacobsohn is clear that financial self-sufficiency alone will not guarantee long-term success for the conservancy movement. "Earning income is not the hardest part. It is learning to run a local institution effectively and efficiently that is the biggest challenge. We are requiring remote rural dwellers, the majority of whom are subsistence farmers, to manage not just wildlife, but also staff, an office, and a vehicle. We are asking them to stick to a constitution, be transparent, communicate with members—do everything that managing a democratic institution involves. These are the conditions towards which NGOs are aiming so that we are no longer required."

MORE WATER, MORE WEALTH
In Darewadi Village

IN DROUGHT-PLAGUED MAHARASHTRA, GOOD WATER MANAGEMENT IS A MATTER OF LIFE and death. Small-scale farmers in the Indian state are dependent on infrequent rainfall to maintain their fields, livestock, and forest-based livelihoods. During the dry season, drinking water is so scarce that supplies are trucked into thousands of villages (D'Souza and Lobo 2004:2). In recent years, development initiatives in the region have focused on village-led watershed management activities, aimed at conserving natural resources and improving livelihoods. Among these is the Indo-German Watershed Development Program (IGWDP),

which has funded 145 projects in 24 districts, successfully mobilizing villagers to regenerate land through tree-planting and water and soil conservation (D'Souza and Lobo 2004:3).

One of the program's more dramatic success stories is Darewadi village, in Ahmednagar, Maharashtra's most drought-prone district. As recently as 1996, the main village and its twelve hamlets were on the verge of desertification. Scarce rainfall supported only 3-4 months of agricultural activity a year, forcing villagers to migrate in search of seasonal work for the rest of the year. Today, farm-based employment is available 9-10 months of the year, and agricultural wages have doubled. More crop varieties are now grown due to extensive new irrigation, and the value of cultivated land has quadrupled (WOTR 2002:4).

Before the watershed was regenerated, Darewadi's 921 residents depended on water deliveries from a tanker truck from April to July. Yet in summer 2004 the village was tanker-free, despite receiving only 350 mm of rain in 2003—100 mm less than its annual average (WOTR 2005).

Inhabitants have also gained in less tangible ways from the self-organization that has driven their village's revival. They have learned new skills and found new social cohesion. The Darewadi project and similar experiments are not perfect: the

role of women can be limited, and landless people may not share equally in the benefits. Nevertheless, Darewadi's undoubted success provides one encouraging model for people-led sustainable development in arid regions, where many of the world's poor live.

Pioneering People-Led Watershed Management

In the 1980's, the Indian government shifted its approach to watershed management in drought-afflicted rural areas. Traditional bureaucratic, top-down projects had often failed due to lack of consultation with or buy-in from local people. In an effort to increase success rates, the government began to encourage programs based on smaller, people-led projects. Among these was the Indo-German Watershed Development Program, launched in 1992.

Co-founded by Father Hermann Bacher, a Jesuit priest, the IGWDP is funded by the German government through the German Agency for Technical Cooperation and the German Bank for Reconstruction. It is implemented by an independent, state-wide NGO, the Watershed Organization Trust (WOTR), in partnership with the Indian government's National Bank for Agriculture and Rural Development (NABARD).

The program funds village-based, participatory watershed development projects, with communities chosen for their low rainfall, geographical position—generally within primary water catchment areas—and social composition. Villages where a few families dominate land ownership are disqualified on the grounds that such power imbalances would deter consensus on developing local land to the benefit of all. To qualify, villages must agree to temporary bans on tree-cutting and grazing on land designated for regeneration. They must also contribute free labor—a common rural practice known as *shramdan*—to cover at least 15-20 percent of project costs (D'Souza and Lobo 2004:4; Lobo and D'Souza 2003:9).

Capacity-building is the program's first priority. In each community, a Village Watershed Committee of local residents is nominated, usually by the village assembly, to make and implement decisions. Villagers also work on a pilot project, learning water and soil conservation techniques, with WOTR or another local NGO providing training, technical organizational, and financial support. After 12 to 18 months, NABARD assumes project oversight, funding scaled-up watershed activities designed by and delivered through the village committee, again with local NGO support (Lobo and D'Souza 2003:6, 15).

By late 2004, the Indo-German Watershed Development Program had spent US$21.9 million funding projects on 165,439 hectares of land, occupied by some 190,000 people (D'Souza and Lobo 2004:3). After 12 years of first-hand experience across Maharashtra, WOTR's co-founder and executive director, Crispino Lobo, summarizes village-based watershed development as "a proven strategy for poverty reduction, augmentation of water resources, livelihood diversification, enhancing well-being, building social capital, and widening the decision-making and opportunity space for women" (D'Souza and Lobo 2004:2).

A Path Out of Poverty

Many of these benefits are apparent in Darewadi, a formerly impoverished and despairing community that now generates year-round employment for a majority of inhabitants.

Back in 1995, with farm work in short supply, Darewadi's 131 households were losing many men to far-flung seasonal work as sugarcane cutters or building laborers. Those who remained often herded sheep, further depleting grazing lands and draining the low water table. The village and its satellite hamlets were surrounded by barren hills, and women walked miles to fetch water and fuelwood. When Father Bacher visited at that time, he concluded that if rejuvenation were possible in Darewadi, it would be possible in any watershed (WOTR 2002:1).

The Darewadi watershed covers 1,535 hectares. Two-thirds is privately owned; the rest is made up of common lands owned by the Maharashtra state government's Forest Department

(WOTR 2002:1). WOTR's first task was to overcome the mistrust of many villagers, especially sheep and goat farmers, including many poorer families, who feared that grazing bans on regenerating land would cut down the available fodder, harming their already fragile livelihoods. Through a series of village meetings, the NGO explained how the temporary bans would allow trees to grow, eventually yielding more fodder and more water for crops.

A compromise was eventually agreed in the village assembly, or *gram sabha*, whereby land closure would proceed in phases as the conservation and planting work progressed and any violators of the ban would pay a fine to the community. It was not an easy compromise to reach, but the villagers were encouraged by the prospect of increased income within a comparatively short period. In addition, most livestock owners are also farmers, and therefore not solely dependent on grazing for income. Another inducement to try the restoration plan came in the form of technical assistance from WOTR, which offered loans and training to livestock owners who wanted to switch from sheep and goats to high-yield milk cows (Lobo 2005c).

Once the villagers had accepted the restoration scheme, WOTR helped them take the necessary official steps to gain state permission and structure the project's management. First they helped the community negotiate a Joint Forest Management agreement with the state Forest Department, legally granting local people the right to work on the state-owned common lands surrounding Darewadi and to own the agricultural produce grown on these lands (Lobo 2005c). Without attention to this question of land use and tenure on state forest lands, a regeneration plan covering the entire watershed would not have been possible, nor would it have been economically attractive enough to gain village support.

Next, the *gram sabha* nominated 24 people to the Village Watershed Committee, which became the registered project authority, legally responsible for managing funds and overseeing development activities. The watershed committee included representatives from all social groups—including landless people and seven women—and from every corner of the scattered community (WOTR 2002:2-3). This was essential, according to Lobo, to create an effective, trusted community institution that could rule by consensus. "What makes our participatory approach work...is involving all stakeholders in arriving at negotiated outcomes that are beneficial or acceptable to all"(Lobo 2005a).

Members of the Village Watershed Committee were assigned tasks by the village assembly. Responsibilities included monitoring grazing bans, organizing paid and voluntary laborers, supervising work and wages, maintaining records, and imposing fines on villagers who broke agreed project rules. Committee members were unpaid, trained by WOTR, and held accountable for fulfilling their duties by the *gram sabha* (Lobo and D'Souza 2003:14-15). They also negotiated with local stakeholders, including the landless, on the specific areas of land to be set aside for phased grazing bans and regeneration. When conflicts arose, they were settled by the committee, sometimes assisted by Forest Department officials, with WOTR taking a back seat (Lobo 2005c).

The Rewards of Regeneration

Five years of regeneration activities followed, including tree and grassland planting and sustainable crop cultivation. Soil and water conservation measures to nurture the regenerating land included the construction of simple water harvesting and irrigation systems such as hillside contour trenches and rainwater-harvesting dams.

The work was carried out by villagers themselves, following training by WOTR field staff in simple conservation-based agricultural practices and management techniques such as land measurement and record-keeping. Wherever possible, the NGO worked with landowning couples, to boost local women's confidence and involvement in decision-making (D'Souza and Lobo 2004:5). Darewadi landowners were also mentored by farmers who had already successfully implemented watershed conservation measures in neighboring villages. Villagers donated 17 percent of total labor costs and earned wages for additional project-related work over and above their *shramdan* (WOTR 2002:2).

The Darewadi project's costs were substantial, totaling 8.7 million rupees when the value of voluntary labor is factored in (WOTR 2002:2). By 2001 the results were apparent. Barren hills and common lands covering 395 hectares had been planted with trees and grasses, with a 65 percent survival rate (D'Souza and Lobo 2004:6). Land under irrigation increased from 197 to 342 hectares, with maize, wheat, and vegetables among successful new crops. Grass fodder for livestock increased 170 percent as a result of the soil and

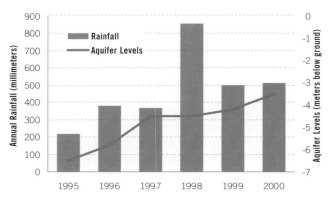

FIGURE 1 ANNUAL RAINFALL AND AQUIFER LEVELS, DAREWADI WATERSHED, 1995-2000

Source: Watershed Organization Trust 2005.

TABLE 1 MORE WATER IN DAREWADI

Impact Indicator	Before Watershed Development, 1996	After Watershed Development, 2001	January 2005
Months requiring delivery of drinking water by tanker truck	February to June	Tanker free	Tanker free
Average depth of water table below ground level	6.5 m	3.5 m	3.1 m
Number of active wells	23	63	67
Electric motors for pumping water	6	52	65
Land under irrigation	197 ha	342 ha	381 ha

Source: Watershed Organization Trust 2005.

water conservation measures (WOTR 2005). (*See Figure 1 and Tables 1 and 2*.)

In response to the grazing bans, many poorer households had sold their sheep and goats. Since the restrictions were lifted in 2001, however, livestock numbers have rebounded. More plentiful fodder has also enabled villagers to raise more valuable hybrid cows with high milk production. Higher-yield crops, milk sales, increased wages, and more days of available work have resulted in a fivefold hike in the village's agricultural income (*see Figure 2*). Signs of increased household wealth and well-being include the arrival of kitchen gardens and individual latrines, as well as televisions, bicycles, and motorcycles.

"Our village has changed totally," says Ramaji B. Phad, a Darewadi sheep owner. "The hills are now covered with trees which we planted at the beginning. The water in wells and the ground water level have increased. The average income of the farmer has increased. People are now able to eat good food like wheat, rice, and dhal" (WOTR 2002:5).

Despite three years of drought since IGWDP funding ended in 2001, the project's benefits are continuing, testifying to the effectiveness of the regeneration and the Village Watershed Committee. The local water table has continued to rise, as have supplies of livestock fodder and the volume of land under irrigation. The availability of agricultural work and wage levels have held steady. In early 2005, 11 villagers acquired telephones (Lobo 2005c).

The transition to self-sufficiency in 2001 was eased by the IGWDP returning to the community the cash equivalent of 50 percent of the value of the village's voluntary labor. The community deposited the money in a maintenance fund for watershed management activities. Contributions from villagers and penalties charged for rule-breaking are also used to top up the fund, and WOTR continues to provide village businesses with microfinance support (Lobo 2005b).

Perhaps most important for the long term are the links that villagers have built up with local government officials. With a new sense of confidence based on their record of achievement, they can now leverage these contacts to seek more development funding. "Before we would not talk in front of outsiders," explains Chimaji Kondaji, deputy chairman of Darewadi's Village Watershed Committee. "[Since the project] we get good cooperation from government departments, who we now approach with ease" (Lobo 2005b).

Improving Women's Lot

The increased availability of wells, subsistence crops, and fodder has reduced women's household labor significantly in Darewadi. Women are typically the chief providers of their families' water, food, fodder, and fuel needs. Women also earned cash as project laborers and have benefited from drudgery-reducing assets made possible by increased incomes, such as kitchen gardens and household toilets (Lobo and D'Souza 2003:16).

However, as work on watershed activities is almost year-round, compared with the seasonal nature of farming duties, many women now work longer hours than before the project. According to Crispino Lobo, "women accept this load because it gives them additional income, which enables them to send their children to school." Becoming breadwinners, he says, also "enhances their status at home."

Empowering women, however, has proved more difficult than improving their material well-being. Faced with traditional rural attitudes about women's subservient roles, the Watershed Organization Trust has taken a soft approach. While strongly urging village assemblies to elect women to Village Watershed Committees, they have not insisted on a 50:50 ratio (D'Souza and Lobo 2004:11). As a result, women generally number no more than one-third of Watershed Committee members in IGWDP projects (Lobo 2005a).

To encourage greater self-confidence and independence, WOTR also trains village women in record-keeping and organizational skills, and encourages them to form savings and credit groups. Darewadi village and its surrounding hamlets

TABLE 2 DAREWADI WATERSHED RESTORATION BENEFITS

Benefit	Before Watershed Development, 1996	After Watershed Development, 2001	January 2005
Cropped area:			
▪ Kharif	490 ha	616 ha	620 ha
▪ Rabi (winter)	310 ha	417 ha	425 ha
▪ Rabi (summer)	0 ha	38 ha	40 ha
Main crops grown	Bajra (pearl millet)	Bajra, onion, tomato, wheat, jowar (sorghum), maize, vegetables	Bajra, onion, tomato, wheat, jowar, maize, vegetables
Waste land	167 ha	17 ha	15 ha
Livestock:			
▪ Crossbred cows	14	113	97
▪ Indigenous cows	170	101	85
▪ Sheep	1017	434	610
▪ Goats	306	132	215
Summer milk production	Insignificant	788 liter/day	550 liter/day
Fodder availability	1054 tons/year	2848 tons/year	3265 tons/year
Agricultural employment	3-4 months/year	9-10 months/year	9-10 months/year
Agricultural wage rate	Rs. 20-30/day	Rs. 40-50/day	Rs. 40-50/day
Value of cropped land	15,000 Rs/acre	65,000 Rs/acre	65,000 Rs/acre
Value of waste land	4,000 Rs/acre	18,000 Rs/acre	20,000 Rs/acre
Biogas units	0	2	2
Gas cylinders	0	32	32
Smokeless chulhas (stoves)	0	54	54
Kitchen gardens	0	30	30
Individual latrines	0	50	50
Televisions	3	76	76
Bicycles	2	122	122
Motorcycles	0	42	45
Tractors	0	2	1

Source: WOTR 2005

now boast eleven such groups as well as an umbrella women's organization, the Samyukta Mahila Samiti (WOTR 2002:3). The women give each other small loans to support basic needs. Bigger loans—for example, to launch Darewadi's women-run dairy—are available through microfinance arranged by WOTR (Lobo and D'Souza 2003:20).

Mixed Blessings for the Poorest

A community's poorest families often receive limited benefits from watershed development, despite their greater need. The landless are unable to take advantage of improved soil and water conditions to plant more crops and vegetables. Those who own only a few sheep or goats may suffer disproportionately from grazing bans imposed on common lands. At the other end of the social scale, by the WOTR's own admission, farmers with the most land have benefited disproportionately in Darewadi and other IGWDP project villages from new consumer items such as televisions, radios, motorcycles, and cooking utensils (D'Souza and Lobo 2004:10).

On the positive side, work on watershed projects can provide sustained wages for poor villagers with no livestock or crops. Families that earn enough to save can then lease, or even buy, small plots of arable land and pull themselves one rung up the economic ladder (Lobo 2005a).

In Darewadi, new agricultural work opportunities and the doubling of hourly wages for such labor have proven a big boon for poor families (Lobo 2005c). *(See Table 1.)* In the mid-1990s, two-thirds of households migrated each year in search of liveli-hoods. Today, people who had moved away are returning. In fact, additional farm laborers are now being drawn from nearby villages to work the new acres of cultivable land (D'Souza and Lobo 2004:11).

In another positive sign for poorer families, sheep and goat ownership has increased since 2001 as villagers benefit from the removal of grazing bans and increased fodder supplies (Lobo 2005c). "People do not have to go outside looking for work now and do not have to starve," says Mrs. Zumbarbai M. Borade, a landless Darewadi resident. "The poor have benefited a lot from this project" (WOTR 2002:6).

The Challenge of Equity

Nevertheless, Darewadi provides a microcosm of the difficul-ties facing Indian authorities and NGOs in trying to ensure

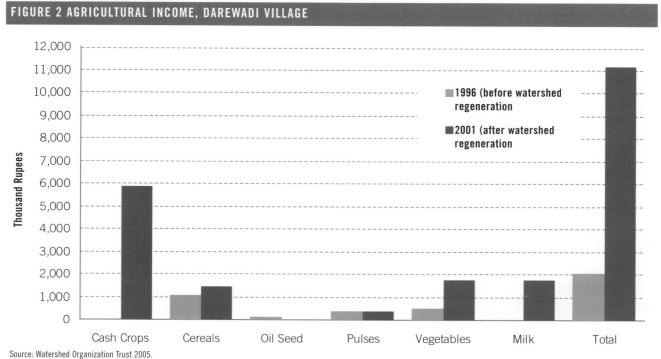

FIGURE 2 AGRICULTURAL INCOME, DAREWADI VILLAGE

Y-axis: Thousand Rupees (0 to 12,000)

Legend:
- 1996 (before watershed regeneration)
- 2001 (after watershed regeneration)

Categories: Cash Crops, Cereals, Oil Seed, Pulses, Vegetables, Milk, Total

Source: Watershed Organization Trust 2005.

that the benefits of development are equally shared. The issue of equity—particularly between landowners and the landless—is perhaps the trickiest problem facing the IGWP and other efforts like it, as they expand their activities across rural India's drylands.

Dr. John Kerr, of the Department of Community, Agriculture, Recreation and Resource Studies at Michigan State University, led a research team that explored the impact of Indian watershed development projects run by IGWDP and other agencies in the Indian states of Maharashtra and Andhra Pradesh. Published in 2002, their report concluded that "by their nature, area development programs offer benefits to landowners, with landless people benefiting indirectly, either through peripheral program activities or trickle-down effects. In fact, watershed projects can actually make women and landless people worse off by restricting their access to resources that contribute to their livelihoods" (Kerr et al. 2002:xi).

The report, based on surveys conducted before Darewadi began its regeneration program, praised IGWDP projects for combating soil erosion and raising water levels, and for their participatory philosophy. "I was really impressed by the IGWDP's approach of consensus-based decision making," recalled Kerr. "Other programs typically require a two-thirds majority and this makes it easy to gang up on poor minorities. The IGWDP works to avoid this" (Kerr 2005). Nevertheless, his report noted that some villagers interviewed had complained of reduced access to common lands for fuel and fodder (Kerr et al. 2002:75).

For his part, Lobo acknowledges that in rural India "the poorest normally do not benefit (at least relative to the better off farmers) from watershed development programs where land holdings are greatly skewed, where social and power relationships are greatly inequitable and discriminatory, and where their concerns, interests, and involvement are ignored in project implementation." Such circumstances, he emphasizes, do not apply to Darewadi (Lobo 2005b).

Addressing these tricky questions of equity and land distribution will require actions on both a local and national scale. Recognizing the benefits of people-led rural development, the Indian Ministries of Agriculture and Rural Development established common guidelines in 2000 for village-based development that would promote equitable distribution of benefits and allow implementing organizations such as NGOs a year to build capacity among local citizens to manage projects themselves (Kerr et al. 2002:80-81).

LEARNING FROM DAREWADI'S WATERSHED REGENERATION

Restoration Can Revitalize Watersheds and Communities. Village-based restoration projects can be an effective route to restoring vital watershed functions and increasing the productivity of local ecosystems. In turn, this can increase farm income and make available more fodder and forest products that directly benefit village livelihoods and build the local economy.

Consensus-Building Is Key to Community Effort. To be effective, watershed restoration requires participation from a wide array of families from across the social spectrum. The Darewadi experience shows that generating consensus among these social groups is not only possible, but also the most practical way to avoid conflicts and promote fairness. If decision-making is based on simple majority (or supermajority) rule, it can easily end up marginalizing the concerns of the poor.

Nongovernmental Organizations Provide Crucial Support. NGOs such as the Watershed Organisation Trust can play both a catalytic and capacity-building role in participatory watershed restoration programs. Experience shows that watershed programs without such an NGO partner do not stand the same chance of success. In Darewadi, WOTR's intervention helped empower, organize, and educate the community, and provided technical help and financial instruments such as microcredit programs to help the community turn increased environmental income into financial strength.

Unequal Access to Land Blocks Equal Distribution of Benefits. The most lucrative benefits of watershed restoration—such as greater access to irrigation—generally accrue to landowners. The landless may also benefit substantially through greater access to wage income and subsistence products from restored common lands, but these benefits tend to be secondary or indirect benefits. Mechanisms such as saving clubs that increase the ability of the poor to lease or purchase private agricultural land, or directly access the products of common lands, can help correct this imbalance of assets. Development of such support services must be a central feature of watershed project design if aiding the poorest is a serious goal.

Forging Links with Government Brings Future Benefits. Perhaps one of the most valuable long-term benefits of Darewadi's watershed management program is the ties it has formed between the community and the local political system and development agencies. Villagers feel they have a new visibility and credibility with state officials, which means that they stand a better chance in the future of benefiting from state-funded economic development programs.

To date, the impact of these broad guidelines has not been measured and analyzed (Lobo 2005b). Yet only if effective means can be found to implement them on the ground—tailored to the particular needs and social circumstances of each region—will the experience of Darewadi's citizens be enjoyed on a wider scale.

REGENERATING WOODLANDS
Tanzania's HASHI Project

U NTIL RECENTLY, THE SHINYANGA REGION JUST SOUTH OF LAKE VICTORIA WAS nick-named the Desert of Tanzania. Its once-abundant woodland had been stripped away over decades, first to eradicate the disease-carrying tsetse fly, then to create cropland and make space for a growing population (Monela et al. 2004:14). Now the acacia and miombo trees are returning, courtesy of the HASHI project, a major restoration effort based on the traditional practice of restoring vegetation in protected enclosures or *ngitili*.

The region-wide HASHI project, whose success was recognized by the UN Development Programme with an Equator Initiative prize in 2002, is run and mainly funded by the Tanzanian government. But its striking success stems from the rich ecological knowledge and strong traditional institutions of the agro-pastoralist Sukuma people who live in the region.

By 2004, 18 years into the project, at least 350,000 hectares of *ngitili* (the Sukuma term for enclosures) had been restored or created in 833 villages, encompassing a population of 2.8 million (Barrow and Mlenge 2004:1; Barrow 2005b). Benefits of the restoration include higher household incomes, better diets, and greater livelihood security for families in the region. Nature has benefited too, with a big increase in tree, shrub, grass, and herb varieties, as well as bird and mammal species (Monela et al 2004:3-4). Table 1 summarizes these wide-ranging benefits. It is drawn from an in-depth study of HASHI's impacts on local livelihoods commissioned by the Tanzanian government and the World Conservation Union (IUCN).

People, Trees, and Livelihoods: A Short History of the HASHI Project

Shinyanga is one of Tanzania's poorest regions, its low hills and plains characterized by long dry summers with only 700 mm of rainfall a year on average. As its woods were cleared from the 1920s onward, land and soil became over-used and degraded, causing a sharp decline in the natural goods on which the Sukuma people had depended for centuries. Women spent more time collecting formerly plentiful fuel wood; grasses to feed livestock became scarcer, as did traditionally harvested wild fruit and medicinal plants.

The region's ecological problems were compounded by a booming human population and by the Sukuma's extensive land-use needs. Nine in ten of Shinyanga's households live by small-scale farming, with families dependent on cropland and livestock pasture for both subsistence farming and cash crops such as cotton, tobacco, and rice (Monela et al. 2004:21-22). Since cattle are highly valued as a liquid asset, many households also kept livestock herds too large for their land to sustain, and burning of woodland to create pasture was common practice.

By the 1970s Shinyanga was under severe ecological strain, its people feeling the consequences in the form of falling incomes and lost livelihoods (Monela et al. 2004:12-13). Early attempts at reforestation launched by Tanzania's government, the World Bank, and other agencies largely failed to stem the loss of indigenous woodland and its impact on communities. Top-down, bureaucratic management of projects meant that villagers had little involvement or stake in the success of these efforts. During the 1970s, the socialist government of President Julius Nyerere also adopted laws that increased communal ownership of rural land and encouraged people to live in discrete villages where services could be better provided—a process called "villagization." Individual *ngitili* enclosures, which many villagers had carefully sustained for food, fodder, fuelwood, and medicines, were no longer encouraged. Indeed, many *ngitili* were destroyed during the period, as the villagization process undermined traditional institutions and practices (Monela et al. 2004:102).

In 1986, Tanzania's government shifted tactics dramatically and launched the people-centered, community-based Shinyanga Soil Conservation Programme, known simply as HASHI (from the Swahili "Hifadhi Ardhi Shinyanga"). The impetus came from President Nyerere himself, who declared Shinyanga the "Desert of Tanzania" after touring the region. By 1987, HASHI was operational and by 1989 it had attracted additional, long-term support from the Norwegian Development Assistance Agency.

The Revival of *Ngitili*

The project's innovative efforts to improve rural livelihoods are based on reviving "*ngitili*," an indigenous natural resource management system (Barrow and Mlenge 2004:1). Traditionally, *ngitili* were used to provide forage for livestock—especially oxen—at the end of the dry season when villagers plough their land. Vegetation and trees are nurtured on fallow lands during the wet season so that livestock fodder supplies are available for dry months.

There are two types of *ngitili*: enclosures owned by individuals or families, and communal enclosures owned and managed in common. Both were originally developed by the Sukuma in response to acute animal feed shortages caused by droughts, the loss of grazing land to crops, and declining land productivity (Barrow and Mlenge 2003:6).

The HASHI project's approach to *ngitili* revival was to work with local people, first to identify areas requiring urgent land restoration, and then to restore them according to customary practice. Field officers, employed by the Division of Forestry and Beekeeping in the Ministry of Natural Resources and Tourism, worked closely with both district government staff and village government authorities—the lowest accountable bodies in Tanzania's government (Barrow 2005b).

Technical guidance and information was also provided by the Nairobi-based International Center for Research in Agro-Forestry (ICRAF), which had researched *ngitili* restoration. ICRAF studies documented appropriate vegetation and management practices, and noted the important role played by traditional knowledge and local institutions in successful land management (Barrow 2005e).

In many villages, HASHI field officers used residual natural seed and root stock to restore *ngitili* enclosures. In others, active

tree planting (first of exotic species, later of the indigenous tree species preferred by local people) was carried out, especially around homesteads. Some of the restored *ngitili* dated back to pre-villagization days. Others were newly created by farmers and villages. In addition to restoring *ngitili*, villagers were encouraged to plant trees around homesteads (particularly fruit and shade trees), field boundaries, and farm perimeters. This helped improve soil fertility and provide firewood, and had the side benefit of helping farmers to stake out and formalize their land rights within villages (Barrow 2005c).

A range of tools were used to educate and empower villagers. These included video, theater, newsletters, and workshops to demonstrate firsthand the links between soil conservation, forest restoration, and livelihood security. Participatory rural appraisal methods helped villagers to identify local natural resource problems and agree on solutions (Kaale et al. 2003:13-14). Farmers and villagers received training in how to get the most out of their *ngitili*. For example, they learned which indigenous species were best suited to enrich farms soils or create dense boundary plantings.

Armed with this powerful combination of traditional and scientific knowledge, villages across Shinyanga gradually revitalized the institution of *ngitili* and broadened its use from simple soil and fodder conservation to production of a wide range of woodland goods and services. Products such as timber, fodder, fuelwood, medicinal herbs, wild fruits, honey, and edible insects enhanced livelihoods and provided a vital safety net during dry seasons and droughts (Barrow and Mlenge 2003:1).

In the early years, restoration efforts proceeded gradually as cautious farmers and communities assessed the benefits and rights which *ngitili* regeneration produced. By the early 1990s, with the project's effectiveness beyond doubt, restoration efforts spread rapidly through the region. In 1986, about 600 hectares of documented *ngitili* enclosures existed in Shinyanga. A survey of 172 sample villages in the late 1990s revealed 18,607 *ngitili* (284 communal, the rest owned by households) covering roughly 78,122 hectares (Kaale et al. 2003:8, Barrow and Mlenge 2004:1). Extrapolating from these figures, project managers estimate that more than 350,000 hectares of land in Shinyanga were in use as *ngitili*, with nine in ten inhabitants of Shinyanga's 833 villages enjoying access to *ngitili* goods and services (Barrow 2005b).

Wendelen Mlenge, longtime manager of the HASHI project (recently renamed the Natural Forest Resources and Agroforestry Center) has closely observed its success. The enthusiasm and commitment with which communities have embraced *ngitili* restoration demonstrates, she says, how "a traditional natural resource management system can [be adapted to] meet contemporary needs" (Barrow and Mlenge 2003:10).

Making It Work:
Traditional and Local Institutions

HASHI's empowering approach was unusual among 1980s rural development programs, but critical to its success. Promoting *ngitili* as the vehicle for land restoration increased local people's ownership over natural resources and their capacity and will to manage them. Likewise, allowing traditional Sukuma institutions and village governments to oversee restoration efforts helped to ensure their region-wide success. While elected village governments officially manage communal *ngitili*, and also decide disputes regarding individually owned *ngitili*, in practice traditional institutions have played an equally important role in most villages (Kaale et al. 2003:14-16; Monela et al. 2004:98).

For example, while each village sets its own rules on *ngitili* restoration and management, most use traditional community guards known as Sungusungu and community assemblies known as Dagashida to enforce them. The Dagashida is led by the Council of Elders which decides what sanctions to impose on individuals caught breaking *ngitili* management rules, for example by grazing livestock on land set aside for regeneration (Monela et al. 2004:98-99).

HASHI field officers have worked to build the capacity and effectiveness of both official and traditional governance institutions. Elected village governments, for example, are increasingly using their powers

to approve by-laws that legally enshrine the conservation of local *ngitili*. Such by-laws, once ratified at the district level, are recognized as legitimate by the national government (Barrow and Mlenge 2003:9, Barrow 2005c).

A 2003 study funded by the World Conservation Union concluded that this twin-track approach had paid off. "Traditional groupings, such as Dagashida and Sungusungu have complemented, rather than conflicted with village government. The blending of the traditional and modern has clearly been an important factor in the success of the restoration" (Kaale et al. 2003:21).

Despite popular support, however, decisions over where to situate *ngitili* and what rules should govern them are not always democratic. While many communities establish communal enclosures through the village assembly—in which every registered adult can vote—others are chosen arbitrarily by village governments without public consultation (Monela et al. 2004:8). "There is no single way of establishing *ngitili* and some are more democratic than others," explains Professor Gerald Monela of the Department of Forest Economics at Tanzania's Sokoine University of Agriculture. In general, he says, devolution of decision-making to village institutions has clearly increased local responsibility for natural resource management and promoted the success of *ngitili* conservation in Shinyanga (Monela 2005).

TABLE 1 IMPROVING LIVELIHOODS THROUGH *NGITILI*: KEY FINDINGS		
Economic value of restored *ngitili*	US$14.00 per person, per month	
National average rural consumption	US$8.50 per person, per month	
Average annual value of 16 major natural resource products harvested from *ngitili* (Bukombe district)	Per household	US$1,190 per year
	Per village	US$700,000 per year
	Per district	US$89.6 million per year
Costs of wildlife damage as a result of forest restoration	US$63 per family per year	
Species of trees, shrubs, and climbers found in restored *ngitili*.	152	
Other flora found	Up to 30 different families of grass and herbs	
Bird and mammal species recorded	145 bird species and 13 mammals	
Reduction in time spent in collecting natural resources	Collection time reduced by:	
	Fuelwood	2-6 hours per day
	Poles	1-5 hours per harvest
	Thatch	1-6 hours per harvest
	Water	1-2 hours per day
	Fodder	3-6 hours per harvest
Percentage of households in seven districts across Shinyanga using *ngitili* products	To diversify diet	22%
	To provide animal fodder and forage	21%
	To collect medicinal products	14%
	To collect fuelwood	61%
	To pay for children's education	36%

Source: Monela et al. 2004:3-4, 53, 61, 67-69

This success has not been lost on Tanzania's other regions, two of which, Mwanza and Tabora, are now adapting and replicating HASHI's empowerment methods (Barrow and Mlenge 2004:2).

Paying Dividends to People

Of the more than 350,000 hectares of land now occupied by restored or newly established *ngitili*, roughly half is owned by groups and half by individuals. Communal enclosures average 164 hectares in size, while individual plots average 2.3 hectares (Kaale et al. 2003:9; Barrow and Mlenge 2004:1).

While the impressive speed of *ngitili*-based reforestation has been apparent for several years, its impact on people's livelihoods and income has only recently been quantified. A major study by a ten-person task force, launched by the Tanzanian government and IUCN in 2004 and directed by Prof. Monela, combined detailed field research among 240 households in 12 villages with market surveys and other data analysis to quantify the HASHI project's benefits (Monela 2005).

The task force estimated the cash value of benefits from *ngitili* in Shinyanga at US$14 per person per month—significantly higher than the average monthly spending per person in rural Tanzania, of US$8.50 (Monela et al 2004:6). Of the 16 natural products commonly harvested from *ngitili*, fuelwood, timber, and medicinal plants were found to be of greatest economic value to households. Other valuable outputs included fodder, thatch-grass for roofing, and wild foods such as bush meat, fruit, vegetables, and honey (Monela et al. 2004:54-56). *(See Table 2.)*

In surveyed villages, up to 64 percent of households reported that they were better off due to the benefits derived from *ngitili*. The task force, headed by Professor Monela, concluded that *ngitili* restoration "demonstrates the importance of tree-based natural resources to the economies of local people" and offers "a significant income source to supplement agriculture to diversify livelihoods in Shinyanga region" (Monela et al. 2004:7,16).

The study also documented the ripple effect of these economic benefits in people's lives. Maintaining *ngitili* has enabled some villagers—mainly through sales of timber and other wood products—to pay school fees, purchase new farm equipment, and hire agricultural labor. Income generated by communal *ngitili* has been used to build classrooms, village offices, and healthcare centers. One farmer, 'Jim' of Seseko

village, reported how he had been able to send his son to secondary school and his daughter to university in Dar es Salaam. "My *ngitili* assists me …I fatten my cattle there and therefore they fetch a good price. Then I use the money to educate my children" (Monela et al. 2004:91).

The new abundance of fruits, vegetables, and edible insects has also improved local health, while easy access to thatched grass has improved housing. Raised water tables due to soil conservation have increased water supplies within villages.

The study also confirms that villagers, particularly women, are saving considerable time by no longer having to walk long distances for fuelwood, fodder, and thatch. *(See Table 1.)* This frees men and women to concentrate on other income-generating activities while also fostering improved child care and school attendance (Monela et al 2004:108). "I now only spend 20 minutes collecting fuel wood. In the past I spent 2-4 hours," reported one Sukuma woman who harvests branches from the family *ngitili* (Barrow and Mlenge 2004:2).

According to Edmund Barrow, Coordinator of Forest and Dryland Conservation and Social Policy at IUCN's Eastern Africa office, the task force findings "demonstrate that natural resource assets are significantly more important in terms of livelihood security and economic benefits than is generally assumed." There are useful lessons to be drawn, he argues, both by Tanzania's government and other comparable countries. "At a time when conservation is increasingly being asked to justify itself in the context of the Millennium Development Goals, the HASHI experience offers detailed insights into the reasons for considering biodiversity conservation as a key component of livelihood security and poverty reduction" (Barrow 2005b; Barrow and Mlenge 2004:1).

The Conservation Dividend

Not only are the restored woodlands important economic assets but, as Table 1 highlights, they are also fostering richer habitats and the recovery of a variety of species. The task force found 152 species of trees, shrubs, and climbers in restored *ngitili*, where recently scrubby wasteland had stood. Small- and medium-sized mammals such as hyenas, wild pigs, deer, hare, and rabbits are also returning, and the task force recorded 145 bird species that had become locally rare or extinct (Monela et al. 2004:3-5).

The returning wildlife has also created problems, with some villages suffering considerable crop damage. Growing hyena populations, for example, are taking a toll on livestock. However, the costs of wildlife damage, which average US$63 per family per year, are greatly outweighed by the economic gains from *ngitili* in most villages (Monela et al. 2004:58-61, 67; Barrow 2005c).

Unequal Distribution of Benefits

Not everyone is benefiting equally from *ngitili* restoration, however. Land use patterns in the region are strongly influenced by Sukuma traditions, with women controlling low-income crops while men control higher-earning livestock and cash crops. The task force found this culture persisting with *ngitili* restoration, with married women rarely owning individual *ngitili* or having a meaningful say in their management (Monela et al 2004: 92). On the other hand, all women have access to communal *ngitili*, a right and resource which has helped them acquire essential household needs such as fuelwood, thatch, and food, and to save time on chores. "Women are better off as a result of *ngitili* revival, despite patriarchal systems, due to their increased access to forest products," argues Professor Monela, the task force chairman (Monela 2005).

Better-off households are also capturing a bigger slice of benefits from reforestation measures than poorer families. The task force reported that differences in land and cattle ownership were the most obvious indicators regarding the scale of benefits reaped, and noted that well-off people were buying additional land from poorer households, thus exacerbating local inequity (Monela et al. 2004:92-93). At the other end of the scale, the poorest households cannot afford individual *ngitili*, although they are entitled to harvest products from communal enclosures, sometimes for a fee.

One impoverished woman, from Mwamnemha village, explained her predicament to a task force researcher: "I do not have a *ngitili* because I do not have money, nor cattle to allow me to buy land. I therefore purchase some of my needs from *ngitili*. If I want to purchase grass for thatching I have to pay 200 shillings [US$ 0.20] per bundle. If I want land for cultivation, I have to rent a piece for 12,000 shillings per acre. I am sometimes given these products free of charge, but this is very rare" (Monela et al. 2004:92).

Despite such problems, there have also been improvements for the poorest. The task force found that *ngitili* were being "used as one of the strategies through which some communities indirectly cushion the vulnerability of households classified as poor...those of the elderly, widows, and households with no assets." Most communities surveyed included families with no cattle as those in need of help, even if they had some land. The task force reported that each village they visited either lent oxen to plough the fields of cattle-less households, or allowed these households free use of products from communal *ngitili*. In the village of Seseko, poor households

TABLE 2 MONEY GROWS ON TREES: VALUE OF *NGITILI* PRODUCTS USED BY HOUSEHOLDS IN BUKOMBE DISTRICT, SHINYANGA, 2004		
Ngitili Product	Percent of Households Using Product in Surveyed Villages	Average Household Value, Per Year (Domestic Use and Sales), in US dollars
Timber	59	71.74
Fuel woods	64	13.09
Poles	29	2.87
Withies	36	8.97
Water	21	34.04
Honey	14	2.39
Bush meat	7	0.72
Edible insects	36	0.48
Mushrooms	36	2.87
Medicinal plants	7	10.76
Thatching materials	36	2.15
Fodder	7	1.15
Vegetables	29	2.15
Fruits	43	2.87
Carpentry	14	1,021.60
Pottery	7	12.91
Total Economic Value, Per Household, Per Year		$1,190.77

Source: Monela et al. 2004:61 Table 3.17

were required to reciprocate by feeding the neighbors who plowed their fields (Monela et al. 2004:95).

Acknowledging the benefits gap between richer and poorer households, the task force warned that additional strategies would be required to prevent social conflicts from erupting and to ensure the long-term sustainability of *ngitili*. In particular, its report concludes, local institutions should make every effort to "enable people to hold on to land resources so that they can maintain *ngitili* and enjoy its products" (Monela et al. 2004:110).

A Fragile Future?

The HASHI project is clearly a success story, drawing attention far beyond Shinyanga's borders. Yet several demographic and land-use trends threaten the continued expansion of *ngitili* as a cornerstone of natural resource management in Tanzania. These include (Monela et al. 2004:103-4,107):

- Scarcity of land and insecurity of tenure;

- Rapidly growing human and livestock populations, which are driving a surge in demand for resources from the still-recovering landscape;

- Damage to livestock and crops caused by growing wildlife populations; in some areas, this threatens to outweigh the benefits gained from *ngitili*;

- Growing, unregulated sales of individually owned *ngitili*.

The government-commissioned task force identified population increase as a particular concern, pointing out that so far "there are not clear indications that the restoration [of *ngitili*] is sustainable" (Monela et al. 2004:107). Shinyanga's population rose from 1.77 million in 1988 to 2.8 million in 2002, and continues to grow by 2.9 percent a year (Monela et al. 2004: 21). As a result, fathers are increasingly dividing their *ngitili* plots between sons, reducing the size and productivity of the plots. Farmers in

Modern and Traditional Institutions Can Be Compatible. Traditional institutions can act as effective vehicles for reducing poverty through environmental regeneration. In Shinyanga, these institutions meshed successfully with the more modern institutions of the popularly elected village councils. Both are necessary for the continued success of *ngitili* restoration.

Local Knowledge Helps Decentralization Succeed. Devolving responsibility for land management to local communities and institutions is often more effective than imposing centralized, top-down solutions. Local or indigenous knowledge of natural resources and traditional institutions and practices can be an invaluable resource, lending crucial site-specific information for management, and improving community buy-in and compliance with management rules. Only when the HASHI project embraced a more participatory and empowering strategy did *ngitili* restoration begin to spread quickly.

Restored Ecosystems Generate Substantial Benefits. Regenerating local ecosystems can deliver significant improvements in livelihood security to rural families dependent on natural resources. *Ngitili* benefits, both subsistence products and cash income, have yielded an increase in family assets and nutrition, as well as generating income for public benefits such as classrooms and health clinics. In this way *ngitili* restoration has contributed directly to achievement of the Millennium Development Goals, improving household incomes, education, and health, while restoring biodiversity and ecosystem integrity.

Inequitable Distribution of Benefits Hurts the Poor. Inequitable power relations between men and women and rich and poor can slant the benefits of *ngitili* restoration away from those who most need them. Without active intervention, the greater productivity that *ngitili* restoration brings will benefit those with more land and assets such as livestock, simply perpetuating existing inequities and wasting some of the potential of *ngitili* for poverty reduction.

Insecure Tenure Discourages Regeneration. Insecurity of tenure can restrain the willingness of both communities and individuals to undertake *ngitili* restoration and to sustainably manage these enclosures. Clearly acknowledging in national law the secure tenure of both private and communal *ngitili* will help insure the future of the HASHI success.

Maswa district, for example, reported in 2004 that the shrinking size of their individually owned *ngitili* had forced them to graze only the neediest animals during the critical dry season.

In addition, there are no constraints on landowners wishing to sell their individually owned *ngitili*, although, because of the village land title system, it is very difficult to sell private land to someone from outside your community. New owners are free to fell the trees and develop the land as they see fit.

The somewhat ambiguous tenure situation of *ngitili* is also a significant concern. Despite popular enthusiasm, the establishment of new *ngitili* is often limited by tenure insecurity—or the perception of insecurity. Although *ngitili* are formally recorded and registered by village governments, their tenure status remains unclear under Tanzanian law. Villages commonly hold a village title deed to all the land within village borders, while households receive a subsidiary title to their privately owned farmland with the village assembly's approval. The remaining land is designated as communal village land, under the management of the village government (Barrow 2005c, d).

These communal lands can be used for communal *ngitili*, but it is not always clear what basis the designation of a village *ngitili* has in law, and therefore what property rights pertain. For example, village governments and assemblies are sometimes wary of officially designating *ngitili* as "protected areas," because they fear the state may appropriate these lands and manage them as public lands at the district or national levels (Barrow 2005d).

Tenure issues can interfere with establishing *ngitili* on private land as well. Private landowners who don't have secure rights to their land are sometimes reluctant to establish or expand *ngitili* for fear of triggering disputes within the community. In some cases, concerted efforts by villagers and local government institutions have overcome tenure problems, with boundary surveys made in order to obtain legally watertight communal and individual land title deeds (Kaale et al. 2003:16). Nevertheless, as pressure on land grows due to rising human and livestock populations, land tenure disputes, trespassing on *ngitili*, and conflicts over grazing rights are all likely to increase.

Designating in law the specific ownership and use-rights that pertain to communal *ngitili* within the overall system of village-owned land could help address the tenure problem, according to Edmund Barrow. Formally recognizing individual and family-owned *ngitili* under Tanzanian law as a separate land management category would also help. Closing these loopholes would help ensure that *ngitili* continue to play a significant and expanding role in villagers' livelihood strategies and income (Barrow 2005c).

Despite these challenges, the multiple benefits of forest restoration are increasingly recognized by Tanzania's government. Since the HASHI project began, new legislation—including the National Land Policy of 1997, the Land Act of 1999, and Village Act of 1999—has supported the formal establishment of *ngitili* and has begun to address the thorny issue of land tenure (Kaale et al. 2003:16). In 1998 Tanzania revised its forest policy, which now emphasizes participatory management of and decentralized control over woodlands, and strongly supports *ngitili*.

Enriching the Benefits Stream

According to Professor Monela's task force, the Tanzanian government can take several additional steps to improve the economic benefits from *ngitili* and thus their anti-poverty impact (Monela et al. 2004:10). These include:

■ Support Better *Ngitili* Management

The state can provide technical help and targeted research specifically aimed at raising *ngitili* productivity. For example, it could help improve fodder productivity by introducing more nutritive and productive tree, shrub, and grass species. And it can research the best methods and timing of cutting and pruning *ngitili* trees to maximize production.

■ Monitor *Ngitili* Trends and Facilitate Lesson-Sharing

The state is in a unique position to offer certain kinds of support that require a national rather than local perspective. For example, using satellite imagery the state could track nationwide changes in land use and biodiversity related to *ngitili* restoration to help HASHI officials understand the macroscale impact of their activities and better target their aid. The state can also mount a national effort to document *ngitili*-related benefits and innovations, helping communities to share their successes and learn from others through public education campaigns and knowledge networks.

■ Expand Markets for *Ngitili* Products

Increasing the income stream from *ngitilis* will help sustain Shinyanga's land-use renaissance by making *ngitilis* even more essential to local livelihoods. One of the most effective ways to do this is to expand the markets for *ngitili* products. The state can help by supporting small-scale processing plants to diversify and add value to *ngitili* products (by making timber into furniture, for example); by removing burdensome regulations and other barriers to *ngitili* expansion and the establishment of local enterprises based on *ngitili* products; and by helping households access local and regional markets for their *ngitili* products by providing relevant and timely market information.

How Tanzania's government responds to these and other challenges facing the *ngitili* restoration movement, remains to be seen. What is not in dispute is a strong national commitment to consolidate the successes of *ngitili* restoration and the benefits it has brought in Shinyanga, and to replicate these, wherever possible, across Tanzania's drylands

This case study was authored by Polly Ghazi, with the collaboration and guidance of Edmund Barrow, Prof. Gerald Monela, and Wendelen Mlenge. Polly Ghazi is a freelance journalist based in London. Edmund Barrow is the coordinator of Forest and Dryland Conservation and Social Policy at the Eastern Africa regional office of The World Conservation Union (IUCN) in Nairobi, Kenya. Prof. Monela is in the Department of Forest Economics at Sokoine University of Agriculture, Morogoro, Tanzania. Wendelen Mlenge is the manager of the Natural Forest Resources and Agroforestry Center, Shinyanga, Tanzania.

BEARING WITNESS
Empowering Indonesian Communities To Fight Illegal Logging

Sustainable livelihoods begin with the ability to exercise control over the natural resources on which one depends. For many forest-dependent people, illegal logging short-circuits this control, robbing them of traditional forest uses and income. But some communities in Indonesia have found a way to fight back to preserve their forest livelihoods. With training in the use of video cameras and film-editing techniques, they have begun to document illegal logging incidents, using the footage to gain media coverage and to lobby for action against corrupt forest practices.

The video training, provided by a pair of environmental NGOs (nongovernmental organizations), has created a network of empowered citizens based in illegal logging hotspots in 15 regions across the archipelago—including Sumatra, Java, Kalimantan, Sulawesi, and West Papua. Some have already put their newfound skills to impressive and effective use, with media and public airings of their films forcing the closure of illegal operations and promoting alternative livelihoods such as bamboo cultivation and fish farming (see examples below).

"One of the propaganda arguments put out by logging companies is that there are no alternative livelihoods for forest communities," says Arbi Valentinus of Telapak, an Indonesian NGO that shares responsibility for the video training program. "In fact it is illegal logging that is disturbing and destroying traditional livelihoods such as mixed crop farming and cultivating rattan, honey, bamboo and herbs used in traditional medicines. Better enforcement against illegal logging helps to secure local livelihoods, reduce corruption, and break communities' dependency on the timber barons" (Valentinus 2004)

Combating the Rise of Illegal Logging

More than 50 million people inhabit Indonesia's rainforests, many pursuing traditional livelihoods including small-plot farming, bamboo harvesting, and fruit and honey collection. In addition to income, forests typically provide a variety of subsis-tence foods, materials, and spiritual and social values. In recent decades, these forests have been increasingly plundered for valuable hardwood that is smuggled overseas, often with the complicity of corrupt officials. Much of this illegal timber finds its way to China, Malaysia, and Singapore on its way to supply Western furniture markets (Schroeder-Wildberg and Carius 2003:24-33; EIA/Telapak 2002:12-15).

Since the fall of former Indonesian President Suharto in 1997, illegal logging and its impact on poor rural forest-dwellers has become a major issue for Indonesia's government, its Western trading partners, and its evolving civil society and media. In part, this reflects the fact that nongovernmental organizations and journalists are now able to comment critically on government policy with less fear of repression. While bureaucratic corruption remains widespread, the Indonesian government at all levels has become more responsive to public scrutiny and civil-society pressure (Anderson and Hidayat 2004:12).

Against this backdrop, two prominent NGOs—the Environmental Investigation Agency (EIA), based in the United Kingdom and the United States, and Telapak, based in Indonesia—began an innovative program to train community-based NGOs to document and disseminate evidence of criminal logging activity in their forests. The project was funded by the UK Department for International Development (DfID) under its Multi Stakeholder Forestry Program, which funds efforts to increase poor forest-dwellers' influence on forest policymaking.

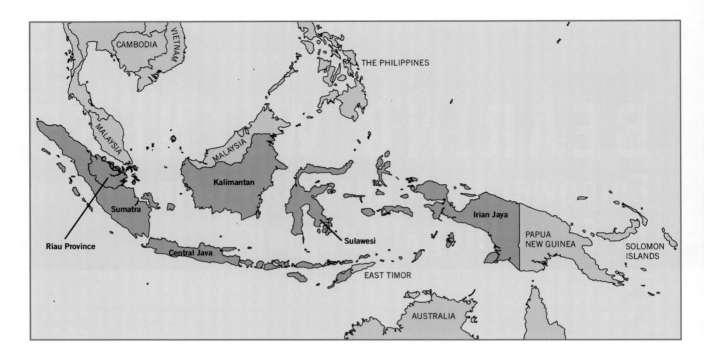

The project was based on the premise that the timber industry offers only short-term benefits to a small minority of Indonesians, and that forest loss means that livelihood alternatives for forest dwellers are dwindling fast, especially for the rural poor (MFP 2000:5; Anderson and Hidayat 2004:12). "Every year, two million hectares of forest disappear, eroding the livelihoods of as many as one million people," says David Brown, a forest economist with DfID. "Meanwhile, only 200,000 people are employed in that segment of the Indonesian log felling and processing industry that operates illegally. Slowing down Indonesia's illegal logging industry will make the forest-linked livelihoods of Indonesians more secure" (Brown 2004).

During the four-and-a-half-year project (2000-2004), Telapak and EIA trained over 300 civil-society representatives from 70 NGO and community groups. Participants were trained in basic camera and video skills, and 13 sets of surveillance and documentation equipment were distributed nationwide as a communal resource. In addition, nine local NGOs were trained in advanced film editing and given computers and software editing facilities. They now serve as regional resource centers for community activists working to fight deforestation and promote sustainable alternative livelihoods. In 2004 some of these regional NGO partners organized their own media training sessions to expand the video network and pass on their video skills to other communities. Total cost of the project was about US$2.3 million.

In setting up the video training, inclusiveness and diversity among the trainees were important guiding principles. Participants represented human rights and women's groups as well as local and regional NGOs working specifically on forestry issues. In each region, attendees were chosen by a local NGO, which in turn was chosen by Telapak. "The groups we trained ranged from informal community groups with a local dignitary as their head to

organized NGOs with 15 staff," explained Dave Currey, EIA director. "We tried to be as inclusive as possible, to encourage those taking part to see illegal logging from a wide social and economic perspective and to encourage networking between civil society groups operating in the same communities. Corruption and intimidation in Indonesia's forests, for example, affects the whole of community life, so you can't discuss illegal logging without talking about human rights, the judicial system, and local governance. We were not prescriptive in how participants used their training. They knew the local conditions and decided themselves how to best use the skills they learned" (Currey 2004).

Praised for Effectiveness

Independent consultants who evaluated the video training project at its completion in 2004 judged it a success. They found

that NGOs and community groups had used their videos and photographs "to inform and influence local and provincial decision-makers," while campaigns these groups had triggered with their work had "helped stop the destruction of forests on which poor people depend" (Anderson and Hidayat 2004:10). Specifically, their publicity and advocacy efforts had helped protect rural communities against illegal logging in Sorong (West Papua), Makassar (South Sulawesi), North Sumatra, Nangroe, Aceh Darussalam, South Kalimantan, Central Kalimantan, Bengkulu, Lampung, Jambi, and Central Java.

The success of the project reached beyond just prevention of illegal encroachment and logging. It also helped support calls for granting communities more management authority over local forests. The independent evaluators found that photos and videos, including interviews with villagers, had helped persuade authorities in several provinces of the rights and management abilities of local communities, and aided local groups in their efforts to secure more favorable forest tenure and management rights (Anderson and Hidayat 2004:13).

The trainees themselves seemed satisfied with their accomplishments. In a questionnaire, 11 of 13 activists trained by EIA and Telapak reported that their subsequent campaigns "had had a direct impact at the village level." One of the benefits was greater activism and solidarity within and among communities around the issue of forest use. In several cases, a group of villages had agreed to work together to protect their local forest from illegal logging.

ILLEGAL LOGGING, LOST LIVELIHOODS

- Indonesia suffers the world's largest annual loss of forest cover. Ministry of Forestry officials estimate that more than 43 million hectares have been degraded, with an average annual deforestation rate of 2.8 million hectares from 1998 to 2002 (Kaban 2005).

- An estimated 70 percent of Indonesia's timber exports are illegal, costing the country US$3.7 billion a year in lost revenue (Saparjadi 2003).

- Middlemen capture most of the profit from illegal logging. Members of illegal logging gangs, often poor forest-dwellers, receive a mere $2.20 per m³ of wood. Timber brokers receive $160 per m³. But Singapore-based exporters of sawn Indonesian hardwood charge US$800 per m³ to ship to Western markets (EIA/Telapak 2002:28).

"A film tells a story better than a printed campaign, it reaches more people," commented Rama Astraatmaja, of Java-based ARuPA, one of the biggest NGOs to receive the video training. "Many homes in Indonesian villages these days have video recorders. Our films tell villagers stories about people with similar situations from other villages. This is something they do not usually see from TV which creates a solidarity feeling among them. Showing film [about illegal logging or non-timber livelihoods] always sparks a discussion. They start to talk about what they have seen, and they…see that the problem is real, and it needs a real solution" (Astraatmaja 2004).

Awareness-raising and campaigning by partner NGOs also reaped success on a larger scale. Nine NGOs reported "a direct impact at district level"—for example, through the introduction of new local government regulations to protect forest areas and limit access to logging companies. Seven reported success at the provincial level, with achievements including the creation by provincial governments of special teams to combat illegal logging. The independent evaluation also identified specific links between EIA/Telapak's empowerment of local communities and efforts to achieve more sustainable nationwide forestry policies, with information on illegal logging feeding into the development of a national forest strategy (Anderson and Hidayat 2004:24).

Unintended Consequences?

While the video vigilance enabled by the project has clearly been effective, activism against illegal logging may also have some unintended consequences. For example, some Indonesian civil society groups are worried that the government, pressed to make some response to illegal logging, may target small-scale community-based loggers, as opposed to larger operations with deeper political and business ties. Some of these small-scale operators claim indigenous rights to forest resources, but their harvest is still considered illegal. For this reason, the wider discussion about illegal logging at a national level has incorporated debate about indigenous rights and tenure (Anderson and Hidayat 2004:3; Astraatmaja 2005; Currey 2005).

In addition, while by far the biggest slice of income from illegal logging is taken by middlemen and timber traders, many poor villagers working on illegal logging crews have benefited from the income it brings. Although the work is often dangerous, it may be more economically attractive than other more sustainable activities—at least for the short time that marketable trees are still available. In 2000, as many as 300 illegal sawmills were estimated to be active in Central Kalimantan alone, giving some idea of the size of the temporary logging economy in that region (Casson 2000:16). In the midst of a logging boom, the web of people drawing income from the logging effort—which includes a variety of jobs from felling, to transport, to milling—may reach well into rural communities (McCarthy 2002:876). Working against illegal logging, then, may cut income for some.

On the other hand, Dave Currey of the Environmental Investigation Agency maintains that any loss of income from shutting down illegal logging pales by comparison to the loss of livelihoods that such illegal operations cause over the longer term. The bigger picture issue, he says, "is that illegal logging is causing widespread poverty—as the DfID Multi-Stakeholder Program explicitly recognizes" (Currey 2004).

The Fruits of Vigilance

Examples of successful forest protection efforts by Indonesian community groups and NGOs, assisted by EIA/Telapak surveillance training and equipment, include:

CENTRAL JAVA
LOCAL VIDEO SURVEILLANCE GROUP: ARuPA

Made up of 14 former forestry students turned environmental activists, ARuPA now acts as a resource hub for forest-based activists across Central Java and has itself trained members of 20 NGOs to document environmental crime and mismanagement.

Using the skills gained through EIA/Telapak training, ARuPA's members documented illegal logging in Java's teak forests by Perhutani, a government-owned forestry company. Their films also featured villagers' complaints about Perhutani's disregard for forest dwellers' rights and were shown to local civil society groups and decision-makers. In 2002, ARuPA's efforts contributed to the revoking of Perhutani's Forest Stewardship Council (FSC) certification by Smartwood, an international timber assessor, which impacted the company's market among Western furniture buyers. Subsequent attempts by the company to regain certification and lost business have failed (Astraatmaja 2004).

ARuPA also uses film to highlight successful examples of alternative, decentralized, sustainable forest-based livelihoods, including community-based forestry management and a Javan community's initiative to plant bamboo after local pine plantations had been clear-cut. "Bamboo forest protects communities from flooding, landslides, and drought—environmental services that could not be provided by the pine forest," says ARuPA spokesman Rama Astraatmaja. After negotiating an informal agreement with the local timber company official, villagers planted bamboo, preserving water supplies for their rice fields and contributing to the village economy by selling bamboo poles.

CENTRAL KALIMANTAN
LOCAL VIDEO SURVEILLANCE GROUP: DAUN

Daun, a regional NGO, campaigns against deforestation in wildlife-rich Tanjung Puting National Park, whose endangered species include clouded leopards, sun bears, and orangutans. Daun's members have used their media training to build public awareness of the destructive impact of illegal logging by showing photographic and video evidence to communities, and then explaining the connection with lost livelihoods. One film distributed among riverside communities living on the park's fringes documented how a local village had successfully developed small-scale fish farming as a sustainable alternative to illegal logging operations.

ILLEGAL LOGGING, LOST LIVELIHOODS

- **The Power of Public Disclosure.** Public disclosure is a powerful tool to motivate action at the local and national scales. Video is a relatively easy route to public exposure, attracting media attention at modest cost and with modest training.

- **An Educational Tool for Alternative Livelihoods.** Video documentation does not have to concentrate on infractions only, but can bring positive messages of alternative livelihood options.

- **A Tool for Community Empowerment.** Use of video or other media tools can empower communities through access to information, which in turn promotes public dialog, shared values, and community activism.

- **Civil Society Groups are Key.** Local community groups are often ideally placed to undertake video surveillance and to deploy the footage locally and to media. Diversity among these groups helps create a more effective network.

- **National and International NGOs are Important Catalysts.** Larger NGOs are well-placed for capacity-building: administering video and media training, and helping to establish a national network for village-level logging surveillance.

- **Adverse Consequences for the Poor.** Targeting illegal logging may benefit forest livelihoods in the long term, but may impose short-term hardships on some community members, particularly the poor, who are dependent on this employment. Supporting communities in the development of income alternatives is important to counterbalance short-term income loss.

SOUTH KALIMANTAN
LOCAL VIDEO SURVEILLANCE GROUP: LPMA

LPMA has produced educational videos both documenting the destructive impact of illegal logging in protected forest in the Meratus area of South Kalimantan, and promoting honey collecting as an alternative way of generating income. The films have been shown to forest communities and to local politicians with the aim (not yet realized) of generating financial support to expand commercial honey collecting.

SUMATRA
LOCAL VIDEO SURVEILLANCE GROUP: ULAYAT

Ulayat, a Sumatran environmental group, documented illegal logging in Bukit Barisan Selatan National Park by Semaku Jaya Sakti, a company owned by the district government. After its compelling visual evidence prompted provincial and national media stories, the park manager sued the logging company, and its director was forced to resign. Ulayat's campaigning also resulted in the Kaur district government creating a forest regulation enabling action against illegal logging.

RIAU
LOCAL VIDEO SURVEILLANCE GROUP: HAKIKI

Hakiki, a regional NGO, documented and publicized evidence that Diamond Raya Timber, a logging concession holder in Riau Province, Sumatra, was logging outside its approved harvesting area. Hakiki then worked with the Riau provincial government to establish the Community Anti-Illegal Logging Network, whose members include provincial authorities, law enforcement officials, NGOs, and three district governments.

VILLAGE BY VILLAGE
Recovering Fiji's Coastal Fisheries

I N THE EARLY 1990s, RESIDENTS OF UCUNIVANUA VILLAGE, ON THE EASTERN COAST OF Fiji's largest island, realized that the marine resources they depended on were becoming scarce. Village elders remembered when a woman could collect several bags of large *kaikoso* clams—a food staple and important source of income—in just a few hours. By the 1990s, however, a woman could spend all day on the mudflats and come home with only half a bag of small clams. The decline of Ucunivanua's marine heritage reflects a larger pattern of depletion repeated throughout the Fiji islands. A combination of greater

commercial fishing and larger local subsistence harvests have left most of Fiji's coastal waters overfished, sometimes heavily so. Rural Fijians, who constitute half of Fiji's population of nearly 900,000, have been hurt. Most of these villagers still lead a traditional subsistence-based livelihood, communally drawing on local marine resources for at least part of their daily protein and income. In the past, the abundance of the marine catch meant a moderate level of affluence and food security. With that abundance gone, the pressure on village economies has mounted, leaving 30-35 percent of rural households in Fiji below the official poverty line.

But Fijians are fighting back, village by village, linked by a network of communities that carefully regulate the use of their coastal waters, slowly restoring their productivity. Although these *locally managed marine areas* (LMMAs) are an innovation of the last decade, they call on a rich tradition of village management of ocean resources. In this new incarnation, traditional local conservation practices are blended with modern methods of monitoring and energized by the full participation of members of the community, who design and implement the marine management plans. The goal is to bolster local incomes and traditions by replenishing local waters—a grassroots approach to rural development.

Ucunivanua was the site of the first locally managed marine area in Fiji, and its results have been dramatic. Since local management began seven years ago, the *kaikoso* clam has once again become abundant, and village incomes have risen significantly. The Ucunivanua project set aside the usual mind-set that only experts know best and that development occurs only when planned by governments. Instead, it let the ultimate choices—the decisions that determine a project's success or failure—rest with the people most dependent on the resources for their livelihoods. The success in Ucunivanua has led to the adoption of LMMAs throughout Fiji, Asia, and the Pacific region (Aalbersberg 2003; Aalbersberg and Tawake 2005; Gell and Tawake 2002; Tawake and Aalbersberg 2002; Tawake et al. 2001).

Locally Managed Marine Areas (LMMAs)

Pacific island communities have long practiced traditional methods of preserving their valuable food sources, such as imposing seasonal bans and temporary no-take areas. These methods have been based on a system of community marine tenure—the right to own or control an inshore area—that has been informally recognized by villagers and local chiefs. Fiji's long-established system of local marine tenure consists of *qoliqolis*, or traditional fishing grounds that are under the control of the communities adjacent to them. *Qoliqolis* have some legal recognition and are officially referred to as "customary fishing rights areas." They are accurately mapped, delineated, and bound by survey lines, with records maintained by the Native Fisheries Commission. There are 385 marine and 25 freshwater *qoliqolis* in Fiji. The resources from these provide livelihoods for approximately 300,000 people living in coastal villages.

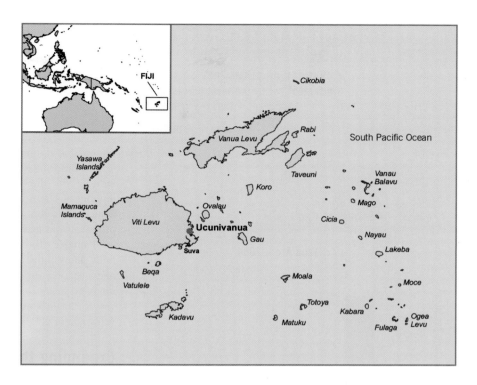

Traditionally, management of *qoliqolis* included temporary closures of these fishing zones, limitations on the number of fishers or the amount of fish they could harvest, restrictions on using certain fishing practices, and the imposition of a *tabu*, or prohibition, on fishing for certain species. In addition, sacred fishing grounds were recognized by communities, and temporary moratoria on fishing were sometimes imposed as part of traditional ceremonies. For example, a 100-day *tabu* on using certain fishing areas was often declared as a token of respect when a high chief died. When the *tabu* ended, villagers harvested fish again and held a large feast to end the mourning period.

Today, many communities maintain such customary practices, with varying levels of compliance. Chiefs are applying this customary *tabu* concept to more practical ends—to protect spawning or overexploited areas and to increase fish stocks—with mounting interest and success. They are linking their traditional practices with modern techniques—assessing fish stocks, measuring potential no-take zones, monitoring the *tabu* area—to establish locally managed marine areas.

Communities set aside at least part of an LMMA as a restricted area, typically 10-15 percent of the village's fishing waters, in order to allow habitat and resources to recover from fishing pressure. The location and size of the *tabu* area is determined by members of the community, depending on how much they feel they can close and still meet their needs. The community may also choose a spot that is easy to police, and not necessarily a rich fishing area. Technical experts may offer their advice to the community on optimal placement of the *tabu* area, but ultimately the community itself has the final say about location. Thus an LMMA is significantly different from a marine reserve or *marine protected area*. In a marine protected area, a central body, often a national government, makes all decisions, often from afar and with little or no local input.

Ucunivanua: One Village's Experiment

The *kaikoso (Anadara antiquate)* a clam found in shallow mudflats and seagrass beds, is the clan totem of the people of Ucunivanua—the community's symbolic animal. It is also a food staple and primary source of income, along with agricultural crops and other marine resources such as octopus. To preserve the *kaikoso*, residents of Ucunivanua began working in the 1990s with the University of the South Pacific (USP) in Suva, Fiji (Tawake et al. 2001). This collaboration began when the son of the high chief of Verata, the district in which Ucunivanua is located, studied land management at USP and asked his teachers there to help address some of the problems in his village.

At the end of two years of workshops and training in environmental education and community planning, the community decided to set up a 24-hectare *tabu* area on the mudflat and seagrass bed directly in front of the Ucunivanua village as an experiment. The hope was that as the clam population recovered in the *tabu* area, more clam larvae would settle in adjacent fishing areas as well, eventually leading to increased clam harvests in these areas—something called a seeding effect.

The village chose a group of 20 men and women to be on the *tabu* area management team. From the outset of the planning process, advisors from USP had requested that the team include equal numbers of adult men, women, and youth—an unusual step in traditional Fijian culture. The *tabu* area management team staked out the boundaries of the proposed protected area. The team then worked with the paramount chief and elders of the village to hold a traditional ceremony declaring the area *tabu* for three years.

FIGURE 1 TRENDS IN CLAM SIZE AND ABUNDANCE, UCUNIVANUA, FIJI

| | NUMBER OF CLAMS (PER 50 M³) | | | |
| | *Tabu* Area | | Adjacent Harvest Site | |
Size Class (cm)	1997	2004	1997	2004
< 2.5	0	3502	1	532
2.5 – 3.5	5	1546	7	622
3.5 – 4.5	12	935	14	385
4.5 – 5.5	13	570	9	221
> 5.5	8	530	1	91

Tabu Area, 2004

Adjacent Harvest Site, 2004

Source: Aalbersberg and Tawake 2005

Here is where modern technique fused with traditional village values. The scientific experts from USP taught team members the skills of monitoring and the basic ideas of sampling and statistics. The team learned how to lay line transects and to sample the clam population at 10-meter inter-

vals along the 500-meter transect line, then record their results and analyze them with simple statistics. Using these skills, the team established a baseline of clam populations in the *tabu* area and in adjacent sites down current. Those baseline calculations were then o be used for comparison with the results of the annual monitoring to follow. In effect, the community learned how to conduct a scientific experiment to see if a locally managed marine area strategy would lead to increased resource yields and better conservation.

Monitoring data gathered by the team in 1997 and 2004 indicate the dimensions of the experiment's success. The number of clams increased dramatically in both the *tabu* and adjacent harvest areas. *(See Figure 1.)* At the start of the project, it was extremely rare to find a clam bigger than 5 cm in diameter. Today, the Ucunivanua community routinely finds clams in the *tabu* area that are over 8 cm in size. Because of its success, the Ucunivanua *tabu* area, which was initially intended to be closed to fishing and collection for just three years, has been extended indefinitely (Tawake and Aalbersberg 2003).

Expanding the LMMA Benefit

The district chief early on in the process had asked that the project include the entire district and not just Ucunivanua. After only one year of local monitoring and reporting at district meetings, the clear benefits of the LMMA strategy at Ucunivanua became apparent to other villages in the Verata district, and they began setting up *tabu* areas. Sawa villagers, for example, imposed a *tabu* on a mangrove island. By counting the "active" holes in the mangroves, they found that the numbers of the mangrove lobster *Thalassina anomala* increased by roughly 250 percent annually, with a spillover effect of roughly 120 percent outside the *tabu* area.

As these results were reported in the local media, villages throughout Fiji facing declines in their inshore fishery approached USP for help in setting up locally managed marine areas in their *qoliqoli*. In Nacamaki village on the island of Gau, one year after creating a *tabu* area the community harvested approximately eight tons of their food totem, the rabbitfish, in one week. This bounty was enough to provide a feast for the entire island—20 villages in three districts, totaling roughly 6,000 people.

While this catch coincided with the high season for rabbitfish, Nacamaki had not seen such abundance in a long time. A 68-year old woman recalled that the last time she saw so many rabbitfish was when she gave birth to her second son 47 years earlier. A testimonial from the Nacamaki village chief illustrates the enthusiasm for LMMA work that has spread throughout Fiji: "The LMMA work that these young guys from USP are doing has changed the attitude of my people to conserve and sustainably manage our resources for our kids. In recognizing this change, our ancestors have released the blessing to us by reviving this tradition."

National and International Collaboration

A concurrent step for advocates of LMMAs—both the technical experts and traditional practitioners—was to work together, first within Fiji and then across Asia and the Pacific, to spread the principles and techniques of locally managed conservation of marine resources.

The Fiji LMMA Network (FLMMA)

The residents and researchers in Ucunivanua were not the only ones in Fiji exploring local solutions to diminishing marine resources in the 1990s. In Cuvu district on the Coral Coast, along a southern stretch of Viti Levu (Fiji's largest island), community members were working with the Foundation for the Peoples of the South Pacific (now Partners in Community Development Fiji) on techniques for setting aside and restoring degraded coral reefs. And in Ono, in the island group of Kadavu, villagers were working with the World Wildlife Fund's South Pacific Programme to find ways to protect and manage blue holes (large deep holes in the middle of a reef). Each of these projects was testing variations of the basic LMMA strategy to see if it could contribute to conservation and local livelihoods under differing conditions.

Team members from these three projects—Ucunivanua, Cuvu, and Ono—joined in 2001 to form the Fiji LMMA

Network (FLMMA), to serve as a forum in which communities with LMMA projects could share methods and results. With the help of the respective project teams, the community members in the network presented the results of their monitoring to fishery policy makers of the Fijian government. While surprised at first to be given scientific findings by villagers, the government representatives grew excited about the idea of adopting Fijian customs to the management of marine resources. The national government has formally adopted the LMMA approach and has designated a division of the Fisheries Department to promote inshore conservation and to work with FLMMA. With FLMMA's assistance, the Fisheries Department has been tasked to conduct resource assessments of all of Fiji's *qoliqolis* and to help develop management plans.

The participatory model used by FLMMA has had additional effects at a national level. The Ministry of Fijian Affairs uses FLMMA's participatory approach for its Community Capacity Building project, which identifies and develops action plans to deal with village problems. Fifteen Fisheries Department extension officers were trained in the network's participatory techniques during a community workshop in June 2002. Members of five government agencies (Fisheries, Fijian Affairs, Environment, Tourism, and the Native Land Trust Board) have formally joined the network to date. Local primary and secondary schools are encouraged to create displays related to LMMA work and even take part in monitoring exercises.

Under current law the Fijian government holds title to the *qoliqolis*, as it does all marine waters. Now, as a direct result of FLMMA's work with local communities, there has been growing pressure for the government to return legal ownership of the country's inshore fishing areas (410 *qoliqolis* in total, equaling roughly 31,000 square kilometers of coastal

147

waters) to their traditional owners—local chiefs. Legislation to do so is now being considered by Fiji's parliament. If the law is enacted, the high chief of an area would hold legal title on behalf of the community, but management decisions would be based on the views of community elders and the needs of the resource users.

Locally, villages have reported that their LMMA experience has given them a greater sense of cohesion and a sharpened ability to identify and address other community problems. Ucunivanua, for example, has raised funds to address two problems they had talked about for years: bringing electricity to the village and working with the central government to build a sea-wall to protect their sacred burial ground. In addition, having a successful resource-management plan enables communities to better negotiate with industry and government. For example, when a Coral Coast hotel asked permission of the *qoliqoli* owners to build a jetty, the community used the opportunity to ask the hotel, in turn, to improve its sewage treatment, since improved reef water quality was a major goal in the village's coastal management plan.

Because some parts of Fiji are days of boat travel away from the capital of Suva, efforts to decentralize operations and extend LMMA work to these remote areas were initiated in 2004. This is being done through the establishment and training of *Qoliqoli* Management Support Teams, composed of provincial government workers, overseas volunteers, and community members trained in LMMA techniques. Community workshops are conducted jointly with experienced LMMA members until the local team is able to work on its own.

This approach has worked well in Kadavu, Fiji's fourth largest island with 33 *qoliqolis*. During 2004 the Qoliqoli Management Support Team under the leadership of the Roko (governor) was able to set up LMMAs in most of the 30 *qoliqolis* that did not have one. The Fisheries Department has indicated a keen interest in formalizing this model for all provinces in Fiji, with hopes that the process will be well on its way by the end of 2005.

To date, nearly 60 LMMAs involving 125 communities with *tabu* areas have been declared in Fiji, covering about 20 percent of the country's inshore fishery. They may designate reefs only or include grass areas and mangroves as well. It is important to keep in mind that the primary reason for these closures is to recover the subsistence and artisanal value of the fishery rather than to restore marine biodiversity, although that is certainly an important side benefit. In their initial planning for an LMMA, communities invariably express the need to generate greater local income, and see a restored fishery as one of the best ways to achieve this. Government also understands that the recovery of the fishery can improve village life and perhaps reduce urban migration.

Beyond Fiji: The LMMA Network

The locally managed marine area approach spread within Fiji and other nations in the Asia-Pacific region through the creation of the LMMA Network, which now has members in Indonesia, Papua New Guinea, Solomon Islands, the Philippines, Palau, and Pohnpei. The network provides a forum for project teams from these nations to share their experiences as they try to determine the right conditions for LMMAs to work.

The network is guided by a group of country LMMA leaders who manage on behalf of local project leaders. The country leaders meet periodically and often include local project representatives. They also arrange inter-country visits,

THE FIJI LMMA NETWORK IN ACTION

Typically, a Locally Managed Marine Area evolves along a well-tested trajectory, with the following steps:

■ Community discussions on goals and expectations

■ Two-day action-planning workshop

■ Community/district adoption of management plan

■ Three-day biological monitoring workshop for projects with newly adopted management plan that can include a no-take zone or restrictions on gears and fishing methods

■ Monitoring in each community within three months of management plan adoption

■ Training in socioeconomic monitoring (usually once biological monitoring is well in place)

■ Actual socioeconomic monitoring in sites where training has taken place

■ Support visits to each site at least every six months

■ Country- or region-wide meetings to discuss how project teams can work together and how adaptive management can be done at the national level such as a 1999 meeting of local representatives from the West Papuan island of Biak, the Solomon Islands, and Fiji. Every three years there is a network-wide gathering that includes community members from each site.

The Process

Once a community in Fiji makes its interest in local marine management known, FLMMA and various partner organizations determine which will be the lead agency, and discussions are held with the community to ensure that the goals of all parties are clear and in harmony. Sometimes the initial planning and education process takes up to a year.

FLMMA teams then offer assistance in three types of workshops: action planning, biological monitoring, and socioeconomic monitoring. The action-planning workshops are adapted from Participatory Learning and Action (PLA) methods and include sessions on mapping the village, understanding historical trends, and analyzing who the local stakeholders are. These sessions serve the dual purpose of exploring resource-management issues and instilling community members with the confidence that they have the capacity to solve their own problems. The workshops then focus on biological and socioeconomic factors such as identification of resource use, threats to local resources, and the root causes of these threats. Finally, the community develops a community action plan, designating what will be done and by whom.

While the establishment of a *tabu* area is usually a central part of a LMMA, the action plan also contains ways to address other issues faced by the community, such as lack of income sources, poor awareness of environmental issues, pollution, and sometimes declining community cohesiveness. Socioeconomic monitoring tests whether these broader problems are being addressed.

There is also ongoing assistance to communities to help them carry out their plans and meet new needs that might arise, such as marking protected area boundaries, publishing LMMA rules, and training fish wardens to protect against poaching.

A key element of success has been the teamwork approach that unites traditional values and modern science. Village workshops are facilitated by government representatives, NGOs, experienced outside community members, and the local university. Questions often arise regarding fisheries regulations, traditional fishing rights, marine biology, pollution, and experiences in other communities. Having a mixed team not only ensures that proper attention is given to each of these issues, but also develops trust and transfers skills among facilitators.

Sustainability and Costs

The estimated cost for the initial suite of community workshops is about $3,000 per site in the first year, $1,000 in the second year, and $500 per year thereafter. The FLMMA has established 71 sites at a cost of approximately $400,000 in outside funding. Many of the costs of FLMMA's work, including workshops, monitoring equipment, and buoys for marking off *tabu* areas, have been met with funding channeled through local NGOs supported by the U.S.-based Packard and MacArthur Foundations.

Most community management plans also include an income-generating aspect. As part of the conservation initiative in Verata, a bioprospecting arrangement was set up with a pharmaceutical company in which the community was paid licensing fees for samples of medicinal plants and marine invertebrates collected in their district. Efforts have been made to ensure that best practice in bioprospecting as outlined by the Convention on Biological Diversity was followed. These activities earned $30,000, which the community put toward a trust fund to sustain their local fisheries work.

At another site, a hotel pays $2 to a community trust fund for each scuba diver that utilizes the village's protected area. This provides an income of roughly $1,000 per year. Another village is "planting" artificial live rock in its *tabu* area to sell to exporters for the aquarium trade after marine life has colonized it. A company makes the artificial live-rock substrate, brings it to the village, and assists in placing it on the reef. Local people need only scrape the rock clean of algae occasionally. Within a year the company harvests the rock with local help. The potential return to the community is $4,000 a year. These sums are not large, but are sufficient to maintain LMMA work once it is established.

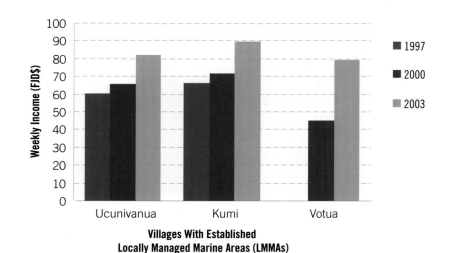

FIGURE 2 HOUSEHOLD INCOME FROM SALES OF MARINE PRODUCTS, FIJI

Villages With Established
Locally Managed Marine Areas (LMMAs)

Source: Aalbersberg and Tawake 2005

LEARNING FROM FIJI'S LOCAL MARINE MANAGEMENT

Small-Scale Projects Can Influence National and International Policy. The success of the early projects at Ucunivanua, Cuvu, and Ono was persuasive. The Fijian government subsequently adopted the LMMA methodology in the national Fisheries Department, while other government departments have applied the program's participatory management techniques. Through the LMMA network, the benefits of local marine management have spread throughout the Pacific region—a demonstration of how community-based ecosystem management can be scaled up for greater poverty reduction.

Success in Marine Conservation Can Promote Broad Economic Growth. As well as conserving marine resources for village consumption, the LMMAs at Ucunivanua and other villages have generated income through commercial sales, bioprospecting, and tourism, demonstrating that ecosystem management can be the first step to broadening the sources of wealth in a rural community. In addition to gaining economic benefits, the villagers participating in local marine management have learned management skills that they have applied to other problems facing the village.

Traditional Management Methods Can Be Fused With Modern Expertise. At Ucunivanua, marine specialists from the University of the South Pacific worked with villagers, and within village traditions, to teach the skills needed for siting a *tabu* area, measuring it, monitoring it, and assessing its recovery. Experts provided the how-to skills, but villagers had the final word on what should be done within the framework of their goals and values.

Traditional Social Norms Can Impede Genuine Participation. For generations, Fijian culture has excluded women and young people from central roles in decision-making, which is traditionally dominated by male elders. Thus, despite a concerted effort to involve the entire village, not all community members participate equally in the Ucunivanua LMMA. A locally managed marine area may have to operate within traditional norms to gain acceptance yet promote participatory equality in ways that challenge those traditional values.

Success Can Bring New Problems. The very success of local marine management—the restoration of fish stocks—has attracted outside fishers to LMMA sites and brought new threats to village resources. The capacity to monitor and protect a *tabu* area requires new capacities from village members, who must take on enforcement duties as fish wardens, battling encroachment through both public education and legal means.

In addition, communities are able to charge more for the annual fishing licenses they sell to outsiders. One of the initial LMMA actions in Verata in 1997 was to put a moratorium on issuing such licenses, of which 60 costing $500 each had been given the previous year. In 2003 chiefs agreed to sell a single license for $30,000. Customary practice allows *qoliqoli* owners to permit outsiders to enter for a specific purpose such as fishing or live-rock harvest. Although issued by the Fisheries Department, the license must be signed by the local chief (Veitayaki, Aalbersberg, and Tawake 2003).

A successful LMMA is, in effect, an alternative income source. The increase in fishery resources not only improves nutrition but also raises household income from market sales. *(See Figure 2.)* Marine resources, on average, make up more than 50 percent of the household income for these villages, and raise these households far above the median income level of F$4000 a year in Fiji.

FLMMA has been recognized with two international awards for its work: the United Nations 2002 Equator Initiative Award for $30,000, and the 2004 Whitley People and Environment Award of £30,000. The funds from these awards were established as trust funds administered by FLMMA to sustain its work. Today FLMMA is a registered charitable trust in Fiji.

Challenges

As successful as many of the LMMAs in Fiji have been in increasing fishery resources, improving habitat, generating income, and promoting community cohesion, there are still problems. Ironically, one is a direct result of the LMMA success: due to higher numbers of fish and other desirable species, outside fishers are drawn to the site to harvest. In addition, non-Fijians continue to fish in the *tabu* areas, as they are either unaware of the *tabu* or do not respect it. In response, FLMMA has supported the training of community members as fish wardens, granting them legal power to apprehend offenders.

A deeper challenge involves working within the social framework in Fiji. Traditional culture does not usually allow for women to be a part of decision-making. This has proven to be a disadvantage, for in Fiji women are often the ones most involved in collecting inshore marine resources and have unique knowledge about them.

In Verata, for example, only the women knew how to locate and accurately count the *kaikoso*. Although women typically collect seafood for the community, the men make the decisions regarding the management of such activities. Continued success of the LMMA movement will require addressing this incongruity. A gender program has recently been introduced in which meetings discussing the progress of the action plan are also held with a local women's group. It is also difficult for young people to participate in decision-making under the traditional societal norms, as they may not have a say among the meeting of elders.

The Way Forward

In response to the challenge of poaching in *tabu* areas, communities are taking a variety of actions, including installing buoys and signs to mark boundaries and having fish wardens trained by the Fisheries Department. Most communities locate their *tabu* areas in plain sight of the village, but others with more distant areas need boats and trained fish wardens empowered to arrest

outsiders coming into their village waters. Usually a boat with a fish warden and other community members will simply approach an encroaching boat and tell it to leave. On occasion, they have apprehended people and confiscated boat and gear.

Another option to protect against encroachment is to gazette protected areas, legally delineating them as no-fishing zones. This would allow police to patrol the area and make arrests. To date, only two of the FLMMA-inspired *tabu* areas have chosen the gazetting route. FLMMA has had meetings with the national government to clarify the steps in the gazetting process and has written this up in the local language.

The Fiji LMMA approach has broadened beyond just helping villages establish *tabu* areas and protect them from outsiders. Its participatory techniques and co-management methods are proving to be effective in improving local governance in general and the delivery of government services. In order to maintain the momentum of this work, FLMMA is continually identifying and addressing needs as they arise and conducting participatory workshops to help local communities to address new challenges.

As FLMMA emphasizes the need to involve all sectors of the community in a project, the inequitable representation of gender and youth needs to be further explored. Efforts are underway to find the best methods for mainstreaming women and youth into projects without violating traditional societal norms. In some communities, youths are encouraged to monitor the LMMAs or develop plays with environmental themes for presentation on special village occasions or at workshops. Women may be involved in waste management, such as composting or monitoring of the marine areas in which they

glean or fish. Holding separate women's meetings has inspired women to participate and discuss issues in a way that they would not when men are present. Having the voices of women heard at the decision-making level of coastal management, however, continues to be a challenge.

LMMA implementation in Fiji has led to increased resources and a corresponding reduction of poverty in rural communities that depend on marine resources. Equally important, the LMMA process has improved community solidarity as well as regional and national policy. The challenge now is to sustain the LMMA movement and decentralize it as it spreads throughout Fiji and other parts of the Pacific .

This case study was authored by Bill Aalbersberg, Alifereti Tawake, and Toni Parras. Bill Aalbersberg is professor of chemistry at the University of the South Pacific and director of the USP Institute of Applied Science. Alifereti Tawake is an assistant project manager at the Institute of Applied Science. Toni Parras is communications specialist of the Locally-Managed Marine Area Network.

The establishment of the Millennium Development Goals and national Poverty Reduction Strategies has raised hopes that governments and multilateral institutions can be mobilized to address world poverty.

GLOBAL DEVELOPMENT POLICIES

MAKING THE MDGs AND PRSPs WORK FOR THE POOR AND THE ENVIRONMENT

IN THE PRECEDING CHAPTERS AND CASE STUDIES WE HAVE approached poverty reduction from the village and local level—the level where ecosystems are accessed for income. We have presented numerous examples of how community-scale projects have improved the livelihoods of the poor by enabling them to manage fisheries, forests, and common lands for income and sustainability.

But the rural village economy we have focused on exists within a national and international framework of economic, legal, and political policies. This special section deals with innovations in poverty policies at these larger scales. In the past five years, two developments have raised hopes that national governments and multilateral institutions can be mobilized to address world poverty: the establishment of the **Millennium Development Goals** (MDGs) and the crafting of national **Poverty Reduction Strategies** (PRSPs). In this section we explore how the concepts of environmental income and pro-poor environmental governance apply to these efforts. A key link between MDG and PRSP processes and the world's poor is the environment. The central question is: Do the Millennium Development Goals and the current crop of Poverty Reduction Strategies incorporate the environment and governance as central features in fighting poverty? And if not, how can they be made to incorporate these themes?

THE MILLENNIUM DEVELOPMENT GOALS

A Break from the Past

In September 2000, the largest-ever gathering of world leaders adopted the United Nations Millennium Declaration. The cornerstone of the Millennium Declaration is a global agenda of eight development goals, known as the Millennium Development Goals (MDGs), for cutting world poverty in half by 2015. The MDGs have been described as "the most broadly supported, comprehensive, and specific poverty reduction targets the world has ever established" and the "fulcrum" on which international development policy pivots (UN Millennium Project 2005:2-4).

In many ways, the MDGs represent an innovative approach to ending poverty worldwide. They constitute a break with business-as-usual in the formulation of international development policy and the delivery of development aid. The MDGs address extreme poverty in many dimensions, including hunger, disease, and lack of adequate shelter, while also committing nations to take action to promote gender equality, education, and environmental sustainability. *(See Table 1.)* The Goals condense and refocus the as-yet-unrealized anti-poverty commitments of the past several decades into an action-oriented agenda.

Perhaps the most important contribution of the MDGs is their infusion of accountability into the global campaign against poverty. The establishment of quantified, time-bound targets and measurable indicators creates a benchmark for tracking progress in reaching the Goals. The requirement for countries to produce periodic MDG progress reports introduces a modicum of transparency that has been conspicuously absent from many international processes.

If these innovative aspects of the MDGs propel them to ultimate success by 2015, the world will look quite different than it might otherwise have looked, given the disappointing development trajectory of the 1990s. Reaching the MDGs and their associated development targets would mean lifting 500 million of the world's people out of extreme poverty, liberating 300 million from the suffering of hunger, and providing 350 million additional people with a reliable, sustainable source of safe drinking water (UN Millennium Project 2005:1).

How is the world faring with efforts to attain the MDGs? The results so far have been mixed. In early 2005, the findings of several monitoring studies were published as part of a five-year stock-taking of MDG progress. These reports generally portray a spotty track record that differs by global region and across the various Goals. With respect to halving income poverty (MDG-1), one study noted that East Asia had already achieved the Goal, and South Asia is on target, but in Sub-Saharan Africa, most countries are in danger of falling far short (IMF and World Bank 2005:2). Another report concluded that much of the sub-Saharan region—faced with continuing hunger and malnourishment as well as high levels of child and maternal mortality—is seriously off track for reaching most of the Goals. Even in Asia, where progress has been most rapid, hundreds of millions of people still live in extreme poverty. Other global regions—such as Latin America, North Africa and the Middle East, and the transitional economies of the former Soviet Union—have mixed records, with slow or no progress on some of the Goals (UN Millennium Project 2005:15). *(See Figure 1.)*

For Environment and Governance, More of the Same

Despite the innovative aspects of the MDG approach, the treatment of the environment and governance in the MDGs harkens back to old, outmoded ways of thinking. The environment is seen as an add-on rather than the essential foundation of all human well-being and economic production. From an operational perspective, environmental sustainability is more of an afterthought than a cross-cutting concept that provides a point of orientation for all of the MDGs.

The seventh of the eight MDGs commits nations to "ensure environmental sustainability," but this vaguely worded goal does little to focus the attention of the world on the central role of the environment in supporting pro-poor economic growth. As currently stated, Millennium Development Goal 7 (MDG-7) may actually be doing more harm than good by making it difficult for nations to perceive, much less act on, crucially important links between poverty reduction and environmental sustainability. Many believe that environmental issues have in fact lost ground in international development circles in the past decade or so, precisely because of the difficulty in pinning down the concept of environmental sustainability in a way that governments can understand and put to use in decision-making. In its current construction, MDG-7 only exacerbates this dilemma.

Focused on the Wrong Nature

To track progress toward reaching MDG-7 on environmental sustainability, the MDG framework establishes three *global targets* and eight *global indicators*. Unfortunately, these targets and indicators fail to capture the aspects of the environment that exert the most powerful impacts on the lives of the poor or that show the most promise for ending extreme poverty.

Target 9, the first of the three MDG environmental targets, calls for countries to "integrate the principles of sustainable development into country policies and programs and reverse the loss of environmental resources." Accompanying this rather vague, general statement are five quantitative indicators. *(See Table 2.)* One of these (Indicator 29: Proportion of population using solid fuels) is directly relevant to how the poor use the environment. But the other Target 9 indicators fail to shed much light on aspects of environmental sustainability that matter most to the poor. Instead, some of the current indicators track issues of global environmental concern, such as per capita carbon

TABLE 1 THE MILLENIUM DEVELOPMENT GOALS

Goal 1: Eradicate extreme poverty and hunger	**Target 1:** Halve, between 1990 and 2015, the proportion of people whose income is less than $1 per day **Target 2:** Halve, between 1990 and 2015, the proportion of people who suffer from hunger
Goal 2: Achieve universal primary education	**Target 3:** Ensure that by 2015 children everywhere, boys and girls alike, will be able to complete a full course of primary schooling
Goal 3: Promote gender equality and empower women	**Target 4:** Eliminate gender disparity in primary and secondary education, preferably by 2005, and in all levels of education no later than 2015
Goal 4: Reduce child mortality	**Target 5:** Reduce by two thirds, between 1990 and 2015, the under-five mortality rate
Goal 5: Improve maternal health	**Target 6:** Reduce by three quarters, between 1990 and 2015, the maternal mortality ratio
Goal 6: Combat HIV/AIDS, malaria, and other diseases	**Target 7:** Have halted by 2015 and begun to reverse the spread of HIV/AIDS **Target 8:** Have halted by 2015 and begun to reverse the incidence of malaria and other major diseases
Goal 7: Ensure environmental sustainability	**Target 9:** Integrate the principles of sustainable development into country policies and programs, and reverse the loss of environmental resources **Target 10:** Halve by 2015 the proportion of people without sustainable access to safe drinking water and basic sanitation **Target 11:** Have achieved by 2020 a significant improvement in the lives of at least 100 million slum dwellers
Goal 8: Develop a global partnership for development	**Target 12:** Develop further an open, rule-based, predictable, nondiscriminatory trading system (includes a commitment to good governance, development, and poverty reduction—both nationally and internationally) **Target 13:** Address the special needs of the Least Developed Countries (includes tariff- and quota-free access for Least Developed Countries' exports, enhanced program of debt relief for heavily indebted poor countries [HIPCs] and cancellation of official bilateral debt, and more generous official development assistance for countries committed to poverty reduction) **Target 14:** Address the special needs of landlocked developing countries and small island developing states (through the Program of Action for the Sustainable Development of Small Island Developing States and 22nd General Assembly provisions) **Target 15:** Deal comprehensively with the debt problems of developing countries through national and international measures in order to make debt sustainable in the long term **Target 16:** In cooperation with developing countries, develop and implement strategies for decent and productive work for youth **Target 17:** In cooperation with pharmaceutical companies, provide access to affordable drugs in developing countries **Target 18:** In cooperation with the private sector, make available the benefits of new technologies, especially information and communications technologies

Source: United Nations 2000a

dioxide emissions and consumption of ozone-depleting chemicals. Others touch on issues of importance to the poor, such as land area covered by forests and land area set aside to protect biodiversity, but do not measure directly the ability of the poor to access key ecosystems as a source of environmental income and sustainable livelihoods or to protect the ecosystems on which they depend from depredation and damage by outside interests and powerful elites.

Targets 10 and 11, the second and third MDG environmental targets, commit nations to "halve by 2015 the proportion of people without sustainable access to safe drinking water and sanitation" and to "have achieved by 2020 a significant improvement in the lives of at least 100 million slum dwellers." These targets and their accompanying indicators are more directly pro-poor, but they too fall short when it comes to establishing broad

markers for progress based on an explicit recognition of ecosystem integrity as the touchstone for sustainability. For instance, under Target 10, countries should focus not just on the numbers of people hooked up to water and sanitation services, but also on the need for integrated water resource planning and policies that take account of a wide range of other considerations. These include water demand, water supply, and water quality issues, as well as water-project impacts on other community objectives and on environmental management goals. Other suitable indicators could focus on governance issues that relate to the poor's access to water, such as the reliability of water service or the pricing of water service relative to income.

At the 2002 World Summit on Sustainable Development in Johannesburg, the international community created additional targets related to environmental sustainability, sometimes referred to as "MDG-Plus" targets. *(See Table 3.)* These targets specifically incorporate pro-poor elements related to sustainable management and use of ecosystems, such as application of the ecosystem approach in conserving biodiversity as well as maintaining or restoring fish stocks to levels that can support sustainable yields.

Realizing that the MDG targets were broad in their outlines, the MDG framers encouraged countries to modify the global MDG-7 targets to suit their local conditions, as well as to establish new, country-specific targets and indicators. A recent UNDP review shows that about half the 100 reporting countries have set one or more MDG-7 targets that modify or

add to the global targets (UNDP 2005a:3). For example, several nations have set specific goals for maintaining or increasing forest cover, or expanding the network of protected areas for biodiversity conservation.

But despite these worthy efforts, countries are not, for the most part, paying sufficient attention to developing and reporting on a broad set of targets and indicators that would accurately gauge their progress toward the goal of MDG-7 of ensuring environmental sustainability. UNDP's analysis of MDG-7 implementation suggests that environmental monitoring and reporting are not being undertaken systematically. Lack of available data is a significant constraint for some

FIGURE 1 PROGRESS TOWARD MDG-1: HALVE EXTREME POVERTY BY 2015

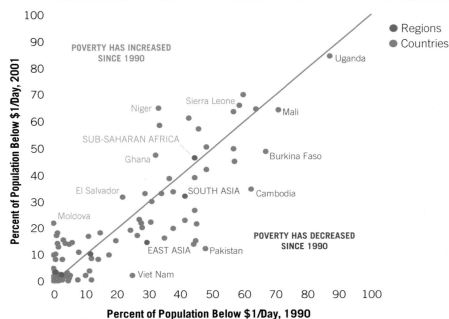

This graph shows changes in poverty from 1990 to 2001. In countries below the line, extreme poverty has decreased during that period. Countries above the line have seen an increase in those living on a dollar a day. Selected outlying countries and regions are identified.

Source: World Bank 2005

TABLE 2 MDG-7 (MILLENNIUM DEVELOPMENT GOAL #7): GLOBAL TARGETS AND INDICATORS

Targets	Indicators
Target 9. Integrate the principles of sustainable development into country policies and programs and reverse the loss of environmental resources	25. Proportion of land area covered by forests 26. Ratio of area protected to maintain biological diversity to surface area 27. Energy use per $1 GDP 28. Carbon dioxide emissions (per capita) and consumption of ozone-depleting chlorofluorocarbons 29. Proportion of population using solid fuels
Target 10. Halve, by 2015, the proportion of people without sustainable access to safe drinking water and sanitation	30. Proportion of population with sustainable access to an improved water source (urban and rural) 31. Proportion of population with access to improved sanitation
Target 11. Have achieved, by 2020, a significant improvement in the lives of at least 100 million slum dwellers	32. Proportion of households with access to secure tenure

Source: United Nations 2000b

TABLE 3 ADDITIONAL TARGETS AGREED TO AT THE WORLD SUMMIT ON SUSTAINABLE DEVELOPMENT	
Biodiversity	■ Encourage by 2010 the application of the ecosystem approach (Paragraph 30) ■ Establish representative marine protected area networks by 2012 (Paragraph 32) ■ Achieve by 2010 a significant reduction in the current rate of loss of biodiversity (Paragraph 44)
Fisheries	■ Maintain or restore fish stocks to a level that can produce a sustainable yield by 2015 (Paragraph 31)
Water	■ Develop integrated water resources management and water efficiency plans by 2005 (Paragraph 26)
Chemical Pollution	■ By 2020, minimize significant adverse effects on human health and the environment associated with the production and use of toxic chemicals, via use of transparent, science-based risk assessment and risk management procedures, and taking account of the precautionary principle (Paragraph 23)

Source: United Nations 2002, Johannesburg Plan of Implementation

countries. But at the same time, many countries have not drawn on existing data from other environment-related efforts, such as National Strategies for Sustainable Development, State of the Environment Reports, and National Biodiversity Action Plans (UNDP 2005b:5).

Getting the Targets and Indicators Right

One of the most important innovations of the MDG approach is its ability to make governments more accountable for their performance in improving human well-being. By stating goals and measuring progress in clear, straightforward language, the MDGs make it easy for civil-society groups to evaluate progress toward human development goals and to issue a public "report card" on a government's success or failure. Unfortunately, the lack of clear, comprehensive targets and indicators for measuring the capacity of ecosystems to provide sustainable environmental income for the poor means that the "accountability effect" of the MDG approach is not yet applicable to the world's environmental goals. Until the environmental framework of the MDGs is fixed, short-run progress towards the other goals is at risk of being unsustainable.

Realigning the MDG framework to correct its environmental shortcomings begins with an acceptance of ecosystems as the key to environmental income, the most direct way that nature affects the poor. This realignment should be guided by the recent findings of the Millennium Ecosystem Assessment, a four-year study conducted by more than 1,300 scientists from 95 countries to ascertain the consequences of ecosystem change for human well-being (MA 2005a). The scientists determined that in all

regions, and particularly in Sub-Saharan Africa, the condition and management of ecosystems is a "dominant factor" affecting the chances of success in fighting poverty. They concluded that the degradation of ecosystems is already a "significant barrier" to achieving the MDGs. In fact, many of the regions facing the biggest hurdles in reaching the MDGs coincide with those experiencing significant ecosystem degradation (MA 2005a:18).

Reconceptualizing Target 9

Reframing MDG-7 requires that the wording of Target 9—not to mention its conceptual underpinnings—should make clear the importance of ecosystems to the poor, and be grounded in an appreciation of the central role of healthy, well-functioning ecosystems in ensuring sustainability.

The current wording of Target 9 has two quite distinct pieces:

Target 9: (1) "Integrate the principles of sustainable development into country policies and programs and (2) reverse the loss of environmental resources."

Both pieces need to be treated separately and reworded. In addition, another component needs to be added to Target 9 to capture the importance of natural resource access to the poor. *(See Table 4 for a summary of suggested changes in the wording and indicators of Target 9, as discussed below.)*

1. Focus on ecosystem capacity
Let's first deal with the second half of Target 9: "reverse the loss of environmental resources." Conceptually, this is the most

TABLE 4 SUGGESTED REWORDING OF MDG-7, TARGET 9

Targets	Indicators
Target 9 (original wording). Integrate the principles of sustainable development into country policies and programs and reverse the loss of environmental resources	■ Proportion of land area covered by forests ■ Ratio of area protected to maintain biological diversity to surface area ■ Energy use per $1 GDP ■ Carbon dioxide emissions (per capita) and consumption of ozone-depleting chlorofluorocarbons ■ Proportion of population using solid fuels
Target 9a (reworded). Maintain or restore the capacity of ecosystems to provide critical ecosystem services, and Integrate the principles of sustainable development into local, national, and international policies and programs	■ Extent and condition of communal fisheries (coastal and inland) ■ Extent and condition of forested areas held in common ■ Watershed conditions on communally held lands (e.g. vegetative cover; water availability; groundwater trends) ■ Soil fertility on private farmlands ■ Land degradation
Target 9b (new). Ensure the poor access to environmental resources and decision-making	■ Proportion of rural households with access to secure tenure ■ Proportion of rural households with access to environmental information (e.g. extension services; pollution or environmental health alerts; environmental impact studies on proposed concessions or developments) ■ Participation in local environmental decision-making

important section of the target. To refocus this section of the target on ecosystems—the primary "environmental resources" used by the poor—the current wording should be replaced with the following: **"maintain or restore the capacity of ecosystems to provide critical ecosystem services."**

As the Millennium Ecosystem Assessment demonstrates, humans have changed ecosystems extensively over the past 50 years. Most ecosystem services are being used unsustainably, and the capacity of ecosystems to deliver these services is being persistently eroded. This growing pressure on ecosystems risks sudden, potentially irreversible changes, such as the collapse of fisheries or the creation of "dead zones" in coastal waters. Also, because the costs of the damage are borne disproportionately by the poor, ecosystem degradation contributes to inequities across social and ethnic groups and is sometimes the principal factor behind poverty and social conflict (MA 2005a:17).

Environmental sustainability, then, is defined by maintaining the ability of ecosystems to deliver the ecosystem services that rich and poor depend on. Some degree of tradeoff between different kinds of ecosystem services is inevitable as human populations expand and as poor people around the world aspire to higher standards of living. However, the key is to ensure that these tradeoffs are managed in ways that preserve the overall integrity of ecosystems and their capacity to provide the full range of services valued by humans.

2. Reconceptualize Target 9 indicators

Indicators for a realigned MDG Target 9 should be focused around those aspects of ecosystem function and integrity that bear most directly on the livelihoods of the poor. For example, the rural poor in developing countries rely on common pool resources to generate significant amounts of environmental income as an

important component of their livelihoods. At least some of the indicators for MDG Target 9 should capture this. Potential indicators that would reflect the state of common pool resources and the associated income opportunities they afford include:

■ extent and condition of communal fisheries (coastal and inland);
■ extent and condition of forested areas held in common;
■ watershed conditions on communally held lands (e.g., vegetative cover and water availability, including groundwater trends).

Cambodia provides an example of good practice here. Officials were thinking along these lines when they created their own MDG-7 targets and indicators, which track communally held resources of direct importance to the rural poor (UNDP 2005c:6). Their indicators include:

■ the proportion of fishing lots released to local communities (targeted to reach 60 percent by 2015, up from 56 percent in 1998), and
■ the number of community-based fisheries (targeted to reach 589 in 2015, up from 264 in 2000).

In addition to tracking common pool resources, Target 9 indicators should acknowledge the reliance poor households place on small-scale farming. Relevant indicators would include:

■ soil fertility (such as nutrient availability or percentage of organic matter in top soil;
■ land degradation (such as salinization; waterlogging; soil loss).

3. Include all institutions; add targets and time-tables

As currently worded, the first half of Target 9 states: "Integrate the principles of sustainable development into country policies and programs." This component of Target 9 should be widened to explicitly encompass key institutions at other levels of governance, including local, provincial, and international agencies. In other words, this section of Target 9 should be worded: **"Integrate the principles of sustainable development into local, national, and international policies and programs."** MDG-7 commits institutions at all levels of governance to make environmental sustainability a reality on the ground, and the wording of Target 9 should clearly reflect this. All such institutions, and not just national-level ones, should be accountable for their performance in this respect, and should report regularly on their progress.

In addition, the general intent of this target needs to be translated into specific, time-framed actions that can be monitored from year to year. Revamping Target 9 to make this element verifiable and time-bound is crucial to the ability of civil society to hold government accountable and exert pressure for improved performance.

4. Add a target that ensures resource access

Target 9, as currently worded, does not capture the importance of access—both physical access to resources as well as access to information and participation in environmental decision-making—to the livelihoods of the poor. The importance of access, manifest in secure tenure and community-level institutions that are poor-friendly, is one of the principal conclusions of Chapter 3. When we say that the MDGs should better reflect the importance of environmental governance to the poor, this is the governance we mean. The "sustainability" that MDG-7 is meant to ensure is only meaningful if the poor share "environ-

mental access"—the combination of physical access and environmental empowerment. This kind of environmental access is the basis of equity in the use of ecosystems—certainly one of the components of sustainability.

Target 9 cannot really accommodate these concepts; they should be captured in a separate Governance Target that could read: **"Ensure the poor access to environmental resources and decision-making."** Such a target would be directed at institutions of governance at all levels: national, sub-national, and international.

Indicators for this target should revolve around:

■ tenure (proportion of rural households with secure tenure to the resources on which their livelihoods are based),
■ access to environmental information (proportion of rural households with access to official information, such as extension services on ecosystem-based agricultural management), and
■ participation in local environmental decisions (indicators of pro-poor decentralization of decision-making on environmental management).

Monitoring and developing indicators of environmental governance is still a relatively new field, and such indicators might have to be adjusted for each nation. However, Cambodia again offers an example of best practice. Officials have set targets and indicators encompassing rural tenure, including an overall target of increasing the proportion of the population in both urban and rural areas with access to land security, as well as increasing the percentage of land parcels having titles in both urban and rural areas from 15 percent in 2000 to 65 percent in 2015 (UNDP 2005c:6).

Encouraging Environment and Governance as Cross-Cutting Themes

Environment and governance must be used as screens and points of orientation for all the other Goals, not just MDG-7. The MDGs are designed to be a collection of interdependent goals that must be pursued in concert with one another. Integrated strategies featuring interventions that advance multiple goals and targets simultaneously will have faster, deeper, more cost-effective, and more lasting impact on human well-being than sequential measures addressing individual goals in isolation. However, all too often, governments operate as if the goals were separate, independent entities, resulting in little coordination or cooperation between various ministries and agencies whose actions bear importantly on the likelihood of reaching MDG targets by 2015.

To be effective, MDG-7 on ensuring environmental sustainability must prompt us to raise questions about how strategies and activities under each of the other goals affect the environment and the long-term capacity of ecosystems to provide the fundamental services required for human survival and well-being. Governments and institutions that fail to recognize this reality and act upon it are at high risk that the investments and reforms they advocate for

reaching one goal are likely to undermine efforts to reach another goal. Nowhere is this more true than in the case of the environmental assets of the poor and the potential for environmental income to contribute to poverty reduction.

An integrated approach to meeting the MDG targets should be focused on improved management of ecosystems and their capacity to sustainably deliver multiple types of ecosystem services (MA 2005b:19.2). A goal-by-goal analysis of the implications of ecosystem conditions for achieving the 2015 MDG targets indicates that most of them depend directly on ecosystem services, including the targets on poverty, hunger, gender equality, child mortality, disease, and sustainable development. Moreover, multiple MDGs depend on the same ecosystem services (MA 2005b:19.4-5).

To reach all the MDGs simultaneously, it is crucially important to look carefully across the board at the required investments in ecosystem services (that is, the continued capacity of ecosystems to provide provisioning, supporting, and regulating services) and the necessary governance reforms and institutional capacity-building. For instance, interventions to reach MDG Target 1 on eradicating extreme poverty must fully explore and integrate the role that ecosystems and their services can play in improving livelihoods. Similarly, efforts to reach

TABLE 5   SOME EXAMPLES OF COUNTRY/CONTEXT-SPECIFIC MDG-7 TARGETS

Global Target 9	Modified or New Targets
Forest cover	▪ Maintain at least 60% of the country under forest cover in perpetuity (Bhutan) ▪ Maintain forest cover at 60% (2000 level) through 2015 (Cambodia) ▪ Increase forest cover from 8.2% in 2000 to 9.0% in 2015 (Mongolia) ▪ Increase afforestation rate from 27% to 35% by 2040 (Romania) ▪ Increase forest cover from 11.9 million ha in 2000 to 12.8 million ha in 2015 (Senegal) ▪ Increase forest cover by 115,000 ha between 2002 and 2006 (Tunisia) ▪ Extend forest cover to 43% by 2010 (Vietnam Nam)
Protected areas	▪ Increase ratio of protected territories from 34.9% in 1990 to 35.9% in 2015 (Bulgaria) ▪ Maintain 23 protected areas (3.3m ha, 1993) and 6 forest-protected areas (1.35m ha) through 2015 (Cambodia) ▪ Increase proportion of areas covered by natural protectorates to 25% by 2015 (Egypt) ▪ Protected areas and reserves to cover 10.8% of the national territory (Gabon) ▪ Increase area protected to maintain biological diversity from 0.2% in 1990 to 1.9% in 2015 (Kyrgyzstan) ▪ Increase land area protected to maintain biological diversity from 13.2% in 2000 to 30% in 2015 (Mongolia) ▪ Increase proportion of protected land area from 2.56% in 1990 to 19% by 2015 (Romania) ▪ Increase area protected for biological diversity from 8% in 1990 to 12% in 2015 (Senegal) ▪ Expand network of national and biosphere reserves and national parks to 10.4% of overall territory (Ukraine)
Energy and climate change	▪ Reduce CO_2 emissions against 1988 baseline in fulfillment of Kyoto Protocol obligations (Bulgaria) ▪ Reduce greenhouse gas emissions by 8% of CO_2 equivalent between 2008 and 2012 (Romania) ▪ Increase use of renewable energy in electricity generation from 29% in 1999 to 33.6% in 2015 (Slovenia) ▪ Increase share of renewable energy to 8% of commercial primary energy by 2011 (Thailand)
Pollution	▪ Decrease total discharge of major pollutants by 10% between 2000 and 2005 (China) ▪ Stabilize ambient air pollution from stationary and mobile sources by 2015 (Ukraine) ▪ Attain national standards in air and water pollution by 2005 (Vietnam)

Source: UNDP 2005b

MDG Target 2 on ending hunger need to be based on an ecosystem-focused analysis of how to most effectively maintain and improve soil fertility, water quality and supply, plant genetic resources, watershed management, and so forth.

To date, however, such assessments have rarely been undertaken in national and international planning for the MDGs. The IMF and World Bank have proposed a five-point agenda for accelerating progress toward the MDGs from which improved environmental management is conspicuously absent (IMF and World Bank 2005:3) Since this agenda was developed with particular reference to Sub-Saharan Africa—where ecosystem degradation is a principal constraint to lasting poverty reduction—the omission seems all the more glaring.

Investments in ecosystem services can produce synergistic effects across several targets: for instance, investments in watershed protection can provide multiple benefits in terms of safe drinking water, reduction of waterborne diseases, and flood protection (MA 2005b:19.39). Improved energy services will be a necessary input for reaching most of the MDGs, and a switch to modern, clean fuels and improved cookstove technology will produce multiple dividends related to improved indoor air quality, better child and maternal health, empowerment of women, and environmental sustainability (MA 2005b:19.40-41).

At the same time, some tradeoffs will be necessary, and it is vital to weigh these with reference to environmental and governance considerations. Although the UN Millennium Project is notable for devoting considerable attention to the role of environmental management in meeting the MDGs, its recommendations for reaching the 2015 targets stop short of fully integrating ecosystems as a cross-cutting orientation. For instance, rapid scale-up of MDG-based investments is a focal point for these recommendations, but they contain no discussion of the need to consider trade-offs in critical areas such as infrastructure development (UN Millennium Project 2005:31-35).

One constraint to a cross-cutting, ecosystems-based approach to reaching the MDGs is the inadequacy of environmental monitoring systems in many parts of the developing world. Documenting and assessing progress toward the 2015 targets and the sustainability of critical ecosystem functioning may require strengthening of monitoring systems for soil fertility, hydrological services (water filtration, aquifer recharging, flood prevention), maintenance of biodiversity, climate regulation, and other key ecosystem services (MA 2005b:19.3). Indicators should reflect how local people value ecosystems, including for food, medicines, cultural purposes, and other uses. Most importantly, indicators need to better capture the impact of extracting a particular bundle of services from an ecosystem on its resilience and capacity to provide future services. Investments in measuring, monitoring, and mapping poverty and ecosystem services will give policymakers at local and national levels access to indicators reflecting the linkages between poverty and the environment, which can be used to shape pro-poor growth strategies.

The slow progress that countries and institutions have made on integrating sustainability into their operations is an indication

not of an idea whose time has passed, but rather of the deep structural changes that it requires. In the context of the MDGs, this means that rich countries and international institutions need to lead by example. New and increased long-term financing mechanisms are needed to strengthen environmental capacities and support integrated, ecosystem-based implementation of the MDGs in developing countries. Countries will likely see faster progress on targets aimed at areas such as hunger, water, and sanitation that respond more directly to increased financial and technical inputs (Clemens et al. 2004:26). The experiences gained in these areas of quick response will be an important foundation for longer-term efforts to design and implement national sustainable development strategies.

POVERTY REDUCTION STRATEGIES (PRSPs)

Also in Need of an Environmental Overhaul

Countries seeking debt relief and concessional loans from the World Bank and the International Monetary Fund (IMF) must prepare a Poverty Reduction Strategy Paper (PRSP)—a document detailing the nation's philosophy and plan for achieving substantive cuts in national poverty. PRSPs have also emerged as a principal policy instrument and process for directing aid from developed countries and international agencies to help developing countries implement the Millennium Development Goals.

Unfortunately, like the Millennium Development Goals, the PRSP process suffers from critical shortcomings when it comes to acknowledging the central role of ecosystems in the lives of the poor, and their potential to reduce rural poverty. Among the current crop of PRSPs, the strategies of most countries fall short of a full commitment to better ecosystem management that benefits the poor. Maximizing environmental income

CORE PRINCIPLES AND KEY ELEMENTS OF THE PRSP APPROACH

The World Bank has set out five core principles underpinning the development and implementation of Poverty Reduction Strategy Papers (PRSPs):

Country-driven and country-owned. PRSPs should involve broad-based participation by civil society and the private sector at all stages, including formulation, implementation, and outcome-based monitoring.

Results-oriented. PRSPs should focus on outcomes that will benefit the poor.

Comprehensive. PRSPs should recognize the multidimensional nature of poverty and the scope of actions needed to effectively reduce poverty.

Partnership-oriented. PRSPs should involve the coordinated participation of development partners, including bilateral and multilateral agencies and nongovernmental organizations.

Based on medium- and long-term perspectives. PRSPs should recognize that sustained poverty reduction will require action over the medium and long terms as well as in the short run.

The Bank also specifies four key areas of content for PRSPs:

1. Macroeconomic and structural policies to support sustainable growth in which the poor participate.

2. Improvements in governance, including public-sector financial management.

3. Appropriate sectoral policies and programs.

4. Realistic costing and appropriate levels of funding for major programs.

opportunities for the poor requires that PRSPs and other formal poverty-reduction plans recognize the importance of their environmental assets, and embody an ecosystem-based perspective to ensure long-term sustainability of rural livelihoods.

A New Approach to Development?

PRSPs were established in 1999 by the World Bank and IMF as a response to the shortcomings of their earlier development approach centered on "structural adjustment"—an approach that made lending contingent on adoption of certain macroeconomic policies that would change the nation's basic economic structure and prime it for growth. Unfortunately, in many countries following the structural adjustment approach, the promised growth either did not appear or did not result in sufficient poverty alleviation. In fact, in many cases, the approach exacerbated existing inequalities, creating a "crisis of legitimacy" surrounding the lending approach of major development institutions by the mid-1990s (Reed 2004:7).

The intent behind PRSPs was to replace the approach in which the World Bank and IMF attempted to mold a nation's development policies along fixed lines as a condition for lending. Instead, the PRSP approach would let countries decide for themselves which development policies to pursue, so long as the policies were aimed at achieving significant, broad-based reductions in poverty and also emphasized governance reforms, including increased transparency and accountability of government decision-making (Oksanen and Mersmann 2003:126).

Six years after their adoption by the World Bank and IMF, PRSPs are now in transition from the preparation stage to implementation. About 70 countries are expected to eventually prepare PRSPs (Levinsohn 2003:2); as of 2004, 53 PRSPs had been produced, including 39 full PRSPs and 14 preliminary versions (Bojö et al. 2004:5). Besides heavily indebted and aid-dependent countries, other countries have also chosen to prepare PRSPs, including many Central European countries as well as middle-income countries like Brazil (Driscoll and Evans 2004a:3).

PRSPs are becoming increasingly important in shaping the planning, policy, and budget priorities of developing countries, as well as in directing the aid flows from richer countries. The PRSP process is credited with focusing the attention of governments and donor agencies on poverty reduction as a central, priority concern rather than a special, marginal activity (Driscoll and Evans 2004b:3). In addition, PRSPs represent a more "upstream" approach to development aid, that is, an approach that redirects donor assistance from specific, discrete projects towards integrated support for sector-wide plans and even general budget support. Already, in eight African countries, up to one-fifth of aid flow is now for general budget support (Chiche and Hervio 2004 in Driscoll and Evans 2004b:5). PRSPs are also intended to draw increased attention to the non-income dimensions of poverty, such as empowerment of poor and marginalized communities, as well as addressing gender disparities (Levinsohn 2003:3).

problems with how the process has actually unfolded in developing countries. Critics say that PRSPs have helped provide general budget support to poor countries without adequate commitments from these countries to specific poverty reduction outcomes, identification of the populations who will benefit from proposed anti-poverty programs, and provisions for monitoring and evaluation of expected outcomes (Reed 2004:9). Others note that, since PRSPs are prerequisites for debt relief and concessional lending, countries have strong incentives to tell donors what they think the donors want to hear rather than what the country is truly committed to doing to help reduce poverty (Tharakan and MacDonald 2004:7). In addition, the initial crop of PRSPs was not very clear about priorities or costs for anti-poverty measures (World Bank and IMF 2003:15,42).

"Mainstreaming" the Environment in PRSPs: The Unfulfilled Promise

Another important criticism of PRSPs has been their failure to adequately "mainstream" environmental issues, that is, to account for the role of resource access and environmental management in the lives of the poor, and their potential contribution to poverty reduction programs. Several studies have assessed the extent to which PRSPs integrate poverty-environment relationships—in general or in specific sectors, such as forestry, biodiversity, and water. In most of these assessments, the texts of PRSPs were analyzed and scores were assigned to indicate whether key issues were mentioned in the PRSP text and how fully these issues were analyzed or discussed.

■ Within the Environment Department of the World Bank, a team of analysts has conducted several studies of environmental mainstreaming in PRSPs (Bojö and Reddy 2002, 2003a, 2003b; Bojö et al. 2004). Based on textual analysis of all available PRSPs, the authors found that the extent of environmental mainstreaming varies widely, with final versions of PRSPs tending to reflect better mainstreaming than initial (so-called interim) versions. They also concluded that issues related to the environmental health targets of the MDGs (safe drinking water and sanitation) receive more attention in PRSPs than do issues of natural resources management.

■ A separate study of forest-related issues in 36 PRSPs (full and interim) found that treatment of forest issues was generally weak. Especially lacking was analysis of causal links between poverty and forest resources, as well as the role of natural resources and ecosystem services in determining human well-being. Given these shortcomings, the PRSPs analyzed included surprisingly many forest-related policies and programs in their agendas for action, most of which were apparently drawn from pre-existing national forest strategies and plans. For example, the PRSPs of Malawi and Mozambique were particularly strong in integrating forest-

How Is the PRSP Approach Faring?

PRSPs improve on the previous, structural adjustment approach of the World Bank and IMF in several important respects. For one, developing-country governments are the principal architects of their own development strategies. They are ostensibly free to decide for themselves how to use external aid flows, which in theory should increase national ownership of the plans and lessen the potential for problems caused by lack of country buy-in. PRSPs are also intended to be subject to continual revision and improvement over the years, serving as an umbrella for coordinating the efforts of various agencies in different economic and social sectors. In addition, the PRSP process was designed to promote increased transparency by governments and international agencies alike, as well as to feature meaningful involvement by civil society in the choice of development priorities (Reed 2004:8).

How well is the PRSP approach working in practice? The reviews are decidedly mixed. Assessments have been undertaken by many different actors, including the World Bank and IMF themselves. The consensus seems to be that PRSP processes have somewhat increased transparency, helped sharpen the focus on investments and institutions designed to reduce poverty, and provided greater opportunities for civil-society input and participation in some countries (Reed 2004:9). Some evidence indicates increased expenditures on health, education, and transport (as a percentage of GDP) in PRSP countries (OED 2004:30), and some assessments point to PRSPs as a catalyst for improvements in public financial management (World Bank and IMF 2003:28,32-33).

However, PRSPs have also been heavily criticized for shortcomings inherent in the PRSP approach as well as

sector activities based on national forest planning processes (Oksanen and Mersmann 2003:123,136-7). *(See Figure 2.)*

■ Assessment of the mainstreaming of biodiversity-related themes in 15 PRSPs found that while declines in biodiversity were analyzed in 12 of the strategies, only one PRSP (Zambia) developed a policy prescription that integrated biodiversity conservation and poverty reduction. Most of the PRSPs analyzed called for efforts to diversify agricultural *species*, but only two PRSPs (Ethiopia and Mozambique) mentioned using different *varieties* of agricultural crops (Bindraban et al. 2004:19, 21). This is an important distinction, since using diverse varieties of the same crop species is a key strategy for reducing agricultural risk by improving disease resistance and enhancing tolerance of harsh environmental conditions.

■ A study of water issues in 10 PRSPs concluded that these issues were inadequately and inconsistently incorporated in PRSPs, especially with respect to integrating the need for close links between strategies for developing additional water-supply and sanitation infrastructure and strategies for managing water resources for productive uses by the poor, including agriculture, small-scale fishing, and small industry (Slaymaker and Newborne 2004:1-2).

Such weaknesses in integrating environmental issues into PRSPs seem to be more often a genuine oversight rather than the result of conscious priority-setting. In a study by the World Bank Environment Department, many PRSPs that scored low for attention to environmental issues were produced by countries where the poverty-environment linkage is strong—places with heavy dependence on natural resources for rural livelihoods, high levels of traditional fuel use, or low levels of access to safe water and sanitation (Bojö and Reddy 2003b:14).

This finding is supported by experiences from the field. For example, reports from Nigeria indicate that environmental concerns were barely mentioned in initial drafts of its "home-grown" version of the PRSP (known as the National Economic Empowerment and Development Strategy, or NEEDS), and efforts were made to incorporate environmental issues only after the draft was distributed to stakeholders, "more or less [as] an afterthought" (Oladipo 2004).

Most assessments concluded that the degree of environmental mainstreaming in PRSPs is strongly influenced by the nature of civil-society participation in their preparation. For

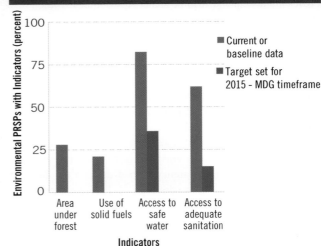

FIGURE 2 PRESENCE OF MDG-7 INDICATORS IN FULL PRSPs

Environmental PRSPs with Indicators (percent)

■ Current or baseline data
■ Target set for 2015 - MDG timeframe

Indicators: Area under forest / Use of solid fuels / Access to safe water / Access to adequate sanitation

A 2004 World Bank assessment of 39 full PRSPs found that, aside from access to safe water and adequate sanitation, most PRSPs did not make use of indicators for MILLENNIUM Development Goal 7 (Environmental Sustainability). Fewer still included targets for future progress.

Source: Bojö et al. 2004

example, the top-scoring cluster of PRSPs in the World Bank studies of environmental mainstreaming also scored high on public participation in PRSP development (Bojö et al. 2004:15).

Many studies also note that inclusion of environmental issues in PRSPs sometimes appears to be driven more by donor concerns rather than domestic political priorities. In several cases, donors have pressed reluctant governments to provide opportunities for significant engagement of civil society in PRSP processes. Indeed, closer relationships between civil society and donors has been an outgrowth of the evolution of PRSP processes in several countries (PRSP Monitoring and Synthesis Project 2002:5).

In the PRSPs of many countries, poverty diagnosis and analysis emphasize technical solutions to poverty-environment issues. Less frequently do PRSPs address more controversial, politically charged issues of access, ownership, control, and rights to environmental resources and how these impact the poor's capacity to derive environmental income from productive assets. However, in a few instances, participation by activist NGOs has begun to shape the content of poverty analysis in PRSPs; for example, the PRSPs of Uganda and Honduras have begun to address issues of access to and control of natural resources in response to concerns expressed in consultations with civil society (Waldman et al. 2005:32).

Another oversight in many PRSPs is the failure to assess the potential impacts of proposed growth policies on environmental sustainability, maintenance of critical ecosystem functioning, and key natural resources relied on by the poor for their livelihoods (Oksanen and Mersmann 2003:137). For example, PRSPs frequently propose incentives to encourage high-input, export-oriented agriculture to stimulate economic growth, yet rarely do they analyze the risks of this approach for harming small-scale rural farmers and weakening their ability to manage local natural resources (Tharakan and MacDonald 2004:25).

The PRSP of Nicaragua refers to intensive production of cash crops, including coffee, for export, but this discussion does not include measures to improve food security or to diversify rural incomes through nonfarm activities (Tharakan and MacDonald 2004:32). The PRSP of Sri Lanka presents goals for rapid economic growth through expansion of cash-crop agriculture, plantation activity, and fisheries, but provides no analysis of the implications of such growth on natural-resource depletion or waste generation (Tharakan and MacDonald 2004:38-9).

Several countries have begun to carry out their PRSPs and thus have been required to submit annual progress reports on PRSP implementation. In general, these annual reports give even less attention to environmental sustainability than the PRSPs themselves. In many cases, policies and programs proposed in a country's PRSP are absent entirely from discussions in its progress reports. Studies by the World Bank found that several countries whose PRSP was very highly rated for environmental mainstreaming submitted annual reports that reflected little progress in implementing environment-related measures (Bojö et al. 2004:19).

Upgrading the Treatment of Environmental Income in PRSPs

PRSPs have become one of the most powerful vehicles for carrying forward a commitment to better ecosystem management that benefits the poor. However, the processes and content of PRSPs in many countries falls far short of the potential. Even among strategies recognized within the development community for a relatively high degree of environmental mainstreaming, PRSPs rarely go far enough in proposing measures that would empower the poor with equitable and sustainable opportunities to derive income from their environmental assets.

ASSESSING ENVIRONMENTAL INCOME OPPORTUNITIES IN PRSPs

To assess the treatment of environmental income opportunities for the poor, *WRR 2005* examined 20 PRSPs that have been touted by the World Bank, the United Nations, and other development experts as the best examples to date of environmental mainstreaming. We found several examples of proposed policies and programs that, if effectively implemented, would genuinely improve the prospects for the poor to derive sustainable income from their environmental assets. Many of these examples are described in the text of this chapter.

Of course, whether these "paper promises" can or will be translated into progress on the ground is the crux of the matter. Our desk study suggests that PRSPs with the most extensive and successful mainstreaming of environment and environmental income opportunities were also the most impeccably presented documents, in some cases perhaps indicating that international consultants, provided through assistance from the donor community, had a large hand in their preparation. The strength of the political will behind these environmental proposals remains to be seen.

What can be done to ensure that PRSPs advance a pro-poor agenda for maximizing sustainable environmental income while maintaining the integrity of critical ecosystem functions? At least seven key issues need to be examined. *(See Framework for Upgrading PRSPs.)* In the discussion below, examples of good practice in crafting PRSPs are highlighted to show that adequate treatment of these issues in PRSPs is both possible and desirable.

1. Ecosystem Orientation and Importance of Environmental Income

PRSPs need to do a better job of recognizing the importance of environmental income and the role it can play in reducing poverty. The approach taken in PRSPs to enhancing rural livelihoods should be based on an awareness of the importance of ecosystems as the ultimate basis for all economic activity and a key contributor to human welfare, and should seek to ensure the long-term sustainability of ecosystem services and the livelihoods derived from them.

FRAMEWORK FOR UPGRADING PRSPs

How should poverty reduction strategies be evaluated for their treatment of environmental income opportunities for the poor? The following questions can shed light on whether PRSPs adequately reflect the importance of environmental income and provide for sustainable and equitable ecosystem management.

ENVIRONMENTAL MAINSTREAMING

1. **Ecosystem orientation and environmental income.** Does the strategy recognize the importance of ecosystems as a source of income for the poor? Does it advocate an ecosystem approach to maintain and enhance this income source?

2. **Sustainability of income over time.** Does the strategy take a long-term approach to natural resource income, stressing sustainable ecosystem management? Does it integrate with existing national sustainability plans?

ENVIRONMENTAL GOVERNANCE

3. **Tenure and access to resources.** Does the strategy address issues of resource access of the poor and recognize their centrality to increasing income security? In particular, does it squarely confront the issue of tenure insecurity and advocate for pro-poor tenure reform?

4. **Decentralization and CBNRM.** Does the strategy address the devolution of power over resource management to competent local authorities, and does it make provision for building the governance capacity and transparency of these local institutions? Does the strategy support community-based natural resource management as an effective form of local empowerment and advocate for its clear recognition in law?

5. **Participation, procedural rights, and gender equality.** Is the strategy grounded in broad-based participation by civil society? Are the priorities identified in the consultation process incorporated into the final strategy? Does the strategy emphasize free and informed consent of communities to economic development activities that entail local environmental impacts? Does the strategy acknowledge and address gender issues?

ENVIRONMENTAL MONITORING AND ASSESSMENT

6. **Environmental monitoring.** Does the strategy include plans for monitoring environmental conditions to track the impacts of economic growth on environmental income and provide the basis for sound ecosystem management?

7. **Targets, indicators, and assessments.** Does the strategy contain quantifiable targets for improving outcomes with respect to the environmental income opportunities of the poor? Does it specify poverty and environmental indicators and how these will be used to shape pro-poor growth strategies? Does it describe plans for assessments to evaluate performance in implementing environment- and governance-related measures to improve the environmental income opportunities of the poor.

One of the strongest PRSPs in terms of recognizing the potential of environmental income for poverty reduction is that of Cambodia. The Cambodian PRSP identifies land, water, agriculture, forests, and fisheries as key to increasing rural incomes and sets out an 11-point program to improve rural livelihoods by increasing income from the development of small-scale aquaculture, establishing and strengthening community forestry, promoting sustainable, community-based management of fishery resources, and improving market access for small-scale farmers and rural producers (Cambodia 2002:v, 53, 61).

Similarly, Bolivia highlights the potential contribution of biodiversity to rural incomes and the economy as a whole. It cites preliminary studies indicating that within 15 years biodiversity-related activities (such as ecotourism, mitigation of climate change, and services related to biotechnology) could increase GDP about 10 percent (Bolivia 2001:133). Biodiversity resources could provide near-term gains to disadvantaged rural populations from projects featuring sustainable use of wild animal species, including vicuna, lizard, and peccary (Bolivia 2001:133). Bolivia also proposes to formally establish non-timber forest activities (e.g., gathering of brazil nuts and cultivation of palms) within the national forest system and municipal forest reserve areas, with the aim of creating new income generation activities for impoverished local communities (Bolivia 2001:134).

However, even among PRSPs that devote significant attention to opportunities for enhancing the poor's environmental income, few refer to the importance of ecosystems as fundamental units for managing natural resources and ensuring long-term environmental sustainability. Of the PRSPs reviewed, only Ghana mentioned the "ecosystem approach" by name and then only in the limited sense of using this approach to restore threatened habitats and ecosystems (Ghana 2003:75).

One exception is Cambodia, which has made some limited efforts to incorporate an ecosystems-based perspective or approach within specific sectors and activities. For instance, the Cambodian PRSP describes a national vision for water resources that explicitly encompasses healthy aquatic ecosystems as well as productive fisheries and provision of safe and affordable drinking water (Cambodia 2002:64). Cambodia also applies the concept of agroecosystems in agricultural development plans, including proposals to set up agricultural research centers in each of the country's principal agroecosystems that would be oriented to small-scale farmers. These centers would conduct research and extension, emphasizing intensification of agricultural production through improved water, soil, and nutrient management, with relatively few external inputs in the form of agrichemicals or improved seeds (Cambodia 2002:56).

2. Sustainability of Income Over Time

A concentration on environmental income is not by itself sufficient if this income stream is not sustainable. Nations thus need to take care that the strategies they promote in their

PRSPs for exploiting natural resources are viable over the long term. PRSPs frequently include expansions of the agriculture, forestry, or fisheries sectors, but rarely look at the implications of these activities for the future health of the resource. For example, of the 20 PRSPs reviewed, several targeted transformation of subsistence agriculture as a key means of reducing rural poverty. In many cases, however, plans for agricultural intensification, modernization, and commercialization did not explicitly address how this transformation could be achieved in ways that would ensure long-term sustainability of agricultural income and protection of the agricultural resource base. Likewise, few PRSPs described detailed plans to generate additional income and employment from forests and fisheries that were explicitly based on improved, sustainable management of these natural resources.

PRSPs might do a better job of incorporating the concepts of sustainability if they were more closely linked to existing environmental planning processes such as a national strategy for sustainability, or a national plan to meet the terms

of the Convention on Biological Diversity. For instance, Nicaragua's PRSP highlights its National Strategy for Sustainable Development, which focuses on the implementation of policies and public investments to ensure more rational use of the country's natural resources. The strategy contains elements addressing several economic sectors and activities, including the Environmental Policy and Action Plan, the Forestry and Development Law, the Fisheries Law, and the Biodiversity Law (Nicaragua 2001:22, 25).

Sri Lanka's PRSP refers to the various environmental strategies and plans it has developed, including a national environmental action plan and a national strategy for sustainable development, as well as planning under international environmental agreements on biodiversity, climate change, and desertification (Sri Lanka 2002:97, 129). The PRSP also mentions revision of other environmental plans, including the national Rain Forest Law, coastal zone management plan, and regional plans for integrated forestry resource management (Sri Lanka 2002:19, 90).

3. Tenure and Access to Resources

Security of tenure, access, and user rights are central to achieving sustainable livelihoods for the rural poor, particularly in providing them with appropriate incentives to manage environmental assets for long-term productivity and income growth. Most PRSPs mention tenure and access to land and other productive resources; however, some treat the subject in only a cursory manner, while others present detailed discussions of tenure-related problems or plans for reform.

PRSPs should clearly identify the role of property and user rights as important factors shaping investments in agricultural productivity and the prospects for expanding rural incomes. More importantly, PRSPs must then indicate how they plan to deal with the nation's particular tenure challenges.

Zambia's PRSP points out that nearly 97 percent of Zambian farmers have no title to the land they cultivate, reducing incentives to invest in land improvements and agriculture-related infrastructure, preventing farmers from having access to credit, and depressing land productivity within a system where smallholders contribute about 60 percent of agricultural output (Zambia 2002:44). The PRSP also links the lack of secure title to disincentives for development of infrastructure for expanded tourism and eco-tourism opportunities (Zambia 2002:67). However, Zambia acknowledges that it has made little progress to date in setting up a land administration system, titling communally owned or state lands, or developing a market for land. The proposed remedy—a review of existing land law and tenure arrangements as well as discussions with traditional communities regarding incentives to open unused land for investment—may be realistic given political and budgetary constraints, but seems unlikely to bring about substantial progress in the foreseeable future (Zambia 2002:58).

On the other hand, Sri Lanka's PRSP presents detailed proposals for far-reaching land reform to provide the poor with greater access to land. The government plans to test a new land

titling program, designed to be fairer and more efficient, which is expected to reduce the cost of titling a parcel of land from US$110 to under $40. Proposed legal reforms would consolidate 25 different laws that directly affect land titling, and alternative dispute mechanisms will be used to resolve issues that prevent titling. Advanced information technologies, including digital mapping and integrated data management, will be used to accelerate land titling and registration and make the land-management system more transparent and accessible (Sri Lanka 2002:62).

Honduras outlines very specific actions, with associated budgets and deadlines, that will be carried out to improve equity and security in the poor's access to land. Key elements include completing a nationwide *cadastre* (survey) of forest and agricultural lands to strengthen the legal basis for land ownership, modernizing the rural property registry to provide a modern tool for guaranteeing the accuracy of land tenure arrangements and land transactions, and an expanded program for titling rural properties for small farmers, ethnic groups, and independent *campesinos* (Honduras 2001:70).

Bolivia plans to regularize the titles to all rural land by 2006, including measures to simplify the procedures for registering land titles and property rights by merging the systems for physical and legal registration of property (Bolivia 2001:110).

4. Decentralization and Community-Based Natural Resource Management

Almost all PRSPs refer to decentralization and its importance for improving governance and reducing poverty. Often the discussion is rather general, however, and mentions only one or two sectors—usually education and health. PRSPs should incorporate analysis of important aspects of decentralization issues that are directly related to natural resources management and opportunities to enhance environmental income for the poor.

Among the current crop of PRSPs, a few contain well-developed discussions of decentralization for the management of environmental resources. A few also outline ways in which the government proposes to work with local people to increase rural income through community-based management of forests, fisheries, and other environmental assets.

Bolivia's PRSP explicitly addresses the implications of decentralization for environmental management. The strategy refers to institution-strengthening initiatives aimed at ensuring that municipal governments will have the capacity to carry out new responsibilities to implement environmental policies and standards. It also highlights the ongoing role of Bolivia's central government in important environment-related planning functions, including the development of diagnostic assessments, resource inventories, and soil and water-use plans, that will influence environmental investments (Bolivia 2001:131-2). Some innovative mechanisms are proposed for financing the environmental activities of local governments, including sharing revenues from a special hydrocarbon tax (Bolivia 2001:149).

Zambia designates development of a decentralization policy a matter of top priority to ensure citizen participation in their own affairs (Zambia 2002:35). The PRSP outlines decentralization measures that will enable communities to benefit from the commercial use of their lands, including shareholding arrangements with investors and tax-sharing arrangements (Zambia 2002:51).

Concerning community-based natural resource management, PRSPs should spell out in detail how the government proposes to work with local people to increase rural incomes through community-based management of forests, fisheries, and other environmental assets. For example, Cambodia notes that it is transitioning from state control to co-management of fisheries with local communities. In response to rising incidence of conflict between commercial fishing operators and subsistence and small-scale family fishers, Cambodia is releasing more than half of the country's fishing lots to local fishing communities. The PRSP notes that this change will empower local people to participate in conservation and management of the fishery resource, giving them an incentive to refrain from illegal fishing practices that have been degrading the aquatic environment (Cambodia 2002:59).

Also outlined in Cambodia's PRSP are initiatives related to community forestry to enhance local community participation in decision-making for forest management. In consultation with local user groups, the government will review the system of fees and permits on NTFPs and work toward removing barriers to marketing NTFPs, especially resin, that can be harvested without damaging the forest (Cambodia 2002:60).

Sri Lanka details several initiatives for community-driven development through sustainable management of natural resources. Community-based reef management projects will be undertaken as part of a 5-year public investment program to minimize coastal erosion, already affecting an estimated 55 percent of the Sri Lankan coast prior to the December 2004 tsunami. Community organizations will prepare coastal management plans, undertake reef stabilization and habitat conservation, implement measures to improve water exchange in affected lagoons, and help develop community fish hatcheries (Sri Lanka 2002:64, 89-90).

The PRSP also highlights plans to involve poor communities in decision-making for protected forests, providing funding to communities to replant degraded forest areas, manage buffer zones, and develop timber farms using conservation-oriented cultivation practices, with a goal of halving the rate of deforestation due to encroachment and illegal forest use (Sri Lanka 2002:90–91). The poor will be encouraged to participate in the development of Sri Lanka's

ecotourism industry by forming community-based organizations in the buffer zones adjacent to national parks and wildlife sanctuaries, which will receive a share of ecotourism earnings and training to assist in wildlife conservation activities (Sri Lanka 2002:91).

Kenya also plans to promote pro-poor tourism by fostering community-based ecotourism in the northern and western areas of the country. The PRSP outlines efforts to strengthen community involvement in wildlife conservation, implement measures to reduce human-wildlife conflict, provide small and medium enterprises with access to credit, review the structure of park tariffs to expand tourism in less-visited parks, and establish certification schemes for environmentally friendly resorts (Kenya 2004:49).

5. Participation, Procedural Rights, and Gender Equality

Guidelines for preparing PRSPs require that these strategies be prepared with extensive input from a broad range of stakeholders and that countries provide detailed explanations of processes used to secure such participation. Evidence to date indicates that PRSP mechanisms to promote participation often emphasize stakeholders that are urban-based, with relatively sophisticated analytical capabilities, and exclude organizations representing largely rural constituents, especially indigenous peoples.

Governments have sometimes barred stakeholders critical of their policies from participating in PRSP consultations (Waldman et al. 2005). Moreover, governments, NGOs, and international donors often have very different ideas of what constitutes "participation." Some governments have sought to limit participation merely to dissemination of information to NGOs and other stakeholders, rather than substantive input. NGOs and some donors have pressed for more authentically democratic exercises in which civil society has opportunities to shape the agenda and contribute meaningfully to the design of PRSPs (PRSP Monitoring and Synthesis Project 2002:2-6). The PRSPs reviewed here varied considerably with respect to the efforts made to involve environmental stakeholders and to incorporate input from civil society.

One of the stronger efforts was that of Cambodia, which devotes an entire chapter of its PRSP to describing its participatory processes, including four national workshops. The chapter also describes consultations held by sector and line ministries, provincial consultations, a forum on monitoring and evaluation aspects, an NGO forum, meetings with the private sector, donor involvement, meetings with parliamentarians, and consultations with trade unions. It also acknowledges the need for ongoing consultations as it prepares subsequent versions of the plan (Cambodia 2002:8-12, 164).

Ghana presents an appendix that lists specific comments offered on various drafts of the PRSP and indicates how these comments were addressed. For instance, environment-related issues that were addressed in response to outside input include:

the need for greater mainstreaming of environment in the PRSP, the imperative to improve natural resources management as a prerequisite to sustainable production, the role of tenure insecurity as a cause of poverty, the importance of small-scale irrigation and access to land to support farmers, and the need to develop alternative sources of energy (Ghana 2003:216-225).

In Rwanda and Vietnam, dissemination of key documents in local languages helped improve awareness of the PRSP process (Bojö and Reddy 2003b:26).

Addressing disparities in women's rights and access to land and other productive assets has been shown to be a fundamental aspect of effective poverty reduction strategies. A few of the PRSPs reviewed presented detailed analysis of the impacts of gender on environmental income opportunities as well as detailed proposals for remedying gender-based inequities in countries where women traditionally have not been accorded equal rights and access to ecosystems.

Cambodia notes that, with women accounting for 65 percent of agricultural labor and 75 percent of fisheries production, poverty reduction cannot succeed unless it addresses the roles and needs of women (Cambodia 2002:127). The PRSP sets an explicit goal of ensuring that women and girls receive full legal protection and education about their legal rights to access to land and natural resources. Equal numbers of women and men are to be included in all consultative processes and on all monitoring and evaluation teams (Cambodia 2002:vii). Cambodia sets a goal of ensuring that women, the primary collectors and users of water, ultimately make up half of all members of water-user associations, and at least 20 percent of such members within three years (Cambodia 2002:113, 128). The government also pledges to address gender disparities through budget allocations as well as policies and programs (Cambodia 2002:136).

Sri Lanka highlights plans for legal reforms to ensure women's equal rights to inherit land and proposes to encourage women's self-employment in small-scale fishing through training and extension activities (Sri Lanka 2002:200,213).

Zambia proposes to mainstream gender in its land policies, including the introduction of legal reforms to provide equal land rights for women and ensure women's access to natural resources. Women's traditional knowledge of sustainable resource use and management will be integrated into the development of environmental management and extension programs, and 30 percent of all land allocations will be reserved for women applicants (Zambia 2002:54, 114).

6. and 7. Environmental Monitoring, Targets, Indicators, and Assessments

PRSPs are notoriously weak in their provisions for monitoring and evaluating the impacts of the policies and programs they propose. In many cases, provisions for monitoring and evaluating environment-related impacts are particularly inadequate.

The World Bank's review of environmental mainstreaming in PRSPs found that few were structured for effective monitoring of progress towards proposed outcomes; that is, few contained realistic, quantified, time-bound, costed targets coupled with a sufficient suite of specific, relevant, quantitative indicators for measuring progress towards these targets (Bojö and Reddy 2003b:25).

Among the PRSPs reviewed, a few clearly identified targets and indicators that will be used to gauge the impact of proposed interventions related to environment and natural resources management. Bolivia presents several targets and indicators related to enhancing environmental income for the poor, including increases in the extent of land brought under secure title. The PRSP proposes to complete the process of securing clear title to rural property in Bolivia by 2006, which would involve regularizing the ownership of more than 7 million ha per year from 2001 to 2006 (Bolivia 2001:183). Other indicators established by Bolivia include annual increases in resources allocated to local communities from the revenues of protected areas, as well as increases in income from sustainable wildlife management programs (Bolivia 2001:186).

Cambodia's PRSP presents an action-plan matrix with numerous strategic objectives, actionable measures, estimated costs, targets and indicators, and the responsible implementing agency. Among the targets and indicators related to environmental income opportunities are increases in the number of land titles issued (including the number of titles held by women) and establishing specific numbers of community forest, fisheries, and small-scale aquaculture projects in various provinces. Quantitative goals are also set for the numbers of women receiving agricultural training on such topics as soil fertility and management, prevention of soil degradation, and safe pesticide use, as well as the percentage of women members in farmers associations (Cambodia 2002:172-80, 229).

Steps toward More Effective PRSPs

One emerging area of debate surrounding PRSPs is whether these strategies will enable countries to successfully meet the MDGs. The UN suggests that existing PRSPs often are not adequate for this purpose and has called for so-called "MDG-based poverty reduction strategies" that are more ambitious, scaled-up, and focused on a longer planning horizon, laying out a path to achievement of the MDGs by 2015. A pivotal step in ramping up PRSPs will be identifying additional sources of capital, since lack of existing capital to finance needed national investments is one of the reasons that interventions described in current PRSPs generally are not ambitious enough to meet the MDGs.

Increased capital to spark poverty-reducing growth could come from various sources, including mobilizing developing countries' own domestic sources of natural wealth as well as expanded development aid and private sector-led trade and investment. Key challenges will be to understand the strategic and policy elements necessary to scale up investment to meet the MDGs and to strike a thoughtful balance between ambition and realism in PRSPs.

To this end, stakeholders could take several important steps toward PRSPs that emphasize scaled-up investment for pro-poor growth while also protecting the ability of ecosystems to provide sustainable services that underlie human well-being and the livelihoods of the poor.

- The World Bank and IMF can support efforts to achieve the MDGs by adapting macroeconomic frameworks for PRSPs according to specific country circumstances. For example, the Bank can encourage countries to work with the poor to invest in ecosystem services such as water resources, soil conservation, and forests and woodlands that generate needed provisioning services such as food, fiber, and fuel. These investments, as shown by the Millennium Ecosystem Assessment, also provide regulating services such as water regulation, erosion control, pest control, and natural-hazard regulation which reduce vulnerability of the poor to damaging effects of drought, floods, loss of soil productivity, and crop failures.

- The United Nations can provide support to developing countries to help them strategically link Poverty Reduction Strategies to efforts to meet the MDGs. This assistance can take several forms, including building national capacities to develop and implement scaled-up investment programs and encouraging the exchange of experiences and lessons learned between countries.

- Developing countries can contribute to the process by ensuring that their PRSP-related efforts emphasize transparency and inclusion and by being accountable for measurable progress in reducing poverty. To this end, monitoring and assessment of poverty and environment outcomes using appropriate data and benchmarks is essential.

- Donor countries can help by ramping up the levels of assistance provided to developing countries to help them reach the MDGs. Development aid needs to be delivered in a stable and predictable manner to facilitate effective planning as well as to avoid destabilizing macroeconomic impacts. Donors should complement development assistance with rapid and significant debt relief to create fiscal "space" for pro-poor, MDG-based investments.

Data
Tables

II

PART

WORLD RESOURCES 2005 Data Tables

Each edition of *World Resources* includes a statistical appendix, a compilation of country-level data culled from a variety of sources. This section presents some of the data required to build a basic picture of the state of the Earth in its human, economic, and environmental dimensions. In an increasingly interdependent, globalized world, a picture of the whole is needed to understand the interactions of human development, population growth, economic growth, and the environment. In addition, *World Resources 2005* provides a selection of data on global poverty and, in particular, on how the poor use natural resources.

The 12 data tables that follow are a subset of a larger online data collection: the *EarthTrends* database of the World Resources Institute. Based on the *World Resources* series, *EarthTrends* is a free, online resource that highlights the environmental, social, and economic trends that shape our world. The website offers the public a comprehensive collection of vital statistics, maps, and graphics viewable by watershed, district, country, region, or worldwide.

General Notes

The *World Resources 2005* data tables present information for 155 countries. These countries were selected from the 191 official member states of the United Nations based on their population levels, land area, and the availability of data. Many more countries are included in the *EarthTrends* online database. Country groupings are based on lists developed by the Food and Agriculture Organization of the United Nations (for developed and developing countries), the World Bank (for low-, medium-, and high-income countries), and the World Resources Institute (for regional classifications). See pages 224-226 for a full listing.

Several general notes apply to all the data tables in the report (except where noted otherwise):

■ ".." in a data column signifies that data are not available or are not relevant (for example, country status has changed, as with the former Soviet republics).

■ Negative values are shown in parentheses.

■ 0 appearing in a table indicates a value of either zero or less than one-half the unit of measure used in the table; (0) indicates a value less than zero and greater than negative one-half.

■ Except where identified by a footnote, regional totals are calculated using regions designated by the World Resources Institute. Totals represent either a summation or a weighted average of available data. Weighted averages of ratios use the denominator of the ratio as the weight. Regional totals are published only if more than 85 percent of the relevant data are available for a particular region. Missing values are not imputed.

■ The regional totals published here use data from all 222 countries and territories in the *World Resources / EarthTrends* database (some of these countries are omitted from the current tables). Regional summations and weighted averages calculated with only the 155 countries listed in these data tables will therefore not match the published totals.

■ Except where identified with a footnote, world totals are presented as calculated by the original data source (which may include countries not listed in WRI's database); original sources are listed after each data table.

■ When available data are judged too weak to allow for any meaningful comparison across countries, the data are not shown. Please review the technical notes for further consideration of data reliability.

■ Comprehensive technical notes are available in the pages following each data table.

EarthTrends: The Environmental Information Portal

Much of the environmental information on the internet is fragmented, buried, or only available at a price. World Resources Institute's *EarthTrends* data portal gathers information from more than 40 of the world's leading statistical agencies, supplemented with WRI-generated maps and analyses, into a single, free repository for rapid searching and retrieving. *EarthTrends* supplements its content with detailed metadata that report on research methodologies and information reliability.

The *EarthTrends* online data source includes more than 40 data tables, similar to those on the following pages. *EarthTrends* also features over 2,000 two-page country profiles that highlight country-level statistics on key topics in sustainable development, as well as hundreds of maps and feature stories. The core of *EarthTrends* is a searchable database with over 600 time-series indicators, spanning 30-plus years: a corpus of statistical knowledge from which the data tables in this volume are drawn.

Two new additions to *EarthTrends* will be of particular interest to readers of this book. *EarthTrends* now features the *EarthTrends Poverty Resource* and the *EarthTrends Global Watersheds Collection*. The *EarthTrends Poverty Resource,* released in December 2004, provides a starting point for research on the nexus of poverty, governance, and ecosystems. It brings together a unique collection of data, maps, and other resources to help readers comprehend and analyze developing world poverty. In addition, the Poverty Resource contains dozens of subnational maps depicting the distribution of poverty and human well-being within countries. The *Global Watersheds Collection,* an updated version of the 1998 report *Watersheds of the World,* provides maps of land cover, population density, and biodiversity for 154 river basins and sub-basins around the world.

Since 2001, *EarthTrends* has remained an authoritative, independent source of information for users in more than 190 countries and territories, demonstrating that carefully compiled web-based information can provide an important basis for decision-making and policy development. The information on *EarthTrends* is varied. While researchers will value the raw data (over 500,000 records), much of the information is available in easy-to-use, printable formats, and can be adapted for educational or policy-oriented presentations.

Additional Data Products

In addition to the main, graphics-intensive site, *EarthTrends* offers users additional ways to access our collection of environmental information.

EarthTrends for Low-Bandwidth Users

In an effort to broaden global access to sustainable development information, WRI has developed a low-bandwidth companion to the *EarthTrends* site. View the entire *EarthTrends* collection of information without high-resolution graphics at **http://earthtrends.wri.org/text.**

World Resources/*EarthTrends* Data CD-ROM

Gain instant, portable access to the EarthTrends database on global conditions and trends with the *EarthTrends* CD-ROM. This time-saving research and reference tool contains all of the economic, population, natural resource, and environmental statistics contained in the *EarthTrends* website and the print edition of *World Resources 2005.* Available for order at **http://www.wristore.com.**

TerraViva! World Resources

Need more power and flexibility in arranging and understanding data? View the World Resources/EarthTrends database through state-of-the-art mapping, analytical, and statistical tools. Compare hundreds of environmental, social, and economic variables, generating maps, graphics, tables, or text as output. Available for order at **http://www.wristore.com.**

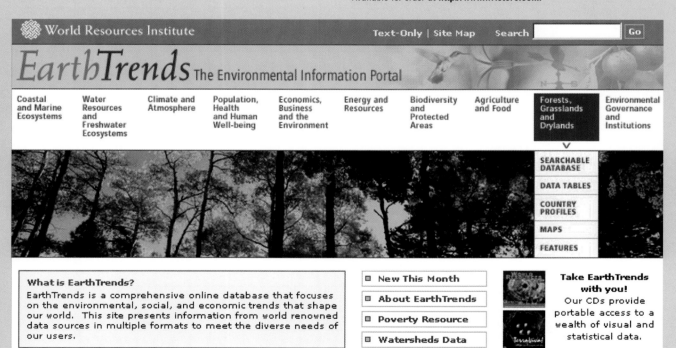

Population and Education

Sources: United Nations Population Division, United Nations Children's Fund, United Nations High Commissioner for Refugees, Global IDP Project, United Nations Educational, Scientific, and Cultural Organization

	Total Population Estimates and Projections (thousands of people) [a]			Percent of Population in Specific Age Groups 2005		Estimated Total Fertility Rate [a] (children per woman) 2000-2005	Estimated Mortality Under Age 5 (per 1000 live births) 2002	Refugees [b] (thousands)		Internally Displaced Persons (thousands) 2004	Estimated Literacy Rate 2004 (percent)		Net School Enrollment (percent) 2001-2002	
	1980	2005	2030	Under 15	65 & Over			Granted Asylum Elsewhere 2003	Repatri- ations 2003		Adults Over Age 15	Youths Ages 15-24	Primary	Secondary
World	4,434,682	6,453,628	8,130,149	28	7	2.7	81	9,672	1,095	25,000	77	89	..	..
Asia (excl. Middle East)	2,477,179	3,624,244	4,436,079	28	7	2.5	..	1,327	9	..	76	91	..	..
Armenia	3,096	3,043	2,786	18	10	1.2	35	13	..	50	99	100	85	85
Azerbaijan	6,161	8,527	10,486	27	7	2.1	105	253	..	570	..	..	80	76
Bangladesh	85,004	152,593	220,321	37	3	3.5	73	6	..	150-520	41	50	87	44
Bhutan	1,318	2,392	4,030	40	4	5.0	94	104	..	..	..	..	..	..
Cambodia	6,613	14,825	23,555	41	3	4.8	138	31	..	..	69	80	86	21
China	998,877	1,322,273	1,450,521	22	8	1.8	38	132	..	..	91	99	93 c	..
Georgia	5,073	5,026	4,258	17	15	1.4	29	12	< 0.5	260	..	..	91	..
India	688,856	1,096,917	1,416,576	32	5	3.0	90	14	..	650	61	..	83 c	..
Indonesia	150,128	225,313	277,567	29	5	2.4	43	13	..	535	88	98	92	48 d
Japan	116,807	127,914	121,017	14	20	1.3	5	< 0.5	..	..	..	..	100	100
Kazakhstan	14,919	15,364	15,258	23	9	2.0	76	7	..	..	99	100	90	84
Korea, Dem People's Rep	17,196	22,876	24,974	25	7	2.0	55	< 0.5	..	..	..	..	100	89
Korea, Rep	38,124	48,182	50,042	19	9	1.4	5	< 0.5	..	..	..	..	90	..
Kyrgyzstan	3,628	5,278	6,711	31	7	2.6	61	3	..	..	..	..	83	31
Lao People's Dem Rep	3,205	5,918	9,282	41	4	4.8	100	10	..	..	66	79	83	31
Malaysia	13,763	25,325	35,191	32	5	2.9	8	< 0.5	..	..	89	97	95	69
Mongolia	1,663	2,667	3,491	30	4	2.4	71	< 0.5	..	..	98	98	87	71
Myanmar	33,705	50,696	61,308	31	5	2.9	108	147	3	600-1,000	85	91	82	35
Nepal	14,881	26,289	40,740	39	4	4.3	87	1	..	100-200	44	63	70 c	..
Pakistan	80,781	161,151	271,600	41	4	5.1	104	24	< 0.5	45	42	54	67 c	..
Philippines	48,088	82,809	113,795	35	4	3.2	37	< 0.5	..	>75	93	95	93	56
Singapore	2,414	4,372	4,934	20	8	1.4	4	< 0.5	..	..	93	100	..	..
Sri Lanka	14,543	19,366	21,670	24	7	2.0	19	122	5	430-500	92	97	100	..
Tajikistan	3,953	6,356	8,548	34	5	3.1	72	59	< 0.5	..	100	100	98	79
Thailand	46,342	64,081	75,424	25	6	1.9	28	< 0.5	..	..	93	98	86	..
Turkmenistan	2,861	5,015	6,825	32	5	2.7	98	1	..	..	99	100	..	..
Uzbekistan	15,952	26,868	35,031	32	5	2.4	68	7	..	3	99	100	..	..
Viet Nam	53,005	83,585	108,374	29	5	2.3	26	363	..	..	90	..	94	65
Europe	692,430	724,720	685,441	16	16	1.4	..	1,098	36	..	99	..	..	..
Albania	2,671	3,220	3,680	27	7	2.3	30	10	..	..	99	99	97 c	74 c
Austria	7,549	8,120	7,911	15	16	1.3	5	< 0.5	..	..	..	..	91 c	88 c
Belarus	9,659	9,809	8,678	15	15	1.2	20	8	..	..	100	100	94	78
Belgium	9,859	10,359	10,512	17	18	1.7	6	< 0.5	..	..	..	..	100 d	..
Bosnia and Herzegovina	3,914	4,209	4,089	16	12	1.3	18	300	14	330	95	100	..	..
Bulgaria	8,862	7,763	6,335	14	16	1.1	16	3	..	..	99	100	93 c	86 c
Croatia	4,377	4,405	3,990	17	17	1.7	8	230	10	11	98	100	88	86
Czech Rep	10,283	10,216	9,608	15	14	1.2	5	7	..	..	..	..	88	89
Denmark	5,123	5,386	5,469	18	15	1.8	4	< 0.5	..	..	..	..	99 d	89 d
Estonia	1,473	1,294	943	15	17	1.2	12	1	..	..	100	100	98 c	92 c
Finland	4,780	5,224	5,253	17	16	1.7	5	< 0.5	..	..	..	..	100 c	95 c
France	53,880	60,711	64,577	18	16	1.9	6	< 0.5	..	..	..	..	100 c	92 c
Germany	78,289	82,560	81,511	14	19	1.4	5	1	..	..	..	..	83	88
Greece	9,643	10,978	10,567	14	19	1.3	5	< 0.5	..	..	..	..	95 c	85 c
Hungary	10,707	9,784	8,636	16	15	1.2	9	3	..	..	..	..	91	92
Iceland	228	294	330	22	12	2.0	4	< 0.5	..	..	..	..	100 c	82 c
Ireland	3,401	4,040	4,762	20	11	1.9	6	< 0.5	..	..	..	..	94 c	82 c
Italy	56,434	57,253	51,546	14	20	1.2	6	< 0.5	..	..	..	..	100 c	88 d
Latvia	2,512	2,265	1,750	14	17	1.1	21	3	..	..	100	100	91 c	89 c
Lithuania	3,413	3,401	2,935	18	15	1.3	9	2	..	..	100	100	97 c	92 c
Macedonia, FYR	1,795	2,076	2,205	21	11	1.9	26	6	2	3	..	..	93 c	..
Moldova, Rep	4,010	4,259	4,011	19	9	1.4	32	11	..	1	99	100	78 c	68
Netherlands	14,150	16,300	17,224	18	14	1.7	5	< 0.5	..	..	..	..	99 c	90 c
Norway	4,086	4,570	4,913	19	15	1.8	4	< 0.5	..	..	..	..	100 c	95 c
Poland	35,574	38,516	36,680	16	13	1.3	9	15	..	..	..	..	98	91 c
Portugal	9,766	10,080	9,721	17	16	1.5	6	< 0.5	..	..	..	..	..	85 c
Romania	22,201	22,228	20,328	16	14	1.3	21	8	..	..	97	98	93 c	80 c
Russian Federation	138,660	141,553	119,713	14	14	1.1	21	96	< 0.5	330	100	100	..	..
Serbia and Montenegro	9,522	10,513	10,094	18	14	1.7	19	297	9	250	..	..	75 c	..
Slovakia	4,976	5,411	5,344	17	12	1.3	9	1	..	..	100	100	87	87
Slovenia	1,832	1,979	1,814	14	15	1.1	5	1	..	..	100	100	93 c	96 c
Spain	37,542	41,184	39,951	14	17	1.2	6	< 0.5	..	..	..	..	100	94
Sweden	8,310	8,895	9,033	17	18	1.6	3	< 0.5	..	..	..	..	100	99
Switzerland	6,319	7,157	6,655	15	17	1.4	6	< 0.5	..	..	..	..	99 c	88 c
Ukraine	50,044	47,782	38,925	15	16	1.2	20	94	..	..	100	100	82	91
United Kingdom	55,530	59,598	64,183	18	16	1.6	7	< 0.5	..	..	..	..	100 c	95 c
Middle East & N. Africa	246,845	448,715	667,291	34	4	3.3	58 e	3,488	705	..	70	85	..	..
Afghanistan	15,117	25,971	49,987	43	3	6.8	257	2,136	646	180-300	..	..	..	..
Algeria	18,740	32,877	44,120	31	4	2.8	49	12	< 0.5	1,000	69	90	95	62
Egypt	43,915	74,878	109,111	34	5	3.3	39	6	..	..	56	73	90	81
Iran, Islamic Rep	39,343	70,675	94,441	30	5	2.3	41	132	4	..	..	..	87	..
Iraq	12,962	26,555	45,338	40	3	4.8	125	368	55	900	..	..	91 d	33 d
Israel	3,764	6,685	8,970	27	10	2.7	6	1	..	150-300	95	100	100	89
Jordan	2,225	5,750	8,643	37	3	3.6	33	1	..	..	91	99	91	80
Kuwait	1,375	2,671	4,198	25	2	2.7	10	1	..	..	83	93	85	77
Lebanon	2,669	3,761	4,692	28	6	2.2	32	25	..	300	..	..	90	..
Libyan Arab Jamahiriya	3,043	5,768	8,123	30	4	3.0	19	2	..	..	82	97	..	..
Morocco	19,382	31,564	42,505	30	5	2.8	43	< 0.5	..	..	51	70	88	31 d
Oman	1,187	3,020	5,223	37	2	5.0	13	< 0.5	< 0.5	..	74	99	75	68
Saudi Arabia	9,604	25,626	43,193	38	3	4.5	28	< 0.5	..	..	78	94	59	53
Syrian Arab Rep	8,959	18,650	28,750	36	3	3.3	28	20	..	200-500	83	95	98	39
Tunisia	6,469	10,042	12,351	26	6	2.0	26	3	..	..	73	94	97	68
Turkey	46,132	73,302	91,920	29	6	2.4	41	186	< 0.5	>1,000	87	96	88	..
United Arab Emirates	1,015	3,106	4,056	24	2	2.8	9	< 0.5	..	..	77	91	81	72
Yemen	8,140	21,480	50,584	48	2	7.0	114	2	< 0.5	..	49	68	67 c	35 d

For more information, please visit http://earthtrends.wri.org/datatables/population

	Total Population Estimates and Projections (thousands of people) [a]			Percent of Population in Specific Age Groups 2005		Estimated Total Fertility Rate [a] (children per woman)	Estimated Mortality Under Age 5 (per 1000 live births)	Refugees [b] (thousands)		Internally Displaced Persons (thousands)	Estimated Literacy Rate 2004 (percent)		Net School Enrollment (percent)	
	1980	2005	2030	Under 15	65 & Over	2000-2005	2002	Granted Asylum Elsewhere 2003	Repatri-ations 2003	2004	Adults Over Age 15	Youths Ages 15-24	Primary 2001-2002	Secondary
Sub-Saharan Africa	377,926	732,512	1,181,279	44	3	5.4	174 e	3,306	345	..	62	77	..	..
Angola	7,048	14,533	28,588	48	3	7.2	260	324	133	450	..	..	30 d	..
Benin	3,459	7,103	12,091	45	3	5.7	156	< 0.5	..	..	40	56	71 d	20 c
Botswana	987	1,801	1,562	39	3	3.7	110	< 0.5	..	..	79	89	81	55 c
Burkina Faso	6,820	13,798	27,910	49	3	6.7	207	1	..	..	13	19	35	8 c
Burundi	4,130	7,319	13,652	45	3	6.8	190	532	82	381	50	66	53	8
Cameroon	8,754	16,564	21,760	41	4	4.6	166	6	< 0.5	..	68	..	..	..
Central African Rep	2,306	3,962	5,475	43	4	4.9	180	35	5	200	49	59	..	..
Chad	4,505	9,117	17,722	47	3	6.7	200	52	1	..	46	70	58	8 d
Congo	1,804	3,921	7,558	47	3	6.3	108	29	2	100	83	98	..	..
Congo, Dem Rep	27,909	56,079	106,988	47	3	6.7	205	453	3	3,400	..	..	..	..
Côte d'Ivoire	8,427	17,165	23,258	40	3	4.7	191	34	17	500-800	..	60	63	..
Equatorial Guinea	219	521	888	44	4	5.9	152	1	< 0.5	..	85	..	85	26 d
Eritrea	2,381	4,456	7,942	45	2	5.4	89	124	10	59	..	..	43	21
Ethiopia	35,688	74,189	127,220	45	3	6.1	171	63	< 0.5	132	42	57	46	15
Gabon	695	1,375	2,044	40	4	4.0	91	< 0.5	..	..	..	..	78 c	..
Gambia	652	1,499	2,338	40	4	4.7	126	1	..	..	..	..	73	28
Ghana	11,043	21,833	32,648	39	3	4.1	97	16	..	..	74	92	60	32
Guinea	4,688	8,788	14,921	44	3	5.8	165	4	..	100	..	..	61	..
Guinea-Bissau	793	1,584	3,154	47	3	7.1	211	1	..	..	..	..	45 d	..
Kenya	16,368	32,849	41,141	40	3	4.0	122	3	< 0.5	350	84	96	70	24
Lesotho	1,277	1,797	1,555	39	5	3.8	87	< 0.5	..	..	81	..	84	22
Liberia	1,869	3,603	6,830	47	2	6.8	235	353	21	500	56	71	70 d	..
Madagascar	9,048	18,409	33,464	44	3	5.7	135	< 0.5	..	..	..	..	69	..
Malawi	6,183	12,572	19,834	47	4	6.1	182	< 0.5	..	..	62	73	81	29
Mali	7,044	13,829	29,572	49	2	7.0	222	< 0.5	..	..	19	24	..	..
Mauritania	1,609	3,069	5,482	43	3	5.8	183	31	..	..	41	50	67	15
Mozambique	12,084	19,495	26,620	44	3	5.6	205	< 0.5	..	..	47	63	60	11
Namibia	1,018	2,032	2,418	43	4	4.6	67	1	< 0.5	..	83	92	78	38
Niger	5,586	12,873	30,337	50	2	8.0	264	1	..	..	17	25	34	5
Nigeria	64,325	130,236	206,696	44	3	5.4	201	24	< 0.5	250	67	89	..	..
Rwanda	5,157	8,607	13,453	45	3	5.7	203	75	23	..	69	85	84	..
Senegal	5,538	10,587	16,926	42	2	5.0	138	8	< 0.5	5	39	53	58	..
Sierra Leone	3,239	5,340	8,206	44	3	6.5	284	71	33	..	..	..	..	..
Somalia	6,487	10,742	24,407	48	2	7.3	225	402	10	375	..	..	..	..
South Africa	29,140	45,323	42,170	32	4	2.6	65	< 0.5	..	..	86	92	90	62 c
Sudan	19,387	35,040	50,525	39	4	4.4	94	606	< 0.5	4,000	60	79	46 d	..
Tanzania, United Rep	18,838	38,365	56,903	44	2	5.1	165	1	< 0.5	..	77	92	54	..
Togo	2,519	5,129	8,117	43	3	5.3	141	11	< 0.5	..	60	77	92	..
Uganda	12,465	27,623	63,953	50	2	7.1	141	35	4	1,600	69	80	..	14 c
Zambia	5,977	11,043	15,224	47	3	5.6	182	< 0.5	< 0.5	..	80	89	66	20
Zimbabwe	7,226	12,963	12,773	42	4	3.9	123	7	..	100-200	90	98	83	40
North America	256,068	332,156	407,530	21	12	2.0	..	< 0.5	..	..	..	..	..	..
Canada	24,516	31,972	36,980	17	13	1.5	7	< 0.5	..	..	..	..	100 c	98 c
United States	231,428	300,038	370,396	21	12	2.1	8	< 0.5	..	..	..	..	93	85
C. America & Caribbean	119,135	186,222	239,093	32	6	2.7	34 e	43	< 0.5	..	86	93	..	..
Belize	144	266	373	36	4	3.2	40	< 0.5	..	..	77	84	96 c	60 c
Costa Rica	2,347	4,327	5,872	28	6	2.3	11	< 0.5	..	..	96	98	91	51
Cuba	9,710	11,353	11,338	19	11	1.6	9	16	..	..	97	100	96	83
Dominican Rep	5,696	8,998	11,290	31	5	2.7	38	< 0.5	..	..	84	92	97	41
El Salvador	4,586	6,709	8,802	34	5	2.9	39	6	< 0.5	..	80	89	89	46
Guatemala	6,820	12,978	21,002	42	4	4.4	49	7	< 0.5	250	70	80	85	29
Haiti	5,453	8,549	11,094	37	4	4.0	123	8	< 0.5	..	52	66	..	..
Honduras	3,568	7,257	10,715	39	4	3.7	42	1	< 0.5	..	80	89	87	..
Jamaica	2,133	2,701	3,380	30	7	2.4	20	< 0.5	..	..	88	95	95	75
Mexico	67,569	106,385	133,591	31	5	2.5	29	2	..	10-12	91	97	99	60
Nicaragua	2,919	5,727	8,929	41	3	3.8	41	4	< 0.5	..	77	86	82	37
Panama	1,949	3,235	4,514	30	6	2.7	25	< 0.5	< 0.5	..	92	97	99	62
Trinidad and Tobago	1,082	1,311	1,327	21	7	1.6	20	< 0.5	..	..	99	100	94	..
South America	242,247	372,042	471,942	29	6	2.5	34 e	48	< 0.5	..	89	96	..	..
Argentina	28,094	39,311	48,611	27	10	2.4	19	1	..	..	97	99	100	81
Bolivia	5,355	9,138	13,275	38	5	3.8	71	< 0.5	< 0.5	..	87	97	94	67 c
Brazil	121,614	182,798	222,078	27	6	2.2	37	< 0.5	..	..	86	94	97	72
Chile	11,147	16,185	20,311	27	8	2.4	12	2	< 0.5	..	96	99	89 c	75 c
Colombia	28,447	45,600	60,843	31	5	2.6	23	38	< 0.5	3,100 d	92	97	87	54
Ecuador	7,961	13,379	17,335	32	5	2.8	29	1	..	..	91	96	99	50
Guyana	761	768	695	29	5	2.3	72	< 0.5	..	..	..	..	98 d	75 c
Paraguay	3,114	6,160	9,890	38	4	3.8	30	< 0.5	..	..	92	96	92	50
Peru	17,324	27,968	37,170	32	5	2.9	39	6	< 0.5	60	85	97	100	66 c
Suriname	355	442	489	30	6	2.5	40	< 0.5	..	..	..	..	97	63
Uruguay	2,914	3,463	3,958	24	13	2.3	15	< 0.5	..	..	98	99	90	72
Venezuela	15,091	26,640	36,991	32	5	2.7	22	1	..	..	93	98	92	57
Oceania	22,808	32,969	41,437	24	10	2.3	..	1	..	..	..	..	..	..
Australia	14,569	20,092	23,833	19	13	1.7	6	< 0.5	..	..	..	..	96	88
Fiji	634	854	982	32	4	2.9	21	1	..	..	93	99	100	76
New Zealand	3,113	3,932	4,457	22	12	2.0	6	< 0.5	..	..	..	..	98	92 c
Papua New Guinea	3,241	5,959	9,075	40	2	4.1	94	< 0.5	..	..	..	..	77	23
Solomon Islands	229	504	850	42	3	4.4	24	< 0.5	..	0.35	..	..	..	..
Developed	1,171,410	1,336,153	1,383,167	18	14	1.6	8 e	1,455	36	..	98	..	..	..
Developing	3,272,787	5,127,115	6,755,472	31	5	2.9	89 e	7,865	1,059	..	75	88	..	..

a. Medium variant population projections; please consult the technical notes for more information. b. Refugees are classified by their country of origin. "Granted asylum elsewhere" refers only to people who have been granted asylum outside of their home country. c. Data are from the 2000-2001 school year. d. Data are from the 1999-2000 school year. e. Regional totals are calculated by UNICEF and combine South America, Central America and the Caribbean; a list of countries classified in each region is available at http://www.unicef.org/files/Table9.pdf. f. Cumulative total since 1985.

Population and Education: Technical Notes

DEFINITIONS AND METHODOLOGY

Total Population refers to estimates and projections of de facto population as of July 1 of the year indicated.

Percent of Population under Age 15 is the proportion of the total population younger than 15 years of age.

Percent of Population Age 65 and Over is the proportion of the total population 65 years of age and older.

Total Fertility Rate is an estimate of the average number of children a woman would have over the course of her entire life if current age-specific fertility rates remained constant during her reproductive years.

The four variables defined above are estimated by the United Nations Population Division (UNPD) for the years 1950-2000 and forecasted based on the assumptions enumerated below for the years 2001-2050.

Past estimates are calculated using census and survey results from all countries. The UNPD compiles, evaluates, and adjusts these data when necessary. Adjustments incorporate data from civil registrations (in developed countries), population surveys (in developing countries), earlier censuses, and, when necessary, population models based on information from similar countries.

The projections reported here assume medium fertility (the "medium-fertility assumption"). All future population projections are based on estimates of the 2000 base-year population and incorporate the three main components of population growth: fertility, mortality, and migration. *Fertility* is estimated by applying age-specific fertility rates to the projected female population using models based on past trends in fertility to project future declines. *Mortality* is projected on the basis of the models of life expectancy that assume a medium pace of mortality decline. For countries affected by the HIV/AIDS epidemic, mortality rates are predicted using a model developed by the Joint United Nations Program on HIV/AIDS (UNAIDS). *Migration* rates are estimated on the basis of past international migration estimates and an assessment of the policy stance of countries with regard to future international migration flows. The UNPD incorporates information on official immigration and emigration, labor migration, undocumented migration, and refugees.

For more information on methodology, see *World Population Prospects,* 2002 Revision. Volume III: Analytical Report. Online at http://www.un.org/esa/population/publications/wpp2002/WPP2002_Vol3.htm.

Mortality under Age 5 is the probability of a child dying between birth and age five expressed per 1,000 live births. Data for estimating mortality of children under age 5 is typically obtained from population census information, civil registration records on deaths of young children, United Nations Childrens' Fund (UNICEF) Multiple Indicator Cluster Surveys (MICS) and Demographic and Health Surveys (DHS). For each country, UNICEF and its partners plotted all data from 1960 to the present on a graph; a curve was fitted through these data using a weighted least-squares regression model.

Refugees Granted Asylum Elsewhere is the number of refugees leaving a country who have been granted asylum status by a foreign government.

Refugees Repatriations is the number of refugees who have successfully returned (repatriated) to their home country.

In both columns, refugees are counted according to their home countries ("country of origin"), not their country of asylum. Data were collected in 2003 but include all persons that have migrated as refugees without returning to their home country. According to Article 1 of the 1951 Convention Relating to the Status of Refugees and the related 1967 Protocol, a refugee is a person who "owing to a well-founded fear of being persecuted for reasons of race, religion, nationality, membership of a particular social group or political opinion, is outside the country

of his nationality and is unable to or, owing to such fear, is unwilling to avail himself of the protection of that country." This variable reflects the number of refugees recognized by the United Nations High Commissioner for Refugees (UNHCR), which generally relies on host government reporting to obtain data, supplemented with information collected by aid workers.

Internally Displaced Persons (IDPs) are defined by the United Nations as "persons or groups of persons who have been forced or obliged to flee or to leave their homes or places of habitual residence, in particular as a result of or in order to avoid the effects of armed conflict, situations of generalized violence, violations of human rights or natural or human-made disasters, and who have not crossed an internationally recognized State border." The UNHCR estimates that globally there are 25 million internally displaced people in over 50 countries. Since they have not crossed into another country, IDPs are generally not afforded the same protections and assistance given to refugees. Estimates are from the Global IDP Project and incorporate a wide variety of sources, including non-governmental organizations (NGOs), academic research, governments, and news agencies.

Literacy Rates measure the proportion of the population in a specific age group who can both read and write with understanding a short, simple statement on their everyday life. **Adult Literacy Rates** refer to all residents of a country or region over the age of 15; **Youth Literacy Rates** evaluate the population of a country between the ages of 15 and 24 in the year specified. Youth literacy rates are increasingly used to gauge the impact of primary education as well as the speed with which illiteracy can be eradicated.

Most literacy data are collected during national population censuses and supplemented by household surveys, labor force surveys, employment surveys, industry surveys, and agricultural surveys when they are available. UNESCO uses these data to graph a logistic regression model. When census and survey data are not available, literacy rates for a specific country are estimated based on neighboring countries with similar characteristics.

Net School Enrollment Ratio (NER) is defined as the enrollment of the official age group for a given level of education expressed as a percentage of the population from the same age group. The theoretical maximum value is 100 percent. A high NER denotes a high degree of participation of the official school-age population. If the NER is below 100 percent, users should not assume that the remaining school-age population is not enrolled in any school; they could be enrolled in school at other grade levels. **Primary Education** is defined by the International Standard Classification of Education (ISCED) as the "beginning of systematic apprenticeship of reading, writing and mathematics." Programs are typically six years long and represent the beginning of compulsory education in many countries. **Secondary education** follows primary education, and is characterized as being subject-oriented with specialized fields of learning. Students achieve a full implementation of basic skills. Programs may be academic, vocational, or technical in nature.

Net enrollment ratio is calculated by dividing the number of pupils enrolled who are of the official age group for a given level of education by the total population of the same age group. National governments provide the United Nations Educational, Scientific, and Cultural Organization (UNESCO) with enrollment data based on a series of electronic questionnaires. When data from national governments are not available or are of inferior quality, UNESCO will estimate enrollment ratios from background data, if available.

FREQUENCY OF UPDATE BY DATA PROVIDERS

UNPD publishes country-level statistics every two years with annual revisions of key estimates. UNICEF and UNHCR publish the most recently available data in an annual report, with more frequent updates online. Education, literacy and IDP data are updated irregularly. Most updates include revisions of past data.

DATA RELIABILITY AND CAUTIONARY NOTES

Total Population, Fertility, and Life Expectancy: Since demographic parameters are estimated on a country-by-country basis, reliability varies among countries. For some developing countries, estimates are derived from surveys rather than censuses, especially when countries lack a civil registration system or have one that does not achieve full coverage of all vital events. Also, for developing countries the availability of detailed information on fertility and mortality is limited and the data on international migration flows are generally inadequate. Although estimates are based on incomplete data and projections cannot factor in unforeseen events (i.e., famine, wars), U.N. demographic models are widely accepted and use well-understood principles, which make these data as comparable, consistent across countries, and reliable as possible.

Mortality Under Age 5: Estimates were calculated based on a wide variety of sources of disparate quality. For information on the underlying data for each country's regressions, refer to the country estimates and new country data available from UNICEF online at http://www.childinfo.org/cmr/kh98meth.html.

Refugees: Since the determination of refugee status varies among countries, UNHCR will estimate numbers in order to provide a normalized dataset. Data are "provisional and subject to change," and accuracy is limited by the politically sensitive nature of refugee estimates and the circumstances under which many refugees live. UNHCR attempts to harmonize the data in order to allow cross-country comparisons.

Internally Displaced Persons: Due to the highly political nature of displacement and the conditions in which many displaced peoples find themselves, accurate data are difficult to collect. While the numbers presented are broad estimates, these data are the best online on the topic.

Adult Literacy Rate: The availability and quality of national statistics on literacy vary widely. National census and survey data are typically collected only once every decade. In addition, many industrialized countries have stopped collecting literacy data in recent years, based on the sometimes incorrect assumption that universal primary education means universal literacy. When census and survey data are not available for a particular country, estimates are sometimes made based on neighboring countries. Actual definitions of adult literacy are not strictly comparable among countries. Some countries equate persons with no schooling with illiterates, or change definitions between censuses. In addition, UNESCO's definition of literacy does not include people who, though familiar with the basics of reading and writing, do not have the skills to function at a reasonable level in their own society.

Net School Enrollment: Even though UNESCO has applied the same methodology to analyze all of the country data, definitions of "schooling" and "enrollment" are not strictly comparable among countries. As net enrollment ratios approach 100 percent, inconsistencies with enrollment and/or population data are more likely to skew the resulting ratios. As a result, some net enrollment ratios are greater than 100 percent. Difficulties also arise when a substantial proportion of students begin school earlier than the prescribed age, or when the reference date for entry into primary education does not coincide with the birthdays of all eligible students.

SOURCES

Total Population, Population by Age Group, and Fertility Rates: United Nations Population Division. 2003. *World Population Prospects: The 2002 Revision.* Dataset on CD-ROM. New York: United Nations. Online at http://www.un.org/esa/population/ordering.htm.

Mortality under Age 5: United Nations Children's Fund (UNICEF). 2004. *State of the World's Children: Girls, Education, and Development.* New York: UNICEF. Online at http://www.unicef.org/sowc04/.

Net Refugee Migration: United Nations High Commissioner for Refugees (UNHCR). 2004. *Global Refugee Trends: Overview of Refugee Populations, New Arrivals, Durable Solutions, Asylum-Seekers and Other Persons of Concern to UNHCR.* Geneva: UNHCR. Online at http://www.unhcr.ch/statistics.

Internally Displaced Persons: Global IDP Project. 2004. *Internal Displacement: A Global Overview of Trends and Developments in 2003.* Geneva: Norwegian Refugee Council. Online at http://www.idpproject.org/global_overview.htm.

Adult Literacy Rate: United Nations Educational, Scientific, and Cultural Organization (UNESCO) Institute for Statistics. *Literacy Rates by Country and by Gender,* July, 2004 Revision. Paris: UNESCO. Online at http://www.uis.unesco.org/.

Net School Enrollment: United Nations Educational Scientific, and Cultural Organization (UNESCO) Institute for Statistics. 2004. *Statistical Tables: Gross and Net Enrollment Ratios.* Paris: UNESCO. Online at http://www.uis.unesco.org/.

POPULATION AND EDUCATION: TECHNICAL NOTES

2 Human Health

Sources: United Nations Population Division, World Health Organization, United Nations Children's Fund, Joint United Nations Programme on HIV/AIDS

	Life Expectancy at Birth (years)		Physicians Per 100,000 Population 1995-2003	Use of Improved Water Source (percent of population) 2002		Use of Improved Sanitation (percent of population) 2002		Malnutrition in Children Under Age Five (1995-2002)		HIV and AIDS Adults Ages 15-49 Living With HIV or AIDS		ART Use Rate (b) (percent) 2002-2003	Tuberculosis Incidence Rate Per 100,000 Population 2002	Malaria Reported Cases Per 100,000 Population 1998-2001	Malaria Percent of Children Under Age 5 Using Treated Bed Nets 1999-2004	Health Care Expenditures Per Capita ($intl)	
	1980-1985	2000-2005		Urban	Rural	Urban	Rural	Underweight Prevalence	Stunting Prevalence	Percent in 2003	Change Since 2001 (a)					Total Spending (c) 2001	Government Spending 2001
World	61.3	65.4	157 d	95	72	81	37	27	31	1.1	8.5	..	142	..	..	629	349
Asia (excl. Middle East)	61.5	67.7	107	93	75	72	31	31	33	0.4	..	..	152	..	..	230	115
Armenia	72.5	72.4	353	99	80	96	61	3	13	0.1	25.0	0.0	77	2	..	273	112
Azerbaijan	68.4	72.2	354	95	59	73	36	7	13	0.1	..	0.0	82	13	1.4	48	32
Bangladesh	50.0	61.4	23	82	72	75	39	48	45	..	..	0.0	221	40	..	58	26
Bhutan	47.7	63.2	5	86	60	65	70	19	40	..	..	..	118	279	..	64	58
Cambodia	52.1	57.4	16	58	29	53	8	45	45	2.6	6.3	3.0	549	399	..	184	27
China	66.6	71.0	164	92	68	69	29	11	16	0.1	27.7	5.0	113	2	..	224	83
Georgia	70.7	73.6	391	90	61	96	69	3	12	0.1	100.0	8.0	85	8	..	108	41
India	54.9	63.9	51	96	82	58	18	47	46	0.9	31.6	2.0	168	192	0.1	80	14
Indonesia	56.2	66.8	16	89	69	71	38	26	..	0.1	93.0	2.7	256	93	0.1	77	19
Japan	76.9	81.6	201	100	100	100	100	..	..	0.1	0.0	..	33	..	..	2,131	1,660
Kazakhstan	67.0	66.3	330	96	72	87	52	4	10	0.2	59.2	1.0	146	..	..	204	123
Korea, Dem People's Rep	69.1	63.1	297	100	100	58	60	21	42	..	..	..	160	516	..	44	32
Korea, Rep	67.2	75.5	181	97	71	..	..	..	..	0.1	48.2	..	91	5	..	948	421
Kyrgyzstan	65.6	68.6	268	98	66	75	51	11	25	0.1	160.0	0.0	142	1	..	108	53
Lao People's Dem Rep	45.8	54.5	59	66	38	61	14	40	41	0.1	112.5	..	170	498	..	51	28
Malaysia	68.0	73.1	70	96	94	..	98	12	..	0.4	24.4	..	95	56	..	345	185
Mongolia	57.5	63.9	267	87	30	75	37	13	25	0.1	150.0	..	209	..	..	122	88
Myanmar	51.8	57.3	30	95	74	96	63	35	34	1.2	18.5	1.0	154	252	..	26	5
Nepal	49.1	59.9	5	93	82	68	20	48	51	0.5	36.4	..	190	29	..	63	19
Pakistan	53.0	61.0	66	95	87	92	35	38	37	0.1	17.7	2.2	181	55	..	85	21
Philippines	62.1	70.0	116	90	77	81	61	28	30	0.1	107.0	3.5	320	45	..	169	76
Singapore	71.8	78.1	140	100	..	100	..	14	11	0.2	20.6	0.0	43	..	..	993	333
Sri Lanka	67.9	72.6	43	99	72	98	89	29	14	0.1	59.1	2.0	54	348	..	122	60
Tajikistan	65.9	68.8	218	93	47	71	47	..	..	0.1	..	0.0	109	186	1.9	43	12
Thailand	65.0	69.3	30	95	80	97	100	19	16	1.5	(9.7)	4.0	128	100	..	254	145
Turkmenistan	63.2	67.1	317	93	54	77	50	12	22	0.1	..	..	94	0	..	245	180
Uzbekistan	66.6	69.7	289	97	84	73	48	19	31	0.1	266.7	0.0	102	0	..	91	68
Viet Nam	58.7	69.2	53	93	67	84	26	33	36	0.4	33.3	1.0	193	86	15.8	134	38
Europe	72.0	74.5	348	100	..	..	..	..	..	0.5	..	..	51	..	..	1,461	1,089
Albania	70.4	73.7	139	99	95	99	81	14	32	..	..	0.0	28	..	..	150	97
Austria	73.1	78.5	324	100	100	100	100	..	..	0.3	1.0	92.6	15	..	..	2,259	1,565
Belarus	70.7	70.1	450	100	100	..	..	..	..	..	..	< 1.0	83	..	..	464	402
Belgium	73.7	78.8	418	100	..	..	..	..	..	0.2	23.5	93.8	14	..	..	2,481	1,779
Bosnia and Herzegovina	70.7	74.0	134	100	96	99	88	4	10	0.1	..	10.0	60	..	..	268	99
Bulgaria	71.2	70.9	338	100	100	100	100	..	..	0.1	..	44.5	48	..	..	303	249
Croatia	70.5	74.2	237	..	..	..	..	1	1	0.1	..	98.7	47	..	..	726	594
Czech Rep	70.7	75.4	343	..	..	..	..	1	2	0.1	19.0	..	13	..	..	1,129	1,032
Denmark	74.6	76.6	366	100	100	..	..	..	..	0.2	8.7	90.9	13	..	..	2,503	2,062
Estonia	69.6	71.7	316	..	..	93	..	..	..	1.1	54.0	32.0	55	..	..	562	437
Finland	73.9	78.0	311	100	100	100	100	..	..	0.1	25.0	94.6	10	..	..	1,845	1,395
France	74.7	79.0	329	100	..	..	..	..	..	0.4	9.1	..	14	..	..	2,567	1,951
Germany	73.8	78.3	362	100	100	..	..	..	..	0.1	4.9	94.7	10	..	..	2,820	2,112
Greece	75.2	78.3	440	..	..	..	..	..	..	0.2	2.3	..	20	..	..	1,522	852
Hungary	69.1	71.9	316	100	98	100	85	2	3	0.1	..	97.0	32	..	..	914	686
Iceland	76.8	79.8	347	100	100	..	..	..	..	0.2	0.0	87.5	3	..	..	2,643	2,191
Ireland	73.1	77.0	237	100	..	..	..	..	..	0.1	18.2	..	13	..	..	1,935	1,471
Italy	74.5	78.7	606	100	..	..	..	..	..	0.5	7.7	72.7	8	..	..	2,204	1,660
Latvia	69.3	71.0	291	..	..	..	..	..	..	0.6	27.1	51.0	78	..	..	509	267
Lithuania	70.8	72.7	403	..	..	..	..	..	..	0.1	18.2	55.0	66	..	..	478	337
Macedonia, FYR	69.6	73.6	219	..	..	..	..	6	7	0.1	0.0	20.0	42	..	..	331	281
Moldova, Rep	64.8	68.9	269	97	88	86	52	3	10	0.2	..	8.3	155	..	..	112	56
Netherlands	76.0	78.3	329	100	99	100	100	..	..	0.2	11.8	96.0	9	..	..	2,612	1,653
Norway	76.0	78.9	356	100	100	..	..	..	..	0.1	11.1	89.6	6	..	..	2,920	2,497
Poland	70.9	73.9	220	100	..	..	..	..	..	0.1	..	92.9	32	..	..	629	452
Portugal	72.2	76.2	324	..	..	..	..	..	..	0.4	4.8	..	47	..	..	1,618	1,116
Romania	69.7	70.5	189	91	16	86	10	6	8	0.1	..	64.4	148	..	..	460	364
Russian Federation	68.3	66.6	417	99	88	93	70	3	13	1.1	62.3	83.3	126	..	..	454	310
Serbia and Montenegro	70.2	73.2	..	99	86	97	77	2	5	0.2	0.0	26.4	38	..	..	616	488
Slovakia	70.6	73.7	325	100	100	100	100	..	..	0.1	..	95.0	24	..	..	681	608
Slovenia	71.2	76.3	219	..	..	..	..	..	..	0.1	0.0	96.3	21	..	..	1,545	1,157
Spain	75.8	79.3	320	..	..	..	..	..	..	0.7	0.0	92.3	30	..	..	1,607	1,147
Sweden	76.3	80.1	305	100	100	100	100	..	..	0.1	6.1	95.0	5	..	..	2,270	1,934
Switzerland	76.2	79.1	352	100	100	100	100	..	..	0.4	8.3	95.0	8	..	..	3,322	1,897
Ukraine	69.1	69.7	297	100	94	100	97	3	15	1.4	20.0	< 1.0	95	..	..	176	119
United Kingdom	74.0	78.2	166 e	100	..	..	..	..	..	0.2	20.5	92.1	12	..	..	1,989	1,635
Middle East & N. Africa	59.2	67.9	121	94	73	90	51	15	23	0.2	43.8 f	..	65	..	..	302	174
Afghanistan	40.0	43.1	19	19	11	16	5	48	52	..	..	0.0	333	1,621	..	34	18
Algeria	60.5	69.7	85	92	80	99	82	6	18	0.1	32.4	..	52	1	..	169	127
Egypt	56.5	68.8	212	100	97	84	56	11	21	0.1	9.1	..	29	0	..	153	75
Iran, Islamic Rep	59.7	70.3	105	98	83	86	78	11	15	0.1	72.2	100.0	29	32	..	422	184
Iraq	62.3	60.7	54	97	50	95	48	16	22	0.1	..	..	167	5	..	97	31
Israel	74.5	79.2	391	100	100	100	..	..	..	0.1	..	..	10	..	..	1,839	1,273
Jordan	63.7	71.0	205	91	91	94	85	5	8	0.1	0.0	21.3	5	..	..	412	194
Kuwait	71.3	76.6	153	..	..	..	..	10	24	..	..	..	26	..	..	612	482
Lebanon	65.9	73.5	325	100	100	100	87	3	12	0.1	40.0	100.0	14	..	..	673	189
Libyan Arab Jamahiriya	62.2	72.8	129	72	68	97	96	5	15	0.3	..	..	21	..	..	239	134
Morocco	58.3	68.7	48	99	56	83	31	9	24	0.1	..	20.7	114	0	..	199	78
Oman	62.7	72.4	126	81	72	97	61	24	23	0.1	30.0	..	12	24	..	343	277
Saudi Arabia	62.6	72.3	140	97	..	100	..	14	20	..	..	..	42	15	..	591	441
Syrian Arab Rep	62.5	71.9	140	94	64	97	56	7	18	0.1	100.0	..	44	0	..	427	187
Tunisia	64.9	72.8	70	94	60	90	62	4	12	0.1	..	..	23	..	..	463	350
Turkey	62.3	70.5	124	96	87	94	62	8	16	..	..	..	32	16	..	294	209
United Arab Emirates	68.6	74.7	202	..	..	100	100	14	17	..	..	..	18	..	..	921	698
Yemen	49.1	60.0	22	74	68	76	14	46	52	0.1	..	..	92	7,600	..	69	24

For more information, please visit http://earthtrends.wri.org/datatables/population

	Life Expectancy at Birth (years) 1980-1985	Life Expectancy at Birth (years) 2000-2005	Physicians Per 100,000 Population 1995-2003	Use of Improved Water Source (percent of population) 2002 Urban	Use of Improved Water Source (percent of population) 2002 Rural	Use of Improved Sanitation (percent of population) 2002 Urban	Use of Improved Sanitation (percent of population) 2002 Rural	Malnutrition Underweight Prevalence	Malnutrition Stunting Prevalence	HIV Adults Ages 15-49 Percent in 2003	HIV Change Since 2001 (a)	ART Use Rate (b) 2002-2003	Tuberculosis Incidence Rate Per 100,000 Population 2002	Malaria Reported Cases Per 100,000 Population 1998-2001	Malaria Percent of Children Under Age 5 Using Treated Bed Nets 1999-2004	Health Care Total Spending (c) 2001	Health Care Government Spending 2001
Sub-Saharan Africa	48.5	46.6	15	82	46	55	26	30	39	7.5	5.0 f	..	359	..	3.2 g	85	36
Angola	40.0	40.1	8	70	40	56	16	31	45	3.9	10.0	< 1.0	336	6,594	2.3	70	44
Benin	49.2	50.6	6	79	60	58	12	23	31	1.9	5.1	2.5	86	11,545	7.4	39	18
Botswana	62.8	39.7	29	100	90	57	25	13	23	37.3	0.0	7.9	657	2,836	..	381	252
Burkina Faso	46.1	45.7	4	82	44	45	5	34	37	4.2	8.0	1.4	157	619	6.5	27	16
Burundi	46.6	40.9	5	90	78	47	35	45	57	6.0	0.0	1.9	359	43,505	1.3	19	11
Cameroon	50.7	46.2	7	84	41	63	33	21	35	6.9	4.0	1.5	188	2,900	1.3	42	16
Central African Rep	46.5	39.5	4	93	61	47	12	24	39	13.5	4.3	< 1.0	338	..	1.5	58	30
Chad	42.3	44.7	3	40	32	30	..	28	29	4.8	5.9	..	222	4,683	0.6	17	13
Congo	56.8	48.2	25	72	17	14	2	14	19	4.9	0.0	..	395	5,880	..	22	14
Congo, Dem Rep	47.1	41.8	7	83	..	43	23	31	38	4.2	5.3	0.0	384	1,414	0.7	12	5
Côte d'Ivoire	50.0	41.0	9	..	..	61	23	21	25	7.0	10.4	2.7	412	2,449	1.1	127	20
Equatorial Guinea	43.8	49.1	25	45	42	60	46	19	39	..	..	6.8	191	..	0.7	106	64
Eritrea	43.3	52.7	3	72	54	34	3	44	38	2.7	0.0	< 1.0	268	5,648	4.2	36	23
Ethiopia	42.7	45.5	3	81	11	19	4	47	52	4.4	16.7	< 1.0	370	621	..	14	6
Gabon	56.3	56.6	29	95	47	37	30	12	21	8.1	21.6	..	248	2,148	..	197	94
Gambia	44.1	54.1	4	95	77	72	46	17	19	1.2	0.0	6.3	230	10,096	14.7	78	39
Ghana	53.6	57.9	9	93	68	74	46	25	26	3.1	3.2	1.8	211	17,143	4.5	60	36
Guinea	40.2	49.1	9	78	38	25	6	23	26	3.2	30.0	..	215	75,386	..	61	33
Guinea-Bissau	39.1	45.3	17	79	49	57	23	25	30	..	..	..	196	2,421	7.4	37	20
Kenya	55.7	44.6	13	89	46	56	43	21	35	6.7	(8.3)	3.0	540	545	4.6	114	24
Lesotho	52.0	35.1	5	88	74	61	32	18	46	28.9	0.0	< 1.0	726	..	..	101	80
Liberia	44.9	41.4	2	72	52	49	7	26	39	5.9	20.0	..	247	26,699	..	127	96
Madagascar	48.0	53.6	9	75	34	49	27	33	49	1.7	32.7	..	234	..	0.2	20	13
Malawi	45.7	37.5	5	96	62	66	42	25	49	14.2	5.2	1.8	431	20,080	35.5	39	14
Mali	44.4	48.6	4	76	35	59	38	33	38	1.9	0.0	2.5	334	741	8.4	30	12
Mauritania	47.4	52.5	14	63	45	64	9	32	35	0.6	50.8	..	188	9,724	4.1	45	33
Mozambique	42.8	38.1	2	76	24	51	14	26	44	12.2	9.1	0.0	436	19,842	..	47	32
Namibia	55.2	44.3	30	98	72	66	14	24	24	21.3	5.3	0.0	751	1,502	3.4	342	232
Niger	40.7	46.2	3	80	36	43	4	40	40	1.2	25.5	..	193	1,693	5.8	22	9
Nigeria	48.1	51.5	27	72	49	48	30	36	43	5.4	6.5	1.5	304	30	1.2	31	7
Rwanda	46.1	39.3	2	92	69	56	38	27	41	5.1	4.5	< 1.0	389	6,510	5	44	24
Senegal	46.3	52.9	8	90	54	70	34	23	25	0.8	7.9	< 1.0	242	11,925	1.7	63	37
Sierra Leone	35.3	34.2	7	75	46	53	30	27	34	..	..	0.0	405	8,943	1.5	26	16
Somalia	43.0	47.9	4	32	27	47	14	26	23	..	..	0.0	405	118	0.3	15	7
South Africa	57.7	47.7	69	98	73	86	44	12	25	21.5	6.3	..	558	61	..	652	270
Sudan	49.1	55.6	16	78	64	50	24	17	..	2.3	26.7	< 1.0	217	12,530	0.4	39	7
Tanzania, United Rep	51.0	43.3	2	92	62	54	41	29	44	8.8	7.1	< 1.0	363	1,207	2.1	26	12
Togo	50.2	49.7	6	80	36	71	15	25	22	4.1	2.1	..	361	9,273	2	45	22
Uganda	47.2	46.2	5	87	52	53	39	23	39	4.1	(13.5)	6.3	377	46	0.2	57	33
Zambia	52.0	32.4	7	90	36	68	32	28	47	16.5	3.8	0.0	668	18,877	6.5	52	28
Zimbabwe	59.6	33.1	6	100	74	69	51	13	27	24.6	0.0	0.0	683	5,410	..	142	64
North America	74.2	77.3	516	100	100	100	100	1	2	0.6	5.3 f	..	5	..	..	4,683	2,151
Canada	75.9	79.3	209	100	99	100	99	..	..	0.3	14.6	..	6	..	..	2,792	1,977
United States	74.0	77.1	549	100	100	100	100	1	2	0.6	5.6	..	5	..	..	4,887	2,170
C. America & Caribbean	66.1	71.5	181	97	76	87	47	10	20	0.8	9.8	..	54	..	..	428	202
Belize	71.2	71.4	105	100	82	71	25	6	..	2.4	25.0	7.7	55	475	..	278	125
Costa Rica	73.5	78.1	173	100	92	89	97	5	6	0.6	9.1	..	15	33	..	562	385
Cuba	73.4	76.7	591	95	78	99	95	4	5	0.1	3.1	..	12	..	..	229	197
Dominican Rep	62.8	66.7	188	98	85	67	43	5	6	1.7	(2.3)	0.0	95	12	..	353	127
El Salvador	56.6	70.7	124	91	68	78	40	12	23	0.7	16.7	..	60	6	..	376	176
Guatemala	58.0	65.8	90	99	92	72	52	24	46	1.1	13.8	46.0	77	307	1.2	199	96
Haiti	51.8	49.5	25	91	59	52	23	17	23	5.6	8.3	..	319	119	..	56	30
Honduras	60.8	68.9	83	99	82	89	52	17	29	1.8	22.9	< 1.0	86	365	..	153	81
Jamaica	71.2	75.7	85	98	87	90	68	6	6	1.2	50.0	< 1.0	8	..	..	253	107
Mexico	67.5	73.4	171	97	72	90	39	8	18	0.3	6.7	92.0	33	5	..	544	241
Nicaragua	59.3	69.5	164	93	65	78	51	10	20	0.2	12.7	0.0	64	201	..	158	77
Panama	70.5	74.7	168	99	79	89	51	7	14	0.9	36.4	..	47	32	..	458	316
Trinidad and Tobago	70.2	71.3	79	92	88	100	100	7	5	3.2	7.7	< 1.0	13	..	..	388	168
South America	64.8	70.2	190	95	64	83	42	6	14	0.6	14.8	..	72	..	..	551	264
Argentina	70.0	74.2	301	97	..	..	..	5	12	0.7	0.0	91.2	46	1	..	1,130	603
Bolivia	53.9	63.9	73	95	68	58	23	10	26	0.1	20.0	< 1.0	234	185	..	125	83
Brazil	63.0	68.1	206	96	58	83	35	6	11	0.7	4.8	100.0	62	225	..	573	238
Chile	70.6	76.1	109	100	59	96	64	1	2	0.3	4.0	..	18	..	..	792	348
Colombia	66.6	72.2	135	99	71	96	54	7	14	0.7	50.0	..	45	482	0.7	356	234
Ecuador	64.3	70.8	148	92	77	80	59	15	27	0.3	5.3	..	137	846	..	177	89
Guyana	61.0	63.2	48	83	83	86	60	14	11	2.5	0.0	0.0	115	3,554	5.5	215	172
Paraguay	67.1	70.9	117	100	62	94	58	5	11	0.5	50.0	50.0	70	48	..	332	127
Peru	61.4	69.8	117	87	66	72	33	7	25	0.5	56.9	19.2	202	305	..	231	127
Suriname	67.1	71.1	45	98	73	99	76	13	10	1.7	25.0	..	68	4,075	2.7	398	240
Uruguay	70.8	75.3	365	98	93	95	85	5	8	0.3	5.5	50.5	29	..	..	971	450
Venezuela	68.6	73.7	194	85	70	71	48	5	13	0.7	40.8	..	42	81	..	386	240
Oceania	70.4	74.6	189	99	52		57	..	..	0.2	29.2 f	..	55	..	..	1,851	1,283
Australia	75.2	79.2	249	100	100	100	100	..	..	0.1	16.7	53.2	6	..	..	2,532	1,719
Fiji	64.7	69.8	34	..	..	99	98	8	3	0.1	20.0	..	30	..	..	224	150
New Zealand	73.7	78.3	223	100	..	..	..	..	..	0.1	16.7	..	11	..	..	1,724	1,324
Papua New Guinea	49.7	57.6	5	88	32	67	41	35	..	0.6	60.0	0.0	254	1,793	..	144	128
Solomon Islands	60.6	69.2	13	94	65	98	18	21	27	..	..	..	91	16,512	..	133	124
Developed	72.4	74.8	361	100	94	100	92 h	..	..	..	..	..	57	..	..	2,221	1,328
Developing	59.6	64.9	99	92	70	73	31	28	32	..	..	..	164	..	..	192	80

a. Measures the percent change in the total number of adults with HIV/AIDS between 2001 and 2003. b. The percent of adults with advanced HIV infection receiving antiretroviral therapy (ART).
c. Includes both personal (private) and government (public) spending on health care. d. Calculated by WRI. e. Data are from 1993. f. Regional totals were calculated by UNAIDS.
g. Calculated by UNICEF. h. Developed country estimates for urban and rural water and sanitation coverage were calculated by WHO.

Human Health: Technical Notes

DEFINITIONS AND METHODOLOGY

Life Expectancy at Birth is the average number of years that a newborn baby is expected to live if the age-specific mortality rates effective at the year of birth apply throughout his or her lifetime.

Physicians per 100,000 Population indicates the density of doctors in a country. "Physician" includes graduates of a faculty or school of medicine who are working in any medical field (including teaching, research, and practice).

Improved Water Source includes any of the following types of drinking water sources: household connections, public standpipes, boreholes, protected dug wells, protected springs, and rainwater collection. To be counted, at least 20 liters per person per day of improved water must be available within one kilometer of a user's dwelling. Examples of unimproved water sources include unprotected wells and springs, vendor-provided water, tanker-provided water, and bottled water. These last examples are considered "unimproved" because they are not consistently available in sufficient quantities. **Improved Sanitation** includes any of the following excreta disposal facilities: connection to a public sewer, connection to a septic tank, pour-flush latrine, simple pit latrine, and ventilated improved pit latrine. Examples of an unimproved sanitation system include open pit latrines, public or shared latrines, and service or bucket latrines.

Data were collected from assessment questionnaires and household surveys and plotted on a graph for each country to show coverage in available years (not necessarily 2002). A trend line was drawn and reviewed by a panel of experts from WHO and UNICEF to determine the level of sanitation and water available in 2002.

Underweight Prevalence, an indicator of malnutrition, refers to the proportion of children under five years of age whose weight-for-age is more than two standard deviations (for moderate underweight) or more than three standard deviations (for severe underweight) below the median weight-for-age of a reference population. **Stunting prevalence,** an indicator of chronic malnutrition, refers to the percentage of children under five whose height-for-age is more than two (moderate stunting) and three (severe stunting) standard deviations from the median of the reference population.

Malnutrition data were obtained from Multiple Indicator Cluster Surveys (MICS), Demographic and Health Surveys (DHS), and other national-level surveys. Where possible, only comprehensive or representative national data have been used.

Adults Ages 15-49 Living With HIV or AIDS is the estimated percentage of people aged 15-49 living with HIV/AIDS. **Change Since 2001** measures the percent change in the total population infected with AIDS or HIV between 2001 and 2003. These estimates include all people with HIV infection, whether or not they have developed symptoms of AIDS, who are alive at the end of the year specified. Data for this age group capture those in their most sexually active years. Measuring infection within this age range also allows greater comparability for populations with different age structures. Estimates for a single point in time and the starting date of the epidemic were used to plot an epidemic curve charting the spread of HIV in a particular country.

Antiretroviral Therapy (ART) Use Rate is the estimated percentage of adults with advanced HIV infection receiving antiretroviral therapy. This therapy can dramatically reduce HIV-related mortality and improve the quality of life of those infected. The estimated number of people receiving treatment is determined by national program-monitoring reports or estimates from local WHO offices. The number of adults with advanced HIV infection is estimated by the Joint United Nations Programme on HIV/AIDS (UNAIDS) to be 15 percent of the total number of infected adults.

Tuberculosis Incidence Rate is the estimated number of new tuberculosis (TB) cases per 100,000 people in the year specified. The estimates include all cases (pulmonary, smear positive, and extrapulmonary). If left untreated, each person with an infectious case of TB will infect 10-15 people every year. It is estimated that TB caused 2 million deaths in 2002 and is now the leading cause of death in people infected with HIV. Data are collected by country using a standard collection form. Initial estimates are derived using surveys of the prevalence of infection and are then refined using a consultative and analytical process involving a panel of epidemiological experts at WHO.

Reported Malaria Cases is the total number of malaria cases reported to the WHO by countries in which malaria is endemic. Most countries report only laboratory confirmed cases, but some countries in Sub-Saharan Africa report clinically diagnosed cases as well. Transmitted to humans by the bite of an infected mosquito, malaria is one of the world's prevalent health crises, killing more than one million people annually. Data on malaria are collected from a variety of surveys, including Routine Health Information Systems (HIS), MICS, DHS, Demographic Surveillance Sites (DSS), and Rolling Back Malaria (RBM) baseline surveys.

Percent of Children Under Age Five Using Treated Bed Nets is the percent of children under age five in each country that sleep under a net treated with an insecticide to ward off mosquitoes, a powerful method of preventing malaria infections. According to UNICEF, the majority of deaths from malaria occur in children under age 5. Data are obtained by UNICEF from DHS, MICS, and other national surveys.

Health Care Spending per Capita is defined as the sum of government and private expenditures on health, expressed on a per-person basis. The estimates are provided in international dollars, which minimizes the consequences of differing price levels among countries. **Government Health Spending** includes all public outlays reserved for the enhancement of the health status of the population and/or the distribution of medical care. Expenditures by all levels of government (national, regional, and local), extrabudgetary agencies, and external resources such as grants are included. The estimates for extrabudgetary expenditure on health include purchase of health goods and services by schemes that are compulsory and government-controlled. **Private Health Spending** is the sum of expenditures by prepaid plans and risk-pooling arrangements, public and private enterprises for medical care and health-enhancing benefits (outside of payment to social security), nonprofit institutions that primarily serve households, and household out-of-pocket spending.

Per capita totals were calculated by WHO using population estimates from the Organization for Economic Co-operation and Development (OECD) and the United Nations Population Division.

Information on government health expenditures are obtained from the OECD, the International Monetary Fund (IMF), national health-accounts reports, government finance data, statistical yearbooks, and public-finance reports. Information for private health expenditures are obtained from national health-accounts reports, statistical yearbooks and other periodicals, official web sites, reports from non-governmental organizations, household surveys, academic studies, government ministries, and professional and trade associations.

FREQUENCY OF UPDATE BY DATA PROVIDERS

Both the UN Population Division and the Joint United Nations Program on HIV/AIDS (UNAIDS) publish country-level statistics every two years with annual revisions of key estimates. UNICEF publishes the most recent available data each year. WHO publishes country-level statistics annually and updates the *Global Atlas of Infectious Diseases* database as new information becomes available.

DATA RELIABILITY AND CAUTIONARY NOTES

Life Expectancy: The United Nations Population Division (UNPD) estimates demographic parameters on a country-by-country basis, so data reliability varies among countries. In some developing countries, census data are not available or are incomplete, and estimates concerning population trends are derived from surveys. Although estimates are based on incomplete mortality data and projections cannot factor in unforeseen events (e.g., famine, wars), UN demographic models are widely accepted and use well-understood qualities, making these data fairly reliable.

Physicians per 100,000 Population: Data reliability varies by country. Due to out-of-date health personnel records, some countries mistakenly include retired physicians or physicians no longer working in the health sector, resulting in overestimates. Also, this indicator speaks solely of the quantity of physicians, not the quality or accessibility of the personnel. It does not show the difference in urban and rural concentrations. The exact definition of "physician" may vary among countries. Some countries may include interns, physicians that are retraining, and those working in the private sector.

Improved Water Sources and Sanitation: These data have become more reliable as WHO and UNICEF shift from provider-based information (national census estimates) to consumer-based information (survey data). Nonetheless, estimates were calculated based on a wide variety of sources of disparate quality, and comparisons among countries should be made with care. Definitions of urban and rural are not consistent across countries. The assessment does not account for intermittent or poor quality of water supplies. WHO emphasizes that these data measure use of an improved water supply and excreta disposal system, but access to sanitary and safe systems cannot be adequately measured on a global scale.

Malnutrition in Children under Five: The data included for these variables cover a wide range of years and sources. Some data refer to periods other than 1995-2002, measure stunting or percentage underweight in a different age range than 0-5, or were collected for only part of a country. Since data are not available for more affluent countries, the regional totals reported here may be larger than the actual averages.

Adults Ages 15-49 Living with HIV or AIDS: While HIV surveillance systems are generally more extensive than those for other diseases, data reliability still varies on a country-by-country basis. The extent of uncertainty depends primarily on the type of epidemic—infection rates for generalized (high-level) epidemics are calculated differently from rates for concentrated (low-level) epidemics—and on the quality, coverage, and consistency of a country's surveillance system. A detailed description of the methods, software, quality of data, and development of ranges for these data was published in the journal Sexually Transmitted Infections in July 2004.

Antiretroviral Therapy Use Rate: The data have been reviewed by UNAIDS and compared with other sources to consolidate validity. The reliability of the national data presented in national reports is dependent on the quality of information provided by the countries themselves. Some countries have very small or highly localized epidemics, so the rates presented here do not necessarily reflect national commitment and action. This indicator does not distinguish between the different types of therapy available nor does it measure the cost, quality, or effectiveness of the treatment. In certain settings, a system may not yet be in place to collect data from community-based organizations, private prescribers, and pharmacies. The estimated proportion of the total infected population with advanced HIV infection (currently 15 percent) may require revision, as the proportion varies according to the stage of the HIV epidemic and the coverage and effectiveness of ART.

Tuberculosis Incidence Rate: Data are reviewed at all levels of WHO, and WHO headquarters attempts to complete any missing responses and resolve any inconsistencies. The quality of the information provided by a particular country is dependent on the quality of its national surveillance system.

Reported Malaria Cases: Malaria infection-rate data are less accurate than estimates of HIV/AIDS or tuberculosis. Data may reflect only a fraction of the true number of malaria cases in a country because of incomplete reporting systems or incomplete coverage by health services, or both. Also, many malaria patients may seek treatment outside of the formal health sector. Case detection and reporting systems vary widely.

Health Care Spending: The estimates provided here should be considered the best estimates of WHO and not the official estimates of its member states. WHO has compared the data to a variety of sources, including inpatient care expenditure and pharmaceutical care expenditure, in an effort to ensure the plausibility of the estimates that have been collected. For further information on data collection and reliability, refer to the World Health Report methodology available at http://www.who.int/whr/2004/en/09_annexes_en.pdf.

SOURCES

Life Expectancy: United Nations Population Division (UNPD). 2003. *World Population Prospects: The 2002 Revision.* Dataset on CD-ROM. New York: United Nations. Online at http://www.un.org/esa/population/ordering.htm.

Physicians Per 100,000 Population, Tuberculosis Incidence Rate, and Reported Malaria Cases: World Health Organization (WHO). 2004. *Global Atlas of Infectious Diseases.* Geneva: WHO. Online at http://globalatlas.who.int/GlobalAtlas/.

Use of Improved Water Source and Sanitation: United Nation's Children's Fund (UNICEF) and World Health Organization (WHO). 2005. *Meeting the MDG Drinking Water and Sanitation Target: A Mid-Term Assessment of Progress.* New York: UNICEF. Online at http://www.unicef.org/wes/mdgreport/who_unicef_WESestimate.pdf.

Malnutrition in Children Under Five: United Nations Children's Fund (UNICEF). 2004. *State of the World's Children: Girls, Education, and Development.* New York: UNICEF. Online at http://www.unicef.org/sowc04/.

Adults Ages 15-49 Living with HIV or AIDS: Joint United Nations Programme on HIV/AIDS (UNAIDS). 2004. *Report on the Global AIDS Epidemic.* Geneva: UNAIDS. Online at http://www.unaids.org/bangkok2004/report.html.

ART Use Rate: Joint United Nations Programme on HIV/AIDS (UNAIDS). 2003. *Progress Report on the Global Response to the HIV/AIDS Epidemic (Follow-up to the 2001 United Nations General Assembly Special Session on HIV/AIDS).* Geneva: UNAIDS. Online at http://www.unaids.org/ungass/en/global/ungass00_en.htm.

Percent of Children Under Age 5 Using Treated Bed Nets: United Nations Children's Fund (UNICEF). 2005. Childinfo.org. New York: UNICEF. Online at http://childinfo.org.

Health Care Spending: World Health Organization (WHO). 2004. *World Health Report.* Geneva: WHO. Online at http://www.who.int/whr/2004/en/09_annexes_en.pdf.

Gender and Development

Sources: United Nations Development Programme, United Nations Human Settlements Programme, United Nations Population Division, United Nations Children's Fund, United Nations Educational, Scientific, and Cultural Organization, Inter-Parliamentary Union

	Gender Empowerment Measure (0-1 scale, 1 = complete equality) 2003	Woman Headed Households as a Percent of Total 1990-99 {a}	Maternity and Family Planning				Education and Literacy			Income and Labor			Parliamentary Seats Held by Women (percent of total) 2004
			Contra-ceptive Prevalence (percent) 1990-2002 {a}	Women With Unmet Family Planning Needs (percent) 1990-2002 {a}	Maternal Mortality Ratio (deaths per 100,000 live births) 2000	Skilled Attendants at Delivery (percent of births) 1995-00	Ratio of Women to Men Enrolled in Secondary Education 2001-02	Literacy Rate (percent) 2000-04 Women	Men	Annual Earned Income (international dollars) 1991-00 {a,b} Women	Men	Female Professional and Technical Workers (percent of total) 1992-01 {a}	
World	..	..	60.9	..	400	58	..	76.6	87.0	..	..	..	15.6
Asia (excl. Middle East)	..	..	64.6	..	..	..	..	78.3	88.3	..	..	..	14.2
Armenia	..	..	60.5	11.8	55	97	106	99.2	99.7	2,564	3,700	..	4.6
Azerbaijan	..	..	55.4	11.5	94	84	98	..	..	2,322	4,044	..	10.5
Bangladesh	0.22	..	53.8	15.3	380	12	109	31.4	50.3	1,150	2,035	25	2.0
Bhutan	..	..	18.8	..	420	24	..	..	..	..	..	..	9.3
Cambodia	0.36	..	23.8	32.6	450	32	59	59.3	80.8	1,622	2,117	33	10.9
China	..	..	83.8	..	56	76	..	86.5	95.1	3,571	5,435	..	20.2
Georgia	0.39	..	40.5	23.8	32	96	108	..	..	1,325	3,283	64	..
India	..	..	48.2	15.8	540	43	74	..	..	1,442	3,820	..	9.3
Indonesia	..	..	57.4	9.2	230	64	100	83.4	92.5	2,138	4,161	..	8.0
Japan	0.53	20.0	55.9	..	10	100	101	..	..	16,977	37,208	46	9.9
Kazakhstan	..	..	66.1	8.7	210	99	98	99.2	99.7	4,247	7,156	..	8.6
Korea, Dem People's Rep	..	..	61.8	..	67	97	..	..	..	..	..	..	..
Korea, Rep	0.38	..	80.5	..	20	100	100	..	..	10,747	23,226	34	5.5
Kyrgyzstan	..	..	59.5	11.6	110	98	101	..	..	1,269	1,944	..	6.7
Lao People's Dem Rep	..	..	32.2	..	650	19	72	55.5	77.4	1,358	2,082	..	22.9
Malaysia	0.52	18.5	54.5	..	41	97	111	85.4	92.0	5,219	13,157	45	16.3
Mongolia	0.43	..	67.4	9.9	110	97	120	97.5	98.0	1,316	1,955	66	10.5
Myanmar	..	..	32.7	..	360	56	93	81.4	89.2	..	..	..	..
Nepal	..	..	39.3	27.8	740	11	74	26.4	61.6	891	1,776	..	6.4
Pakistan	0.42	..	27.6	32.0	500	20	..	28.5 j	53.4 j	915	2,789	26	20.8
Philippines	0.54	..	46.5	19.8	200	58	110	92.7	92.5	3,144	5,326	62	17.2
Singapore	0.65	..	62.0	..	30	100	..	88.6	96.6	15,822	31,927	43	16.0
Sri Lanka	0.28	..	66.1	..	92	97	..	89.6	94.7	2,570	4,523	49	4.4
Tajikistan	..	..	33.9	..	100	71	82	99.3	99.7	759	1,225	..	12.4
Thailand	0.46	..	72.2	..	44	99	..	90.5	94.9	5,284	8,664	55	9.6
Turkmenistan	..	..	61.8	10.1	31	97	..	98.3 j	99.3 j	3,274	5,212	..	26.0
Uzbekistan	..	..	67.2	13.7	24	96	97	98.9	99.6	1,305	1,983	..	7.2
Viet Nam	..	..	78.5	4.8	130	70	93	86.9 j	93.9 j	1,888	2,723	..	27.3
Europe	..	..	69.1	..	..	..	..	99.0	99.5	..	..	..	19.1
Albania	..	..	57.5	..	55	99	..	98.3	99.2	3,442	6,185	..	5.7
Austria	0.77	33.1	50.8	..	4	100 j	96	..	..	15,410	43,169	48	30.6
Belarus	..	..	50.4	..	35	100	105	99.6	99.8	4,405	6,765	..	18.4
Belgium	0.81	26.2	78.4 c	2.1 d	10	100 j	112	..	..	18,528	37,180	48	33.9
Bosnia and Herzegovina	..	..	47.5	..	31	100	..	91.1	98.4	..	..	..	12.3
Bulgaria	..	..	41.5	..	32	..	98	98.1	99.1	5,719	8,627	..	26.3
Croatia	0.56	..	..	..	8	100	101	97.1	99.3	7,453	13,374	51	17.8
Czech Rep	0.59	..	72.0	8.0 d	9	99	102	..	..	11,322	20,370	52	15.7
Denmark	0.85	..	78.0 d,j	..	5	100 j	105	..	..	26,074	36,161	51	38.0
Estonia	0.59	54.2	70.3	..	63	..	102	99.8	99.8	9,777	15,571	68	18.8
Finland	0.82	..	77.4 j	..	6	100 j	111	..	..	21,645	30,970	52	37.5
France	..	..	74.6	5.7 d	17	99 j	101	..	..	19,923	33,950	..	11.7
Germany	0.80	30.6	74.7	..	8	100 j	99	..	..	18,763	35,885	49	31.4
Greece	0.52	..	..	..	9	..	..	..	..	10,892	25,601	48	..
Hungary	0.53	..	77.4	4.2 d	16	..	101	..	..	10,307	17,465	62	9.8
Iceland	0.82	..	..	..	0	..	106	..	..	22,716	36,043	55	30.2
Ireland	0.71	26.3	..	..	5	100	110	..	..	21,056	52,008	52	14.2
Italy	0.58	..	60.2 c	7.4 d	5	..	96	..	..	16,702	36,959	45	10.3
Latvia	0.59	..	48.0	10.6 d	42	100	101	99.7	99.8	7,685	11,085	66	21.0
Lithuania	0.51	..	46.6	12.1 d	13	..	99	99.6	99.6	8,419	12,518	70	10.6
Macedonia, FYR	0.52	..	..	..	23	97	98	..	..	4,599	8,293	51	18.3
Moldova, Rep	0.47	..	62.4	6.7 d	36	99	103	98.6	99.6	1,168	1,788	64	12.9
Netherlands	0.82	42.8	78.5	..	16	100	97	..	..	20,358	38,266	48	35.1
Norway	0.91	34.3	73.8 e, j	..	16	100 j	103	..	..	31,356	42,340	49	36.4
Poland	0.61	35.2	49.4	..	13	99 j	..	..	..	8,120	13,149	60	20.7
Portugal	0.64	19.8	66.3 j	..	5	100	..	..	..	13,084	24,373	51	19.1
Romania	0.47	..	63.8	4.5 d	49	98	101	96.3	98.4	4,837	8,311	56	9.3
Russian Federation	0.47	..	..	..	67	99	100	99.5	99.7	6,508	10,189	64	8.0
Serbia and Montenegro	..	21.8	58.3 f	..	11	99	..	..	..	..	..	..	7.9
Slovakia	0.61	23.1	74.0 d	..	3	..	101	99.7	99.7	10,127	15,617	61	19.3
Slovenia	0.58	..	73.8	..	17	100 j	101	99.6	99.7	14,084	22,832	55	12.2
Spain	0.72	..	80.9	3.0 d	4	..	106	..	..	13,209	29,971	46	30.5
Sweden	0.85	37.0	78.0 d, j	..	2	100 j	121	..	..	23,781	28,700	50	45.3
Switzerland	0.77	..	82.0 c	..	7	..	94	..	..	20,459	40,769	45	24.8
Ukraine	0.41	..	67.5	14.9	35	100	100	99.5	99.8	3,429	6,493	64	5.3
United Kingdom	0.70	25.3	84.0 g	..	13	99	125	..	..	19,807	32,984	44	17.3
Middle East & N. Africa	..	..	51.8	..	220 i	70 i	..	61.6	80.5	..	..	..	..
Afghanistan	..	..	4.8	..	1900	12	..	..	..	..	..	..	..
Algeria	..	..	64.0	..	140	92	107	59.6	78.0	2,684	8,794	..	..
Egypt	0.27	..	56.1	11.2	84	61	93	43.6 j	67.2 j	1,963	5,216	30	3.6
Iran, Islamic Rep	0.31	..	72.9	..	76	90	95	70.4 j	83.5 j	2,835	9,946	33	..
Iraq	..	..	13.7 j	..	250	72	..	..	..	..	..	..	..
Israel	0.61	29.5	68.0 h	..	17	99 j	99	93.4	97.3	14,201	26,636	54	15.0
Jordan	..	..	55.8	11.0	41	97	101	85.9	95.5	1,896	6,118	..	7.9
Kuwait	..	..	50.2	..	5	98	106	81.0	84.7	7,116	20,979	..	0.0
Lebanon	..	..	61.0	..	150	89	109	..	..	2,552	8,336	..	2.3
Libyan Arab Jamahiriya	..	..	39.7	..	97	94	106	70.7	91.8	..	..	..	..
Morocco	..	..	50.3	16.1	220	40	..	38.3	63.3	2,153	5,354	..	..
Oman	..	..	23.7	..	87	95	99	65.4	82.0	4,056	18,239	..	..
Saudi Arabia	0.21	..	31.8	..	23	91 j	89	69.5	84.1	3,825	18,616	31	0.0
Syrian Arab Rep	..	..	36.1	..	160	76	89	74.2	91.0	1,549	5,496	..	12.0
Tunisia	..	..	60.0	..	120	90	104	63.1	83.1	3,615	9,933	..	11.5
Turkey	0.29	..	63.9	10.1	70	81	77	78.5	94.4	4,757	7,873	31	4.4
United Arab Emirates	..	..	27.5	..	54	96	106	80.7	75.6	..	..	25	0.0
Yemen	0.12	..	20.8	38.6	570	22	..	28.5	69.5	387	1,274	15	0.3

For more information, please visit http://earthtrends.wri.org/datatables/population

| | Gender Empowerment Measure (0-1 scale, 1 = complete equality) 2003 | Woman Headed Households as a Percent of Total 1990-99 {a} | Maternity and Family Planning | | | | Education and Literacy | | | Income and Labor | | | Parliamentary Seats Held by Women (percent of total) 2004 |
| | | | Contraceptive Prevalence (percent) 1990-2002 {a} | Women With Unmet Family Planning Needs (percent) 1990-2002 {a} | Maternal Mortality Ratio (deaths per 100,000 live births) 2000 | Skilled Attendants at Delivery (percent of births) 1995-00 | Ratio of Women to Men Enrolled in Secondary Education 2001-02 | Literacy Rate (percent) 2000-04 | | Annual Earned Income (international dollars) 1991-00 {a,b} | | Female Professional and Technical Workers (percent of total) 1992-01 {a} | |
								Women	Men	Women	Men		
Sub-Saharan Africa	..	..	20.2	22.4	940 i	42 i	..	54.4	69.8	..	..	..	13.5
Angola	..	..	6.2	..	1700	45	81	..	..	1,627	2,626	..	15.5
Benin	..	..	18.6	27.2	850	66	46	25.5	54.8	876	1,268	..	7.2
Botswana	0.56	..	40.4	..	100	94	107	81.5	76.1	5,353	10,550	52	17.0
Burkina Faso	..	5.2	11.9	4.4	1000	31	67	8.1 j	18.5 j	855	1,215	..	11.7
Burundi	..	..	15.7	..	1000	25	75	43.6	57.7	561	794	..	18.5
Cameroon	..	..	19.3	13.0	730	60	81	59.8	77.0	1,235	2,787	..	8.9
Central African Rep	..	..	27.9	16.2	1100	44	..	33.5	64.7	889	1,469	..	..
Chad	..	..	7.9	9.4	1100	16	..	37.5	54.5	760	1,284	..	5.8
Congo	..	..	..	..	510	..	73	77.1	88.9	707	1,273	..	10.6
Congo, Dem Rep	..	..	31.4	..	990	61	..	..	..	467	846	..	10.2
Côte d'Ivoire	..	..	15.0	43.4	690	63	58	..	..	818	2,222	..	8.5
Equatorial Guinea	..	..	..	..	880	65	..	..	..	16,852	42,304	..	5.0
Eritrea	..	..	8.0	27.0	630	21	67	..	..	654	1,266	..	22.0
Ethiopia	..	..	8.1	35.8	850	6	65	33.8	49.2	516	1,008	..	7.8
Gabon	..	..	32.7	28.0	420	86	..	..	..	4,937	8,351	..	11.0
Gambia	..	15.9	9.6	..	540	55	70	..	..	1,263	2,127	..	13.2
Ghana	..	..	22.0	23.0	540	44	83	65.9	81.9	1,802	2,419	..	9.0
Guinea	..	..	6.2	24.2	740	35	..	..	..	1,569	2,317	..	19.3
Guinea-Bissau	..	..	7.6	..	1100	35	..	..	..	465	959	..	..
Kenya	..	..	39.0	23.9	1000	44	88	78.5	90.0	962	1,067	..	7.1
Lesotho	..	29.4	30.4	..	550	60	127	90.3	73.7	1,357	3,578	..	17.0
Liberia	..	..	6.4 j	..	760	51	..	39.3	72.3	..	..	..	..
Madagascar	..	..	18.8	25.6	550	46	..	..	..	534	906	..	6.4
Malawi	..	..	30.6	29.7	1800	56	74	48.7	75.5	427	626	..	9.3
Mali	..	..	8.1	28.5	1200	41	..	11.9 j	26.7 j	635	1,044	..	10.2
Mauritania	..	..	8.0	31.6	1000	57	76	31.3	51.5	1,581	2,840	..	4.4
Mozambique	..	..	5.6	6.7	1000	44	63	31.4	62.3	840	1,265	..	30.0
Namibia	0.57	..	28.9	22.0	300	78	114	82.8	83.8	4,262	8,402	55	21.4
Niger	..	..	14.0	16.6	1600	16	63	9.3	25.1	575	1,005	..	1.2
Nigeria	..	..	15.3	17.5	800	42	..	59.4	74.4	562	1,322	..	5.8
Rwanda	..	..	13.2	37.0	1400	31	93	63.4	75.3	968	1,570	..	45.0
Senegal	..	19.6	12.9	32.6	690	58	68	29.7	49.0	1,140	2,074	..	19.2
Sierra Leone	..	..	4.3	..	2000	42	..	..	..	337	815	..	14.5
Somalia	..	..	..	..	1100	34	..	..	..	..	..	..	..
South Africa	..	37.8	56.3	15.0	230	84	108	85.3	86.7	6,371	14,202	..	27.8
Sudan	..	..	8.3	26.0	590	86 j	..	49.1	70.8	867	2,752	..	9.7
Tanzania, United Rep	..	..	25.4	21.8	1500	36	..	69.2	85.2	467	660	..	21.4
Togo	..	..	25.7	32.3	570	49	45.4	45.4	74.3	941	2,004	..	7.4
Uganda	..	..	22.8	24.4	880	39	79	59.2	78.8	1,088	1,651	..	24.7
Zambia	..	..	34.2	18.3	750	43	78	73.8	86.3	571	1,041	..	12.0
Zimbabwe	..	32.8	53.5	12.9	1100	73	89	86.3	93.8	1,757	3,059	..	10.0
North America	..	..	76.2	..	..	..	..	..	..	..	..	..	18.1
Canada	0.79	46.6	74.7	..	6	98	99	..	..	22,964	36,299	54	23.6
United States	0.77	29.0	76.4	..	17	99	98	..	..	27,338	43,797	55	14.0
C. America & Caribbean	..	..	64.4	..	190 i	82 i	..	84.8	88.3	..	..	..	21.4
Belize	0.46	..	46.7	..	140	83	..	77.1	76.7	2,376	9,799	52	9.3
Costa Rica	0.66	..	75.0	..	43	98	103	95.9	95.7	4,698	12,197	28	35.1
Cuba	..	..	73.3	..	33	100	99	96.8	97.0	..	..	..	36.0
Dominican Rep	0.53	32.8	64.7	12.5	150	98	125	84.4	84.3	3,491	9,694	49	15.4
El Salvador	0.45	..	59.7	8.2	150	90	100	77.1	82.4	2,602	7,269	46	10.7
Guatemala	..	..	38.2	23.1	240	41	93	62.5	77.3	2,007	6,092	..	8.2
Haiti	..	..	27.4	39.8	680	24	..	50.0	53.8	1,170	2,089	..	9.1
Honduras	0.36	..	61.8	7.0	110	56	..	80.2	79.8	1,402	3,792	36	5.5
Jamaica	..	..	65.9	..	87	95	104	91.4	83.8	3,169	4,783	..	13.6
Mexico	0.56	16.3	68.4	..	83	86	107	88.7	92.6	4,915	12,967	40	21.2
Nicaragua	..	29.4	68.6	14.7	230	67	117	76.6	76.8	1,520	3,436	..	20.7
Panama	0.49	22.3	58.2 j	..	160	90	107	91.7	92.9	3,958	7,847	49	9.9
Trinidad and Tobago	0.64	..	38.2	..	160	96	109	97.9	99.0	5,916	13,095	51	25.4
South America	..	..	74.4	8.1	190 i	82 i	..	88.8	90.0	..	..	..	14.7
Argentina	0.65	22.4	..	..	82	98	106	97.0	97.0	5,662	15,431	53	31.3
Bolivia	0.52	18.1	53.4	26.1	420	69	97	80.7	93.1	1,559	3,463	40	17.8
Brazil	..	23.1	76.7	7.3	260	88	111	86.5	86.2	4,594	10,879	62	9.1
Chile	0.46	..	..	..	31	100	..	95.6	95.8	5,442	14,256	52	10.1
Colombia	0.50	24.4	76.9	6.2	130	86	111	92.2	92.1	4,429	8,420	50	10.8
Ecuador	0.49	..	65.8	10.0	130	69	100	89.7	92.3	1,656	5,491	44	16.0
Guyana	..	..	37.3	..	170	86	..	..	..	2,439	6,217	..	20.0
Paraguay	0.42	..	57.4	11.3	170	71	102	90.2	93.1	2,175	6,641	54	9.6
Peru	0.52	..	68.9	10.2	410	59	93	80.3	91.3	2,105	7,875	44	18.3
Suriname	..	..	42.1	..	110	85	139	..	..	..	..	51	17.6
Uruguay	0.51	29.2	..	..	27	100	114	98.1	97.3	5,367	10,304	52	11.5
Venezuela	0.44	..	..	..	96	94	116	92.7	93.5	3,125	7,550	61	9.7
Oceania	..	..	64.1	..	..	..	..	..	..	..	..	..	12.4
Australia	0.81	..	76.1 j	..	8	100	99	..	..	23,643	33,259	55	26.5
Fiji	0.34	..	..	..	75	100	106	91.4 j	94.5 j	2,838	7,855	9	5.9
New Zealand	0.77	..	74.9	..	7	100	..	..	..	18,168	26,481	52	28.3
Papua New Guinea	..	..	25.9	..	300	53	78	..	..	1,586	2,748	..	0.9
Solomon Islands	..	..	..	..	130	85	..	..	..	1,239	1,786	..	0.0
Developed	..	..	68.7	..	..	..	..	98.6 k	99.1 k	..	..	..	18.5
Developing	..	..	59.4	..	440	55 i	..	69.4 k	83.4 k	..	..	..	13.6

a. Data are for the most recent year available within the range of dates shown. b. Excludes agricultural wages. c. Including some cases of sterilization for non-contraceptive reasons. d. Data pertain to all sexually active women. e. Data pertain to women born in 1945, 1950, 1955, 1960, 1965, or 1968. f. Data pertain to former Yugoslavia, excluding the province of Kosovo and Metohija. g. Data exclude Northern Ireland. h. Data pertain only to the Jewish population. i. Regional totals are calculated by UNICEF and combine South America, Central America, and the Caribbean. j. Data refer to years or periods other than those specified in the column heading. k. Regional totals were calculated by UNESCO.

Gender and Development: Technical Notes

DEFINITIONS AND METHODOLOGY

Gender Empowerment Measure is a composite index that quantifies women's opportunities. The measure is calculated from three components. *Political participation and decision-making power* is measured by the proportional share, by gender, of parliamentary seats. *Economic participation and decision-making power* is measured by (a) the proportional share, by gender, of positions as legislators, senior officials, and managers; and (b) the proportional share, by gender, of professional and technical positions. *Power over economic resources* is measured by the estimated earned income for women and men, in US dollars adjusted for purchasing power parity (PPP). Variables in these three areas are weighted equally and indexed by their relationship to the ideal scenario (i.e., 50-50 distribution between genders is considered the ideal for representation in parliaments). The gender empowerment measure for a particular country is presented on a scale of 0-1, with higher numbers representing greater levels of equality.

Woman-Headed Households is the percent of occupied housing units whose members acknowledge a woman as the head of the household. In many countries, female-headed households suffer from a lower and more precarious tenure status than male-headed households, which leads to greater insecurity for themselves and their dependents. Data were collected primarily through census data and household surveys. In other cases, data may come from specific housing studies carried out by different UN groups. Public housing boards, housing financial institutions, real-estate agencies, and nongovernmental organizations have also supplied data when census or household data were unavailable.

Contraceptive Prevalence Rate is the percentage of women of reproductive age (15-49 years) in a marital or consensual union who are currently using contraception.

Women with Unmet Family Planning Needs is the percentage of fertile women who are not using contraception and report that they do not want children or want their next child with a delay of two years or more. Contraception includes both modern (sterilization, the pill, condoms, vaginal barrier methods, etc.) and traditional (periodic or prolonged abstinence, withdrawal, etc.) methods. Data were compiled primarily from surveys based on nationally representative samples of women aged 15-49. The surveys used for data compilation include Demographic and Health Surveys (DHS), UNICEF's Multiple Indicator Cluster Surveys (MICS), and Family Health Surveys (FHS).

Maternal Mortality Ratio is the annual number of deaths of women from pregnancy-related causes, either when pregnant or within 42 days of birth or termination of pregnancy. Measured per 100,000 live births, it quantifies the risk of death once a woman has become pregnant. Women in countries with both high fertility and high maternal mortality run the highest lifetime risks of death as a result of childbearing. (Reduction of maternal mortality is one the United Nations' MILLENNIUM Development Goals.) Estimates of maternal mortality were obtained by UNICEF from a variety of sources, including government reporting, household surveys, and DHS.

Skilled Attendants At Delivery is the percentage of births attended by physicians, nurses, midwives, or primary health care workers trained in midwifery skills. Women are most in need of skilled care during delivery and the immediate postpartum period, when roughly three-quarters of all maternal deaths occur. Multiple Indicator Cluster Surveys (MICS), developed by UNICEF with partners in 1997, were used by governments in 66 countries to collect the data presented here. Demographic and Health Surveys (DHS) provided relevant data to UNICEF for more than 35 additional countries. For the majority of remaining countries, national governments provided non-MICS data. Where no reliable official figures exist, estimates have been made by UNICEF. Where possible, only comprehensive or representative national data have been used.

Ratio of Women to Men Enrolled in Secondary Education represents the ratio of female to male gross enrollment in secondary schooling. A ratio of 100 indicates equality in representation. Lower numbers represent a higher percentage of male than female enrollment. The data are for the 2001-2002 school year. The ratio is calculated by WRI by dividing the gross enrollment of males by that of females for secondary education. The result is multiplied by 100 to produce the final ratio. UNICEF calculates gross enrollment data by dividing the number of pupils enrolled in a given level of education, regardless of age, by population in the relevant official age group, and then multiplying by 100 to produce a ratio.

Literacy Rate, shown here for both men and women, is generally defined as the percentage of the population aged 15 years and over who can both read and write, with understanding, a short, simple statement on their everyday life. This indicator can be used to measure the achievement of literacy programs and the effectiveness of primary education. According to UNESCO, "literacy represents a potential for further intellectual growth and contribution to economic-socio-cultural development of society." Adult literacy correlates with GNP per capita, life expectancy, fertility rates, infant mortality, and urbanization. Most literacy data are collected during national population censuses. Typically, censuses are held only once in a decade, so UNESCO supplements these data with household surveys, labor force surveys, employment surveys, industry surveys, and agricultural surveys when they are available.

Annual Earned Income, shown here for both men and women, is an estimate of the annual earning power available to workers in the nonagricultural sector. Data are reported in 2002 international dollars adjusted for purchasing power parity (PPP). Direct measures of income disaggregated by gender are unavailable for most countries. In order to calculate this indicator, UNDP uses a ratio of female nonagricultural wage to the male non-agricultural wage, male and female shares of the economically active population, total male and female population, and GDP per capita (PPP). These data are obtained from the World Bank's World Development Indicators and the United Nations Population Division.

Female Professional and Technical Workers is women's share of total positions defined according to the International Standard Classification of Occupations (ISCO-88) Major Group 2. This classification includes physical, mathematical and engineering science professionals, life science and health professionals, teaching professionals and other (business, social science, legal, religious) professionals. Values were calculated by UNDP on the basis of occupational data from the International Labor Organization (ILO) LABORSTA database. The ILO receives these data from country labor surveys.

Parliamentary Seats Held by Women is calculated based on the total number of seats in parliament and the number of seats occupied by women. When there is both an upper house and a lower house of parliament, the total number of women in both houses is divided by the total number of seats in both houses. Data are current as of April 1, 2004. The Inter-Parliamentary Union compiles these data based on information provided by national parliaments.

FREQUENCY OF UPDATE BY DATA PROVIDERS

The Gender Empowerment Index and labor data are published annually by UNDP in the *Human Development Report*. Literacy and education data are compiled annually by UNESCO. UNICEF publishes maternal health indicators in its annual *State of the World's Children*. Household data are released by UN-Habitat in its Human Settlement Statistics database approximately every five years. Data on world contraceptive use are updated every two years. The Inter-Parliamentary Union updates its Women in Parliament data set monthly to reflect elections.

DATA RELIABILITY AND CAUTIONARY NOTES

Gender Empowerment Measure: This index is calculated for the purposes of comparing across countries, so data must be obtained from international datasets, limiting the variables that can be used for the calculation. Without these constraints, other variables that are more detailed could have been used to measure more accurately the political, professional, and economic empowerment of women.

Women-Headed Households: Data reliability varies on a country-by-country basis. Data for women-headed households are limited and were collected over a 15-year period. The reader should use caution when comparing across countries.

Contraceptive Prevalence Rate and Women with Unmet Family Planning Needs: The data refer only to women ages 15-49 who are married or in a consensual union. Information on single men or women is not as widely available, although it constitutes a significant proportion of contraceptive use (or lack thereof).

Maternal Mortality Ratio: The purpose of these estimates is to draw attention to the existence and likely dimensions of the problem of maternal mortality. The data are not intended to serve as precise estimates. The margins of uncertainty associated with these values are large and the estimates cannot be used to monitor trends.

Skilled Attendants at Delivery: The data included for this variable cover a wide range of years and sources. Some data refer to periods other than 1995-2002. Comparisons between countries should be made with caution due to the resulting potential for variability in data quality and timing for individual countries.

Ratio of Women to Men Enrolled in Secondary Education: While UNESCO keeps the most complete global data set on enrollment levels, problems do remain. The availability and quality of national school enrollment statistics vary widely, particularly for developing countries. Even though UNESCO has applied the same methodology to analyze all of the country data, definitions of "schooling" and "enrollment" are not strictly comparable among countries.

Literacy Rate: The availability and quality of national statistics on literacy varies widely, particularly for developing countries. When census and survey data are not available for a particular country, estimates need to be made based on neighboring countries. Even when census and survey data are available, they are typically collected only once every decade. In addition, many industrialized countries have stopped collecting literacy data in recent years, based on the assumption, sometimes incorrect, that universal primary education means universal literacy. Even though UNESCO has applied the same methodology to analyze all of the country data, actual definitions of adult literacy are not strictly comparable among countries. Some countries assume that persons with no schooling are illiterate, or change definitions between censuses. In addition, UNESCO's definition of literacy does not include people who, though familiar with the basics of reading and writing, do not have the skills to function at a reasonable level in their own society. Practices for identifying literates and illiterates during actual census enumeration may also vary, and errors in literacy self-declaration can affect data reliability. Therefore, users should exercise caution when making cross-country comparisons.

Annual Earned Income: Since direct measures of income disaggregated by gender are unavailable for most countries, this indicator is calculated by UNDP from wage figures including both men and women, estimates of the size of the labor force by gender, and ratios of male-to-female income.

Female Professional and Technical Workers: The collection and reporting of labor statistics is governed by a well-defined set of standards developed through a number of international agreements. The ILO applies rigorous quality standards to the data it receives. However, as is the case with all large datasets that rely on government reporting, there are likely to be some irregularities.

SOURCES

Gender Empowerment Measure, Annual Earned Income, and Female Professional and Technical Workers: United Nations Development Programme (UNDP). 2004. *Human Development Report,* Tables 24 and 25. New York: UNDP. Available in print and online at http://hdr.undp.org/reports/global/2004/.

Woman-Headed Households: United Nations Human Settlements Programme (UN-HABITAT). 2001. *Global Report on Human Settlements: Statistical Annexes.* Table A-4. Nairobi: UN-HABITAT. Online at http://www.unchs.org/habrdd/statprog.htm.

Contraceptive Prevalence Rate and Women With Unmet Family Planning Needs: United Nations Population Division. 2004. *World Contraceptive Use.* New York: UN. Online at http://www.un.org/esa/population/publications/contraceptive2003/WallChart_CP2003.pdf.

Skilled Attendants At Delivery, Maternal Mortality Ratio: United Nations Children's Fund. 2004. *State of the World's Children: Girls, Education, and Development,* Table 8. New York: UNICEF. Available in print and online at http://www.unicef.org/sowc04/.

Ratio of Women to Men Enrolled in All Levels of Education and Literacy Rates: United Nations Educational, Scientific, and Cultural Organization (UNESCO) Institute for Statistics. 2004. *World Statistical Tables.* Paris: UNESCO. Online at http://www.uis.unesco.org/.

Parliamentary Seats Held by Women: Inter-Parliamentary Union (IPU). 2004. *Women in National Parliaments.* Geneva: IPU. Online at http://www.ipu.org/wmn-e/classif.htm .

4 Income and Poverty

Sources: World Bank, United Nations Development Programme

	GDP Per Capita PPP (int'l $) 2002	National Poverty Rates (percent)				International Poverty Rates (international dollars)						Income Inequality		Unemployment Rate 2000-2002 (d)	Human Development Index (e) (1 = most developed) 2002	Human Poverty Index (100 = highest poverty) 2002
		Survey Year	Total	Urban	Rural	Survey Year	Percent of Population Living on Less Than (a) $1/day	$2/day	Poverty Gap (b) (percent) $1/day	$2/day		Survey Year	Gini Index (c) (0 = perfect equality)			
World	7,880	..	..	..	..	..	..	..	..	..		..	..	..	0.73	..
Asia (excl. Middle East)	4,684	..	..	..	..	..	..	..	..	..		..	..	4.6	..	..
Armenia	3,117	1998-99	53.7	60.4	44.8	1998 f	12.8	49.0	3.3	17.3		1998 f	37.9		0.75	..
Azerbaijan	3,207	2001	49.6	..	..	2001 f	3.7	9.1	< 1.0	3.5		2001 f	36.5	1.3	0.75	..
Bangladesh	1,695	2000	49.8	36.6	53.0	2000 f	36.0	82.8	8.1	36.3		2000 f	31.8	3.3	0.51	42.2
Bhutan	..	..	..	..	..	..	..	..	..	..		..	..		0.54	..
Cambodia	2,001	1997	36.1	21.1	40.1	1997 f	34.1	77.7	9.7	34.5		1997 f	40.4	1.8	0.57	42.6
China	4,577	1998	4.6	< 2.0	4.6	2001 f	16.6	46.7	3.9	18.4		2001 f	44.7	3.1	0.75	13.2
Georgia	2,307	1997	11.1	12.1	9.9	2001 f	2.7	15.7	0.9	4.6		2001 f	36.9	11.0	0.74	..
India	2,681	1999-00	28.6	24.7	30.2	1999-00 f	34.7	79.9	8.2	35.3		1999-00 f	32.5	..	0.60	31.4
Indonesia	3,228	1999	27.1	..	..	2002 f	7.5	52.4	0.9	15.7		2002 f	34.3	6.1	0.69	17.8
Japan	26,937	..	..	..	..	..	..	..	..	..		1993 g	24.9	5.4	0.94	11.1
Kazakhstan	5,814	1996	34.6	30.0	39.0	2001 f	< 2.0	8.5	< 0.5	1.4		2001 f	31.3		0.77	..
Korea, Dem People's Rep	..	..	..	..	..	..	..	..	..	..		..	..		..	..
Korea, Rep	17,161	..	..	..	..	1998 g	< 2.0	< 2.0	< 0.5	< 0.5		1998 f	31.6	3.1	0.89	..
Kyrgyzstan	1,622	1999	64.1	49.0	69.7	2001 f	< 2.0	27.2	< 0.5	5.9		2001 f	29.0	8.6	0.70	..
Lao People's Dem Rep	1,765	1997-98	38.6	26.9	41.0	1997-98 f	26.3	73.2	6.3	29.6		1997 f	37.0		0.53	40.3
Malaysia	9,130	1989	15.5	..	..	1997 g	< 2.0	9.3	< 0.5	2.0		1997 g	49.2	3.9	0.79	..
Mongolia	1,709	1995	36.3	38.5	33.1	1995 f	13.9	50.0	3.1	17.5		1998 f	44.0		0.67	19.1
Myanmar	..	..	..	..	..	..	..	..	..	..		..	..		0.55	25.4
Nepal	1,382	1995-96	42.0	23.0	44.0	1995 f	37.7	82.5	9.7	37.5		1995-96 f	36.7		0.50	41.2
Pakistan	1,941	1998-99	32.6	24.2	35.9	1998 f	13.4	65.6	2.4	22.0		1998-99 f	33.0	7.8	0.50	41.9
Philippines	4,171	1997	36.8	21.5	50.7	2000 f	14.6	46.4	2.7	17.2		2000 f	46.1	9.8	0.75	15.0
Singapore	24,006	..	..	..	..	..	..	..	..	..		1998 g	42.5	3.4	0.90	6.3
Sri Lanka	3,560	1995-96	25.0	15.0	27.0	1995-96 f	6.6	45.4	1.0	13.5		1995 f	34.4	8.2	0.74	18.2
Tajikistan	981	..	..	..	..	1998 f	10.3	50.8	2.6	16.3		1998 f	34.7		0.67	..
Thailand	7,009	1992	13.1	10.2	15.5	2000 f	< 2.0	32.5	< 0.5	9.0		2000 f	43.2	1.8	0.77	13.1
Turkmenistan	5,049	..	..	..	..	1998 f	12.1	44.0	2.6	15.4		1998 f	40.8		0.75	..
Uzbekistan	1,661	2000	27.5	22.5	30.5	2000 f	21.8	77.5	5.4	28.9		2000 f	26.8		0.71	..
Viet Nam	2,305	1993	50.9	25.9	57.2	1998 f	17.7	63.7	3.3	22.9		1998 f	36.1		0.69	20.0
Europe	18,097	..	..	..	..	..	..	..	..	..		..	..	7.8	..	..
Albania	4,270	2002	25.4	..	29.6	2002 f	< 2.0	11.8	< 0.5	2.0		2002 f	28.2	22.7	0.78	..
Austria	29,220	..	..	..	..	..	..	..	..	..		1997 g	30.0	3.6	0.93	..
Belarus	5,518	2000	41.9	..	..	2000 f	< 2.0	< 2.0	< 0.5	0.1		2000 f	30.4	2.3	0.79	..
Belgium	27,569	..	..	..	..	..	..	..	..	..		1996 g	25.0	6.9	0.94	12.4 h
Bosnia and Herzegovina	5,777	2001-02	19.5	13.8	19.9	..	..	..	..	..		2001 f	26.2		0.78	..
Bulgaria	7,253	2001	12.8	..	..	2001 f	4.7	16.2	1.4	5.7		2001 g	31.9	19.4	0.80	..
Croatia	10,286	..	..	..	..	2000 f	< 2.0	< 2.0	< 0.5	< 0.5		2001 f	29.0	15.2	0.83	..
Czech Rep	15,794	..	..	..	..	1996 g	< 2.0	< 2.0	< 0.5	< 0.5		1996 g	25.4	7.3	0.87	..
Denmark	30,943	..	..	..	..	..	..	..	..	..		1997 g	24.7	4.3	0.93	9.1 h
Estonia	12,255	1995	8.9	6.8	14.7	1998 f	< 2.0	5.2	< 0.5	0.8		2000 g	37.2	12.6	0.85	..
Finland	26,186	..	..	..	..	..	..	..	..	..		2000 g	26.9	9.0	0.94	8.4 h
France	26,921	..	..	..	..	..	..	..	..	..		1995 g	32.7	8.9	0.93	10.8 h
Germany	27,102	..	..	..	..	..	..	..	..	..		2000 g	28.3	8.6	0.93	10.3 h
Greece	18,718	..	..	..	..	..	..	..	..	..		1998 g	35.4	9.6	0.90	..
Hungary	13,869	1997	17.3	..	..	1998 g	< 2.0	7.3	< 0.5	1.7		1999 f	24.4	5.8	0.85	..
Iceland	29,749	..	..	..	..	..	..	..	..	..		..	..	3.2	0.94	..
Ireland	36,360	..	..	..	..	..	..	..	..	..		1996 g	35.9	4.2	0.94	15.3 h
Italy	26,429	..	..	..	..	..	..	..	..	..		2000 g	36.0	9.0	0.92	11.6 h
Latvia	9,202	..	..	..	..	1998 f	< 2.0	8.3	< 0.5	2.0		1998 g	32.4	12.8	0.82	..
Lithuania	10,313	..	..	..	..	2000 f	< 2.0	13.7	< 0.5	4.2		2000 f	31.9	13.8	0.84	..
Macedonia, FYR	6,483	..	..	..	..	1998 f	< 2.0	4.0	< 0.5	0.6		1998 f	28.2	31.9	0.79	..
Moldova, Rep	1,478	1997	23.3	..	26.7	2001 f	22.0	63.7	5.8	25.1		2001 f	36.2	7.3	0.68	..
Netherlands	29,105	..	..	..	..	..	..	..	..	..		1994 g	32.6	3.1	0.94	8.2 h
Norway	36,596	..	..	..	..	..	..	..	..	..		2000 g	25.8	3.9	0.96	7.1 h
Poland	10,934	1993	23.8	..	..	1999 g	< 2.0	< 2.0	< 0.5	< 0.5		1999 f	31.6	19.9	0.85	..
Portugal	18,282	..	..	..	..	1994 g	< 2.0	< 0.5	< 0.5	< 0.5		1997 g	38.5	5.1	0.90	..
Romania	6,556	1994	21.5	20.4	27.9	2000 f	2.1	20.5	0.6	5.2		2000 f	30.3	6.6	0.78	..
Russian Federation	8,269	1994	30.9	..	..	2000 f	6.1	23.8	1.2	8.0		2000 f	45.6	8.9	0.80	..
Serbia and Montenegro	..	..	..	..	..	..	..	..	..	..		..	..	22.3	..	..
Slovakia	12,892	..	..	..	..	1996 g	< 2.0	2.4	< 0.5	0.7		1996 g	25.8	18.6	0.84	..
Slovenia	18,615	..	..	..	..	1998 f	< 2.0	< 2.0	< 0.5	< 0.5		1998-99 g	28.4	5.9	0.90	..
Spain	21,457	..	..	..	..	..	..	..	..	..		1990 g	32.5	11.4	0.92	11.0 h
Sweden	26,048	..	..	..	..	..	..	..	..	..		2000 g	25.0	5.2	0.95	6.5 h
Switzerland	30,008	..	..	..	..	..	..	..	..	..		1992 g	33.1	2.9	0.94	..
Ukraine	4,887	1995	31.7	..	..	1999 g	2.9	45.7	0.6	16.3		1999 f	29.0	11.1	0.78	..
United Kingdom	26,155	..	..	..	..	..	..	..	..	..		1999 g	36.0	5.1	0.94	14.8 h
Middle East & North Africa	5,994	..	..	..	..	..	2.4	29.9	..	..		..	..	..	..	..
Afghanistan	..	..	..	..	..	..	..	..	..	..		..	..		..	..
Algeria	5,783	1998	12.2	7.3	16.6	1995 f	< 2.0	15.1	< 0.5	3.8		1995 f	35.3	29.8	0.70	21.9
Egypt	3,813	1999-00	16.7	..	..	2000 f	3.1	43.9	0.5	11.3		1999 f	34.4	9.0	0.65	30.9
Iran, Islamic Rep	6,701	..	..	..	..	1998 f	< 2.0	7.3	< 0.5	1.5		1998 f	43.0		0.73	16.4
Iraq	..	..	..	..	..	..	..	..	..	..		..	..		..	..
Israel	19,532	..	..	..	..	..	..	..	..	..		1997 g	35.5	10.3	0.91	..
Jordan	4,223	1997	11.7	..	..	1997 f	< 2.0	7.4	< 0.5	1.4		1997 f	36.4	13.2	0.75	7.2
Kuwait	16,320	..	..	..	..	..	..	..	..	..		..	..	0.8	0.84	..
Lebanon	4,755	..	..	..	..	..	..	..	..	..		..	..		0.76	9.5
Libyan Arab Jamahiriya	..	..	..	..	..	..	..	..	..	..		..	..		0.79	15.3
Morocco	3,810	1998-99	19.0	12.0	27.2	1999 f	< 2.0	14.3	< 0.5	3.1		1998-99 f	39.5		0.62	34.5
Oman	13,337	..	..	..	..	..	..	..	..	..		..	..		0.77	31.5
Saudi Arabia	12,845	..	..	..	..	..	..	..	..	..		..	..		0.77	15.8
Syrian Arab Rep	3,527	..	..	..	..	..	..	..	..	..		..	..	11.2	0.71	13.7
Tunisia	6,763	1995	7.6	3.6	13.9	2000 f	< 2.0	6.6	< 0.5	1.3		2000 f	39.8		0.75	19.2
Turkey	6,365	..	..	..	..	2000 f	< 2.0	10.3	< 0.5	2.5		2000 f	40.0	10.6	0.75	12.0
United Arab Emirates	..	..	..	..	..	..	..	..	..	..		..	..	2.3	0.82	..
Yemen	870	1998	41.8	30.8	45.0	1998 f	15.7	45.2	4.5	15.0		1998 f	33.4		0.48	40.3

For more information, please visit http://earthtrends.wri.org/datatables/economics

	GDP Per Capita PPP (int'l $) 2002	National Poverty Rates (percent)			International Poverty Rates (international dollars)	Percent of Population Living on Less Than (a)		Poverty Gap (b) (percent)		Income Inequality	Gini Index (c) (0 = perfect equality)	Unemployment Rate 2000-2002 (d)	Human Development Index (e) (1 = most developed) 2002	Human Poverty Index (100 = highest poverty) 2002
		Survey Year	Total	Urban	Rural	Survey Year	$1/day	$2/day	$1/day	$2/day	Survey Year				
Sub-Saharan Africa	1,779	..	..	..	..		46.5	78.0	..	..		..	..	..	..
Angola	2,208	..	..	..	..	..	..	..	..	..	..	..	..	0.38	..
Benin	1,073	1995	33.0	..	..	..	..	..	..	..	..	..	..	0.42	45.7
Botswana	7,928	..	..	..	..	1993 f	23.5	50.1	7.7	22.8	1993 f	63.0	15.8	0.59	43.5
Burkina Faso	1,112	1998	45.3	16.5	51.0	1998 f	44.9	81.0	14.4	40.6	1998 f	48.2	..	0.30	65.5
Burundi	635	1990	..	43.0	36.0	1998 f	58.4	89.2	24.9	51.3	1998 f	33.3	..	0.34	45.8
Cameroon	2,037	2001	40.2	22.1	49.9	2001 f	17.1	50.6	4.1	19.3	2001 f	44.6	..	0.50	36.9
Central African Rep	1,171	..	..	..	..	1993 f	66.6	84.0	38.1	58.4	1993 f	61.3	..	0.36	47.7
Chad	1,029	1995-96	64.0	63.0	67.0	..	..	..	..	..	..	..	..	0.38	49.6
Congo	979	..	..	..	..	..	..	..	..	..	..	..	..	0.49	31.9
Congo, Dem Rep	621	..	..	..	..	..	..	..	..	..	..	..	..	0.37	42.9
Côte d'Ivoire	1,520	..	..	..	..	1998 f	15.5	50.4	3.8	18.9	1998 f	45.2	..	0.40	45.0
Equatorial Guinea	..	..	..	..	..	..	..	..	..	..	..	..	..	0.70	32.7
Eritrea	909	1993-94	53.0	..	..	..	..	..	..	..	..	..	..	0.44	41.8
Ethiopia	745	1999-00	44.2	37.0	45.0	1999-00 f	26.3	80.7	5.7	31.8	2000 f	30.0	..	0.36	55.5
Gabon	6,595	..	..	..	..	..	..	..	..	..	..	..	..	0.65	..
Gambia	1,571	1998	..	48.0	61.0	1998 f	59.3	82.9	28.8	51.1	1998 f	38.0	..	0.45	45.8
Ghana	2,141	1998	39.5	18.6	49.9	1999 f	44.8	78.5	17.3	40.8	1999 f	30.0	..	0.57	26.0
Guinea	2,098	1994	40.0	..	..	..	..	..	..	..	1994 f	40.3	..	0.43	..
Guinea-Bissau	705	..	..	..	..	..	..	..	..	..	1993 f	47.0	..	0.35	48.0
Kenya	1,018	1997	52.0	49.0	53.0	1997 f	23.0	58.6	6.0	24.1	1997 f	44.5	..	0.49	37.5
Lesotho	2,423	..	..	..	..	1995 f	36.4	56.1	19.0	33.1	1995 f	63.2	..	0.49	47.9
Liberia	..	..	..	..	..	..	..	..	..	..	..	..	..	..	..
Madagascar	744	1999	71.3	52.1	76.7	1999 f	49.1	83.3	18.3	44.0	2001 f	47.5	..	0.47	35.9
Malawi	581	1997-98	65.3	54.9	66.5	1997-98 f	41.7	76.1	14.8	38.3	1997 f	50.3	..	0.39	46.8
Mali	976	1998	63.8	30.1	75.9	1994 f	72.8	90.6	37.4	60.5	1994 f	50.5	..	0.33	58.9
Mauritania	1,683	2000	46.3	25.4	61.2	2000 f	25.9	63.1	7.6	26.8	2000 f	39.0	..	0.47	48.3
Mozambique	1,061	1996-97	69.4	62.0	71.3	1996 f	37.9	78.4	12.0	36.8	1996-97 f	39.6	..	0.35	49.8
Namibia	6,128	..	..	..	..	1993 g	34.9	55.8	14.0	30.4	1993 g	70.7	33.8	0.61	37.7
Niger	806	1989-93	63.0	52.0	66.0	1995 f	61.4	85.3	33.9	54.8	1995 f	50.5	..	0.29	61.4
Nigeria	919	1992-93	34.1	30.4	36.4	1997 f	70.2	90.8	34.9	59.0	1996-97 f	50.6	..	0.47	35.1
Rwanda	1,224	1993	51.2	..	..	1983-85 f	35.7	84.6	7.7	36.7	1983-85 f	28.9	..	0.43	44.7
Senegal	1,594	1992	33.4	..	40.4	1995 f	26.3	67.8	7.0	28.2	1995 f	41.3	..	0.44	44.1
Sierra Leone	523	1989	68.0	53.0	76.0	1989 f	57.0	74.5	39.5	51.8	1989 f	62.9	..	0.27	..
Somalia	..	..	..	..	..	..	..	..	..	..	..	..	..	..	..
South Africa	10,152	..	..	..	..	1995 f	7.1	23.8	1.1	8.6	1995 f	59.3	29.5	0.67	31.7
Sudan	1,936	..	..	..	..	..	..	..	..	..	..	..	..	0.51	31.6
Tanzania, United Rep	579	2000-01	35.7	..	38.7	1993 f	19.9	59.7	4.8	23.0	1993 f	38.2	..	0.41	36.0
Togo	1,486	1987-89	32.3	..	..	..	..	..	..	..	..	..	..	0.50	38.0
Uganda	1,413	1997	44.0	..	..	..	..	..	..	..	1999 f	43.0	..	0.49	36.4
Zambia	839	1998	72.9	56.0	83.1	1998 f	63.7	87.4	32.7	55.4	1998 f	52.6	..	0.39	50.4
Zimbabwe	..	1995-96	34.9	7.9	48.0	1990-91 f	36.0	64.2	9.6	29.4	1995 f	56.8	..	0.49	52.0
North America	35,138	..	..	..	..	..	..	..	..	..	..	..	5.9	..	..
Canada	29,484	..	..	..	..	..	..	..	..	..	1998 g	33.1	7.7	0.94	12.2 h
United States	35,746	..	..	..	..	..	..	..	..	..	2000 g	40.8	5.8	0.94	15.8 h
C. America & Caribbean	7,347	..	..	..	..	..	..	..	..	..	..	..	3.0	..	..
Belize	6,538	..	..	..	..	..	..	..	..	..	..	..	..	0.74	16.7
Costa Rica	8,817	1992	22.0	19.2	25.5	2000 g	2.0	9.5	0.7	3.0	2000 g	46.5	6.4	0.83	4.4
Cuba	..	..	..	..	..	..	..	..	..	..	..	..	3.3	0.81	5.0
Dominican Rep	6,644	1998	28.6	20.5	42.1	1998 g	< 2.0	< 2.0	< 0.5	< 0.5	1998 g	47.4	15.6	0.74	13.7
El Salvador	4,887	1992	48.3	43.1	55.7	2000 g	31.1	58.0	14.1	29.7	2000 g	53.2	6.2	0.72	17.0
Guatemala	4,058	2000	56.2	27.1	74.5	2000 g	16.0	37.4	4.6	16.0	2000 g	48.3	..	0.65	22.5
Haiti	1,623	1995	..	..	66.0	..	..	..	..	..	..	..	..	0.46	41.1
Honduras	2,597	1993	53.0	57.0	51.0	1998 g	23.8	44.4	11.6	23.1	1999 g	55.0	3.8	0.67	16.6
Jamaica	3,982	2000	18.7	..	25.1	2000 f	< 2.0	13.3	< 0.5	2.7	2000 f	37.9	..	0.76	9.2
Mexico	8,972	1988	10.1	..	..	2000 g	9.9	26.3	3.7	10.9	2000 g	54.6	2.4	0.80	9.1
Nicaragua	2,486	1998	47.9	30.5	68.5	2001 f	45.1	79.9	16.7	41.2	2001 g	55.1	11.2	0.67	18.3
Panama	6,166	1997	37.3	15.3	64.9	2000 g	7.2	17.6	2.3	7.4	2000 g	56.4	13.2	0.79	7.7
Trinidad and Tobago	9,446	1992	21.0	24.0	20.0	1992 g	12.4	39.0	3.5	14.6	1992 g	40.3	..	0.80	7.7
South America	7,333	..	..	..	..	..	..	..	..	..	..	..	11.5	..	..
Argentina	11,083	1998	..	29.9	..	2001 g	3.3	14.3	0.5	4.7	2001 g	52.2	17.8	0.85	..
Bolivia	2,459	1999	62.7	..	81.7	1999 f	14.4	34.3	5.4	14.9	1999 f	44.7	5.2	0.68	14.4
Brazil	7,752	1990	17.4	13.1	32.6	2001 g	8.2	22.4	2.1	8.8	2001 g	58.5	9.4	0.78	11.8
Chile	9,796	1998	17.0	..	..	2000 g	< 2.0	9.6	< 0.5	2.5	2000 g	57.1	7.8	0.84	4.1
Colombia	6,493	1999	64.0	55.0	79.0	1999 g	8.2	22.6	2.2	8.8	1999 g	57.6	17.9	0.77	8.1
Ecuador	3,583	1994	35.0	25.0	47.0	1998 g	17.7	40.8	7.1	17.7	1998 f	43.7	11.0	0.74	12.0
Guyana	4,224	1998	35.0	..	..	1998 g	< 2.0	6.1	< 0.5	1.7	1999 f	43.2	..	0.72	12.9
Paraguay	4,657	1991	21.8	19.7	28.5	1999 g	14.9	30.3	6.8	14.7	1999 g	56.8	..	0.75	10.6
Peru	5,012	1997	49.0	40.4	64.7	2000 g	18.1	37.7	9.1	18.5	2000 g	49.8	8.7	0.75	13.2
Suriname	..	..	..	..	..	..	..	..	..	..	..	..	..	0.78	..
Uruguay	7,767	..	..	..	..	2000 g	< 2.0	3.9	< 0.5	0.8	2000 g	44.6	17.2	0.83	3.6
Venezuela	5,368	1989	31.3	..	..	1998 g	15.0	32.0	6.9	15.2	1998 g	49.1	12.8	0.78	8.5
Oceania	21,348	..	..	..	..	..	..	..	..	..	..	..	5.9	..	..
Australia	28,262	..	..	..	..	..	..	..	..	..	1994 g	35.2	6.0	0.95	12.9 h
Fiji	5,242	..	..	..	..	..	..	..	..	..	..	..	..	0.76	21.3
New Zealand	21,742	..	..	..	..	..	..	..	..	..	1997 g	36.2	5.2	0.93	..
Papua New Guinea	2,366	1996	37.5	16.1	41.3	..	..	..	..	..	1996 f	50.9	..	0.54	37.0
Solomon Islands	1,654	..	..	..	..	..	..	..	..	..	..	..	..	0.62	..
High Income {i}	28,480	..	..	..	..	..	..	..	..	..	..	..	6.2	0.93	..
Middle Income {i}	5,800	..	..	..	..	..	..	..	..	..	..	..	4.9	0.76	..
Low Income {i}	2,110	..	..	..	..	..	..	..	..	..	..	..	..	0.56	..

a. Measures the percent of the population living below $1.08 a day and $2.15 a day at 1993 international prices. b. The Poverty Gap measures both the breadth and severity of poverty below thresholds of $1.08 a day and $2.15 a day at 1993 international prices. c. The Gini Index measures the equality of income distribution within the population (0 = perfect equality; 100 = perfect inequality). d. Data are for the most recent year in the listed range. e. According to the UNDP, the Human Development Index measures "average achievement in three basic dimensions of human development—a long and healthy life, knowledge, and a decent standard of living." f. Ranked by per capita consumption or expenditures. g. Ranked by per capita income. h. For OECD countries, a separate Human Poverty Index is used (see notes). i. Regional totals for high-, middle-, and low- income countries are calculated by the original data providers.

Income and Poverty: Technical Notes

DEFINITIONS AND METHODOLOGY

Gross Domestic Product (GDP) Per Capita is the total annual output of a country's economy divided by the population of the country for that year. GDP is the final market value of all goods and services produced in a country in a given year, equal to total consumer, investment, and government spending. Dollar figures for GDP are converted to international dollars using purchasing power parity (PPP) rates and are not adjusted for inflation. An international dollar buys roughly the same amount of goods and services in each country.

PPP rates account for the local prices of goods and services, allowing GDP estimates to be adjusted for cost of living and more accurately compared across countries. PPP rates are estimated through extrapolation and regression analysis using data from the International Comparison Programme (ICP). Computation of the PPP involves deriving implicit quantities from national accounts expenditure data and specially collected price data and then revaluing the implicit quantities in each country at a single set of average prices. GDP data for most developing countries are collected from national statistical organizations and central banks by visiting and resident World Bank missions. The data for high-income economies are from the OECD.

The **Survey Year** shows the years in which the surveys used to collect national poverty data, international poverty data, and income inequality data were administered.

National Poverty Rates show the percent of a country's population living below a nationally established poverty line. Estimates include total poverty rates and rates in both urban and rural areas. Values are calculated on a country-by-country basis according to the needs of the poor in a given country. Data for the National Poverty Rates are derived from surveys prepared for the World Bank and conducted between 1985 and 2002. Surveys asked households to report either their income, or, preferably, their consumption levels. These nationally representative household surveys were conducted by national statistical offices, private agencies under the supervision of government, or international agencies. The level of income that is used to determine national poverty lines varies among countries. As the cost of living is frequently higher in urban areas, the urban poverty line is higher than the rural poverty line in the same country.

International Poverty Rates data are based on nationally representative primary household surveys conducted by national statistical offices, or by private agencies under the supervision of government or international agencies and obtained from government statistical offices and World Bank country departments. Surveys were conducted between 1985 and 2002. PPP exchange rates, such as those from the Penn World Tables or the World Bank, are used because they take into account local prices and goods and services not traded internationally. In past years, the World Bank has calculated poverty estimates using PPPs from the Penn World Tables. Beginning in 2002 the World Bank used 1993 consumption PPP estimates produced at the Bank.

Population Living Below $1/day is the percentage of the population of a country living on less than $1.08 a day at 1993 international prices, equivalent to $1 in 1985 prices when adjusted for purchasing power parity. This amount is calculated as the consumption level necessary to basic life maintenance, and income below this level is referred to as "extreme poverty." **Population Living Below $2/day** is the percentage of the population of a country living on less than $2.15 a day at 1993 international prices, equivalent to $2 in 1985 prices when adjusted for purchasing power parity.

Poverty Gap measures both the breadth and severity of poverty below thresholds (poverty lines) of $1.08/day and $2.15/day at 1993 international prices (equivalent to $1 and $2 respectively in 1985 prices, adjusted for purchasing power parity). Measured as a percentage, the indicator shows the "poverty deficit" of the country's population, where the poverty deficit is the per capita amount of resources that would be needed to bring all poor people to the poverty line through perfectly targeted cash transfers.

For example, a greater proportion of the population in Laos is living on less than $2/day than in El Salvador—73 percent vs. 58 percent. While Laos has a greater breadth (incidence) of poverty, the poverty in El Salvador is more severe, so the two countries both have poverty gaps that approach 30 percent. It would require the same investment in both countries relative to the total population in each to bring the entire population to the poverty line: 30% x $2/day = $0.60/day per capita.

In technical terms, the poverty gap is defined as the mean distance from the poverty line expressed as a percentage of the poverty line, counting the distance of the non-poor as zero. It is calculated by dividing the average income shortfall by the poverty line. For example, in a country with a poverty line of $1/day and three average daily incomes—$1.60, $0.90, and $0.50—the poverty gap would be 20 percent. (Three shortfalls—$0.00, $0.10, and $0.50—are averaged to yield a mean shortfall of $0.20, and the resulting poverty gap is $0.20/$1.00 = 20 percent)

The **Gini Index** measures income inequality by quantifying the deviation of income or consumption distribution from perfect equality. A score of zero implies perfect equality while a score of 100 implies perfect inequality. If every person in a country earned the same income, the Gini Index would be zero; if all income was earned by one person, the Gini Index would be 100. The Gini Index is calculated by compiling income (or expenditure) distribution data. For developing countries, the Gini Index is compiled from household survey data; for high-income countries the index is calculated directly from the Luxemburg Income Study database, using an estimation method consistent with that applied for developing countries. Once compiled, income or expenditure distribution data are plotted on a Lorenz curve, which illustrates the cumulative percentages of total income received against the cumulative number of recipients, starting with the poorest individual or household. The Gini Index is calculated as the area between the Lorenz curve and a hypothetical (45-degree) line of absolute equality, expressed as a percentage of the maximum area under the line.

Unemployment Rate is defined as the percentage of the total labor force which is simultaneously without work, available to work, and actively seeking work. Definitions may vary among countries. The World Bank receives its data on national unemployment rates from the International Labour Organization's (ILO) Bureau of Statistics. The ILO compiles this information from a combination of sources, including labor force surveys, national estimates, social insurance statistics, and employment office statistics. The information presented here is the annual average of the monthly, quarterly, or biannual unemployment estimates.

The **Human Development Index** is comprised of three sub-indices that measure health and lifespan, education and knowledge, and standard of living. It attempts to describe achievement of development goals related to quality of life using data that can be compared across countries and time. It is aggregated from 4 indicators: *life expectancy, adult literacy, the gross school enrollment index,* and *GDP per capita. Life expectancy* is the average number of years that a newborn baby is expected to live using current age-specific mortality rates. *Adult literacy* is defined as the percentage of the population aged 15 years and over which can both read and write, with understanding, a short, simple statement on their everyday life. The *gross enrollment index* measures school enrollment, regardless of age, as a percentage of the official school-age population. *Gross Domestic Product (GDP)* per capita measures the total annual output of a country's economy per person. These four indicators are classified in three separate categories—life expectancy, education, and GDP—which are indexed independently and then weighted equally to calculate the final index. More information is available at http://hdr.undp.org.

The **Human Poverty Index** is a composite indicator that describes a population's deprivation from three development goals related to quality of life: health, literacy, and sufficient standard of living. The index is scaled from 0-100, with 100 representing the highest possible level of poverty.

Data presented here are from two separate surveys. Non-OECD countries are evaluated using the "HP-1" index based on four indicators: probability at birth of not surviving to age 40 (1/3 total index value), adult illiteracy rate (1/3 total index value), children underweight for age (1/6 total index value), and population without access to an improved water source (1/6 total index value). OECD countries are evaluated using the "HP-2" index with four different indicators: probability at birth of not surviving to age 60, adults lacking functional literacy skills, population below income poverty line, and long-term unemployment. The four OECD indicators are weighted equally in calculating the final index. For more information, see http://hdr.undp.org.

FREQUENCY OF UPDATE BY DATA PROVIDERS

Human Development Index and **Human Poverty Index** data are published annually by the United Nations Development Programme (UNDP) in the *Human Development Report*. **Poverty Rates** and **Income Inequality** data are updated irregularly as surveys are conducted in individual countries; new survey results are compiled and released annually in the World Bank's World Development Indicators. **GDP Per Capita** and **Unemployment Rates** are updated annually in World Development Indicators.

DATA RELIABILITY AND CAUTIONARY NOTES

GDP per capita (PPP): While the World Bank produces the most reliable global GDP estimates available, many obstacles inhibit data collection and compilation of accurate information. Informal economic activities sometimes pose a measurement problem, especially in developing countries, where much economic activity may go unrecorded. Obtaining a complete picture of the economy requires estimating household outputs produced for local sale and home use, barter exchanges, and illicit or deliberately unreported activity. Technical improvements and growth in the services sector are both particularly difficult to measure. Purchasing power parity (PPP) rates are based on price surveys that do not include a full selection of goods and services, and not all countries participate in the International Comparison Program. The World Bank is in the process of developing updated PPP estimates from new price surveys
.

National Poverty Rates: National poverty lines are based on the calculation of the minimum income necessary to purchase a fixed amount of essential food and non-food items. Since these needs vary by nation, the poverty rates in this category are not comparable among countries, and, unlike international poverty rates, should not be used for comparison. However, national poverty rates can provide a more complete sense of poverty in a nation by describing poverty levels unique to each country and showing the differences between urban and rural areas.

International Poverty Rates: The quality of surveys underlying these estimates varies, and even similar surveys may not be strictly comparable. For example, surveys can be based on either household consumption or household income. Consumption data are considered to be more accurate and accord better with the standard of living, but when consumption data are not available, surveys based on household income are used. Household consumption can also differ widely, for example, based on the number of distinct categories of consumer goods they identify. Comparisons across countries at different levels of development pose a

potential problem because of differences in the relative importance of consumption of nonmarket goods. The local market value of all in-kind consumption (including consumption from own production, particularly important in underdeveloped rural economies) should be included in the measure of total consumption expenditure. Similarly, the imputed profit from production of nonmarket goods should be included in income. This is not always done, though such omissions were a far bigger problem in surveys before the 1980s. Most survey data now include valuations for consumption or income from own production. Nonetheless, valuation methods vary. For example, some surveys use the price in the nearest market, while others use the average farm gate selling price.

Although the $1/day and $2/day poverty lines are commonly used, there exists an ongoing debate as to how well they capture poverty across nations. Values should be treated as rough statistical approximations of the number of people earning or consuming at a given level rather than a certain prognosis of how many people are poor. International poverty rates do not capture other elements of poverty, including lack of access to health care, education, safe water, or sanitation.

Income Inequality: Values are derived in part from household surveys that measure expenditure in different countries. Despite recent improvements in survey methodology and consistency in the type of data collection, income distribution indicators are still not strictly comparable across countries. Surveys can differ in the type of information requested—for example, whether income or consumption is used. The distribution of income is typically more unequal than the distribution of consumption. Even where two surveys request income information, definitions of income may vary. Consumption is usually a much better welfare indicator, particularly in developing countries. The households that are surveyed can differ in size and in the extent of income sharing among members, and individuals within a household may differ in age and consumption needs. Differences among countries in these respects may bias comparisons of distribution.

Unemployment Rate: Though the quality of the underlying data compiled by the ILO varies and differences in national reporting standards do exist, the final estimates should be considered generally accurate. The ILO has developed a rigorous accounting procedure, and balances government reports with employment office statistics as well as its own surveys and the knowledge of in-country experts.

Human Development Index and Human Poverty Index: These two indices have been constructed specifically to use data from respected sources and calculated in a fashion as to allow for time-series analysis and cross-country comparisons. Ultimately, there is some degree of subjectivity in the creation of any index of this sort, but the data underlying the index can be considered reliable. For a discussion of the collection of international statistics and their limitations, see the "Note on Statistics in the Human Development Report" in the Technical Notes and Definitions appendix of the Human Development Report 2004.

SOURCES

GDP, National Poverty Rates, International Poverty Rates, Income Inequality, and Unemployment Rates: World Bank. 2004. World Development Indicators Online. Washington, DC: The World Bank. Available at http://www.worldbank.org/data/onlinedbs/onlinedbases.htm.

Human Development and Human Poverty Indices: United Nations Development Programme. 2004. *Human Development Report 2004.* New York: United Nations. Available at http://hdr.undp.org/reports/global/2004/.

Economics and Financial Flows

Sources: World Bank, United Nations Conference on Trade and Development

	Gross Domestic Product (GDP), Constant 1995 $US						Financial Flows (million current $US)			Workers' Remittances as a Percent of Gross National Income (GNI) 2002	Average Annual Inflation (b) (percent) 1998-2003
	Total (million dollars) 2002	Average Annual Growth Rate (percent) 1992-2002	Per Capita (dollars) 2002	Distribution by Sector (percent)			Cross-Border Mergers and Acquisitions (net inflows) (a) 2003	Foreign Direct Investment (net inflows) 2002	Official Development ment Assistance and Aid 2002		
				Agriculture 2002	Industry 2002	Services 2002					
World	35,065,010	2.8	5,708	4	28	68 c	..	630,827	69,815	..	..
Asia (excl. Middle East)	9,182,585	2.6	2,738	6	33	61 c	..	91,267	13,009	0.28	..
Armenia	4,591	5.4	777	26	37	37	25	111	293	0.42	1.6
Azerbaijan	4,132	1.2	638	16	52	32	1,387	1,392	349	2.78	(0.3) d
Bangladesh	53,751	5.0	396	23	26	51	437	47	913	5.57	3.5
Bhutan	494	7.0	580	34	37	29	..	0	73	..	3.5
Cambodia	4,062	4.8	395	36	28	36	0.3	54	487	3.19	1.1
China	1,206,605	9.0	944	15	51	34	2,174	49,308	1,476	0.14	(0.0)
Georgia	2,783	2.1	861	21	23	56	1 e	165	313	1.41	7.4 d
India	517,843	6.0	493	23	27	51	(414)	3,030	1,463	1.68	4.1
Indonesia	224,386	2.5	1,060	17	44	39	2,029	(1,513)	1,308	0.84	10.3
Japan	5,608,145	1.1	45,029	1	31	68 c	2,506	9,087	..	0.02	(0.6)
Kazakhstan	28,009	0.4	1,933	9	39	53	337	2,583	188	0.47	8.6
Korea, Dem People's Rep	..	..	..	..	..	..	..	..	267	..	..
Korea, Rep	680,293	5.3	14,937	4	34	63	3,095	..	(82)	..	2.8
Kyrgyzstan	2,055	0.7	459	38	23	39	5 e	5	186	2.77	11.6
Lao People's Dem Rep	2,640	6.3	477	51	23	26 c	..	25	278	..	26.1
Malaysia	116,937	5.3	4,811	9	47	44	(3,601)	3,203	86	..	1.7
Mongolia	1,077	2.8	442	30	16	54	7 e	78	208	5.29	6.2
Myanmar	..	..	..	..	..	..	417 e	129	121	..	24.7
Nepal	5,803	4.6	242	41	21	38	..	10	365	3.06	3.8
Pakistan	76,385	3.4	521	23	23	53	..	823	2,144	5.81	3.6
Philippines	95,570	3.7	1,209	15	33	53	229	1,111	..	0.23	4.6
Singapore	113,486	6.1	27,533	0	35	65	(3,252)	6,097	7	..	0.6
Sri Lanka	16,909	4.6	899	20	26	54	76	242	344	8.01	8.8
Tajikistan	2,863	(3.0)	271	29	25	46	..	9	168	7.10	..
Thailand	183,981	2.5	3,000	9	43	48	(121)	900	296	..	1.2
Turkmenistan	9,909	1.5	911	25	44	30 c	..	100	41	..	..
Uzbekistan	13,341	2.3	693	35	22	44	21 e	65	189	..	..
Viet Nam	33,203	7.4	413	23	39	38	14	1,400	1,277	..	1.4
Europe	11,451,996	2.1	16,010	2	28	69	..	402,391	9,024	..	..
Albania	3,420	5.8	1,114	25	19	56	2	135	317	14.19	2.7
Austria	272,562	2.2	34,044	2	32	66	371	886	..	0.18	1.9
Belarus	15,684	2.0	2,118	11	37	52	2 e	247	39	..	93.7
Belgium	323,356	2.4	31,094	1	27	72	15	..	..	..	2.0
Bosnia and Herzegovina	6,886	..	1,671	18	37	45	0.1 e	293	587	13.70	..
Bulgaria	13,634	0.3	1,742	13	28	59	383	600	381	..	6.2
Croatia	24,288	3.6	5,500	8	29	62	581	981	166	3.24	3.3
Czech Rep	58,107	2.0	5,695	4	40	57	1,615	9,323	393	..	2.8
Denmark	210,690	2.6	39,661	3	27	71	(1,340)	6,410	..	..	2.5
Estonia	6,790	3.7	4,315	5	30	65	3	285	69	0.10	3.9
Finland	169,358	4.0	32,284	3	33	64	2,957	8,156	..	..	2.1
France	1,822,901	2.2	30,790	3	25	72	8,718	52,020	..	0.06	1.6
Germany	2,706,380	1.5	32,826	1	30	69	5,489	37,296	..	..	1.4
Greece	150,494	3.0	14,162	7	22	70	572	53	..	0.95	3.3
Hungary	58,300	3.4	5,903	4	31	65	160	854	471	0.08	7.9
Iceland	9,041	3.7	31,385	..	..	..	(147)	125	..	..	4.7
Ireland	116,935	8.6	30,551	3	42	54 c	(1,516)	24,697	..	0.06	4.3
Italy	1,229,818	1.8	21,396	3	29	69	10,597	14,699	..	0.03	2.5
Latvia	7,238	3.4	3,033	5	25	71	12	382	86	0.03	2.4
Lithuania	9,244	2.5	2,999	7	31	62	135	713	147	0.27	0.6
Macedonia, FYR	4,928	0.8	2,432	12	30	57	0.2	77	277	2.65	3.3
Moldova, Rep	3,103	(4.0)	488	24	23	53	19 e	111	142	0.09	18.3
Netherlands	503,046	3.0	31,287	3	26	71	674	28,534	..	..	3.1
Norway	176,295	3.2	40,043	2	38	60	5,276	1,008	..	..	2.5
Poland	145,305	4.8	4,557	3	30	66	273	4,131	1,160	0.62	5.3
Portugal	131,930	3.0	13,034	4	30	66 c	1,625	4,235	..	2.47	3.4
Romania	36,010	0.6	1,652	13	38	49	492	1,144	701	0.02	32.7
Russian Federation	393,851	(0.8)	3,273	6	34	60	(884)	3,009	1,301	0.08	26.3
Serbia and Montenegro	14,932	0.1 f	1,798	..	..	..	863 e	475	1,931	17.97	..
Slovakia	24,852	3.9	4,655	4	29	67	160	4,012	189	..	8.1
Slovenia	24,553	4.1	12,326	3	36	61	(14)	1,865	171	0.08	7.6
Spain	736,495	3.2	18,050	3	30	66	(428)	21,284	..	0.66	3.2
Sweden	286,614	2.7	33,665	2	28	70	(107)	11,828	..	0.08	1.7
Switzerland	339,642	1.3	46,554	..	..	..	2,977	3,599	..	0.06	1.0
Ukraine	50,566	(4.7)	1,028	15	38	47	191	693	484	0.35	13.2
United Kingdom	1,354,618	2.9	22,974	1	26	73	(25,556)	28,180	..	..	2.1
Middle East & N. Africa	744,095 i	1.7 g	2,666	13	32	55	..	..	9,145	1.42	..
Afghanistan	..	..	..	52	24	24	..	..	1,285	..	..
Algeria	51,888	2.6	1,665	10	53	37	3	1,065	361	..	2.2
Egypt	82,939	4.7	1,253	17	33	50	2,198	647	1,286	2.96	2.9
Iran, Islamic Rep	117,104	3.5	1,819	12	39	49	..	37	116	..	14.7
Iraq	..	..	..	..	..	..	..	..	116	..	..
Israel	106,383 j	4.6 h	16,676	..	..	..	(549)	1,649	754	..	2.7
Jordan	8,589	3.7	1,662	2	26	72	990	56	534	21.05	1.4
Kuwait	27,282 i	3.4 g	11,598	..	..	..	(441)	7	5	..	1.7
Lebanon	12,736	3.3	2,922	12	21	67	98	257	456	5.50	..
Libyan Arab Jamahiriya	..	..	..	..	..	..	(430)	..	10	..	(5.1) d
Morocco	43,761	3.0	1,455	16	30	54	1,624	428	636	8.29	1.5
Oman	15,940	3.9	6,147	..	..	..	(125)	40	41	..	(0.7)
Saudi Arabia	141,592 i	1.3 g	7,562	5	51	44	(473)	..	27	..	(0.6)
Syrian Arab Rep	13,618	3.5	805	24	29	47	..	225	81	..	(0.8) d
Tunisia	25,253	4.7	2,573	10	29	60	..	795	475	5.49	2.6
Turkey	204,869	2.8	2,947	13	24	63	275	1,037	636	1.11	49.2
United Arab Emirates	..	..	17,520	..	..	..	(36)	..	4	..	..
Yemen	5,838	5.4	330	15	40	44	..	114	584	14.10	9.7

For more information, please visit http://earthtrends.wri.org/datatables/economics

DATA TABLE 5: ECONOMICS AND FINANCIAL FLOWS

	Gross Domestic Product (GDP), Constant 1995 $US						Financial Flows (million current $US)			Workers' Remittances as a Percent of Gross National Income (GNI) 2002	Average Annual Inflation (b) (percent) 1998-2003
	Total (million dollars) 2002	Average Annual Growth Rate (percent) 1992-2002	Per Capita (dollars) 2002	Distribution by Sector (percent)			Cross-Border Mergers and Acquisitions (net inflows) (a) 2003	Foreign Direct Investment (net inflows) 2002	Official Development Assistance and Aid 2002		
				Agriculture 2002	Industry 2002	Services 2002					
Sub-Saharan Africa	393,001	3.1	593	17	29	53	..	7,826	17,507	..	
Angola	8,305	5.2	623	8	68	24	..	1,312	421	..	175.5
Benin	2,872	5.0	443	36	14	50	..	41	220	2.70	2.8
Botswana	7,245	5.7	3,983	2	47	50	..	37	38	..	7.9
Burkina Faso	3,051	4.5	284	31	18	51	..	8	473	1.52	1.8
Burundi	1,012	(1.6)	143	49	19	31	..	0	172	..	8.8
Cameroon	11,038	3.6	710	44	19	37	..	86	632	..	1.6 d
Central African Rep	1,331	3.0	332	57	22	21	..	4	60	..	2.6
Chad	2,017	3.3	238	38	17	45	..	901	233	..	3.8
Congo	2,560	1.9	700	6	63	30	..	331	420	0.05	1.5
Congo, Dem Rep	4,660	(3.4)	90	58	19	23	..	32	807	..	276.8 d
Côte d'Ivoire	11,941	3.4	776	26	20	53	..	230	1,069	..	3.0
Equatorial Guinea	742	24.2	2,444	9	86	5	..	323	20	..	
Eritrea	716	5.0	160	12	25	63	..	21	230	..	
Ethiopia	8,334	5.5	122	42	11	47	..	75	1,307	0.51	1.8
Gabon	5,685	2.6	4,323	8	46	46	..	123	72	..	
Gambia	509	3.7	356	26	14	60	..	43	61	..	3.9 d
Ghana	8,671	4.2	437	36	24	40	55	50	653	0.79	22.9
Guinea	4,861	4.3	633	24	37	39	1	0	250	0.48	
Guinea-Bissau	241	0.1	187	62	13	25	..	1	59	..	2.7
Kenya	10,172	2.1	323	16	19	65	(2)	50	393	..	6.4
Lesotho	1,205	3.7	552	16	43	41	..	81	76	0.19	
Liberia	657	17.2	197	..	..	..	(37)	(65)	52	..	..
Madagascar	3,562	2.6	215	32	13	55	5 e	8	373	..	9.3
Malawi	1,744	3.8	157	37	15	49	..	6	377	0.05	23.3
Mali	3,548	4.6	327	34	30	36	..	102	472	3.30	1.9
Mauritania	1,451	4.4	533	21	29	50	..	12	355	..	4.2
Mozambique	4,229	8.3	223	23	34	43	88 e	406	2,058	..	11.3
Namibia	4,398	3.9	2,411	11	31	58	67	..	135	0.10	9.4
Niger	2,387	3.3	209	40	17	43	..	8	298	..	1.7
Nigeria	32,953	2.3	254	37	29	34	..	1,281	314	..	12.2
Rwanda	2,405	4.2	295	42	22	37	..	3	356	0.38	2.9
Senegal	6,287	4.7	618	15	22	63	..	93	449	..	1.6
Sierra Leone	862	(2.9)	165	53	32	16	..	5	353	..	4.9
Somalia	..	..	..	..	..	..	..	(0)	194	..	
South Africa	182,280	2.7	4,201	4	32	64	995	739	657	..	6.3
Sudan	11,507	6.0	335	39	18	43	768 e	633	351	7.36	8.7 k
Tanzania, United Rep	7,179	3.9	213	44	16	39	2	240	1,233	..	
Togo	1,545	3.1	320	40	22	38	..	75	51	4.13	2.0
Uganda	8,597	6.7	363	32	22	46	..	150	638	6.15	3.1
Zambia	4,292	1.5	422	22	26	52	..	197	641	..	24.0 d
Zimbabwe	6,771	1.2	521	17	24	59	..	26	201	..	77.0 d
North America	9,962,239	3.5	31,089	2	23	75 c	..	60,134	..	..	
Canada	741,060	3.6	23,621	..	..	..	(10,884)	20,501	..	..	2.4
United States	9,221,179	3.5	31,891	2	23	75 c	(12,726)	39,633	..	..	2.5
C. America & Caribbean	473,654	2.7	3,009	6	27	68	..	18,609	2,254	2.48	
Belize	817	4.2	3,568	15	20	65	..	25	22	1.71	1.1
Costa Rica	15,479	4.6	3,938	8	29	62	11	662	5	1.32	10.3
Cuba	..	..	..	..	..	..	..	..	61	..	
Dominican Rep	18,388	6.2	2,128	12	33	55	..	961	157	9.71	9.9
El Salvador	11,501	3.8	1,758	9	30	61	417	208	233	14.31	2.3
Guatemala	18,532	3.8	1,552	22	19	58	..	110	249	7.51	6.6
Haiti	2,851	0.8	338	27	16	57	..	6	156	..	15.5
Honduras	4,806	2.8	716	13	31	56	..	143	435	11.35	9.5
Jamaica	5,682	0.1	2,107	6	31	63	..	481	24	16.03	7.6
Mexico	374,729	3.2	3,721	4	26	70	(4,127)	14,622	136	1.64	7.9
Nicaragua	..	..	497	18	25	57	..	174	517	9.88	7.7
Panama	11,288	3.8	3,418	6	14	80	(120)	57	35	0.72	1.0
Trinidad and Tobago	7,206	4.2	5,526	2	41	58	87	737	(7)	..	4.2
South America	1,643,751	2.3	4,093	8	26	66	..	26,319	2,386	0.65	..
Argentina	249,542	1.3	6,842	11	32	57	1,788	785	0	..	6.6
Bolivia	8,240	3.5	952	15	33	52	..	677	681	1.05	2.4
Brazil	810,244	2.7	4,642	6	21	73	2,206	16,566	376	0.34	8.1
Chile	84,689	5.0	5,441	9	34	57	56	1,713	(23)	..	3.2
Colombia	99,472	2.0	2,276	14	30	56	35	2,023	441	3.03	8.2
Ecuador	223,511	1.8	1,796	9	28	63	273	1,275	216	7.49	39.7
Guyana	724	3.5	950	31	29	41	0.3 e	44	65	7.75	5.2 d
Paraguay	9,382	1.5	1,701	22	28	50	..	(22)	57	1.52	9.3
Peru	64,305	4.0	2,380	8	28	64	156	2,391	491	1.30	2.2
Suriname	447	2.9	1,905	11	20	69	..	..	12	1.53	42.1
Uruguay	18,469	1.2	5,447	9	27	64	9	177	13	0.24	8.8
Venezuela	74,732	0.4	2,978	3	43	54	164	690	57	..	19.7
Oceania	567,617	3.7	18,031	4	26	70 c	..	17,585	1,319	..	
Australia	485,640	4.0	24,455	4	26	71 c	(4,836)	16,622	..	..	3.4
Fiji	2,396	2.7	2,736	16	27	57	1	77	34	..	2.4
New Zealand	73,613	3.2	18,947	..	..	..	1,199	823	..	0.41	2.1
Papua New Guinea	4,600	1.1	879	27	39	33	82	50	203	..	12.9
Solomon Islands	234	(1.3)	534	..	..	..	..	(7)	26	..	8.3
High Income {l}	28,547,160	2.6	29,541	2	27	71 c	..	483,001	1,852	..	..
Middle Income {l}	5,864,176	3.4	1,979	9	34	56	..	133,443	27,370	..	..
Low Income {l}	979,032	5.0	431	26	26	48	..	14,640	27,652	..	..

a. Equal to the value of sales minus purchases for all cross-border mergers & acquisitions (M&As). b. Based on the Consumer Price Index (CPI). c. Sectoral GDP data for these countries and regions are from 2001. d. Average annual growth from 1998-2002. e. Data are for cross-border sales only; purchases are either equal to zero or data are unavailable. f. For the time period 1995-2002. g. For the time period 1992-2001. h. For the time period 1992-2000. i. Values are from 2001. j. Values are from 2000. k. Average annual growth from 1998-2001. l. With the exception of FDI inflows regional aggregates for low-, middle-, and high-income countries are obtained directly from the World Bank, not calculated from a list of countries by WRI.

Economics and Financial Flows: Technical Notes

DEFINITIONS AND METHODOLOGY

Gross Domestic Product (GDP), Constant 1995 Dollars is the sum of the value added by all producers in an economy. Data are expressed in millions of U.S. dollars. Currencies are converted to dollars using the International Monetary Fund's (IMF) average official exchange rate for 2002. Gross domestic product estimates at purchaser values (market prices) include the value added in the agriculture, industry, and service sectors, plus taxes and minus subsidies not included in the final value of the products. It is calculated without making deductions for depreciation of fabricated assets or for depletion of natural resources. To obtain series of constant price data that one can compare over time, the World Bank rescales GDP and value added by industrial origin to a common reference year, currently 1995.

National accounts indicators for most developing countries are collected from national statistical organizations and central banks by visiting and resident World Bank missions. The data for high-income economies are obtained from the Organisation for Economic Cooperation and Development (OECD) data files (see the OECD's monthly *Main Economic Indicators*). Additional data are obtained from the United Nations Statistics Division's *National Accounts Statistics: Main Aggregates and Detailed Tables* and *Monthly Bulletin of Statistics*.

Average Annual Growth Rate of GDP is the average percentage growth of a country or region's economy for each year between (and including) 1992 and 2002. WRI assumes compound growth and uses the least-squares method to calculate average annual percent growth. The least squares method works by fitting a trend line to the natural logarithm of annual GDP values. The slope (m) of this trend line is used to calculate the annual growth rate (r) using the equation $r = e^m - 1$. The growth rate is an average rate that is representative of the available observations over the entire period. It does not necessarily match the actual growth rate between any two periods.

Gross Domestic Product Per Capita is the total annual output of a country's economy divided by the mid-year population. GDP per capita values are obtained directly from the World Bank.

Distribution of GDP by Sector is the percent of total output of goods and services that are a result of value added by a given sector. These goods and services are for final use occurring within the domestic territory of a given country, regardless of the allocation to domestic and foreign claims. Value added is the net output of a sector after adding up all outputs and subtracting intermediate inputs. The industrial origin of value added is determined by the International Standard Industrial Classification (ISIC) revision 3. The ISIC is a classification system for economic activity developed and maintained by the United Nations.

Agriculture corresponds to ISIC divisions 1-5 and includes forestry and fishing. **Industry** corresponds to ISIC divisions 10-45 and comprises the mining, manufacturing, construction, electricity, water, and gas sectors. **Services** correspond to ISIC divisions 50-99 and include value added in wholesale and retail trade (including hotels and restaurants); transport; and government, financial, professional, and personal services such as education, health care, and real estate services. Value added from services is calculated as total GDP less the portion from agriculture and industry, so any discrepancies that may occur in the GDP distribution by sector calculation will appear here.

Cross-Border Mergers and Acquisitions (M&As) are defined as the joining of two firms or the takeover of one by another when the parties involved are based in different national economies. Data are presented here as the net inflows of M&A capital (sales less purchases) and are in millions of U.S. dollars.

The United Nations Conference on Trade and Development (UNCTAD) obtains these data from Thomson Financial Securities Data Company. Data are reported at the time of transaction and recorded by the governments of both the target firm and the purchasing firm. WRI calculates net inflows by subtracting the total value of purchases of firms within a country from total value of acquisitions made by firms within that country. Transaction amounts are recorded at the time of transfer, rather than contract.

Foreign Direct Investment (FDI) is private investment in a foreign economy to obtain a lasting management interest (10 percent or more of voting stock) in an enterprise. The IMF defines FDI in its *Balance of Payments Manual* as the sum of equity investment, reinvestment of earnings, and inter-company loans between parent corporations and foreign affiliates. Data are in million current U.S. dollars. FDI became the dominant means for funds transfer from rich to poor countries after the liberalization of global financial markets in the 1970s and accounts for more than one-half of financial flows to developing countries. Data are based on balance of payments information reported by the IMF, supplemented by data from the OECD and official national sources.

Official Development Assistance (ODA) and Aid includes concessions by governments and international institutions to developing countries to promote economic development and welfare. The data shown here record the actual receipts of financial resources or of goods or services valued at the cost to the donor, less any repayments of loan principal during the same period. Values are reported in million current US dollars. Grants by official agencies of the members of the Development Assistance Committee (DAC) of the OECD are included, as are loans with a grant element of at least 25 percent, and technical cooperation and assistance. The data on development assistance are compiled by the DAC and published in its annual statistical report, *Geographical Distribution of Financial Flows to Aid Recipients,* and the DAC annual *Development Co-operation Report.*

WRI calculates **Remittances as a Percent of GNI** by dividing workers' remittances by Gross National Income. Both values are originally in current U.S. dollars, and the quotient is expressed as a percentage.

Workers' remittances include the transfer of earned wages by migrant workers to their home country. It includes all transfers by migrants who are employed or intend to remain employed for more than a year in another economy in which they are considered residents. Transfers made by self-employed workers are not considered remittances, as this indicator attempts to describe money raised through labor rather than entrepreneurial activity. Since 1980, recorded remittance receipts to low- and middle-income countries have increased six-fold.

Average Annual Inflation Rate is the average annual percentage change in consumer prices between (and including) 1998 and 2003. The inflation rates shown here are based on the Consumer Price Index (CPI), which measures the change in cost to the average consumer of acquiring a basket of goods and services, using the Laspeyres formula. WRI assumes compound growth and uses the least-squares method to calculate average annual percent growth. The least squares method works by fitting a trend line to the natural logarithm of annual consumer price values. The slope (m) of this trend line is used to calculate the annual growth rate (r) using the equation $r = e^m - 1$. The growth rate is an average rate that is representative of the available observations over the entire period. It does not necessarily match the actual growth rate between any two periods.

FREQUENCY OF UPDATE BY DATA PROVIDERS

The World Bank publishes *World Development Indicators* each year in April. Data for this table were taken from the 2004 on-line edition, which typically include values through 2002 or 2003. UNCTAD updates the *World Investment Report* annually.

DATA RELIABILITY AND CAUTIONARY NOTES

Gross Domestic Product: The World Bank produces the most reliable global GDP estimates available. Informal economic activities sometimes pose a measurement problem, however, especially in developing countries, where much economic activity may go unrecorded. Obtaining a complete picture of the economy requires estimating household outputs produced for local sale and home use, barter exchanges, and illicit or deliberately unreported activity. Technical improvements and growth in the services sector are both particularly difficult to measure. How consistent and complete such estimates will be depends on the skill and methods of the compiling statisticians and the resources available to them. Because values are measured in U.S. dollars, these data do not account for differences in purchasing power among countries.

Mergers and Acquisitions: Values are calculated based on the year that a deal closes, not at the time a deal is announced. M&A values may be paid out over more than one year. Data are accepted "as is" from national surveys. Some underreporting of data may occur, though as all transactions are registered in both the country of the purchasing firm and the targeting firm, this is likely to be uncommon.

Foreign Direct Investment: Because of the multiplicity of sources, definitions, and reporting methods, data may not be comparable across countries. (Data do not include capital raised locally, which has become an important source of financing in some developing countries.) In addition, data only capture cross-border investment flows when equity participation is involved and thus omit non-equity cross-border transactions. For a more detailed discussion, please refer to the World Bank's *World Debt Tables 1993-1994,* volume 1, chapter 3.

Official Development Assistance: Data are not directly comparable, since the ODA figures do not distinguish among different types of aid, which can affect individual economies in different ways. Because data are based on donor-country reports, they may not match aid receipts recorded in developing and transition economies. According to the World Bank, "the nominal values used here may overstate the real value of aid to the recipient." The purchasing power of foreign aid can decrease when price and exchange rates fluctuate, grants are tied to specific policy restrictions, or technical assistance pays for the work of firms in other countries.

Worker Remittances: Data on worker remittances are reported by the countries receiving the transfers. Variations in reporting standards do exist, particularly in determining the residency status of a worker.

Inflation Rate: Data are based on CPIs, which are updated frequently and based on the prices of explicit goods and services. However, the weights used in calculating CPIs are derived from household expenditure surveys, which can vary in quality and frequency across countries. The definition of a household, the specific "basket" of goods chosen, and the geographic location of a survey can vary across countries and within a specific country over time. According to the World Bank, these data are "useful for measuring consumer prices within a country, [but] consumer price indexes are of less value in making comparisons across countries."

SOURCES

GDP, Financial Flows (excluding M&A data), Remittances, and Inflation data: The World Bank, Development Data Group. 2004. World Development Indicators 2004 online. Washington, D.C.: The World Bank. Available at http://www.world bank.org/data/onlinedbs/onlinebases.htm.

Mergers and Acquisitions: United Nations Conference on Trade and Development (UNCTAD). 2004. *World Investment Report 2004: The Shift Towards Services.* Annex tables B.7 "Cross-border M&A sales by region/economy of seller" and B.8 "Cross-border M&A purchases by region/economy of purchaser." New York and Geneva: United Nations. Available at http://www.unctad.org/Templates/Page.asp?intItemID= 1465&lang=1.

ECONOMICS AND FINANCIAL FLOWS: TECHNICAL NOTES

Institutions and Governance

Sources: Polity IV Project, Transparency International, World Bank, International Telecommunications Union, Privacy International, Freedom House

	Governance Indices			Regulatory Barriers to Starting a Business, 2004		Government Expenditures (as a percent of Gross Domestic Product)			Access to Information		
	Level of Democracy (-10 - 10, 10 = most democratic) 2002	Political Competition (0 - 5, 5 = most competitive) 2002	Corruption Perceptions Index (0 - 10, 10= least corrupt) 2003	Average Number of Days to Incorporate	Percent of GNI Per Capita (a) Required to Incorporate	Public Health 2000	Public Education (b) 2000	Military 2000	Digital Access Index (1 - 100, 100= most access) 2002	Status of Freedom of Information (FOI) Legislation 2005	Press Freedom Index (0 - 100, 0= most free) 2004
World	..	..	..	50	79	5.4	4.1	2.3	..	..	..
Asia (excl. Middle East)	..	..	..	..	..	4.5	..	1.4	..	..	..
Armenia	5	4	3.0	25	7	3.2	2.9	3.6	30	Law Enacted	64
Azerbaijan	-7	2	1.8	123	15	0.7	3.9	2.6	24	Pending Effort	71
Bangladesh	6	3	1.3	35	91	1.6	2.5	1.4	18	Pending Effort	68
Bhutan	-8	2	..	62	11	3.5	5.2	..	13	..	68
Cambodia	2	4	..	94	480	1.7	1.8	3.5	17	..	63
China	-7	1	3.4	41	15	2.0	..	2.1	43	..	80
Georgia	5	3	1.8	25	14	1.1	2.2	0.6	37	Law Enacted	54
India	9	4	2.8	89	50	0.9	4.1	2.3	32	Law Enacted c	41
Indonesia	7	4	1.9	151	131	0.6	1.5	1.1	34	Pending Effort	55
Japan	10	5	7.0	31	11	6.0	3.6	1.0	75	Law Enacted	18
Kazakhstan	-6	2	2.4	25	11	2.1	..	0.8	41	..	74
Korea, Dem People's Rep	-9	1	..	..	..	1.8	..	..	..	..	98
Korea, Rep	8	4	4.3	22	18	2.6	3.8	2.8	82	Law Enacted	29
Kyrgyzstan	-3	2	2.1	21	12	2.0	2.9	1.8	32	..	71
Lao People's Dem Rep	-7	1	..	198	19	1.5	2.3	2.0	15	..	82
Malaysia	3	3	5.2	30	25	1.8	6.2	1.7	57	..	69
Mongolia	10	5	..	20	8	4.4	..	2.5	35	..	36
Myanmar	-7	1	1.6	..	..	0.3	1.3	2.3	17	..	95
Nepal	-4	3	..	21	74	1.6	3.7	0.9	19	..	65
Pakistan	-5	2	2.5	24	36	1.0	1.8	4.4	24	Law Enacted c	59
Philippines	8	4	2.5	50	20	1.7	3.5	1.1	43	Pending Effort d	34
Singapore	-2	2	9.4	8	1	1.3	..	4.7	75	..	64
Sri Lanka	6	3	3.4	50	11	1.8	..	4.5	38	Pending Effort	53
Tajikistan	-1	3	1.8	..	..	0.9	..	1.2	21	Law Enacted e	73
Thailand	9	4	3.3	33	7	2.1	5.4	1.5	48	Law Enacted	39
Turkmenistan	-9	1	..	..	..	3.0	..	3.8	37	..	95
Uzbekistan	-9	1	2.4	35	17	2.8	..	..	31	Law Enacted e	84
Viet Nam	-7	1	2.4	56	29	1.5	..	..	31	..	82
Europe	..	..	..	..	..	6.5	..	2.0	..	..	..
Albania	7	4	2.5	47	32	2.4	..	1.2	39	Law Enacted	49
Austria	10	5	8.0	29	6	5.6	5.8	0.8	75	Law Enacted	23
Belarus	-7	2	4.2	79	25	4.6	..	1.3	49	..	84
Belgium	10	5	7.6	34	11	6.2	..	1.4	74	Law Enacted	9
Bosnia and Herzegovina	..	..	3.3	54	46	3.1	..	9.5	46	Law Enacted	48
Bulgaria	9	4	3.9	32	10	4.0	..	2.7	53	Law Enacted	35
Croatia	7	4	3.7	49	14	7.8	..	2.9	59	Law Enacted	37
Czech Rep	10	5	3.9	40	11	6.5	4.4	2.0	66	Law Enacted	23
Denmark	10	5	9.5	4	0	6.8	8.3	1.5	83	Law Enacted	8
Estonia	6	3	5.5	72	8	4.5	..	1.6	67	Law Enacted	17
Finland	10	5	9.7	14	1	5.0	5.9	1.3	79	Law Enacted	9
France	9	5	6.9	8	1	7.1	5.8	2.6	72	Law Enacted	19
Germany	10	5	7.7	45	6	8.0	4.5	1.5	74	Pending Effort	16
Greece	10	5	4.3	38	35	5.3	3.8	4.9	66	Law Enacted	28
Hungary	10	5	4.8	52	23	5.1	4.9	1.7	63	Law Enacted	20
Iceland	..	..	9.6	..	..	7.8	6.0	..	82	Law Enacted	8
Ireland	10	5	7.5	24	10	4.7	4.3	0.7	69	Law Enacted	16
Italy	10	5	5.3	13	16	6.0	4.6	2.1	72	Law Enacted	33
Latvia	8	4	3.8	18	18	3.5	5.9	1.0	54	Law Enacted	17
Lithuania	10	5	4.7	26	4	4.4	..	1.8	56	Law Enacted	18
Macedonia, FYR	9	4	2.3	48	12	5.1	..	2.1	48	Pending Effort	53
Moldova, Rep	8	3	2.4	30	19	2.9	4.0	0.4	37	Law Enacted	63
Netherlands	10	5	8.9	11	13	5.5	..	1.6	79	Law Enacted	12
Norway	10	5	8.8	23	3	6.5	6.8	1.8	79	Law Enacted	9
Poland	9	4	3.6	31	21	4.2	5.0	1.9	59	Law Enacted	19
Portugal	10	5	6.6	78	14	6.2	5.8	2.1	65	Law Enacted	14
Romania	8	4	2.8	28	7	5.2	..	2.5	48	Law Enacted	47
Russian Federation	7	4	2.7	36	7	3.7	2.9	3.6	50	Pending Effort f	67
Serbia and Montenegro	7	4	2.3	51	10	5.9	..	5.9	45	Law Enacted g	40
Slovakia	9	4	3.7	52	6	5.1	4.1	1.7	59	Law Enacted	21
Slovenia	10	5	5.9	61	12	6.1	..	1.2	72	Law Enacted	19
Spain	10	5	6.9	108	17	5.3	..	1.2	67	Law Enacted	19
Sweden	10	5	9.3	16	1	7.1	..	2.1	85	Law Enacted	8
Switzerland	10	5	8.8	20	8	5.9	..	1.1	76	Law Enacted c	9
Ukraine	7	4	2.3	34	18	2.9	4.2	3.6	43	Law Enacted	68
United Kingdom	10	5	8.7	18	1	5.9	..	2.5	77	Law Enacted	19
Middle East & N. Africa	..	..	..	..	..	3.5	..	5.9	..	..	..
Afghanistan	-66	-66	..	..	..	2.7	..	..	..	..	72
Algeria	-3	3	2.6	26	27	2.7	..	3.5	37	..	63
Egypt	-6	2	3.3	43	63	1.8	..	2.5	40	..	76
Iran, Islamic Rep	3	3	3.0	48	7	2.7	4.4	3.9	43	..	79
Iraq	-9	1	2.2	..	..	1.0	..	..	..	..	66
Israel	10	5	7.0	34	6	5.7	7.3	8.2	70	Law Enacted	28
Jordan	-2	4	4.6	36	52	3.8	..	9.0	45	..	63
Kuwait	-7	2	5.3	35	2	2.7	..	8.0	51	..	57
Lebanon	-66	-66	3.0	46	132	..	3.0	5.4	48	..	66
Libyan Arab Jamahiriya	-7	1	2.1	..	..	1.5	..	..	42	..	94
Morocco	-6	2	3.3	11	12	1.6	5.0	4.1	33	..	61
Oman	-8	2	6.3	34	5	2.4	..	10.6	43	..	74
Saudi Arabia	-10	1	4.5	64	70	3.3	..	10.6	44	..	80
Syrian Arab Rep	-7	1	3.4	47	34	2.2	..	5.5	28	..	80
Tunisia	-4	3	4.9	14	11	4.6	6.8	1.7	41	..	80
Turkey	7	3	3.1	9	26	4.4	3.5	5.0	48	Law Enacted	52
United Arab Emirates	..	1	5.2	54	27	2.7	..	2.5	64	..	75
Yemen	-2	3	2.6	63	269	1.4	10.0	5.4	18	..	67

For more information, please visit http://earthtrends.wri.org/datatables/governance

DATA TABLE 6: INSTITUTIONS AND GOVERNANCE

	Governance Indices			Regulatory Barriers to Starting a Business, 2004		Government Expenditures (as a percent of Gross Domestic Product)			Access to Information		
	Level of Democracy (-10 - 10, 10 = most democratic) 2002	Political Competition (0 - 5, 5 = most competitive) 2002	Corruption Perceptions Index (0 - 10, 10= least corrupt) 2003	Average Number of Days to Incorporate	Percent of GNI Per Capita (a) Required to Incorporate	Public Health 2000	Public Education (b) 2000	Military 2000	Digital Access Index (1 - 100, 100= most access) 2002	Status of Freedom of Information (FOI) Legislation 2005	Press Freedom Index (0 - 100, 0= most free) 2004
Sub-Saharan Africa	..	..	..	63	225	2.7	..	1.9	..	..	..
Angola	-3	3	1.8	146	885	1.9	2.7	4.9	11	Law Enacted e	66
Benin	6	4	..	32	197	1.8	3.1	..	12	..	30
Botswana	9	4	5.7	108	11	3.7	..	3.7	43	Pending Effort	30
Burkina Faso	0	4	..	135	153	1.8	..	..	8	..	39
Burundi	0	3	..	43	192	2.0	3.4	6.0	10	..	75
Cameroon	-4	3	1.8	37	183	1.1	3.2	1.4	16	..	67
Central African Rep	5	3	..	14	205	2.1	..	..	10	..	64
Chad	-2	3	..	75	344	2.4	..	1.5	10	..	74
Congo	-4	2	2.2	67	318	1.4	..	..	17	..	54
Congo, Dem Rep	-77	-77	..	155	603	1.4	..	..	12	..	80
Côte d'Ivoire	4	3	2.1	58	134	1.0	4.6	..	13	..	65
Equatorial Guinea	-5	2	..	..	..	1.3	0.6	..	20	..	89
Eritrea	-7	2	..	..	..	3.7	..	..	13	..	89
Ethiopia	1	3	2.5	32	77	1.1	4.8	9.8	10	Pending Effort	66
Gabon	-4	2	..	..	..	1.6	3.9	..	34	..	62
Gambia	-5	2	2.5	..	..	2.9	2.7	1.1	13	..	63
Ghana	6	4	3.3	85	88	2.4	..	1.0	16	Pending Effort	28
Guinea	-1	3	..	49	208	1.8	1.9	1.5	10	..	71
Guinea-Bissau	5	3	..	..	..	3.4	..	4.4	10	..	63
Kenya	8	4	1.9	47	53	2.1	6.3	1.6	19	Pending Effort	60
Lesotho	8	3	..	92	58	4.9	10.0	3.1	19	Pending Effort	40
Liberia	0	3	..	..	..	3.2	..	..	..	..	75
Madagascar	7	4	2.6	44	65	1.6	3.2	1.2	15	..	41
Malawi	5	4	2.8	35	141	3.0	..	0.9	15	Pending Effort	52
Mali	6	3	3.0	42	187	1.8	..	2.5	9	..	27
Mauritania	-6	2	..	82	141	2.7	..	..	14	..	64
Mozambique	6	4	2.7	153	96	3.8	..	2.4	12	Pending Effort	45
Namibia	6	4	4.7	85	19	4.8	..	3.4	39	Pending Effort	34
Niger	4	0	..	27	396	1.5	2.8	1.1	4	..	56
Nigeria	4	0	1.4	44	95	0.4	..	0.8	15	Pending Effort	53
Rwanda	-4	2	..	21	317	3.0	2.8	3.8	15	..	82
Senegal	8	4	3.2	57	113	2.6	3.2	1.4	14	..	37
Sierra Leone	5	3	2.2	26	..	2.6	..	3.6	10	..	58
Somalia	-77	-77	..	..	..	1.2	..	..	..	..	80
South Africa	9	4	4.4	38	9	3.6	..	1.5	45	Law Enacted	24
Sudan	-6	2	2.3	..	..	1.1	..	3.0	13	..	85
Tanzania, United Rep	2	3	2.5	35	187	2.1	..	..	15	Pending Effort	50
Togo	-2	3	..	53	229	1.5	4.8	..	18	..	78
Uganda	-4	2	2.2	36	131	3.1	..	2.2	17	Pending Effort	44
Zambia	1	3	2.5	35	23	2.9	..	0.6	17	Pending Effort	63
Zimbabwe	-7	2	2.3	96	305	3.8	..	4.9	29	Law Enacted h	89
North America	..	..	..	..	..	5.8	4.9	3.0	..	..	..
Canada	10	5	8.7	3	1	6.4	5.2	1.2	78	Law Enacted	15
United States	10	5	7.5	5	1	5.8	4.9	3.1	78	Law Enacted	13
C. America & Caribbean	..	..	..	..	..	2.7	..	..	..	..	..
Belize	..	..	4.5	..	..	2.4	6.2	..	47	Law Enacted	22
Costa Rica	10	5	4.3	77	26	4.7	4.4	..	52	..	19
Cuba	-7	1	4.6	..	..	6.1	8.5	..	38	..	96
Dominican Rep	8	4	3.3	78	25	2.2	..	..	42	Law Enacted	39
El Salvador	7	4	3.7	115	128	3.6	2.5	0.7	38	Pending Effort	42
Guatemala	8	4	2.4	39	63	2.2	1.7	0.8	38	Pending Effort	62
Haiti	-2	3	1.5	203	176	2.5	..	..	15	..	79
Honduras	7	4	2.3	62	73	3.2	..	..	29	Pending Effort	52
Jamaica	9	4	3.8	31	15	2.9	6.3	..	53	Law Enacted	17
Mexico	8	4	3.6	58	17	2.6	..	0.5	50	Law Enacted	36
Nicaragua	8	3	2.6	45	170	3.7	..	1.3	19	Pending Effort	37
Panama	9	5	3.4	19	25	5.3	5.0	..	47	Law Enacted	45
Trinidad and Tobago	..	..	4.6	..	..	1.8	3.8	..	53	Law Enacted	25
South America	..	..	..	..	..	3.4	..	1.5	..	..	..
Argentina	8	4	2.5	32	16	4.9	4.6	1.3	53	Pending Effort f	35
Bolivia	9	4	2.3	59	174	3.5	5.5	1.5	38	Pending Effort f	37
Brazil	8	4	3.9	155	12	3.1	3.8	1.3	50	Pending Effort	36
Chile	9	4	7.4	27	10	2.9	3.9	2.8	58	Pending Effort	23
Colombia	7	3	3.7	43	27	3.7	4.8	3.4	45	Law Enacted	63
Ecuador	6	3	2.2	92	47	2.2	..	..	41	Law Enacted	42
Guyana	6	3	..	..	..	4.2	..	..	43	..	20
Paraguay	7	3	1.6	74	158	3.0	4.9	1.0	39	Pending Effort	54
Peru	9	4	3.7	98	36	2.6	..	2.0	44	Law Enacted	34
Suriname	..	..	..	..	..	6.3	..	..	46	..	18
Uruguay	10	5	5.5	45	48	5.1	2.8	1.1	54	Pending Effort	26
Venezuela	6	3	2.4	116	15	3.4	..	1.1	47	..	68
Oceania	..	..	..	..	..	6.2	4.9	1.6	..	..	..
Australia	10	5	8.8	2	2	6.2	4.7	1.7	74	Law Enacted	14
Fiji	5	3	..	64	25	2.6	6.0	2.1	43	Pending Effort	29
New Zealand	10	5	9.5	12	0	6.2	6.0	1.3	72	Law Enacted	10
Papua New Guinea	10	5	2.1	56	31	3.8	2.3	0.8	26	Pending Effort	25
Solomon Islands	..	..	..	35	44	4.6	3.5	..	17	..	30

a. Gross national income. b. May include subsidies for private or religious schools. c. Law is not yet implemented. d. Extensive access is available through the national constitution. e. Limited implementation. f. Executive order implementing FOI adopted. g. Laws in Montenegro still pending. h. This law is primarily used to supress media, while its FOIA provisions are unused.

Key to Indices: **Level of Democracy (Polity IV):** Scaled from -10 to 10, -10 represents a fully autocratic regime, 10 a fully democratic regime. -66 represents an interruption in government due to foreign occupation. -77 signifies a period of interregnum after a collapse of centralized political authority.
Political Competition (Polity IV): Assigned a value from 0 to 5: 0 = unregulated, 1 = most repressed (least competitive), and 5 = most competitive (least repressed).
Corruption Perceptions Index (Transparency International): Scaled from 0 (most corrupt) to 10 (least corrupt).
Digital Access Index (International Telecommunications Union): Scaled from 0 to 100, 100 represents highest access.
Press Freedom Index (Freedom House): Scaled from 1 to 100. 1-30 = Free, 31-60 = Partly Free, 61-100 = Not Free.

Institutions and Governance: Technical Notes

DEFINITIONS AND METHODOLOGY

The **Level of Democracy** is a scale measuring the degree to which a nation is either autocratic or democratic. A score of plus 10 indicates a strongly democratic state; a score of minus 10 a strongly autocratic state. A democratic government possesses fully competitive political participation, institutionalized constraints on executive power, and guarantee of civil liberties to all citizens. An autocratic system sharply restricts or suppresses competitive political participation, and its chief executives are chosen by an elite group and exercise power with few institutionalized constraints.

The **Level of Political Competition** measures the extent to which alternate preferences for policy and leadership can be pursued in the political arena. On a scale of 0-5, one of the following categories is assigned to a country: (0) "Not Applicable" is used for a political system without stable groups. (1) "Repressed" is assigned to totalitarian party systems, authoritarian military dictatorships, and despotic monarchies—any regime where oppositional activity is not permitted outside of the ruling party. Repressed regimes also have the power and ability to carry out systematic repression. (2) "Suppressed" political systems contain some limited political competition outside of government; however, peaceful political competition and large classes of people are excluded from the political process. (3) "Factional" polities contain parochial or ethnic-based political factions that compete for influence in order to promote agendas that favor the interests of group members over common interests. (4) "Transitional" arrangements accommodate competing interests, but some factionalism associated with parochial interests may still be present. (5) "Competitive" systems are characterized by relatively stable and enduring political groups with regular competition and voluntary transfer of power. Small parties or political groups may, however, be restricted.

The Level of Democracy and Political Competition indices are reported by the Polity IV Project of the Center for International Development & Conflict Management. The Polity IV indices are compiled by a panel of experts using multiple historical sources for each country, combined with reference to a variety of standard sources.

The **Corruption Perceptions Index (CPI)** measures the degree to which corruption—the abuse of public office for private gain—is perceived to exist among public officials and politicians. Ratings range in value from 10 (least corrupt) to 0 (most corrupt). CPI is a composite index compiled by Transparency International from the results of 17 surveys reported by 13 different independent institutions.

Regulatory Barriers to Starting a Business measure the average amount of time and money necessary to register and incorporate a new business venture in the largest city of a given country. These two indicators are measured in days and as a percent of the per capita gross national income (GNI). Governments differ significantly in the requirements they set for these processes. Broadly speaking, higher values represent regulatory environments that stifle the creation of new enterprises.

Data are obtained from the World Bank's Doing Business Database. World Bank staff collect this information in an extensive investigative process involving surveys and the input of local experts. Surveys are sent to lawyers working as business retainers in the country of interest. Respondents are asked to list the steps required to begin a business and to estimate both the cost and amount of time required to perform each. Respondents' answers are compared and normalized in order to present a clear picture of the regulations surrounding the start of a business as well as shortcuts and common methods used for compliance. Survey results are corroborated by other in-country experts in business law and practice.

Government Expenditures as a percent of gross domestic product (GDP) roughly indicate the economic importance of public health, public education, and military activities on national economies.

Public Health Expenditure consists of recurrent and capital spending from government (both central and local) budgets, external borrowings and grants (including donations from international agencies and nongovernmental organizations), and social (or compulsory) health insurance funds. The estimates of health expenditure come mostly from the World Health Organization's (WHO) *World Health Report 2003* and its subsequent updates, and from the OECD for its member countries, supplemented by World Bank poverty assessments and country-sector studies. Data are also drawn from the World Bank and the International Monetary Fund.

Public Education Expenditure consists of public spending on public education plus subsidies to private education at the primary, secondary, and post-secondary levels. Foreign aid for education is excluded. Education expenditure estimates are provided to the World Bank by the Institute for Statistics of the United Nations Educational, Scientific, and Cultural Organization (UNESCO). UNESCO compiles its data from annual financial reports of central or federal governments and state or regional administrations.

Military Expenditure is defined by the Stockholm International Peace Research Institute (SIPRI) as "all current and capital expenditure on: (a) the armed forces, including peacekeeping forces; (b) defense ministries and other government agencies engaged in defense projects; (c) paramilitary forces, when judged to be trained and equipped for military operations; and (d) military space activities." Expenditures include the cost of procurements, personnel, research and development, construction, operations, maintenance, and military aid to other countries. Civil defense, veteran's benefits, demobilization, and destruction of weapons are not included as military expenditures. SIPRI obtains military expenditure data from several sources. Primary sources include national budget documents, defense white papers, public finance statistics, and responses to surveys. Surveys are administered by either SIPRI, the United Nations, or the Organization for Security and Co-operation in Europe (OSCE). Secondary sources include data published by the North Atlantic Treaty Organization (NATO), the International Monetary Fund (IMF), the *Europa Yearbook,* and country reports of the Economist Intelligence Unit.

The Digital Access Index reflects the ability of each country's population to take advantage of internet communication technologies. It is a composite score of eight variables describing availability of infrastructure, affordability of access, educational level, quality of information and communication technology (ICT) services, and Internet usage. The index is calculated by the International Telecommunications Union (ITU). ITU receives data on information technology from governments and industry associations. Data on education and literacy rates are provided by UNESCO's Institute for Statistics.

Freedom of Information (FOI) Legislation requires disclosure of government records to the public. There are now 48 countries with comprehensive FOI laws, plus a dozen or so countries with FOI-related constitutional provisions that can be used to access information. Data are collected by Privacy International on a country-by-country basis and were last updated in February 2005. ".." in a data column signifies countries with no FOI legislation or no available data.

The **Press Freedom Index** is defined by Freedom House as "the degree to which each country permits the free flow of information," measured on a scale of 1 to 100. Countries with a score between 1 and 30 are considered to have a "free" media; 31 to 60, "partly free"; and 61 to 100, "not free." Freedom House emphasizes that this survey does not measure press responsibility; rather, it measures the degree of freedom in the flow of information. Data are collected from overseas correspondents, staff travel, international visitors, the findings of human rights organizations, specialists in geographic and geopolitical areas, the reports of governments, and a variety of domestic and international news media. The final index measures three separate categories of influence on the media: national laws and administrative decisions; censorship and intimidation; and quotas, licensing biases, or government funding.

FREQUENCY OF UPDATE BY DATA PROVIDERS

All variables are updated annually except for the Digital Access Index, which was most recently released by ITU in November, 2003.

DATA RELIABILITY AND CAUTIONARY NOTES

Many of the data in this table are index calculations and therefore contain an unavoidable amount of subjectivity. Indices typically measure ideas and behaviors rather than discrete physical quantities. While these data can illustrate rough comparisons and trends over time, rigid score comparisons and rankings are discouraged.

Level of Democracy and Political Competition: The Polity IV data are subject to substantial cross-checking and inter-coder reliability checks. The least reliable calculations are typically the most recent, due to "the fluidity of real-time political dynamics and the effects this immediacy may have on the assignment of Polity codes in a semi-annual research cycle."

Corruption Perceptions Index (CPI): CPI is based solely on the perceptions of local residents, expatriates, business people, academics, and risk analysts. Hard empirical data such as cross-country comparisons of prosecutions or media reporting are not used because they may measure the extent of anti-corruption efforts instead of the extent of actual corruption.

Regulatory Barriers to Starting a Business: The data have been subject to a rigorous series of quality-control measures in order to ensure accuracy and comparability across countries. However, problems do remain. Data only measure the time and expense of starting an enterprise in the largest city of each country. Only businesses who employ more than 50 people or have more than five local owners are included. Smaller enterprises that are not measured here may have the most difficulty navigating bureaucratic and legal requirements. These data also assume the ability of the business to hire a lawyer well-versed in the regulations regarding the starting of a business, a service not available to many smaller entrepreneurs.

Public Health Expenditure: The values reported here represent the product of an extensive effort by WHO, OECD, and the World Bank to produce a comprehensive data set on national health accounts. Nonetheless, there are some difficulties with the data. Few developing countries have health accounts that are methodologically consistent with national accounting procedures. Data on public spending at the sub-national level is not aggregated in all countries, making total public expenditure on health care difficult to measure. WHO cautions that these data should only be used for an "order of magnitude" estimate, and that specific cross-country comparisons should be avoided.

Public Education Expenditure: Recent data are preliminary. In some cases data refer only to a ministry of education's expenditures, excluding other ministries and local authorities that spend a part of their budget on educational activities. Spending on religious schools, which constitutes a large portion of educational spending in some developing countries, may be included. The World Bank cautions that these data do not measure the effectiveness or levels of attainment in a particular educational system.

Military Expenditure: The entire data set has been carefully compiled with extensive analysis by a single provider, SIPRI, which makes these data fairly reliable. When a time series is not available, or a country's definition of military expenditure differs from SIPRI's, estimates are made based on analysis of official government budget statistics. Estimates are always based on empirical evidence, not assumptions or extrapolations. SIPRI cautions that military expenditure does not relate directly to military capability or security.

Status of Freedom of Information Legislation: While the FOI data have been thoroughly researched, there are unavoidable difficulties in assigning each country to one of three categories. Some countries have laws guaranteeing access, but the laws are not enforced. Others guarantee access to government documents in specific categories, excluding access in other categories. A more thorough description of each country's policies is available at http://www.privacyinternational.org/issues/foia/foia-survey.html.

Press Freedom Index: Freedom House has been reviewing press freedom since 1979; the Press Freedom Survey emerged in its current form in 1994. The data are reproducible and the index components are clear. The data are considered to be reliable; nonetheless, there is an unavoidable amount of subjectivity in any index calculation.

SOURCES:

Level of Democracy and Political Competition: Polity IV Project. 2003. *Polity IV Project: Political Regime Characteristics and Transitions.* College Park: University of Maryland. Available at http://www.bsos.umd.edu/cidcm/inscr/polity/index.htm.

Corruption Perceptions Index: Transparency International. 2003. *2003 Corruption Perceptions Index*, Table 1. Berlin: Transparency International. Available at http://www.transparency.org/pressreleases_archive/2003/2003.10.07.cpi.en.html.

Regulatory Barriers to Starting a Business: The World Bank, Rapid Response Research Group. 2004. Doing Business Database. Washington, D.C.: The World Bank. Available at http://rru.worldbank.org/DoingBusiness/ExploreTopics/StartingBusiness/CompareAll.aspx.

Government Expenditures: The World Bank Development Data Group. World Development Indicators Online. Washington, DC: The World Bank. Available at http://worldbank.org/data/onlinedbs/onlinedbases.htm.

Digital Access Index: International Telecommunications Union (ITU). 2003. *World Telecommunication Development Report.* Available at http://www.itu.int/newsarchive/press_releases/2003/30.html.

Freedom of Information Legislation: Banisar, David. 2005. *Freedom of Information and Access to Government Records Around the World.* Washington, DC: Privacy International.

Press Freedom Index: Freedom House. 2004. *The Annual Survey of Press Freedom 2004.* New York: Freedom House. Available at http://www.freedomhouse.org/research/pfsratings.xls.

Energy

Sources: International Energy Agency, World Health Organization, BP plc

	Total From All Sources (1000 metric toe)		Per Capita (kgoe)	Consumption by Source (percent), 2001					Population Relying on Solid Fuels {b} (percent)	Electricity Consumption Per Capita (kWh)	Percent of Population With Access	Proven Fossil Fuel Reserves (million metric toe)			Net Fuel Imports {c} (1000 metric toe)
	1991	2001	2001	Fossil Fuels	Solid Biomass	Nuclear	Hydro-electric	Other Renew-ables {a}	2000	2001	2000	Coal 2003	Oil 2003	Natural Gas 2003	2001
World	8,706,507	10,029,096	1,631	79.5	10.4	6.9	2.2	0.7	56 d	2,326	73	501,172	156,700	158,198	..
Asia (excl. Middle East)	2,215,374	3,145,549	890	75.3	18.2	4.2	1.6	0.5	75	1,087	70	..	..	..	684,754
Armenia	..	2,297	744	75.2	0.0	22.6	3.6	0.0	66	1,017	..	..	..	..	1,727
Azerbaijan	..	11,582	1,408	98.5	0.0	0.0	1.0	0.0	37	2,105	..	..	959	1,233	(7,955)
Bangladesh	12,572	20,410	145	61.7	37.9	0.0	0.4	0.0	> 95	99	20	..	..	306	4,276
Bhutan	..	..	..	..	..	..	..	..	< 5	..	..	..	..	..	..
Cambodia	..	..	..	..	..	..	..	..	> 95	..	16	..	..	..	..
China	873,087	1,139,369	887	78.6	18.8	0.4	2.1	0.1	80	1,069	99	58,900	3,238	1,641	3,583
Georgia	..	2,413	462	52.1	26.7	0.0	19.8	0.4	71	1,204	..	..	..	..	1,146
India	379,440	531,453	514	59.3	38.5	0.9	1.2	0.0	81	408	43	55,597	741	769	90,862
Indonesia	99,944	152,304	711	66.2	31.6	0.0	0.6	1.7	50	423	53	2,053	613	2,301	(80,835)
Japan	446,399	520,729	4,091	80.9	0.7	16.0	1.4	0.7	< 5	8,096	100	515	..	..	417,093
Kazakhstan	..	40,324	2,596	97.4	0.2	0.0	1.7	0.0	51	3,312	..	21,667	1,233	1,710	(43,679)
Korea, Dem People's Rep	31,299	20,440	912	90.6	4.9	0.0	4.5	0.0	68	760	20	300	..	..	1,291
Korea, Rep	100,390	194,780	4,132	83.6	0.1	15.0	0.2	0.0	< 5	5,607	100	52	..	..	164,442
Kyrgyzstan	..	2,235	447	59.1	0.2	0.0	47.8	0.0	> 95	1,439	..	..	..	..	983
Lao People's Dem Rep	..	..	..	..	..	..	..	..	95	..	..	..	..	..	..
Malaysia	26,222	51,608	2,197	94.2	4.7	0.0	1.2	0.0	29	2,824	97	..	524	2,165	(25,719)
Mongolia	..	..	..	..	..	..	..	..	67	..	90	..	..	..	..
Myanmar	10,505	12,159	252	21.3	77.4	0.0	1.3	0.0	> 95	94	5	..	..	328	(3,108)
Nepal	5,999	8,416	350	12.8	84.9	0.0	1.9	0.4	> 95	67	15	..	..	..	1,070
Pakistan	44,819	64,506	441	59.3	37.2	0.9	2.5	0.0	76	379	53	755	..	675	16,331
Philippines	28,268	42,151	546	54.1	23.1	0.0	1.4	21.3	85	517	87	..	..	..	21,935
Singapore	14,464	29,158	7,103	99.8	0.0	0.0	0.0	0.0	< 5	7,677	100	..	..	..	47,477
Sri Lanka	5,600	7,923	423	43.7	52.9	0.0	3.4	0.0	89	288	62	..	..	..	3,577
Tajikistan	..	3,036	494	56.4	0.0	0.0	39.8	0.0	> 95	2,172	..	..	..	..	1,655
Thailand	46,447	75,542	1,227	81.9	17.1	0.0	0.7	0.0	72	1,563	82	423	90	393	35,782
Turkmenistan	..	15,309	3,243	101.0	0.0	0.0	0.0	0.0	50	1,400	..	..	75	2,610	(34,979)
Uzbekistan	..	50,650	2,001	98.8	0.0	0.0	1.0	0.0	79	1,796	..	..	81	1,665	(5,068)
Viet Nam	24,824	39,356	497	37.8	58.3	0.0	4.0	0.0	> 95	332	76	100	338	207	(11,157)
Europe	..	3,606,369	3,621	84.2	2.0	10.5	2.4	0.3	16	5,598	..	..	..	..	44,742
Albania	1,862	1,715	549	65.8	7.5	0.0	17.8	0.1	76	1,123	..	..	..	..	808
Austria	26,701	30,721	3,790	77.5	9.0	0.0	11.7	0.6	< 5	7,419	100	..	..	..	20,034
Belarus	..	24,415	2,445	92.7	3.7	0.0	0.0	0.0	11	2,995	..	..	..	..	20,152
Belgium	51,651	59,001	5,743	76.5	0.6	20.5	0.1	0.1	< 5	8,272	100	..	..	..	51,174
Bosnia and Herzegovina	..	4,359	1,072	88.0	4.1	0.0	10.0	0.0	74	1,876	..	..	..	..	1,174
Bulgaria	22,631	19,476	2,424	73.3	2.8	26.2	0.8	0.0	31	3,854	..	908	..	..	9,666
Croatia	..	7,904	1,778	86.1	3.7	0.0	6.8	0.0	16	2,938	..	..	..	..	3,850
Czech Rep	42,916	41,396	4,036	90.6	0.9	9.3	0.4	0.2	< 5	5,891	100	2,597	..	..	11,485
Denmark	19,854	19,783	3,706	88.7	5.0	0.0	0.0	2.3	< 5	6,492	100	..	170	85	(6,111)
Estonia	..	4,697	3,472	89.7	11.4	0.0	0.0	0.0	34	4,766	..	..	..	..	1,763
Finland	29,582	33,815	6,518	56.9	18.7	17.6	3.4	0.1	< 5	15,687	100	..	..	..	18,319
France	239,982	265,570	4,459	53.9	3.6	41.3	2.4	0.3	< 5	7,401	100	19	..	..	139,392
Germany	349,219	351,092	4,263	84.1	1.3	12.7	0.5	0.6	< 5	6,852	100	29,667	..	186	216,864
Greece	22,286	28,704	2,622	94.5	3.3	0.0	0.6	0.7	< 5	4,686	100	958	..	..	21,866
Hungary	27,362	25,340	2,542	82.7	1.3	14.6	0.1	0.0	26	3,426	100	366	..	..	13,511
Iceland	2,123	3,363	11,800	27.1	0.0	0.0	16.8	56.0	< 5	26,947	100	..	..	..	956
Ireland	10,604	14,981	3,876	98.4	1.0	0.0	0.3	0.4	< 5	5,917	100	..	..	..	13,792
Italy	156,817	171,998	2,990	91.9	1.0	0.0	2.3	2.0	< 5	5,318	100	..	106	198	142,337
Latvia	..	4,297	1,828	61.3	29.3	0.0	5.7	0.0	19	2,193	..	..	..	..	2,607
Lithuania	..	8,023	2,303	58.3	8.2	37.2	0.3	0.0	42	2,687	..	..	..	..	4,113
Macedonia, FYR	..	2,608	1,282	89.9	5.7	0.0	2.1	0.9	58	2,799	..	..	..	..	979
Moldova, Rep	..	3,140	734	92.1	1.9	0.0	0.2	0.0	72	940	..	..	..	..	2,908
Netherlands	70,332	77,214	4,831	95.0	0.7	1.3	0.0	0.3	< 5	6,659	100	..	1,350	1,500	30,064
Norway	22,188	26,607	5,921	54.3	5.0	0.0	38.9	0.1	< 5	25,595	100	..	1,350	2,215	(201,565)
Poland	98,482	90,570	2,343	95.6	4.2	0.0	0.2	0.0	37	3,227	100	14,153	..	104	10,151
Portugal	17,301	24,732	2,465	86.2	7.6	0.0	4.9	0.5	< 5	4,145	100	..	..	..	22,013
Romania	51,476	36,841	1,642	86.6	5.8	3.9	3.5	0.0	45	2,041	..	486	123	280	9,246
Russian Federation	..	621,349	4,289	90.9	0.6	5.8	2.4	0.0	7	5,319	..	68,699	9,500	42,300	(365,972)
Serbia and Montenegro	..	16,061	1,523	86.6	5.0	0.0	6.2	0.0	70	2,869	..	..	..	..	5,033
Slovakia	19,147	18,717	3,470	73.3	1.4	24.1	2.3	0.2	24	5,005	100	..	..	..	11,856
Slovenia	..	6,838	3,440	70.8	5.9	20.0	4.8	0.1	< 5	6,007	..	..	..	..	3,623
Spain	94,662	127,381	3,116	80.3	2.9	13.0	2.8	0.7	< 5	5,501	100	287	..	..	100,320
Sweden	48,185	51,054	5,762	34.5	14.9	36.8	13.3	0.3	< 5	16,021	100	..	..	..	18,477
Switzerland	25,317	28,019	3,906	59.1	1.9	25.0	12.7	0.7	< 5	8,026	100	..	..	..	16,379
Ukraine	..	141,577	2,872	85.2	0.2	14.0	0.7	0.0	56	2,767	..	16,809	..	999	58,412
United Kingdom	218,742	235,158	3,994	88.5	0.4	10.0	0.1	0.4	< 5	6,171	100	833	595	567	(22,602)
Middle East & N. Africa	378,681	577,251	1,487	96.9	1.8	0.0	0.8	0.3	17	1,848	87	..	..	..	(1,016,784)
Afghanistan	..	..	..	..	..	..	..	..	> 95	..	2	..	..	..	..
Algeria	25,217	29,438	957	99.7	0.3	0.0	0.0	0.0	< 5	723	98	..	1,425	4,071	(115,502)
Egypt	32,425	48,012	695	94.7	2.8	0.0	2.5	0.0	23	1,114	94	..	508	1,580	(7,438)
Iran, Islamic Rep	75,352	120,000	1,785	99.0	0.7	0.0	0.4	0.0	< 5	1,689	98	..	17,952	24,021	(126,024)
Iraq	15,545	28,476	1,193	99.7	0.1	0.0	0.2	0.0	< 5	1,471	95	..	15,520	2,798	(94,820)
Israel	12,102	21,193	3,433	97.6	0.0	0.0	0.0	3.0	< 5	6,459	100	..	..	..	20,865
Jordan	3,538	5,116	987	98.1	0.1	0.0	0.1	1.3	10	1,373	95	..	..	..	4,922
Kuwait	4,784	16,368	6,956	100.0	0.0	0.0	0.0	0.0	< 5	15,818	100	..	13,292	1,401	(91,991)
Lebanon	2,883	5,435	1,537	95.0	2.3	0.0	0.5	0.1	< 5	1,824	95	..	..	..	5,141
Libyan Arab Jamahiriya	13,791	15,992	2,995	99.1	0.9	0.0	0.0	0.0	< 5	3,968	100	..	4,688	1,183	(58,285)
Morocco	7,053	11,006	372	93.9	4.0	0.0	0.7	0.2	11	570	71	..	..	..	10,648
Oman	5,956	9,984	3,714	100.0	0.0	0.0	0.0	0.0	< 5	3,247	94	..	756	851	(55,799)
Saudi Arabia	71,407	110,586	4,844	100.0	0.0	0.0	0.0	0.0	< 5	5,886	98	..	36,089	6,010	(364,198)
Syrian Arab Rep	13,037	13,955	822	93.8	0.0	0.0	6.1	0.0	19	1,539	86	..	311	270	(20,422)
Tunisia	5,447	8,243	857	84.6	15.2	0.0	0.1	0.0	29	1,046	95	..	65	..	1,641
Turkey	52,505	72,458	1,046	86.6	8.7	0.0	2.8	1.4	11	1,509	95	1,322	..	..	45,608
United Arab Emirates	20,833	32,624	11,332	100.0	0.0	0.0	0.0	0.0	< 5	12,279	96	..	12,954	5,454	(105,249)
Yemen	3,033	3,560	191	97.8	2.2	0.0	0.0	0.0	66	127	50	..	92	431	(19,029)

For more information, please visit http://earthtrends.wri.org/datatables/energy

| | Energy Consumption | | | | | | | | Population Relying on Solid Fuels {b} (percent) 2000 | Electricity | | Proven Fossil Fuel Reserves (million metric toe) | | | Net Fuel Imports {c} (1000 metric toe) 2001 |
| | Total From All Sources (1000 metric toe) | | Per Capita (kgoe) 2001 | Consumption by Source (percent), 2001 | | | | | | Con-sumption Per Capita (kWh) 2001 | Percent of Population With Access 2000 | | | | |
	1991	2001		Fossil Fuels	Solid Biomass	Nuclear	Hydro-electric	Other Renew-ables {a}				Coal 2003	Oil 2003	Natural Gas 2003	
Sub-Saharan Africa	..	..	..	..	..	..	..	..	76	..	24	..	..	..	..
Angola	6,361	8,454	662	30.3	68.7	0.0	1.0	0.0	> 95	101	12	..	1,201	..	(34,979)
Benin	1,703	2,028	318	..	71.2	0.0	0.0	0.0	89	65	22	..	..	..	511
Botswana	..	..	..	..	..	..	..	..	65	..	22	..	..	..	..
Burkina Faso	..	..	..	..	..	..	..	..	> 95	..	13	..	..	..	..
Burundi	..	..	..	..	..	..	..	..	> 95	..	..	..	..	..	..
Cameroon	5,079	6,445	418	16.3	79.0	0.0	4.6	0.0	77	173	20	..	31	..	(6,046)
Central African Rep	..	..	..	..	..	..	..	..	> 95	..	..	..	..	..	..
Chad	..	..	..	..	..	..	..	..	95	..	..	..	..	..	..
Congo	1,082	931	263	29.2	64.9	0.0	3.1	0.0	67	134	21	..	214	..	(12,763)
Congo, Dem Rep	12,116	15,039	302	4.4	93.0	0.0	3.3	0.0	> 95	82	7	..	..	..	(562)
Côte d'Ivoire	4,543	6,497	404	32.5	66.6	0.0	..	0.0	93	194	50	..	..	..	509
Equatorial Guinea	..	..	..	..	..	..	..	..	83	..	..	..	..	..	..
Eritrea	..	771	200	..	68.9	0.0	0.0	0.0	> 95	46	17	..	..	..	244
Ethiopia	15,614	19,161	285	..	93.1	0.0	0.8	0.0	> 95	25	5	..	..	..	1,171
Gabon	1,359	1,702	1,327	39.9	55.7	0.0	4.5	0.0	34	907	31	..	324	..	(13,071)
Gambia	..	..	..	..	..	..	..	..	> 95	..	..	..	..	..	..
Ghana	5,512	8,180	408	26.5	66.3	0.0	6.9	0.0	95	348	45	..	..	..	2,172
Guinea	..	..	..	..	..	..	..	..	> 95	..	..	..	..	..	..
Guinea-Bissau	..	..	..	..	..	..	..	..	95	..	..	..	..	..	..
Kenya	12,535	15,377	495	17.7	78.2	0.0	1.3	2.7	85	118	8	..	..	..	2,801
Lesotho	..	..	..	..	..	..	..	..	85	..	5	..	..	..	..
Liberia	..	..	..	..	..	..	..	..	83	..	..	..	..	..	..
Madagascar	..	..	..	..	..	..	..	..	> 95	..	8	..	..	..	..
Malawi	..	..	..	..	..	..	..	..	> 95	..	5	..	..	..	..
Mali	..	..	..	..	..	..	..	..	> 95	..	..	..	..	..	..
Mauritania	..	..	..	..	..	..	..	..	69	..	..	..	..	..	..
Mozambique	7,167	7,687	422	6.0	88.3	0.0	9.8	0.0	87	272	7	..	..	..	473
Namibia	652	1,159	601	65.5	15.2	0.0	10.2	0.0	83	1,334	34	..	..	..	759
Niger	..	..	..	..	..	..	..	..	> 95	..	..	..	..	..	..
Nigeria	74,241	95,444	810	21.9	77.5	0.0	0.6	0.0	67	86	40	..	4,635	4,497	(110,304)
Rwanda	..	..	..	..	..	..	..	..	> 95	..	..	..	..	..	..
Senegal	2,235	3,179	330	44.5	55.5	0.0	0.0	0.0	79	137	30	..	..	..	1,446
Sierra Leone	..	..	..	..	..	..	..	..	92	..	..	..	..	..	..
Somalia	..	..	..	..	..	..	..	..	< 5	..	..	..	..	..	..
South Africa	95,393	107,738	2,426	85.5	11.9	2.6	0.2	0.0	28	4,546	66	33,013	..	..	(32,589)
Sudan	10,583	13,525	421	18.9	80.3	0.0	0.8	0.0	< 5	68	30	..	94	..	(8,025)
Tanzania, United Rep	10,007	13,917	391	6.9	91.5	0.0	1.6	0.0	> 95	61	11	..	..	..	938
Togo	1,005	1,422	303	..	74.3	0.0	0.0	0.0	> 95	109	9	..	..	..	323
Uganda	..	..	..	..	..	..	..	..	> 95	..	4	..	..	..	..
Zambia	5,597	6,423	608	10.2	81.5	0.0	10.9	0.0	87	591	12	..	..	..	575
Zimbabwe	9,768	9,882	775	36.3	57.4	0.0	2.6	0.0	67	813	40	335	..	..	886
North America	2,152,179	2,529,598	7,929	85.3	2.5	9.1	1.8	0.8	< 5	13,416	100	..	..	..	510,372
Canada	208,832	248,184	7,999	77.0	4.2	8.1	11.5	0.0	< 5	16,787	100	3,350	2,308 e	1,498	(129,563)
United States	1,943,347	2,281,414	7,921	86.2	2.3	9.2	0.8	0.9	< 5	13,053	100	121,962	4,184	4,711	639,935
C. America & Caribbean	175,649	214,218	1,265	82.7	11.1	1.1	1.7	3.2	37	1,409	85	..	..	..	(53,415)
Belize	..	..	..	..	..	..	..	..	< 5	..	..	..	..	..	..
Costa Rica	2,097	3,481	867	50.8	11.0	0.0	14.0	24.8	58	1,598	96	..	..	..	1,783
Cuba	13,530	13,651	1,215	75.6	24.0	0.0	0.0	0.4	42	1,153	97	..	..	..	7,467
Dominican Rep	4,164	7,810	920	81.0	18.4	0.0	0.6	0.0	48	897	67	..	..	..	6,325
El Salvador	2,797	4,269	676	44.7	32.7	0.0	2.3	19.4	65	579	71	..	..	..	1,886
Guatemala	4,656	7,313	624	44.7	53.3	0.0	2.3	0.0	73	365	67	..	..	..	2,149
Haiti	1,580	2,088	257	..	72.7	0.0	1.1	0.0	82	31	34	..	..	..	547
Honduras	2,431	3,236	489	51.8	41.1	0.0	6.3	0.0	66	524	55	..	..	..	1,836
Jamaica	2,955	4,009	1,540	87.9	11.9	0.0	0.2	0.0	47	2,352	90	..	..	..	3,557
Mexico	129,294	152,273	1,516	88.3	5.4	1.5	1.6	3.2	22	1,809	95	690	2,285	374	(76,813)
Nicaragua	2,184	2,792	537	44.8	48.2	0.0	0.6	6.3	72	335	48	..	..	..	1,274
Panama	1,610	3,180	1,058	78.9	14.6	0.0	6.8	0.0	37	1,358	76	..	..	..	2,653
Trinidad and Tobago	5,730	8,693	6,718	99.7	0.3	0.0	0.0	0.0	< 5	3,982	99	..	265	663	(9,185)
South America	290,832	382,156	1,089	70.9	14.9	1.5	11.3	1.6	25	1,639	90	..	..	..	(181,696)
Argentina	46,421	57,601	1,535	85.8	5.2	3.2	5.5	0.0	< 5	2,126	95	..	440	598	(24,854)
Bolivia	2,878	4,271	504	78.9	16.8	0.0	4.4	0.0	61	411	60	..	..	732	(2,667)
Brazil	134,792	185,083	1,064	60.3	20.3	2.0	12.4	3.3	27	1,794	95	3,976	1,456	221	37,916
Chile	14,106	23,801	1,544	74.4	17.7	0.0	7.8	0.0	15	2,648	99	..	..	..	15,737
Colombia	25,254	29,245	683	72.8	17.9	0.0	9.4	0.0	36	781	81	4,305	206	101	(44,296)
Ecuador	6,289	8,727	692	84.6	8.4	0.0	7.0	0.0	28	654	80	..	649	..	(13,460)
Guyana	..	..	..	..	..	..	..	..	< 5	..	..	..	..	..	..
Paraguay	3,161	3,756	670	27.8	57.9	0.0	103.8 f	0.1	64	841	75	..	..	..	1,063
Peru	9,770	12,113	459	68.4	18.7	0.0	12.5	0.4	40	704	73	..	129	222	2,677
Suriname	..	..	..	..	..	..	..	..	69	..	..	..	..	..	..
Uruguay	2,441	2,703	803	59.1	15.5	0.0	29.3	0.0	< 5	1,940	98	..	..	..	1,953
Venezuela	45,720	54,856	2,216	89.5	1.0	0.0	9.5	0.0	< 5	2,729	94	319	11,239	3,735	(155,765)
Oceania	..	..	..	..	..	..	..	..	..	..	..	..	..	..	..
Australia	86,717	115,627	5,975	94.2	4.1	0.0	1.2	0.3	< 5	10,316	100	41,547	560	2,294	(134,092)
Fiji	..	..	..	..	..	..	..	..	< 5	..	..	..	..	..	..
New Zealand	13,671	18,294	4,795	70.3	4.4	0.0	10.1	13.0	< 5	8,828	100	202	..	..	3,308
Papua New Guinea	..	..	..	..	..	..	..	..	> 95	..	..	..	51	385	..
Solomon Islands	..	..	..	..	..	..	..	..	< 5	..	..	..	..	..	..
Developed	..	6,112,050	4,600	83.9	2.4	10.4	2	0.7	14	7578.3	..	..	..	..	1,105,717
Developing	2,789,194	3,911,044	828	73.6	21.7	1.4	2	0.7	67	896.2	67	..	..	..	(1,071,719)

One **toe** equals one ton of oil equivalent; one **kgoe** equals one kilogram of oil equivalent.
a. Other renewables refer to biogas, liquid biomass, geothermal, solar, wind, and wave energy. b. Solid fuels include biomass and fossil fuels burned directly by a household. c. Net Fuel Imports are equal to imports minus exports and includes crude oil, petroleum products, coal and coal products, and natural gas. d. World totals are calculated by WRI. e. Includes an official estimate of oil sands under active development. f. Paraguay exports significant amounts of the hydroelectricity listed here to neighboring countries.

Energy: Technical Notes

DEFINITIONS AND METHODOLOGY

Total Energy Consumption is the amount of primary energy from all sources (coal, nuclear, hydroelectric, etc.) used annually by a particular country or region. Consumption equals indigenous production plus imports minus exports, stock changes, and energy delivered to international marine bunkers. Energy losses from transportation, friction, heat, and other inefficiencies are included here. The original source material published by the International Energy Agency (IEA) refers to these values as Total Primary Energy Supply (TPES). To facilitate comparisons among different sources of energy, the heat content of all energy commodities is presented in metric tons of oil equivalent (toe), which measures the energy contained in a metric ton (1000 kg) of crude oil. One toe is equal to 10^7 kilocalories, 41.868 gigajoules, or 11,628 kilowatt-hours (kWh).

Basic energy statistics are collected by the IEA from a variety of sources. In OECD member countries, national administrations fill out five annual questionnaires. In non-OECD countries, statistics are collected from the distribution of questionnaires, communication with international organizations such as the United Nations, co-operation with national statistical bodies, and direct contact with energy consultants and companies. If data are not available from any of these sources, they are estimated by the IEA. The energy produced by fossil fuels is calculated using conversion factors per unit mass of fuel (e.g., 10,000 kcal/kg of oil). Since energy sources such as coal and crude oil may vary in quality, the IEA uses specific conversion factors supplied by national administrations for the main categories of energy sources and uses (i.e., production, imports, exports). The energy produced by non-fossil fuels is more complicated to measure; the IEA must first assume a primary form of energy to measure using global or regional efficiency averages, and then calculate the primary energy equivalent. Please refer to the original source for further information on the variables and collection methodologies.

Energy Consumption Per Capita is the amount of energy, as defined above, consumed on average by each person, expressed in kilograms of oil equivalent (kgoe). This variable was calculated by dividing total consumption by population figures from the United Nations Population Division.

Energy Consumption by Source data show the amount of energy consumed in five different categories as a percentage of total consumption:

Fossil Fuels include crude oil and natural gas liquids, petroleum products, coal and coal products, and natural gas. Coal and coal products include hard coal, lignite, patent fuel, coke, blast furnace gas, coke-oven gas, brown coal briquettes (BKB), and peat. Oil and natural gas products include crude oil, natural gas liquids, refinery feedstocks, petroleum products, natural gas, gas works gas, and other hydrocarbons. The inclusion of petroleum products accounts for domestic processing of crude oil as well as assorted petroleum imports. Petroleum products refer to refinery gas, ethane, liquified petroleum gas, aviation gasoline, motor gasoline, jet fuels, kerosene, gas/diesel oil, heavy fuel oil, naphtha, white spirit, lubricants, bitumen, paraffin waxes, petroleum coke, and other products.

Solid Biomass includes any plant matter used directly as a fuel or converted into other forms before combustion, including wood; vegetal waste including wood waste and crop waste used for energy; animal materials and wastes; sulphite lyes (also known as black liquor, this is a sludge that contains the lignin digested from wood for paper making); and other solid biomass. Inputs to charcoal production are included here. However, since charcoal is a secondary product, the IEA excludes final charcoal production numbers to avoid double counting.

Nuclear includes all energy produced by nuclear power plants from nuclear fission. The consumption data shown here assume an average thermal efficiency of 33 percent.

Hydroelectric shows the energy content of the electricity produced in hydro power plants. The output from pumped storage plants is not included in these values.

Other Renewables include energy from biogas, liquid biomass, geothermal, solar, ocean, and wave systems. *Biogas energy* is produced by the fermentation of animal dung, human sewage or crop residues. *Liquid biomass energy* is produced from bio-additives such as ethanol (alcohol). *Geothermal technologies* use the heat of the earth to generate energy. *Solar energy* includes the production of electricity from solar photovoltaic cells as well as the production of both electricity and heat from solar thermal energy. Passive solar energy for the direct heating, cooling, and lighting of dwellings or other buildings is not included here. *Ocean energy* includes the production of electricity from the mechanical energy of ocean waves and tides or from the thermal energy (heat) stored in the ocean. *Wind energy* uses the mechanical energy of the wind for generating electricity.

Population Relying on Solid Fuels measures the percentage of the total population that burns solid fuels in their households. Solid fuels include coal or biomass such as dung, charcoal, wood, or crop residues. The World Health Organization (WHO) measures the prevalence of solid fuel usage because the burning of solid fuels in traditional stoves causes high levels of indoor air pollution, emitting dangerous pollutants such as carbon monoxide and particulates.

Electricity Consumption per Capita measures the average kilowatt-hours (kWh) of electrical power generated per person in a particular country or region. Public electricity plants, private electricity plants, and combined heat and power (CHP) plants are all included. Electricity output from crude oil and natural gas liquids is not included here. Electricity consumption equals production and imports minus exports and distribution losses.

Population with Access to Electricity is defined as the percentage of the total population that has electrical power in their home. It includes commercially sold electricity, both on and off the grid. For those countries where access to electricity has been assessed through government surveys, it also includes self-generated electricity.

Proved Fossil Fuel Reserves are generally measured as quantities that geological and engineering information indicates with reasonable certainty can be recovered in the future from known reservoirs under existing economic and operating conditions. In order to facilitate comparisons among different sources of energy, fossil fuel reserves estimates have been converted to metric tons of oil equivalent (toe). A toe measures the energy contained in a metric ton (1000 kg) of crude oil. **Coal** reserves include anthracite, bituminous, sub-bituminous, and lignite coal. The standard conversion factors for one ton of oil equivalent are 1.5 tons of anthracite and bituminous coal and 3 tons of sub-bituminous and lignite coal. **Oil** includes gas condensate and natural gas liquids (NGLs) as well as crude oil. Estimates were converted to metric tons of oil equivalent by BP, the data provider, using individual country conversion factors. **Natural Gas** was converted using the standard conversion factor of 0.9 million metric tons of oil equivalent per billion cubic meters of natural gas.

Net Fuel Imports measures the amount of fossil fuel that enters the national territorial boundaries of a country, whether or not customs clearance has taken place, minus the amount that leaves via export. Fossil fuel includes crude oil and natural gas liquids, petroleum products, coal and coal products, and natural gas. Quantities of crude oil and oil products imported under processing agreements (i.e., refining on account) are included. Quantities of oil in transit are excluded. Re-exports of oil imported for processing within bonded areas are shown as exports of product from the processing country to the final destination. Petroleum products refer to refinery gas, ethane, liquified petroleum gas, aviation gasoline, motor gasoline, jet fuels, kerosene, gas/diesel oil, heavy fuel oil, naphtha, white spirit, lubricants, bitumen, paraffin waxes, petroleum coke, and other petroleum products. Natural gas and gas-works gas are included. Natural gas is reported as coming from the country of origin. Coal imports includes all coal, both primary (including hard coal and lignite/brown coal) and derived fuels (including patent fuel, coke-oven coke, gas coke, BKB, coke oven gas, and blast furnace gas). Peat is also included. In most cases, coal in transit is not included. Regional totals include goods imported from other countries belonging to the same region. Consequently, these totals by no means represent a region's net imports or net exports.

FREQUENCY OF UPDATE BY DATA PROVIDERS

IEA and BP update their energy data annually. WHO updates their information every two years. These updates also often include revisions of past data. Data may therefore differ from those reported in past editions of the World Resources Report.

DATA RELIABILITY AND CAUTIONARY NOTES

Energy
The data on energy balances are based primarily on well-established and institutionalized accounting methodologies and are therefore considered reliable. One exception is fuelwood and other biomass fuels, which are estimated by the IEA based on small sample surveys or other incomplete information. Energy production estimates from nuclear power and renewable sources (hydroelectric, solar, geothermal, and wind power) are calculated using a number of assumptions about primary energy forms and plant efficiencies. As a result, these values may be less reliable than estimates of energy produced from fossil fuels, and the share of renewables in total energy consumption may appear different here than it would from other providers.

IEA data do not distinguish between "no data" (denoted in these tables with "..") and zero values. WRI has distinguished between the two where possible, but some values represented as zero should probably be indicated by ".." and vice versa.

Proven Fossil Fuel Reserves
Every effort is made to come up with a consistent series for reserves based on a common definition; however, in reality, different countries use different methodologies, and the data have varying levels of reliability. Since energy sources such as coal may vary in quality, converting the estimates into toe using standard conversion factors, rather than country specific conversion factors, introduces a level of uncertainty to the reserve estimates shown here.

Percent of Population Relying on Solid Fuels
The estimates of household solid fuel use were compiled with the help of several studies conducted over the past decade. It has been assumed that patterns in solid fuel use have not changed dramatically over this time period.

SOURCES

Energy and Electricity Consumption and Net Inputs: International Energy Agency (IEA). 2003. *Energy Balances of OECD Countries (2003 Edition)* and *Energy Balances of non-OECD Countries (2003 Edition)*. Paris: Organization for Economic Cooperation and Development (OECD). Electronic database online at http://data.iea.org/ieastore/default.asp.

Access to Electricity: International Energy Agency (IEA). 2002. *World Energy Outlook: Energy and Poverty.* Paris: International Energy Agency (IEA). Online at http://www.worldenergyoutlook.org.

Solid Fuel Use: World Health Organization (WHO). 2004. *World Health Report,* Annex Table 7. Geneva: World Health Organization (WHO). Online at http://www.who.int/whr/2004/en/09_annexes_en.pdf.

Proven Reserves Data: BP plc. 2004. *Statistical Review of World Energy.* London: BP plc. Online at http://www.bp.com/statisticalreview2004.

Climate and Atmosphere

Sources: World Resources Institute, International Energy Agency, United Nations Framework Convention on Climate Change

| | Carbon Dioxide (CO$_2$) Emissions {a} | | | | Cumulative CO$_2$ Emissions (million metric tons) | | CO$_2$ Emissions by Sector (as a percent of total CO$_2$ emissions) | | | Emissions (in million metric tons CO$_2$ equivalent) of | | | Total GHG Emissions {c} | Kyoto Protocol Status |
| | Total | | Per Capita | | | | | | | | | | | |
	(million metric tons) 2000	(percent change since 1990)	(metric tons per person) 2000	(percent change since 1990)	From Fossil Fuels & Cement 1950-2000	From Land-Use Change 1950-2000	Trans-portation 2000	Industry & Construc-tion 2000	Elec-tricity 2000	Methane 2000	Nitrous Oxide 2000	Fluori-nated Gases {b} 2000	(million metric tons CO$_2$ equivalent) 2000	(year ratified, n.r. = not ratified) {d}
World	23,895.7	12.7	3.9	(2.3)	781,501	315,122	24.1	18.5	38.3	5,948.2	3,402.9	374.3	33,309	..
Asia (excl. Middle East)	7,837.0	35.1	2.2	17.9	175,087	163,621	13.3	24.7	40.1	2,149.9	1,395.9	123.3	11,471	..
Armenia	3.7	(44.5)	1.2	(36.7)	219	..	13.9	34.2	38.9	2.8	0.3	0.0	7	2003
Azerbaijan	29.5	(39.1)	3.6	(46.3)	1,630	..	5.2	17.2	49.8	11.9	0.8	0.2	42	2000
Bangladesh	29.9	105.6	0.2	63.2	433	(273)	10.8	35.4	31.6	47.6	44.8	0.0	122	2001
Bhutan	0.4	203.1	0.2	150.7	4	0	..	..	..	1.1	0.3	0.0	2	2002
Cambodia	0.5	18.8	0.0	(10.9)	18	1,658	..	..	..	68.0	1.2	0.0	69	2002
China	3,473.6	39.3	2.7	26.2	71,662	38,909	6.9	29.0	41.8	802.9	644.7	45.6	4,942	2002
Georgia	6.2	(35.2)	1.2	(32.7)	321	..	27.3	13.5	27.8	4.4	1.1	0.0	12	1999
India	1,008.0	63.7	1.0	36.3	18,195	(1,191)	12.2	21.8	51.8	445.3	399.0	1.8	1,837	2002
Indonesia	286.0	96.8	1.4	69.4	4,213	75,740	22.7	21.0	22.6	169.2	38.7	0.5	495	2004
Japan	1,224.7	12.3	9.6	9.2	37,155	5,008	21.8	20.3	35.7	21.8	37.0	50.3	1,333	2002 e
Kazakhstan	123.7	(51.7)	7.9	(48.1)	8,469	..	5.4	26.4	47.8	27.3	7.8	0.2	159	n.r.
Korea, Dem People's Rep	168.3	(19.2)	7.6	(27.6)	4,987	313	2.5	61.3	16.4	33.5	6.5	0.2	209	2005
Korea, Rep	470.0	85.4	10.0	69.7	6,971	867	20.2	19.1	32.6	25.0	16.1	14.4	525	2002
Kyrgyzstan	4.8	(55.7)	1.0	(60.4)	362	..	13.3	21.1	41.7	2.2	0.1	0.0	7	2003
Lao People's Dem Rep	0.4	78.8	0.1	39.3	11	698	..	..	..	6.2	0.1	0.0	7	2003
Malaysia	123.6	120.3	5.4	70.9	1,714	20,654	26.2	23.1	25.5	30.4	13.3	0.6	169	2002
Mongolia	7.3	(27.1)	2.9	(35.3)	248	69	..	..	..	8.2	12.1	0.0	28	1999
Myanmar	8.9	108.1	0.2	78.1	217	12,571	37.5	18.8	26.6	61.1	12.5	0.0	82	2003
Nepal	3.2	235.0	0.1	163.5	34	3,648	26.0	35.0	0.6	16.4	11.3	0.0	32	n.r.
Pakistan	106.0	62.7	0.7	26.6	1,833	1,292	24.7	26.2	32.6	94.7	84.6	0.2	285	2005
Philippines	75.3	77.5	1.0	43.4	1,507	2,803	33.5	13.3	32.5	34.2	20.8	0.6	133	2003
Singapore	61.1	103.4	15.2	52.8	913	1	9.8	4.1	39.7	1.2	0.9	0.9	64	n.r.
Sri Lanka	11.2	167.6	0.6	142.3	202	873	52.8	10.1	26.6	13.3	2.9	0.0	28	2002
Tajikistan	4.5	(67.5)	0.7	(71.6)	448	..	46.7	0.0	14.0	1.4	0.1	2.3	8	n.r.
Thailand	171.7	93.5	2.8	72.7	2,377	1,407	28.3	22.8	35.0	75.9	13.1	0.6	261	2002
Turkmenistan	34.6	(18.0)	7.4	(35.2)	1,441	..	4.3	0.0	25.8	27.1	0.6	0.0	62	1999
Uzbekistan	121.0	(16.7)	4.9	(31.4)	4,992	..	8.7	16.4	29.9	46.2	13.5	0.1	181	1999
Viet Nam	47.5	147.6	0.6	108.9	854	(1,440)	32.5	26.4	22.8	68.1	12.9	0.1	130	2002
Europe	6,071.0	(18.3)	8.3	(19.0)	292,323	14,591	13.1	13.5	33.8	987.1	518.9	77.9	7,638	..
Albania	3.1	(55.1)	1.0	(52.6)	183	26	47.8	15.9	8.0	0.5	0.1	0.0	4	2005
Austria	64.4	8.1	7.9	3.1	2,465	45	28.3	25.4	21.1	9.7	2.8	1.1	79	2002 e
Belarus	59.6	(40.5)	5.9	(39.1)	3,358	45	10.5	16.3	53.1	21.6	8.3	0.1	79	n.r. e
Belgium	125.0	13.7	12.2	10.5	5,626	..	20.4	28.4	20.9	11.7	13.3	0.9	148	2002 e
Bosnia and Herzegovina	14.3	(41.6)	3.6	(36.8)	620	0	12.7	14.4	63.2	1.4	0.6	0.6	17	n.r.
Bulgaria	44.7	(43.0)	5.5	(38.6)	2,774	(17)	12.5	22.9	56.4	10.0	18.5	0.2	62	2002 e
Croatia	19.2	(39.9)	4.3	(34.5)	733	(4)	25.3	20.5	23.5	3.8	3.4	0.2	26	n.r. e
Czech Rep	124.1	(19.3)	12.1	(19.0)	6,744	(1)	11.1	20.5	52.1	10.8	8.2	0.4	143	2001 e
Denmark	51.3	2.0	9.6	(1.5)	2,490	8	23.9	10.9	46.4	6.0	9.3	0.5	66	2002 e
Estonia	14.9	(39.7)	10.9	(30.2)	833	16	10.8	7.3	72.3	2.4	0.4	0.0	22	2002 e
Finland	56.6	4.5	10.9	0.6	2,000	241	22.0	21.2	39.8	4.3	7.3	0.3	69	2002 e
France	363.5	(3.6)	6.1	(7.8)	18,619	52	39.3	21.6	12.0	59.3	72.3	7.6	512	2002 e
Germany	837.4	(15.2)	10.2	(18.1)	47,002	188	20.7	15.8	39.0	62.7	60.5	11.0	989	2002 e
Greece	92.2	21.6	8.5	13.4	2,084	(51)	22.7	12.5	51.5	10.9	11.2	2.4	120	2002 e
Hungary	56.9	(18.2)	5.7	(15.3)	3,033	6	16.2	14.1	40.3	11.3	12.9	0.4	76	2002 e
Iceland	2.2	8.5	7.9	(1.9)	81	..	29.2	35.6	0.0	0.3	0.1	0.2	3	2002 e
Ireland	42.8	29.8	11.2	19.5	1,186	(36)	25.8	12.9	38.6	12.9	9.8	0.5	67	2002 e
Italy	446.6	7.0	7.8	5.5	14,625	(5)	26.5	18.7	32.1	37.0	43.5	7.6	531	2002 e
Latvia	6.5	(55.4)	2.7	(49.0)	483	28	33.6	16.4	42.7	2.6	1.2	0.1	10	2002 e
Lithuania	11.6	(47.9)	3.3	(44.3)	747	23	27.2	18.0	34.4	5.9	3.5	0.1	15	2003 e
Macedonia, FYR	8.9	(11.1)	4.4	(16.2)	359	..	11.7	12.3	70.5	1.3	1.1	0.0	11	n.r.
Moldova, Rep	6.7	(65.0)	1.6	(64.3)	629	..	7.8	7.6	61.1	2.6	1.6	0.0	11	2003
Netherlands	174.8	10.4	11.0	3.8	6,370	2	19.1	20.6	31.6	21.6	17.2	4.5	216	2002 e
Norway	35.3	21.7	7.9	15.4	1,203	(18)	33.8	22.8	1.1	7.1	5.1	3.1	51	2002 e
Poland	303.8	(15.2)	7.9	(16.4)	15,873	52	8.7	17.1	53.8	47.2	23.9	0.5	382	2002 e
Portugal	64.8	48.8	6.5	47.1	1,254	(95)	30.5	21.3	35.5	14.3	8.1	0.3	79	2002 e
Romania	90.7	(48.5)	4.0	(46.8)	5,842	82	11.0	22.0	47.3	36.1	7.2	1.7	125	2001 e
Russian Federation	1,540.4	(32.1)	10.6	(30.9)	76,722	13,838	11.6	13.9	56.6	298.7	51.5	14.5	1,919	2004 e
Serbia and Montenegro	44.4	(27.7)	4.2	(30.5)	1,688	3	12.4	16.6	61.1	9.5	6.1	0.8	59	n.r.
Slovakia	36.9	(35.4)	6.9	(37.0)	2,303	22	11.4	29.7	40.5	4.2	3.2	0.3	46	2002 e
Slovenia	15.1	11.3	7.6	7.3	498	8	26.6	19.5	37.6	2.5	2.0	0.2	19	2002 e
Spain	304.9	35.1	7.5	30.3	7,662	(115)	32.3	19.3	32.5	39.6	30.1	7.4	381	2002 e
Sweden	48.8	(2.0)	5.5	(5.3)	3,017	257	48.2	23.8	13.7	7.1	7.1	0.7	64	2002 e
Switzerland	41.8	(6.0)	5.8	(10.4)	1,733	11	37.2	17.8	5.3	5.0	3.7	0.6	50	2003 e
Ukraine	348.4	(44.7)	7.0	(42.2)	21,048	..	4.9	27.6	27.9	153.5	19.9	0.5	517	2004 e
United Kingdom	558.2	(3.3)	9.5	(6.4)	29,791	(21)	24.4	12.2	33.4	51.1	43.8	8.6	660	2002 e
Middle East & N. Africa	1,531.5	58.6	3.8	27.2	27,645	3,035	17.9	20.9	30.4	458.3	175.9	5.0	2,163	..
Afghanistan	0.9	(65.7)	0.0	(77.7)	74	427	..	..	..	13.2	7.5	0.0	22	n.r.
Algeria	74.2	21.3	2.5	0.3	1,531	115	11.3	9.7	24.9	28.5	9.2	0.4	112	2005
Egypt	127.1	42.1	1.9	16.9	2,417	136	22.4	30.6	27.5	34.3	16.0	0.5	178	2005
Iran, Islamic Rep	297.9	59.1	4.5	35.8	5,528	565	22.9	20.4	22.0	96.9	43.8	0.2	439	n.r.
Iraq	78.5	31.1	3.4	(2.1)	1,704	9	36.6	23.2	23.8	14.4	6.5	0.0	100	n.r.
Israel	62.7	70.7	10.4	27.5	1,177	6	18.6	8.9	57.8	11.4	1.7	1.5	77	2004
Jordan	15.5	51.5	3.1	(2.1)	268	1	24.7	15.0	36.5	7.9	0.2	0.1	24	2003
Kuwait	58.5	173.6	26.0	160.9	1,167	0	9.6	25.7	37.8	9.9	0.2	0.3	69	2005
Lebanon	15.6	127.4	4.5	77.3	330	33	27.8	18.8	40.6	1.3	1.1	0.1	18	n.r.
Libyan Arab Jamahiriya	42.3	48.5	8.1	22.1	885	37	25.3	12.3	32.1	9.6	2.5	0.0	54	n.r.
Morocco	33.2	59.9	1.1	35.0	651	98	6.0	16.6	37.5	10.0	15.7	0.0	58	2002
Oman	25.0	131.0	9.6	63.3	255	0	11.8	30.9	33.0	3.7	1.0	0.1	30	2005
Saudi Arabia	266.1	75.8	12.0	31.4	4,081	0	11.7	10.3	25.4	54.4	8.7	0.7	330	2005
Syrian Arab Rep	51.3	51.8	3.1	16.6	878	6	11.6	21.7	31.9	9.7	9.4	0.2	71	n.r.
Tunisia	20.2	40.4	2.1	21.1	394	184	22.8	23.7	34.6	4.8	5.2	0.1	30	2003
Turkey	223.9	48.7	3.3	25.5	4,085	1,395	17.2	27.3	36.5	97.4	40.6	0.5	356	n.r. e
United Arab Emirates	72.3	66.6	25.6	20.2	1,028	..	8.0	43.0	45.1	35.2	0.1	0.2	108	2005
Yemen	10.4	34.8	0.6	(10.7)	246	18	51.3	5.6	17.4	8.7	5.6	0.0	25	2004

For more information, please visit http://earthtrends.wri.org/datatables/climate

| | Carbon Dioxide (CO₂) Emissions (a) | | | | Cumulative CO₂ Emissions (million metric tons) | | CO₂ Emissions by Sector (as a percent of total CO₂ emissions) | | | Emissions (in million metric tons CO₂ equivalent) of | | | Total GHG Emissions (c) (million metric tons CO₂ equivalent) 2000 | Kyoto Protocol Status (year ratified, n.r. = not ratified) (d) |
| | Total | | Per Capita | | | | | | | | | | | |
	(million metric tons) 2000	(percent change since 1990)	(metric tons per person) 2000	(percent change since 1990)	From Fossil Fuels & Cement 1950-2000	From Land-Use Change 1950-2000	Trans-portation 2000	Industry & Construc-tion 2000	Elec-tricity 2000	Methane 2000	Nitrous Oxide 2000	Fluori-nated Gases (b) 2000		
Sub-Saharan Africa	492.1	19.7	0.8	(8.3)	13,867	39,934	..	..	..	498.7	350.6	8.5	1,323	..
Angola	4.9	9.3	0.4	(17.5)	123	507	20.1	42.0	10.4	15.8	6.1	0.0	26	n.r.
Benin	1.7	325.4	0.3	216.7	20	1,030	60.3	9.9	3.3	3.3	2.7	0.0	7	2002
Botswana	4.0	85.9	2.3	45.9	52	560	..	..	..	7.0	4.8	0.0	15	2003
Burkina Faso	1.1	8.9	0.1	(18.0)	19	18	..	..	..	8.8	11.7	0.0	21	2005
Burundi	0.2	23.7	0.0	8.6	5	207	..	..	..	1.8	1.2	0.0	3	2001
Cameroon	3.4	12.2	0.2	(13.4)	75	2,193	62.3	7.4	1.0	11.8	9.8	2.3	27	2002
Central African Rep	0.3	44.4	0.1	14.9	7	255	..	..	..	6.6	5.1	0.0	11	n.r.
Chad	0.1	(9.1)	0.0	(32.0)	6	99	..	..	..	9.6	8.7	0.0	18	n.r.
Congo	0.8	(10.2)	0.2	(34.9)	28	281	59.5	10.8	0.0	3.2	1.7	..	5	n.r.
Congo, Dem Rep	2.5	(42.5)	0.1	(55.6)	153	9,025	26.4	37.4	1.1	32.9	17.2	0.0	53	2005
Côte d'Ivoire	7.1	131.3	0.5	82.6	133	2,592	18.2	8.8	30.9	6.5	2.9	0.0	16	n.r.
Equatorial Guinea	0.7	512.0	1.6	374.3	5	126	..	..	..	0.3	0.2	0.0	1	2000
Eritrea	0.6	..	0.2	..	6	..	33.3	6.7	23.3	0.0	..	0.0	1	n.r.
Ethiopia	3.6	42.0	0.1	5.7	73	240	55.5	27.1	0.6	47.5	12.2	0.0	59	2005
Gabon	1.5	21.5	1.2	(8.0)	69	104	27.3	25.2	29.4	3.8	1.8	0.0	7	n.r.
Gambia	0.3	46.6	0.2	4.4	6	(7)	..	..	..	0.7	0.5	0.0	1	2001
Ghana	5.9	85.9	0.3	44.5	125	794	52.0	14.2	10.4	7.1	7.4	0.2	20	2003
Guinea	1.3	32.1	0.2	0.0	40	297	..	..	..	5.7	2.4	0.0	9	2000
Guinea-Bissau	0.3	36.8	0.2	1.5	6	32	..	..	..	0.9	0.8	0.0	2	n.r.
Kenya	10.2	39.9	0.3	8.1	242	339	41.3	9.7	25.2	21.5	22.6	0.0	53	2005
Lesotho	0.2	35.5	0.1	19.2	3	0	..	..	..	1.2	1.5	0.0	3	2000
Liberia	0.4	(8.8)	0.1	(33.9)	35	1,120	..	..	..	1.2	0.8	0.0	2	2002
Madagascar	2.5	161.9	0.2	94.9	46	1,713	..	..	..	18.9	11.6	0.0	32	2003
Malawi	0.8	30.1	0.1	7.8	26	760	..	..	..	3.6	2.3	0.0	6	2001
Mali	0.6	34.9	0.0	2.1	15	228	..	..	..	12.0	13.8	0.0	25	2002
Mauritania	3.1	19.1	1.2	(8.6)	53	..	..	..	..	4.4	6.4	0.0	14	n.r.
Mozambique	1.2	16.9	0.1	(11.7)	92	264	68.3	5.7	0.8	11.1	3.2	0.0	15	2005
Namibia	1.9	..	1.0	..	18	65	63.1	7.5	1.6	4.5	4.2	0.0	10	2003
Niger	1.2	14.1	0.1	(19.0)	26	20	..	..	..	6.5	5.0	0.0	12	2004
Nigeria	48.1	20.4	0.4	(9.7)	1,054	5,540	42.9	12.7	12.3	72.5	41.6	0.3	163	n.r.
Rwanda	0.6	12.9	0.1	(1.3)	12	212	..	..	..	2.2	1.2	0.0	4	2004
Senegal	3.9	62.0	0.4	26.7	86	102	35.0	16.6	37.0	8.4	6.6	0.0	19	2001
Sierra Leone	0.6	71.8	0.1	58.5	22	379	..	..	..	2.6	0.9	0.0	4	n.r.
Somalia	..	..	..	..	..	148	..	..	..	..	..	..	..	n.r.
South Africa	344.6	16.8	7.8	(2.2)	10,165	49	10.4	17.4	53.8	37.4	25.8	5.4	413	2002
Sudan	5.9	5.4	0.2	(16.6)	166	867	48.1	15.1	23.3	46.6	47.1	0.1	96	2004
Tanzania, United Rep	2.7	16.7	0.1	(13.5)	89	414	53.9	22.2	20.4	31.7	27.1	0.0	59	2002
Togo	1.6	117.7	0.4	65.0	21	245	31.0	52.4	4.8	2.1	2.3	0.0	6	2004
Uganda	1.4	77.4	0.1	29.8	37	1,118	..	..	..	12.4	12.9	0.0	27	2002
Zambia	1.9	(35.6)	0.2	(49.4)	168	6,697	42.1	42.7	3.5	11.2	5.5	0.0	18	n.r.
Zimbabwe	14.1	(5.2)	1.1	(21.6)	468	1,349	15.9	22.1	38.2	11.0	8.6	0.1	33	n.r.
North America	6283.5	18.2	19.9	6.1	229,327	(21,005)	30.1	12.1	40.7	736.8	487.4	137.4	7,599	..
Canada	521.4	22.1	16.9	9.9	17,275	5,194	29.1	18.2	25.5	123.4	57.5	11.3	675	2002 e
United States	5762.1	17.9	20.2	5.8	212,052	(26,199)	30.2	11.5	42.1	613.4	430.0	126.1	6,924	n.r. e
C. America & Caribbean	507.5	28.6	3.0	7.8	12,276	13,469	27.6	18.3	32.9	161.7	50.5	4.7	725	..
Belize	0.8	165.9	3.4	106.1	10	949	..	..	..	0.2	0.2	0.0	1	2003
Costa Rica	5.2	67.5	1.3	31.1	104	439	64.5	17.8	1.3	3.6	3.6	0.1	12	2002
Cuba	31.4	(5.7)	2.8	(10.5)	1,151	(399)	6.4	45.2	39.9	9.1	9.3	0.2	50	2002
Dominican Rep	19.9	102.1	2.4	70.8	317	0	35.2	7.7	34.3	5.9	4.3	0.0	30	2002
El Salvador	6.6	148.1	1.1	104.4	111	184	46.7	20.9	20.6	3.2	2.2	0.1	12	1998
Guatemala	10.1	124.0	0.9	71.7	168	2,514	43.7	14.5	25.5	6.2	5.2	0.1	22	1999
Haiti	1.4	35.6	0.2	17.3	31	89	49.6	20.6	13.5	3.4	2.6	0.0	7	2005
Honduras	5.0	97.9	0.8	49.1	89	782	40.8	26.8	23.4	4.9	3.5	0.0	14	2000
Jamaica	10.3	40.8	4.0	29.3	268	117	19.1	5.5	54.1	1.3	1.3	0.0	13	1999
Mexico	385.1	24.7	3.9	4.9	9,238	4,300	28.1	15.9	33.2	111.7	10.0	4.1	511	2000
Nicaragua	3.6	54.2	0.7	16.3	82	2,385	41.9	11.3	40.7	5.3	4.0	0.0	13	1999
Panama	5.7	110.7	1.9	72.2	141	2,110	38.7	18.5	17.4	3.3	2.7	0.0	12	1999
Trinidad and Tobago	18.1	45.2	14.0	36.9	384	..	9.6	40.9	22.5	3.1	0.3	0.0	22	1999
South America	796.9	42.0	2.3	21.0	20,753	91,234	35.4	25.7	13.4	639.0	369.3	11.4	1,812	..
Argentina	139.0	31.1	3.7	15.0	4,322	2,448	32.2	15.3	19.4	86.7	63.4	0.7	287	2001
Bolivia	11.7	110.0	1.4	68.2	201	3,723	25.0	7.3	10.6	21.3	5.8	0.0	39	1999
Brazil	327.9	53.3	1.9	32.8	7,323	60,946	40.8	30.6	9.2	297.2	207.7	8.3	842	2002
Chile	54.8	72.9	3.6	48.7	1,204	687	30.5	21.7	26.1	14.5	7.5	0.1	77	2002
Colombia	64.0	23.3	1.5	2.4	1,800	4,715	31.4	33.0	11.9	55.5	41.2	0.2	161	2001
Ecuador	20.7	58.8	1.7	31.2	414	2,616	47.0	16.9	11.9	16.2	2.9	0.1	40	2000
Guyana	1.6	44.1	2.1	38.7	60	1,551	..	..	..	1.4	0.8	0.0	4	2003
Paraguay	3.7	70.8	0.7	31.7	68	916	84.9	7.9	0.6	12.3	10.2	0.0	26	1999
Peru	28.2	44.1	1.1	20.8	847	8,316	35.1	30.1	11.6	19.6	21.9	0.1	70	2002
Suriname	2.2	24.0	5.3	17.3	72	0	..	..	..	0.9	0.4	0.0	4	n.r.
Uruguay	6.4	50.1	1.9	39.6	252	(1,084)	41.1	15.0	7.3	18.3	0.7	0.1	26	2001
Venezuela	136.7	24.1	5.6	(0.4)	4,190	6,399	26.9	26.1	14.3	95.1	6.9	1.8	237	2005
Oceania	369.1	26.4	12.3	8.8	10,224	6,362	..	..	..	155.0	43.4	..	578	..
Australia	332.4	25.8	17.4	10.9	9,184	1,321	22.8	15.9	51.7	113.2	27.0	5.3	491	n.r. e
Fiji	0.7	(13.8)	0.9	(23.3)	26	12	..	..	..	1.0	1.1	..	3	1998
New Zealand	32.6	37.4	8.6	22.0	924	686	39.3	30.4	16.7	36.2	12.4	0.7	73	2002 e
Papua New Guinea	2.4	0.7	0.5	(22.4)	66	4,314	..	..	..	3.9	2.3	0.0	9	2002
Solomon Islands	0.2	6.2	0.4	(22.6)	4	19	..	..	..	0.1	0.1	0.0	0	2003
Developed	14679.5	(2.0)	11.2	(6.5)	598,135	655	23.7	15.3	40.8	2,067.1	1,134.3	281.5	18,102	..
Developing	9268.5	47.5	1.9	25.6	186,721	310,586	16.1	24.5	36.1	3,741.0	2,265.7	92.8	15,285	..

All emissions data are expressed in terms of carbon dioxide (CO₂) equivalent.
a. CO₂ emissions from land-use change are not included here. **b.** Fluorinated gas ('F' gas) emissions include hydrofluorocarbons (HFCs), perfluorocarbons (PFCs), and sulfur hexafluoride (SF₆). **c.** Total emissions of all greenhouse gases (GHGs) include CO₂ emissions from fossil fuels and cement manufacture plus emissions of methane, nitrous oxide, and fluorinated gases. **d.** Status of countries as of July, 2005. **e.** Indicates Annex I (developed) countries, which are subject to different restrictions under the Kyoto Protocol.

Climate and Atmosphere: Technical Notes

DEFINITIONS AND METHODOLOGY

Total Carbon Dioxide (CO_2) Emissions measures the mass of carbon dioxide produced during combustion of solid, liquid, and gaseous fuels, as well as from gas flaring and the manufacture of cement. Data are expressed in million metric tons. CO_2 emissions from land-use change are not included here. These estimates do not include bunker fuels used in international transportation. Where values were originally in given in mass of carbon, WRI multiplied by 3.664 (the ratio of the molecular mass of CO_2 to that of carbon) to convert to mass of CO_2.

CO_2 Emissions Per Capita measures the mass of CO_2 produced per person for a country or region, in metric tons. WRI calculates per capita emissions with population estimates from the United Nations Population Division (2002 revision).

Data on carbon dioxide emissions are obtained from the World Resources Institute's Climate Analysis and Indicators Tool (CAIT). In order to provide the most complete and accurate data set, CAIT compiles data from the International Energy Agency (IEA), the Carbon Dioxide Information Analysis Center (CDIAC), and the Energy Information Agency (EIA). Fossil fuel emissions estimates for 131 countries are available from the IEA and reported in CAIT. WRI used CDIAC data on fossil fuel emissions for the 53 countries that lack IEA data. (Data for Lesotho were obtained from the EIA.) Data on emissions from cement manufacturing were obtained from CDIAC for all countries and added to the fossil-fuel emissions totals by WRI. A complete country-by-country listing of source and notes can be found at http://cait.wri.org/cait.php?page=notes&chapt=2.

Emissions are calculated by the IEA using the Intergovernmental Panel on Climate Change (IPCC) Reference Approach. CDIAC estimates are derived from energy statistics obtained from United Nations Statistical Office questionnaires and supplemented by official national statistical publications. The U.S. Energy Information Administration (EIA) estimates CO_2 emissions by country and year, based on energy balances.

Cumulative CO_2 Emissions from Fossil Fuels and Cement, 1950-2000 represents the total mass of CO_2 produced in all years from 1950 to 2000 as a result of the combustion of solid, liquid, and gaseous fuels, as well as from gas flaring and the manufacture of cement. CO_2 emissions from land use change are not included here. These estimates do not include bunker fuels used in international transportation. To estimate cumulative emissions in recently formed countries, WRI apportions emissions estimates based on current emissions and historical emissions from former countries and territories.

Cumulative CO_2 Emissions from Land-Use Change, 1950-2000 represents the total mass of carbon dioxide (CO_2) absorbed or emitted into the atmosphere between 1950 and 2000 as a result of man-made land-use changes (for example, deforestation, shifting cultivation, and vegetation re-growth on abandoned croplands and pastures). Positive values signify a positive net flux ("source") of CO_2, indicating that carbon dioxide has been released into the atmosphere. Negative values signify a negative net flux ("sink") of CO_2, indicating that carbon dioxide has been absorbed as a result of the re-growth of previously removed vegetation. Data include emissions from living and dead vegetation disturbed at the time of clearing or harvest, emissions from wood products (including fuel wood), and emissions from the oxidation of organic matter in the soil in years following initial cultivation. Ecosystems that are not directly affected by human activities such as agriculture and forestry are not included in these totals. The net flux of CO_2 for each country was calculated by R.A. Houghton at the Woods Hole Research Center based on regional fluxes. WRI calculated cumulative carbon emissions from land-use change using annual country-level data. For more information, refer to "Data Note: Emissions (and Sinks) of Carbon from Land-Use Change," online at http://cait.wri.org.

Carbon Dioxide Emissions by Sector shows the proportion of total CO_2 emissions from fossil fuel burning contributed by transportation, industry, and electricity production. The **Transportation** sector includes fossil fuel emissions from road, rail, air, and other forms of transportation, and agricultural vehicles while they are on highways. Data do not include international aviation or ship emissions. The **Industry and Construction** sectors include fossil fuel emissions in all industries and construction. The **Electricity** sector includes fossil fuel emissions from public electricity generation, combined heat and power generation, and heat plants. Emissions from electricity and heat production for use by the producer (autoproduction) for public or private activities are included here.

The emissions figures presented here are calculated by the IEA using the IPCC Sectoral Approach and default emission factors from the Revised 1996 IPCC Guidelines for National Greenhouse Gas Inventories and the IEA energy balances.

Methane Emissions measures the total release of methane (CH_4) into the earth's atmosphere that results from human activities such as agricultural and industrial methane production. Values are expressed in thousand metric tons of CO_2 equivalent using the global warming potential (GWP), which allows the different gases to be compared on the basis of their effective contributions. One kilogram of methane is 23 times as effective at trapping heat in the earth's atmosphere as a single kilogram of CO_2 (using a time horizon of 100 years).

Nitrous Oxide Total Emissions represents the total release of nitrous oxide (N_2O) into the earth's atmosphere that results from human activities such as agriculture, biomass burning, industrial activities, and livestock management. Values are expressed in thousand metric tons of CO_2 equivalent using the GWP, which allows the different gases to be compared on the basis of their effective contributions. The global warming potential of one kilogram of N_2O is nearly 300 times that of a single kilogram of CO_2 (using a time horizon of 100 years).

Fluorinated Gases Emissions represents the total release of hydrofluorocarbons (HFCs), perfluorocarbons (PFCs), and sulfur hexafluoride (SF_6) into the earth's atmosphere. These three groups of fluorinated gases ("f-gases") persist in the atmosphere for thousands of years. *Hydrofluorocarbons* are a by-product of HFC-23 and HCFC-22 (IPCC Source Categories 2E and 2F), which are used in the production of aerosols, refrigeration/AC compounds, solvents, foams, fire extinguishing compounds, semiconductors, and flat-panel displays. *Perfluorocarbons* are produced in the manufacture of semiconductors and as a byproduct of CF_4 and C_2F_6 in primary aluminum production (IPCC Source Categories 2C, 2E, and 2F). *Sulfur Hexafluoride* emissions are generated from magnesium processing, semiconductor production, and the use and manufacture of gas insulated switchgear in electricity distribution networks (IPCC Source Categories 2C and 2F). Values are expressed in thousand metric tons of CO_2 equivalent using the global warming potential (GWP), which allows the different gases to be compared on the basis of their effective contributions. The global warming potential of one kilogram of a fluorinated gas is several thousand times that of a single kilogram of CO_2 (using a time horizon of 100 years).

Most of the **Methane, Nitrous Oxide, and Fluorinated Gas** data shown here were compiled by WRI from *Non-CO_2 Gases Economic Analysis and Inventory*. This data set was prepared by the U.S. Environmental Protection Agency (EPA), covers 90 countries, and accounts for close to 90 percent of global emissions. The remaining data were either obtained from the EDGAR database of the Dutch National Institute of Public Health and the Environment (RIVM) or estimated by WRI based on regional totals and figures for earlier years. A complete listing of sources by country is available at http://cait.wri.org/cait.php?page=notes&chapt=2.

Total GHG Emissions include the total mass of carbon dioxide (CO_2) emitted from fossil fuel and cement manufacturing plus the CO_2 emissions equivalent of methane (CH_4), nitrous oxide (N_2O), hydrofluorocarbons (HFCs), perfluorocarbons (PFCs), and sulfur hexafluoride (SF_6) in the year 2000. Data shown here exclude CO_2 from land-use change.

Kyoto Protocol Status indicates the year that a country ratified the Kyoto Protocol to the United Nations Framework Convention on Climate Change (UNFCCC). Ratification (or its equivalents of acceptance, approval, or accession) binds the state to observe the treaty. The Kyoto Protocol was established in 1997 by the third session of the Conference of Parties (COP-3) to the UNFCCC. Upon ratification, Annex I (industrialized) countries commit themselves to reducing their collective emissions of six greenhouse gases by at least 5 percent from 1990 levels during the first commitment period, which is 2008-2012. Compared to emissions levels that would be expected by 2010 without emissions-control measures, the Protocol target represents a 30 percent cut. Under the Protocol, both developed and developing countries agree to limit emissions and promote adaptation to future climate change, submit information on their national climate-change program and inventories, promote technology transfer, cooperate on scientific and public research, and promote public awareness and education. The Protocol came into force on February 16, 2005, following ratification by Russia in November, 2004. More information is available in *A Guide to the Climate Change Convention Process,* online at http://unfccc.int/resource/process/guideprocess-p.pdf.

FREQUENCY OF UPDATE BY DATA PROVIDERS

Carbon dioxide emissions, cumulative emissions, and non-CO_2 greenhouse gas emissions are updated by WRI's CAIT tool when new data are available; most CO_2 emissions data are updated annually, while non-CO_2 GHG emissions are updated intermittently by RIVM and the EPA. Sectoral emissions data are updated by the IEA every year; as of spring, 2005, data are available from the original source through 2002. Sectoral emissions data from 2000 are included here to enable direct comparisons with the emissions data in this table.

DATA RELIABILITY AND CAUTIONARY NOTES

CO_2 Emissions: The IPCC Reference Approach (used here for most emissions estimates) can overestimate emissions because it uses energy supply data rather than combustion data. In a few cases, the estimates shown here differ significantly (by more than 5 percent) from those reported by individual countries or by the UNFCCC. This is because some countries use different energy figures than the IEA and WRI or treat bunker fuels differently. Other countries calculate emissions with specific calorific values instead of the averages used by the IEA.

Emissions data are synthesized by WRI from three different data sets, which presents both advantages and disadvantages. On the one hand, "filling" the gaps from different data sources improved the ability to make cross-country comparisons and related analyses. Yet comparability can be endangered when data points from different sources (using different methodologies) are placed side-by-side. For a complete discussion of CAIT's methodology, see http://cait.wri.org/downloads/cait_ghgs.pdf.

Cumulative CO_2 Emissions from Land-Use Change: CO_2 emissions estimates from land-use change are considerably less reliable than other CO_2 and GHG emissions estimates; as a result, data should be treated as order-of-magnitude estimates. The data provider states that yearly flux estimates are uncertain on the order of ±150 percent for large fluxes, and ±50 million tons of carbon per year for estimates near zero. The cumulative emissions presented here, however, are more accurate than the data for individual years. More information is available at: http://cait.wri.org/downloads/DN-LUCF.pdf.

CO_2 Emissions by Sector: Data shown in these columns are calculated using the IPCC Sectoral Approach, which surveys actual consumption of fossil fuels by each sector in order to calculate emissions. Other columns in the table have been calculated using the IPCC Reference Approach. While in theory the numbers should be identical, in practice there are minor variations between the data produced by the two methodologies.

Methane, Nitrous Oxide, and Fluorinated Gas Emissions: Generally, estimates of non-CO_2 GHG emissions are less certain than CO_2 emissions estimates. Estimates of nitrous oxide emissions are less certain than methane and fluorinated gas estimates. This data set provides a sound basis for comparability, however, since the methods used are comparable to IPCC methodologies, the global totals comply with budgets used in atmospheric studies, and the data were based on international information sources.

The data presented here may not match the official methane emissions estimates submitted by countries to the UNFCCC. In most cases, however, the differences are not substantial. In the year 2000, WRI estimated methane and nitrous oxide emissions for some countries (accounting for about 10 percent of all emissions); these estimates should be considered rough approximations.

SOURCES

Total and Cumulative Emissions: World Resources Institute. 2005. Climate Analysis Indicators Tool (CAIT), version 2.0. Washington D.C.: World Resources Institute. Online at http://cait.wri.org.

CO_2 Emissions by Sector: International Energy Agency (IEA). 2003. *CO_2 Emissions from Fossil Fuel Combustion* (2003 Edition). Paris: Organization for Economic Cooperation and Development (OECD). Database online at http://data.iea.org/ieastore/default.asp.

Kyoto Protocol, Year Ratified: United Nations Framework Convention on Climate Change (UNFCCC). 2005. *Kyoto Protocol Status of Ratification.* Bonn: UNFCCC. Online at http://unfccc.int/files/essential_background/kyoto_protocol/application/pdf/kpstats.pdf.

9 Water Resources and Fisheries

Source: Food and Agriculture Organization of the United Nations

| | Actual Renewable Water Resources [a] | | Annual Water Withdrawals | | Withdrawals by Sector (percent), 2000 [b] | | | Inland and Marine Fisheries Production (thousand metric tons) [c] | | | | Trade in Fish and Fisheries Products (million $US) [c] 2000-2002 | | Number of Fishers 2000 | Fish Protein as a Percent of Animal Protein Supply 2002 |
| | | | | | | | | Capture | | Aquaculture | | | | | |
	Total (km³)	Per Capita (m³ per person)	Total (km³) 2000	Per Capita (m³ per person) 2000	Agriculture	Industry	Domestic	1990-1992	2000-2002	1990-1992	2000-2002	Imports	Exports		
World	..	8,549	3,802.3	633	70	20	10	84,529.0	93,650.8 d	14,074.7 d	37,694.7 d	60,312.2	56,520.1	34,501,411	15
Asia (excl. Middle East)	..	4,079	2,147.5	631	81	12	7	34,528.9	44,189.1	11,745.9	33,275.1	22,301.9	19,051.0	28,890,352	..
Armenia	11	3,450	3.0	949	66	4	30	2.2	0.8	3.4	1.1	3.0	0.7	244	1
Azerbaijan	30	3,585	17.2	2,114	68	28	5	36.1	13.7	1.7	0.2	1.6	2.2	1,500	1
Bangladesh	1,211	8,089	79.4	576	96	1	3	684.2	1,058.8	210.1	718.8	6.2 e	328.3 e	1,320,480	52
Bhutan	95	40,860	0.4	204	95	1	4	0.3	0.3	0.0	0.0	..	..	450	..
Cambodia	476	32,876	4.1	311	98	1	2	106.3	372.9	7.2	14.3	3.2	27.9	73,425	57
China	2,830	2,206	630.3	494	68	26	7	7,449.7	16,690.0	7,206.8	26,132.7	1,927.0	4,029.1	12,233,128	19
Georgia	63	12,481	3.6	685	59	21	20	66.9	2.2	1.4	0.1	1.4	0.3	1,900	1
India	1,897	1,754	645.8	635	86	5	8	2,867.6	3,799.4	1,212.6	2,084.6	23.1	1,351.8	5,958,744	14
Indonesia	2,838	12,749	82.8	391	91	1	8	2,704.3	4,300.8	522.6	855.6	88.2	1,536.6	5,118,571	57
Japan	430	3,365	88.4	696	62	18	20	8,598.8	4,715.7	808.7	797.7	14,204.2	786.3	260,200	45
Kazakhstan	110	7,116	35.0	2,238	82	17	2	70.7	27.7	8.7	0.7	16.5	15.2	16,000	2
Korea, Dem People's Rep	77	3,387	9.0	405	55	25	20	406.0	208.1	56.7	64.7	25.8	138.2	129,000	27
Korea, Rep	70	1,454	18.6	397	48	16	36	2,321.9	1,828.6	364.9	294.9	1,619.9	1,195.9	176,928	40
Kyrgyzstan	21	3,952	10.1	2,048	94	3	3	0.3	0.1	0.9	0.1	1.4	0.0	154	1
Lao People's Dem Rep	334	57,638	3.0	567	90	6	4	18.6	31.2	10.4	50.6	2.0	0.1	15,000	40
Malaysia	580	23,316	9.0	392	62	21	17	966.3	1,270.6	65.8	158.4	335.9	359.6	100,666	38
Mongolia	35	13,232	0.4	178	52	28	20	0.1	0.2	..	..	0.4	0.1	0	0
Myanmar	1,046	20,870	33.2	699	98	1	1	731.6	1,183.1	14.0	113.8	1.4	210.4	610,000	46
Nepal	210	8,171	10.2	433	96	1	3	5.5	17.1	10.1	16.2	0.3	0.4	50,000	4
Pakistan	223	1,415	169.4	1,187	96	2	2	504.0	604.7	11.8	13.8	0.3	136.7	272,273	3
Philippines	479	5,884	28.5	377	74	9	17	1,875.4	1,961.2	391.8	423.9	89.0	396.4	990,872	39
Singapore	1	139	..	..	..	..	..	10.6	3.8	2.1	4.9	509.8	380.0	364	..
Sri Lanka	50	2,602	12.6	678	95	2	2	185.9	290.9	5.5	9.3	73.2	106.3	146,188	51
Tajikistan	16	2,537	12.0	1,965	92	5	4	0.2	0.1	3.1	0.1	0.2	..	200	0
Thailand	410	6,459	87.1	1,429	95	2	2	2,664.2	2,950.3	338.7	702.4	947.7	4,027.6	354,495	40
Turkmenistan	25	5,004	24.6	5,308	98	1	2	38.4	12.6	2.2	0.0	0.2	0.3	611	3
Uzbekistan	50	1,904	58.3	2,342	93	2	5	5.8	3.2	21.7	4.8	1.8	0.1	4,800	0
Viet Nam	891	10,805	71.4	914	68	24	8	826.1	1,483.0	164.4	515.9	44.9	1,764.2	1,000,000	29
Europe	..	10,655	400.3	581	33	52	15	19,025.1	15,773.3	1,470.1	2,064.1	23,051.7	19,356.0	855,333	12
Albania	42	13,056	1.7	551	62	11	27	5.3	3.5	2.1	0.5	6.5	7.0	1,590	2
Austria	78	9,569	2.1	261	1	64	35	0.5	0.4	3.1	2.5	177.6	11.9	2,300	4
Belarus	58	5,887	2.8	278	30	46	23	1.8	2.4	13.3	6.1	91.6	18.3	5,000	8
Belgium	18	1,770	..	..	..	..	..	39.5	29.7	0.8	1.7	1,030.7	520.2	544	..
Bosnia and Herzegovina	38	8,958	..	..	..	..	..	2.0	2.5	..	4.7	15.6	0.2	3,500	4
Bulgaria	21	2,721	10.5	1,296	19	78	3	41.1	9.5	7.9	3.0	14.7	5.8	1,483	2
Croatia	106	23,890	..	..	..	..	..	26.7	20.3	6.8	8.4	62.4	62.5	65,151	9
Czech Rep	13	1,286	2.6	250	2	57	41	..	4.8	..	19.6	84.0	31.0	2,243	5
Denmark	6	1,116	1.3	238	42	26	32	1,726.9	1,495.5	42.4	39.1	1,781.8	2,762.9	6,711	10
Estonia	13	9,794	0.2	120	5	39	56	266.6	106.6	1.0	0.3	45.7	112.0	13,346	13
Finland	110	21,093	2.5	479	3	84	14	140.6	150.5	18.6	15.4	129.6	15.3	5,879	14
France	204	3,371	40.0	674	10	74	16	595.1	620.3	250.6	256.0	3,082.0	1,067.7	26,113	9
Germany	154	1,866	47.1	572	20	68	12	259.7	213.8	78.6	56.4	2,343.5	1,098.0	4,358	6
Greece	74	6,764	7.8	712	81	3	16	141.2	94.2	14.1	93.6	319.2	221.3	19,847	11
Hungary	104	10,579	7.6	763	32	59	9	11.1	6.8	15.4	12.5	48.3	5.1	4,900	2
Iceland	170	582,192	0.2	543	0	66	34	1,375.8	2,031.0	2.7	3.9	65.2	1,309.5	6,100	29
Ireland	52	13,003	1.1	296	0	77	23	232.9	305.0	27.2	58.3	121.5	407.7	8,478	6
Italy	191	3,336	44.4	771	45	37	18	391.4	295.4	161.4	205.3	2,719.2	392.7	48,770	11
Latvia	35	15,507	0.3	124	12	33	55	341.4	126.1	1.9	0.4	43.5	93.0	6,571	7
Lithuania	25	7,276	0.3	76	7	15	78	330.3	127.0	4.5	1.9	78.5	57.4	4,700	27
Macedonia, FYR	6	..	..	..	..	..	..	0.2	0.2	1.0	1.3	6.7	0.1	8,472	3
Moldova, Rep	12	..	2.3	539	33	58	9	0.9	0.4	5.1	1.3	7.3	0.2	40	8
Netherlands	91	5,608	7.9	500	34	60	6	415.5	492.7	68.9	62.3	1,241.8	1,522.5	3,743	11
Norway	382	83,919	2.2	489	10	67	23	2,015.3	2,710.0	147.5	518.6	627.9	3,488.7	23,552	26
Poland	62	1,598	16.2	419	8	79	13	452.9	221.7	28.7	34.7	334.0	247.2	8,640	12
Portugal	69	6,821	11.3	1,125	78	12	10	310.3	192.9	5.9	8.1	914.3	284.2	25,021	21
Romania	212	9,512	23.2	1,031	57	34	9	86.3	7.3	29.7	9.9	38.8	2.4	8,519	2
Russian Federation	4,507	31,653	76.7	527	18	63	19	6,481.5	3,611.6	156.4	88.5	333.9	1,437.9	316,300	13
Serbia and Montenegro	209	..	..	..	..	..	..	3.0	1.2	2.3	2.7	35.1	0.3	1,429	1
Slovakia	50	9,266	..	..	..	..	..	1.5	..	0.9	34.7	2.0	215	5
Slovenia	32	16,080	..	..	..	..	..	3.9	1.8	0.9	1.2	28.7	6.0	231	4
Spain	112	2,711	35.6	874	68	19	13	1,086.7	1,006.9	199.2	296.2	3,640.4	1,777.8	75,434	18
Sweden	174	19,581	3.0	335	9	54	37	265.2	315.1	8.1	5.7	748.4	522.7	2,783	14
Switzerland	54	7,468	2.6	359	2	74	24	3.2	1.6	1.2	1.1	358.3	3.1	522	7
Ukraine	140	2,898	37.5	755	52	35	12	667.0	339.4	67.7	30.9	101.1	31.7	120,000	13
United Kingdom	147	2,474	9.5	163	3	75	22	788.0	726.2	55.9	167.3	2,249.4	1,305.9	17,847	10
Middle East & N. Africa	..	1,505	324.6	807	86	6	8	2,096.7	3,048.9	117.7	525.5	827.6	1,354.7	746,955	10
Afghanistan	65	2,608	23.3	1,087	98	0	2	1.1	0.9	..	..	..	..	1,500	..
Algeria	14	443	6.1	201	65	13	22	88.5	127.0	0.2	0.4	11.9	5.0	26,151	6
Egypt	58	794	68.7	1,013	78	14	8	272.6	412.7	62.5	353.1	147.1	1.6	250,000	23
Iran, Islamic Rep	138	1,970	72.9	1,097	91	2	7	267.7	348.4	23.1	60.0	30.9 f	48.1 f	138,965	7
Iraq	75	2,917	42.7	1,839	92	5	3	18.1	16.8	2.7	1.7	0.1	0.0	12,000	..
Israel	2	255	2.0	338	63	7	31	6.7	5.2	14.0	21.2	135.9	7.5	1,535	7
Jordan	1	157	1.0	202	75	4	21	0.4	0.5	0.0	0.5	25.5	1.2	721	6
Kuwait	0	8	0.4	198	52	3	45	4.8	5.9	0.0	0.3	16.7	3.6	670	6
Lebanon	4	1,189	1.4	394	67	1	33	1.6	3.8	0.1	0.5	48.3	0.2	9,825	8
Libyan Arab Jamahiriya	1	106	4.8	919	89	3	8	26.5	33.4	0.1	0.1	9.8	10.1	9,500	9
Morocco	29	934	12.8	438	90	2	8	571.9	958.5	0.6	1.6	10.4	913.4	106,096	17
Oman	1	337	1.4	518	91	2	7	115.2	131.0	0.0	0.0	8.1	62.0	28,003	..
Saudi Arabia	2	96	17.3	782	89	1	10	42.3	51.4	2.2	7.0	123.2	9.8	25,360	6
Syrian Arab Rep	26	1,441	19.9	1,205	95	2	3	4.0	8.0	3.7	6.2	56.5	0.0	11,292	3
Tunisia	5	459	2.7	286	82	2	16	86.7	96.9	0.9	1.8	16.3	88.8	50,815	13
Turkey	229	3,171	37.5	550	74	11	15	394.5	532.6	7.6	69.1	37.1	93.7	33,614	11
United Arab Emirates	0	49	2.3	818	68	9	23	94.2	105.2	0.0	0.0	98.3	52.9	15,543	12
Yemen	4	198	6.6	368	95	1	4	79.8	138.7	..	..	5.9	38.0	12,200	16

For more information, please visit http://earthtrends.wri.org/datatables/freshwater

| | Actual Renewable Water Resources (a) | | Annual Water Withdrawals | | Withdrawals by Sector (percent), 2000 (b) | | | Inland and Marine Fisheries Production (thousand metric tons) (c) | | | | Trade in Fish and Fisheries Products (million $US) (c) 2000-2002 | | Number of Fishers 2000 | Fish Protein as a Percent of Animal Protein Supply 2002 |
	Total (km³)	Per Capita (m³ per person)	Total (km³) 2000	Per Capita (m³ per person) 2000	Agriculture	Industry	Domestic	Capture 1990-1992	Capture 2000-2002	Aquaculture 1990-1992	Aquaculture 2000-2002	Imports	Exports		
Sub-Saharan Africa	..	6,322	113.4	173	88	4	9	4,126.4	5,159.6	25.4	63.1	812.1	1,862.1	1,995,694	20
Angola	184	13,070	0.3	28	61	16	22	121.3	250.6	..	..	17.5	22.4	30,364	34
Benin	25	3,585	0.3	40	74	11	15	35.3	37.1	..	0.0	7.2	2.3	61,793	21
Botswana	14	8,022	0.1	81	43	19	38	1.0	0.1	..	..	6.9	0.0	2,620	3
Burkina Faso	13	933	0.8	66	88	0	11	7.2	8.5	0.0	0.0	1.4	0.1	8,300	8
Burundi	4	509	0.2	37	82	1	17	20.8	11.8	0.0	0.1	0.1	0.2	7,030	17
Cameroon	286	17,520	1.0	65	74	8	18	70.7	114.4	0.1	0.2	23.7	0.5	24,500	34
Central African Rep	144	36,912	0.0	6	4	19	77	13.2	15.0	0.2	0.1	0.3	0.2	5,410	9
Chad	43	4,857	0.2	30	80	1	19	70.0	84.0	..	..	0.3	0.0	300,000	15
Congo	832	217,915	0.0	11	10	30	59	44.4	43.3	..	0.2	19.2	2.2	10,500	43
Congo, Dem Rep	1,283	..	0.4	7	31	16	52	171.7	214.6	0.7	2.6	33.5	0.4	108,400	43
Côte d'Ivoire	81	4,794	0.9	59	65	12	23	88.3	76.4	0.2	1.0	154.3	125.7	19,707	..
Equatorial Guinea	26	51,282	0.1	232	1	16	83	3.6	3.5	..	..	4.2	0.7	9,218	..
Eritrea	6	1,466	0.3	82	95	1	4	..	9.9	..	..	0.2	1.3	14,500	11
Ethiopia	110	1,519	2.6	40	93	6	1	4.6	14.5	0.0	0.0	0.2	0.0	6,272	2
Gabon	164	121,392	0.1	102	40	11	48	22.0	43.7	0.0	0.2	12.4	13.5	8,258	33
Gambia	8	5,472	0.0	24	67	11	22	21.5	36.4	0.0	0.0	0.7	2.8	2,000	61
Ghana	53	2,489	0.5	27	48	15	37	393.9	423.6	0.4	5.7	100.4	74.8	230,000	64
Guinea	226	26,218	1.5	187	90	2	8	49.5	100.2	0.0	0.0	6.6	2.0	10,707	43
Guinea-Bissau	31	20,156	0.1	81	91	1	9	5.2	5.0	..	..	0.2	4.4	2,500	6
Kenya	30	932	1.6	52	64	6	30	187.2	174.9	1.2	0.8	4.2	37.8	59,565	8
Lesotho	3	1,678	0.1	30	19	41	40	0.0	0.0	0.0	0.0	..	..	60	0
Liberia	232	66,533	0.1	36	56	15	28	8.3	11.5	0.0	0.0	2.1	0.1	5,143	26
Madagascar	337	18,826	15.0	937	96	2	3	102.3	136.4	0.7	7.7	10.0	106.9	83,310	17
Malawi	17	1,401	1.0	88	81	5	15	68.9	41.6	0.2	0.6	0.4	0.2	42,922	26
Mali	100	7,458	6.9	582	99	0	1	69.3	103.3	0.0	0.5	1.8	0.4	70,000	13
Mauritania	11	3,826	1.7	642	88	3	9	66.6	81.5	..	..	1.0	99.0	7,944	9
Mozambique	216	11,266	0.6	36	87	2	11	32.5	34.8	0.0	0.2	7.6	98.9	20,000	17
Namibia	18	8,921	0.3	142	63	5	33	374.6	587.4	0.0	0.1	16.5	334.6	2,700	14
Niger	34	2,710	2.2	204	95	1	4	3.0	20.2	0.0	0.0	0.6	2.4	7,983	3
Nigeria	286	2,252	8.0	70	69	10	21	287.5	458.2	13.3	26.9	197.6	17.6	481,264	29
Rwanda	5	613	0.1	10	39	14	48	3.2	6.9	0.1	0.4	0.1	..	5,690	8
Senegal	39	3,811	1.6	169	90	4	6	334.9	393.7	0.0	0.1	1.0	245.5	55,547	44
Sierra Leone	160	30,960	0.4	86	93	2	5	63.6	77.6	0.0	0.0	4.1	13.7	17,990	61
Somalia	14	1,309	3.3	378	100	0	0	24.1	19.4	..	..	0.1	3.1	18,900	..
South Africa	50	1,106	15.3	348	73	10	17	574.4	720.0	4.3	4.1	56.1	291.1	10,500	9
Sudan	65	1,879	37.3	1,187	97	1	3	33.2	56.3	0.2	1.2	0.6	0.3	27,700	2
Tanzania, United Rep	91	2,416	2.0	57	93	1	6	357.1	331.1	0.4	0.4	0.4	107.4	92,529	27
Togo	15	2,930	0.2	36	47	8	45	13.0	22.1	0.1	0.4	10.9	6.3	14,120	40
Uganda	66	2,472	0.3	13	39	15	45	241.6	220.7	0.1	2.7	0.1	54.8	57,862	23
Zambia	105	9,630	1.7	167	76	8	16	66.4	65.6	2.5	4.2	1.9	0.4	23,833	22
Zimbabwe	20	1,547	2.6	207	86	5	10	23.1	13.0	0.1	2.2	4.9	3.4	1,804	4
North America	..	19,992	525.3	1,663	38	48	14	6,908.1	6,071.6	409.1	628.6	11,651.6	6,345.6	303,784	7
Canada	2,902	91,419	46.0	1,494	12	69	20	1,471.7	1,026.2	44.9	151.0	1,371.2	2,883.9	8,696	10
United States	3,069	10,333	479.3	1,682	41	46	13	5,291.4	4,866.7	364.2	477.5	10,268.5	3,210.5	290,000	6
C. America & Caribbean	..	6,924	100.7	603	75	6	18	1,753.9	1,989.7	50.1	147.4	455.2	1,525.4	446,390	9
Belize	19	71,111	0.1	519	0	89	11	2.3	30.4	0.2	4.2	2.3	18.6	1,872	18
Costa Rica	112	26,447	2.7	681	53	17	29	16.8	34.4	1.6	12.7	25.0	129.9	6,510	4
Cuba	38	3,365	8.2	732	69	12	19	147.0	46.6	9.8	27.0	36.4	86.2	11,865	14
Dominican Rep	21	2,367	3.4	405	66	2	32	16.4	14.2	0.6	2.8	60.7	1.5	9,286	13
El Salvador	25	3,815	1.3	205	59	16	25	10.6	21.0	0.4	0.5	9.2	26.4	24,534	6
Guatemala	111	8,788	2.0	176	80	13	6	6.7	28.6	1.0	5.7	10.5	25.4	17,275	3
Haiti	14	1,663	1.0	123	94	1	5	5.1	5.0	..	..	5.9	3.6	4,700	9
Honduras	96	13,513	0.9	133	81	11	8	16.5	12.8	4.4	12.4	13.0	72.8	21,000	2
Jamaica	9	3,513	0.4	159	49	17	34	16.0	5.7	3.3	5.1	47.5	8.5	23,465	17
Mexico	457	4,357	78.2	791	77	5	17	1,297.3	1,388.6	24.6	67.9	165.1	659.1	262,401	8
Nicaragua	197	35,142	1.3	256	83	3	14	5.2	24.8	0.1	5.8	6.6	72.6	14,502	8
Panama	148	46,579	0.8	279	28	5	66	155.2	260.2	3.7	3.1	14.6	304.8	13,062	8
Trinidad and Tobago	4	2,938	0.3	237	6	27	67	12.3	10.6	0.0	0.0	9.2	10.8	7,297	14
South America	..	47,044	164.4	474	68	12	19	15,272.4	16,314.5	198.1	868.6	568.9	5,231.8	784,051	6
Argentina	814	20,941	29.1	784	74	9	16	632.9	928.4	0.4	1.5	58.5	810.7	12,320	4
Bolivia	623	69,378	1.4	167	83	3	13	5.7	5.9	0.3	0.4	6.7	0.0	7,754	3
Brazil	8,233	45,573	59.3	345	62	18	20	762.9	798.6	24.6	210.1	271.3	289.3	290,000	4
Chile	922	57,639	12.5	824	64	25	11	5,851.3	4,122.9	49.5	501.1	49.8	1,867.4	50,873	9
Colombia	2,132	47,469	10.7	254	46	4	50	119.9	131.6	15.6	63.9	74.8	177.4	129,410	5
Ecuador	432	32,747	17.0	1,367	82	5	12	282.1	499.2	100.5	66.2	10.4	651.6	162,870	6
Guyana	241	314,211	1.6	2,163	97	1	2	39.6	50.1	0.1	0.6	2.4	55.9	6,571	38
Paraguay	336	55,833	0.5	89	72	9	20	14.5	25.0	0.1	0.1	1.4	0.1	4,469	4
Peru	1,913	69,395	20.1	776	82	10	8	7,089.7	9,137.2	5.9	8.2	20.9	1,136.1	66,361	25
Suriname	122	277,904	0.7	1,565	93	3	4	8.3	18.4	0.0	0.4	3.5	9.0	3,628	22
Uruguay	139	40,419	3.1	941	96	1	2	120.1	109.0	0.0	0.0	13.9	104.0	4,023	4
Venezuela	1,233	47,122	8.4	345	47	7	45	335.2	430.1	1.3	16.0	55.4	130.4	44,302	..
Oceania	..	54,637	26.2	900	72	10	18	817.5	1,104.2	58.4	122.3	643.2	1,793.6	85,324	9
Australia	492	24,708	23.9	1,250	75	10	15	221.8	193.1	14.4	35.3	529.5	933.5	13,800	7
Fiji	29	33,707	0.1	85	78	11	11	29.1	43.6	0.0	1.7	21.5	38.1	8,985	30
New Zealand	327	83,760	2.1	558	42	9	49	394.8	556.9	42.9	83.0	55.4	671.6	1,928	12
Papua New Guinea	801	137,252	0.1	14	1	43	56	26.4	122.8	0.0	0.0	7.4	68.3	16,000	..
Solomon Islands	45	91,039	..	..	..	..	..	49.7	28.8	0.0	0.0	5.0	15.0	11,000	76
Developed	..	11,514	1,221.2	956	46	40	14	35,555.2	27,917.4	2,806.4	3,641.1	49,698.5	28,159.2	1,467,401	12
Developing	..	7,762	2,583.9	545	81	11	8	48,719.3	65,694.4	11,281.5	34,059.6	10,704.1	28,378.4	32,640,482	18

a. Although data were obtained from FAO in 2004, they are long-term averages originating from multiple sources and years. For more information, please consult the original source at http://www.fao.org/waicent/faoinfo/agricult/agl/aglw/aquastat/water_res/index.htm. b. Sectoral withdrawal data may not add up to 100 percent because of rounding. c. Figures are three-year averages for the range of years specified. d. World totals were calculated by WRI. e. Year ending 30 June. f. Year beginning 20-23 March.

Water Resources and Fisheries: Technical Notes

DEFINITIONS AND METHODOLOGY

Actual Renewable Water Resources, measured in cubic kilometers per year (km³/year), gives the maximum theoretical amount of water actually available for each country, although in reality a portion of this water may be inaccessible to humans. Actual renewable water resources are defined as the sum of internal renewable resources (IRWR) and external renewable resources (ERWR), taking into consideration the quantity of flow reserved to upstream and downstream countries through formal or informal agreements or treaties and possible reduction of external flow due to upstream water abstraction. IRWR include the average annual flow of rivers and the recharge of groundwater (aquifers) generated from endogenous precipitation—the precipitation occurring within a country's borders. ERWR represent the portion of the country's renewable water resources that is not generated within the country. ERWR include inflows from upstream countries (groundwater and surface water) and a portion of the water of border lakes or rivers.

Per Capita Actual Renewable Water Resources are measured in cubic meters per person per year (m3/person/year). Per capita actual water resources were calculated by WRI using population data from the United Nations Population Division for the year 2004.

Annual Water Withdrawals, measured in cubic kilometers per year, is the gross amount of water extracted from any source, either permanently or temporarily, for a given use. It can be either diverted towards distribution networks or directly used. It includes consumptive use, conveyance losses, and return flow. Total water withdrawal is the sum of estimated water use by the agricultural, domestic, and industrial sectors. It does not include precipitation.

Per Capita Annual Withdrawals were calculated by WRI using national population data from the UN Population Division for the year 2000.

Withdrawals by Sector, expressed as a percentage, refers to the proportion of water used for one of three purposes: agriculture, industry, or domestic uses. All water withdrawals are allocated to one of these three categories. **Agricultural** uses of water primarily include irrigation and, to a lesser extent, livestock. **Industrial** use measures consumption by self-supplied industries not connected to any distribution network for manufacturing, cooling machinery and equipment, producing energy, cleaning and washing manufactured goods, and as a solvent. **Domestic** uses include drinking water plus water withdrawn for homes, municipalities, commercial establishments, and public services (e.g., hospitals).

Freshwater resources data were provided by AQUASTAT, a global database of water statistics maintained by the Food and Agriculture Organization of the United Nations (FAO). AQUASTAT collects its information from a number of sources—national water resources and irrigation master plans; national yearbooks, statistics, and reports; and national or international surveys.

When possible, FAO cross-checks information between countries to improve assessments in countries where information is limited. When several sources give different or contradictory figures, preference is always given to information collected at national or sub-national level. This preference is based on the assumption that no regional information can be more accurate than studies carried out at the country level. Unless proven inaccurate, official rather than unofficial sources were used. In the case of shared water resources, a comparison between countries was made to ensure consistency at river-basin level.

Inland and Marine Fisheries Production, Capture data refer to the nominal catch of fish, crustaceans, molluscs, aquatic mammals, and other aquatic animals taken for commercial, industrial, recreational, and subsistence purposes from marine, brackish, and inland waters. The harvest from aquaculture and other kinds of farming are excluded. Statistics for aquatic plants are also excluded from country totals. Total capture production includes freshwater fish (carp, tilapias, etc.), diadromous fish (river eels, salmon, etc.), marine fish (flounders, cods, redfishes, tunas, mackerels, sharks, etc.) crustaceans (lobster, shrimp, etc.), and molluscs (oyster, clams, squid, etc.). Data include all quantities caught and landed for both food and feed purposes but exclude catch discarded at sea.

Inland and Marine Fisheries Production, Aquaculture data refer to the harvest of fish, molluscs, crustaceans, and other aquatic animals cultivated in marine, inland, or brackish environments. Data do not include capture production. Statistics for aquatic plants are also excluded. Aquaculture is defined by FAO as "the farming of aquatic organisms, including fish, molluscs, crustaceans, and aquatic plants. Farming implies some form of intervention in the rearing process to enhance production, such as regular stocking, feeding, protection from predators, etc. [It] also implies ownership of the stock being cultivated." Aquatic organisms that are exploitable by the public as a common property resource are not included in aquaculture production.

Production of fish, crustaceans, and molluscs is expressed in live weight, the nominal weight of the aquatic organisms at the time of harvest. For a more detailed listing of the species mentioned above, refer to the original source at http://www.fao.org/waicent/faostat/agricult/fishitems-e-e.html.

Most fisheries statistics are collected by FAO from questionnaires sent to national fisheries agencies. When these data are missing or considered unreliable, FAO estimates fishery production based on regional fishery organizations, project documents, industry magazines, or statistical interpolations. Regional totals represent a sum of available data and may be incomplete.

Trade in Fish and Fisheries Products measures the value of all fisheries products, excluding non-edible shells and aquatic plants, entering (referred to as imports) or leaving (referred to as exports) a country's borders each year through trade. The totals reported here incorporate the same species as the FAO's Yearbook of Fishery Statistics (ftp://ftp.fao.org/fi/stat/summary/default.htm). The value of this trade is expressed in millions of U.S. dollars.

In accordance with internationally recommended practice, import statistics include fish caught by foreign fishing craft, whether or not processed on board, landed in domestic ports; export statistics include fish caught by domestic fishing craft, whether or not processed on board, landed in foreign ports. As such, land-bound countries can therefore export marine fish and fish products. Exports are generally on a free-on-board basis (i.e., not including insurance or freight costs). Regional totals are calculated by adding up imports or exports of each country included in that region. The regional totals should not be taken as a net trade for that region, since much trade occurs intra-regionally.

Number of Fishers includes the number of people employed full or part-time in commercial and subsistence fishing (both personnel on fishing vessels and on shore), operating in freshwater, brackish, and marine areas, and in aquaculture production activities. Data on people employed in fishing and aquaculture are collected by the FAO through annual questionnaires submitted to the national reporting offices of the member countries. When possible, other national and regional published sources are also used to estimate figures.

Fish Protein as a Percent of Animal Protein Supply is defined as the quantity of protein from both freshwater and marine fish, seafood, and derived products available for human consumption as a percentage of all available animal protein. FAO calculates per capita protein supply for all products, including fish, in its collection of Supply/Utilization Accounts (SUAs) and food balance sheets. For each product, the SUA traces supplies from production, imports, and stocks to its utilization in different forms—addition to stocks; exports; animal feed; seed; processing for food and non-food purposes; waste (or losses); and lastly as food available for human consumption, where appropriate. For more detailed information, please refer to the following article: "Supply Utilization Accounts and Food Balance Sheets in the Context of a National Statistical System," maintained on-line by FAO at http://www.fao.org/es/ESS/Suafbs.htm.

FREQUENCY OF UPDATE BY DATA PROVIDERS

Most freshwater data are not available in a time series and are updated intermittently; the global data set maintained on-line by AQUASTAT contains data collected over a time span of up to 30 years. Fisheries production and trade data are updated annually by the Fishery Information, Data and Statistics Unit (FIDI) of FAO. Number of fishers data are updated by FIDI every 2-4 years. The FAO updates the data on fish protein annually; the most recent updates incorporated in these tables are from July 2004.

DATA RELIABILITY AND CAUTIONARY NOTES

Water Resources and Withdrawals: While AQUASTAT represents the most complete and careful compilation to date of statistics on country-level water resources, the quality of the primary information on which it relies varies. Information sources are numerous but rarely complete. Some governments will keep internal water resources information confidential because they are competing for water resources with bordering countries. Many instances of water scarcity are highly localized and are not reflected in national statistics. In addition, the accuracy and reliability of information vary greatly among regions, countries, and categories of information, as does the year in which the information was gathered. All data should be considered order-of-magnitude estimates.

Actual Renewable Water Resources: Exchanges between countries are complicated when a river crosses the same border several times. Part of the incoming water flow may thus originate from the same country in which it enters, making it necessary to calculate a "net" inflow to avoid double counting of resources. In addition, the water that is actually accessible to humans for consumption is often much smaller than the total renewable water resources indicated in the data table.

Actual Renewable Water Resources Per Capita: Water resources data are from a different set of years than the population data used in the calculation. While the water resources data are usually long-term averages, inconsistencies may arise when combining it with 2000 population data. For more information about the collection methodology and reliability of the UN population data, please refer to the notes accompanying the Demographics and Education table.

Total Fisheries Production and Trade in Fish and Fisheries Products: While FISHSTAT provides the most extensive global time series of fishery statistics since 1950, there are some problems associated with the data. Country-level data are often submitted with a 1-2 year delay. Statistics from smaller artisanal and subsistence fisheries are particularly sparse. While these statistics provide a good overview of regional fisheries trends, data should be used with caution and supplemented with estimates from regional organizations, academic literature, expert consultations, and trade data. For more information, consult *Fishery Statistics Reliability and Policy Implications,* published by the FAO Fisheries Department and available on-line at http://www.fao.org/DOCREP/FIELD/006/Y3354M/Y3354M00.HTM.

Number of Fishers data are gross estimates. Many countries do not submit data on fishers, or submit incomplete information; some countries have occasionally omitted fish farmers from the total or included subsistence and sport fishers, as well as family members living on fishing. Apart from the gaps and the heavy presence of estimates due to non-reporting, the information provided by national statistical offices may not be strictly comparable due to the utilization of different definitions and methods in the assessment of the number of people engaged in fishing and aquaculture. FAO recognizes that these statistics are incomplete and may not accurately reflect the current level of employment in the fishing sector.

Fish Protein as a Percent of Total Protein Supply: Food supply is different from actual consumption. Figures do not account for discards (including bones) and losses during storage and preparation. Supply data should only be used to assess food security if they are combined with an analysis of food availability and accessibility. Nonetheless, the data are subject to "vigorous consistency checks." According to FAO, the food supply statistics, "while often far from satisfactory in the proper statistical sense, do provide an approximate picture of the overall food situation in a country and can be useful for economic and nutritional studies, for preparing development plans and for formulating related projects." For more information see *Food Balance Sheets: A Handbook,* maintained on-line by FAO at http://www.fao.org/DOCREP/003/X9892E/X9892E00.htm.

SOURCES

Renewable Water Resources and Water Withdrawals: Food and Agriculture Organization of the United Nations (FAO), Water Resources, Development and Management Service. 2003. AQUASTAT Information System on Water and Agriculture. Rome: FAO. Available at http://www.fao.org/waicent/faoinfo/agricult/agl/aglw/aquastat/main/index.stm.

Population Data (for per capita calculations): United Nations Population Division. 2003. World Population Prospects: The 2002 Revision. New York: United Nations. Data set on CD-ROM.

Total Fisheries Production and Trade in Fish and Fisheries Products: Food and Agriculture Organization of the United Nations (FAO), Fishery Information, Data and Statistics Unit. 2004. FISHSTAT Plus: Universal software for fishery statistical time series, Version 2.3. Rome: FAO. Available at http://www.fao.org/fi/statist/FISOFT/FISHPLUS.asp.

Number of Fishers: Food and Agriculture Organization of the United Nations (FAO), Fishery Information, Data and Statistics Unit (FIDI). 2000. Rome: FAO. More information available at http://www.fao.org/fi/statist/fisoft/fishers.asp.

Fish Protein as a Percent of Total Animal Protein Supply: Food and Agriculture Organization of the United Nations (FAO). FAOSTAT on-line statistical service. 2004. Rome: FAO. Available at http://apps.fao.org.

Biodiversity

Sources: United Nations Environment Programme - World Conservation Monitoring Centre, Ramsar Convention Bureau, United Nations Educational, Scientific, and Cultural Organization, International Union for Conservation of Nature and Natural Resources

	Protected Areas					Number of Known and Threatened Species						Net Legal Trade in Selected Wildlife Products as Reported by CITES (c)		
	All Areas Under IUCN Management Categories I-V, 2004 (a)		Marine Areas, IUCN Categories I-VI, Number 2004	Wetlands of International Importance, Number 2005	Biosphere Reserves, Number 2004	Mammals		Birds		Plants (b)				
	Total Area (1000 ha)	Percent of Total Land Area				Known Species 2004	Number Threatened 2003	Known Species 2004	Number Threatened 2003	Known Species 2004	Number Threatened 2003	Live Primates 2002	Live Parrots 2002	Animal Skins (d) 2002
World	806,722 e	6.1 e	3,459 e	1,420	459	4,629 f	..	10,000 g	..	270,000 h	..	..	..	..
Asia (excl. Middle East)	191,450	7.9	661	145 i	67	..	..	..	..	..	..	(19,001)	43,634	(723,299)
Armenia	299	10.1	..	2	..	78	9	302	12	3,553	1	..	..	0
Azerbaijan	394	4.6	3	3	..	82	11	364	11	4,300	0	2	(1)	0
Bangladesh	66	0.5	5	2	..	131	22	604	23	5,000	12	..	335	0
Bhutan	1,181	29.6	..	..	..	92	21	625	18	5,468	7	..	..	0
Cambodia	3,750	20.5	2	3	1	127	23	521	24	..	31	..	..	(1)
China	105,527	11.3	41	30	26	502	80	1,221	82	32,200	443	(14,322)	(53,326)	45,767
Georgia	290	4.2	2	2	..	98	11	268	8	4,350	0	4	(5)	670
India	15,291	4.9	120	19	4	422	85	1,180	79	18,664	246	4	75	(95)
Indonesia	8,607	4.5	116	2	6	667	146	1,604	121	29,375	383	(3,250)	15,817	(873,858)
Japan	3,123	8.4	164	13	4	171	37	592	53	5,565	12	5,978	17,489	292,287
Kazakhstan	7,742	2.9	1	2	..	145	15	497	23	6,000	1	12	3	0
Korea, Dem People's Rep	316	2.6	..	2	2	105	12	369	22	2,898	3	4	59	45,256
Korea, Rep	350	3.6	7	2	2	89	12	423	34	2,898	0	194	48	30,095
Kyrgyzstan	608	3.1	..	1	2	58	6	207	4	4,500	1	..	..	0
Lao People's Dem Rep	..	..	..	..	..	215	30	704	21	8,286	19	..	..	0
Malaysia	1,366	4.1	67	4	..	337	50	746	40	15,500	683	196	3,791	(491,605)
Mongolia	20,992	13.5	..	11	4	140	13	387	22	2,823	0	..	..	0
Myanmar	174	0.3	1	1	..	288	39	1,047	41	7,000	38	(2)	3	0
Nepal	1,127	7.6	..	4	..	203	29	864	31	6,973	7	..	2	(2)
Pakistan	3,509	4.0	5	19	1	195	17	625	30	4,950	2	..	(476)	(3)
Philippines	1,513	5.1	38	4	2	222	50	590	70	8,931	212	(2,654)	(591)	11
Singapore	3	5.2	2	..	..	73	3	400	10	2,282	54	10	29,328	81,980
Sri Lanka	637	9.6	19	3	3	123	21	381	16	3,314	280	5	199	0
Tajikistan	2,603	18.3	..	5	..	76	7	351	9	5,000	2	..	..	0
Thailand	6,516	12.7	19	10	4	300	36	971	42	11,625	84	310	15,650	103,742
Turkmenistan	1,883	4.0	..	1	1	103	12	318	13	..	0	..	..	0
Uzbekistan	2,050	4.6	..	1	1	91	7	343	16	4,800	1	..	20	0
Viet Nam	1,099	3.4	12	1	4	279	41	837	41	10,500	145	(5,142)	2	(133,885)
Europe	137,694	6.1	761	788 i	172	..	..	..	..	..	..	9,783	137,082	1,429,081
Albania	56	2.0	7	2	..	73	1	303	9	3,031	0	..	..	0
Austria	2,346	28.0	..	17	5	101	5	412	8	3,100	3	7	868	7,969
Belarus	1,304	6.3	..	7	3	71	6	226	4	2,100	0	8	..	1
Belgium	83	2.7	2	9	..	92	9	427	10	1,550	0	1,135	(2,138)	64
Bosnia and Herzegovina	27	0.5	..	1	..	78	8	312	8	..	1	..	(2)	0
Bulgaria	593	5.4	1	10	16	106	12	379	11	3,572	0	(1)	26	36
Croatia	339	6.0	18	4	1	96	7	365	9	4,288	0	11	56	26
Czech Rep	196	2.5	..	11	7	88	6	386	9	1,900	4	31	(24,481)	8
Denmark	933	21.8	72	38 j	1	81	4	427	10	1,450	3	(1)	(905)	2,917
Estonia	350	7.6	..	11	1	67	4	267	3	1,630	0	4	0	130
Finland	1,044	3.1	14	11	2	80	3	421	10	1,102	1	(1)	1	81
France	1,624	3.0	83	22 j	10	148	16	517	15	4,630	2	3,373	30,981	272,532
Germany	10,445	29.3	40	32	14	126	9	487	14	2,682	12	705	3,602	266,995
Greece	239	1.8	14	10	2	118	11	412	14	4,992	2	269	17,170	2,343
Hungary	821	8.8	..	23	5	88	7	367	9	2,214	1	37	(610)	(2,744)
Iceland	476	4.7	9	3	..	33	7	305	0	377	0	..	97	1
Ireland	78	1.1	12	45	2	63	4	408	8	950	1	(2)	42	2
Italy	2,160	7.2	55	46	8	132	12	478	15	5,599	3	241	51,086	524,785
Latvia	818	12.7	1	6	1	68	4	325	8	1,153	0	(2)	1	43
Lithuania	592	9.2	3	5	..	71	5	227	4	1,796	0	12	236	0
Macedonia, FYR	180	7.1	..	1	..	89	9	291	9	3,500	0	..	(176)	0
Moldova, Rep	47	1.4	..	2	..	50	4	203	8	1,752	0	..	98	0
Netherlands	175	4.9	10	49 j	1	95	9	444	11	1,221	0	819	(15,041)	45
Norway	1,952	6.1	18	37 j	..	83	9	442	6	1,715	2	(1)	1,849	32
Poland	3,417	11.0	6	8	9	110	12	424	12	2,450	4	19	649	196
Portugal	399	4.4	26	12	1	105	15	501	15	5,050	15	11	19,732	0
Romania	476	2.0	8	2	3	101	15	365	13	3,400	1	44	16	79
Russian Federation	90,223	5.4	47	35	34	296	43	645	47	11,400	7	146	780	1,338
Serbia and Montenegro	327	3.2	2	5	2	96	10	381	10	4,082	1	550	(1,241)	220
Slovakia	357	7.3	..	13	4	87	7	332	11	3,124	2	12	(621)	41
Slovenia	293	14.4	2	2	2	87	7	350	7	3,200	0	..	878	456
Spain	4,059	8.0	38	49	27	132	20	515	20	5,050	14	101	34,436	304,775
Sweden	4,364	9.8	95	51	1	85	5	457	9	1,750	3	(3)	(784)	6
Switzerland	1,185	28.7	..	11	2	93	4	382	8	3,030	2	(13)	174	55,422
Ukraine	1,937	3.3	17	33	6	120	14	325	13	5,100	1	5	1,264	160
United Kingdom	3,731	15.3	153	159 j	9	103	10	557	10	1,623	13	2,266	17,798	(8,970)
Middle East & N. Africa	33,360	2.7	91	77 i	26	..	..	..	..	..	..	194	40,945	63,360
Afghanistan	219	0.3	..	..	..	144	12	434	17	4,000	1	..	..	0
Algeria	11,864	5.1	4	26	6	100	12	372	11	3,164	2	..	3	0
Egypt	4,536	4.6	17	2	2	118	6	481	17	2,076	2	..	39	55,111
Iran, Islamic Rep	10,376	6.4	7	22	9	158	21	498	18	8,000	1	..	(1)	0
Iraq	1	0.0	..	..	..	102	9	396	18	..	0	..	(1)	0
Israel	379	18.4	19	2	1	115	13	534	18	2,317	0	(250)	9,873	(464)
Jordan	913	10.2	1	1	1	93	7	397	14	2,100	0	265	4,980	0
Kuwait	0	0.0	4	..	..	23	1	358	12	234	0	..	2,618	0
Lebanon	4	0.3	1	4	..	70	5	377	10	3,000	1	20	1,415	1,651
Libyan Arab Jamahiriya	122	0.1	3	2	..	87	5	326	7	1,825	1	78	3	0
Morocco	326	0.8	4	4	2	129	12	430	13	3,675	2	(3)	7	19
Oman	22	0.1	4	..	..	74	12	483	14	1,204	6	..	384	0
Saudi Arabia	3,922	2.0	3	..	..	94	9	433	17	2,028	3	28	7,790	3,108
Syrian Arab Rep	..	..	..	1	..	82	3	350	11	3,000	0	..	1	0
Tunisia	28	0.2	2	1	4	78	10	360	9	2,196	0	18	75	15
Turkey	571	0.7	14	9	..	145	15	436	14	8,650	3	34	2,211	3,847
United Arab Emirates	0	0.0	..	..	..	30	5	268	11	..	0	2	1,112	60
Yemen	..	..	..	..	1	74	6	385	14	1,650	159	..	..	12

For more information, please visit http://earthtrends.wri.org/datatables/biodiversity

	All Areas Under IUCN Management Categories I-V, 2004 (a)		Marine Areas, IUCN Categories I-VI, Number 2004	Wetlands of International Importance, Number 2005	Biosphere Reserves, Number 2004	Mammals		Birds		Plants (b)		Live Primates 2002	Live Parrots 2002	Animal Skins (d) 2002
	Total Area (1000 ha)	Percent of Total Land Area				Known Species 2004	Number Threatened 2003	Known Species 2004	Number Threatened 2003	Known Species 2004	Number Threatened 2003			
Sub-Saharan Africa	142,025	5.9	153	102 i	50	..	..	..	..	..	..	(8,916)	(198,174)	(383,039)
Angola	5,271	4.2	4	..	..	296	11	930	20	5,185	26	(1)	(4)	0
Benin	778	6.7	..	2	2	159	6	485	2	2,500	14	..	2	(2,500)
Botswana	10,499	18.1	..	1	..	169	6	570	9	2,151	0	2	50	4
Burkina Faso	3,135	11.5	..	3	2	129	6	452	2	1,100	2	..	0	0
Burundi	146	5.4	..	1	..	116	7	597	9	2,500	2	..	(6)	0
Cameroon	3,456	7.4	2	..	3	322	42	936	18	8,260	334	(3)	(16,490)	(20)
Central African Rep	7,320	11.8	..	..	2	187	11	663	3	3,602	15	(1)	(10)	(4)
Chad	11,494	9.0	..	2	..	104	12	531	5	1,600	2	1	2	(43,538)
Congo	4,861	14.1	..	1	2	166	14	597	4	6,000	35	..	(8,201)	0
Congo, Dem Rep	11,868	5.1	..	2	3	430	29	1,148	30	11,007	65	..	(5,966)	0
Côte d'Ivoire	1,953	6.1	3	1	2	229	23	702	11	3,660	105	(4)	(4,017)	0
Equatorial Guinea	455	16.8	3	3	..	153	17	418	6	3,250	61	..	..	0
Eritrea	501	4.1	..	..	..	70	9	537	7	..	3	..	..	0
Ethiopia	5,518	4.9	..	..	..	288	35	839	20	6,603	22	..	(1)	(207)
Gabon	80	0.3	2	3	1	166	11	632	5	6,651	107	6	(28)	(5)
Gambia	1	0.0	5	1	..	133	3	535	2	974	4	60	..	0
Ghana	1,104	4.6	..	6	1	249	15	729	8	3,725	117	(11)	2	(6)
Guinea	51	0.2	..	12	4	215	18	640	10	3,000	22	(27)	(10,068)	(10)
Guinea-Bissau	..	..	..	1	1	101	5	459	1	1,000	4	(3)	(4)	0
Kenya	3,485	6.0	11	4	6	407	33	1,103	28	6,506	103	1	(1)	(2,461)
Lesotho	7	0.2	..	1	..	59	3	311	7	1,591	1	..	..	0
Liberia	129	1.3	1	1	..	183	20	576	11	2,200	46	..	(1,656)	(1)
Madagascar	1,404	2.4	7	3	3	165	49	262	34	9,505	276	2	(3,754)	(8,036)
Malawi	1,059	8.9	..	1	1	207	7	658	13	3,765	14	..	6	(60)
Mali	4,532	3.6	..	1	1	134	12	624	5	1,741	6	..	(12,750)	(56,413)
Mauritania	250	0.2	5	3	..	94	7	521	5	1,100	0	..	0	0
Mozambique	3,285	4.2	6	1	..	228	12	685	23	5,692	46	..	(19)	(291)
Namibia	3,214	3.9	4	4	..	192	10	619	18	3,174	24	2	828	(101)
Niger	9,694	8.2	..	7	2	123	10	493	2	1,460	2	(7)	1	0
Nigeria	3,254	3.6	..	1	1	290	25	899	9	4,715	170	(3)	0	(4)
Rwanda	194	7.7	..	..	1	206	13	665	9	2,288	3	..	..	0
Senegal	2,096	10.7	7	4	3	191	11	612	5	2,086	7	(1)	(20,245)	(5)
Sierra Leone	145	2.0	..	1	..	197	12	626	10	2,090	47	..	(100)	0
Somalia	180	0.3	1	..	..	182	15	642	13	3,028	17	..	..	0
South Africa	6,460	5.3	27	17	4	320	29	829	36	23,420	75	(678)	(114,898)	(49,156)
Sudan	8,616	3.5	1	..	2	302	16	952	10	3,137	17	(90)	(154)	(107,111)
Tanzania, United Rep	13,786	14.6	8	4	3	375	34	1,056	37	10,008	239	(844)	(39)	(1,384)
Togo	429	7.5	..	2	..	175	7	565	2	3,085	10	(24)	(508)	(1,500)
Uganda	1,763	7.3	..	2	1	360	29	1,015	15	4,900	38	3	(24)	(2)
Zambia	6,366	8.4	..	2	..	255	11	770	12	4,747	8	3	100	(27,609)
Zimbabwe	3,103	7.9	..	..	..	222	8	661	10	4,440	17	1	(465)	(88,934)
North America	131,738	6.7	659	57 i	60	..	..	..	..	..	..	20,739	36,241	(25,113)
Canada	52,069	5.3	219	36	13	211	16	472	19	3,270	1	1,209	3,473	(12,497)
United States	79,664	8.4	399	21	47	468	40	888	71	19,473	240	19,530	32,759	(12,616)
C. America & Caribbean	6,041	2.2	397	101 i	32	..	..	..	..	..	..	(1,525)	(2,370)	595,983
Belize	633	28.6	22	1	..	147	5	544	3	2,894	30	(2)	1	0
Costa Rica	477	9.3	21	11	2	232	13	838	18	12,119	110	4	1,918	0
Cuba	96	0.9	36	6	6	65	11	358	18	6,522	163	(3)	(20,103)	0
Dominican Rep	1,113	22.9	14	1	1	36	5	224	16	5,657	30	57	526	0
El Salvador	..	..	3	1	..	137	2	434	3	2,911	25	(7)	(6)	(1)
Guatemala	594	5.4	3	4	2	193	7	684	10	8,681	85	7	2,270	0
Haiti	7	0.3	..	..	..	41	4	271	15	5,242	28	..	..	0
Honduras	529	4.7	18	5	1	201	10	699	6	5,680	111	..	1,429	0
Jamaica	0	0.0	4	1	..	35	5	298	12	3,308	208	..	12	0
Mexico	1,205	0.6	37	55	16	544	72	1,026	57	26,071	261	341	12,152	602,606
Nicaragua	777	6.0	5	8	2	181	6	632	8	7,590	39	2	(5,038)	(4)
Panama	483	6.5	14	4	2	241	17	904	20	9,915	195	..	2,580	(6,629)
Trinidad and Tobago	24	4.8	9	1	..	116	1	435	2	2,259	1	..	308	0
South America	106,018	5.9	196	76 i	40	..	..	..	..	..	..	(1,518)	(46,218)	(917,236)
Argentina	5,911	2.1	29	13	11	375	32	1,038	55	9,372	42	3	(16,517)	(230,030)
Bolivia	12,082	11.1	..	8	3	361	26	1,414	30	17,367	70	2	..	(33,720)
Brazil	32,866	3.9	82	8	5	578	74	1,712	120	56,215	381	(4)	983	2,769
Chile	2,650	3.5	27	9	7	159	22	445	32	5,284	40	13	167	103
Colombia	9,786	8.6	13	3	5	467	39	1,821	86	51,220	222	3	9	(547,545)
Ecuador	2,308	9.3	4	11	3	341	34	1,515	69	19,362	..	1	..	1
Guyana	486	2.3	..	..	..	237	13	786	3	6,409	23	(918)	(12,264)	(1,000)
Paraguay	1,391	3.5	..	6	1	168	11	696	27	7,851	10	..	(6,552)	(91,317)
Peru	4,010	3.1	3	10	3	441	46	1,781	94	17,144	274	(298)	(3,301)	(197)
Suriname	1,846	12.7	7	1	..	203	12	674	0	5,018	27	(318)	(9,859)	0
Uruguay	30	0.2	4	2	1	118	6	414	24	2,278	1	2	(1,004)	(83)
Venezuela	31,357	34.2	19	5	1	353	26	1,392	25	21,073	67	(4)	2,120	(16,217)
Oceania	58,396	6.9	541	74 i	12	..	..	..	..	..	..	247	(11,136)	(38,122)
Australia	51,895	6.7	339	64	12	376	63	851	60	15,638	56	266	(95)	(10,147)
Fiji	16	9.9	15	..	..	15	5	112	13	1,518	66	..	18	(1)
New Zealand	6,401	24.0	76	5	..	73	8	351	74	2,382	21	(24)	(1,459)	106
Papua New Guinea	7	0.0	14	2	..	260	58	720	33	11,544	142	..	(9,594)	(28,080)
Solomon Islands	..	..	1	..	..	72	20	248	21	3,172	16	..	..	0
Developed	353,555	6.3	2,010	963 i	..	..	..	..	..	..	..	35,832	84,241	1,637,264
Developing	454,467	5.9	1,430	464 i	..	..	..	..	..	..	..	(35,821)	(84,241)	(1,635,648)

a. Extent of protected areas may include marine components that artificially inflate the percentage of land area protected. b. Total plant species refer to vascular plants only. Threatened plant species include both vascular plants and mosses. c. CITES trade is expressed as the balance of imports minus exports; negative numbers represent net exports. d. Trade in animal skins includes the skins of crocodiles, wild cats, lizards, and snakes. e. Global totals were calculated by WRI. f. Global estimate is from Wilson and Reeder's *Mammal Species of the World*, 1993. g. Estimate from Birdlife International's *Avibase* database. h. 1992 estimate from *Scientific American*. i. Transboundary sites may be included more than once in regional totals. See technical notes for full details. j. Includes sites in overseas territories.

Biodiversity: Technical Notes

VARIABLE DEFINITIONS AND METHODOLOGY

A **Protected Area** is defined by the World Conservation Union (IUCN) as "an area of land and/or sea especially dedicated to the protection and maintenance of biological diversity, and of natural and associated cultural resources, and managed through legal or other effective means." Since September 2002 the World Database on Protected Areas (WDPA) consortium has been working to produce an improved and updated database, available to the public and maintained by the United Nations Environment Programme-World Conservation Monitoring Centre (UNEP-WCMC). The WDPA contains summary information for over 100,000 sites, including the legal designation, name, IUCN Management Category, size in hectares, location (latitude and longitude), and year of establishment. WRI calculated protected area data using the 2004 WDPA database.

IUCN categorizes protected areas by management objective and has identified six distinct categories of protected areas. WRI has calculated **Total Area** in thousand hectares and **Percent of Land Protected** for categories I-V.

Category Ia. Strict nature reserve: a protected area managed mainly for scientific research and monitoring; an area of land and/or sea possessing some outstanding or representative ecosystems, geological or physiological features, and/or species.

Category Ib. Wilderness area: a protected area managed mainly for wilderness protection; a large area of unmodified or slightly modified land and/or sea retaining its natural character and influence, without permanent or significant habitation, which is protected and managed so as to preserve its natural condition.

Category II. National park: a protected area managed mainly for ecosystem protection and recreation; a natural area of land and/or sea designated to (a) protect the ecological integrity of one or more ecosystems for present and future generations; (b) exclude exploitation or occupation inimical to the purposes of designation of the area; or (c) provide a foundation for spiritual, scientific, educational, recreational, and visitor opportunities, all of which must be environmentally and culturally compatible.

Category III. Natural monument: a protected area managed mainly for conservation of specific natural features; an area containing one or more specific natural or natural/cultural features that is of outstanding or unique value because of its inherent rarity, representative or aesthetic qualities, or cultural significance.

Category IV. Habitat/species management area: a protected area managed mainly for conservation through management intervention; an area of land and/or sea subject to active intervention for management purposes so as to ensure the maintenance of habitats and/or to meet the requirements of specific species.

Category V. Protected landscape/seascape: a protected area managed mainly for landscape/seascape conservation and recreation; an area of land, with coast and sea as appropriate, where the interaction of people and nature over time has produced an area of distinct character with significant aesthetic, ecological, and/or cultural value, and often with high biological diversity.

Category VI. Managed mainly for the sustainable use of natural ecosystems. These areas contain predominantly unmodified natural systems, managed to ensure long-term protection and maintenance of biological diversity, while also providing a sustainable flow of natural products and services to meet community needs.

IUCN defines a **Marine Protected Area** (MPA) as: "any area of intertidal or subtidal terrain, together with its overlying water and associated flora and fauna, historical and cultural features, which has been reserved by law or other effective means to protect part or all of the enclosed environment."

These MPAs include areas that are fully marine or littoral. "Littoral" is defined as any site which is known to incorporate at least some intertidal area.

Many MPAs have large terrestrial areas. The extent of the marine portion of most protected areas is rarely documented. The degree of protection varies from one country to another, and may bear little relationship to the legal status of any site. The total number of marine areas in IUCN categories I-VI is shown in this table.

Wetlands of International Importance, or Ramsar sites, are defined under the Wetlands Convention, signed in Ramsar, Iran, in 1971. In order to qualify as a Ramsar site, an area must have "international significance in terms of ecology, botany, zoology, limnology or hydrology." The Convention on Wetlands is an intergovernmental treaty that provides the framework for national action and international cooperation for the conservation and wise use of wetlands and their resources. As of January 2005 there were 1420 Ramsar sites in 146 countries with an overall extent of 123,914,362 hectares.

Biosphere Reserves are terrestrial and coastal environments recognized under United Nations Educational, Scientific, and Cultural Organization's (UNESCO's) Man and the Biosphere Programme. Selected for their value to conservation, they are intended to foster the scientific knowledge and skills necessary for improving the balance between people and nature, and for promoting sustainable development. Ideally, biosphere reserves perform three main roles: (a) conservation in situ of natural and semi-natural ecosystems and landscapes; (b) the establishment of demonstration areas for ecologically and socio-culturally sustainable resource use; and (c) the provision of logistic support for research, monitoring, education, training, and information exchange. Biosphere reserves normally consist of three elements: a minimally disturbed core area for conservation and research; a buffer zone where traditional land uses, research, and ecosystem rehabilitation may be permitted; and a transition area. Biosphere reserves are nominated by national governments and remain under the sovereign jurisdiction of the state where they are located. As of November 2004 there were 459 biosphere reserves in 97 countries.

The **Total Number of Known Species** refers to the total number of a particular type of species in a given country. Data on **known mammals** exclude marine mammals. Data on **known birds** include only birds that breed in that country, not those that migrate or winter there. The number of **known plants** includes higher plants only: ferns and fern allies, conifers and cycads, and flowering plants.

The number of known species is collected by WCMC from a variety of sources, including, but not limited to, national reports from the Convention on Biodiversity, other national documents, independent studies, and other texts. Data are updated on a continual basis as they become available; however, updates vary widely by country. While some countries (WCMC estimates about 12) have data that were updated in the last six months, other species estimates have not changed since the data were first collected in 1992.

The **Number of Threatened Species** listed for all countries includes all species that are "critically endangered, endangered, or vulnerable" as defined by the IUCN, but excludes introduced species, species whose status is insufficiently known (categorized by IUCN as "data deficient"), those known to be extinct, and those for which status has not been assessed (categorized by IUCN as "not evaluated"). Species are classified as vulnerable or endangered if they face a risk of extinction in the wild in the immediate future (critically endangered), in the near-term (endangered), or in the medium-term (vulnerable). Threat categories are assigned based on total population size, distribution, and rates of decline. **Threatened birds** include breeding bird species plus all species that are known to migrate or winter in a given country. Where possible, **threatened mammals** include marine mammals.

Net Legal Trade in Selected Wildlife Products is the balance of imports minus exports of live primates, live parrots, and animal skins reported by the Convention on International Trade in Endangered Species of Wild Fauna and Flora (CITES). Negative values represent net exports. **Live primates** includes all species of monkeys, apes, and prosimians listed under CITES that were traded live in 2002. **Live parrots** includes individuals from the Psittaciformes species listed under CITES that were traded live in 2002. **Animal skins** includes whole skins of all crocodile, cat, lizard, and snake species that were traded in 2002. Data are obtained from trade records submitted by parties to the CITES convention and compiled by the secretariat in the CITES Trade Database.

International trade in wildlife and wildlife products, worth billions of dollars annually, causes serious declines in the numbers of many species of animals and plants. In response, CITES entered into force in 1975 with the purpose of protecting wildlife against overexploitation and preventing international trade from threatening species with extinction. Species are listed in appendices to CITES according to their degree of rarity and the threat posed by trade. International trade in either the listed species themselves or in products derived from the species requires permits or certificates for export, import, and re-export.

FREQUENCY OF UPDATE BY DATA PROVIDERS

Protected Areas data are updated annually by the WDPA. Wetlands of International Importance and Biosphere Reserves information is updated several times a year as new sites are added. Data for Known Species are updated when new information is provided to WCMC (see above). Threatened Species data are updated by IUCN on a continual basis. Species trade data are published in annual reports; the data presented here were published in 2004.

DATA RELIABILITY AND CAUTIONARY NOTES

Protected Areas: Due to variations in consistency and methodology of collection, data on protected areas are highly variable among countries. Some countries update their information with greater regularity or have more accurate data on extent of coverage. Many countries have an underreported number and/or extent of protected areas within their borders. Please see http://parksdata.conserveonline.org for the latest revision.

Biosphere Reserves and Wetlands of International Importance: Reserves can be conterminous or overlapping. Regional wetland totals may include some double counting of sites that are contained in more than one country. A full listing of these sites is available at http://www.unesco.org/mab/BR-WH.htm and at http://www.unesco.org/mab/BR-Ramsar.htm.

Number of Known Species: Values are preliminary estimates based on a compilation of available data from a large variety of sources. They are not based on species checklists. Data have been collected over the last decade without a consistent approach to taxonomy. This can result in significant variations in data quality among countries. Additionally, while the number of species in each country does change, not all countries have been updated; some data may not reflect recent trends. At best, only about 2% of the total species of the world are represented in the UNEP-WCMC Species Database. For this reason, it is important to recognize that numbers of known species in this table are vast underestimates of the actual species worldwide. Data for plant species are less reliable and consistent than data for birds and mammals. Global estimates were not obtained from UNEP-WCMC; see below for citations.

Number of Species Threatened: The total number of threatened species in species groups worldwide are frequently underestimated. For all species groups, there are many species that have yet to be described and whose status is yet unknown. In addition, while threat assessments have been conducted for all described species of mammals and birds, only a small portion of described plant species have been assessed.

Net Legal Trade in Selected Wildlife Products: Data on net exports and net imports as reported by CITES correspond to legal international trade and are based on permits issued, not actual items traded. Figures may be overestimates if not all permits are used that year. Some permits issued in one year are used at a later date;

therefore, numbers of exports and imports may not match exactly for any given year. Species traded within national borders and illegal trade in wildlife and wildlife products are not reflected in these figures. CITES trade data also do not reflect legal trade between non-CITES members. In addition, data on mortality of individuals during capture or collection, transit, or quarantine are also not reflected in these numbers.

SOURCES

Protected Areas (IUCN management categories, marine protected areas): United Nations Environment Programme - World Conservation Monitoring Centre (UNEP-WCMC). 2004. World Database on Protected Areas (WDPA). CD-ROM. Cambridge, U.K. Available at http://sea.unepwcmc.org/wdbpa/download/wdpa2004/index.html.

Ramsar Sites (Wetlands of International Importance): Ramsar Convention Bureau, Gland, Switzerland. Available at http://ramsar.org/sitelist.pdf.

Biosphere Reserves: United Nations Educational, Scientific, and Cultural Organization (UNESCO), Man and the Biosphere Programme, UNESCO-MAB Biosphere Reserve Directory, available at http://www.unesco.org/mab/wnbr.htm.

Known Species of Mammals, Plants, and Breeding Birds: United Nations Environment Programme-World Conservation Monitoring Centre (UNEP-WCMC). 2004. Species Data (unpublished, September 2004). Cambridge, England: UNEP-WCMC. Web site available at http://www.unep-wcmc.org.

Known Species of Mammals, Global Total: Wilson, D. E., and D. M. Reeder (eds). 1993. *Mammal Species of the World*. Washington, DC: Smithsonian Institution Press.

Known Species of Birds, Global Total: LePage, D. 2004. *Avibase: The World Bird Database*. Port Rowan, Ontario: Bird Studies Canada. Available on-line at http://www.bsc-eoc.org/avibase/avibase.jsp.

Known Species of Plants, Global Total: May, RM. 1992. "How many species inhabit the Earth?" *Scientific American* 267(4), 18-24.

Threatened Species of Mammals, Plants and Birds: World Conservation Union (IUCN). 2003. 2003 *IUCN Red List of Threatened Species*. Cambridge, UK: IUCN. Available at http://www.redlist.org/info/tables/table5.html.

International Legal Net Trade Reported by CITES: United Nations Environment Programme-World Conservation Monitoring Centre (UNEP-WCMC). 2004. *Convention on International Trade in Endangered Species of Wild Flora and Fauna (CITES) annual report data, World Conservation Monitoring Centre (WCMC) CITES Trade Database*. Cambridge, U.K. Available at http://www.cites.org.

Land Use and Human Settlements

Sources: Food and Agriculture Organization of the United Nations, University of Maryland, United Nations Environment Programme, United Nations Population Division, World Bank, United Nations Human Settlements Programme

	Total Land Area (1000 ha) 2002	Forested MODIS Satellite (a) Imagery, 2000 >50% Cover	Forested MODIS Satellite (a) Imagery, 2000 >10% Cover	Forested FAO (b) Estimates, >10% Cover 2000	Forested FAO (b) Estimates, >10% Cover 1990	Arable and Permanent Cropland 2002	Arable and Permanent Cropland 1992	Permanent Pasture 2002	Permanent Pasture 1992	Dry-lands (c)	Population Density (people per km²) 2000	Urban Population as a Percent of Total 2000	Urban Population as a Percent of Total 1990	Living in Cities With More Than 100,000 People 2002	Living in Cities With More Than 1 Million People 2002	Percent of Urban Population Living in Slum Conditions 2001
World	13,066,880	24	50	29	30	12	12	27	26	..	45	47	43	..	..	32
Asia (excl. Middle East)	2,406,300	21	38	20	20	21	20	34	34	..	135	35	30	19	12	40
Armenia	2,820	9	23	12	10	20	20	30	24	98	104	65	67	56	47	2
Azerbaijan	8,260	8	27	13	11	24	22	32	26	84	94	51	54	29	25	7
Bangladesh	13,017	11	35	9	8	65	64	5	5	0	958	23	20	13	10	85
Bhutan	4,700	61	73	64	64	4	3	9	7	0	44	8	6	0	0	44
Cambodia	17,652	47	82	52	55	22	22	8	8	0	73	17	13	11	8	72
China	932,742	15	31	17	15	17	14	43	43	34	133	36	27 e	17	11	38
Georgia	6,949	42	67	43	43	15	16	28	30	34	76	53	55	38	28	9
India	297,319	11	44	20	19	57	57	4	4	60	309	28	26	19	11	56
Indonesia	181,157	78	100	55	62	19	16	6	7	3	111	42	31	24	16	23
Japan	36,450	71	87	64	64	13	14	1	1	0	336	65	63	..	..	6
Kazakhstan	269,970	1	4	4	4	8	13	69	69	99	6	56	57	34	8	30
Korea, Dem People's Rep	12,041	..	..	68	68	22	21	0	0	0	185	60	58	34	14	1
Korea, Rep	9,873	59	76	63	63	19	21	1	1	0	472	80	74	78	69	37
Kyrgyzstan	19,180	2	9	5	4	7	7	49	47	55	25	34	38	20	0	52
Lao People's Dem Rep	23,080	76	98	53	55	4	4	4	3	0	22	19	15	3	0	66
Malaysia	32,855	82	97	59	66	23	23	1	1	0	70	62	50	40	19	2
Mongolia	156,650	3	8	7	7	1	1	83	78	65	2	57	57	31	0	65
Myanmar	65,755	61	86	51	59	16	15	0	1	..	70	28	25	16	10	26
Nepal	14,300	34	71	26	32	23	17	12	12	9	160	14	9	7	5	92
Pakistan	77,088	1	7	3	3	29	27	6	6	83	179	33	31	24	17	74
Philippines	29,817	50	89	19	22	36	33	5	4	0	252	59	49	28	20	44
Singapore	67	11	29	3	3	3	3	..	..	0	6478	100	100	0	0	0
Sri Lanka	6,463	33	91	30	35	30	29	7	7	24	283	21	21	14	13	14
Tajikistan	13,996	0.1	3	3	3	8	7	23	25	40	43	26	32	15	0	56
Thailand	51,089	28	82	29	31	38	40	2	2	7	119	31	29	17	14	2
Turkmenistan	46,993	0.0	0.3	8	8	4	3	65	66	100	10	45	45	25	0	2
Uzbekistan	41,424	0.0	2	4	4	12	12	54	55	99	56	37	40	29	13	51
Viet Nam	32,549	43	86	30	28	27	21	2	1	0	236	24	20	17	12	47
Europe	2,260,099	32	65	45	45	13	14	8	8	..	31	73	72	..	..	6
Albania	2,740	16	67	34	37	26	26	16	15	0	108	42	36	15	0	7
Austria	8,273	55	75	46	45	18	18	23	24	0	97	66	66	..	..	6
Belarus	20,748	47	70	45	33	28	30	15	15	..	48	70	66	47	18	6
Belgium (d)	3,282	24	48	23	22	26	24	21	211	0	310	97	96	..	..	15
Bosnia and Herzegovina	5,120	57	92	44	44	21	20	20	23	0	78	43	39	20	0	8
Bulgaria	11,063	29	66	33	31	32	39	16	16	53	73	69	66	33	15	6
Croatia	5,592	44	81	32	31	28	24	28	19	0	79	58	54	23	0	8
Czech Rep	7,728	41	68	33	33	43	..	13	..	13	130	74	75	26	13	6
Denmark	4,243	13	48	11	10	54	60	9	5	0	124	85	85	..	..	6
Estonia	4,239	74	94	46	43	15	27	2	6	0	30	69	71	36	0	12
Finland	30,459	50	96	65	65	7	8	0	0	0	15	61	61	..	..	6
France	55,010	26	61	28	27	36	35	18	20	0	108	76	74	..	..	6
Germany	34,895	36	62	30	30	34	34	14	15	5	231	88	85	..	..	4
Greece	12,890	16	62	27	25	30	31	36	41	45	83	60	59	..	..	6
Hungary	9,210	18	61	20	19	52	54	12	13	46	108	64	62	38	26	6
Iceland	10,025	3	35	0	0	0	0	23	23	..	3	92	91	..	..	6
Ireland	6,889	25	62	9	7	16	15	48	49	0	54	59	57	..	..	1
Italy	29,411	26	58	33	32	38	40	15	15	21	191	67	67	..	..	6
Latvia	6,205	70	95	45	43	30	28	10	13	0	37	67	70	43	0	6
Lithuania	6,268	45	75	31	30	48	49	8	7	0	54	67	68	40	0	6
Macedonia, FYR	2,543	28	69	35	35	24	26	25	25	37	79	59	58	28	0	8
Moldova, Rep	3,288	5	44	10	9	65	67	12	11	100	127	46	47	30	0	31
Netherlands	3,388	13	42	9	9	28	27	30	31	0	383	64	60	..	..	9
Norway	30,625	24	61	27	26	3	3	1	0	0	14	76	72	..	..	6
Poland	30,629	31	60	29	28	46	48	13	13	19	124	62	61	35	15	6
Portugal	9,150	11	70	40	34	30	33	16	9	29	109	53	47	..	..	14
Romania	22,987	34	66	27	26	43	43	21	21	38	94	55	53	33	10	19
Russian Federation	1,688,850	32	65	50	50	7	8	5	5	22	9	73	73	49	23	6
Serbia and Montenegro	10,200	31	65	28	28	37	40	18	21	..	103	52	51	25	16	5
Slovakia	4,808	49	73	44	41	32	..	18	..	0	110	57	57	12	0	6
Slovenia	2,014	69	89	55	54	10	12	15	16	0	98	51	51	13	0	6
Spain	49,944	13	48	28	27	37	40	23	21	69	81	76	75	..	..	6
Sweden	41,162	56	90	60	60	7	7	1	1	0	20	83	83	..	..	6
Switzerland	3,955	40	67	29	28	11	11	28	29	0	174	68	68	..	..	6
Ukraine	57,935	16	52	16	15	58	59	14	13	65	82	67	67	41	19	6
United Kingdom	24,088	21	57	12	11	24	27	46	48	0	242	89	89	..	..	6
Middle East & N. Africa	1,291,988	1	3	2	2	8	8	28	24	..	31	58	54	39	24	36
Afghanistan	65,209	0.1	1	2	2	12	12	46	46	94	33	22	18	18	9	99
Algeria	238,174	0.1	1	1	1	3	3	13	13	21	13	57	51	32	12	12
Egypt	99,545	0.0	0.5	0	0	3	3	..	..	8	68	42	43	38	28	40
Iran, Islamic Rep	163,620	1	2	4	4	10	11	27	27	90	40	64	56	46	26	44
Iraq	43,737	0.0	1	2	2	14	13	9	9	100	53	68	70	63	34	57
Israel	2,171	0.3	9	6	4	20	20	7	7	69	287	92	90	81	62	2
Jordan	8,893	0.0	0.2	1	1	4	4	8	9	72	56	79	72	58	47	16
Kuwait	1,782	..	..	0	0	1	0	8	8	92	126	96	95	69	69	3
Lebanon	1,023	1	26	3	4	31	30	2	1	59	334	87	83	66	53	50
Libyan Arab Jamahiriya	175,954	0.0	0.1	0	0	1	1	8	8	23	3	85	80	94	62	35
Morocco	44,630	0.2	5	7	7	21	22	47	47	92	65	56	48	36	16	33
Oman	30,950	0.0	0.1	0	0	0	0	3	3	14	8	76	62	47	0	61
Saudi Arabia	214,969	0.0	0.0	1	1	2	2	79	56	24	10	86	78	5	0	20
Syrian Arab Rep	18,378	0.1	4	2	2	29	30	45	44	98	89	50	49	41	27	1
Tunisia	15,536	0.3	3	3	3	32	31	31	29	94	58	63	58	25	17	4
Turkey	76,963	7	28	13	13	37	36	17	16	77	88	65	59	44	26	43
United Arab Emirates	8,360	0.0	0.0	4	3	3	1	4	3	0	34	85	83	81	50	2
Yemen	52,797	0.0	1	1	1	3	3	30	30	30	34	25	21	17	9	65

For more information, please visit http://earthtrends.wri.org/datatables/forests

	Total Land Area (1000 ha) 2002	Forested MODIS Satellite {a} Imagery, 2000 >50% Cover 2000	Forested >10% Cover 2000	FAO {b} Estimates, >10% Cover 2000	FAO >10% Cover 1990	Arable and Permanent Cropland 2002	Arable and Permanent Cropland 1992	Permanent Pasture 2002	Permanent Pasture 1992	Dry-lands {c}	Population Density (people per km²) 2000	Urban Population as a Percent of Total 2000	Urban Population as a Percent of Total 1990	Percent of Population Living in Cities With More Than 100,000 People 2002	Percent of Population With More Than 1 Million People 2002	Percent of Urban Population Living in Slum Conditions 2001
Sub-Saharan Africa	2,362,209	18	52	20	22	8	7	35	35	..	27	34	28	22	13	73
Angola	124,670	25	83	56	57	3	3	43	43	19	10	33	26	24	20	83
Benin	11,062	0.3	94	24	30	25	16	5	5	88	55	42	35	28	0	84
Botswana	56,673	0.1	21	21	23	1	1	45	45	100	3	50	42	0	0	61
Burkina Faso	27,360	0.0	32	26	26	16	13	22	22	100	43	17	14	10	0	77
Burundi	2,568	8	95	3	9	53	51	39	33	0	225	9	6	5	0	65
Cameroon	46,540	57	91	50	55	15	15	4	4	13	32	49	40	25	18	67
Central African Rep	62,298	58	98	37	37	3	3	5	5	20	6	41	38	21	0	92
Chad	125,920	0.4	18	10	11	3	3	36	36	68	6	24	21	9	0	99
Congo	34,150	70	94	65	65	1	1	29	29	0	10	52	48	22	0	90
Congo, Dem Rep	226,705	72	99	58	60	3	3	7	7	0	21	30	28	30	19	50
Côte d'Ivoire	31,800	21	98	22	30	22	19	41	41	..	49	44	40	36	24	68
Equatorial Guinea	2,805	89	94	62	66	8	8	4	4	0	16	45	35	23	0	87
Eritrea	10,100	0.0	3	13	14	5	..	69	..	83	32	19	16	22	0	70
Ethiopia	100,000	9	52	4	5	11	10	20	41	58	59	15	13	5	4	99
Gabon	25,767	87	97	82	82	2	2	18	18	0	5	81	68	49	0	66
Gambia	1,000	2	73	43	39	26	16	46	45	97	116	26	25	15	0	67
Ghana	22,754	12	91	27	32	28	19	37	37	66	82	44	37	20	13	70
Guinea	24,572	25	98	28	30	6	6	44	44	14	33	33	25	20	19	72
Guinea-Bissau	2,812	45	108	61	67	19	15	38	38	6	38	32	24	20	0	93
Kenya	56,914	3	37	29	31	9	8	37	37	68	53	36	25	16	9	71
Lesotho	3,035	0.5	62	0	0	11	11	66	66	0	59	18	17	9	0	57
Liberia	9,632	81	99	31	38	6	6	21	21	0	26	45	42	43	43	56
Madagascar	58,154	19	76	20	22	6	6	41	41	23	27	26	24	12	8	93
Malawi	9,408	7	90	22	28	26	21	20	20	0	96	15	12	9	0	91
Mali	122,019	0.1	13	11	11	4	2	25	25	80	10	30	24	12	9	93
Mauritania	102,522	0.0	0.0	0	0	0	0	38	38	46	3	58	44	23	0	94
Mozambique	78,409	20	95	38	39	6	5	56	56	38	22	32	21	19	9	94
Namibia	82,329	0.0	4	10	11	1	1	46	46	91	2	31	27	11	0	38
Niger	126,670	0.0	0.2	1	2	4	3	9	8	62	9	21	16	11	0	96
Nigeria	91,077	7	59	15	19	36	36	43	44	58	124	44	35	35	18	79
Rwanda	2,467	11	90	12	17	56	48	19	26	0	293	14	5	4	0	88
Senegal	19,253	2	39	32	34	13	12	29	30	94	48	47	40	35	24	76
Sierra Leone	7,162	54	99	15	20	8	8	31	31	0	62	37	30	26	22	96
Somalia	62,734	0.1	12	12	13	2	2	69	69	80	14	33	29	21	12	97
South Africa	121,447	3	38	7	7	13	12	69	68	66	36	56	49	39	29	33
Sudan	237,600	3	24	25	28	7	6	49	47	67	13	36	27	26	18	86
Tanzania, United Rep	88,359	11	85	41	42	6	5	40	40	..	37	32	22	14	7	92
Togo	5,439	2	90	9	13	48	40	18	18	34	80	33	29	15	0	81
Uganda	19,710	18	95	17	21	37	35	26	26	16	97	12	11	5	5	93
Zambia	74,339	20	91	42	53	7	7	40	40	16	14	35	39	36	16	74
Zimbabwe	38,685	3	78	49	57	9	8	44	44	67	32	34	29	28	18	3
North America	1,879,066	29	55	24	23	12	12	13	14	..	16	79	75	27	13 f	6
Canada	922,097	36	62	25	25	5	5	2	2	16	3	79	77	58 f	31 f	6
United States	915,896	23	49	23	23	19	20	26	26	41	30	79	75	27 f	8 f	6
C. America & Caribbean	264,826	27	66	29	33	16	15	38	37	..	64	67	64	41	26	24
Belize	2,280	73	92	59	74	4	4	2	2	0	11	48	48	0	0	62
Costa Rica	5,106	59	97	39	42	10	10	46	46	0	77	59	54	36	36	13
Cuba	10,982	29	90	21	19	34	39	26	25	11	101	75	74	..	..	2
Dominican Rep	4,838	30	89	28	28	33	32	43	43	5	171	58	55	47	32	38
El Salvador	2,072	34	95	6	9	44	41	38	31	0	295	58	49	32	27	35
Guatemala	10,843	53	98	26	31	18	16	24	23	0	105	45	41	22	21	62
Haiti	2,756	8	82	3	6	40	40	18	18	3	289	36	30	23	21	86
Honduras	11,189	51	98	48	53	13	17	13	13	0	58	44	40	33	20	18
Jamaica	1,083	58	96	30	34	26	22	21	22	31	235	52	52	35	0	36
Mexico	190,869	21	56	28	31	14	14	42	41	69	51	75	73	54	32	20
Nicaragua	12,140	44	95	25	34	18	13	40	40	0	39	56	53	33	25	81
Panama	7,443	57	96	38	45	9	9	21	20	0	39	56	54	34	34	31
Trinidad and Tobago	513	60	91	50	55	24	24	2	2	4	251	74	69	31	0	32
South America	1,752,020	44	81	50	52	7	7	29	29	..	19	80	74	54	36	36
Argentina	273,669	9	40	12	13	13	11	52	52	53	13	90	87	64	42	33
Bolivia	108,438	49	74	48	50	3	2	31	31	..	8	62	56	39	31	61
Brazil	845,942	49	93	64	66	8	7	23	22	15	20	81	75	54	36	37
Chile	74,880	25	41	21	21	3	4	17	17	21	20	86	83	70	36	9
Colombia	103,870	66	104	44	45	4	5	40	39	17	37	75	69	54	36	22
Ecuador	27,684	53	83	37	42	11	11	18	18	63	44	60	55	50	35	26
Guyana	19,685	91	102	79	81	3	3	6	6	0	4	36	33	30	0	5
Paraguay	39,730	37	95	57	60	8	6	55	55	55	13	55	49	25	0	25
Peru	128,000	58	72	51	53	3	3	21	21	37	20	73	69	48	28	68
Suriname	15,600	85	89	86	86	0	0	0	0	0	3	74	65	..	..	7
Uruguay	17,502	4	97	7	4	8	7	77	77	0	19	92	89	51	51	7
Venezuela	88,205	56	96	54	57	4	4	21	21	49	27	87	84	58	37	41
Oceania	849,088	10	30	24	23	6	6	49	51	..	4	73	70	..	..	4
Australia	768,230	4	24	20	20	6	6	52	55	86	3	91	85	..	..	2
Fiji	1,827	..	..	45	46	16	14	10	10	0	45	49	42	21	0	68
New Zealand	26,799	43	73	29	28	13	13	52	52	0	14	86	85	..	..	1
Papua New Guinea	45,286	89	99	66	69	2	2	0	0	1	12	13	13	7	0	19
Solomon Islands	2,799	82	90	88	89	3	3	1	1	0	15	16	14	0	0	8
Developed	5,462,781	25	51	31	30	12	12	22	22	..	23	72	70	25	15	8
Developing	7,623,524	23	49	25	26	12	11	30	29	..	60	40	35	25	15	43

a. 500 km resolution imagery processed by the Global Land Cover Facility (GLCF) at the University of Maryland. b. Forest Resource Assessment by the United Nations Food and Agriculture Organization of the United Nations (FAO) c. Drylands area is determined using aridity zones; arid, semi-arid and dry sub-humid zones are included. Hyper-arid (bare sand deserts) are excluded. Climate data from 1950 to 1981 were analyzed to produce these estimates. d. Land area data includes Luxembourg. e. Data for 1990 and 2000 do not include Hong Kong or Macau. f. Data are from national censuses.

Land Use and Human Settlements: Technical Notes

DEFINITIONS AND METHODOLOGY

Total Land Area is measured in thousand hectares and excludes the area under inland water bodies. Inland water bodies generally include major rivers and lakes. Data on land area were provided to the Food and Agriculture Organization (FAO) by the United Nations Statistical Division.

Forested Area is calculated by WRI as a percentage of total land area using data from MODIS satellite imagery analyzed by the Global Land Cover Facility (GLCF) at the University of Maryland and from FAO's *Global Forest Resources Assessment 2000* (FRA 2000).

MODIS Satellite Imagery identifies the percent of tree crown cover for each 500-meter pixel image of land area based on one year of MODIS photography. Data were aggregated to country-level by the GLCF at the request of WRI. The values presented here show the percentage of total land area with more than 10 percent or 50 percent of the ground covered by tree crowns.

The Food and Agriculture Organization (FAO) Estimates are drawn from *FRA 2000*. Forest area includes both natural forests, composed primarily of native tree species, and plantations, forest stands that are established artificially. If no other land use (such as agro-forestry) predominates, any area larger than 0.5 hectares with tree crowns covering more than 10 percent of the ground is classified as a forest. Forest statistics are based primarily on forest inventory information provided by national governments; national gathering methodologies can be found at http://www.fao.org/forestry/fo/fra/index.jsp. FAO harmonized these national assessments with the 10-percent forest definition mentioned above. In tropical regions, national inventories are supplemented with high resolution Landsat satellite data from a number of sample sites covering a total of 10 percent of the tropical forest zone. Where only limited or outdated inventory data were available, FAO used linear projections and expert opinion to fill in data gaps. If no forest statistics existed for 1990 and 2000, FAO projected forward or backward in time to estimate forest area in the two reference years.

Arable and Permanent Cropland is calculated by WRI as a percent of total land area. Arable land is land under temporary crops (double-cropped areas are counted only once), temporary meadows for mowing or pasture, land under market and kitchen gardens, and land temporarily fallow (less than five years). Abandoned land resulting from shifting cultivation is not included in this category. Permanent cropland is land cultivated with crops that occupy the land for long periods and need not be replanted after each harvest, such as cocoa, coffee, and rubber; this category includes land under trees grown for wood or timber. Wherever possible, data on agricultural land use are reported by country governments in questionnaires distributed by FAO. However, a significant portion of the data is based on both official and unofficial estimates.

Permanent Pasture is calculated by WRI as a percent of total land area. Permanent pasture is land used long-term (five years or more) for herbaceous forage crops, either cultivated or growing wild. Shrublands and savannas may be classified in some cases as both forested land and permanent pasture.

Drylands is calculated by WRI as the percent of total land area that falls within three of the world's six aridity zones—the arid, semi-arid, and dry sub-humid zones. The United Nations Convention to Combat Desertification (UNCCD) adopted this definition of drylands in order to identify areas where efforts combating land degradation should be focused and methods for attaining sustainable development should be promoted. The world is divided into six aridity zones based on the aridity index—the ratio of mean annual precipitation (PPT) to mean annual potential evapotranspiration (PET). Drylands of concern to the UNCCD include those lands with an aridity index between .05 and .65 (excluding polar and sub-polar regions).

Ratios of less than .05 indicate hyper-arid zones, or true deserts. Ratios of 0.65 or greater identify humid zones. The areas with an aridity index between .05 and .65 encompass the arid, semi-arid, and dry sub-humid areas. See the UNCCD's website at http://www.unccd.int/main.php for more information. Climatic data from 1950 to 1981 were used to define aridity zone boundaries for the globe with a resolution of about 50 km.

Population Density is calculated by WRI as the number of persons per square kilometer of land area using FAO land-area data shown in the first column. Population data are from the United Nations Population Division.

Urban Population as a Percent of Total is the proportion of a country's total population that resides in areas defined as urban in each of the countries of the world. These definitions vary slightly from country to country. Many countries define an urban area by the total number of inhabitants in a population agglomeration. Typically the threshold for considering a region urban is between 1,000 and 10,000 inhabitants. Other countries specify several of their cities or provinces as urban, and the remaining population is defined as rural. Estimates of the proportion of the population living in urban areas are obtained from national sources. Censuses and population registers are the most common sources of those counts. Once values of the urban proportion at the national level are established, they are applied to estimates and projections of the total national population from *World Population Prospects: The 2002 Revision.*

Percent of Population Living in Cities with More Than 100,000 and 1 Million People indicates population distribution and levels of urbanization within a country. WRI calculated percentages from the *Urban Population in World Bank Regions by City Size* data set and total population figures from the UN Population Division. Urban population data were primarily collected from national statistical offices, international organizations such as the United Nations, and the World Gazetteer web site. Data from national census bureaus in several OECD countries (Canada, United States) were added to complement this data set.

Percent of Urban Population Living in Slum Conditions is the proportion of a country's urban population that is living in households classified as slum dwellings. A slum household is defined by the United Nations Human Settlements Program (UN-HABITAT) as a group of individuals living under the same roof that lacks one or more of the following conditions: "secure tenure status, adequate access to improved water, adequate access to improved sanitation and other infrastructure, structural quality of housing, and sufficient living area."

While the same methodology was used to determine the slum population in all countries, data sources vary. Where available, household surveys, such as Demographic and Health Surveys (DHS) and Multiple Indicator Cluster Surveys (MICS), were the common sources of data. An effort was made to ensure that households were not counted twice, in the event that they lacked more than one of the indicators. In the absence of household surveys, or when household surveys did not provide answers for the desired indicators, the slum populations were estimated. Estimates were derived from a statistical model using available country data and the Human Development Index (HDI) of the United Nations Development Programme (UNDP).

FREQUENCY OF UPDATE BY DATA PROVIDERS

Total Land Area, Arable and Permanent Cropland Area, and Permanent Pasture data are updated annually by the FAO. Population data are updated every two years by the United Nations Population Division. Forested Land Area based on Modis Satellite Imagery was released by the GLCF in 2002. The *FRA* is published by the FAO every 5 years; data in this table are from the 2000 release. Drylands Area data were prepared in 1991; no update is planned. Data on urban population by city size are updated continually by the World Bank. Urban Population Living in Slum Conditions is the first global compilation of such data.

DATA RELIABILITY AND CAUTIONARY NOTES

Land-area data are intended for broad estimations only and not for strict comparisons. Land-area classification is inherently subjective; experts often express different opinions on the criteria for categorizing ecosystem and use types, and the resolution of the underlying satellite and survey information can vary widely among data sets. In addition, the information on land-area types shown here is from different sources and represents different time periods. They are not intended to represent exclusive land-cover types; some degree of overlap is present.

Forest Cover: As shown in the table, forest cover estimates differ widely based on collection methodology and classification used. FAO uses a more complex definition of forests than is used in the MODIS data set, requiring that there be 10 percent tree cover and that forestry be the predominant land use in the survey area. Thus some areas with tree cover of more than 10 percent may not be counted as forest if the predominant land use is determined to be agriculture, urban settlement, or some other nonforestry use. Because the MODIS tree-cover data set makes no such distinction, the tree cover in the "10 percent and above" categories will sum to a larger area than the FAO forest area for most countries.

MODIS Satellite Imagery: Following publication of the Global Land Cover Characteristics (GLCC) database by GLCF, a number of scientific teams assessed the accuracy of the GLCC's approach by comparing the results with higher-resolution satellite imagery. These teams found that the accuracy of the GLCF's approach was, depending on the assessment approach, in a range from 60 to nearly 80 percent, meaning that the assessment teams' classification of a given area agreed with the GLCF's classification between 60 and 80 percent of the time.

FAO Estimates: FAO acknowledges that the quality of primary data available remains poor, particularly for tropical countries, open woodland areas, and non-production forests. In most tropical countries, forests are not monitored comprehensively or frequently enough to map their extent accurately or to track their rate of change. In the absence of inventory data for specific dates (1990 and 2000), FAO's latest estimates of forest area and change over time are often based on projections and expert opinion and thus remain educated guesses. Just one or two satellite images appear to have been the prime source of new information for some countries with poor inventory data. Open woodlands are difficult to monitor by remote sensing techniques, and government forestry agencies tend not to survey them as part of normal forest inventories. Non-production forests are not included in these totals, even though many appear to meet the FAO definition of forests. While the quality of data from developed countries is generally better than from developing countries, problems still arise with estimates because of differences in national forestry definitions and systems of measurement, and the use of different reference periods. In northern countries, the boundary between forest and tundra is vague. For a discussion of some data reliability issues associated with *FRA 2000,* see http://pdf.wri.org/fra2000.pdf.

Drylands: The accuracy of land-area totals is limited by the 50-kilometer resolution of the data set. The climate data set was derived from a limited number of field observations. Actual boundaries between aridity zones are neither abrupt nor static, making delineated borders somewhat artificial. The data should therefore be considered useful as a general indicator of the extent of drylands within each country, rather than as an exact depiction of the climatic situation on the ground. Alternative methods for measuring extent of drylands area include use of soil moisture and agricultural production systems, although these methods may also be subject to similar problems such as low-resolution data, limited field observations, and subjectivity when delineating exact boundaries on the ground.

Percent of Urban Population Living in Slum Conditions: UN-HABITAT's definition of slum conditions, described above, may not always measure living conditions with sufficient precision. Sub-national coverage for the household surveys varies as does the international coverage for the different indicators. Despite these drawbacks, this is the most reliable global data set available on this complex issue.

SOURCES

Total Land Area and Cropland Area: Food and Agriculture Organization of the United Nations (FAO). 2004. FAOSTAT on-line statistical service. Rome: FAO. Available at http://apps.fao.org.

Forested Area, Modis Satellite Imagery: University of Maryland Global Land Cover Facility (GLCF). 2002. MODIS 500m Vegetation Continuous Fields Percent Tree Cover. Available at http://glcf.umiacs.umd.edu/data/.

Forested Area, FAO Estimates: Food and Agriculture Organization of the United Nations (FAO). 2001. *Global Forest Resources Assessment 2000—Main Report.* Rome: FAO. Available at http://www.fao.org/forestry/fo/fra/index.jsp.

Dryland Area: U. Deichmann and L. Eklundh. 1991. *Global Digital Data Sets for Land Degradation Studies: A GIS Approach.* GRID Case Study Series No. 4. Nairobi, Kenya: United Nations Environment Program/Global Resource Information Database (UNEP/GRID).

Population Density: United Nations Population Division. 2003. World Population Prospects: The 2002 Revision. Dataset on CD-ROM. New York: United Nations. Available at http://www.un.org/esa/population/ordering.htm.

Urban Population: United Nations Population Division. 2004. World Urbanization Prospects: The 2003 Revision. Urban and Rural Areas Dataset (POP/DB/WUP/Rev.2003/ Table A.7). Data set in digital form. Available at http://www.un.org/esa/population/ ordering.htm. New York: United Nations.

Population by City Size: The World Bank Group. 2004. *Urban Population in World Bank Regions by City Size.* Washington, DC: World Bank. Available at http://www.worldbank.org/urban/env/population-regions.htm.

Population Living in Slum Conditions: United Nations Human Settlements Program (UN-HABITAT). 2003. *Slums of the World: The Face of Urban Poverty in the New Millennium?* Nairobi: UN-HABITAT. Available at http://www.unhabitat.org/ publication/slumreport.pdf.

Food and Agriculture

Source: Food and Agriculture Organization of the United Nations, International Federation of Organic Agriculture Movements, United States Department of Agriculture

	Agricultural Land (a) (000 ha) 2002	Irrigated Cropland as a Percent of Total 2002	Organic Cropland as a Percent of Total 2003	Labor (workers per ha) 2001	Fertilizer (kg/ha) 2001	Mechanization (tractors per 000 ha) 2001	Water Withdrawals (meters³/ha) 2000	Per Capita Food Production Index (1999-2001=100) 1983	Per Capita Food Production Index (1999-2001=100) 2003	Cereals Received as Food Aid (000 metric tons) 2002	Net Cereal Imports (b) as a Percent of Consumption 2002	Cereal Fed to Livestock as a Percent of Total Consumption 2003	Calorie Supply Per Capita (kilocalories /person/day) 2002	Share of Calorie Supply From Animal Products (percent) 2002
World	1,534,466	18.1	..	0.87	90.1	17.5	..	87.1	101.4	8,610	..	36.9	2,804	16.7
Asia (excl. Middle East)	500,878	34.2	..	2.02	139.0	12.3	..	..	..	2,182	..	20.6	2,682	14.3
Armenia	560	50.0	..	0.36	8.9	32.7	3,464	..	114.6	16	46.1	29.2	2,268	16.1
Azerbaijan	2,009	72.4	0.20	0.50	6.1	15.0	6,108	91.8	118.3	5	21.5	21.6	2,575	14.6
Bangladesh	8,429	54.5	..	4.58	170.8	0.7	8,999	91.8	97.8	353	6.6	0.0	2,205	3.1
Bhutan	165	24.2	..	5.83	..	..	2,500	119.4	76.2	0	22.5	..	..	..
Cambodia	3,807	7.1	..	1.22	..	0.5	1,052	89.6	99.9	25	3.4	..	2,046	9.4
China {c}	153,956	35.7	0.06	3.29	227.6 e	7.2	3,149	52.1	109.1	..	(1.4)	28.1	2,951	20.9
Georgia	1,064	44.1	..	0.48	26.3	16.1	2,005	..	112.3	18	48.3	39.3	2,354	17.6
India {d}	170,115	33.6	0.03	1.57	102.1	9.0	3,291	83.0	98.4	128	(5.5)	4.9	2,459	7.7
Indonesia	33,700	14.3	0.09	1.48	78.5 e	2.1	2,254	76.2	104.2	204	11.5	7.4	2,904	4.3
Japan	4,762	54.7	0.10	0.54	282.4	423.0	11,435	112.9	95.7	..	67.6	45.8	2,761	20.7
Kazakhstan	21,671	10.8	..	0.06	2.3	2.3	1,321	..	107.5	..	(47.4)	47.2	2,677	25.6
Korea, Dem People's Rep	2,700	54.1	..	1.21	100.5 e	25.9	2,480	108.7	106.0	975	26.5	..	2,142	6.5
Korea, Rep	1,877	60.6	0.05	1.20	379.4 e	106.5	..	76.7	92.4	..	65.0	46.3	3,058	15.6
Kyrgyzstan	1,411	76.0	..	0.38	18.8	18.0	6,587	..	99.0	2	11.5	39.8	2,999	19.6
Lao People's Dem Rep	1,001	17.5	0.01	2.15	12.8	1.1	..	68.9	112.6	6	1.4	..	2,312	7.1
Malaysia	7,585	4.8	..	0.24	149.1	5.7	736	60.8	108.4	..	69.0	41.4	2,881	18.1
Mongolia	1,200	7.0	..	0.26	2.7	4.2	195	132.4	95.8	..	58.2	..	2,249	39.7
Myanmar	10,611	18.8	..	1.71	9.0 e	1.0	3,110	84.2	116.2	..	(3.6)	4.9	2,937	4.8
Nepal	3,294	34.5	0.00	3.33	22.7	1.4	3,307	88.1	99.3	..	0.3	..	2,453	6.5
Pakistan {d}	22,120	80.5	0.08	1.14	132.9	14.5	7,407	78.8	97.9	1	(13.6)	3.9	2,419	18.1
Philippines	10,700	14.5	0.02	1.18	73.4 e	1.1	2,099	95.5	106.1	68	19.6	23.7	2,379	15.7
Singapore	2	..	..	..	..	32.5	..	893.0	71.0	..	..	14.1	..	..
Sri Lanka	1,916	33.3	0.65	2.02	127.7 e	4.2	6,280	115.4	100.1	81	29.0	..	2,385	7.1
Tajikistan	1,057	68.0	..	0.77	11.4	28.4	12,745	..	120.6	121	37.2	12.9	1,828	9.2
Thailand	19,367	25.6	0.02	1.12	92.0 e	11.4	4,597	90.2	103.2	1	(26.5)	..	2,467	12.0
Turkmenistan	1,915	94.0	..	0.38	54.0	26.1	14,182	..	98.1	..	..	18.3	2,742	15.4
Uzbekistan	4,827	88.7	..	0.62	149.1	35.2	11,210	..	103.4	119	3.8	18.6	2,241	17.5
Viet Nam	8,895	33.7	0.08	3.30	225.9 e	18.4	6,615	64.7	113.8	60	(5.5)	10.0	2,566	12.1
Europe	303,993	8.3	..	0.10	73.4	36.1	..	..	107.5 f	96	..	51.3	3,331	27.7
Albania	699	48.6	..	1.07	26.8 e	11.4	1,522	89.6	105.0	25	44.9	..	2,848	28.6
Austria	1,462	0.3	11.60	0.13	148.1	224.5	14	96.7	91.7	..	(9.7)	..	3,673	33.1
Belarus	5,730	2.3	..	0.11	121.5	11.5	134	..	110.9	..	11.9	50.8	3,000	26.2
Belgium	..	..	1.45	..	..	..	..	..	96.8	..	52.6	..	3,584	30.5
Bosnia and Herzegovina	1,093	0.3	..	0.11	38.8	26.2	..	..	83.8	54	28.2	62.2	2,894	13.5
Bulgaria	3,583	16.5	0.00	0.06	43.2 e	6.7	425	145.2	101.0	3	(25.0)	39.1	2,848	24.5
Croatia	1,588	0.3	0.00	0.10	110.7	1.5	..	..	92.6	..	(8.3)	71.1	2,799	19.2
Czech Rep	3,305	0.7	5.09	0.14	119.2 e	28.6	17	..	90.5	..	(1.6)	..	3,171	27.0
Denmark	2,284	19.6	6.65	0.05	134.2	53.5	234	87.5	101.4	..	(12.5)	..	3,439	38.1
Estonia	631	0.6	3.00	0.12	42.6	79.7	7	..	107.5	..	25.4	..	3,002	27.0
Finland	2,208	2.9	7.00	0.06	135.1	88.2	30	124.9	101.6	..	(6.0)	..	3,100	37.5
France	19,583	13.3	1.70	0.04	213.3	64.5	200	99.4	93.0	..	(55.0)	..	3,654	37.1
Germany	11,997	4.0	4.10	0.08	217.4	85.8	775	101.0	93.2	..	(22.2)	..	3,496	30.6
Greece	3,846	37.2	0.86	0.20	111.9 e	64.9	1,621	100.1	95.9	..	22.0	..	3,721	21.8
Hungary	4,804	4.8	1.70	0.10	94.5 e	23.6	511	115.5	95.3	..	(44.7)	..	3,483	32.6
Iceland	7	..	0.70	..	.. e	1288.4	29	129.7	104.3	..	..	..	3,249	41.5
Ireland	1,123	..	0.70	0.15	562.2	144.8	0	89.8	92.4	..	24.6	..	3,656	31.1
Italy	11,064	24.9	8.00	0.12	128.1	148.2	1,849	106.8	91.4	..	25.9	..	3,671	25.9
Latvia	1,861	1.1	0.81	0.08	35.0	30.1	19	..	111.0	..	(8.6)	..	2,938	28.2
Lithuania	2,989	0.2	0.25	0.07	54.2	34.2	6	..	109.6	..	(6.1)	..	3,325	26.3
Macedonia, FYR	612	9.0	..	0.19	36.4	88.2	..	..	91.1	..	29.1	44.9	2,655	21.8
Moldova, Rep	2,143	14.0	..	0.22	14.9	19.1	..	..	102.8	..	(24.9)	59.7	2,806	16.2
Netherlands	949	59.5	2.19	0.26	443.5	159.4	2,853	101.5	92.6	..	68.3	..	3,362	34.2
Norway	871	14.6	3.13	0.12	200.3	151.1	259	118.5	97.5	..	25.7	68.0	3,484	33.0
Poland	14,226	0.7	0.36	0.30	110.0 e	91.4	94	111.4	97.5	..	0.3	..	3,375	26.1
Portugal	2,705	24.0	2.20	0.23	76.9	62.5	3,258	68.2	97.4	..	64.8	..	3,741	29.1
Romania	9,899	31.1	0.27	0.16	37.2 e	16.6	1,339	124.2	106.2	1	(3.4)	59.2	3,455	20.5
Russian Federation	125,300	3.7	0.00	0.06	12.7	6.2	108	..	110.4	1	(16.9)	49.0	3,072	22.3
Serbia and Montenegro	3,724	0.8	0.30	0.26	66.7	109.2	..	..	97.7	0	(8.0)	65.6	2,678	35.0
Slovakia	1,559	11.7	2.20	0.17	74.5 e	14.7	..	..	91.0	..	(1.5)	..	2,889	27.5
Slovenia	198	1.5	1.91	0.09	357.0	562.6	..	..	106.4	..	37.3	..	3,001	32.1
Spain	18,715	20.2	2.28	0.07	122.3	48.4	1,331	74.4	106.5	..	28.4	..	3,371	27.8
Sweden	2,682	4.3	6.09	0.05	98.5	61.2	98	115.1	99.7	..	(11.8)	..	3,185	33.7
Switzerland	433	5.8	10.00	0.36	225.5	256.9	114	112.5	99.2	..	32.5	59.0	3,526	33.8
Ukraine	33,457	6.8	0.58	0.11	14.2	9.5	588	..	95.6	12	(53.8)	45.8	3,054	20.5
United Kingdom	5,803	2.9	4.22	0.09	327.9	87.7	47	107.0	96.8	..	2.1	..	3,412	30.6
Middle East & N. Africa	100,520	28.7	..	0.51	66.8	17.2	..	..	..	2,232	..	33.2	3,110	9.9
Afghanistan	8,054	29.6	..	0.74	2.3	0.1	2,836	..	..	388	..	..	..	..
Algeria	8,265	6.8	..	0.31	12.8 e	11.4	481	76.2	109.7	43	73.8	25.4	3,022	9.9
Egypt	3,400	100.0	0.19	2.52	392.0	26.8	16,364	68.6	95.7	11	34.1	32.7	3,338	7.6
Iran, Islamic Rep	17,088	43.9	..	0.38	80.1 e	14.3	..	72.6	106.7	10	24.1	21.2	3,085	9.5
Iraq	6,090	57.9	..	0.10	105.0 e	9.8	7,108	..	..	1,333	..	16.1	..	..
Israel	424	45.8	0.90	0.16	210.8	57.8	3,055	124.8	99.2	..	75.8	66.7	3,666	21.8
Jordan	400	18.8	..	0.48	55.9 e	14.4	1,896	110.0	121.9	205	91.4	49.8	2,674	9.2
Kuwait	15	86.7	..	0.93	..	5.9	23,333	56.7	103.9	..	114.4	42.9	3,010	17.4
Lebanon	313	33.2	0.07	0.14	187.1 e	26.5	2,757	78.1	96.1	48	81.6	40.0	3,196	17.0
Libyan Arab Jamahiriya	2,150	21.9	..	0.05	34.0 e	15.8	1,987	107.7	95.4	..	91.3	20.9	3,320	10.4
Morocco	9,283	14.5	0.14	0.44	37.1 e	4.6	1,180	80.3	116.7	4	43.8	27.1	3,052	7.7
Oman	81	76.5	..	..	..	1.9	15,340	107.9	86.7	..	84.2	..	..	..
Saudi Arabia	3,794	42.7	..	0.19	101.1 e	2.6	4,075	72.7	100.7	..	62.9	69.9	2,845	13.7
Syrian Arab Rep	5,421	24.6	0.00	0.28	54.9	18.4	3,537	115.2	112.5	5	7.5	34.7	3,038	13.6
Tunisia	4,908	7.8	0.36	0.19	20.4 e	7.2	445	87.0	89.2	..	90.6	36.4	3,238	10.7
Turkey	28,523	18.3	0.14	0.55	63.4 e	33.3	1,044	97.3	95.2	..	5.0	36.0	3,357	22.5
United Arab Emirates	266	28.6	..	0.31	147.1	1.5	6,371	32.7	52.5	..	84.5	12.8	3,225	9.5
Yemen	1,669	30.0	..	1.80	10.2	4.1	3,786	99.8	98.9	184	91.3	0.9	2,038	7.0

For more information, please visit http://earthtrends.wri.org/datatables/agriculture

	Land			Intensity of Agricultural Inputs				Per Capita Food Production Index (1999-2001 =100)		Food Aid, Security, and Nutrition				
	Agricultural Land {a} (000 ha) 2002	Irrigated Cropland as a Percent of Total 2002	Organic Cropland as a Percent of Total 2003	Labor (workers per ha) 2001	Fertilizer (kg/ha) 2001	Mechan- ization (tractors per 000 ha) 2001	Water Withdrawals (meters³/ha) 2000	1983	2003	Cereals Received as Food Aid (000 metric tons) 2002	Net Cereal Imports {b} as a Percent of Consumption 2002	Cereal Fed to Livestock as a Percent of Total Consumption 2003	Calorie Supply Per Capita (kilocalories /person/day) 2002	Share of Calorie Supply From Animal Products (percent) 2002
Sub-Saharan Africa	182,680	3.7	..	1.02	11.4	1.3	..	92.4	97.4 f	3,145	..	7.0	2,262	6.6
Angola	3,300	2.3	..	1.27	..	3.1	64	91.9	104.1	217	42.7	..	2,083	8.5
Benin	2,815	0.4	0.00	0.68	13.7	0.1	84	62.4	99.0	6	16.5	..	2,548	4.4
Botswana	380	0.3	..	0.94	12.3	15.8	161	162.2	100.4	..	168.2	12.2	2,151	18.1
Burkina Faso	4,400	0.6	..	1.34	0.4	0.5	179	72.8	108.6	21	7.3	4.8	2,462	4.6
Burundi	1,351	5.5	..	2.40	2.8	0.1	153	117.0	98.8	55	7.2	..	1,649	2.1
Cameroon	7,160	0.5	0.09	0.52	7.3 e	0.1	102	103.0	105.0	0	20.3	..	2,273	5.7
Central African Rep	2,024	..	..	0.63	0.3	0.01	1	88.9	101.5	5	21.1	..	1,980	9.9
Chad	3,630	0.6	..	0.76	4.8	0.05	53	92.0	101.4	16	5.5	..	2,114	6.6
Congo	240	0.4	..	2.60	21.0	3.0	18	125.8	97.6	14	102.6	..	2,162	6.1
Congo, Dem Rep	7,800	0.1	..	1.66	0.2	0.3	14	151.0	89.6	45	23.7	0.0	1,599	2.2
Côte d'Ivoire	6,900	1.1	..	0.42	9.2 e	0.6	82	83.2	91.8	13	43.3	1.9	2,631	4.1
Equatorial Guinea	230	..	..	0.59	..	0.7	4	96.6	90.4	..	..	..	..	..
Eritrea	503	4.2	..	2.87	10.9 e	0.9	574	..	74.6	184	471.3	2.7	1,513	5.4
Ethiopia	10,671	1.8	..	2.10	11.8 e	0.3	231	..	99.6	1,219	7.4	1.1	1,857	4.9
Gabon	495	3.0	..	0.42	0.6	3.0	104	119.3	95.4	..	68.5	..	2,637	12.7
Gambia	255	0.8	..	2.11	3.1	0.2	91	133.2	65.5	7	49.1	0.0	2,273	5.6
Ghana	6,331	0.2	0.16	0.95	5.3	0.6	43	57.7	107.6	43	18.2	3.2	2,667	4.5
Guinea	1,540	6.2	..	2.23	2.1	0.4	919	97.1	103.6	32	26.0	..	2,409	3.6
Guinea-Bissau	548	3.1	..	0.92	4.4	0.03	286	83.4	93.6	6	38.1	..	2,024	6.5
Kenya	5,162	1.7	0.00	2.34	29.1 e	2.4	223	96.6	94.2	84	22.2	1.9	2,090	11.9
Lesotho	334	0.3	..	0.84	34.0	6.0	31	119.9	104.2	38	240.7	6.8	2,638	4.3
Liberia	600	0.5	..	1.33	..	0.5	101	141.0	84.8	37	74.0	..	1,900	2.9
Madagascar	3,550	30.7	..	1.63	2.5	1.0	4,089	128.6	94.0	40	5.2	..	2,005	9.5
Malawi	2,440	1.2	0.01	1.98	11.7	0.6	362	82.4	79.5	156	17.9	2.3	2,155	2.7
Mali	4,700	2.9	..	0.99	8.9	0.6	1,469	104.0	96.3	7	4.7	1.5	2,174	9.6
Mauritania	500	9.8	..	1.28	5.8 e	0.8	3,000	109.1	97.6	63	..	0.0	2,772	17.5
Mozambique	4,435	2.4	..	1.82	5.9	1.4	133	99.7	98.1	95	27.8	1.0	2,079	2.3
Namibia	820	0.9	..	0.38	0.4	3.8	205	134.4	90.7	41	123.4	..	2,278	15.9
Niger	4,500	1.5	..	1.00	1.1	0.03	462	115.4	99.8	17	8.7	2.7	2,130	5.1
Nigeria	33,000	0.7	..	0.49	7.1	1.0	179	62.4	97.0	13	14.1	1.8	2,726	3.2
Rwanda	1,385	0.4	..	2.99	0.2	0.1	25	126.4	103.4	20	8.7	7.4	2,084	2.9
Senegal	2,500	2.8	0.10	1.26	12.0	0.3	598	72.2	86.0	2	58.4	0.0	2,280	9.1
Sierra Leone	600	5.0	..	1.86	0.5	0.1	643	137.3	96.6	50	52.8	0.0	1,936	3.8
Somalia	1,071	18.7	..	2.57	0.5	1.6	3,075	..	..	16	..	5.0	..	..
South Africa	15,712	9.5	0.05	0.11	48.5 e	4.6	708	94.6	100.1	21	11.4	34.4	2,956	12.2
Sudan	16,653	11.7	..	0.46	5.1 e	0.7	2,195	89.7	102.0	126	25.0	7.4	2,228	20.4
Tanzania, United Rep	5,100	3.3	0.14	2.93	1.6 e	1.5	374	129.3	97.3	51	7.7	2.2	1,975	6.3
Togo	2,630	0.7	..	0.45	7.3	0.03	30	93.0	96.2	..	16.0	13.9	2,345	3.4
Uganda	7,200	0.1	1.39	1.29	0.8	0.7	17	114.0	99.1	113	6.4	4.4	2,410	6.2
Zambia	5,289	0.9	0.06	0.58	6.9 e	1.1	250	107.6	102.7	35	75.8	3.4	1,927	4.9
Zimbabwe	3,350	3.5	..	1.08	45.4 e	7.2	670	95.5	85.1	174	61.7	8.5	1,943	7.7
North America	223,951	10.4	..	0.02	99.0	24.8	..	82.8	97.5 f	..	..	62.5	3,756	27.6
Canada	45,879	1.7	1.30	0.01	53.6 e	16.0	118	87.1	95.2	..	(47.5)	72.0	3,589	26.7
United States	178,068	12.6	0.23	0.02	110.7	27.1	1,105	82.3	97.8	..	(40.5)	61.3	3,774	27.7
C. America & Caribbean	42,178	19.3	..	0.40	66.9	10.6	..	..	..	415	..	45.1	2,878	17.1
Belize	102	2.9	1.30	0.25	45.2	11.6	2	67.7	94.0	..	31.7	..	2,869	20.7
Costa Rica	525	20.6	3.11	0.62	223.2 e	13.3	2,834	72.4	88.5	..	81.6	54.7	2,876	20.0
Cuba	3,788	23.0	0.16	0.17	46.1 e	19.3	1,264	128.3	107.9	1	61.8	..	3,152	12.3
Dominican Rep	1,596	17.2	0.40	0.37	61.1 e	1.2	1,404	138.2	102.6	..	61.4	57.1	2,347	14.8
El Salvador	910	4.9	0.31	0.85	80.4 e	3.8	934	88.2	95.1	70	40.8	33.9	2,584	13.2
Guatemala	1,905	6.8	0.33	1.03	107.6 e	2.3	844	85.1	95.5	118	46.1	29.4	2,219	9.2
Haiti	1,100	6.8	..	1.98	12.7	0.1	1,022	151.6	98.8	144	61.2	2.0	2,086	7.0
Honduras	1,428	5.6	0.06	0.54	106.1	3.6	486	114.6	101.1	27	52.4	42.8	2,356	14.4
Jamaica	284	8.8	0.26	0.93	73.4	10.8	730	86.4	97.8	..	80.8	33.8	2,685	14.6
Mexico	27,300	23.2	0.20	0.31	68.3 e	11.9	2,210	94.2	100.8	..	31.8	47.5	3,145	19.4
Nicaragua	2,161	4.3	0.14	0.18	8.9 e	1.3	393	107.0	110.7	55	19.6	30.6	2,298	7.8
Panama	695	5.0	0.24	0.36	42.0 e	7.2	357	126.9	98.5	..	51.5	32.1	2,272	23.9
Trinidad and Tobago	122	3.3	..	0.40	14.3 e	22.1	139	100.1	114.3	..	97.7	34.8	2,732	15.8
South America	126,594	8.3	..	0.21	78.7	10.4	..	76.0	107.5 f	289	..	52.4	2,851	21.2
Argentina	35,000	4.5	1.70	0.04	24.6 e	8.6	791	83.8	99.6	..	(174.9)	38.6	2,992	29.9
Bolivia	3,106	4.2	1.04	0.49	3.7	1.9	524	63.7	110.0	77	27.3	36.5	2,235	16.2
Brazil	66,580	4.4	0.24	0.19	102.9 e	12.1	562	68.5	114.2	..	12.8	62.3	3,050	22.1
Chile	2,307	82.4	1.50	0.43	209.1 e	23.5	3,468	67.5	102.0	..	31.4	50.9	2,863	21.4
Colombia	3,850	23.4	0.24	0.87	145.9	4.9	1,082	87.7	98.7	..	48.6	35.4	2,585	16.0
Ecuador	2,985	29.0	0.74	0.42	117.1 e	4.9	4,653	68.6	103.5	63	23.5	40.0	2,754	18.2
Guyana	510	29.4	0.01	0.11	25.5 e	7.1	3,226	65.0	105.2	26	(22.8)	8.1	2,692	16.0
Paraguay	3,115	2.2	0.38	0.23	21.5	5.3	147	81.4	107.4	..	(3.6)	3.0	2,565	22.1
Peru	4,310	27.7	0.42	0.71	74.7 e	3.1	3,900	66.8	105.7	124	38.7	40.6	2,571	13.1
Suriname	67	76.1	0.28	0.45	83.6	19.9	9,194	149.1	104.1	..	(12.5)	..	2,652	13.1
Uruguay	1,340	13.5	4.00	0.14	86.7 e	24.6	2,264	92.2	101.8	..	(18.9)	15.0	2,828	29.7
Venezuela	3,408	16.9	..	0.23	88.0 e	14.4	1,168	99.1	91.6	..	37.4	23.1	2,336	17.4
Oceania	53,664	5.4	..	0.06	59.9	7.2	..	90.4	98.7 f	..	..	62.5	..	..
Australia	48,600	5.2	2.20	0.01	47.1	6.2	356	85.3	95.9	..	156.4	64.8	3,054	33.8
Fiji	285	1.1	0.04	0.46	35.1	24.6	190	86.2	96.1	..	93.5	..	2,894	16.4
New Zealand	3,372	8.5	0.33	0.05	267.2	22.5	270	88.2	110.4	..	29.9	41.6	3,219	33.0
Papua New Guinea	870	..	0.41	2.22	13.7	1.3	1	103.4	98.0	..	85.2	..	..	..
Solomon Islands	75	..	..	2.27	..	0.1	..	121.1	96.7	..	85.6	..	2,265	7.5
Developed	635,324	10.7	..	0.07	79.9	30.5	..	100.1	98.5 f	397	..	56.3	3,314	26.3
Developing	904,850	23.2	..	1.42	98.6	8.3	..	73.4	103.8 f	7,962	..	23.8	2,674	13.5

a. Excludes land used for permanent pasture. b. Net cereal imports are calculated as imports minus exports; negative values denote countries that are net exportes of cereal. Includes food received as food aid. Values do not account for changes in cereal stocks. As a result, some numbers may be negative or greater than 100. c. Data for China generally include Taiwan. d. Data for Kashmir-Jammu are generally included under India and excluded from Pakistan. Data for Sikkim are included under India. e. Data are collected from July 1, 2001 to June 30, 2002. f. Regional totals are obtained directly from FAO, so regional definitions may vary slightly from those used by WRI.

Food and Agriculture: Technical Notes

DEFINITIONS AND METHODOLOGY

Agricultural Land, in thousand hectares, is the total area of all arable and permanent cropland. Arable land is land under temporary crops (those that are sown and harvested in the same agricultural year), temporary meadows for mowing or pasture, land under market and kitchen gardens, and land temporarily fallow (less than five years). Abandoned land resulting from shifting cultivation is not included under this category. Permanent cropland is land cultivated with crops that occupy the land for long periods and need not be replanted after each harvest, including land under trees grown for wood or timber. Land in permanent pasture is not included here.

Irrigated Cropland as a Percent of Total refers to the proportion of agricultural land equipped to provide water to crops. These include areas equipped for full and partial control irrigation, spate irrigation areas, and equipped wetland or inland valley bottoms.

Organic Cropland as a Percent of Total shows the portion of agricultural land converted to certified organic agriculture or in the process of conversion. Definitions of organic agriculture vary among countries. According to the International Federation of Organic Agriculture Movements (IFOAM), "Organic agriculture is an agricultural production system that promotes environmentally, socially, and economically sound production of food and fibers, and excludes the use of synthetically compounded fertilizers, pesticides, growth regulators, livestock feed and additives, and genetically modified organisms." Data are obtained directly from IFOAM. The data shown here include pastures used for grazing. Data on land under organic management are a result of surveys undertaken between October and December of 2003 and research conducted by IFOAM. Experts from member organizations, certification bodies, and other institutions were asked to contribute statistics.

Intensity of Agricultural Inputs: Labor shows the labor input intensity of agricultural systems per hectare of agricultural land. WRI calculates labor intensity by dividing the number of agricultural workers by agricultural land area. Agricultural workers include all economically active persons engaged in agriculture, hunting, forestry, or fishing. According to the International Labor Organization (ILO), the economically active population "comprises all persons of either sex who furnish the supply of labor for the production of economic goods and services." The ILO derives the labor estimates from population censuses and sample surveys of the economically active population. When country data are missing, the ILO estimates figures from similar neighboring countries or by using special models of activity rates. The UN Food and Agriculture Organization (FAO) provided the annual figures used for these calculations through interpolating and extrapolating the ILO's decennial series.

Intensity of Agricultural Inputs: Fertilizer measures the mass in kilograms of the nutrients nitrogen (N), potash (K_2O), and phosphate (P_2O_5) consumed annually per hectare of cropland. Some countries report data based on the fertilizer year; i.e., 2001 data actually encompassed July 1, 2001 to June 30, 2002. Data are collected through the FAO fertilizer questionnaire, with support from the Ad Hoc Working Party on Fertilizer Statistics.

Intensity of Agricultural Inputs: Mechanization shows the number of tractors used in agriculture per thousand hectares of arable and permanent cropland. WRI calculates the intensity of tractor use with FAO's estimates on agricultural land area and the total number of tractors for each country. Tractors generally refer to total wheeled and crawler tractors, excluding garden tractors. Tractor intensity is useful for understanding the nature of production systems, as tractors tend to be used in areas with flatter lands and scarce labor. Information on agricultural machinery is reported to FAO by country governments through surveys.

Intensity of Agricultural Inputs: Water Withdrawals measures the volume of water used in the agricultural sector per square hectare of arable and permanent cropland. Water use for agriculture is defined as the water withdrawals that are attributed to the agricultural sector, used primarily for irrigation. WRI calculates water intensity using water-use data from FAO's AQUASTAT information system and agricultural land-use data from the FAOSTAT database. To estimate agricultural water use, an assessment has to be made both of irrigation water requirements and of water withdrawal for agriculture. AQUASTAT collects its information from a number of sources, including national water resources and irrigation master plans; national yearbooks, statistics and reports; reports from FAO; international surveys; and results from surveys made by national or international research centers.

The **Per Capita Food Production Index** shows the food output, excluding animal feed, of a country's agriculture sector relative to the base period 1999-2001. The per capita food production index covers all edible agricultural products that contain nutrients; coffee and tea are excluded. For a given year and country, the index is calculated by taking the disposable average output of all food commodities in terms of weight or volume during the period of interest and dividing that year's output by the average of the 1999-2001 output, and then multiplying by 100. In other words, the index values shown in this table indicate per capita food production levels larger than 1999-2001 levels if their values are larger than 100. Data shown here are for 1983 and 2003.

Cereals Received as Food Aid represents the total shipments of cereals transferred to recipient countries on a total-grant basis or on highly concessional terms. Cereals include wheat, barley, maize, rye, oats, millet, sorghum, rice, buckwheat, alpiste/canary seed, fonio, quinoa, triticale, wheat flour, and the cereal component of blended foods. To facilitate comparisons between deliveries of different commodities, processed and blended cereals are converted into their grain equivalent with specific conversion factors. Information on food aid shipments is provided to the FAO by the World Food Program (WFP).

Net Cereal Imports as a Percent of Consumption indicates whether countries are able to produce sufficient grain for domestic consumption. It is calculated by dividing the sum of net imports (imports minus exports) by total cereal consumption (production plus imports, minus exports). Cereals imported as food aid are included in net imports. This variable does not account for changes in cereal stocks. As a result, some numbers may be negative or greater than 100. Cereals include wheat, barley, maize, rye, oats, millet, sorghum, rice, buckwheat, alpiste/canary seed, fonio, quinoa, triticale, wheat flour, and the cereal component of blended foods. Import and export data have, for the most part, been supplied to FAO by governments, national publications and, most frequently, FAO questionnaires.

Cereal Fed to Livestock as a Percent of Total Consumption is calculated by dividing the total feed grain consumed by total domestic grain consumed. Grains include wheat, rice, corn, barely, sorghum, millet, rye, oats, and mixed grains. Grain consumption includes all domestic use during the local marketing year of the individual country. It is the sum of feed, food, seed, and industrial uses. Data are collected from a variety of sources. Whereas the FAO is required to use official country estimates, the USDA supplements official estimates with data collected from other sources. The international portion of the USDA data is updated with input from agricultural attachés stationed at U.S. embassies around the world, U.S. Foreign Agricultural Service (FAS) commodity analysts, and country and commodity analysts with the USDA's Economic Research Service (ERS). WRI calculates the percentage shown here from USDA grain consumption and feed estimates.

Calorie Supply Per Capita refers to the amount of available food per person per day, expressed in kilocalories. Share of Calorie Supply from Animal Products refers to the percent of available food that is derived from animal products, including all types of meat and fish; animal fats and fish oils; edible offal; milk, butter, cheese, and cream; and eggs and egg products. FAO compiles statistics on apparent food consumption based on Supply/Utilization Accounts (SUAs) maintained in FAOSTAT, its online statistical service. SUAs are time-series data using statistics on supply and utilization. For each food product, the SUA traces supplies from production, imports, and stocks to utilization in different forms—addition to stocks, exports, animal feed, seed, processing for food and non-food purposes, waste (or losses), and lastly, as food available to the population. For internal consistency, total food supply equals total utilization. FAO derives caloric values by applying the appropriate food composition factors to the quantities of the processed commodities, rather than examining primary commodities. Per capita supplies are derived from the total supplies available for human consumption by dividing the quantities of food by the total population actually partaking of the food supplies during the reference period.

FREQUENCY OF UPDATE BY DATA PROVIDERS

Data from FAO are updated annually, with the exception of production data, which are updated three times each year, and trade data, which are updated semiannually. Data on international organic agriculture was first published by IFOAM in 1998 and are updated annually. The USDA's Foreign Agricultural Service updates international grain production estimates every month.

DATA RELIABILITY AND CAUTIONARY NOTES

Agricultural Land and Irrigated Cropland: Data are compiled from various sources (national publications, FAO questionnaires, international publications, etc.). As a result, definitions and coverage do not always conform to FAO recommendations and may not always be completely consistent across countries.

Organic Cropland as a Percent of Total: Data for organic agriculture are collected by IFOAM from a variety of sources, including member organizations, certification bodies, and other institutions. Data collection methods vary depending on the institution and the country. Figures for percent of total agricultural land under organic management are calculated by IFOAM. Data on total agricultural land used in these calculations are different from those provided by FAO for total arable and permanent cropland.

Labor: Values vary widely among and within countries according to labor scarcity, production technologies, and costs of energy and machinery. The annual figures for total number of agricultural workers were obtained by interpolating and extrapolating past trends (1950-2000) taken from ILO decennial population series. As a result, fluctuations in the labor force may not be captured in annual figures. Labor intensity may be overestimated in countries with substantial fishing or forestry industries, since the total agricultural labor force includes some workers engaged in these activities.

Fertilizer: Data are excluded for some countries with a relatively small area of cropland, such as Iceland and Singapore. In these cases, the calculation of fertilizer consumed per hectare of cropland yields an unreliable number.

Mechanization: Data collection methods differ across countries, resulting in varying degrees of reliability. Some caution should be used in interpreting tractors-in-use figures because the data do not account for variations in the size and horsepower of different tractors.

Water Withdrawals: While AQUASTAT represents the most complete and careful compilation of water resources statistics to date, freshwater data are generally of poor quality. Sources of information vary but are rarely complete. Access to information on water resources is still sometimes restricted for reasons related to political sensitivity at the regional level. The accuracy and reliability of the information vary greatly among regions and countries. Data are typically collected in different years for different countries and interpolated or extrapolated to a single year.

Per Capita Food Production Index: Indices are not directly measured; they are derived from a set of formulas and algorithms. The calculation therefore contains an unavoidable amount of subjectivity. Reliability is limited by the accuracy and precision of agricultural production and price data. While these data can illustrate rough comparisons and trends over time, rigid score comparisons and rankings are discouraged. The country-level indices reported here may differ from other calculations of agricultural production due to varying concepts of production, coverage, weights, time reference of data, and methods of calculation.

Cereals Received as Food Aid: Data on shipments and receipts of food aid are governed by established accounting procedures and are generally considered to be reliable. These measurements represent the amount of cereals distributed to recipient countries; they are not a measure of consumption.

Cereal Fed to Livestock as a Percent of Total Consumption: As with any large and complex data set, there are numerous difficulties involved with maintaining accuracy and standardizing reporting standards across countries and commodities. In general, these data should be considered accurate, but users should exercise the usual caution in attempting to create reliable cross-country comparisons.

Calorie Supply: Figures shown here represent only the average calorie supply available for the population as a whole and do not necessarily indicate what is actually consumed by individuals. Even if data are used as approximations of per capita consumption, it is important to note that there is considerable variation in consumption among individuals. Food supply data are only as accurate as the underlying production, trade, and utilization data.

SOURCES

Total Agricultural Land, Irrigation, Labor, Fertilizer, Mechanization, Food Production Indices, Food Aid, and Calorie Supply: Food and Agriculture Organization of the United Nations (FAO). 2004. FAOSTAT on-line statistical service. Rome: FAO. Available at http://apps.fao.org.

Organic Cropland as a Percent of Total: Yussefi, M. and Willer, H. (editors). 2004. The World of Organic Agriculture—Statistics and Emerging Trends—2004. Tholey-Theley, Germany: IFOAM. Available at http://www.ifoam.org.

Water Withdrawals: Food and Agriculture Organization of the United Nations (FAO), Water Resources, Development and Management Service. 2003. AQUASTAT Information System on Water and Agriculture: Review of World Water Resources by Country. Rome: FAO. Available at http://www.fao.org/waicent/faoinfo/agricult/agl/aglw/aquastat/water_res/index.htm.

Cereal Fed to Livestock: United States Department of Agriculture (USDA), Economic Research Service, Foreign Agricultural Service (FAS). 2004. Production, Supply and Distribution Data on-line. Washington, DC: USDA. Available at http://www.fas.usda.gov/psd/.

REGIONS

Classifications by the World Resources Institute

ASIA
(excluding the Middle East)
Armenia
Azerbaijan
Bangladesh
Bhutan
Brunei Darussalam
Cambodia
China
Georgia
Hong Kong
India
Indonesia
Japan
Kazakhstan
Korea, Dem People's Republic
Korea, Republic
Kyrgyzstan
Lao People's Dem Republic
Macau
Malaysia
Maldives
Mongolia
Myanmar
Nepal
Pakistan
Philippines
Singapore
Sri Lanka
Taiwan
Tajikistan
Thailand
Timor-Leste
Turkmenistan
Uzbekistan
Viet Nam

EUROPE
Albania
Andorra
Austria
Belarus
Belgium
Bosnia and Herzegovina
Bulgaria
Channel Islands
Croatia
Czech Republic
Denmark
Estonia
Faeroe Islands
Finland
France
Germany
Gibraltar
Greece
Hungary
Iceland
Ireland
Isle of Man
Italy
Latvia
Liechtenstein
Lithuania
Luxembourg
Macedonia, FYR
Malta
Moldova, Republic
Monaco
Netherlands
Norway
Poland
Portugal
Romania
Russian Federation
San Marino
Serbia and Montenegro
Slovakia
Slovenia
Spain
Sweden
Switzerland
Ukraine
United Kingdom

MIDDLE EAST AND NORTH AFRICA
Afghanistan
Algeria
Bahrain
Cyprus
Egypt
Iran, Islamic Republic
Iraq
Israel
Jordan
Kuwait
Lebanon
Libyan Arab Jamahiriya
Morocco
Oman
Palestinian Territories
Qatar
Saudi Arabia
Syrian Arab Republic
Tunisia
Turkey
United Arab Emirates
Western Sahara
Yemen

SUB-SAHARAN AFRICA
Angola
Benin
Botswana
Burkina Faso
Burundi
Cameroon
Cape Verde
Central African Republic
Chad
Comoros
Congo
Congo, Dem Republic
Côte d'Ivoire
Djibouti
Equatorial Guinea
Eritrea
Ethiopia
Gabon
Gambia
Ghana
Guinea
Guinea-Bissau
Kenya
Lesotho
Liberia
Madagascar
Malawi
Mali
Mauritania
Mauritius
Mozambique
Namibia
Niger
Nigeria
Réunion
Rwanda
Saint Helena
Sao Tome and Principe
Senegal
Seychelles
Sierra Leone
Somalia
South Africa
Sudan
Swaziland
Tanzania
Togo
Uganda
Zambia
Zimbabwe

NORTH AMERICA
Bermuda
Canada
Greenland
Saint Pierre and Miquelon
United States

CENTRAL AMERICAN AND CARRIBEAN
Antigua and Barbuda
Aruba
Bahamas
Barbados
Belize
British Virgin Islands
Cayman Islands
Costa Rica
Cuba
Dominica
Dominican Republic
El Salvador
Grenada
Guadeloupe
Guatemala
Haiti
Honduras
Jamaica
Martinique
Mexico
Netherlands Antilles
Nicaragua
Panama
Puerto Rico
Saint Kitts and Nevis
Saint Lucia
Saint Vincent and Grenadines
Trinidad and Tobago
Turks and Caicos Islands
Virgin Islands

SOUTH AMERICA
Argentina
Bolivia
Brazil
Chile
Colombia
Ecuador
Falkland Islands
French Guiana
Guyana
Paraguay
Peru
Suriname
Uruguay
Venezuela

OCEANIA
American Samoa
Australia
Cook Islands
Fiji
French Polynesia
Guam
Kiribati
Marshall Islands
Micronesia, Fed States
Nauru
New Caledonia
New Zealand
Niue
Northern Mariana Islands
Palau
Papua New Guinea
Samoa
Solomon Islands
Tonga
Vanuatu

DEVELOPING AND DEVELOPED WORLD

Classifications by the Food and Agriculture Organization of the United Nations

DEVELOPING

Afghanistan
Algeria
American Samoa
Angola
Antigua and Barbuda
Argentina
Aruba
Bahamas
Bahrain
Bangladesh
Barbados
Belize
Benin
Bermuda
Bhutan
Bolivia
Botswana
Brazil
British Virgin Islands
Brunei Darussalam
Burkina Faso
Burundi
Cambodia
Cameroon
Cape Verde
Cayman Islands
Central African Republic
Chad
Chile
China
Colombia
Comoros
Congo
Congo, Dem Republic
Cook Islands
Costa Rica
Côte d'Ivoire
Cuba
Cyprus
Djibouti
Dominica
Dominican Republic
Ecuador
Egypt
El Salvador
Equatorial Guinea
Eritrea
Ethiopia
Falkland Islands
Fiji
French Guiana
French Polynesia
Gabon
Gambia
Ghana
Greenland
Grenada
Guadeloupe
Guam

Guatemala
Guinea
Guinea-Bissau
Guyana
Haiti
Honduras
Hong Kong
India
Indonesia
Iran, Islamic Republic
Iraq
Jamaica
Jordan
Kenya
Kiribati
Korea, Dem People's Republic
Korea, Republic
Kuwait
Lao People's Dem Republic
Lebanon
Lesotho
Liberia
Libyan Arab Jamahiriya
Macau
Madagascar
Malawi
Malaysia
Maldives
Mali
Marshall Islands
Martinique
Mauritania
Mauritius
Mexico
Micronesia, Fed States
Mongolia
Morocco
Mozambique
Myanmar
Namibia
Nauru
Nepal
Netherlands Antilles
New Caledonia
Nicaragua
Niger
Nigeria
Niue
Northern Mariana Islands
Oman
Pakistan
Palau
Palestinian Territories
Panama
Papua New Guinea
Paraguay
Peru
Philippines
Puerto Rico
Qatar

Réunion
Rwanda
Saint Helena
Saint Kitts and Nevis
Saint Lucia
Saint Pierre and Miquelon
Samoa
Sao Tome and Principe
Saudi Arabia
Senegal
Seychelles
Sierra Leone
Singapore
Solomon Islands
Somalia
Sri Lanka
Saint Vincent and Grenadines
Sudan
Suriname
Swaziland
Syrian Arab Republic
Taiwan
Tanzania
Thailand
Timor-Leste
Togo
Tonga
Trinidad and Tobago
Tunisia
Turkey
Turks and Caicos Islands
Uganda
United Arab Emirates
Uruguay
Vanuatu
Venezuela
Viet Nam
Virgin Islands
Western Sahara
Yemen
Zambia
Zimbabwe

DEVELOPED

Albania
Andorra
Armenia
Australia
Austria
Azerbaijan
Belarus
Belgium
Bosnia and Herzegovina
Bulgaria
Canada
Channel Islands
Croatia
Czech Republic
Denmark
Estonia

Faeroe Islands
Finland
France
Georgia
Germany
Gibraltar
Greece
Hungary
Iceland
Ireland
Isle of Man
Israel
Italy
Japan
Kazakhstan
Kyrgyzstan
Latvia
Liechtenstein
Lithuania
Luxembourg
Macedonia, FYR
Malta
Moldova, Republic
Monaco
Netherlands
New Zealand
Norway
Poland
Portugal
Romania
Russian Federation
San Marino
Serbia and Montenegro
Slovakia
Slovenia
South Africa
Spain
Sweden
Switzerland
Tajikistan
Turkmenistan
Ukraine
United Kingdom
United States
Uzbekistan

LOW-, MIDDLE-, AND HIGH-INCOME

Classifications by the World Bank

LOW INCOME

Afghanistan
Angola
Azerbaijan
Bangladesh
Benin
Bhutan
Burkina Faso
Burundi
Cambodia
Cameroon
Central African Republic
Chad
Comoros
Congo
Congo, Dem Republic
Côte d'Ivoire
Equatorial Guinea
Eritrea
Ethiopia
Gambia
Georgia
Ghana
Guinea
Guinea-Bissau
Haiti
India
Indonesia
Kenya
Korea, Dem People's Republic
Kyrgyzstan
Lao People's Dem Republic
Lesotho
Liberia
Madagascar
Malawi
Mali
Mauritania
Moldova, Republic
Mongolia
Mozambique
Myanmar
Nepal
Nicaragua
Niger
Nigeria
Pakistan
Papua New Guinea
Rwanda
Sao Tome and Principe
Senegal
Sierra Leone
Solomon Islands
Somalia
Sudan
Tajikistan
Tanzania
Timor-Leste
Togo
Uganda
Uzbekistan
Viet Nam
Yemen
Zambia
Zimbabwe

MIDDLE INCOME

Albania
Algeria
American Samoa
Argentina
Armenia
Belarus
Belize
Bolivia
Bosnia and Herzegovina
Botswana
Brazil
Bulgaria
Cape Verde
Chile
China
Colombia
Costa Rica
Croatia
Cuba
Czech Republic
Djibouti
Dominica
Dominican Republic
Ecuador
Egypt
El Salvador
Estonia
Fiji
Gabon
Grenada
Guatemala
Guyana
Honduras
Hungary
Iran, Islamic Republic
Iraq
Jamaica
Jordan
Kazakhstan
Kiribati
Latvia
Lebanon
Libyan Arab Jamahiriya
Lithuania
Macedonia, FYR
Malaysia
Maldives
Marshall Islands
Mauritius
Mexico
Micronesia, Fed States
Morocco
Namibia
Northern Mariana Islands
Oman
Palau
Palestinian Territories
Panama
Paraguay
Peru
Philippines
Poland
Romania
Russian Federation
Saint Kitts and Nevis
Saint Lucia
Saint Vincent and Grenadines
Samoa
Saudi Arabia
Serbia and Montenegro
Seychelles
Slovakia
South Africa
Sri Lanka
Suriname
Swaziland
Syrian Arab Republic
Thailand
Tonga
Trinidad and Tobago
Tunisia
Turkey
Turkmenistan
Ukraine
Uruguay
Vanuatu
Venezuela
Western Sahara

HIGH INCOME

Andorra
Antigua and Barbuda
Aruba
Australia
Austria
Bahamas
Bahrain
Barbados
Belgium
Bermuda
Brunei Darussalam
Canada
Cayman Islands
Channel Islands
Cyprus
Denmark
Faeroe Islands
Finland
France
French Guiana
French Polynesia
Germany
Greece
Greenland
Guadeloupe
Guam
Hong Kong
Iceland
Ireland
Isle of Man
Israel
Italy
Japan
Korea, Republic
Kuwait
Liechtenstein
Luxembourg
Macau
Malta
Martinique
Monaco
Netherlands
Netherlands Antilles
New Caledonia
New Zealand
Norway
Portugal
Puerto Rico
Qatar
Réunion
San Marino
Singapore
Slovenia
Spain
Sweden
Switzerland
United Arab Emirates
United Kingdom
United States
Virgin Islands

ACKNOWLEDGMENTS

World Resources 2005 is the result of a unique partnership between the United Nations Environmental Programme (UNEP), the United Nations Development Programme (UNDP), the World Bank, and the World Resources Institute (WRI). It is the only instance where UN agencies, a multilateral financial institution, and an NGO work together to determine the content, conclusions, and recommendations of a major environmental report.

For this eleventh edition in the *World Resources* series, the *World Resources* staff gives special thanks to the governments of Norway and Finland through the Trust Fund for Environmentally and Socially Sustainable Development, the Netherlands Ministry of Foreign Affairs, the Swedish International Development Cooperation Agency (SIDA), the United States Agency for International Development (USAID), and the MacArthur Foundation for their generous financial support of *World Resources 2005* and *Earth Trends*, the companion website to the *World Resources* series.

We thank our Norwegian colleagues at UNEP/GRID-Arendal for their contributions of energy, ideas, and content. We are grateful to our colleagues in the Poverty Environment Partnership (PEP), an informal network of bilateral aid agencies, development banks, UN agencies, and NGOs Their advice and the concepts embodied in the PEP publication "Linking Poverty Reduction and Environmental Management" were important inputs for this volume. Likewise, we acknowledge the intellectual contributions of Jon Anderson and his colleagues at USAID, whose publication "Nature, Wealth, and Power: Emerging Best Practice for Revitalizing Rural Africa" formed one of the foundations of our thinking.

Individual Contributions

Many individuals contributed to the development of this report by providing written drafts, careful review of manuscripts, data, or expert advice. While final responsibility for the contents rests with the *World Resources* staff, the report reflects valuable contributions from all of the following individuals. In particular, we wish to thank Mirjam Schomaker (consultant) of UNEP, Kirk Hamilton of The World Bank, Charles McNeill of UNDP, and Otto Simonett (UNEP/GRID-Arendal) for coordinating the input of colleagues from their organizations. We also wish to acknowledge the important intellectual contributions made by Paul Steele of the United Kingdom Department for International Development (DFID), Jon Anderson (USAID), Jan Bojö (World Bank), and Peter Hazelwood (UNDP). In addition, we appreciate the tireless writing and editing efforts of Polly Ghazi, Karen Holmes, and Wendy Vanasselt. Below we detail the individual efforts of our many writers, contributors, and reviewers:

Part I The Wealth of the Poor

Chapter 1 Nature, Power, and Poverty
Main Text: *Lead Writers:* Paul Steele (consultant), Greg Mock (WRI)
   Contributors: Yumiko Kura (consultant)
Box 1.1: *Lead Writer:* Emily Cooper (WRI)
Box 1.2: *Lead Writer:* Emily Cooper (WRI)
Box 1.3: *Lead Writer:* Emily Cooper (WRI)
Box 1.4: *Lead Writers:* Amy Cassara (WRI), Daniel Prager (WRI), Paul Steele (consultant)

Chapter Editor: Greg Mock (WRI)
Reviewers: Jon Anderson (USAID), Anna Ballance (DFID), Jan Bojö (World Bank), Dr Shelton Davis (Georgetown University), Polly Ghazi (consultant), Kirk Hamilton (World Bank), David Jhirad (WRI), Onesmus Mugyenyi (ACODE), Urvashi Narain (RFF), Thierry Oliveira (UNEP), Jennifer Potter (Seattle Initiative for Global Development), Mirjam Schomaker (UNEP consultant), Michael Toman (IADB), Dan Tunstall (WRI)

Chapter 2 Ecosystems and Livelihoods of the Poor
Main Text: *Lead Writers:* Daniel Prager (WRI), Greg Mock (WRI)
   Contributors: Emily Cooper (WRI), Robert Soden (WRI), John Virden (World Bank)
Box 2.1: *Lead Writer:* Daniel Prager (WRI)
   Contributor: Valerie Thompson (WRI)
Box 2.2: *Lead Writer:* Robert Soden (WRI)

Chapter Editor: Greg Mock (WRI)
Reviewers: Edmund Barrow (IUCN), Jan Bojö (World Bank), Patti Kristjanson (ILRI), Urvashi Narain (RFF), Mirjam Schomaker (UNEP consultant), Charlie Shackleton (Rhodes University), Sheona Shackleton (Rhodes University), Paul Steele (consultant), Dan Tunstall (WRI)

Chapter 3 The Role of Governance
Main Text: *Lead Writers:* Antonio LaViña (WRI), Karen Holmes (consultant)
   Contributors: Wendy Vanasselt (consultant)
Box 3.1: *Lead Writer:* Karen Holmes (consultant)
Box 3.2: *Lead Writers:* Karen Holmes (consultant), Emily Cooper (WRI)
Box 3.3: *Lead Writer:* Antonio LaViña (WRI)
   Contributor: Smita Nakhooda (WRI)

Chapter Editor: Greg Mock (WRI)
Reviewers: Anna Ballance (DFID), John Bruce (World Bank), Max Everest-Phillips (DFID), Mirjam Schomaker (UNEP consultant), Dan Tunstall (WRI)

Chapter 4
Four Steps to Greater Environmental Income
Main Text: *Lead Writer:* Greg Mock (WRI)
    Contributors: Antonio LaViña (WRI),
    Karen Holmes (consultant), Emily Cooper (WRI),
    Wendy Vanasselt (Consultant)
Box 4.1: *Lead Writer:* Polly Ghazi (consultant)
Box 4.2: *Lead Writers:* Emily Cooper (WRI),
    Polly Ghazi (consultant)
Box 4.3: *Lead Writer:* Allen Hammond (WRI)
Box 4.4: *Lead Writer:* Emily Cooper (WRI)
Box 4.5: *Lead Writer:* David Jhirad (WRI)

Chapter Editor: Greg Mock (WRI)
Reviewers: Jon Anderson (USAID), Anna Ballance (DFID),
    Charles McNeill (UNDP), Mirjam Schomaker (UNEP
    consultant), Paul Steele (consultant), Dan Tunstall (WRI)

Chapter 5
Turning Natural Assets into Wealth: Case Studies
Namibia
Lead Writer: Polly Ghazi (consultant)
Contributors: Dr Margaret Jacobsohn (IRDNC),
    Chris Weaver (WWF)

Editor: Greg Mock (WRI)
Reviewers: Jon Anderson (USAID), Sushenjit Bandyopadhyay
    (World Bank), Peter Croal (Southern African Institute for
    Environmental Assessment), Dr Margaret Jacobsohn
    (IRDNC), Mirjam Schomaker (UNEP consultant), Otto
    Simonett (UNEP/GRID-Arendal), Dan Tunstall (WRI),
    Peter Veit (WRI), Chris Weaver (WWF)

Darewadi, India
Lead Writer: Polly Ghazi (consultant)
Contributors: Crispino Lobo (WOTR)

Editor: Greg Mock (WRI)
Reviewers: Salif Diop (UNEP), Dr John Kerr (Michigan State
    University), Crispino Lobo (WOTR), Mirjam Schomaker
    (UNEP consultant), Amita Shah (Gujarat Development
    Research), Anju Sharma (UNEP), Dan Tunstall (WRI)

Tanzania
Lead Writer: Polly Ghazi (consultant)
Co-Authors: Edmund Barrow (IUCN), Wendelin Mlenge
    (NAFRAC), Prof Gerald Monela (Sokoine University
    of Agriculture)

Editor: Greg Mock (WRI)
Reviewers: Jon Anderson (USAID), Edmund Barrow (IUCN),
    Kirk Hamilton (World Bank), Mirjam Schomaker (UNEP
    consultant), Dan Tunstall (WRI)

Indonesia
Lead Writer: Polly Ghazi (consultant)
Contributors: Julian Newman (EIA)

Editor: Greg Mock (WRI)
Reviewers: Rama Astraatmaja (Arupa), David Brown (DFID),
    Dave Currey (EIA), Julian Newman (EIA),
    Mirjam Schomaker (UNEP consultant), Otto Simonett
    (UNEP/GRID-Arendal), Fred Stolle (WRI),
    Dan Tunstall (WRI)

Fiji
Lead Writers: Toni Parras (LMMA Network),
    Bill Aalbersberg (USP Institute of Applied Science),
    Alifereti Tawake (USP Institute of Applied Science)

Editors: Peter Whitten (WRI), Greg Mock (WRI)
Reviewers: John Parks (NOAA), Robert Pomeroy (University of
    Connecticut), Mirjam Schomaker (UNEP consultant),
    John Virdin (World Bank)

Special Section: Global Development Policies
Lead Writers: Karen Holmes (consultant),
    Norbert Henninger (WRI)
Contributors: Greg Mock (WRI), Dan Tunstall (WRI)
Chapter Editor: Greg Mock (WRI)
Reviewers: Jan Bojö (World Bank), Charles McNeill (UNDP),
    Mirjam Schomaker (UNEP consultant),
    Paul Steele (consultant)

Part I Graphics:
Daniel Prager (WRI), Robert Soden (WRI),
Amy Cassara (WRI)

Part II Data Tables

Project Manager: Amy Cassara (WRI)
Data Team Advisor: Dan Tunstall (WRI)
Lead Writers: Amy Cassara (WRI), Robert Soden (WRI),
    Daniel Prager (WRI)
Contributors: Abigail Moy (WRI), Jonathan St. John (WRI),
    Brianna Peterson (WRI), Rajiv Sharma (WRI),
    Claudio Tanca (WRI), Abigail Nugent (WRI)

1. **Population and Education**
2. **Human Health**
3. **Gender and Development**
4. **Income and Poverty**
Reviewers: Alan Brewster (Yale University), Nada Chaya (PAI),
    Robert Johnston (UNDP), Dan Tunstall (WRI),
    Tessa Wardlaw (UNICEF)

5. Economics and Financial Flows
Reviewers: Christian Averous (OECD), Katharine Bolt
(University of East Anglia), Rashid Hassan
(University of Pretoria), Saeed Ordoubadi (World Bank),
Amanda Sauer (WRI), Dan Tunstall (WRI)

6. Institutions and Governance
Reviewers: David Banisar (Privacy International),
Carl Bruch (ELI), Marianne Fernagut
(UNEP/GRID-Arendal)

7. Energy, 8. Climate and Atmosphere
Reviewers: Kevin Baumert (WRI), Tim Herzog (WRI),
Niklas Höhne (ECOFYS), Matt Markoff (University of
Washington), Karen Treanton (IEA)

9. Water Resources and Fisheries
Reviewers: Karen Frenken (FAO), Yumiko Kura (consultant),
Eriko Hoshino (World Bank), Sandra Postel (Global Water
Policy), Carmen Revenga (TNC)

10. Biodiversity
Reviewers: Robert Hoft (CBD), Hillary Masundire (IUCN),
Frederik Schutyser (IUCN), Alfred O. Yeboah (CBD)

11. Land Use and Human Settlements
Reviewers: Tony Janetos (Heinz Foundation), David Kaimowitz
(CIFOR), Marc Levy (CIESIN), Martin Raithelhuber
(UN-HABITAT), Jeff Tschirley (FAO)

12. Food and Agriculture
Reviewers: Marianne Fernagut (UNEP/GRID-Arendal),
Suzie Greenhalgh (WRI), Siet Meijer (World Bank),
Mindy Selman (WRI)

Additional Thanks

The staff of World Resources also wishes to extend thanks to the
following individuals for their various contributions:

Jill Blockhus, John Bruce, Jane Kibbassa, Priya Shyamsundar,
Stephano Pagiola, John Virdin, and Sushenjit Bandyopadhyay
from the World Bank; Marion Cheatle, Jacquie Chenje,
Timothy Kasten, Thierry Oliveira, and Anju Sharma from
UNEP; Gelila Terrefe and Peter Hazelwood from UNDP; Jon
Anderson from USAID; Urvashi Narain from Resources for the
Future; Anna Ballance and Max Everest-Philips from DFID;
Carmen Revenga from The Nature Conservancy; Ashok
Khosla from Development Alternatives; Owen Cylke and David
Reed from the WWF Macroeconomics Program Office; Peter
Veit, Jesse Ribot, Frances Seymour, Philip Angell, Oretta
Tarkhani, and Paul Mackie from WRI.

References

Chapter 1

Main Text

- Agarwal, A., and S. Narain. 1999. "Community and Household Water Management: The Key to Environmental Regeneration and Poverty Alleviation." Presented at EU-UNDP Conference, Brussels, February 1999. Online at http://www.undp.org/seed/pei/publication/water.pdf.
- Alternatives to Slash-and-Burn (ASB) Programme. 2003. "Forces Driving Tropical Deforestation." Policy Brief 6. Nairobi, Kenya: ASB. Online at http://www.asb.cgiar.org/PDFwebdocs/PolicyBrief6.pdf.
- Bardhan, P. 1991. "A Note on Interlinked Rural Economic Arrangements." In *The Economic Theory of Agrarian Institutions,* ed. P. Bardhan, 237-242. Oxford, UK: Clarendon Press.
- Barr, C. 1998. "Bob Hasan, The Rise of Akpindo and the Shifting Dynamics of Control in Indonesia's Forestry Sector." *Indonesia* 65:1-36. Online at http://epublishing.library.cornell.edu/Dienst/Repository/1.0/Disseminate/seap.indo/1106953918/body/pdf?userid=&password=.
- Beck, T., and C. Nesmith. 2001. "Building on Poor People's Capacities: The Case of Common Property Resources in India and West Africa." *World Development* 29(1):119-133.
- Béné, C. 2003. "When Fishery Rhymes with Poverty: A First Step Beyond the Old Paradigm in Small-Scale Fisheries." *World Development* 31(6):949-975.
- Benjaminsen, T. 2000. "Conservation Policies in the Sahel, Policies and People in Mali, 1990-1998." In *Producing Nature and Poverty in Africa,* eds. V. Broch-Due and R. Schroeder, 94-108. Uppsala: Nordiska Afrikainstitutet.
- Bojö, J., and R. Reddy. 2003. *Poverty Reduction Strategies and the Millennium Development Goal on Environmental Sustainability: Opportunities for Alignment.* World Bank Environment Department Paper No. 92. Washington, DC: World Bank.
- Bojö, J., K. Green, S. Kishore, S. Pilapitiya, and R. Reddy. 2004. *Environment in Poverty Reduction Strategies and Poverty Reduction Support Credits.* World Bank Environment Department Paper No. 102. Washington, DC: World Bank.
- Borsuk, R. 2003. "Suharto Crony Stays Busy Behind Bars: 'Bob' Hasan Starts Business, Pulls Strings at Olympics." *The Wall Street Journal* (August 13).
- Brown, K., and S. Rosendo. 2000. "Environmentalists, Rubber-Tappers and Empowerment: The Politics of Extractive Reserves." *Development and Change* 31:201-227.
- Bruns, B., A. Mingat, and R. Rakotomalala. 2003. *Achieving Universal Primary Education by 2015: A Chance for Every Child.* Washington, DC: World Bank. Online at http://www.wds.worldbank.org/servlet/WDS_IBank_Servlet?pcont=details&eid=000094946_03082204005065.
- Cairncross, S., D. O'Neill, A. McCoy, and D. Sethi. 2003. "Health, Environment and the Burden of Disease; A Guidance Note." London: United Kingdom Department for International Development.
- Cambodia, Royal Government of (Cambodia PRSP). 2002. National Poverty Reduction Strategy 2003-2005. Online at http://www.imf.org/External/NP/prsp/2002/khm/01/index.htm.
- Chen, S., and M. Ravallion. 2004. "How Have the World's Poorest Fared Since the Early 1980s?" Policy Research Working Paper 3341. Washington, DC: World Bank. Online at http://econ.worldbank.org/files/36297_wps3341.pdf.
- Dei, G. 1992. "A Ghanian Rural Community: Indigenous Responses to Seasonal Food Supply Cycles and the Socio-Economic Stresses of the 1990s." *In Development from Within: Survival in Rural Africa,* eds. D. Fraser Taylor and F. Mackenzie, 58-81. London: Routledge.
- DeNavas-Walt, C., B. Proctor, and R. Mills. 2004. *Income, Poverty, and Health Insurance Coverage in the United States: 2003.* Current Population Report P60-226. Washington, DC: U.S. Census Bureau. Online at http://www.census.gov/prod/2004pubs/p60-226.pdf.
- Dollar, D. 2004. "Globalization, Poverty, and Inequality Since 1980." WPS3333. Washington, DC: World Bank. Online at http://wdsbeta.worldbank.org/external/default/WDSContentServer/IW3P/IB/2004/09/28/000112742_20040928090739/Rendered/PDF/wps3333.pdf.
- Duraiappah, A. 1998. "Poverty and Environmental Degradation: A Review and Analysis of the Nexus." *World Development* 26(12):2169-2179.
- Duraiappah, A. 2004. *Exploring the Links: Human Well-Being, Poverty and Ecosystem Services.* Nairobi, Kenya: United Nations Environment Programme and International Institute for Sustainable Development. Online at http://www.unep.org/dpdl/poverty_environment/PDF_docs/economics_exploring_the_links.pdf.
- Economy, E. 2005. "China's Environmental Movement." Testimony before the Congressional Executive Commission on China, Roundtable on Environmental NGOs in China, February 7, 2005. Washington, DC: Council on Foreign Relations. Online at http://www.cfr.org/pub7770/elizabeth_c_economy/chinas_environmental_movement.php#.
- Ellis, F., and G. Bahiigwa. 2003. "Livelihoods and Rural Poverty Reduction in Uganda." *World Development* 31(6):997-1013.
- Food and Agriculture Organization of the United Nations (FAO). 2002. *Report of the Consultation on Integrating Small-Scale Fisheries in Poverty Reduction Planning in West Africa.* Rome: FAO. Online at http://www.sflp.org/ftp/dload/frpt15.pdf.
- Food and Agriculture Organization of the United Nations (FAO). 2004. *The State of Food and Agriculture 2003-2004: Agricultural Biotechnology—Meeting the Needs of the Poor?* Rome: FAO. Online at http://www.fao.org/WAICENT/FAOINFO/ECONOMIC/ESA/en/pubs_sofa.htm.
- Food and Agriculture Organization of the United Nations (FAO). 2005. "Special Event on Impact of Climate Change, Pests and Diseases on Food Security and Poverty Reduction: Background Document." Paper presented to the 31st Session of the Committee on World Food Security. Rome: FAO.
- Glewwe, P., M. Gragnolati, and H. Zaman. 2000. "Who Gained from Vietnam's Boom in the 1990's? An Analysis of Poverty and Inequality Trends." Working Paper No. 2275. Washington, DC: World Bank.
- Goldin, I., H. Rogers, and N. Stern. 2002. *The Role and Effectiveness of Development Assistance: Lessons from World Bank Experience.* Washington, DC: World Bank. Online at http://wbln0018.worldbank.org/eurvp/web.nsf/Pages/Paper+by+Ian+Goldin/$File/GOLDIN.PDF.
- Hufbauer, G. 2003. "Polarization in the World Economy." *The Milken Institute Review* First Quarter 2003:26-36.
- Intergovernmental Panel on Climate Change (IPCC). 2001. "Climate Change 2001: Impacts, Adaptation and Vulnerability." Contribution of Working Group I to the Third Assessment Report of the Intergovernmental Panel on Climate Change, eds. J. McCarthy, O. Canziani, N. Leary, D. Dokken and K. White. Cambridge: Cambridge University Press.
- International Food Policy Research Institute (IFPRI). 2004. *Ending Hunger in Africa: Prospects for the Small Farmer.* Washington, DC: IFPRI. Online at http://www.ifpri.org/pubs/ib/ib16.pdf.
- International Fund for Agricultural Development (IFAD). 2001. *Rural Poverty Report 2001.* Rome: International Fund for Agricultural Development. Online at http://www.ifad.org/poverty/index.htm.
- International Monetary Fund (IMF). 2004. *Report on the Evaluation of Poverty Reduction Strategy Papers (PRSPs) and the Poverty Reduction and Growth Facility (PRGF).* Washington, DC: IMF. Online at http://www.imf.org/External/NP/ieo/2004/prspprgf/eng/.
- Irz, X., L. Lin, C. Thirtle, and S. Wiggins. 2001. "Agricultural Productivity Growth and Poverty Alleviation." *Development Policy Review* 19(4):449-466.
- Jodha, N. 1986. "Common Property Resources and Rural Poor in Dry Regions of India." *Economic and Political Weekly* 21(27):1169-1181.
- Kakwani, N. 2004. "Pro-Poor Growth in Asia." *In Focus* January 2004:5-6. Online at http://www.undp.org/povertycentre/newsletters/infocus1jan04eng.pdf.
- Kaufmann, D., A. Kraay, and P. Zoido-Lobaton. 1999. "Governance Matters." Policy Research Working Paper No. 2196. Washington, DC: World Bank. Online at http://www.worldbank.org/wbi/governance/pubs/govmatters.htm.
- Kerr, J., G. Pangare, and V. Pangare. 2002. "Watershed Development Projects in India: An Evaluation." Research Report 127. Washington, DC: International Food Policy Research Institute. Online at http://www.ifpri.org/pubs/abstract/127/rr127.pdf.
- Kura, Y., C. Revenga, E. Hoshino, and G. Mock. 2004. *Fishing for Answers: Making Sense of the Global Fish Crisis.* Washington, DC: World Resources Institute.

■ Kurien, J. 1992. "Ruining the Commons and Responses of the Commoners: Coastal Over-Fishing and Fishworkers' Actions in Kerala State, India." In *Grassroots Environmental Action,* eds. G. and J. Vivian, 221-258. London, UK: Routledge.

■ Lampietti, J., and J. Dixon. 1995. *To See the Forest for the Trees: A Guide to Non-Timber Forest Benefits.* Environmental Economics Series, Paper No. 013. Washington, DC: World Bank.

■ Lenselink, N. 2002. "Participation in Artisanal Fisheries Management for Improved Livelihoods in West Africa: A Synthesis of Interviews and Cases from Mauritania, Senegal, Guinea and Ghana." FAO Fisheries Technical Paper No. 432. Rome: Food and Agriculture Organization of the United Nations. Online at http://www.fao.org/DOCREP/ 005/Y4281E/Y4281E00.HTM.

■ Lvovsky, K. 2001. "Health and Environment." Environment Strategy Paper No.1. Washington, DC: World Bank. Online at http://www-wds.worldbank.org/servlet/ WDS_IBank_Servlet?pcont=details&eid=000094946_0205040403117.

■ Macro International. 2005. MEASURE DHS STATcompiler. Online at http://www .measuredhs.com.

■ Macro International and Central Statistical Office, Zimbabwe. 2000. *Zimbabwe Demographic and Health Survey 1999.* Calverton, Maryland, USA: Macro International and Central Statistical Office.

■ McNeill, J. 2000. *Something New Under the Sun—An Environmental History of the Twentieth Century.* New York: W.W. Norton & Co.

■ Meinzen-Dick, R., and M. Di Gregorio. 2004. "Collective Action and Property Rights for Sustainable Development: Overview." In *Collective Action and Property Rights for Sustainable Development,* eds. R. Meinzen-Dick and M. DiGregorio, 3-4. 2020 Vision for Food, Agriculture and the Environment, Focus 11, Policy Brief No.1. Washington, DC: International Food Policy Research Institute. Online at http://www.ifpri.org/2020/focus/focus11/focus11.pdf.

■ Millennium Ecosystem Assessment (MA). 2005. *Ecosystems and Human Well-Being: Synthesis.* Washington, DC: Island Press.

■ Morris, J. 2002. *Bitter Bamboo and Sweet Living: Impacts of NTFP Conservation Activities on Poverty Alleviation and Sustainable Livelihoods.* Prepared for IUCN's 31-C Project on Poverty Alleviation, Livelihood Improvement and Ecosystem Management. IUCN The World Conservation Union. Online at http://www.iucn.org/themes/fcp/ publications/files/3ic_cs_lao.pdf.

■ Narayan, D., R. Patel, K. Schafft, A. Rademacher, and S. Koch-Schulte. 2000. *Voices of the Poor: Can Anyone Hear Us?* New York: Oxford University Press for The World Bank.

■ Narayan, D., and P. Petesch. 2002. Voices of the Poor: From Many Lands. New York: Oxford University Press for the World Bank.

■ ORC Macro and Committee for Population, Family and Children, Vietnam. 2003. *Vietnam Demographic and Health Survey 2002.* Calverton, Maryland, USA: Macro International and Committee for Population, Family and Children.

■ ORC Macro and International Institute for Population Sciences (IIPS). 2000. *National Family Health Survey (NFHS-2), 1998–99: India.* Mumbai: IIPS.

■ Ostrom, E. 1990. *Governing the Commons. The Evolution of Institutions for Collective Action.* The Political Economy of Institutions and Decisions Series, eds. J. Alt and D. North. Cambridge, UK: Cambridge University Press.

■ Pagiola, S., K. von Ritter, and J. Bishop. 2004. *Assessing the Economic Value of Conservation.* Environment Department Paper No. 101. Washington, DC: World Bank, IUCN World Conservation Union, and Nature Conservancy.

■ Ravallion, M., and S. Chen. 2004. "China's (Uneven) Progress Against Poverty." Policy Research Working Paper 3408. Washington, DC: World Bank. Online at http://econ.worldbank.org/files/38741_wps3408.pdf.

■ Reed, D. 2001. *Poverty is Not a Number, The Environment is Not a Butterfly.* Washington, DC: WWF Macroeconomics Policy Office.

■ Reed, D. 2004. *Analyzing the Political Economy of Poverty and Ecological Disruption.* Washington, DC: WWF Macroeconomics Program Office. Online at http://www.panda.org/downloads/policy/analyticalapproach_cufa.pdf.

■ Roosevelt, F. 1941. "State of the Union, January 6, 1941: Four Freedoms." Presidential address to the U.S. Congress. Online at http://millercenter.virginia.edu/ scripps/diglibrary/prezspeeches/roosevelt/fdr_1941_0106.html.

■ Sachs, J. 2003. "The Strategic Significance of Global Inequality." In *Environmental Change and Security Project Report,* ed. G. Dabelko, 27-35. Washington, DC: Woodrow Wilson International Center for Scholars.

■ Shaban, R., D. Abu-Ghaida, and A.-S. Al-Naimat. 2001. *Poverty Alleviation in Jordan: Lessons for the Future.* Washington, DC: World Bank. Online at http://www-wds .worldbank.org/servlet/WDSContentServer/WDSP/IB/2001/08/04/000094946_ 01072504014634/Rendered/PDF/multi0page.pdf.

■ Siegel, P., and P. Diouf. 2004. "New Approaches to Shared Objectives." PowerPoint presentation. Dakar, Senegal: World Wildlife Fund West African Marine Ecoregion.

■ Smith, L., and I. Urey. 2002. *Agricultural Growth and Poverty Reduction: A Review of Lessons From the Post-Independence and Green Revolution Experience in India.* United Kingdom Department for International Development. Online at http://www.imperial.ac.uk/agriculturalsciences/research/sections/aebm/projects/ poor_ag_downloads/indiaback.pdf.

■ Steele, P. 2005. Personal Communication. E-mail. June 7, 2005.

■ Thomas, V., M. Dailami, A. Dhareshwar, D. Kaufmann, N. Kishor, R. López, and Y. Wang. 2000. *The Quality of Growth.* Washington, DC: World Bank. Online at http://www.worldbank.org/wbi/qualityofgrowth/.

■ Thornton, P., R. Kruska, N. Henninger, P. Kristjanson, R. Reid, F. Atieno, A. Odero, and T. Ndegwa. 2002. *Mapping Poverty and Livestock in the Developing World.* Nairobi: International Livestock Research Institute. Online at http://www.ilri.cgiar.org/ InfoServ/Webpub/fulldocs/mappingPLDW/index.htm.

■ Timmer, P. 1988. "Agricultural Transformation." *In Handbook of Development Economics,* Volume 1, eds. H. Chenery and T. Srinivasan, 275-332. Elsevier Science.

■ Transparency International. 2002. *Corruption in South Asia: Insights and Benchmarks from Citizen Feedback Surveys in Five Countries.* Berlin: Transparency International. Online at http://www.transparency.org/pressreleases_archive/2002/dnld/south_asia_report.pdf.

■ United Kingdom Department for International Development (DFID). 1999. *Sustainable Livelihoods Guidance Sheets.* London: DFID. Online at www.livelihoods.org.

■ United Kingdom Department for International Development (DFID), European Commission, United Nations Development Program, and World Bank. 2002. *Linking Poverty Reduction and Environmental Management: Policy Challenges and Opportunities.* Washington, DC: World Bank.

■ United Nations (UN). 1945. *Charter of the United Nations.* New York: UN. Online at http://www.un.org/aboutun/charter/.

■ United Nations (UN). 2002. *Report of the World Summit on Sustainable Development.* Johannesburg, South Africa, August 26-September 4, 2002. A/CONF.199/20. Online at http://daccessdds.un.org/doc/UNDOC/GEN/N02/636/93/PDF/N0263693.pdf?OpenElement.

■ United Nations Children's Fund (UNICEF). 2005. *Meeting the MDG Drinking Water and Sanitation Target: A Mid-Term Assessment of Progress.* New York: UNICEF.

■ United Nations Development Programme (UNDP). 1996. *Human Development Report 1996: Economic Growth and Human Development.* New York: UNDP. Online at http://hdr.undp.org/reports/global/1996/en/.

■ United Nations Development Programme (UNDP), and European Commission (EC). 1999. *Attacking Poverty While Improving the Environment: Towards Win-Win Policy Options.* New York: UNDP-EC Poverty and Environment Initiative. Online at http:// www.undp.org/seed/pei.

■ United Nations Development Programme (UNDP). 2005. "Monitoring Country Progress Towards MDG7: Ensuring Environmental Sustainability." UNDP Practice Note. New York: UNDP. Online at http://www.undp.org/fssd/sustdevmdg.htm.

■ United Nations General Assembly (UN). 1992. "Rio Declaration on Environment and Development." Report of the United Nations Conference on Environment and Development, Rio de Janeiro, June 3-14, 1992. A/CONF.151/26 (Vol. I). New York: UN. Online at http://www.un.org/documents/ga/conf151/aconf15126-1annex1.htm.

■ United Nations General Assembly (UN). 2001. *Road Map Towards the Implementation of the United Nations Millennium Declaration.* A/56/326. New York: UN.

■ United States Agency for International Development (USAID), in collaboration with Center for International Forestry Research, Winrock International, World Resources

Institute, and International Resources Group. 2002. *Nature, Wealth and Power: Emerging Best Practice for Revitalizing Rural Africa.* Washington, DC: USAID.

■ United States Census Bureau. 2001. *Poverty in the United States: 2000.* Washington, DC: United States Census Bureau. Online at http://www.census.gov/prod/2001pubs/p60-214.pdf.

■ Vaughan, K., S. Mulonga, J. Katjiuna, and N. Branston. 2003. "Cash from Conservation. Torra Community Tastes the Benefits: A Short Survey and Review of the Torra Conservancy Cash Payout to Individual Members." Wildlife Integration for Livelihood Diversification Project (WILD) Working Paper 15. Windhoek, Namibia: Namibia Directorate of Environmental Affairs and United Kingdom Department for International Development.

■ Wines, M., and S. LaFraniere. 2004. "Hut by Hut, AIDS Steals Life in a Southern Africa Town." *New York Times* (28 November):1.

■ World Bank. 2001a. *Poverty and Income Distribution in a High Growth Economy. The Case of Chile 1987-98,* Volume I. Report No. 22037-CH. Washington, DC: World Bank.

■ World Bank. 2001b. *Making Sustainable Commitments: An Environment Strategy for the World Bank.* Washington, DC: World Bank.

■ World Bank. 2003. *Reaching the Rural Poor: A Renewed Strategy for Rural Development.* Washington, DC: World Bank.

■ World Bank. 2004. *World Development Indicators Online.* Online at http://www.worldbank.org/data/onlinedbs/onlinedbases.htm.

■ World Bank. 2005. *World Development Indicators 2005.* Washington, DC: World Bank.

■ World Health Organization (WHO). 2004. *World Health Report 2004: Changing History.* Geneva: WHO. Online at http://www.who.int/whr/2004/en.

■ World Resources Institute (WRI), United Nations Development Programme, United Nations Environment Programme, and World Bank. 2000. *World Resources 2000-2001: People and Ecosystems—The Fraying Web of Life.* Washington, DC: WRI.

■ World Resources Institute (WRI), United Nations Development Programme, United Nations Environment Programme, and World Bank. 2003. *World Resources 2002-2004: Decisions for the Earth—Balance, Voice, and Power.* Washington, DC: WRI.

■ World Wildlife Fund, and Rossing Foundation. 2004. "Living in a Finite Environment Project. End of Project Report for Phase II: August 12, 1999-September 30, 2004." Draft Report, October 2004. Washington, DC: United States Agency for International Development.

■ Xu, J., E. Katsigris, and T. White, eds. 2002. *Implementing the Natural Forest Protection Program and the Sloping Land Conversion Program: Lessons and Policy Recommendations.* China Council for International Cooperation on Environment and Development.

■ Yardley, J. 2004. "Rivers Run Black, and Chinese Die of Cancer." *The New York Times* (September 13):1.

Box 1.1

■ Barrett, C., and B. Swallow. 2003. "Dynamic Poverty Traps and Rural Livelihoods." Working Paper 2003-44. Department of Applied Economics and Management, Cornell University. Online at http://aem.cornell.edu/research/researchpdf/wp0344.pdf.

■ Chen, S., and M. Ravallion. 2004. "How Have the World's Poorest Fared Since the Early 1980s?" Policy Research Working Paper 3341. Washington, DC: World Bank. Online at http://econ.worldbank.org/files/36297_wps3341.pdf.

■ Coudouel, A., J. Hentschel, and Q. Wodon. 2002. "Poverty Measurement and Analysis." In *The PRSP Sourcebook,* 29-74. Washington, DC: World Bank.

■ Deaton, A. 2004. *Measuring Poverty.* Princeton University. Online at http://www.wws.princeton.edu/%7Erpds/downloads/deaton_povertymeasured.pdf.

■ Demographic and Health Surveys. 2005. MEASURE DHS STATcompiler. Online at http://www.measuredhs.com.

■ Hulme, D., K. Moore, and A. Shepherd. 2001. "Chronic Poverty: Meanings and Analytical Frameworks." Working Paper 2. Manchester, UK: University of Manchester, Chronic Poverty Research Centre.

■ Joint United Nations Programme on HIV/AIDS (UNAIDS). 2004. *Report on the Global AIDS Epidemic. Geneva: UNAIDS.* Online at http://www.unaids.org/bangkok2004/report.html.

■ Kryger, T. 2005. "Poverty Rates by Electorate." Research Note No. 49: 2004-05. Canberra: Parliament of Australia. Online at http://www.aph.gov.au/library/pubs/

RN/2004-05/05rn49.htm.

■ Narayan, D., R. Chambers, M.K. Shah, and P. Petesch. 2000a. *Voices of the Poor: Crying Out for Change.* New York: Oxford University Press for The World Bank.

■ Narayan, D., R. Patel, K. Schafft, A. Rademacher, and S. Koch-Schulte. 2000b. *Voices of the Poor: Can Anyone Hear Us?* New York: Oxford University Press for The World Bank.

■ Narayan, D., and P. Petesch. 2002. *Voices of the Poor: From Many Lands.* New York: Oxford University Press for The World Bank.

■ Ravallion, M., G. Datt, and D. van de Walle. 1991. "Quantifying Absolute Poverty in the Developing World." *Review of Income and Wealth* 37(4):345-361.

■ Ritakallio, V. 2002. "Trends of Poverty and Income Inequality in Cross-National Comparison." *European Journal of Social Security* 4(2):151-177. Online at http://www.lisproject.org/publications/liswps/272.pdf.

■ Sen, A. 1999. *Development as Freedom.* New York: Knopf.

■ United Nations Children's Fund (UNICEF). 2004. *State of the World's Children: Girls, Education, and Development.* New York: UNICEF. Online at http://www.unicef.org/sowc04/.

■ United Nations Development Programme (UNDP). 2004. *Human Development Report 2004.* New York: UNDP. Online at http://hdr.undp.org/.

■ United Nations Educational Scientific and Cultural Organization (UNESCO) Institute for Statistics. 2004. *World Education Indicators.* Paris: UNESCO. Online at http://www.uis.unesco.org/.

■ United Nations Population Division. 2003. *World Population Prospects: The 2002 Revision.* Dataset on CD-ROM. New York: United Nations.

■ World Bank. 1990. *World Development Report 1990: Poverty.* New York: Oxford University Press.

■ World Bank. 2001. *World Development Report 2000-2001: Attacking Poverty.* New York: Oxford University Press.

■ World Bank. 2002. *Bolivia Poverty Diagnostic 2000.* Washington D.C. World Bank Poverty Reduction and Economic Management Sector Unit.

■ World Bank. 2004a. *World Development Indicators Online.* Online at http://www.worldbank.org/data/onlinedbs/onlinedbases.htm.

■ World Bank. 2004b. *PovcalNet Online.* Online at http://iresearch.worldbank.org/PovcalNet/jsp/index.jsp.

Box 1.2

■ Lee, H. 2000. *Poverty and Income Distribution in Argentina: Patterns and Changes.* Report No. 19992-AR. Background Paper No.1 for "Poor People in a Rich Country: A Poverty Report for Argentina." Washington, DC: World Bank.

■ Narayan, D., R. Patel, K. Schafft, A. Rademacher, and S. Koch-Schulte. 2000a. *Voices of the Poor: Can Anyone Hear Us?* New York: Oxford University Press for The World Bank.

■ Narayan, D., R. Chambers, M. Shah, and P. Petesch. 2000b. *Voices of the Poor: Crying Out for Change.* New York: Oxford University Press for The World Bank.

■ National Bureau of Statistics of Tanzania. 2002. *Household Budget Survey 2000/01.* Dar es Salaam, Tanzania. Online at http://www.tanzania.go.tz/hbs/HomePage_HBS.html.

■ Rutherford, S. 2002. "Money Talks: Conversations with Poor Households in Bangladesh about Managing Money." Working paper number 45. Manchester, UK: University of Manchester Institute for Development Policy and Management. Online at http://idpm.man.ac.uk/publications/archive/fd/fdwp45.pdf.

■ United States Department of Labor. 2004. *Consumer Expenditures in 2002.* Report 974. Washington, DC: Bureau of Labor Statistics. Online at http://www.bls.gov/cex/csxann02.pdf.

■ World Bank. 2001. *Kingdom of Morocco Poverty Update, Volume II: Statistical Annex.* Report No. 21506-MOR. Washington, DC: World Bank.

■ Yemtsov, R. 1999. "Technical Paper 1: The Profile of Poverty in Georgia." In Georgia, *Poverty and Income Distribution, Volume II: Technical Papers,* 1-52. Washington, DC: World Bank.

Box 1.3

■ "Food for Thought." *The Economist* (July 31):67-69.

■ Barrett, C., and J. McPeak. 2003. *Poverty Traps and Safety Nets.* Background paper for

"Poverty, Inequality and Development: A Conference in Honor of Erik Thorbecke," Ithaca, NY, October 10-11, 2003. On-line at http://www.saga.cornell.edu/images/wp154.pdf.

■ Bechu, N. 1998. "The Impact of Aids on the Economy of Families in Cote d'Ivoire: Changes in Consumption Among AIDS-Affected Households." *In Confronting AIDS: Evidence from the Developing World: Selected Background Papers for the World Bank Policy Research Report,* eds. M. Ainsworth, L. Fransen and M. Over, 2-3. European Commission, United Kingdom, and AIDS Analysis Africa.

■ Blakely, T., S. Hales, C. Kieft, N. Wilson, and A. Woodward. 2004. "Distribution of Risks by Poverty." In *Comparative Quantification of Health Risks: Global and Regional Burden of Disease Attributable to Selected Major Risk Factors,* eds. M. Ezzati, A. Lopez, A. Rodgers and C. Murray, 1942-2128. Geneva: World Health Organization. Online at http://www.who.int/publications/cra/

■ Cairncross, S., D. O'Neill, A. McCoy, and D. Sethi. 2003. "Health, Environment and the Burden of Disease: A Guidance Note." London: United Kingdom Department for International Development.

■ Demeke, M. 1993. "The Potential Impact of HIV/AIDS on the Rural Sector of Ethiopia." Unpublished manuscript.

■ Desai, M., S. Mehta, and K. Smith. 2004. Indoor Smoke from *Solid Fuels: Assessing the Environmental Burden of Disease at National and Local Levels.* WHO Environmental Burden of Disease Series, No. 4. Geneva: World Health Organization.

■ Ezzati, M., A. Rodgers, A. Lopez, S. Vander Hoorn, and C. Murray. 2004. "Mortality and Burden of Disease Attributable to Individual Risk Factors." In *Comparative Quantification of Health Risks: Global and Regional Burden of Disease Attributable to Selected Major Risk Factors,* eds. M. Ezzati, A.Lopez, A. Rodgers and C. Murray, 2141-2165. Geneva: World Health Organization. Online at http://www.who.int/publications/cra/chapters/volume2/2141-2166.pdf.

■ Food and Agriculture Organization of the United Nations (FAO), International Fund for Agricultural Development, and The World Food Program. 2002. *Reducing Poverty and Hunger: The Critical Role of Financing for Food, Agriculture and Rural Development.* Paper prepared for the International Conference on Financing for Development, Monterrey, Mexico, March 18-22. Rome: FAO. Online at ftp://ftp.fao.org/docrep/fao/003/y6265e/y6265e.pdf.

■ Gordon, B., R. Mackay, and E. Rehfuess. 2004. *Inheriting the World: Atlas of Children's Environmental Health and the Environment.* Geneva: World Health Organization. Online at http://www.who.int/ceh/publications/atlas/en/.

■ Hamilton, P. 2003. "Struggling to Survive Poverty. A Survey of Small Farmers' Coping Strategies in Rural Kenya." *Enable. Newsletter of the Association for Better Land Husbandry* 16. Online at http://www.taa.org.uk/Enable/EnableJan2003.htm.

■ International Energy Agency (IEA). 2002. *World Energy Outlook 2002.* Paris: IEA. Online at http://www.worldenergyoutlook.org/weo/pubs/weo2002/EnergyPoverty.pdf.

■ Krishna, A., P. Kristjanson, A. Odero, and W. Nindo. 2004. "Escaping Poverty and Becoming Poor in Five Kenyan Villages." Submitted to *Development in Practice.*

■ Lawson, D. 2004. "The Influence of Ill Health on Chronic and Transient Poverty: Evidence from Uganda." CPRC Working Paper No 41. Manchester, UK: Chronic Poverty Research Centre.

■ McMichael, A., D. Campbell-Lendrum, C. Corvalan, K. Ebi, A. Githeko, J. Scheraga, and A. Woodward, eds. 2003. *Climate Change and Human Health: Risks and Responses.* Geneva: World Health Organization.

■ Narayan, D., R. Chambers, M.K. Shah, and P. Petesch. 2000. *Voices of the Poor: Crying Out for Change.* New York: Oxford University Press for The World Bank.

■ Narayan, D., and P. Petesch. 2002. *Voices of the Poor: From Many Lands.* New York: Oxford University Press for The World Bank.

■ Stover, J., and L. Bollinger. 1999. *The Economic Impact of AIDS.* The Policy Project. Online at http://www.policyproject.com/pubs/SEImpact/SEImpact_Africa.pdf.

■ Tibaijuka, A. 1997. "AIDS and Economic Welfare in Peasant Agriculture: Case Studies from Kagabiro Village, Kagera Region, Tanzania. " *World Development;* 25(6):963-975.

■ Transparency International. 2002. *Corruption in South Asia: Insights and Benchmarks from Citizen Feedback Surveys in Five Countries.* London: Transparency International.

■ Warwick, H., and A. Doig. 2003. "Smoke: the Killer in the Kitchen." Rugby, United Kingdom: ITDG. Online at http://www.itdg.org/?id=smoke_report_home.

■ World Bank. 2001. *World Development Report 2000-2001: Attacking Poverty.* New York: Oxford University Press.

■ World Bank. 2004. *World Development Report 2004: Making Services Work for Poor People.* Washington, DC: World Bank.

■ World Health Organization (WHO). 2001. *Iron Deficiency Anaemia: Assessment, Prevention and Control.* Geneva: WHO. Online at http://www.who.int/nut/documents/ida_assessment_prevention_control.pdf.

■ World Health Organization (WHO). 2002. *World Health Report 2002: Reducing Risks, Promoting Healthy Life.* Geneva:WHO. Online at http://www.who.int/whr/2002/en/.

■ World Resources Institute (WRI), in collaboration with United Nations Environment Programme, United Nations Development Programme and the World Bank. 1998. *World Resources 1998-99: Environmental Change and Human Health.* Washington DC: WRI.

Box 1.4

■ Anderson, K. 2004. "The Challenge of Reducing Subsidies and Trade Barriers." Policy Research Working Paper 3415. Washington, DC: World Bank. Online at http://wdsbeta.worldbank.org/external/default/WDSContentServer/IW3P/IB/2004/10/14/000160016_20041014091046/Rendered/PDF/WPS3415.pdf.

■ Catholic Agency for Overseas Development (CAFOD). 2003. "The Cancún WTO Ministerial Meeting, September 2003: What happened? What does it mean for development?" Online at http://www.cafod.org.uk/archive/policy/CAFOD_Cancun_Analysis.pdf.

■ Environmental Working Group. 2005. *Cotton Subsidies in the United States.* Farm Subsidy Database. Online at http://www.ewg.org/farm/progdetail.php?fips=00000&yr=2003&progcode=cotton&page=conc.

■ Food and Agriculture Organization of the United Nations (FAO). 2002. "Dependence on Single Agricultural Commodity Exports in Developing Countries: Magnitude and Trends." In *FAO Papers on Selected Issues Related to the WTO Negotiations on Agriculture,* 219-239. Rome: FAO. Online at ftp://ftp.fao.org/docrep/fao/004/Y3733E/Y3733E00.pdf.

■ Food and Agriculture Organization of the United Nations (FAO). 2004. Follow-up to the World Food Summit and "World Food Summit: Five Years Later—Regional Dimensions." Twenty-Eighth FAO Regional Conference for Latin America and the Caribbean, Guatemala City, Guatemala, April 26-30, 2004.

■ Greenhill, R., and P. Watt. 2005. *RealAid: An Agenda for Making Aid Work.* Johannesburg: ActionAid International. Online at http://www.actionaidusa.org/Action%20Aid%20Real%20Aid.pdf.

■ Maurer, C. 2003. "The Transition from Fossil Fuel to Renewable Energy Systems: What Role for Export Credit Agencies?" Paper prepared for the German Advisory Council on Global Change, Berlin, Germany. Washington, DC: World Resources Institute. Online at http://www.wbgu.de/wbgu_jg2003_ex05.pdf.

■ Murphy, S., M. Ritchie, and M. Lake. 2004. "United States Dumping on World Agricultural Markets." Cancun Series Paper, No. 1. Minneapolis: Institute for Agriculture and Trade Policy. Online at http://www.tradeobservatory.org/library.cfm?RefID=26018.

■ Oxfam. 2002. *Global Finance Hurts the Poor: Analysis of the Impact of North-South Private Capital Flows on Growth, Inequality and Poverty.* Boston: Oxfam America. Online at http://www.oxfamamerica.org/newsandpublications/publications/research_reports/art2613.html.

■ United Nations Conference on Trade and Development (UNCTAD). 2003. "FDI and Development: Policy Issues Related to the Growth of FDI in Services." Prepared for Eighth Session of Commission on Investment, Technology, and Related Finacial Issues, Geneva, January 26-30, 2004. Online at http://www.unctad.org/en/docs/c2d55_en.pdf.

■ United Nations Conference on Trade and Development (UNCTAD). 2004. *The Least Developed Countries Report 2004.* New York and Geneva: United Nations. Online at http://www.unctad.org/en/docs/ldc2004_en.pdf.

■ United Nations Development Programme (UNDP). 2003. *Human Development Report 2003.* New York: UNDP. Online at http://hdr.undp.org/reports/global/2003/.

■ United Nations Millennium Project. 2005. *Investing in Development: A Practical Plan to Achieve the Millennium Development Goals.* New York: United Nations. Online at http://www.unmillenniumproject.org/reports/fullreport.htm.

■ World Bank. 2004. *PovcalNet Online*. Online at http://iresearch.worldbank.org/PovcalNet/jsp/index.jsp.

■ World Bank. 2005. *World Development Indicators* 2005. Washington, DC: World Bank.

Chapter 2

Main Text

■ Adhikari, B. 2003. "Property Rights and Natural Resources: Socio-Economic Heterogeneity and Distributional Implications of Common Property Resource Management." Working Paper No. 1-03. Kathmandu, Nepal: South Asian Network for Development and Environmental Economics.

■ Ahmed, M., N. Hap, L. Vuthy, and M. Tiongco. 1998. *Socio-Economic Assessment of Freshwater Capture Fisheries of Cambodia*. Report on a Household Survey. Phnom Penh, Cambodia: Mekong River Commission.

■ Angelsen, A., and S. Wunder. 2003. "Exploring the Forest-Poverty Link: Key Concepts, Issues and Research Implications." CIFOR Occasional Paper No. 40. Bogor, Indonesia: Center for International Forestry Research. Online at http://www.cifor.cgiar.org/publications/pdf_files/OccPapers/OP-40.pdf.

■ Arnold, M., G. Köhlin, R. Persson, and G. Shepherd. 2003. "Fuelwood Revisited: What Has Changed in the Last Decade?" CIFOR Occasional Paper No. 39. Jakarta, Indonesia: Center for International Forestry Research.

■ Aryal, B. 2002. "Are Trees for the Poor? A Study from Budongo Forest, Uganda." Thesis, Master of Science in Development and Resource Economics. As, Norway: Agricultural University of Norway.

■ Asher, M., P. Bhandari, K. Ramnarayan, and E. Theophilus. 2002. "Livelihoods in Transition: Agriculture in the Alpine Village of Malla Johar, Western Himalaya." Presented at the International Symposium on Mountain Farming, Mussorie, Uttaranchal, India. Agar, Malwa, India: Foundation for Ecological Security.

■ Bahamondes, M. 2003. "Poverty-Environment Patterns in a Growing Economy: Farming Communities in Arid Central Chile, 1991-99." *World Development* 31(11):1947-1957.

■ Bayer, T. 2003. "Mariculture: Alleviating Poverty in Coastal Tanzania." Paper prepared for the Second International Tropical Marine Ecosystems Management Symposium, Manila, The Philippines, March 24-27, 2003.

■ Beck, T., and C. Nesmith. 2001. "Building on Poor People's Capacities: The Case of Common Property Resources in India and West Africa." *World Development* 29(1):119-133.

■ Béné, C. 2003. "When Fishery Rhymes with Poverty: A First Step Beyond the Old Paradigm in Small-Scale Fisheries." *World Development* 31(6):949-975.

■ Botha, J., E. Witkowski, C. Shackleton, and D. Fairbanks. 2004. "Socio-Economic Differentiation in the Trade of Wildlife Species for Traditional Medicines in the Lowveld, South Africa: Implications for Resource Management." *International Journal of Sustainable Development and World Ecology* 11:280-297.

■ Burke, L., and J. Maidens. 2005. *Reefs at Risk in the Caribbean*. Washington, DC: World Resources Institute.

■ Bye, R. 1993. "Non-Timber Forest Products in Mexico." Background paper for the forest and natural resource conservation review of Mexico. Washington, DC: World Bank.

■ Campbell, B., S. Jeffrey, W. Kozanayi, M. Luckert, M. Mutamba, and C. Zindi. 2002. *Household Livelihoods in Semi-Arid Regions: Options and Constraints*. Bogor, Indonesia: Center for International Forestry Research. Online at http://www.cifor.cgiar.org/publications/pdf_files/Books/Household.pdf.

■ Cavendish, W. 2000. "Empirical Regularities in the Poverty-Environment Relationship of Rural Households: Evidence from Zimbabwe." *World Development* 28(11):1979-2003.

■ Cavendish, W. 1998. "The Complexity of the Commons: Environmental Resource Demands in Rural Zimbabwe." Centre for the Study of African Economies Working Paper Series, WPS/99-8. Online at http://www.csae.ox.ac.uk/workingpapers/pdfs/9908text.PDF.

■ Chambers, R., and G. Conway. 1991. "Sustainable Rural Livelihoods: Practical Concepts for the 21st Century." Discussion Paper 296. Brighton, U.K.: Institute of Development Studies. Online at http://www.livelihoods.org/static/rchambers_NN13.html.

■ Chopra, K. 2001. "Wastelands and Common Property Land Resources." *Seminar* 499:24-31. Online at http://www.india-seminar.com/semframe.htm.

■ Cooke, P. 1998. "The Long-Term Effect of Environmental Degradation on Women in the Hills of Nepal." Preliminary draft. Washington, DC: International Food Policy Research Institute.

■ Degen, P., F. Van Acker, N. van Zalinge, N. Thuok, and L. Vuthy. 2000. "Taken for Granted: Conflicts Over Cambodia's Freshwater Fish Resources." Presented at the Eighth Conference of the International Association for the Study of Common Property, Bloomington, Indiana, May 31-June 4. Online at http://dlc.dlib.indiana.edu/archive/00000245/.

■ Dei, G. 1992. "A Ghanian Rural Community: Indigenous Responses to Seasonal Food Supply Cycles and the Socio-Economic Stresses of the 1990s." In *Development from Within: Survival in Rural Africa,* eds. D. Fraser Taylor and F. Mackenzie, 58-81. London: Routledge.

■ Delgado, C., M. Rosegrant, H. Steinfeld, S. Ehui, and C. Courbois. 1999. "Livestock to 2020: The Next Food Revolution." Discussion Paper No. 28. 2020 Vision for Food, Agriculture, and the Environment International Food Policy Research Institute, Food and Agricultural Organization of the United Nations, International Livestock Research Institute. Online at http://www.ifpri.org/2020/dp/dp28.pdf.

■ Dorward, A. 2002. "A Typology of Malawian Rural Households." Working paper, Institutions and Economic Policies for Pro-Poor Agricultural Growth. Wye, England: Imperial College.

■ Ellis, F. 1998. "Household Strategies and Rural Livelihood Diversification." *Journal of Development Studies* 35(1):1-38.

■ Fisher, M. 2004. "Household Welfare and Forest Dependence in Southern Malawi." *Environment and Development Economics* 9:135-154.

■ Food and Agriculture Organization of the United Nations (FAO). 2000a. *Indonesia Fishery Profile*. Rome: FAO. Online at http://www.fao.org/fi/fcp/en/IDN/profile.htm.

■ Food and Agriculture Organization of the United Nations (FAO). 2000b. *The State of the Food and Agriculture 2002*. Rome: FAO. FAO. Online at http://www.fao/documents/show_cdr.asp?url_file+/docrep/x4400e/x4400e00.htm

■ Food and Agriculture Organization of the United Nations (FAO). 2002. *The State of the World Fisheries and Aquaculture 2002*. Rome: FAO.

■ Food and Agriculture Organization of the United Nations (FAO), and United Kingdom Department for International Development (DFID). 2002. "Report of the Consultation on Integrating Small-Scale Fisheries in Poverty Reduction Planning in West Africa, Cotonou, November 12-14, 2002." Sustainable Fisheries Livelihoods Programme in West Africa SFLP/FR/15. Contonou, Benin: FAO and DFID. Online at http://www.sflp.org/ftp/dload/frpt15.pdf.

■ Food and Agriculture Organization of the United Nations (FAO). 2004. *FAOSTAT Online Statistical Service*. FAO: Rome. Online at http://apps.fao.org.

■ Haggblade, S., P. Hazell, I. Kirsten, and R. Mkandawire. 2004. "African Agriculture: Past Performance, Future Imperatives." Brief 1 in *Building on Successes in African Agriculture*, ed. S. Haggblade. 2020 Vision for Food, Agriculture, and the Environment Initiative, Focus 12. Washington, DC: International Food Policy Research Institute.

■ Heffernan, C., F. Misturelli, L. Nielsen, D. Pilling, and F. Fuller. 2002. *Livestock and the Poor: Understanding the Perceptions and Realities of Livestock-based Livelihoods*. Reading, UK: Livestock Development Group, University of Reading.

■ Heffernan, C., F. Misturelli, and L. Nielsen. 2001. *Restocking and Poverty Alleviation: Perceptions and Realities of Livestock-Keeping Among Poor Pastoralists in Kenya*. Reading, U.K.: Veterinary Epidemiology and Economics Research Unit, University of Reading.

■ High, C., and S. Shackleton. 2000. "The Comparative Value of Wild and Domestic Plants in Home Gardens of a South African Rural Village." *Agroforestry Systems* 48:141-156.

■ Hoon, V. 2003. "A Case Study From Lakshadweep." In *Poverty and Reefs*. Vol. 2: Case Studies, eds. E. Whittingham, J. Campbell and P. Townsley, 187-226. DFID, IMM Ltd, IOC/UNESCO.

■ Horemans, B. 1998. *The State of Artisinal Fisheries in West Africa in 1997*. IDAF/WP/122. Cotonou, Benin: Programme for the Integrated Development of Artisinal

Fisheries in West Africa, Food and Agriculture Organization of the United Nations.

■ Hussein, K. 2002. *Livelihoods Approaches Compared: A Multi-Agency Review of Current Practice.* London: United Kingdom Department for International Development and Overseas Development Institute. Online at http://www.livelihoods.org/info/docs/LAC.pdf.

■ International Energy Agency (IEA). 2002. *World Energy Outlook 2002.* Paris: IEA. Online at http://www.worldenergyoutlook.org/weo/pubs/weo2002/EnergyPoverty.pdf.

■ International Fund for Agricultural Development (IFAD), Danish International Development Agency, and World Bank. 2004. *Livestock Services and the Poor: A Global Initiative. Collecting, Coordinating and Sharing Experiences.* Rome: IFAD. Online at http://www.ifad.org/lrkm/book/english.pdf.

■ Jodha, N. 1995. "Common Property Resources and Dynamics of Rural Poverty in India's Dry Regions." *Unasylva: International Journal of Forestry and Forest Industries* No. 180, 46(1):23-30. Online at http://www.fao.org/documents/show_cdr.asp?url_file=/docrep/v3960e/v3960e00.htm.

■ Jodha, N. 1986. "Common Property Resources and Rural Poor in Dry Regions of India." *Economic and Political Weekly* 21(27):1169-1181.

■ Kantai, P. 2002. "Hot and Dirty." *EcoForum* 25(4):16-22.

■ Kebede, B. 2002. "Land Tenure and Common Pool Resources in Rural Ethiopia: A Study Based on Fifteen Sites." *African Development Review* 14:113-149.

■ Kerapeletswe, C., and J. Lovett. 2001. "The Role of Common Pool Resources in Economic Welfare of Rural Households." Working paper. York, England: University of York. Online at http://dlc.dlib.indiana.edu/archive/00000472/.

■ Khalil, S. 1999. "Economic Valuation of the Mangrove Ecosystem Along the Karachi Coastal Areas." In *The Economic Value of the Environment: Cases from South Asia,* ed. J.E. Hecht. London: IUCN World Conservation Union. Online at http://www.uicn.org/themes/marine/pdf/mangrove.pdf.

■ Kristjanson, P., A. Krishna, M. Radeny, and W. Nindo. 2004. "Pathways Out of Poverty in Western Kenya and the Role of Livestock." Working Paper No.14. Rome: Pro-Poor Livestock Policy Initiative, International Livestock Research Institute, Food and Agriculture Organization of the United Nations. Online at http://www.ilri.org/data/newshilight/04Kristjanson_PathwaysOutOfPovertyInWesternKenya_Final_FAO.pdf.

■ Kumar, S., and D. Hotchkiss. 1988. "Consequences of Deforestation for Women's Time Allocation, Agricultural Production, and Nutrition in Hill Areas of Nepal." Research Report 69. Washington, DC: International Food Policy Research Institute. Online at http://www.ifpri.org/pubs/abstract/69/rr69.pdf.

■ Kura, Y., C. Revenga, E. Hoshino, and G. Mock. 2004. *Fishing for Answers: Making Sense of the Global Fish Crisis.* Washington, DC: World Resources Institute.

■ Lampietti, J., and J. Dixon. 1995. *To See the Forest for the Trees: A Guide to Non-Timber Forest Benefits.* Environmental Economics Series: Paper No. 013. Washington, DC: World Bank.

■ Maltsoglou, I., and K. Taniguchi. 2004. "Poverty, Livestock and Household Typologies in Nepal." Working Paper No.13. Rome: Pro-Poor Livestock Policy Initiative, International Livestock Research Institute, Food and Agriculture Organization of the United Nations. Online at http://www.fao.org/ag/againfo/projects/en/pplpi/project_docs.html.

■ Millennium Ecosystem Assessment. 2003. *Ecosystems and Human Well-Being: A Framework for Assessment.* Washington, DC: Island Press. Online at http://www.millenniumassessment.org/en/Products.EHWB.aspx#downloads.

■ Mogaka, H., G. Simons, J. Turpie, L. Emerton, and F. Karanja. 2001. "Economic Aspects of Community Involvement in Sustainable Forest Management in Eastern and Southern Africa." Nairobi: IUCN The World Conservation Union, Eastern Africa Regional Office.

■ Molnar, A., S. Sherr, and A. Khare. 2004. *Who Conserves the World's Forests? Community-Driven Strategies to Protect Forests and Respect Rights.* Washington, DC: Forest Trends and Ecoagriculture Partners. Online at http://www.forest-trends.org/documents/publications/Who%20Conserves_long_final%202-14-05.pdf.

■ Murphy, C., and H. Suich. 2004. "Basket Cases: Individual Returns from Common Property Resources." Paper prepared for the Tenth Biennial Conference of the International Association for the Study of Common Property, Oaxaca, Mexico, August 9-13, 2004. Online at http://dlc.dlib.indiana.edu/archive/00001448/00/Murphy_Basket_040527_Paper227.pdf.

■ Nankhuni, F., and J. Findeis. 2003. "Natural Resource Collection Work and Children's Schooling in Malawi." Presented at the 25th International Conference of Agricultural Economists, Durban, South Africa, August 16-22, 2003. Online at http://www.iaae-agecon.org/conf/durban_papers/papers/077.pdf.

■ Narain, U. 2005. Fellow, Resources for the Future. Personal communication. E-mail. May 2005.

■ Narain, U., S. Gupta, and K. van't Veld. 2005. "Poverty and the Environment: Exploring the Relationship Between Household Incomes, Private Assets, and Natural Assets." Draftpaper. Washington, DC: Resources For the Future (RFF).

■ Neumann, R., and E. Hirsch. 2000. *Commercialisation of Non-Timber Forest Products: Review and Analysis of Research.* Bogor, Indonesia: Center for International Forestry Research (CIFOR).

■ Pro-Poor Livestock Policy Initiative (PPLPI). 2003. "Livestock—A Resource Neglected in Poverty Reduction Strategy Papers." Policy Brief. Rome: International Livestock Research Institute, Food and Agriculture Organization of the United Nations. Online at http://www.fao.org/ag/againfo/projects/en/pplpi/docarc/pb_wp1.pdf.

■ Quereshi, M., and S. Kumar. 1998. "Contributions of Common Lands to Household Economies in Haryana, India." *Environmental Conservation* 25(4):342-353.

■ Reddy, S., and S. Chakravarty. 1999. "Forest Dependence and Income Distribution in a Subsistence Economy: Evidence from India." *World Development* 27(7):1141-1149.

■ Rengasamy, S., J. Devavaram, R. Prasad, and E. Arunodaya. 2003. "A Case Study from the Gulf of Mannar." In *Poverty and Reefs,* Volume II: Case Studies, eds. E. Whittingham, J. Campbell and P. Townsley, 113-146. Paris, France: DFID-IMM-IOC/UNESCO.

■ Ruiz-Pérez, M., B. Belcher, R. Achdiawan, M. Alexiades, C. Aubertin, J. Caballero, B. Campbell, C. Clement, T. Cunningham, A. Fantini, H. de Foresta, C. García Fernández, K. Gautam, P. Hersch Martínez, W. de Jong, K. Kusters, M. Kutty, C. López, M. Fu, M. Martínez Alfaro, T. Nair, O. Ndoye, R. Ocampo, N. Rai, M. Ricker, K. Schreckenberg, S. Shackleton, P. Shanley, T. Sunderland, and Y. Youn. 2004. "Markets Drive the Specialization Strategies of Forest Peoples." *Ecology and Society* 9(2). Online at http://www.ecologyandsociety.org/vol9/iss2/art4/.

■ Shackleton, C. 2005. Senior Lecturer and Research Associate, Rhodes University, Grahamstown, South Africa. Personal communication. E-mail. May 4, 2005.

■ Shackleton, C., J. Botha, and P. Emanuel. 2003. "Productivity and Abundance of *Sclerocarya birrea* subsp. *caffra* in and around Rural Settlements and Protected Areas of the Bushbuckridge Lowveld, South Africa." *Forests, Trees and Livelihoods* 13(217-232).

■ Shackleton, C., and S. Shackleton. 2004. "The Importance of Non-Timber Forest Products in Rural Livelihood Security and as Safety Nets: A Review of Evidence from South Africa." *South African Journal of Science* 100:658-664.

■ Shackleton, C., S. Shackleton, and B. Cousins. 2001. "The Role of Land-Based Strategies in Rural Livelihoods: The Contribution of Arable Production, Animal Husbandry and Natural Resource Harvesting." *Development Southern Africa* 18(5):581-604.

■ Shackleton, S., C. Shackleton, and B. Cousins. 2000a. "Re-Valuing the Communal Lands of Southern Africa: New Understanding of Rural Livelihoods." ODI Natural Resource Perspectives No 62. London: Overseas Development Institute. Online at http://www.odifpeg.org.uk/publications/policybriefs/nrp/nrp-62.pdf.

■ Shackleton, S., C. Shackleton, and B. Cousins. 2000b. "The Economic Value of Land and Natural Resources to Rural Livelihoods: Case Studies from South Africa." In *At the Crossroads: Land and Agrarian Reform in South Africa into the 21st Century,* ed. B. Cousins, 35-67. Cape Town, South Africa: NLC, PLAAS, and the University of the Western Cape.

■ Shackleton, S., C. Shackleton, T. Netshiluvhi, B. Geach, A. Ballance, and D. Fairbanks. 2002. "Use Patterns and Value of Savanna Resources in Three Rural Villages in South Africa." *Economic Botany* 56(2):130-146.

■ Shanley, P., A. Pierce, S. Laird, and S. Guillén. 2002. *Tapping the Green Market: Management and Certification of Non-Timber Forest Products.* Sterling, Virginia: Stylus Publishing, LLC.

■ Shylajan, C., and G. Mythili. 2003. "Community Dependence on Protected Forest Areas: A Study on Valuation of Non-Wood Forest Products in a Region in India." *Sri Lankan Journal of Agricultural Economics* 5:97-122.

- Solesbury, W. 2003. "Sustainable Livelihoods: A Case Study of the Evolution of DFID Policy." Working Paper No. 217. London: Overseas Development Institute. Online at http://www.odi.org.uk/publications/working_papers/wp217.pdf.
- Spencer, D. 2001. "Will They Survive? Prospects for Small Farmers in Sub-Saharan Africa." Summary note for conference "Sustainable Food Security for All by 2020," Bonn, Germany, September 4-6, 2001. 2020 Vision for Food, Agriculture, and the Environment Initiative. Washington, DC: International Food Policy Research Institute.
- Sverdrup-Jensen, S. 2002. "Fisheries in the Lower Mekong Basin: Status and Perspective." MRC Technical Paper No. 6. Phnom Penh, Cambodia: Mekong River Commission.
- Taylor, F., S. Mateke, and K. Butterworth. 1996. "A Holistic Approach to the Domestication and Commercialization of Non-Timber Forest Products." In *International Conference on Domestication and Commercialization of Non-Timber Forest Products in Agroforestry Systems*, eds. R. Leakey, A. Temu, M. Melnyk and P. Vantomme, 75-85. Non-Wood Forest Products 9. Rome: Food and Agriculture Organization of the United Nations. Online at http://www.fao.org/documents/show_cdr.asp?url_file=///docrep/w3735e/w3735e00.htm.
- Tefft, J. 2004. "Mali's White Revolution—Smallholder Cotton from 1960 to 2003." Brief 5 in *Building on Successes in African Agriculture,* ed. S. Haggblade. 2020 Vision for Food, Agriculture, and the Environment Initiative, Focus 12. Washington, DC: International Food Policy Research Institute.
- Tewari, D., and J. Campbell. 1996. "Increased Development of Nontimber Forest Products in India: Some Issues and Concerns." *Unasylva: International Journal of Forestry and Forest Industries* 47(187):26-31. Online at http://www.fao.org/documents/show_cdr.asp?url_file=/docrep/w2149E/w2149e06.htm.
- Thornton, P., R. Kruska, N. Henninger, P. Kristjanson, R. Reid, F. Atieno, A. Odero, and T. Ndegwa. 2002. *Mapping Poverty and Livestock in the Developing World.* Nairobi, Kenya: International Livestock Research Institute.
- Twine, W., D. Moshe, T. Netshiluvhi, and V. Siphungu. 2003. "Consumption and Direct-Use Values of Savanna Bio-Resources Used by Rural People in Mametja, a Semi-Arid Area of Limpopo Province, South Africa." *South African Journal of Science* 99:467-473.
- United Kingdom Department for International Development (DFID). 1999. *Sustainable Livelihoods Guidance Sheets.* London: DFID. Online at http://www.livelihoods.org.
- United Kingdom Department for International Development (DFID). 2000. An Analysis of Poverty and Aquatic *Resources Use Focusing Especially on the Livelihoods of the Poor in Cambodia.* Bangkok: DFID South East Asia, Aquatic Resources Management Programme. Online at http://www.streaminitiative.org/Library/pdf/DFID/CambodiaPovertyReport_01.pdf.
- Vadivelu, G. 2004. *Common Pool Resources in India—New Evidence on the PPR-CRP Hypothesis.* Paper prepared for the Tenth Biennial Conference of the International Association for the Study of Common Property. Oaxaca, Mexico, August 9-13 2004.
- Vedeld, P., A. Angelsen, E. Sjaastad, and G.K. Berg. 2004. *Counting on the Environment: Forest Incomes and the Rural Poor.* Environmental Economics Series, Paper No. 98. Washington, DC: World Bank. Online at http://lnweb18.worldbank.org/essd/envext.nsf/44ByDocName/CountingontheEnvironmentForestIncomesandtheRuralPoor2004/$FILE/CountingontheEnvironmentForestIncomesandtheRuralPoor.pdf.
- Whittingham, E., J. Campbell, and P. Townsley, eds. 2003. Poverty and Reefs. Vol2: Case Studies. Paris, France: DFID-IMM-IOC/UNESCO.
- Wickens, G. 1991. "Management Issues for Development of Non-Timber Forest Products." *Unasylva: International Journal of Forestry and Forest Industries* 42(165):3-8. Online at http://www.fao.org/documents/show_cdr.asp?url_file=/docrep/u2440E/u2440E00.htm.
- Wilson, J., P. Muchave, and A. Garrett. 2003. "A Case Study from Mozambique." In *Poverty and Reefs,* Volume II: Case Studies, eds. E. Whittingham, J. Campbell and P. Townsley, 73-112. DFID-IMM-IOC/UNESCO.
- World Bank. 2002. *The Environment and the Millennium Development Goals.* Washington, DC: World Bank. Online at http://www.wds.worldbank.org/servlet/WDSContentServer/WDSP/IB/2002/09/24/000094946_0209060414432/Rendered/PDF/multi0page.pdf.
- World Bank. 2004. *Saving Fish and Fishers: Toward Sustainable and Equitable Governance of the Global Fishing Sector.* Report No. 29090-GLB. Washington, DC: World Bank, Agriculture and Rural Development Department.

Box 2.1
- Millennium Ecosystem Assessment (MA). 2005a. *Ecosystems and Human Well-Being: Synthesis.* Washington, DC: Island Press.
- Millennium Ecosystem Assessment (MA). 2005b. "Marine Systems." *Current State and Trends: Findings of the Condition and Trends Working Group.* Vol. 1 Ecosystems and Human Well-Being, Chapter 25. Final draft. Washington, DC: Island Press.

Box 2.2
- Stoian, D. 2003. "Making the Best of Two Worlds: Rural and Peri-Urban Livelihood Options Sustained by Non-Timber Forest Products from the Bolivian Amazon." Presented at the conference "Rural Livelihoods, Forests, and Biodiversity," Bonn, Germany, 19-22 May, 2003. Online at http://www.catie.ac.cr/bancoconocimiento/C/CeCoEco_Publicaciones_2004/BONN_2003_Paper_Stoian.pdf.

Chapter 3

Main Text
- Alden Wily, L., A. Akida, O. Haule, H. Haulle, S. Hozza, C. Kavishe, S. Luono, P. Mamkwe, E. Massawe, S. Mawe, D. Ringo, M. Makiya, M. Minja, and A. Rwiza. 2000. "Community Management of Forests in Tanzania—A Status Report at the Beginning of the 21st Century." *Forests, Trees and People Newsletter* 42 (June 2000):36-45.
- Alden Wily, L. 2004. "Can We Really Own the Forest? A Critical Examination of Tenure Development in Community Forestry in Africa." Presented at the Tenth Conference of the International Association for the Study of Common Property, Oaxaca, Mexico, August 9-13, 2004. Online at http://dlc.dlib.indiana.edu/archive/00001513/.
- Antinori, C., and D.B. Bray. 2004. *Concepts and Practices of Community Forest Enterprises: Economic and Institutional Perspectives from Mexico.* Presented at the Tenth Conference of the International Association for the Study of Common Property, Oaxaca, Mexico, August 9-13, 2004.
- Asante, F., and J. Ayee. 2004. *Decentralization and Poverty Reduction.* Legon, Ghana: Institute of Statistical, Social, and Economic Research (ISSER). Online at http://www.isser.org/Decentralization_Asante_Ayee.pdf.
- Baviskar, A. 2004. "Between Micro-Politics and Administrative Imperatives: Decentralisation and the Watershed Mission in Madhya Pradesh, India." In *Democratic Decentralization Through a Natural Resource Lens: Experiences from Africa, Asia and Latin America,* eds. A. Larson and J. Ribot. Special issue of the *European Journal of Development Research* 16(1): 26-40. Online at http://pdf.wri.org/eaa_decentralization_ejdr_final_chap2.pdf.
- Boyle, A., and M. Anderson. 1996. *Human Rights Approaches to Environmental Protection.* Oxford: Clarendon Press.
- Bruce, J. 1998a. "Review of Tenure Terminology." Tenure Brief No.1:1-8.
- Bruce, J. 1998b. "Learning from Comparative Experience with Agrarian Reform." Presented at International Conference on Land Tenure in the Developing World, Cape Town, South Africa, January 27-29, 1998.
- Bruce, J. 2000. "African Tenure Models at the Turn of the Century: Individual Property Models and Common Property Models." *Land Reform, Land Settlement and Cooperatives* 2000(1):17-27. Online at ftp://ftp.fao.org/sd/sda/sdaa/LR00/02-Land.pdf.
- Bruce, J. 2004. "Strengthening Property Rights for the Poor." In *Collective Action and Property Rights for Sustainable Development,* eds. R. Meinzen-Dick and M. Di Gregorio, 33-34. Washington, DC: International Food Policy Research Institute. Online at http://www.ifpri.org/2020/focus/focus11/focus11_16.pdf.
- Bruce, J. 2005. Senior Counsel, Legal Department, World Bank. Personal communication. E-mail. April 20, 2005.
- Bruce, J., M. Freudenberger, and T. Ngaido. 1995. "Old Wine in New Bottles: Creating New Institutions for Local Land Management." Deutsche Gesellschaft fur Technische Zusammenarbeit (GTZ). Online at http://scholar.google.com/scholar?hl=en&lr=

&q=cache:DueUeyZf2EgJ:www.gtz.de/lamin/download/tenure/old_wine.pdf+ngaido+conflict+tenure.

- Carter, M. 2003. "Designing Land and Property Rights Reform for Poverty Alleviation and Food Security." *Land Reform* 2003(2):45-57. Online at ftp://ftp.fao.org/docrep/fao/006/j0415T/j0415T00.pdf.

- Chapman, R., T. Slaymaker, and J. Young. 2003. *Livelihoods Approaches to Information and Communication in Support of Rural Poverty Elimination and Food Security.* London: United Kingdom Department of International Development and Food and Agriculture Organization of the United Nations.

- Crook, R., and A. Sverrisson. 2001. "Decentralization and Poverty-Alleviation in Developing Countries: A Comparative Analysis or, is West Bengal Unique?" IDS Working Paper 130. Brighton, U.K.: Institute for Development Studies. Online at http://www.ids.ac.uk/ids/bookshop/wp/wp130.pdf.

- De Soto, H. 2000. *The Mystery of Capital: Why Capitalism Triumphs in The West and Fails Everywhere Else.* New York, NY: Basic Books.

- Deininger, K. 2003. *Land Policies for Growth and Poverty Reduction.* Washington, DC and Oxford: World Bank and Oxford University Press.

- Deininger, K., G. Feder, G. Gordillo de Anda, and P. Munro-Faure. 2003. "Land Policy to Facilitate Growth and Poverty Reduction." *Land Reform, Land Settlement and Cooperatives* 2003(3):5-18. Online at ftp://ftp.fao.org/docrep/fao/006/y5026E/y5026E00.pdf.

- Djogo, T., and R. Syaf. 2003. "Decentralization without Accountability: Power and Authority over Local Forest Governance in Indonesia." Honolulu, Hawaii, and Bangkok, Thailand: East-West Center and Regional Community Forestry Training Center.

- Economic and Social Research Council Global Environmental Change Program. 2001. "Environmental Justice: Rights and Means to a Healthy Environment for All." Special Briefing No. 7. Brighton, U.K.: University of Sussex. Online at http://www.foe.co.uk/resource/reports/environmental_justice.pdf.

- Elbow, K., R. Furth, A. Knox, K. Bohrer, M. Hobbs, S. Leisz, and M. Williams. 1998. "Synthesis of Trends and Issues Raised by Land Tenure Country Profiles of West African Countries, 1996." In *Country Profiles of Land Tenure: Africa 1996*, ed. J. Bruce, 2-18. Research Paper No. 130. Madison, Wisconsin: Land Tenure Center, University of Wisconsin. Online at http://agecon.lib.umn.edu/cgi-bin/pdf_view.pl?paperid=1153&ftype=.pdf.

- Ellis, F., M. Kutengule, and A. Nyasulu. 2003. "Livelihoods and Rural Poverty Reduction in Malawi." *World Development* 31(9):1495-1510.

- Encarta Online Encyclopedia. 2005. Online at http://encarta.msn.com/media_701500404/Languages_Spoken_by_More_Than_10_Million_People.html.

- Feder, G. 2002. "The Intricacies of Land Markets: Why the World Bank Succeeds in Economic Reform through Land Registration and Tenure Security." Conference of the International Federation of Surveyors, Washington, DC, April 19-26, 2002.

- Food and Agriculture Organization of the United Nations (FAO). 2002. "Land Tenure and Rural Development." FAO Land Tenure Studies No. 3. Rome: FAO. Online at http://www.fao.org/documents/show_cdr.asp?url_file=/DOCREP/005/Y4307E/Y4307E00.HTM.

- Girishankar, N., L. Hammergren, M. Holmes, S. Knack, B. Levy, J. Litvack, N. Manning, R. Messick, J. Rinne, and H. Sutch. 2002. "Governance." In *Poverty Reduction Strategy Sourcebook.*, ed. J. Klugman, pp. 269-299. Washington, D.C.: World Bank. Online at http://povlibrary.worldbank.org/files/4105_chap8.pdf.

- Global Reach. 2005. *Global Internet Statistics: Sources and References.* Online at http://global-reach.biz/globstats/refs.php3.

- Hardin, G. 1968. "The Tragedy of the Commons." Science 162(3859):1243-1248. Online at http://faculty.bennington.edu/~kwoods/classes/global%20change/readings/tragedy%20of%20the%20commons.pdf.

- He, Jun. 2005. "Forest Governance: Local Perspectives of Multi-Level Decision-Making." Presentation at WRI by head of Watershed Governance Program, Center for Biodiversity and Indigenous Knowledge (Kunming, China), February 24, 2005. Washington, DC: World Resources Institute.

- International Council on Human Rights Policy (IHCRP). 2002. *Local Rule: Decentralization and Human Rights.* Versoix, Switzerland: IHCRP.

- Internet World Stats—Usage and Population Statistics. 2005. *Internet Users by Language: Top 10 Languages Used in the Internet.* Online at http://internetworld-stats.com/stats7.htm.

- Jensen, M. 2000. "Common Sense and Common-Pool Resources: Researchers Decipher How Communities Avert the Tragedy of the Commons." *BioScience* 50(8):638-644.

- Johnson, N., J. Belsky, V. Benavides, M. Goebel, A. Hawkins, and S. Waage. 2001. "Global Linkages to Community-Based Ecosystem Management in the United States." *Journal of Sustainable Forestry* 12(3/4):35-63.

- Kaufmann, D, A. Kraay, and M. Mastruzzi. 2005. *Governance Matters IV: Governance Indicators for 1996–2000.* Washington, DC: World Bank. Online at http://www.worldbank.org/wbi/governance/pubs/govmatters4.html.

- Kebede, B. 2002. "Land Tenure and Common Pool Resources in Rural Ethiopia: A Study Based on Fifteen Sites." *African Development Review* 14(1):113-149.

- La Viña, A. 2002. "The Future of CBNRM in the Philippines: The Impact and Challenge of Global Change on Philippine Natural Resources Policy." Presented at the Ninth Conference of the International Association for the Study of Common Property, Victoria Falls, Zimbabwe, June 17-21, 2002.

- Larson, A., and J. Ribot. 2004. "Democratic Decentralization Through a Natural Resource Lens." Special issue of the *European Journal of Development Research* 16(1).

- Lynch, O., and K. Talbot. 1995. *Balancing Acts: Community Based Forest Management and National Law in Asia and the Pacific.* Washington DC: World Resources Institute.

- Manor, J. 2004. "User Committees: A Potentially Damaging Second Wave of Decentralisation?" In *Democratic Decentralisation through a Natural Resource Lens,* eds. A. Larson and J. Ribot, 183-203. *European Journal of Development Research,* No. 16, Vol 1, Spring.

- McCarthy, J. 2002. "Turning in Circles: District Governance, Illegal Logging, and Environmental Decline in Sumatra, Indonesia." *Society and Natural Resources* 15:867-886.

- Mearns, R. 2004. "Decentralization, Rural Livelihoods, and Pasture-Land Management in Post-Socialist Mongolia." In *Democratic Decentralisation through a Natural Resource Lens,* eds. A. Larson and J. Ribot. Special issue of the *European Journal of Development Research* 16(1):133-152.

- Meinzen-Dick, R., A. Knox, F. Place, and B. Swallow, eds. 2002. *Innovation in Natural Resource Management: The Role of Property Rights and Collective Action in Developing Countries.* Washington DC: International Food Policy Research Institute.

- Meinzen-Dick, R., R. Pradhan, and M. Di Gregorio. 2004. "Understanding Property Rights." In *Collective Action and Property Rights for Sustainable Development,* eds. R. Meinzen-Dick and M. DiGregorio, 7-8. 2020 Vision for Food, Agriculture and the Environment, Focus 11, Policy Brief No. 3. Washington, DC: International Food Policy Research Institute. Online at http://www.ifpri.org/2020/focus/focus11/focus11.pdf.

- Moser, C. 2004. "Rights, Power, and Poverty Reduction." *Power, Rights, and Poverty: Concepts and Connections,* Washington, DC and London: World Bank and United Kingdom Department for International Development.

- Mukhopadhyay, M. 2003. "Engendering Governance Institutions." *Governing for Equity: Gender, Citizenship and Governance.*

- Namara, A., and X. Nsabagasani. 2003. "Decentralization and Wildlife Management: Devolving Rights or Shedding Responsibility? Bwindi Impenetrable National Park, Uganda." Environmental Governance in Africa Working Paper No. 9. Washington, DC: World Resources Institute. Online at http://pdf.wri.org/eaa_wp9.pdf.

- Narayan, D., ed. 2002. *Empowerment and Poverty Reduction: A Sourcebook.* Washington DC: World Bank. Online at http://siteresources.worldbank.org/INTEMPOWERMENT/Resources/486312-1095094954594/draft.pdf.

- Ngaido, T., and N. McCarthy. 2004. "Institutional Options for Managing Rangelands." In *Collective Action and Property Rights for Sustainable Development,* eds. R. Meinzen-Dick and M. Di Gregorio, 19-20. Washington, DC: International Food Policy Research Institute. 2020 Focus 11, Policy Brief No. 2. Online at http://www.ifpri.org/2020/focus/focus11/focus11.pdf.

- Ostrom, E. 1990. "Governing the Commons. The Evolution of Institutions for Collective Action." In *The Political Economy of Institutions and Decisions,* eds. J. Alt and D. North. Cambridge, UK: Cambridge University Press.

- Ostrom, E., J. Burger, C. Field, R. Norgaard, and D. Policansky. 1999. "Revisiting the Commons: Local Lessons, Global Challenges." *Science* 284(5412):278-282. Online at http://www.soc.duke.edu/~pmorgan/ostrom.htm.

- Pacheco, P. 2004. "What Lies behind Decentralization? Forest, Powers and Actors in Lowland Bolivia." In *Democratic Decentralisation through a Natural Resource Lens*, eds. A. Larson and J. Ribot. Special issue of the *European Journal of Development Research* 16(1): 85-102. Online at http://pdf.wri.org/eaa_decentralization_ejdr_final_chap6.pdf.

- Petkova, E., C. Maurer, N. Henninger, and F. Irwin. 2002. Closing the Gap: *Information, Participation, and Justice in Decision-Making*. Washington, DC: World Resources Institute.

- Reddy, M., and M. Bandhii. 2004. "Participatory Governance and Institutional Innovation: A Case of Andhra Pradesh Forestry Project (JFM)." Presented at the Tenth Conference of the International Association for the Study of Common Property, Oaxaca, Mexico, August 9-13, 2004.

- Ribot, J. 2004. *Waiting for Democracy: The Politics of Choice in Natural Resource Decentralization*. Washington, DC: World Resources Institute (WRI).

- Ribot, J. 2002. *African Decentralization: Local Actors, Powers and Accountability*. Democracy, Governance and Human Rights Paper No. 8. Geneva: United Nations Research Institute for Social Development Programme on Democracy, Governance and Human Rights, and International Development Research Center. Online at http://www.unrisd.org/unrisd/website/document.nsf/0/3345ac67e6875754c1256d12003e6c95/$FILE/ribot.pdf.

- Riddell, J. 2000. *Contemporary Thinking on Land Reform*. SD-Dimensions. Rome: Food and Agriculture Organization (FAO). Online at http://www.caledonia.org.uk/land/fao.htm.

- Rukuni, M. 1999. "Land Tenure, Governance and Prospects for Sustainable Development in Africa." Policy Brief No. 6. Washington, DC: Natural Resources Policy Consultative Group for Africa. June 1999.

- Serageldin, M., J. Driscoll, L. San Miguel, L. Valenzuela, C. Bravo, E. Solloso, C. Solá-Morales, and T. Watkin. 2003. *Assessment of Participatory Budgeting in Brazil*. Center for Urban Development Studies, Harvard University. Washington, D.C.: Inter-American Development Bank. Online at http://www.iadb.org/sds/doc/participatorybudget.pdf.

- Shyamsundar, P., E. Araral, and S. Weeartne. 2004. *Devolution of Resource Rights, Poverty, and Natural Resource Management—A Review*. Environment Department Paper No. 104. Washington DC: World Bank.

- Sibanda, S. 2000. "Poverty and Democratic Participation: A Pyramidal Construct of Democratic Needs." Presented at the Workshop on Democracy, Poverty, and Social Exclusion: Is Democracy the Missing Link? Addis Ababa, Ethiopia, May 15-16, 2000. Online at http://www.dpmf.org/poverty-silindiwe.html.

- Sivanna, N. 1990. *Panchayati Raj Reforms and Rural Development*. Allahabad, India: Chugh Publications.

- United Cities and Local Governments (UCLG). 2003. *Survey of Women in Local Decision Making*. Online at www.iula.org [gender/women statistics].

- Westergaard, K. 1986. *People's Participation , Local Government and Rural Development: The Case of West Bengal, India*. Research Report No. 8. Copenhagen: Centre for Development Research (CDR).

- White, A., and A. Martin. 2002. *Who Owns the World's Forests?* Washington, DC: Forest Trends and Center for International Environmental Law. Online at http://www.cbnrm.net/pdf/white_a_001_foresttenure.pdf.

- World Bank. 2005. *Doing Business Database*. Online at http://rru.worldbank.org/DoingBusiness/.

- World Resources Institute (WRI), United Nations Development Programme, United Nations Environment Programme, and the World Bank. 2000. *World Resources 2000-2001: People and Ecosystems—The Fraying Web of Life*. Washington, DC: WRI. Online at http://governance.wri.org/pubs_description.cfm?PubID=3027.

- World Resources Institute (WRI), United Nations Development Programme, United Nations Environment Programme, and World Bank. 2003. *World Resources 2002-2004: Decisions for the Earth—Balance, Voice, and Power*. Washington, DC: WRI. Online at http://governance.wri.org/pubs_description.cfm?PubID=3764.

Box 3.1

- Alinon, K. 2002. "The End of the Coercive Protected Area Policy in Northern Togo: Can a Local Management Scheme be an Alternative in Sustaining Common Wild Resources?" Presented at the Ninth Conference of the International Association for the Study of Common Property, Victoria Falls, Zimbabwe, June 17-21, 2002. Online at http://dlc.dlib.indiana.edu/archive/00000781/.

- Ayudhaya, P., and H. Ross. 1998. "From Conflicting to Shared Visions for a Commons: Stakeholder's Visions for Integrated Watershed Management in Thailand's Highlands." Presented at the Seventh Conference of the International Association for the Study of Common Property, Vancouver, British Columbia, Canada, June 10-14, 1998. Online at http://dlc.dlib.indiana.edu/archive/00000010/.

- Food and Agriculture Organization of the United Nations (FAO). 2002. "Land Tenure and Rural Development." FAO Land Tenure Studies No. 3. Rome: FAO. Online at ftp://ftp.fao.org/docrep/fao/005/y4307E/y4307E00.pdf.

- Hasler, R. 2002. "Political Ecologies of Scale and the Okavango Delta: Hydro-Politics, Property Rights and Community Based Wildlife Management." Presented at the Ninth Conference of the International Association for the Study of Common Property, Victoria Falls, Zimbabwe, June 17-21, 2002.

- Hue, L. 2002. Land Allocation, "Social Differentiation, and Mangrove Management in a Village of Northern Vietnam." Presented at the Ninth Conference of the International Association for the Study of Common Property, Victoria Falls, Zimbabwe, June 17-21, 2002.

- Kinch, J. 2003. "Marine Tenure and Rights to Resources in the Milne Bay Province, Papua New Guinea." Presented at the conference "Traditional Lands in the Pacific Region: Indigenous Common Property Resources in Convulsion or Cohesion," Brisbane, Australia, September 7-9, 2003. Online at http://dlc.dlib.indiana.edu/archive/00001213/.

- Kumar, K., J. Kerr, and P. Choudhury. 2004. "Tenure and Access Rights as Constraints to Community Watershed Development in Orissa, India." Presented at the Tenth Conference of the International Association for the Study of Common Property, Oaxaca, Mexico, August 9-13, 2004.

- Lynch, O., and K. Talbot. 1995. *Balancing Acts: Community Based Forest Management and National Law in Asia and the Pacific*. Washington DC: World Resources Institute.

- Pereira, H. 2000. "The Emergence of Common Property Regimes in Amazonian Fisheries." Presented at the Eighth Conference of the International Association for the Study of Common Property, Bloomington, Indiana, USA, May 31-June 4, 2000.

- Rahman, M., A. Islam, S. Halder, and D. Capistrano. 1998. "Benefits of Community Managed Wetland Habitat Restoration: Experimental Results from Bangladesh." Presented at the Seventh Conference of the International Association for the Study of Common Property, Vancouver, British Columbia, Canada, June 10-14, 1998.

- Schlager, E., and E. Ostrom. 1992. "Property-Rights Regimes and Natural Resources: A Conceptual Analysis." *Land Economics* 68:249-262.

Box 3.2

- Alden Wily, L. 2002. "Participatory Forest Management in Africa: An Overview of Progress and Issues." Keynote paper presented at the Second International Workshop on Participatory Forest Management in Africa, Arusha, Tanzania, February 18-23, 2002. Online at http://www.cbnrm.net/pdf/aldenwily_l_002_cfm.pdf.

- Alden Wily, L., A. Akida, O. Haule, H. Haulle, S. Hozza, C. Kavishe, S. Luono, P. Mamkwe, E. Massawe, S. Mawe, D. Ringo, M. Makiya, M. Minja, and A. Rwiza. 2000. "Community Management of Forests in Tanzania—A Status Report at the Beginning of the 21st Century." *Forests, Trees and People Newsletter* 42:36-45.

- Alternatives to Slash-and-Burn (ASB) Programme. 2001. "Putting Community-Based Forest Management on the Map." Policy Brief 2. Nairobi: ASB. Online at http://www.asb.cgiar.org/PDFwebdocs/PolicyBrief2.pdf.

- Cortave, M. 2004. *ACOFOP's Experiences in the Sustainable Forest Management of the Maya Biosphere Reserve, Petén, Guatemala*. PowerPoint presentation at the Forest Trends workshop "Forests: A Resource for Development," Tegucigalpa, Honduras, May 11-13, 2004. Association of Forest Communites of Petén (ACOFOP). Online at http://www.forest-trends.org/documents/meetings/Honduras_2004/acofop-venezuelaAK_smaller.pdf.

- Down To Earth. 2002. "A Midsummer Dream." *Down to Earth* 11(3).
- Fujita, Y., and K. Phanvilay. 2004. "Land and Forest Allocation and its Implication on Forest Management and Household Livelihoods: Comparison of Case Studies from CBNRM Research in Central Laos." Presented at the Tenth Conference of the International Association for the Study of Common Property, Oaxaca, Mexico, August 9-13, 2004. Online at http://www.iascp2004.org.mx/downloads/paper_105b.pdf.
- Ghate, R. 2003. "Ensuring 'Collective Action' in 'Participatory' Forest Management." Working Paper No. 3-03. Kathmandu, Nepal: South Asian Network for Development and Environmental Economics.
- Kaimowitz, D., P. Pacheco, J. Johnson, Iciar Pávez, C. Vallejos, and R. Vélez. 1999. *Local Governments and Forests in the Bolivian Lowlands*. Rural Development Forestry Network Paper 24b. London: Overseas Development Institute. Online at http://www.odifpeg.org.uk/publications/rdfn/24/rdfn-24b.pdf.
- Malla, Y. 2000. "Impact of Community Forestry Policy on Rural Livelihoods and Food Security in Nepal." *Unasylva: International Journal of Forestry and Forest Industries* 51(202):37-45.
- Malleson, R. 2001. *Opportunities and Constraints for 'Community-Based' Forest Management: Findings from the Korup Forest, Southwest Province, Cameroon*. Network Paper 25g. London: Rural Development Forestry Network. United Kingdom Department for International Development and Overseas Development Institute. Online at http://www.odifpeg.org.uk/publications/rdfn/25/rdfn-25g-ii.pdf.
- Molnar, A., S. Sherr, and A. Khare. 2004. *Who Conserves the World's Forests? Community-Driven Strategies to Protect Forests and Respect Rights*. Washington, DC: Forest Trends and Ecoagriculture Partners. Online at http://www.forest-trends.org/documents/publications/Who%20Conserves_long_final%202-14-05.pdf.
- Neupane, H. 2003. "Contested Impact of Community Forestry on Equity: Some Evidence from Nepal." *Journal of Forest and Livelihood* 2(2):55-61. Online at http://www.forestaction.org/journal_articles/hari_neupane8_vol2_2.PDF.
- Shilling, J., and J. Osha. 2003. Paying for Environmental Stewardship: Using Markets and Common-Pool Property to Reduce Rural Poverty While Enhancing Conservation. Washington, DC: World Wildlife Fund. Online at http://www.wwf.dk/db/files/mpopaying_env_stewardship.pdf.
- Smith, W. 2005. "Mapping Access to Benefits in Cameroon Using Commodity Chain Analysis: A Case Study of the Azobe Timber Chain." Cambridge, UK: University of Cambridge.
- Varshney, V. 2003. "Forests Are the Main Source of Herbs: Interview with John F. Kharshiing, Chairperson, Khasi School of Medicine." *Down to Earth* 12(7):46.
- World Resources Institute (WRI), United Nations Development Programme, United Nations Environment Programme, and World Bank. 2003. *World Resources 2002-2004: Decisions for the Earth—Balance, Voice, and Power*. Washington, DC: WRI. Online at http://pubs.wri.org/pubs_description.cfm?PubID=3764.

Box 3.3

- Bass, S., P. Parikh, R. Czebiniak, and M. Filbey. 2003. *Prior Informed Consent and Mining: Promoting the Sustainable Development of Local Communities*. Washington, DC: Environmental Law Institute. Online at http://www.elistore.org/reports_detail.asp?ID=10965&topic=Mining.
- Casas, A. 2004. "Prior Informed Consent in the Convention on Biological Diversity—Bonn Guidelines: National Implementation in Colombia." *Sustainable Development Law and Policy, Special Issue: Prior Informed Consent* IV(2):27-28.
- Commonwealth of Australia. 1976. "Aboriginal Land Rights (Northern Territory) Act 1976." In *Commonwealth Consolidated Acts,* 2001, ed. A.L.I. Institute. Canberra. Online at http://www.atns.net.au/biogs/A000007b.htm.
- Congress of the Philippines. 1997. "The Indigenous Peoples Rights Act of 1997." In *A Divided Court: Case Materials from the Constitutional Challenge to the Indigenous Peoples' Rights Act of 1997,* ed. A. Ballesteros. Quezon City, The Philippines: Legal Rights and Natural Resources Center-Kasama sa Kalikasan.
- Extractive Industries Review (EIR). 2003. *Striking a Better Balance: The Final Report of the Extractive Industries Review.* Washington, DC: World Bank Group. Online at http://web.worldbank.org/WBSITE/EXTERNAL/TOPICS/EXTOGMC/0,,contentMDK:20306686~menuPK:592071~pagePK:148956~piPK:216618~theSitePK:336930,00.html.
- Goodland, R. 2004. "Free, and Prior Informed Consent and the World Bank Group." *Sustainable Development Law and Policy, Special Issue: Prior Informed Consent* IV(2):66-74.
- Kamijyo, M. 2004. "The 'Equator Principles': Improved Social Responsibility in the Private Finance Sector." *Sustainable Development Law and Policy, Special Issue: Prior Informed Consent* IV(2):35-39.
- MacKay, F. 2004. "Indigenous Peoples' Right to Free, Prior and Informed Consent and the World Bank's Extractive Industries Review." *Sustainable Development Law and Policy, Special Issue: Prior Informed Consent* IV(2):43-65.
- Permanent Forum on Indigenous Issues. 2005. *Report of the International Workshop on Methodologies Regarding Free, Prior and Informed Consent and Indigenous Peoples.* New York: United Nations Permanent Forum on Indigenous Issues. Online at http://www.un.org/Docs/journal/asp/ws.asp?m=E/C.19/2005/3.
- Perrault, A. 2004. "Facilitating Prior Informed Consent in the Context of Genetic Resources and Traditional Knowledge." *Sustainable Development Law and Policy, Special Issue: Prior Informed Consent* IV(2):21-26.
- Tebtebba (Indigenous Peoples' International Centre for Policy Research and Education). 2002. *Indigenous Peoples and Sustainable Development.* Submitted to the Multi Stakeholder Dialogue of the WWSD PrepCom 2, New York, January 28-February 8, 2002. Baguio City, The Philippines: Tebtebba. Online at http://www.tebtebba.org/tebtebba_files/wssd/wssdippaper.html.
- World Bank. 2004. *Striking A Better Balance, the World Bank Group and Extractive Industries: The Final Report of the Extractive Industries Review, World Bank Group Management Response.* Washington, DC: World Bank. Online at http://siteresources.worldbank.org/INTOGMC/Resources/finaleirmanagementresponse.pdf.
- World Commission on Dams (WCD). 2000. *Dams and Development: A New Framework for Decision-Making.* The Report of the World Commission on Dams. London: Earthscan Publications Ltd.

Chapter 4

Main Text

- Adewusi, H. 2004. "Potential for Development and Conservation of *Dacryodes edulis* in Sakpoba Forest Reserve, Edo State, in the Niger Delta Area of Nigeria." In *Forest Products, Livelihoods and Conservation: Case-Studies of Non-Timber Forest Product Systems,* eds. T. Sunderland and O. Ndoye, 133-147. Bogor, Indonesia: Centre for International Forestry Research (CIFOR). Online at http://www.cifor.cgiar.org/publications/pdf_files/Books/NTFPAfrica/Chapter7-Chapter13.PDF.
- Agarwal, A., and S. Narain. 1999. "Community and Household Water Management: The Key to Environmental Regeneration and Poverty Alleviation." Presented at EU-UNDP Conference, Brussels, February 1999. Online at http://www.undp.org/seed/pei/publication/water.pdf.
- Alden Wily, L., and S. Mbaya. 2001. *Land, People and Forests in Eastern and Southern Africa at the Beginning of the 21st Century: The Impact of Land Relations on the Role of Communities in Forest Future.* Nairobi: IUCN-EARO. Online at http://www.iucn.org/places/earo/pubs/forest/LANDPEOP.PDF.
- Bacon, C. 2002. "The Story of Nicaragua's Coffee Quality Improvement Project: An Independent Evaluation for Thanksgiving Coffee Company." Online at http://www.agroecology.org/people/chrisbacon/summary.pdf.
- Barber, C., and V. Pratt. 1997. *Sullied Seas: Strategies for Combating Cyanide Fishing in Southeast Asia and Beyond.* Washington, DC: World Resources Institute and International Marinelife Alliance. Online at http://pubs.wri.org/pubs_description.cfm?PubID=2770.
- Bruce, J., M. Freudenberger, and T. Ngaido. 1995. *Old Wine in New Bottles: Creating New Institutions for Local Land Management.* Deutsche Gesellschaft fur Technische Zusammenarbeit (GTZ). Online at http://www2.gtz.de/dokumente/bib/00-0590.pdf.

- Carter, M. 2003. "Designing Land and Property Rights Reform for Poverty Alleviation and Food Security." *Land Reform* 2003(2):45-57. Online at ftp://ftp.fao.org/docrep/fao/006/j0415T/j0415T00.pdf.

- Chater, S. 2003. "Balancing Rainforest Conservation and Poverty Reduction." ASB Policy Brief 5. Nairobi, Kenya: Alternatives to Slash and Burn Programme. Online at http://www.asb.cgiar.org/PDFwebdocs/Policybrief5..pdf.

- Deininger, K. 2003. *Land Policies for Growth and Poverty Reduction.* Washington, DC and Oxford: The World Bank and Oxford University Press.

- Elbow, K., R. Furth, A. Knox, K. Bohrer, M. Hobbs, S. Leisz, and M. Williams. 1998. "Synthesis of Trends and Issues Raised by Land Tenure Country Profiles of West African Countries, 1996." In *Country Profiles of Land Tenure: Africa 1996,* ed. J. Bruce, 2-18. Research Paper No. 130. Madison, Wisconsin: Land Tenure Center, University of Wisconsin. Online at http://agecon.lib.umn.edu/cgi-bin/pdf_view.pl?paperid=1153&ftype=.pdf.

- Fernandez, A. 2003. *People's Institutions Managing Natural Resources in the Context of a Watershed Strategy.* Bangalore, India: MYRADA.

- Fitter, R., and R. Kaplinsky. 2001. *Who Gains from Product Rents as the Coffee Market Becomes More Differentiated? A Value Chain Analysis.* IDS Bulletin Paper. Sussex, UK: Institute of Development Studies (IDS), University of Sussex. Online at http://www.ids.ac.uk/ids/global/pdfs/productrents.pdf.

- Food and Agriculture Organization of the United Nations (FAO). 2002a. *Land Tenure and Rural Development.* FAO Land Tenure Studies No. 3. Rome: FAO. Online at ftp://ftp.fao.org/docrep/fao/005/y4307E/y4307E00.pdf.

- Food and Agriculture Organization of the United Nations (FAO). 2002b. *Information on Fisheries Management in Samoa.* FAO Country Profiles and Mapping Information System. Rome: FAO. Online at http://www.fao.org/fi/fcp/en/WSM/body.htm.

- Food and Agriculture Organization of the United Nations (FAO). 2005. *Milk and Dairy Products, Post-Harvest Losses and Food Safety in Sub-Saharan Africa and the Near East (PFL).* Website. Online at http://www.fao.org/ag/againfo/projects/en/pfl/home.html.

- Gabriel, A., and B. Hundie. 2004. *Farmers' Post-Harvest Grain Management Choices Under Liquidity Constraints and Impending Risks: Implications for Achieving Food Security Objectives in Ethiopia.* Presented at the Second International Conference on the Ethiopian Economy, Addis Ababa, Ethiopia, June 3-5, 2004. Online at http://eeaecon.org/EEA/conferences/papers/Abebe%20HaileGabriel%20and%20Bekele%20Hunde%20-%20postharvest_abebe.pdf.

- Gresser, C., and S. Tickell. 2002. *Mugged. Poverty in Your Coffee Cup.* Oxfam International. Online at http://www.maketradefair.com/assets/english/mugged.pdf.

- Grieg-Gran, M., and J. Bishop. 2004. "How Can Markets for Ecosystem Services Benefit the Poor?" In *The Millennium Development Goals and Conservation—Managing Nature's Wealth for Society's Health,* ed. D. Roe, 55-72. London: International Institute for Environment and Development (IIED). Online at http://www.iied.org/docs/mdg/MDG2-ch4.pdf.

- International Fund for Agricultural Development (IFAD). 2004. Rural Finance Policy. Rome: IFAD. Online at http://www.ifad.org/pub/basic/finance/ENG.pdf.

- International Livestock Research Institute (ILRI). 2003. *Milk and Dairy Products, Post-Harvest Losses and Food Safety in Sub-Saharan Africa and the Near East—Regional Approaches to National Challenges. Phase 1 Synthesis Report.* Rome: Food and Agriculture Organization of the United Nations. Online at http://www.fao.org/ag/againfo/projects/en/pfl/documents.html.

- Kellert, S., J. Mehta, S. Ebbin, and L. Lichtenfeld. 2000. "Community Natural Resource Management: Promise, Rhetoric, and Reality." *Society and Natural Resources* 13:705-715. Online at http://www.ksu.edu/bsanderc/avianecology/kellert2000.pdf.

- Kerr, J. 2002a. "Watershed Development, Environmental Services, and Poverty Alleviation in India." *World Development* 30(8):1387-1400.

- Kerr, J. 2002b. "Sharing the Benefits of Watershed Management in Sukhomajri, India." In *Selling Forest Environmental Services: Market-based Mechanisms for Conservation and Development,* eds. S. Pagiola, J. Bishop and N. Landell-Mills, 53-63. London: Earthscan Publications Ltd.

- Kerr, J., G. Pangare, and V. Pangare. 2002. *Watershed Development Projects in India: An Evaluation.* Research Report 127. Washington, DC: International Food Policy Research Institute (IFPRI). Online at http://www.ifpri.org/pubs/abstract/127/rr127.pdf.

- King, M., and U. Fa'asili. 1999. "Community-Based Management of Subsistence Fisheries in Samoa." *Fisheries Management and Ecology* (6):133-144.

- Kumar, S. 2002. "Does Participation in Common Pool Resource Management Help the Poor? A Social Cost-Benefit Analysis of Joint Forest Management in Jharkhand, India." *World Development* 30(5):763-782.

- Landell-Mills, N., and I. Porras. 2002. *Silver Bullet or Fools' Gold? A Global Review of Markets for Forest Environmental Services and Their Impact on the Poor.* Instruments for Sustainable Private Sector Forestry Series. London: International Institute for Environment and Development (IIED). Online at http://www.iied.org/docs/flu/psf/psf_silvbullet.pdf.

- Manasseh, K., and G. Chopra. 2004. "India: World Bank Supports National Highway Systems Improvements in Uttar Pradesh and Bihar." *World Bank News Release* #251, December 21. Washington, DC: Online at http://www.worldbank.org.in/WBSITE/EXTERNAL/COUNTRIES/SOUTHASIAEXT/INDIAEXTN/0,,contentMDK:20298357~menuPK:295603~pagePK:141137~piPK:141127~theSitePK:295584,00.html.

- Marshall, E., A. Newton, and K. Schreckenberg. 2003. "Commercialisation of Non-Timber Forest Products: First Steps in Analysing the Factors Influencing Success." *International Forestry Review* 5(2):128-137.

- May, P. 1992. "Building Institutions and Markets for Non-Wood Forest Products from the Brazilian Amazon." *Unasylva: International Journal of Forestry and Forest Industries,* 42. Rome: Food and Agriculture Organization of the United Nations. Online at http://www.fao.org/documents/show_cdr.asp?url_file=/docrep/u2440E/u2440E00.htm.

- Mayers, J., and S. Vermeulen. 2002. *Company-Community Forestry Partnerships: From Raw Deals to Mutual Gains?* Instruments for Sustainable Private Sector Forestry Series. London: International Institute for Environment and Development (IIED). Online at http://www.poptel.org.uk/iied/docs/flu/psf_cmpny_prtnrship.pdf.

- Millennium Ecosystem Assessment (MA). 2005a. *Ecosystems and Human Well-Being: Synthesis Report.* Washington, DC: Island Press.

- Millennium Ecosystem Assessment (MA). 2005b. *Ecosystems and Human Well-Being: Biodiversity Synthesis.* Washington, DC: World Resources Institute.

- Miranda, M., I. Porras, and M. Moreno. 2003. *The Social Impacts of Payments for Environmental Services in Costa Rica. A Quantitative Field Survey and Analysis of the Virilla Watershed.* London: International Institute for Environment and Development (IIED). Online at http://www.iied.org/eep/pubs/documents/MES1.pdf.

- Morduch, J., and B. Haley. 2002. *Analysis of the Effects of Microfinance on Poverty Reduction.* NYU Wagner Working Paper No. 1014. New York: New York University. Online at http://www.nyu.edu/wagner/public_html/cgi-bin/workingPapers/wp1014.pdf.

- Morris, J. 2002. *Bitter Bamboo and Sweet Living: Impacts of NTFP Conservation Activities on Poverty Alleviation and Sustainable Livelihoods.* Prepared for IUCN's 31-C Project on Poverty Alleviation, Livelihood Improvement and Ecosystem Management. IUCN The World Conservation Union. Online at http://www.iucn.org/themes/fcp/publications/files/3ic_cs_lao.pdf.

- Munsiari, S. 2003. "WAIGA: A Journey from Local Initiative to Van Panchayat." Working Paper 1. Anand, India: Foundation for Ecological Security (FES).

- Neumann, R., and E. Hirsch. 2000. *Commercialisation of Non-Timber Forest Products: Review and Analysis of Research.* Bogor, Indonesia: Center for International Forestry Research (CIFOR). Online at http://www.cifor.cgiar.org/publications/pdf_files/mgntfp3.pdf.

- Pagiola, S. 2002. "Paying for Water Services in Central America: Learning from Costa Rica." In *Selling Forest Environmental Services: Market-Based Mechanisms for Conservation and Development,* eds. S. Pagiola, J. Bishop and N. Landell-Mills, 31-51. London: Earthscan Publications Ltd.

- Pagiola, S., A. Arcenas, and G. Platais. 2003. "Ensuring the Poor Benefit from Systems of Payments for Environmental Services." Presented at the Workshop on Reconciling Rural Poverty Reduction and Resource Conservation: Identifying Relationships and Remedies. Cornell University, Ithaca, NY, May 2-3, 2003.

- Reddy, V., M. Reddy, S. Galab, J. Soussan, and O. Springate-Baginski. 2004. "Participatory Watershed Development in India: Can it Sustain Rural Livelihoods?" *Development and Change* 35(2):297-326.

- Ribot, J. 1998. "Theorizing Access: Forest Profits Along Senegal's Charcoal Commodity Chain." *Development and Change* (29):307-341.
- Riddell, J. 2000. *Contemporary Thinking on Land Reform.* SD-Dimensions. Rome: Food and Agriculture Organization of the United Nations. Online at http://www.caledonia.org.uk/land/fao.htm.
- Rodriguez, C. 2004. "The Environmental Services Payment Program: An Alternative to Financial Sustainability for Sustainable Development." PowerPoint Presentation. Costa Rica Ministry of Environment and Energy.
- Rosa, H., S. Kandel, and L. Dimas. 2003. *Compensation for Environmental Services and Rural Communities: Lessons from the Americas and Key Issues for Strengthening Community Strategies.* San Salvador: The Salvadoran Research Program on Development and Environment (PRISMA). Online at http://www.prisma.org.sv/pubs/CES_RC_En.pdf.
- Samperio, D. 2002. A Fair Grind: Mexico. New York: UNDP Equator Initiative. Online at http://www.tve.org/ho/doc.cfm?aid=910.
- Scherr, S., A. White, and D. Kaimowitz. 2002. *Making Markets Work for Forest Communities.* Washington, DC and Bogor, Indonesia: Forest Trends and Center for International Forestry Research.
- Scherr, S., A. White, and D. Kaimowitz. 2003. *A New Agenda for Forest Conservation and Poverty Reduction: Making Forest Markets Work for Low-Income Producers.* Washington, DC: Forest Trends. Online at http://www.cifor.cgiar.org/publications/pdf_files/Books/A%20New%20Agenda.pdf.
- Shanley, P., A. Pierce, S. Laird, and S. Guillen. 2002. *Tapping the Green Market: Management and Certification of Non-Timber Forest Products.* Sterling, Virginia: Stylus Publishing, LLC.
- Shyamsundar, P., E. Araral, and S. Weerartne. 2004. *Devolution of Resource Rights, Poverty, and Natural Resource Management—A Review.* Environment Department Paper No. 104. Washington, DC: World Bank.
- Southey, S. 2004. *Project Documentation, Kalinga Mission for Indigenous Children and Youth Development, Inc. (KAMICYDI).* UNDP Equator Initiative. Online at http://www.globalgiving.com/pfil/774/projdoc.doc.
- Tognetti, S. 2001. *Creating Incentives for River Basin Management as a Conservation Strategy—A Survey of the Literature and Existing Initiatives.* Washington, DC: WWF-US.
- United Nations Housing Rights Programme (UNHRP). 2005. *Indigenous Peoples' Right to Adequate Housing: A Global Overview.* Report No. 7. Nairobi: United Nations Human Settlements Programme. Online at http://www.unhabitat.org/programmes/housingpolicy/pubvul.asp
- United States Agency for International Development (USAID). 2004. *USAID Quality Coffee Program Helps Gain Fame for Nicaraguan Coffee and Higher Incomes for Farmers.* USAID Nicaragua. Online at http://www.usaid.org.ni/ssoct04_1.html.
- United States Agency for International Development (USAID). 2005. *Natural Resource Management in Namibia.* Website. Online at www.usaid.org.na/project.asp?proid=3#top.
- Waldman, L., with contributions from A. Ballance, R. Benítez Ramos, A. Gadzekpo, O. Mugyenyi, Q. Nguyen, G. Tumushabe, and H. Stewart. 2005. *Environment, Politics, and Poverty: Lessons from a Review of PRSP Stakeholder Perspectives. Synthesis Review.* Study initiated under the Poverty and Environment Partnership (PEP) and jointly funded and managed by CIDA, DFID, and GTZ.
- White, A., and A. Martin. 2002. *Who Owns the World's Forests?* Washington, DC: Forest Trends and Center for International Environmental Law. Online at http://www.cbnrm.net/pdf/white_a_001_foresttenure.pdf.
- World Resources Institute (WRI). 2005. "FOODNET Uganda." Digital Dividend Project Summary. Washington, DC: WRI. Online at http://wriws1.digitaldividend.org/wri/app/navigate?_action=opencapsule&_form=default&dbId=1602801%3afcc3edcad7%3a-7fd2%3a3f-692c-7.
- World Resources Institute (WRI), United Nations Development Programme, United Nations Environment Programme, and World Bank. 2003. *World Resources 2002-2004: Decisions for the Earth—Balance, Voice, and Power.* Washington, DC: WRI. Online at http://governance.wri.org/pubs_description.cfm?PubID=3764.

Box 4.1

- Capitania del Alto y Bajo Izogog (CABI). 2004. "Equator Prize Submission to UN Development Program's Equator Initiative." Santa Cruz: CABI.
- Noss, A. 2005. Conservation Zoologist and Coordinator, Chaco Landscape program, Wildlife Conservation Society. Personal Communication. E-mail. April 18, 21, 2005.
- Roach, J. 2004. "Unique Bolivia Park Begun by Indigenous People." *National Geographic News* (January 13, 2004). Online at http://news.nationalgeographic.com/news/2004/2001/0113_040113_chacopark.html.
- Winer, N. 2003. "Co-Management of Protected Areas, the Oil and Gas Industry and Indigenous Empowerment—The Experience of Bolivia's Kaa-Iya del Gran Chaco." *Policy Matters* 12:181-191.
- Winer, N. 2001. "Bolivia Case Study: Kaa Iya del Gran Chaco." Report prepared for IUCN The World Conservation Union.

Box 4.2

- Bacon, C. 2005. "Confronting the Coffee Crisis: Can Fair Trade, Organic, and Specialty Coffees Reduce Small-Scale Farmer Vulnerability in Northern Nicaragua?" *World Development* 33(3):497-511.
- Darjeeling Ladenla Road Prerna (RCDC). 1996. *Economic and Social Survey Report on Dabaipani, Harsing and Yangkhoo.* Darjeeling, India: RCDC.
- Down to Earth. 2004. "24/7 Water Supply." *Down to Earth* (August 15):44.
- Fairtrade Labelling Organizations International (FLO). 2004. "Fairtrade Standards for Coffee." Online at http://www.fairtrade.net/pdf/sp/english/Coffee%20SP%20versionJune04.pdf.
- Fairtrade Labelling Organizations International (FLO). 2005. "Facts and Figures." FLO website. Online at http://www.fairtrade.net/sites/impact/facts.html.
- Howard, K. 2005. Sales Manager, Equal Exchange. Personal Communication. Interview. January 5, 2005.
- International Coffee Organization (ICO). 2005. *Historical Data: Prices Paid to Growers in Exporting Member Countries (Monthly).* Database. Online at http://www.ico.org/historical.asp.
- Murray, D., L. Raynolds, and P. Taylor. 2003. *One Cup at a Time: Poverty Alleviation and Fair Trade Coffee in Latin America.* Fort Collins, Colorado: Colorado State University, Fair Trade Research Group. Online at http://www.colostate.edu/Depts/Sociology/FairTradeResearchGroup/.
- Rice, R. 2001. Smithsonian Migratory Bird Center. Personal Communication. E-mail. June 11, 2001.
- Taylor, P. 2002. *Poverty Alleviation Through Participation in Fair Trade Coffee Networks: Synthesis of Case Study Research Question Findings.* Fort Collins, Colorado: Colorado State University and the Community and Resource Development Program, Ford Foundation. Online at http://www.colostate.edu/Depts/Sociology/FairTradeResearchGroup/doc/pete.pdf.
- Tea Promoters of India (TPI). 1999. "Small Farmers Scheme, Mineral Springs, Dabaipani: Yearly Report." Calcutta, India: TPI.
- Valencia, A. 2001. "Birds and Beans: The Changing Face of Coffee Production." *EarthTrends,* Features. Washington, DC: World Resources Institute. Online at http://earthtrends.wri.org/pdf_library/features/bio_fea_coffee.pdf.
- Young, G. 2003. *Fair Trade's Influential Past and the Challenges of its Future.* Brussels, Belgium: King Baudouin Foundation. Online at http://www.kbs-frb.be.

Box 4.3

- Annamalai, K., and S. Rao. 2003. *What Works: ITC's e-Choupal and Profitable Rural Transformation.* Washington, DC: World Resources Institute (WRI).
- e-Choupal. 2005. e-Choupal Website. ITC Ltd. Online at http://www.echoupal.com/.

Box 4.4

- Echavarría, M. 2002. *Water User Associations in the Cauca Valley: A Voluntary Mechanism to Promote Upstream-Downstream Cooperation in the Protection of Rural*

Watersheds. Land-Water Linkages in Rural Watersheds Case Study Series. Rome, Italy: Food and Agriculture Organization of the United Nations. Online at http://www.fao.org/ag/agl/watershed/watershed/papers/papercas/paperen/colombia.pdf

- IUCN The World Conservation Union. 2003. "Chiapas, Mexico." IUCN, Global Partnership on Forest Landscape Restoration. Online at http://www.unep-wcmc.org/forest/restoration/globalpartnership/docs/Mexico.pdf.

- Phillips, G., G. Hellier, and R. Tipper. 2002. *The Plan Vivo System: Verification Status Review.* Edinburgh, UK: The Edinburgh Centre for Carbon Management, Ltd. Online at http://www.eccm.uk.com/climafor/PVS%20Verification%20Report.PDF.

- Rosa, H., S. Kandel, and L. Dimas. 2003. *Compensation for Environmental Services and Rural Communities: Lessons from the Americas and Key Issues for Strengthening Community Strategies.* San Salvador: The Salvadoran Research Program on Development and Environment (PRISMA). Online at http://www.prisma.org.sv/pubs/CES_RC_En.pdf.

- Scherr, S., A. White, A. Khare, M. Inbar, and A. Molar. 2004. *For Services Rendered: The Current Status and Future Potential of Markets for the Ecosystem Services Provided by Tropical Forests.* ITTO Technical Series No. 21. International Tropical Timber Organization. Online at http://www.itto.or.jp/live/Live_Server/724/TS21e.pdf.

Box 4.5

- Annamalai, K., and S. Rao. 2003. *What Works: ITC's e-Choupal and Profitable Rural Transformation.* Washington, DC: World Resources Institute (WRI).

- Aulisi, A., A. Farrell, J. Pershing, and S. VanDeveer. 2005. *Greenhouse Gas Emissions Trading in U.S. States: Observations and Lessons from the OTC NOx Budget Program.* WRI White Paper. Washington, DC: World Resources Institute. Online at http://pdf.wri.org/nox_ghg.pdf.

- Ellerman, A., P. Joskow, R. Schmalensee, J. Montero, and E. Bailey. 2000. *Markets for Clean Air: the U.S. Acid Rain Program.* Cambridge: Cambridge University Press.

- International Energy Agency (IEA). 2004. *World Energy Outlook 2004.* Paris: IEA.

- Kura, Y., C. Revenga, E. Hoshino, and G. Mock. 2004. *Fishing for Answers: Making Sense of the Global Fish Crisis.* Washington, DC: World Resources Institute. Online at http://pubs.wri.org/pubs_description.cfm?PubID=3866.

- Millennium Ecosystem Assessment (MA). 2005. *Ecosystems and Human Well-Being: Synthesis.* Washington, DC: Island Press. Online at http://www.millenniumassessment.org/en/products.aspx.

- National Research Council (NRC). 1999. *Sharing the Fish: Toward a National Policy on Individual Fishing Quotas.* Washington, DC: National Academy Press.

- Soros, G. 2005. "Transparency Can Alleviate Poverty." *Financial Times* (March 17):43

- World Trade Organization (WTO). 2003. *Annual Report 2003.* Geneva: WTO. Online at http://www.wto.org/english/res_e/reser_e/annual_report_e.htm.

- World Wildlife Fund (WWF). 2005. *AREAS Project: Technology.* WWF. Online at http://www.worldwildlifefund.org/action/areasproject/technology.cfm.

Chapter 5: Case Studies

Namibia

- Adams, P. 2004. Community Liaison Officer, Torra Conservancy, Namibia. Personal Communication. Interview. October 2004.

- Baker, L. 2003. "Torra Conservancy Pays Dividends to Members." *The Namibian* (January 9). Online at http://www.usaid.org.na/pdfdocs/0103Torra%0120Conservancy%0120Dividends.pdf.

- Bandyopadhyay, S., M. Humavindu, P. Shyamsundar, and L. Wang. 2004. "Do Households Gain from Community-Based Natural Resource Management? An Evaluation of Community Conservancies in Namibia." Policy Research Working Paper 3337. Washington, DC: World Bank.

- Barnes, J. 2004. "Namibian CBNRM Program." PowerPoint presentation. Washington, DC: United States Agency for International Development.

- Florry, P. 2004. Manager, Damaraland Camp, Torra Conservancy, Namibia. Personal Communication. E-mail. October.

- Hamilton, K. 2004. Lead Economist, Environment Department, World Bank. Personal Communication. Interview. October.

- Jacobsohn, M. 2004. Co-Director, Integrated Rural Development and Nature Conservation. Personal Communication. E-mail. October.

- Long, S. 2001. "Disentangling Benefits, Livelihoods, Natural Resource Management and Managing Revenue from Tourism: The Experience of Torra Conservancy, Namibia." Wildlife Integration for Livelihood Diversification (WILD) Project Working Paper 3. Online at http://www.dea.met.gov.na/met/programmes/Wild/WILDworkingpapers1-5/WP%203%20-%20Disentangling%20Benefits.pdf.

- Long, S. ed. 2004. *Livelihoods and CBNRM in Namibia: The Findings of the WILD (Wildlife Integration for Livelihood Diversification) Project.* Final Technical Report of the Wildlife Integration for Livelihood Diversification Project (WILD). Prepared for the Directorates of Environmental Affairs and Parks and Wildlife Management, Ministry of Environment and Tourism. Windhoek: Government of the Republic of Namibia. Online at http://www.dea.met.gov.na/met/programmes/Wild/wildfinalrpt.htm.

- Sullivan, S. 2001. "How Sustainable is the Communalizing Discourse of 'New' Conservation? The Masking of Difference, Inequality and Aspiration in the Fledgling 'Conservancies' of Namibia." In *Conservation and Mobile Indigenous Peoples: Displacement, Forced Settlement and Sustainable Development,* eds. D. Chatty and M. Colchester, 158-187. Oxford: Berghahn Press.

- United States Agency for International Development (USAID). 2005. *Natural Resource Management in Namibia.* Website. Online at www.usaid.org.na/project.asp?proid=3#top.

- Vaughan, K., S. Mulonga, J. Katjiuna, and N. Branston. 2003. "Cash from Conservation. Torra Community Tastes the Benefits: A Short Survey and Review of the Torra Conservancy Cash Payout to Individual Members." Wildlife Integration for Livelihood Diversification Project (WILD) Working Paper 15. Online at http://www.dea.met.gov.na/met/programmes/Wild/WILDworkingpapers13-16/WP%2015%20%20Torra%20cash%20payouts.pdf.

- Weaver, C. 2004. Director, WWF-LIFE Program, Namibia. Personal Communication. Telephone Interview. October.

- World Wildlife Fund (WWF), and Rossing Foundation. 2004. *Living in a Finite Environment (LIFE) Project. End of Project Report for Phase II: August 12, 1999-September 30, 2004.* Draft report, October 2004. Washington, DC: United States Agency for International Development.

Darewadi

- D'Souza, M., and C. Lobo. 2004. "Watershed Development, Water Management and the Millennium Development Goals." Presented at the Watershed Summit, Chandigarh, November 25-27, 2004. Ahmednagar, India: Watershed Organization Trust.

- Kerr, J., G. Pangare, and V. Pangare. 2002. *Watershed Development Projects in India: An Evaluation.* Research Report 127. Washington, DC: International Food Policy Research Institute. Online at http://www.ifpri.org/pubs/abstract/127/rr127.pdf.

- Kerr, J. 2005. Assistant Professor, Department of Community, Agriculture, Recreation and Resource Studies, Michigan State University. Personal Communication. E-mail. February 20, 2005.

- Lobo, C. 2005a. Executive Director, Watershed Organization Trust. Personal Communication. E-mail. January 15, 2005

- Lobo, C. 2005b. Executive Director, Watershed Organization Trust. Personal Communication. E-mail. February 1, 2005.

- Lobo, C. 2005c. Executive Director, Watershed Organization Trust. Personal Communication. E-mail. March 17, 2005.

- Lobo, C., and M. D'Souza. 2003. "Qualification and Capacity-Building of NGOs and Village Self-Help Groups for Large-Scale Implementation of Watershed Projects: The Experience of the Indo-German Watershed Development Programme in Maharashtra." Revised version of a paper published in *Journal of Rural Development* 18(4). Ahmednagar, India: Watershed Organization Trust.

- Watershed Organization Trust (WOTR). 2002. *Darewadi Watershed Project.* Project summary paper. Ahmednagar, India: WOTR. On-line at http://www.wotr.org.

■ Watershed Organization Trust (WOTR). 2005. "Darewadi Project Benefits 1996-2005." Unpublished table.

Indonesia

■ Anderson, P., and A. Hidayat. 2004. *Evaluation of the Performance of the EIA-Telapak Project: Building Capacity of NGOs to Work on Illegal Logging Issues in Indonesia.* Report to the Multi-Stakeholder Forestry Programme (MFP). Jakarta: MFP.

■ Astraatmaja, R. 2004. Campaigner, ARuPA, Central Java, Indonesia. Personal Communication. Interview. December 14, 2004.

■ Astraatmaja, R. 2005. Campaigner, ARuPA, Central Java, Indonesia. Personal Communication. E-mail. February 3, 2005.

■ Brown, D. 2004. Forest Economist, Multi-Stakeholder Forestry Programme. Personal Communication. Interview. December 21, 2004.

■ Casson, A. 2000. "Illegal Tropical Timber Trade in Central Kalimantan, Indonesia." Draft paper prepared for the Programme on the Underlying Causes of Deforestation, Centre for International Forestry (CIFOR). Bogor, Indonesia: CIFOR.

■ Currey, D. 2004. Director, Environmental Investigation Agency. Personal Communication. Interview. December 14, 2004.

■ Currey, D. 2005. Director, Environmental Investigation Agency. Personal Communication. Interview. January 28, 2005.

■ Environmental Investigation Agency (EIA)/Telapak Indonesia. 2002. *Timber Trafficking: Illegal Logging in Indonesia, South East Asia, and International Consumption of Illegally Sourced Timber.* London: EIA.

■ Kaban, H. 2005. Minister of Forestry. Speech to the Consultative Group on Indonesia. January 19, 2005, Jakarta.

■ McCarthy, J.F. 2002. "Turning in Circles: District Governance, Illegal Logging, and Environmental Decline in Sumatra, Indonesia." *Society and Natural Resources* 15:867-886.

■ Multi-Stakeholder Forestry Programme (MFP). 2000."Strengthening Decentralised Institutional Arrangements and Policy Mechanisms for Sustainable and Equitable Forest Management in Indonesia." Draft Programme Memorandum PRC (00) 20. Jakarta: MFP. Online at http://www.mfp.or.id/new/mfp.php.

■ Saparjadi, K. 2003. Director General of Forest Protection and Nature Conservation, Indonesian Ministry of Forestry. Quoted in "Indonesia Losing $3.7 Billion Annually From Illegally Sourced Timber." *Asia Pulse* (18 June).

■ Schroeder-Wildberg, E., and A. Carius. 2003. *Illegal Logging, Conflict and the Business Sector in Indonesia.* Berlin: InWEnt—Capacity Building International.

■ Valentinus, A. 2004. Coordinator, Forest Programs and Campaigns, Telapak and Environmental Investigation Agency. Personal Communication. E-mail. December 18, 2004.

Tanzania

■ Barrow, E., and W. Mlenge. 2003. "Trees as Key to Pastoralist Risk Management in Semi-Arid Landscapes in Shinyanga, Tanzania and Turkana, Kenya." Presented at the CIFOR-FLR conference, Bonn, Germany, May 2003.

■ Barrow, E., and W. Mlenge. 2004. *Ngitili for Everything—Woodland Restoration in Shinyanga, Tanzania.* Dar es Salaam: The United Republic of Tanzania Ministry of Natural Resources and Tourism and IUCN The World Conservation Union, Eastern Africa Regional Office.

■ Barrow, E. 2005a. Coordinator, Forest Conservation and Social Policy, Eastern Africa Regional Office, IUCN The World Conservation Union. Personal Communication. E-mail. January 24, 2005.

■ Barrow, E. 2005b. Coordinator, Forest Conservation and Social Policy, Eastern Africa Regional Office, IUCN The World Conservation Union. Personal Communication. E-mail. January 26, 2005.

■ Barrow, E. 2005c. Coordinator, Forest Conservation and Social Policy, Eastern Africa Regional Office, IUCN The World Conservation Union. Personal Communication. E-mail. February 11, 2005.

■ Barrow, E. 2005d. Coordinator, Forest Conservation and Social Policy, Eastern Africa

Regional Office, IUCN The World Conservation Union. Personal Communication. E-mail. February 14, 2005.

■ Barrow, E. 2005e. Coordinator, Forest Conservation and Social Policy, Eastern Africa Regional Office, IUCN The World Conservation Union. Personal Communication. E-mail. March 23, 2005.

■ Kaale, B., W. Mlenge, and E. Barrow. 2003. "The Potential of Ngitili for Forest Landscape Restoration in Shinyanga Region: A Tanzanian Case Study." Working Paper. Dar es Salaam: Natural Forest Resources and Agroforestry Center.

■ Monela, G., S. Chamshama, R. Mwaipopo, and D. Gamassa. 2004. *A Study on the Social, Economic and Environmental Impacts of Forest Landscape Restoration in Shinyanga Region, Tanzania.* Draft. Dar-es-Salaam: The United Republic of Tanzania Ministry of Natural Resources and Tourism, Forestry and Beekeeping Division, and IUCN The World Conservation Union, Eastern Africa Regional Office.

■ Monela, G. 2005. Assistant Lecturer, Department of Forest Economics, Sokoine University of Agriculture, Morogoro, Tanzania. Personal Communication. E-mail. February 8, 2005.

Fiji

■ Aalbersberg, B. 2003. "The Role of Locally-managed Marine Areas (LMMAs) in the Development of Ecotourism in Fiji." IAS Technical Report No. 2003/03.

■ Aalbersberg, B., and A. Tawaki. 2005. Unpublished data. Personal communication. E-mail. June 2005.

■ Gell, F., and A. Tawake. 2002. "Community-based Closed Areas in Fiji." In *The Fishery Effects of Marine Reserves and Fishery Closures,* eds. F. Gell and C. Roberts, 60-63, in press. York, UK: University of York. Online at www.worldwildlife.org/oceans/fishery_effects.pdf.

■ Tawake, A., and W. Aalbersberg. 2002. "Community-Based Refugia Management in Fiji." IAS Technical Report No. 2002/08. Suva, Fiji: Institute of Applied Science, University of the South Pacific.

■ Tawake, A., J. Parks, P. Radikedike, W. Aalbersberg, V. Vuki and N. Salasfsky. 2001. "Harvesting Clams and Data: Involving Local Communities in Implementing and Monitoring a Marine Protected Area. A Case Study from Fiji." *Conservation Biology in Practice,* Fall 2001.

■ Veitayaki, J., B. Aalbersberg, and A. Tawake. 2003. "Net Gains." *Between the Lines: Equator Initiative Newsletter.* September Issue 3, 5-6. Online at http://www.undp.org/equatorinitiative/pdf/BetweenTheLinesIssuethree.pdf.

Special Section

■ Bindraban, P., H. Aalbers, H. Moll, I. Brouwer, A. Besselink, and V. Grispen. 2004. *Biodiversity, Agro-Biodiversity, International Trade and Food Safety in CCA and PRSP Country Reports: Major Issues of Development in the UN System of Common Country Assessments and World Bank Poverty Reduction Strategy Papers.* Report No. 76. Wageningen, the Netherlands: Wageningen University and Plant Research International.

■ Bojö, J., and R. Reddy. 2002. *Poverty Reduction Strategies and Environment: A Review of 40 Interim and Full Poverty Reduction Strategy Papers.* World Bank Environment Department Paper No. 86. Washington, DC: World Bank.

■ Bojö, J., and R. Reddy. 2003a. *Poverty Reduction Strategies and the Millennium Development Goal on Environmental Sustainability: Opportunities for Alignment.* World Bank Environment Department Paper No. 92. Washington, DC: World Bank.

■ Bojö, J., and R. Reddy. 2003b. *Status and Evolution of Environmental Priorities in the Poverty Reduction Strategies.* World Bank Environment Department Paper No. 93. Washington, DC: World Bank.

■ Bojö, J., K. Green, S. Kishore, S. Pilapitiya, and R. Reddy. 2004. *Environment in Poverty Reduction Strategies and Poverty Reduction Support Credits.* World Bank Environment Department Paper No. 102. Washington, DC: World Bank.

■ Bolivia, Republic of (Bolivia PRSP). 2001. *Poverty Reduction Strategy Paper.* Online at http://www.imf.org/external/NP/prsp/2001/bol/01/Index.htm.

■ Cambodia, Royal Government of (Cambodia PRSP). 2002. *National Poverty Reduction Strategy 2003-2005*. Online at http://www.imf.org/External/NP/prsp/2002/khm/01/index.htm.

■ Chiche, M., and G. Hervio. 2004. *Budget Support Donor Groups Summary Analysis*. Report by European Commision Co-Chair of the Budget Support Working Group of the Strategic Partnership with Africa. Brussels: European Commission.

■ Clemens, M., C. Kenny, and T. Moss. 2004. "The Trouble with the MDGs: Confronting Expectations of Aid and Development Success." Working Paper Number 40. Washington, DC: Center for Global Development. Online at http://www.cgdev.org/docs/cgd_wp040Rev2.pdf.

■ Driscoll, R., and A. Evans. 2004a. *The PRSP Process and DFID Engagement: Summary of Progress 2003*. London: Overseas Development Institute. Online at http://www.prspsynthesis.org/synthesis9_engagement.pdf.

■ Driscoll, R., and A. Evans. 2004b. *Second Generation Poverty Reduction Strategies*. Report prepared for the PRSP Monitoring and Synthesis Project. London: Overseas Development Institute. Online at http://www.prspsynthesis.org/synthesis10.pdf.

■ Ghana, Republic of (Ghana PRSP). 2003. *Ghana Poverty Reduction Strategy 2003-2005: An Agenda for Growth and Prosperity*. Online at http://www.imf.org/external/pubs/ft/scr/2003/cr0356.pdf.

■ Honduras, Government of (Honduras PRSP). 2001. *Poverty Reduction Strategy Paper*. Online at http://www.imf.org/External/NP/prsp/2001/hnd/01/index.htm.

■ International Monetary Fund (IMF), and World Bank. 2005. *Global Monitoring Report 2005: Millennium Development Goals: From Consensus to Momentum*. Washington, DC: IMF and World Bank. Online at http://web.worldbank.org/WBSITE/EXTERNAL/TOPICS/GLOBALMONITORINGEXT/0,,pagePK:64022007~theSitePK:278515,00.html.

■ Kenya, Republic of (Kenya PRSP). 2004. *Investment Programme for the Economic Recovery Strategy for Wealth and Employment Creation 2003-2007*. Online at http://www.imf.org/external/pubs/ft/scr/2005/cr0511.pdf.

■ Levinsohn, J. 2003. *The World Bank's Poverty Reduction Strategy Paper Approach: Good Marketing or Good Policy?* G-24 Discussion Paper Series, No. 21. New York: United Nations Conference on Trade and Development (UNCTAD) and Center for International Development, Harvard University. Online at http://www.unctad.org/en/docs/gdsmdpbg2420032_en.pdf.

■ Millennium Ecosystem Assessment (MA). 2005a. *Ecosystems and Human Well-Being: Synthesis*. Washington, DC: Island Press.

■ Millennium Ecosystem Assessment (MA). 2005b. "Implications for Achieving the Millennium Development Goals." In *Policy Responses: Findings of the Responses Working Group*. Vol. 3: Ecosystems and Human Well-Being, Chapter 19: Final draft. Washington, DC: Island Press.

■ Nicaragua, Government of (Nicaragua PRSP). 2001. *A Strengthened Growth and Poverty Reduction Strategy*. Online at http://www.imf.org/External/NP/prsp/2001/nic/01/073101.pdf.

■ Oksanen, T., and C. Mersmann. 2003. "Forests in Poverty Reduction Strategies: An Assessment of PRSP Processes in Sub-Saharan Africa." In *Forests in Poverty Reduction Strategies: Capturing the Potential*, eds. T. Oksanen, B. Pajari and T. Tuomasjukka, 121-155. EFI Proceedings No. 47. Tuusula, Finland: European Forest Institute (EFI). Online at http://www.efi.fi/attachment/f5d80ba3c1b89242106f2f97ae8e3894/241e80d8e1b2b0919426d5a82060db7e/Proc_47.pdf.

■ Oladipo, E. 2004. "Sustainable Development Advisor, UNDP Nigeria." Posting to UNDP e-discussion: Mainstreaming Environment into the PRS. May 28, 2004.

■ Operations Evaluation Department (OED). 2004. *The Poverty Reduction Strategy Initiative: An Independent Evaluation of the World Bank's Support Through 2003*. Washington, DC: World Bank. Online at http://www.worldbank.org/oed/prsp/index.html.

■ PRSP Monitoring and Synthesis Project. 2002. *Synthesis Note 3: Assessing Participation in PRSPs in Sub-Saharan Africa*. London: Overseas Development Institute and United Kingdom Department for International Development. Online at http://www.prspsynthesis.org/synthesis3.pdf.

■ Reed, D. 2004. *Analyzing the Political Economy of Poverty and Ecological Disruption*.

■ Washington, DC: WWF Macroeconomics Program Office. Online at http://www.panda.org/news_facts/publications/policy/publication.cfm?uNewsID=14913&uLangId=1.

■ Slaymaker, T., and P. Newborne. 2004. *Implementation of Water Supply and Sanitation Programmes Under PRSPs: Synthesis of Research Findings from Sub-Saharan Africa*. London: Overseas Development Institute and WaterAid. Online at http://www.odi.org.uk/wpp/publications_pdfs/Watsan_PRSP_text_ResearchReport.pdf.

■ Sri Lanka, Government of (Sri Lanka PRSP). 2002. *Regaining Sri Lanka: Vision and Strategy for Accelerated Development*. Online at http://www.imf.org/External/NP/prsp/2002/lka/01/120502.pdf.

■ Tharakan, P., and M. MacDonald. 2004. *Developing and Testing a PRSP Evaluation Methodology*. Washington, DC: WWF Macroeconomic Program Office. Online at http://www.panda.org/downloads/policy/prspfinal.pdf.

■ United Nations. 2000a. *United Nations Millennium Development Goals*. Online at http://www.un.org/millenniumgoals/.

■ United Nations. 2000b. "Millennium Development Goal #7 (MDG 7): Global Targets and Indicators." Online at http://www.undp.org/mdg/abcs.html#Goals.

■ United Nations Development Programme (UNDP). 2005a. *Environmental Sustainability in 100 Millennium Development Goal Country Reports*. New York: UNDP.

■ United Nations Development Programme (UNDP). 2005b. "Monitoring Country Progress Towards MDG7: Ensuring Environmental Sustainability." Practice Note. New York: UNDP. Online at http://www.undp.org/fssd/sustdevmdg.htm.

■ United Nations Development Programme (UNDP). 2005c. *Synthesis of Environmental Sustainability (MDG7) for 100 Millennium Development Goal Country Reports*. New York: UNDP. Online at http://www.undp.org/fssd/sustdevmdg.htm.

■ United Nations Millennium Project. 2005. Investing in Development: *A Practical Plan to Achieve the Millennium Development Goals*. New York: Earthscan. Online at http://www.unmillenniumproject.org/reports/fullreport.htm.

■ Waldman, L., with contributions from A. Ballance, R. Benítez Ramos, A. Gadzekpo, O. Mugyenyi, Q. Nguyen, G. Tumushabe, and H. Stewart. 2005. *Environment, Politics, and Poverty: Lessons from a Review of PRSP Stakeholder Perspectives. Synthesis Review*. Study initiated under the Poverty and Environment Partnership (PEP), and jointly funded and managed by Canadian International Development Agency, United Kingdom Department for International Development, and Deutsche Gesellschaft fur Technische Zusammenarbeit.

■ World Bank. 2001. *A Sourcebook for Poverty Reduction Strategy Papers*. Washington, DC: World Bank. Online at http://web.worldbank.org/WBSITE/EXTERNAL/TOPICS/EXTPOVERTY/EXTPRS/0,,contentMDK:20175742~pagePK:210058~piPK:210062~theSitePK:384201,00.html.

■ World Bank. 2005. *World Development Indicators 2005*. Washington, DC: World Bank.

■ World Bank and International Monetary Fund (IMF). 2003. *Poverty Reduction Strategy Papers: Detailed Analysis of Progress in Implementation*. Washington, DC: World Bank. Online at http://www.imf.org/external/np/prspgen/2003/091503.pdf.

■ Zambia, Government of (Zambia PRSP). 2002. *Zambia Poverty Reduction Strategy Paper 2002-2004*. Online at http://www.imf.org/External/NP/prsp/2002/zmb/01/033102.pdf.

PHOTO CREDITS

Chapter 1: (8) Alston Taggart; (15) IFAD/F. Mattioli; (22) IFAD/C. Nesbitt; (27) C. Gibson/M. Rice/Heat Dust & Dreams

Chapter 2: (32) IFAD/R. Chalasani; (46) Andre Bartschi/wildtropix.com

Chapter 3: (54) IFAD/S. Beccio; (57) Andrew Katona; (60) IFAD/R. Chalasani; (63) IFAD/R. Grossman; (64) Andrew Katona; (67) IFAD/R. Mattioli; (68) IFAD/R. Chalasani; (77) Andrew Katona

Chapter 4: (88) IFAD/A. Hossain; (101) Alston Taggart; (104) Alston Taggart; (108) Andrew Katona; (110) IFAD/G. Mintapradja

Chapter 5: (112) IFAD/R. Faidutti; (114) C. Gibson/M. Rice/Heat Dust & Dreams; (117) C. Gibson/M. Rice/Heat Dust & Dreams; (118) C. Gibson/M. Rice/Heat Dust & Dreams; (119) C. Gibson/M. Rice/Heat Dust & Dreams; (120) C. Gibson/M. Rice/Heat Dust & Dreams; (121) C. Gibson/M. Rice/Heat Dust & Dreams; (122) C. Gibson/M. Rice/Heat Dust & Dreams; (123) C. Gibson/M. Rice/Heat Dust & Dreams; (124) Watershed Organization Trust; (126) Watershed Organization Trust; (127) Watershed Organization Trust; (128) Watershed Organization Trust; (130) Watershed Organization Trust; (131) Edmund Barrow; (134) Edmund Barrow; (136) Edmund Barrow; (138) Edmund Barrow; (139) A. Ruwindrijarto/Telapak/Environmental Investigation Agency (140) A. Ruwindrijarto/Telapak/Environmental Investigation Agency; (141, left) Paul Redman/Telapak/Environmental Investigation Agency; (141 right) Telapak/Environmental Investigation Agency; (142) Mardi Minangsari/Telapak/Environmental Investigation Agency; (143) Campbell Plowden/Environmental Investigation Agency; (144) Toni Parras; (147) Toni Parras; (148) Toni Parras; (151) Alifereti Tawake

Special Section: (171) Andrew Katona

Index

A

Access
 Access Principles (Rio Declaration), 71
 common pool resources, 40–41
 as determinant of rural wealth, 16
 effectiveness of efforts to improve, 71
 to financing and credit, 86, 98–99, 109
 governance issues, 3–4, 19, 23, 70–71, 75–76
 to information, 56, 71, 73–75, 159
 to justice, 71, 76–77
 Millennium Development Goals, 159
 obstacles to, 71, 74
 in poverty reduction strategy papers, 165, 167–168, 170
 privatization of resources, 42
 women's, 75–76, 170
 See also Tenure
Accountability
 in democratic processes, 69
 in governance, 64, 69, 73
 information needs for, 73–74
 in Millennium Development Goals, 154, 157
Africa
 agricultural economy, 4, 31, 35
 common pool resources, 40
 fisheries incomes, 35
 Millennium Development Goals, 154
 poverty trends, 7, 10
 See also specific country
Agriculture
 climate change and, 16
 economic significance of, for poor, 35, 39, 45
 ecosystem management to improve, 81–82
 environmental income and, 34, 35, 39, 45
 export economy, 35
 fair-trade certification, 94–95
 Green Revolution, 18–19, 45
 information needs of rural poor, 73, 75
 organic products, 95, 100–101
 productivity, 17
 product losses in storage and processing, 99
 strategies for poverty reduction, 18–19
 trade and subsidization policies, 30–31
 watershed management in India and, 127
 woodlands management in Tanzania and, 131, 136
AIDS/HIV, 10–11, 22
Argentina, 14
Asia
 Millennium Development Goals, 154
 See also specific country

B

Bangladesh, 68–69
 household spending patterns, 14
Bioprospecting, 72, 149–150
Bolivia, 63, 67, 87, 105
 environmental income, 46
 poverty profile, 6
 poverty reduction strategy papers, 166, 168–169, 170
Botswana
 common pool resources, 40
 environmental income, 44
Brazil, 25, 75, 98, 104
 environmental income, 48
 payment for environmental service programs, 108

C

Cambodia, 27, 159
 common pool resources, 40
 environmental income, 49
 fisheries, 38, 158
 poverty reduction strategy papers, 166, 169, 170
Cameroon, 67, 86
Caribbean countries. *See* Latin America and Caribbean
Chad, 50
Children
 educational attainment, 52
 health risks for, 21
 household responsibilities, 52
 malnutrition effects, 21
 Millennium Development Goals, 154
Chile, 25
 poverty trends, 10
China
 experimental land reforms, 86
 poverty trends, 7, 10, 11
Climate change, 13, 16, 22
Coffee, 94, 98, 99
Colombia, 69
 payment for environmental services in, 106, 107
Co-management partnerships, 93–96
Commercialization and marketing
 commodity chain, 99
 cooperatives, 94–95, 99–100
 fair-trade certification, 94–95, 100
 information needs, 73, 97, 102–103
 infrastructure needs, 97
 niche products and services, 17–18
 obstacles to improving environmental income, 97
 organic products, 94–95, 100–101
 private sector partnerships, 101–104
 problems of ecosystem commercialization, 105
 product processing strategies, 99
 training and support, 97

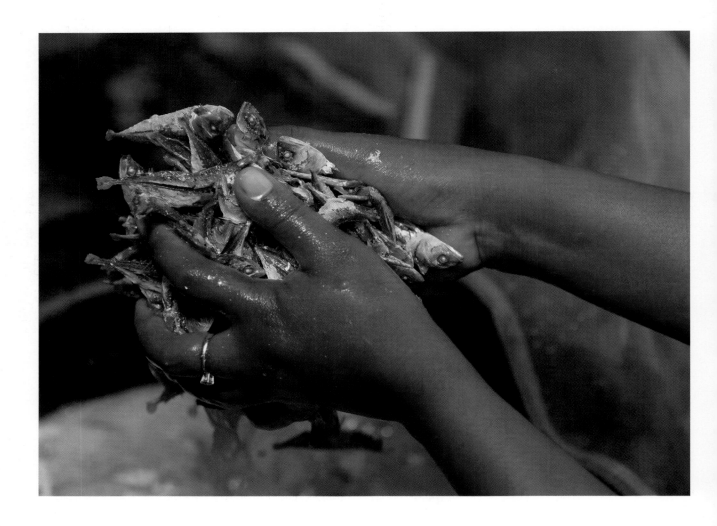